Budd

# THE IRONY OF REGULATORY REFORM

# THE IRONY
# OF
# REGULATORY REFORM

The Deregulation of American Telecommunications

## ROBERT BRITT HORWITZ

New York     Oxford
OXFORD UNIVERSITY PRESS
1989

Oxford University Press

Oxford   New York   Toronto
Delhi   Bombay   Calcutta   Madras   Karachi
Petaling Jaya   Singapore   Hong Kong   Tokyo
Nairobi   Dar es Salaam   Cape Town
Melbourne   Auckland
and associated companies in
Berlin   Ibadan

Published by Oxford University Press, Inc.
200 Madison Avenue, New York, New York 10016

Oxford is a registered trademark of Oxford University Press

Library of Congress Cataloging-in-Publication Data

Horwitz, Robert Britt.
The irony of regulatory reform: the deregulation of American
telecommunications / Robert Britt Horwitz.
p.     cm.     Bibliography: p. Includes index.
ISBN 0-19-505445-8
1. Telecommunication—United States—Deregulation.
2. Telecommunication policy—United States. I. Title.
HE7781.H67 1988      384'.041—dc19      88-5962 CIP

9 8 7 6 5 4 3 2 1
Printed in the United States of America
on acid-free paper

*For my father and to the memory of my mother*

# Preface

Deregulation was one of the political buzzwords of the early 1980s. The Reagan Administration came to power on a platform dedicated to reducing the size of government and removing government from the economy. Rhetorically defended as "getting the government off the backs of the people," deregulation promised to dismantle onerous regulatory controls and restore to businessmen the freedom of action they had lost to government bureaucrats. Unleashed entrepreneurialism would lower inflation, raise productivity, and reverse the sagging fortunes of American industry in the increasingly competitive world economy. And proponents declared deregulation morally right because it constituted a rollback of the arbitrary power of the state in favor of individual initiative and liberty.

But the actual politics of deregulation had already turned out to be far more complex than this rhetoric suggested, and their course was replete with paradoxes. Whereas the prime targets of the Reagan Administration were the regulatory agencies dealing with social issues, like the Environmental Protection Agency and Occupational Safety and Health Administration, deregulation affected primarily agencies that had rationalized economic activities in industries such as transportation and telecommunications. The latter were agencies spawned or expanded by the New Deal: the Federal Communications Commission, the Civil Aeronautics Board, the Interstate Commerce Commission. Ironically, notwithstanding general business hostility toward much regulation, only those industries whose principal players generally desired continued regulatory oversight got deregulation. Moreover, the dismantling of economic regulation had already been initiated before Reagan came to power.

This book explores the deregulation phenomenon through the concrete prism of the history of the regulation and deregulation of American telecommunications. Telecommunications is a particularly interesting industry to study, not only because of its tremendous technological transformation during the past two decades and the fact that it constitutes the modern public sphere, but also because of its basic role in anchoring the so-called "post-industrial" society. Indeed, one of the reasons put forward for the deregulation of telecommunications was that this key industry had to be unshackled so that the United States could properly enter the "information age."

Regulation was not always held in contempt. After all, the system of regulation was largely responsible for the stabilization, growth, and universalization of telephone and broadcast industries in the United States. Traditional economic regulation functioned, in today's argot, as a successful "industrial policy." This is not to say, of course, that regulation was without its problems. The regulation of telecommunications by the Federal Communications Commission often functioned as a form of protection, if not cartel management, for the established players of the telecommunication industry. The difficulty in assessing regulation rests in the difficulty of trying to identify the public interest in an intricate system of private enterprise and state controls. It is the task of this book to unveil the complex mosaic of forces—regulatory, economic, political, legal, and technological—that undermined the traditional regulation of telecommunications and eventuated in deregulation and the break-up of AT&T.

I would like to acknowledge the assistance of the many people whose help made this book possible. Egon Bittner, George Ross, and Yale Braunstein provided much help in the early phases of the study. Joel Greifinger, Carmen Sirianni, Chandra Mukerji, and Peter Irons read parts of the ever-changing manuscript along the way and provided much-needed suggestions and criticisms. The late readings provided by Daniel Hallin, Barbara Tomlinson, and George Lipsitz helped me finalize changes at a time when I was desperate to finish. The close and critical readings the entire manuscript received from Brian Winston and Dan Schiller were invaluable. I had the benefit of research and bibliographic assistance from A. Margot Gordon, Dennis Costa, and Wai-Teng Leong. I would also like to thank the reference librarians at UCSD's Central Library, including Elliot Kanter, Paul Zarins, Sharon Anderson, and Larry Cruz.

Special thanks go to the following friends: Michael Schudson, who commented on more drafts of chapters than he probably would have liked; Priscilla Long, whose close copyedit of the near-final version was as wonderful and generous a gesture as it was helpful; Lew Friedland, without whose counsel, discussion, and criticism the manuscript would have suffered incalculably; and Libby Brydolf, who suffered with me through the many drafts and agonies with equanimity, close reading, and wise suggestions.

*La Jolla*                                                                              R.B.H.
*April 1988*

# Contents

# THE IRONY OF REGULATORY REFORM

# CHAPTER

## 1

• • •

# Telecommunications and Their Deregulation: An Introduction

The telecommunications revolution, we are told, has arrived. Telecommunications used to mean the telephone, a mature, rather dull, and highly regulated industry dominated by the staid Bell System. For most of us, the technology of the telephone was so good and reliable, and its uses so set and inflexible, that it was functionally forgotten. For corporate users, telecommunications represented just another mundane cost of doing business. Telecommunications also encompassed broadcasting, a more glitzy endeavor than telephone to be sure, but one primarily characterized by a remarkable stability of three commercial television networks that aired mostly imitative and inoffensive entertainment programs, along with one poorly funded public network.

Today the very term telecommunications may be too confining. The once stable, noncompetitive businesses of telephone service and equipment manufacturing have become dynamic and highly competitive. Telephone technology has merged with that of the computer to vastly enhance the capabilities of both. The resulting fusion, sometimes labeled ''information technology,'' has become a vibrant, burgeoning industry, reconfiguring business practices and permitting corporations to slash operating costs and automate the workplace. Some government policy-makers have pronounced information technology the United States' most important industry. Likewise, broadcasting has been so transformed by satellites, the abundance of cable television, and videotape technology, that the traditionally limited television system seems nearly a thing of the past. There are now sports channels, news

3

channels, movie channels, "adult" channels, Christian channels, Spanish language channels, and so on.

While many of these changes reflect a grand profusion of technological innovation, perhaps the more interesting phenomenon is the less apparent transformation of the state—deregulation—which has accompanied and abetted this technological "revolution." The changes in telecommunications have emerged as much from changes in their regulatory treatment as they have from technological innovation. This book examines the framework within which the telecommunications industry has been structured, and how that framework changed. It seeks to answer the question: how and why were American telecommunications deregulated?

The American telecommunications industry is being deregulated after more than fifty years of close government oversight. In broadcasting, some of the changes are fundamental. Commercial broadcasters, once subject to many "public interest" regulatory controls, such as a requirement for public information programming, an obligation to ascertain the broadcast needs of the community, and recommendations on the maximum amount of advertising, are no longer constrained by such rules. The famous "Fairness Doctrine," which obligated broadcasters to air issues of controversy and to be balanced in that coverage, is now officially moribund. The period of license tenure for a radio frequency has been extended from three years to seven; for a television frequency from three years to five. The ceiling on the number of broadcast stations a single corporate entity may own has been raised from a total of seven AM, seven FM radio stations, and seven television outlets, to twelve of each. By the mid-1980s talk echoed in the Senate Commerce Committee and at the Federal Communications Commission about complete First Amendment protection for any and all "publishers," print or electronic. The aim of such proposals is to completely dismantle any remaining regulatory controls over broadcasting, particularly the rules which require broadcasters to operate as "public trustees."

Ancillary broadcast services, long restricted by regulations favoring conventional broadcasting, have been given a green light. The most important of these was cable television. For years, regulations hindered the expansion of cable television and restricted the type of signals and programs cable operators could purvey. These restrictions began to be dismantled in the mid-1970s. Cable has grown quickly since. Historic restrictions on pay television were removed, and new programming sources have emerged. By the late 1970s the FCC went so far as to promote new broadcast services.

Common carriers such as the telephone system have experienced even greater changes. Long considered a "natural monopoly," the telephone system was closely regulated under the watchful eye of the Federal Communications Commission and state public utilities commissions. Regulatory controls made competition impossible. In exchange for monopoly status, telephone companies were obliged to extend service to all. Through the control of telephone rates, regulatory policies facilitated internal cross-subsidies to expand telephone service and keep particular rates low. The telephone system was united by the giant, vertically integrated American Telephone and Telegraph Company (AT&T), operator of the only long-distance network and of local telephone service in most major metropolises. But, beginning as early as the late 1950s, the FCC allowed a certain amount of competition in specialized business services. Liberalized entry extended to domestic communication satellites in the early 1970s, and, most important, to long-distance telephone service by the late 1970s. In 1982 the structure of regulated telecommunications was massively transformed by the break-up of AT&T. A divestiture agreement between AT&T and the Justice Department severed AT&T of its local telephone service companies. AT&T, historically confined to the provision of regulated telecommunications services, was now free to compete with computer giants such as IBM in global information technology markets. The break-up of AT&T has become the single most important event in the deregulation of American industry.

## The Context of Deregulation

Yet telecommunication is not alone in experiencing a fundamental change in its regulatory treatment. It joins the ranks of several other industries that have been wholly or partially deregulated since the late 1970s. These include commercial airlines, railroads, trucking, intercity busing, banking, and (to a far lesser degree) oil and natural gas. Given the widespread growth of the regulatory state in the twentieth century, how are we to understand this phenomenon of deregulation? Deregulation runs against the traditional understanding of government regulation as a means of rationalizing the economy and/or of safeguarding the public interest. We commonly think of government regulation as the modern means of coordinating highly complex social activities in ways that the market cannot. One traditionally accepted argument is that capitalists, acting on their own, pursuing the logic of profit maximization, cannot adequately safeguard the conditions which allow their industry—when taken as a whole—to flourish. Some businesses are regulated because their inordinate market power enables them to abuse other businesses and/or the public. The coercive, regulatory power of the state limits the choices of individual capitalists in the long-term interest of both the industry and the public. Is deregulation, then, a gross betrayal of the public interest, a strategy on the part of capital to reappropriate the power it once lost to democratic reforms?

Or is deregulation a response to the dubious efficacy or even failure of government action? Government interference in the economy is claimed to irreparably disrupt the allocative beneficence of the self-regulating, self-equilibrating market. Indeed, regulatory agencies often are said to be "captured" by the regulated parties, which then utilize the state apparatus for private ends. Regulatory agencies protect businesses from competition. Does deregulation represent the "coming to senses" of an increasingly bureaucratized state apparatus, dismantling itself in favor of more workable market controls?

In another popular account, the deregulation of *telecommunications* is taken to be a consequence of the revolution in technology. In this view, new technologies such as cable television and satellite delivery overwhelmed the traditional formulae of broadcast regulation. The advent of digital encoding (a method of breaking down information into a code of binary numbers) and the melding of the computer with telephone switching caused the dissolution of the legal boundary between the regulated telecommunications industry and the unregulated computer industry. In other words, the "information revolution" caused or necessitated deregulation. This idea is a variant of technological determinism: it sees technology as self-generative and social change as technologically driven.

In my view, all such theories of deregulation are decidedly incomplete. For deregulation can only be understood in larger contexts. Telecommunication is just one of several American industries to be deregulated since the mid-1970s. Hence its deregulation cannot be explained with reference to internal telecommunications issues or technological factors alone. Deregulation went beyond telecommunications, but was confined to a specific type of industry under a specific type of regulatory control. This points to the need to look toward regulatory structures.

Deregulation was a political process, whereby the economic and political problems enveloping certain industries (but not others) turned a surprisingly heterogeneous political coalition against continued regulation. Joined within that coalition were two political logics usually diametrically opposed to each other—conservative free market economic theory and a left-liberal theory of political participation. Each "logic" attacked regulation from the standpoint of its own theoretical position. Liberals and public interest groups, seeing in traditional regulatory agencies evidence of "capture" by the very firms under regulation, came to advocate deregulation as a solution to entrenched corporate power. Conservatives and free market economists, seeing in regulatory agencies vast bureaucracies whose arbitrariness engendered economic inefficiency and artificial protectionism, also came to advocate deregulation. In various of these industries, the empirical example of an unregulated service provided the ideologically diverse regulatory reform coalition with a powerful model that legitimated competition as a practice which fulfilled the values of both efficiency and equity. The industries under regulation fought hard for continued regulation, but could not overcome the politics of reform.

It is only when the phenomenon is situated in this context that one can grasp one of the great ironies of contemporary deregulation. The prevalent business-inspired rhetoric of "getting government off the backs of the people" notwithstanding, deregulation has most strongly affected those regulatory agencies whose actions historically have been *least* odious to business. The agencies long criticized as having been "captured" by their regulated clients and serving those clients' narrow interests are precisely the agencies which are deregulating. Deregulation has affected primarily the industry-specific regulatory agencies created during the New Deal, such as the Civil Aeronautics Board (CAB) and Federal Communications Commission (FCC). Some industries, like airlines and trucking, were deregulated over the hostile and vociferous objections of the major corporate players and powerful unions of those industries. In contrast, the agencies universally reviled by business, such as the Occupational Safety and Health Administration (OSHA), the Environmental Protection Agency (EPA), and the National Highway Traffic Safety Administration (NHTSA), though cut back and to some degree subverted under a hostile Reagan Administration, have not deregulated. In short, the conditions were not there for a heterogeneous political coalition to support the deregulation of the so-called "social" regulatory agencies. But they were there for deregulation of price-and-entry regulated infrastructure industries.

The industries that have undergone deregulation—airlines, trucking, railroads, telecommunications, banking, oil, and natural gas—have something very important in common. They are "infrastructures," the basic services which underlie all economic activity. They are central to the circulation of capital and the flow of commerce. Historically, regulatory agencies have exercised administrative controls over infrastructure industries as part of the state's effort to construct a national arena for commerce and to stabilize the essential services upon which commerce depends. The type of regulatory controls exercised over these industries are known as "price-and-entry" controls. Agencies determined how many and which firms would compete in a given market, and set the basic prices that firms could charge. They substituted administrative decisions for market controls.

The deregulated industries share another characteristic. With the exception of the Interstate Commerce Commission, which began regulating the nation's railroads in the late 1880s, all were brought under regulation around the time of the Depression and New Deal. The agencies are industry-specific—each agency has jurisdiction over a particular industry only. While the main goal of New Deal regulatory agencies was to safeguard commerce, they also secured basic social equity. The "obligation to serve," a principle rooted in the old common law, was an essential feature of the regulation of infrastructure services.

I argue that the regulation of telecommunications, like that of other infrastructure industries, did serve the "public interest." However, the notion of the public interest embodied in the policies of the key government player, the Federal Communications Commission, was so conservative and narrow, and its range of available regulatory options so constrained, that these policies did indeed protect the principal parties of the telecommunications industry, as many critics have charged. Traditional regulation of telecommunications exhibited a typically New Deal cautious guardianship over industries and firms deemed central to commerce. The public interest character of the regulation of infrastructure industries for the most part was exhibited in that facilitation of commerce.

The regulation of infrastructure industries has been inherently conservative in other respects. The nature of price-and-entry regulatory structures is to construct operating boundaries and barriers to entry. In theory this permits existing firms to provide services essential to commerce wittout experiencing the destabilizing effects of competition. In short, price-and-entry regulation creates cartels. In so doing, the regulatory structures also facilitate socially valued "cross-subsidy" arrangements. For instance in telephony, long-distance rates supposedly were used to keep local rates low in order to encourage the universal expansion of the telephone network. Similar cross-subsidy arrangements were established in all infrastructure industries brought under regulation. However, because of these very arrangements, there always exist incentives for certain classes of consumers—primarily large corporate users—to drop out of or "bypass" the regulated system, and for would-be entrepreneurial entrants to service those users. In periods of high, sustained inflation, regulation generally exacerbates bypass incentives. The agencies grant the regulated industries price hikes which, under traditional cross-subsidy arrangements, hit large corporate users proportionately more. Technological innovations— particularly in telecommunications—provide potential bypassers with additional incentives and with the means to drop out of the regulated system. Dissatisfied corporate users and potential competitors may form an alliance that pressures the regulated industry in the regulatory arena.

The regulatory agency generally responds to technological innovations and by-pass demands as unwelcome challenges to the organizational "settledness," or even to the integrity of the agency itself. The agency often responds to such challenges conservatively, clinging to its tried and true formulae and policies and acting to safeguard the regulated system. The regulated parties also act to thwart challenge and to protect the status quo. It was this conservative dynamic of protectionism that aroused the ire of both left-liberals and conservative free market ideologues in the period of the late 1970s, a period when the political agenda had shifted from regulatory activism to one that questioned the efficacy of regulation.

## Regulation: Elements of a Theory

This book examines regulation and deregulation through the prism of American telecommunications. Most studies of American communications focus on either broadcasting or telephone, rarely on both. Conventional studies tend to be either economic or anecdotal histories of the respective industries, with an occasional bow to law and regulation. Or, they are policy analyses, steeped in the byzantine complexities of agency decisions, but bereft of a larger theoretical context. Yet the interrelation between the telephone and broadcast industries is not only important for an understanding of the process of regulation, but central to how deregulation came about in telecommunications. At another level, studies that look only at the deregulation of telecommunications miss the links to other deregulated industries—and hence miss the broad reasons for the deregulation phenomenon. This book examines both broadcast and telephone industries. It looks at regulation and deregulation in other industries. It situates the analysis of regulation and deregulation within the theoretical context of the relationship between the state and the economy in the American setting.

Telecommunication is a particularly interesting infrastructure because it not only is crucial for commerce, but also constitutes the public realm of ideas and discussion, and hence implicates the range of issues surrounding freedom of speech. This leads to two important subthemes. The first relates to telephony, and involves the tensions surrounding the benefits and drawbacks of a regulated monopoly infrastructure in a capitalist economy. The second relates to broadcasting, and deals with tensions among private ownership of the means of communication, the notion of a free and diverse marketplace of ideas, and the First Amendment quandary of regulatory controls.

As should be clear already, this book analyzes deregulation as the consequence of a mosaic of forces, of structures in interaction over time. The key piece in that moving mosaic (if such a mixed metaphor is permitted) is the nature of regulation itself, for it is through and in and against the traditional price-and-entry regulatory structures that the interplay of economic, technological, legal, and ideological forces took shape. The interplay of those forces constituted the conditions upon which political choices came to be made.

The importance of regulatory structures might be appreciated by contextualizing the role of technological innovation. An important factor in telecommunications deregulation, technological innovation was not an independent, abstract force, but a concrete dynamic situated within entrepreneurial opportunities, political discourse, and, most important, regulatory constraints. What is important about technology was how specific innovations reconfigured the internal balance of entrepreneurial interests—a balance created and maintained within regulatory policies and formulae. This dynamic of technological change *within* regulatory constraints became crucial, for example, as the FCC attempted to meet the demands of large telecommunications users for better service and freer options. The small policy changes initiated by these users' demands chipped away at the AT&T monopoly and the regulatory formulae which legitimized that monopoly. They inadvertently set in motion additional forces which culminated in the break-up of AT&T.

Hence I argue that an adequate understanding of deregulation must rest upon a historically rooted theory of regulation that accounts both for the genesis of agencies and for actual agency operations. Regulation emerged in the twentieth century as a political institution to address new, systemic economic and social problems. Regulation in many ways is the hallmark of the modern "interventionist" state. It is part and parcel of the dynamic of national development by private enterprise but directed in some fashion by the state. The long regime of regulatory oversight of infrastructures provided a rational foundation for economic growth and development—within a capitalist economic framework, of course.

To begin to address the question of deregulation, one must understand why regulatory agencies arose, what they do, and why they traditionally regulate particular kinds of industries such as telecommunications. The key is the role of the state in a capitalist economy. And this role lies at the heart of the question of the meaning of that ubiquitous, but maddeningly vague term of regulation, the "public interest." In all state action, of which regulation is one, the definition of the public interest is crucial; it is a sort of black box whose meaning or representation is the terrain of struggle.

The emergence of regulatory agencies constituted the building of *national* administrative structures in a state which had been institutionally localistic and court-centered. For much of the 19th century, the dispersed structure of American state power permitted an active judiciary to direct the course of economic development. Judicial activism facilitated the establishment of quasi-infrastructural services in the early part of the century, largely by means of eminent domain law and the granting of exclusive franchises to the builders of bridges, roads, or canals. Once the infrastructure was in place, judicial action favored business risk-taking (and consequently capitalist economic growth). With the exception of land grants and certain other subsidies, the economy was established by mid-century as a sphere largely beyond political intervention. This pattern changed by the 1890s, because the triumph of laissez-faire had created a general crisis of social control. Regulatory agencies grew in response to the needs and great changes fostered by the rise of the large national corporation.

But regulatory agencies are not of a piece. Central to my theory is the notion that agencies have different functions and different scopes of activity, which generally correspond to the historical conditions surrounding their creation. The particular nature of inter-business and wider political conflicts dictated the emergence of three different *types* of regulatory bodies, generally corresponding to three historical periods of origin.

Progressive Era (approximately from 1900 to World War I) legislation created regulatory bodies largely in response to popular political activism. These bodies were designed to relieve the economic and social instability caused by the large corporation and its tremendous transformation of social and economic life. These agencies were concerned mainly with the *general* character of economic activity. The antitrust division of the Department of Justice (formed in the aftermath of the Sherman Act) and the Federal Trade Commission (established along with the Clayton Act of 1914) dealt with broad matters of monopoly and competition. The Federal Reserve System sought to control the exchange and circulation of money. The Interstate Commerce Commission, although literally an exception to this categorization (because it regulated a single industry), upon closer examination fits rather well. This is due to the absolutely pivotal importance of the railroad for the conduct of commerce in the late 19th and early 20th century.

New Deal agencies such as the Civil Aeronautics Board and the Federal Communications Commission sought to create strong price and entry controls in *specific* markets, with the purpose of establishing stable cartels. This "industry-specific" type of regulation grew in response to the anarchy of the market during the Depression, and was vigorously sought after by various industries. The form of regulatory action introduced by the price-and-entry agencies is often labeled in the economics literature "producer protection." Both Progressive Era and New Deal regulation established federal political structures which functioned in two interrelated ways. First, by providing an extra-market policing function, regulatory agencies helped to rationalize corporate capitalism. Second, regulatory agencies provided an administrative framework within which important interest groups, primarily large corporations, could bargain, settle conflicts, and legally collude under state imprimatur.

The agencies of the 1960s and early 1970s, established in large part in response to liberal reform movements during and just after the Great Society, dealt with the *social* impact of businesses, not with their economic behavior *per se*. These new agencies were to regulate *all* industries, not specific ones. In contrast to the producer orientation of the Progressive Era and New Deal types of regulation, the Great Society agencies were oriented largely toward the values of consumers and the interests of those left out of producer-oriented interest representation. The Environmental Protection Agency and Occupational Safety and Health Administration are the best known of the "social" regulatory agencies.

However, the origin of an institution is different from the set of reasons and structures by which that institution operates or is maintained over time. I argue that there is a fundamental distinction between genesis and operationality. Although regulatory agencies should be differentiated according to the temporal political alignment of social and economic forces reflected in their creation, and according to their function, all regulatory agencies are situated within the same field of institutional power, and all regulatory agencies are united under the rubric of administrative law. Similar forces of institutional constraint, bureaucratic organization, and procedure affect all agencies.

Regulatory agencies constitute a new structure of federal political power in the American political system; they represent a mixture of legislative, executive, and judicial functions, able on the one hand to be flexible and informal and on the other hand to formulate hard and fast rules. In theory this flexibility permits regulatory oversight to be continuous and substantive. But regulatory agencies do not fundamentally alter the traditionally dispersed system of political power in the United States. The agency is generally the weakest player situated in an already constituted terrain of political power—including the pragmatic fact of actual functioning of the industry brought under regulation. Precisely because regulatory agencies do *not* centralize political power—agencies cannot direct economic production and they must vie with the many other layers of institutionalized governmental power at local, state, and federal levels—"bureaucratism" is endemic to them. This bureaucratism is seen in numerous time delays, in wrangling over jurisdiction, and in the multiple hearings at various institutional levels which any proposed regulation undergoes. The forces which engender bureaucratism in regulatory agencies push agencies to regulate conservatively.

Regulatory agencies may properly be seen as a mechanism of rationalization in advanced capitalism, but they are only occasionally successful at this. Their overall lack of power means they might serve as a forum to allow oligopolistic industries to police themselves, or, alternatively, they might punish some corporations for "externalities" (indirect, or spillover effects of business activity, such as pollution), but they usually are unable to act as planning bodies. Institutional and organizational factors are of critical importance in understanding how a regulatory agency actually operates. This relation between the originally conceived function of a specific regulatory agency and the bureaucratic constraints that mold its actual operation must be considered in any analysis of regulation.

## Telecommunications as Infrastructure

Why are some industries, like telecommunications, regulated while others are not? Put a different way, why are some industries considered to be imbued with a public function or affected with a "public interest?" Notwithstanding the fact that some (perhaps much) regulation at first glance seems to serve private, rather than public interests, this is not true of *all* forms of regulation. Certain industries, and certain types of industries, appear historically always imbued with something larger, something more general than private interest. This "something" is what we intuitively understand as the public interest.

Telecommunication constitutes one of the four essential modes or channels that permit trade and discourse among members of a society, the other three being transportation, energy utilities, and the system of currency exchange, or money. Transportation, energy, and telecommunication industries provide the services upon which all economic activity (beyond the level of self-sufficiency) depends. Money, at bottom a representation of value and the means of exchange of value, also is crucial for economic intercourse beyond the level of barter. These services are "connective" institutions. They are the channels for trade and discourse which bind together a community, society, or nation. They are central to the circulation of capital and literally constitute both the foundation and the limit for the overall economic functioning of a society. This is why transportation, energy, telecommunications, and currency systems are called infrastructures. They are the structures below or underneath.

As I suggested earlier, the construction and maintenance of infrastructures usually have been the responsibility of governments. A central contention of this study is that infrastructure industries are always the focus of direct state intervention, whether by way of promotion, subsidy, or regulation. This has been true in the Anglo-American context since 13th-century English common law courts declared certain kinds of occupations to be possessed of a special status—the so-called "common callings." Even in the United States, where the liberal tradition has meant that energy, transportation, communications, and even financial services—like all other capitalist enterprises—are private commercial ventures, government has been closely involved in their creation, maintenance, and oversight. In the 19th century, the state's involvement rested in acts of promotion and subsidy, and the extensive use of eminent domain law in the effort to establish quasi-public infrastructural services. In the 20th century the state's involvement has been the imposition of regulation and the establishment of complex systems of administrative control over these services.

Both governmental assistance and the imposition of regulatory controls were central to the establishment and ongoing operation of the American telecommunications system. State actions helped private corporations establish telecommunication services. Throughout its early years, the telegraph industry received critical infusions of federal and state subsidies. Congress legitimized telephony as a "natural monopoly," and established regulatory oversight to facilitate both the expansion of the nationwide telephone network and the reduction of business risk. Federal intervention facilitated the emergence of radio in the United States, first by constructing a patent pool among the major corporate patent holders of radio technology and later by engineering the formation of the Radio Corporation of American (RCA). The Federal Communications Commission, established in 1934, was given a wide mandate to oversee wire and wireless communications. The FCC attended to the public interest in telecommunications largely by protecting the existing structures of telephony and broadcasting (and the corporations which provided those services). Federal regulation stabilized the chaotic use of the radio airwaves for commercial broadcasters and oversaw a system of guaranteed fair rate of return for wired common carriers.

The legal principle upon which state intervention in these industries has rested is the commerce clause of the Constitution: "The Congress shall have Power . . . to regulate Commerce with foreign Nations, and among the several States. . . ."[1] This is important. If there is a *general* concept of the public interest informing state intervention into infrastructure industries, it is a commerce-based concept. State intervention in infrastructure industries generally has meant the creation of a national trading area where goods and services can circulate freely. To facilitate the actual circulation of goods and services, government imposed *common carrier* regulatory controls on the means of circulation.

As it emerged in transportation law in the late 19th century, the main principle of common carrier law was that a carrier must allow nondiscriminatory, that is, fair and equitable, access to its service at just and reasonable prices. Nondiscrimination would ensure that carriers would *serve* the needs of commerce rather than inhibit commerce. Part of the provision of nondiscriminatory access to their services meant that common carriers were mandated to interconnect their lines with other carriers. Most often, common carriers were characterized by economies of scale and were granted monopoly franchises. Among other things, such franchises granted the right to take private property for public use, through eminent domain. These legal tools facilitated the construction of an overall network. Regulatory oversight would ensure nondiscriminatory service and "fair" rates. Regulation thus took advantage of certain efficiencies deriving from the monopolistic organization of capital while presumably protecting against the abuses that monopoly power could bring. The key to common carrier law—and the regulation of infrastructure industries generally—rests in the fact that it satisfies the contradictory demand for a unified plan of national development within a system of private property.

## Telecommunications and the Public Interest

But state support and regulatory oversight did not simply help establish and protect telecommunication corporations and their services. They also secured certain broader public interest goals, goals linked to democratically based principles of fairness and equity. Telephone and telegraph companies were legally obliged to provide service to all, at fair and reasonable rates—known as "universal service." In part because of such obligations, the American telephone network traditionally was universal and efficient, and the service was comparatively inexpensive for the customer. It is significant that telephony achieved these ends as a government-regulated monopoly.

Broader public interest or equity-based values were attached to broadcasting as well. Broadcasters, though given licenses to monopolize a given radio frequency, were not to view that license as a property right. The airwaves were deemed the property of all the people of the United States, and the holders of broadcast licenses were required to operate as public trustees. Ultimately, broadcast regulation was founded upon a public domain argument, that the airwaves were a natural resource held in common—much like waterways. The state acted to protect and safeguard that commonly held resource. The public domain rationale rested upon a (now debated) scientific judgment as to the limited nature of the electromagnetic resource. Because not everyone who wished to engage in broadcasting could do so, government had to select individual licensees from a pool of prospective applicants. In a very real sense, the government endowed certain private parties with immense public benefits. Because of this, the broadcast licensee technically was deemed a "public trustee," and had to fulfill certain "affirmative" obligations.

The common carrier principle is really little more than a *commerce-based* notion of the public interest. As it was applied to telegraphy and telephony, common carrier law meant simply the guaranteed access to the means of transmission. Even when common carriage entailed, as it did in telephony, a policy which obliged carriers to extend service to all, this also can be considered to some degree a commerce-based policy. It allowed and encouraged the expansion of communication necessary for the free flow of commerce. The fact that people were given access to the telecommunications infrastructure was essentially a logical extension of expanding the marketplace.

Nonetheless, the fulfillment of the commerce function was responsible for the wider public interest accomplishment of making the telephone essentially a public utility, available (in principle) to all citizens. In this sense, even as it facilitates commerce, common carrier law embraces principles broader than commerce. The obligation to serve and not to discriminate among customers—rooted in the old common law—clearly embody principles of social equity.

There is another way in which commerce is not the only fundamental principle which underlies the regulation of telecommunications. Telecommunication is a peculiar infrastructure because it is a primary medium for the circulation of ideas and information, a realm where, in principle, political life can be discussed openly in accordance with the standards of critical reason. The regulation of telecommunications is more complicated and interesting than that of transportation, for example, precisely because in principle it safeguards the democratic right of freedom of speech.

There *is* a historical and logical—but uneasy—connection between the capitalist orientation to the market (that is to say, contractual freedom, lumped under what I have called the commerce principle) and wider civil freedoms (for our purposes here, the principle of freedom of speech and the creation of a "free marketplace of ideas"). After all, classical liberalism sought to carve out spheres of behavior free from control by the state. This primarily entailed the freedom to fashion contracts and engage in commercial activity. Contractual freedom rested upon the legal privilege granted an individual to *autonomously* regulate his/her relations with others by his/her own transactions.[2] This is why contracts are, in a sense, private law-making. The recognized autonomy of the individual in contractual behavior logically extended to the individual in other spheres of conduct, including the sphere of speech and ideas. Indeed, for a time the bourgeoisie's historic struggle for contractual freedom went hand in hand with the struggle for individual rights of speech and print. In Europe, the bourgeoisie promoted the development of a public sphere in opposition to the traditionalist and hierocratic forms of feudal authority. The Bill of Rights to the United States Constitution, cast within the natural law theory so intimately connected to the bourgeois revolution, protected speech and press from governmental intrusions. Both in Europe and America, the spread of private, partisan newspapers and journals in the late 18th and early 19th century constructed a sphere of public opinion which mediated between society and the state.[3]

The abstract connection between early capitalism and free speech had a concrete form as well. The marketplace in early capitalism often was both the site for the circulation of commodities *and* the site where public discourse took place. Central to the theory of freedom of speech are the notions that only in a free and open "marketplace" of ideas can a citizenry exercise democratic prerogative, and only in such an open marketplace can "truth" prevail.[4] The liberal separation of the state from the private realm of ideas was indeed essential to the creation of an independent public sphere. But this separation facilitates a democratic public sphere only to a degree, a fact that underscores one of the great tensions between liberalism and democracy. Just as concrete factors affect competition in the *economic* marketplace, the marketplace of ideas is greatly affected, if not essentially determined, by the available means of communication. The public sphere constructed by assembly in marketplaces and by a profusion of partisan newspapers is far different from a public sphere constructed by and within great and often centralized institutions of mass communication.

The liberal model of freedom of speech stops at the limit of commerce. The model assumes that a democratic public sphere will emerge consequent to the unimpeded, private actions of speech-entrepreneurs. But the results of the state's noninterference in the public sphere is much less clear when the means of communication are complicated, consolidated, and not generally accessible. The public sphere constituted by media of electronic communication greatly extend the public sphere and vastly expand the amount of information available, but at the same time create difficult problems of power. Because access to the modern public sphere was (and is) restricted to those with the capital to own a newspaper or operate a broadcast station, this mode of communication is essentially one of expanded *monologue,* with only indirect feedback mechanisms. While those with wealth can disseminate their views, the First Amendment "right" of most citizens is merely to listen and read. Yet a free marketplace of ideas implies *dialogue.* In short, the nature of the media of communication and the terms of access to them greatly affect the actual marketplace of ideas. If we take the liberal theory of the marketplace of ideas seriously, the limited access to centralized media constitutes a limit on self-government and substantive free speech.

The dilemma of broadcast regulation was this: how to safeguard the use of an important, technologically scarce, medium of commerce while maintaining the separation of the state from the private realm of ideas, *and* at the same time also facilitate a democratic public sphere? The solution was for a regulatory body to license would-be broadcasters, and suggest (not impose) broad and vague (not specific or concrete) principles of public interest licensee behavior.

The paradox of the liberal conception of the public interest in telecommunications, as embodied both in common carrier law and in broadcast regulation, is that it is inescapably bound to the commerce origin. The free speech function of communications media was assumed protected by safeguarding the commerce function of the telecommunications infrastructure. Because a free market in ideas is assumed to result from the absence of government interference, there has never been a viable ideology of positive government action to facilitate the exchange of ideas. The FCC assumed that a diversity of owners of broadcast media would result in a diversity of ideas. And yet the commerce-rooted imposition of common carrier law in telecommunications did indirectly serve broader free speech interests. Because of the commerce function of the telegraph and the telephone, access to those services was to be nondiscriminatory. The nondiscrimination principle indirectly served free speech interests by establishing the separation of the control of the means of communication (the "conduit") from the content of the traffic which went over those lines. Although less clear-cut and far less complete, the common carrier principle also applied to broadcasting. The broadcaster was legally obliged to air programs on controversial matters of public policy and to be balanced in that coverage. When a broadcaster permitted a candidate for public office to use the airwaves, that broadcaster had to open the frequency to all candidates.[5] These obligations might be considered quasi-common carrier in nature.

## Deregulation and the Public Interest

I argue that it is largely a commerce-based concept of the public interest which underlay the traditional system of telecommunications regulation. But regulation had powerful equity-based ramifications as well. Universal telephone service came to embody a principle that access to information and to the means of communication is part of being a citizen. Universal telephone service allows individuals to be part of the fabric of national life, if only due to a legally embedded principle of mandatory access to the equipment at cheap rates. Likewise, the scarcity rationale for the regulation of broadcasting created a public interest goal beyond the technical problem of allocating the electromagnetic spectrum, to wit, that the diversity of viewpoints and speech opportunities is crucial to a good society and a democratic polity. The principle of keeping content distinct from conduit, embedded in antitrust and regulatory "separations" policies, is, in a sense, a technologically rooted protection of freedom of speech. Separations policies constructed institutional boundaries between communications services: broadcasters were kept distinct from common carriers, telephone companies could not engage in telegraphy, AT&T could not enter the data processing industry. Notwithstanding the original commerce-based intentions underlying the system of telecommunications regulation, broader conceptions of the public interest came to be attached to that regulatory system *post hoc*.

Yet, historically, the application of the conceptions of "universal and nondiscriminatory service," the "marketplace of ideas," and "diversity of viewpoints" was always tremendously problematic in the traditional regime of telecommunications regulation. Indeed, as the ensuing chapters will show, regulation barely secured these broader ends of equity and fairness. Sometimes, in attempting to secure such public interest ends, regulation actually sabotaged them. The irony is that these broader notions of the public interest were "attached" to specific technologies and, further, to the regulatory protection of such technologies. As the technologies themselves change and the separation between them becomes more problematic, the broader notions of the public interest lose their material and legal moorings. This underscores the other great irony of deregulation. Liberals and public interest groups backed deregulation in large part because they saw "regulation as usual" as a form of regulatory "capture." The dissolution of regulatory protectionism and the forces unleashed therefrom served, however, to undercut the historic connections between particular telecommunications technologies and the broader notions of the public interest. The broader public interest goals became subsumed and redefined under the ideological rubrics of technological expansion and unbridled competition.

The deregulation of various industries underscores an important contemporary transformation of the concept of the public interest which goes well beyond the technological changes in telecommunications. I have noted that it is the New Deal, industry-specific, price-and-entry agencies which are deregulating. Traditional economic regulation created, at one and the same time, a complex system of producer cartels and service-based entitlements. Congress established the price-and-entry regulatory agencies to bring order, or "rationality," to various industries during the Depression. Such agencies were given authority over a single industry which was burdened by some destabilizing condition. Railroads, trucking, and airlines were beset by too much competition; telephony was burdened with problems of monopoly; radio broadcasting suffered from an absence of general technical operating rules; speculative banking practices undermined financial institutions. Regulatory agencies established how many and which firms could enter into business, set general pricing levels, and formulated rules specific to the operation of an industry, such as which routes a certain trucking firm would service or which radio frequency a licensee would inhabit.

In fulfilling the goal to stabilize these various industries, the price-and-entry regulatory agencies created structures of mutual benefit—or cartels—among the major interests (often including organized labor) in any particular industry. Industries and markets were "saved" precisely by not permitting marketplace controls to function freely. Regulation substituted administrative rationality and informal political decision-making for market rationality. Price-and-entry regulation constituted a form of state intervention which not only stabilized certain key industries but, in the process, fulfilled certain broad New Deal social policies as well. Regulation brought order to these industries, fixing stable market shares and prices. In so doing, it facilitated the broad unionization of those industries (which could be seen also as fulfilling the Keynesian macroeconomic goal of stimulating aggregate demand). Lastly, such regulation constructed a sort of service-based entitlement system. Regardless of profit potential, buses, trucks, and airlines had to serve out-of-the-way areas; local telephone service was made cheap and universally available; broadcasters had to fulfill (however nominally) the obligations of a public trustee. Regulation compelled that rates be skewed to facilitate the expansion of service. This generally entailed internal cross-subsidies that favored poor and out-of-the-way customers. In short, regulation constructed a reasonably stable system of mutual compromises and benefits to major corporations, organized labor, and even consumers. Deregulation undermines this complex set of benefits.

Deregulation serves to dismantle the easy functioning of regulation-enforced cartels. It permits the resurgence of competition and the anarchistic play of market forces. How such a political phenomenon could come to pass is very surprising, because the regulatory *control* of competition brought business certainty and relatively assured benefits to the parties of the various cartels. It is not generally in the interest of the major beneficiaries of an arrangement to seek alteration of the arrangement. Indeed, as if to underscore this point, the powerful interests of the deregulated industries generally opposed deregulation. Another factor favoring maintenance of the regulatory status quo is the bureaucratic nature of the regulatory agency itself. It is often asserted that regulatory bodies, like most bureaucratic organizations, tend not to shrink or dismantle themselves. Indeed, a frequent criticism aimed at regulators and agencies is that they try to expand their purviews and budgets. With deregulation, however, regulators surrender their expertise to the workings of the market. More shocking still, some agencies actually initiated the deregulatory process themselves.

A key cause of deregulation is the divergence over time of administrative rationality and economic rationality. Regulatory structures and formulae tend to reflect an internal balance of interests within a regulated industry. This is largely because the basic business and functional institutional patterns are set *before* the advent of regulatory controls. Regulation usually recapitulates these patterns and applies the coercive authority of the state to make them work. Over time, changes in the larger economic environment and technological innovation may alter the balance of interests in and around a regulated industry, but the regulatory structures and formulae may not adapt to these changes.

In theory, the informal, discretionary nature of regulation permits an agency to adapt to new circumstances. In practice, regulation tends to be conservative. In the case of the FCC, the Commission clung to familiar definitions and policies long after their applicability had become ambiguous. The agency, beset with many problems and conflicts, often clings to established rules and policies. Regulatory rules may make administrative, but not economic sense. Moreover, if the regulatory arena becomes too contentious, if the struggle between interests is too basic, the agency experiences additional pressures to become more formalistic. Regulatory delay and irrationality reach a point where business decisions are made uncertain. Regulated parties flee the regulatory arena for relief. New policy forums may then disrupt the settledness of regulatory conservatism.

To describe this process in historical terms, the liberal-left regulatory activism of the Great Society period not only produced new regulatory agencies, but pushed the older agencies to become more open to democratic (or at least non-industry) demands. The traditional regulatory arena, long protective of (if sometimes also bothersome to) the major regulated interests, waxed inordinately contentious and politicized. This phenomenon pushed agencies to become more formalistic, more prone to time delays and drawn-out judicial challenges. In a period of high inflation, regulatory activism helped modify rate increases such that large service users paid a higher proportional share of the "cross-subsidy." These pressures magnified the economic incentives for large users to bypass the regulated system and for new entrepreneurs to offer unregulated services that would sidestep the regulated industry's delicate system of producer cartels and service entitlements. In response, the traditional regulatory agencies enacted new rules to thwart such bypass.

Corporations, reeling under new obligations, costs, and time delays imposed by the new social regulatory agencies, counterattacked. They formed lobbying groups and foundations, and commissioned reports decrying the "overregulated" society. Corporations attempted to tie the decline of US economic productivity to excessive regulation. One effect of this corporate attempt to alter the reigning political discourse was to open up a greater space for the analyses of academic economists of regulation, who had been writing about the inefficiencies of regulation for years. In a strange sort of way, the corporate effort succeeded *and* failed. With the backdrop of a crisis in public institutions consequent to Watergate and the economic "stagflation'' of the 1970s, corporations largely succeeded in transforming a generalized populist dissatisfaction with government (including regulation) to a critique *of* regulation. But the regulatory agencies most affected were not the new social regulatory agencies so reviled by business. Rather, they were those agencies most criticized by academic economists—the New Deal price-and-entry agencies.

Notwithstanding the usual conservatism of regulation, political dynamics and technological innovation and changes in political culture can alter the conservative tenor of "regulation as usual." By the mid-1970s an ideologically diverse political coalition—including free-market economists located in key positions in the Ford Administration, historically pro-regulation liberals such as Senators Edward Kennedy and Philip Hart, and consumer advocate Ralph Nader—had emerged to reform regulation. Early reform stirrings coalesced around commercial airlines and the Civil Aeronautics Board. Despite vociferous opposition from the airline industry and nearly 40 years of CAB precedent, commercial air transport was deregulated. Early successes with airline deregulation (lower prices and reputedly higher efficiency) created further political impetus to deregulate other transportation carriers and other infrastructure services.

Telecommunication was affected greatly by the general environment of deregulation, yet in some ways both broadcasting and common carriage had already experienced changes which made them ripe for the deregulation impulse. The regulation of broadcasting had long been characterized by the protection of the conventional services of AM radio and VHF television from competitive entry. Although the FCC formulated various structural and content controls on broadcasters, their efficacy in securing "public interest" broadcasting was dubious. The broadcast reform movement set out to change this.

The broadcast reform movement (the communications "wing" of the many liberal activist consumer groups of the Great Society period, consisting of a loose coalition of liberal, often minority-group organizations dedicated to altering the broadcast system) utilized three identifiable strategies in the late 1960s and early 1970s. The most widespread of these was that of conducting challenges to the license renewals of existing broadcast stations. Petitions to deny license renewal were filed on the basis that such stations had not fulfilled their obligation to broadcast in the public interest. Reform groups were greatly assisted in this endeavor by the judicial expansion of legal "standing." This expansion enabled parties without property interests to argue before regulatory agencies. The second strategy entailed a call for the right of limited, but mandatory citizen access to broadcast frequencies. This included demands for airtime to respond to "controversial" advertisements, such as cigarette ads. Last, the reform movement initiated (or at least picked up and gave loud voice to) a new discourse on the potential of "new technologies" to alleviate the endemic problems of broadcasting. In particular, this discourse focused on cable television as a technology that could create a "wired democracy," able to transcend the limited and commercial system of conventional broadcasting.

License renewal challenges and access demands caused short-term but severe regulatory problems for broadcasters, and caused them to flee the regulatory arena toward Congress for relief. Congress took up broadcast industry demands for license renewal relief in hearings which by 1976 became bound to the broader (ultimately unsuccessful) effort to rewrite the Communications Act. At the same time, the broadcast reform movement's "new technologies" discourse, resonating with the material interests of non-broadcast entrepreneurs, slowly pushed the FCC away from its traditional policies of protection. Broadcast deregulation emerged from an unexpected combination of new technologies and mutually contradictory rules designed to protect conventional television broadcasting. The advent of satellite-delivered programs to cable operators caused contradictions in the regulations designed to restrict cable television. The subsequent inadvertent relaxation of conflicting regulations provided the FCC with a real-world case for judging whether broadcasters were, in fact, being injured by cable. When broadcasters could not show that they were injured by the relaxation of specific cable rules, the FCC, now taken with the general notion of regulatory reform, relaxed more of the rules. In addition, a crucial court case in 1977 established that certain other FCC rules designed to protect broadcasters were unconstitutional. By the late 1970s, the FCC had moved from the New Deal cautious guardian model of regulation, to one which worked actively to liberalize entry in the broadcast business.

The common carrier area had been dominated by a vertically integrated AT&T monopoly which was protected by the FCC. AT&T controlled long-distance telephony, was the local service monopolist in most metropolises, and supplied all of its equipment needs through its own manufacturing subsidiary. By the mid-1970s, however, the internal balance of interests in the industry had shifted—partly due to the entrepreneurial opportunities created by technological innovation and partly to economic incentives to bypass the regulated system. Again, technology is not an independent, abstract force, but a dynamic situated within contexts of entrepreneurial opportunities and regulatory constraints. Underlying this shift were two important factors: one, longstanding antitrust problems over AT&T's vertical monopoly, and two, the needs of a powerful community of large telecommunications users which was inadequately served by AT&T and wanted freedom from AT&T-imposed options.

AT&T, so adept at providing universal telephone service, was always suspected of using its vertical monopoly to internally manipulate its prices in order to raise profits. Such antitrust considerations resulted in the 1956 confinement of AT&T to the provision of regulated common carrier telecommunications only. The large, vertical monopolistic structure also was responsible for the company's inability to satisfy the more specific needs of large telecommunication consumers in the post-World War II period of business expansion. In response to the demands of these large users, the FCC opened special small parts of the Bell monopoly's operating environment to competition. These small entry "liberalizations" were permitted only because AT&T could not serve specialized users adequately. They were not intended or envisioned to open up AT&T's monopoly. Nevertheless, the FCC could neither foresee nor control the consequences of its actions. Entry liberalization encouraged the emergence of new technologies and new players into telecommunications common carriage, notably in "private lines" (special lines dedicated between two points, used increasingly for data carriage) and "terminal equipment" (telephone instruments and switching systems). Over the years, these new players (particularly the MCI Corporation) and large users would push continuously at the borders of the Bell System with new technologies and new services.

Such developments had two inadvertent but serious ramifications. First, they raised serious issues of public policy regarding the appropriate boundary between regulated and unregulated activities. And second, they placed AT&T's rate structure in potential jeopardy. These antitrust and liberalized entry matters became inexorably intertwined in the mid- to late 1970s. In 1974 the Justice Department filed an antitrust suit against AT&T, charging that the company had used its regulated profits to practice predatory pricing in competitive markets.

Faced with new competitive players and unclear regulatory boundaries, AT&T found its external operating environment and its policy arena, both for decades remarkably stable and certain, becoming increasingly unstable and uncertain. By 1976, partly at AT&T's urging, and partly the result of the deregulation environment, the policy-making arena opened to include Congress in an attempt to rewrite the 1934 Communications Act. Soon, however, all branches of government were engaged in efforts to formulate new national telecommunications policy—a process likened by AT&T's Chairman Charles L. Brown to "nothing less than a three-ring circus."

What began as a complex antitrust case in 1974 inadvertently became by 1981 a closed policy forum within which various economic and political concerns could be joined. In the context of Reagan Administration Justice Department negotiations, the need to solve pressing contradictions in domestic telecommunications common carriage could be reconciled with large users' demands for telecommunications options, with AT&T's desire to be freed of regulatory barriers, with national security considerations, and, finally, with the growing concern to protect and enhance American global interest in information technology.

The transformation of the concept of the public interest posed by the deregulation of these industries involves a shift away from a concern with stability and a kind of social equity to a concern with market controls and economic efficiency. In this regard, the deregulation of telecommunications commands particular attention. For, again, it involves not only the usual issues of political economy in the spheres of commerce and antitrust, but is characterized centrally by issues of public utility and free speech as well.

The divestiture of AT&T, and the relaxation of regulatory controls over broadcasting in particular, pose important questions about the nature of the modern public sphere. The foreseeable outcome of the divestiture of AT&T is increasing telecommunications options for business and the decline of the principle of universal service. The deregulation of broadcasting threatens to collapse the First Amendment's protection of messages to mean complete freedom for media owners only. Diversity and a free marketplace of ideas are declared to be delivered by the unfettered market. Telecommunications deregulation thus creates a distinctly modern political and philosophical paradox: how to guarantee meaningful freedom of speech in an age of information abundance. There are also basic questions about deregulation's effect on commerce. Given that a planned and stable telecommunications infrastructure was crucial to economic development and the free flow of commerce, will the opening of that infrastructure to competition secure similar results?

# Theories of Regulation

Theories of regulation spring from two main sources: welfare economics and political theory. Welfare economics refers to the belief in the capability of state intervention to secure both socially desirable economic redistributions and general economic efficiency. Traditional theories of regulation invariably center themselves around a concept of the "public interest" which is rooted in welfare economics. This concept of the public interest strikes an uneasy balance between elements of a command, or government-directed, economy and classical liberalism's doctrine of preserving a strict separation between the state and private property. The public interest legitimates limited state intervention in the marketplace, even though in theory the marketplace operates best without interference.

From political theory come various models of political dynamics that purport to explain the genesis of regulation and the behavior of regulatory agencies. Theories of regulation rooted in political theory are generally "private interest" theories. They assert that regulatory agencies serve private interests, whether those be the industries regulated or the regulators themselves.

The literature on regulation is extensive and sometimes confusing. It spans several disciplines, mainly history, political science, and law, and, more recently, economics and sociology as well. Historical studies examine the legislative debates and other circumstances surrounding the origin of regulation, attempting to discover what groups or coalitions initiated regulation, and who was served by it. Legal studies discuss the legislative mandates of agencies and the history of judicial treatment of agency actions. These histories, though important in their own right, generally tell us little about what regulation actually did or does. Economic theories tend to focus on the empirically approachable outcomes of specific regulatory processes, tested by assumptions of market efficiency. Finding that regulation often does not live up to its welfare economics rationale, these economic studies often move quickly, however, to functionalist, generally unwarranted theoretical conclusions as to the general "purpose" or "function" of regulation. Studies from political science sometimes steer a middle course, looking at origins and attempting to follow the analysis into operations. Most often, these studies propose theories of private interest to account for regulatory origin and practice. Sociological analyses tend to study regulatory agencies as complex organizations.

The difficulties of reconciling perspectives derive from the differences in approaches and in evidence considered. As Thomas K. McCraw suggests, the method of historians is distinctively empirical; economists use a theory-oriented testing of market efficiency; and political scientists and lawyers center on due process, legitimacy, and reform.[1] These orientations vary in conception as to what the public interest actually is, as well as in conception of the underlying model of the state. Neither conception is always made explicit and theoretical. I group theories of regulation under five general, ideal-typical categories: "public interest" theory, regulatory failure or "perverted" public interest theory, conspiracy theory, organizational behavior theory, and capitalist state theory.

To understand regulation, in my view, genesis and operationality can and must be separated but reunited at some later level of analysis. The *creation* of any specific regulatory body is wedded to the historical circumstances surrounding it, most important, the state of the industry and whether or not its internal market controls function to secure rational risk-taking, and whether or not the social and economic consequences of industry actions kindle popular ferment. How a regulatory agency *operates* once established, though not unrelated to the mandate of its creation, is a separate issue, resting upon complexes of organizational behavior and institutional constraints. Moreover, the dynamic of regulatory operation itself may change through time, due to historically altering relations within the industry, and changes within or without the agency itself. Conflation of genesis and operationality, also known as the "fallacies of origin and effect," is a major deficiency of much of the literature.[2] Yet any new theory of regulation and deregulation is indebted to, and also departs from, previous perspectives. Here follows a brief survey of the major theories, and their strengths and weaknesses. This survey is a necessary springboard into the theory offered in the chapter which follows.

## *"Public Interest" Theory*

The oldest of the theories regarding government regulation of business is the so-called "public interest" theory. Public interest theory lies behind both the "official" view of legislative intent and the many scholarly analyses which look at the history of regulatory origin. Broadly, this perspective holds that regulation is established in response to the conflict between private corporations and the general public. The creation of regulatory agencies is viewed as the concrete expression of the spirit of democratic reform. The agencies are seen as institutional manifestations of the victory of "the people" in their successful struggle against various corporate special interests. Stimulated by market failures and especially monopolistic abuses by corporations, popular clamor induced government to limit corporate prerogatives and to take control of some market activities. Made necessary by the unprecedented complexities of industrial technology and large-scale capitalism, regulatory commissions take as their guide, in the words of Charles Francis Adams, an early champion of railroad regulation, the "interests of the community." Informed regulators would harmonize the community's general interest with the specific needs of business.[3]

Historically, public interest theory went through two main phases. The early phase might be characterized as the "Granger" period, referring to the anti-monopoly activism of the agrarian social movements of the late 19th century—the largest of which was the Order of Patrons of Husbandry, or the Grange. For the most part, the farmers' movement was social and educational, and sought to preserve a localized and personalized agricultural society. The Granger movement did not have a coherent *political* program, but its demands reflected the farmers' distrust of business. Believing that carriers and middlemen robbed them of their just compensation, farmers argued that railroads and grain elevators should be placed under public authority. The agitation of these movements in the early 1870s helped induce local and state legislation to regulate railroad, warehouse, and grain elevator rates.

The role of farmer activism has been overemphasized in many historical accounts of the political events of the 1870s. The regulatory legislation of that period—the "Granger Laws"—was in large part the result of earlier *sectional* disputes over discriminatory railroad and warehouse rates. Legislative control over railroad and warehouse rates was a response to the disruption of traditional patterns of trade by the emerging interstate railroad system. Localities sought rate regulation in order to alleviate the effects of discriminatory rates on trade. In this effort, older mercantile and commercial interests often led the struggle for controls over railroad and warehouse corporations.[4]

Nevertheless, because of the broad anti-monopoly sentiment which informed such state legislation, it is appropriate to label that political perspective "Granger" public interest theory. Crucial to the Granger public interest perspective was an amalgam of traditional assumptions regarding economics, politics and society, and a new supposition regarding power. These assumptions were that competition was good, in the sense that competing economic units allocated goods and services efficiently and equitably. Monopoly was evil not only because it was inequitable but because concentrated economic power ramified into social and political power as well. Finally, political power was "public" power, to be used legitimately to curb monopolistic abuses.

In the Granger formulation, the public interest derives from the standpoint of the individual *producer,* who is taken to be the founding unit of the good society. This embodied the Jeffersonian ideal of the independent small holder, which lay at the basis of the traditional American conception of a democratic society. The Grange perspective held that by the late 19th century, corporate productive power had begun to displace the small independent producer in political, as well as economic importance. This perspective (adopted in many respects by the later Populist movement) reflected a profound distrust by local communities of the "alien" nature of large capital. Accordingly, the danger of the "trusts" and of economic power in general was perceived originally as a *moral,* rather than a purely economic issue. The legislative debates surrounding the passage of the 1887 Interstate Commerce Act and the 1890 Sherman Antitrust Act convey this moral fervor.[5]

In the subsequent pursuance of antitrust and railroad legislation, a contradiction soon became apparent between economic efficiency and political equity. The productive might and capacity of the industrial corporation had to be reckoned with. As the industrial corporation began to restructure the economy and society, the older moral vision of the independent producer (tied to a now declining agricultural social system) had to compete with a new and rising ideology which esteemed the economic efficiency of large-scale industrial production. Indeed, in the early decades of the 20th century, an ideology of "efficiency" came to command a normative power as a type of morality.[6] The early 20th century debate over "good versus bad trusts" reveals the ascendance of this ideology of industrial efficiency.

The second phase of public interest theory, the "Progressive" phase, reflected the altered economic conditions created by the large corporation. The efficiencies of the corporation essentially created the modern mass consumer. Public interest theory registered a shift from a conception of regulation as protecting the individual as *producer* to protecting the individual as *consumer.* Regulation sought then to maintain the economic scale of the giant corporation while "curbing its abuses."[7] In the view of Progressive public interest theory, regulation was imposed by government to correct inefficient or inequitable market practices. Where monopoly reigned, regulation would act to restore some degree of competition. In those instances where economies of scale made "natural" monopolies necessary or possible, the regulatory agency would function as a watchdog for the general welfare through the oversight of rates and profit levels.

In the perspective of the Progressives, then, democratic governmental power reconciled the tension between the needs of powerless consumers and the productive might of the corporation. This perspective can be found in the writings of Progressive Era intellectual reformers such as Walter Lippmann, Herbert Croly, and Walter Weyl, and is also evident in many of the official justifications of the policies of Theodore Roosevelt and Woodrow Wilson.[8] The Progressive public interest perspective informs the theoretical basis of an entire generation of American historians. From Benjamin Parke DeWitt through William Allen White, Charles and Mary Beard, Vernon L. Parrington, to Arthur Schlesinger, Jr., one finds similar versions of the history of reform as a successful moral drama in which the people, armed with democratic values, defeat the forces of corruption, exploitation, and privilege inherent in the "trusts."[9] Progressive public interest theory did not jettison the moral tenor of its earlier Granger phase, it merely shifted the subject of protection from the independent producer to the consumer. Progressive public interest theory essentially became the official ideology of the interventionist state. Over the years, the theory expanded its scope from the justification of narrow economic regulation to embrace the vision of the federal government as the protector of the weak, the poor, and the powerless. Again, the notion of the public interest which implicitly underlies this theory is its identification with the interests of consumers.[10]

Progressive public interest theory abounds with faith in the administrative process not only to protect powerless consumers, but also to effect rationality and fairness in the economy generally. Regulatory agencies are able to do this because of impersonal, nonpartisan, scientific expertise vested in a body which is continually in session. In the words of Joseph B. Eastman, Interstate Commerce Commissioner and later Federal Coordinator of Transportation from 1933–1936,

> Public regulation used to be thought of merely as a means of protecting the public against extortionate charges. It has that purpose, but it also has a much wider sphere of usefulness. It is needed for the welfare of the industry itself, to promote order and stability, prevent exploitation, and curb destructive competition and waste. The public served needs it, not only as protection against extortionate charges, but to prevent unjust discriminations, promote safety, reliability, and responsibility of service at known and stable rates, reduce expense both direct and overhead, and avoid a financial demoralization which in the end is as destructive to the public interest as it is to the private investors. . . . Our regulation in the past has operated too much on the cure basis, dealing with complaints after they arise but forestalling them. National planning has been conspicuous by its absence.[11]

Public interest theory treats the creation of regulatory agencies as the victorious result of the people's struggle with private corporate interests. Agencies employ the positive power of the state to take advantage of economic efficiencies and serve the general welfare, and in so doing, regulation protects the consumer from corporate abuses. Progressive public interest theory thus marries regulation as political response to corporate power with regulation as welfare economics. Regulation can curb abusive business practices *and* promote greater economic efficiency at the same time. The underlying conception of the state is a sort of positive pluralism. A neutral state can be mobilized through struggle to create administrative apparatuses which will serve the democratic public interest. Such apparatuses subsequently institutionalize within the state a "countervailing power" to powerful private interests. And such apparatuses "work" because they are nonpartisan and scientific.[12]

The strength of the public interest approach is that, when sophisticated, it is grounded in historical understandings about the origins of some regulatory agencies.[13] The theory is beset by some large problems, however. First, it generally places a Progressivist gloss on all regulatory agencies. In reality, some agencies were established not in response to the democratic demands of an abused public, but in response to the pleas of particular industries for protection and subsidy. Second, because public interest theory is tied to a pluralist theory of power, it slights the structural importance of the economy and of economic power. Hence, the identification of the "public interest" as the *consumers'* interest cannot account for the complexity of actual regulatory goals and practice. Much regulation is designed to benefit industry. Indeed, most regulation is designed to facilitate *commerce:* the benefits of regulation to consumers or industry are bound up in the facilitation of commerce. This latter point indicates a singular failing of the theory: it fails to look at what regulation accomplishes once an agency is established. As I will argue, it is vitally important to look at the conditions of the genesis of an agency, its mandated goals, and the dynamics of regulatory operation.

## Regulatory Failure, or "Perverted" Public Interest Theory

That public interest theory remains the yardstick by which regulation is measured can be seen in the mammoth literature assessing regulatory failure. In this perspective, the public interest is posited as either a theoretical standard or as a historical fact of a regulatory agency's birth. Subsequent *behaviors* of agencies are found to betray or "pervert" the public interest standard, as measured by various criteria such as democratic due process, economic efficiency, or bureaucratic rationality. The perversion of the public interest is seen in the many studies which assert that regulation has tended to serve the private interests of the industries under regulation. Again, this theory rests on the same below-the-surface assumptions as does public interest theory. This is why, as a whole, this literature is so strident and condemnatory of regulatory behavior. Regulatory failure theorists are public interest theorists betrayed.

This theoretical perspective marks an advance over public interest theory, in my view, because it confronts the rhetoric of public interest with the reality of empirical fact. The regulatory failure literature studies what regulation actually does. Much of it does a fine job describing the microprocesses of regulatory practice. After "exposing" the failure of regulation, these studies attempt to explain why the perversion of the public interest happens. Here we find many different explanations often related to different political orientations. Whereas the proponents of public interest theory tend to be political liberals, regulatory failure theorists run the political gamut, from free-market conservatives, to the epigones of consumer activist Ralph Nader, to neo-Marxists.

The most frequently cited general reason for the perversion of the public interest is the overidentification of the regulatory agency with the industry it regulates. Indeed, this is the most common analysis of the regulation of broadcasting by the FCC. There are various explanations for this phenomenon, but most are "influence" models. They postulate that the regulated industries come to exercise (undue) influence on regulatory agencies. I see three basic types of influence models: "instrumental," "structural," and "capture." These, of course, are ideal-types, and many arguments do not fit neatly into a single category.

"Instrumental" explanations focus primarily on personnel factors. In this perspective, the failure of agencies to live up to their public interest mandates has to do with the specific orientation of key agency bureaucrats. The standard explanation points to a "revolving door" between industry and regulatory agency for experts and high-level administrators.[14] There are varied interpretations of what this empirical fact means. Because industry and regulatory officials are drawn from the same social class, one assumption is that they share a fundamental outlook regarding the proper relation between business and government.[15] The argument does not have to rest on social origins. Put simply, because regulators are drawn in large part from the regulated industry, they tend to conceive the purposes of regulation with the industry's mind's-eye. Another such interpretation posits the eventual "venality" of regulators. Venality is said to derive from factors ranging from outright bribes (or, more often, industry solicitude toward regulators) to the future-orientation of regulators seeking to safeguard their employment opportunities in the regulated industry.[16]

Other instrumentalist explanations point to the political and social-psychological contexts of regulators' working lives. Some analyses find regulators uniquely vulnerable to various political pressures. Pressures from Congressmen who are self-serving and/or who serve the interests of powerful regulated constituents may force regulators to become compliant.[17] Regulators must meet frequently with representatives of the regulated industries and require good working relations with them. In fact, the regulator's sense of professionalism is mediated primarily through his/her relations with industry counterparts. Thus regulators have a built-in incentive to reduce interpersonal conflict. Eventually, the regulators come to see the problems and options of regulation in industry terms.[18]

Notwithstanding the descriptive accuracy of these assertions, their theoretical contribution is less clear. Instrumental explanations are weak, in my view, because they rest on the personal motivation and behavior of individual regulators. It seems highly unlikely that regulators, who possess such wide latitude of discretion, would act in the same manner across the regulatory spectrum over such a long period of time. Surely there must have existed "good" regulators. What explains the persistence of regulatory failure during the tenure of competent bureaucrats? More "structural" explanations seem more appropriate.

Structural analysis refers to the relationship between *institutions* which restrict and channel the possible options of the individuals who make decisions within those institutions. Thus, a structural explanation of regulator-regulatee "like-mindedness" might argue that industries can influence the selection of agency appointments through the political spoils system. Because appointments to regulatory agencies are considered political plums without serious political liabilities, presidents use the appointments to reward and retain the political support of important regulated industries. In other words, because agency appointments are so tied in to the political spoils system, industry can indirectly influence the composition of a regulatory agency.

A standard structural argument is that the regulated industries possess far greater resources than do the agencies (or other parties) in terms of personnel, money, and political influence. Arguing one's case in administrative or judicial arenas is so expensive that those parties with the most resources can be expected to prevail in most instances and over the long run. Usually poorly funded, agencies must depend on industry for technical information and expertise, and on Congress for their budgets. Compounding this (or perhaps, as a result of this), agencies are reactive—the regulated parties set the agency's agenda. In the case of the FCC, industry lobbying power is said to be magnified by the particular nature of the regulated industry. AT&T, at one time the largest corporation in the world, is infinitely more powerful than the FCC in terms of resources, intelligent attorneys and engineers, and political influence.[19] Because broadcasters have their fingers on the very means of publicity, local politicians are highly responsive to broadcasters' views, and the legislators make these known to the subordinate FCC.[20]

A major subset of the structural regulatory failure literature is the government-sponsored investigations of regulatory performance. There is a virtual industry of these reports.[21] For all of their differences in underlying political sentiment, all the reports found that regulation had failed in similar respects. They generally place the onus of such failure upon bureaucratic irrationality. Often they do not explicitly claim that regulation serves the interests of the regulated parties. That inference is left unsaid. The reports simply claim that regulatory agencies do not fulfill their missions and public interest goals, and that they fail to formulate clear and consistent policies.[22] All the government reports berate regulatory agencies for inefficiency and for failing to analyze and plan. The reasons postulated for this general incompetence include the observation that, ordinarily, public service doesn't attract good people; or that high agency turnover rate and insufficient funding prevent the establishment of an ongoing knowledgeable bureaucracy which can develop continuous, coherent policy; or that public agencies tend not to develop sufficient organizational capacities. The 1949 Hoover Commission Report, for example, argued that the quality of appointees was the single most crucial factor in the success or failure of regulatory agencies.

These reports and their recommendations are flawed, in my view, because they imply that the failings of regulatory agencies are due to their misorganization and poor leadership. The first Hoover Commission Report, for example, railed on about the FCC's failure to delegate authority. The report assailed the Commissioners' preoccupation with minor matters because this prevented them from devoting the necessary time and thought to the more basic issues of regulation. Such structural explanations of bureaucratic incompetence usually rest on instrumentalist fears of personnel corruption and subpar job performance. The analytical flaws of these government reports are underscored by the distinctly varied recommendations offered to remedy the problem. Nearly all reports agree that there is a problem of too much outside influence over regulatory agencies. Some suggest the problem is that agencies are not independent enough, particularly in the sense that their inadequate operating budgets force them to rely on the industry for information and expertise.[23] Recommendations to increase commissioner tenure or to separate executive from judicial functions in commissions largely seek to insulate agencies from outside influence—including politics and politicians. Conversely, other reports conclude that agencies are prone to industry influence precisely because they are too far removed from political oversight.[24] They recommend reforms which would allow closer Congressional or Executive control over agencies. Some reports recommend that agency ''management'' capacities be enhanced by increasing the power of the agency chairman.[25]

Perhaps the most influential of the perverted public interest theories, and one which pulls elements from instrumental and structural explanations, is ''capture'' theory. Capture theory is stronger than other perverted public interest theories. Whereas other theories claimed that, by various means, regulated parties come to exercise influence on agencies and commissioners, capture theory asserts that agencies are taken over or ''captured'' by regulated industries. Capture is, in the last analysis, an influence model as well, but the strength and completeness of this influence make it qualitatively different. The implication of capture theory is that a captured agency *systematically* favors the private interests of regulated parties and *systematically* ignores the public interest.

The paragon of capture theory is Marver Bernstein's life cycle of agencies model, formulated in *Regulating Business by Independent Commission*. Bernstein postulated a history of regulatory agency evolution. His model poses four periods in the historical life of any regulatory agency, a pattern metaphorically equivalent to a human life cycle: gestation, youth, maturity, and old age. The gestation period finds aggrieved groups demanding legislative redress, culminating in vague, compromise legislation that creates a regulatory agency. In its youthful stage, the new agency operates with the benefit of a supportive public environment. Despite the vagueness of its mandate, the young agency is crusading and aggressive in dealing with problems and the industry generally. The agency is staffed by young, inexperienced professionals, eager to do their jobs and establish their reputations. Relations with regulated parties are generally hostile.

As the agency matures, the brouhaha which created it subsides, and the agency adjusts to the conflicts it faces. Without sustained public support or much Congressional interest, the agency adapts to its new environment. Operating budgets do not rise very quickly and the "young Turk" staffers tend to leave the agency. The agency transforms itself from a policeman to a manager. Personnel turnover is high and expertise falls. The agency comes to rely on routine and precedent, and seeks to maintain good relations with its industry. As the agency hits old age, it becomes a bureaucratic morass which, because of precedent, serves to protect its industry.[26] The age variable seems crucial to Bernstein's and roughly similar life-cycle capture models.[27]

The Bernstein model and capture theory generally are descriptively alluring. They suggest that regulatory impetus and operations change historically—that where agencies have been created by popular reform, some process unfolds whereby they come to serve other interests. This basic argument is not new. Other classic confirmations of the main tenets of capture theory are G. Cullom Davis' description of the transformation of the Federal Trade Commission in the 1920s and Samuel P. Huntington's analysis of the early Interstate Commerce Commission.[28] One of the earliest statements of the essence of capture theory is the oft-quoted 1892 letter of Attorney General Richard Olney to the president of the Chicago, Burlington and Quincy Railroad. In this simple and bald letter, Olney sought to dissuade railroad leaders from their efforts to exterminate the fledgling Interstate Commerce Commission. Olney proposed instead that the railroads "utilize" the agency.[29]

The problem with Bernstein's model, and perhaps with capture theory in the generic, is that it is *quasi*-history. The relatively unitary treatment of agencies ignores the different circumstances surrounding, and reasons for, their creation.[30] Also, the theory is causally imprecise about agency behavioral stage progression. Bernstein's stages of an agency's "life" evolve according to natural law. The impreciseness of causation and definitiveness of evolution seem partially due to the questionable biological metaphor.[31]

On the other hand, Bernstein's model provides helpful suggestions for a more complete theory. If (some) agencies move from a public interest orientation to a regulated interest orientation, one of the reasons, according to Bernstein, is a shift in political alignment and/or change in the larger political climate. In Bernstein's model a crisis or scandal can initiate a return to the beginning of the cycle. Regulation to some degree responds to the "political agenda." As I see it, this correctly underscores the importance of political dynamics to regulatory practice.

Two of Bernstein's observations are of particular importance for my theory. His work suggests that regulatory agencies face broad policy dilemmas because of the conflicting demands—for instance, to promote and to police—mandated by originating legislation. Also, Bernstein identifies the formalism of agency procedures and the conservative reliance on precedent as major features of the operations of the mature regulatory agency.

The problem of the vague and conflicting legislative mandate is central to Theodore Lowi's version of capture theory in his influential book, *The End of Liberalism*. Lowi claims that the compromise legislation which marked the founding of many regulatory agencies called for contradictory goals, to be resolved (or avoided and masked) by ceding tremendous discretionary power to the agencies. Upon close examination, Lowi found many regulatory statues devoid of any meaningful guidelines beyond a perfunctory and abstract proscription to regulate in the public interest. Unclear, internally inconsistent mandates along with the delegation of vast discretionary power created a new source of power both for the extension of government into spheres of life from which it had been absent and for interest groups to seize and manipulate. Claiming that pluralism and interest group politics have worked only too well, Lowi sees regulatory agencies as brokers of state power and largesse. They constitute centers of private power within the state.

He constructs a fascinating and complex analysis which finds administrative discretionary power increasing as newer regulatory bodies are created to deal with more abstract, general, and systemic aspects of economic activity.[32] Lowi lays out a functional typology of regulatory actions and purviews. It establishes that all agencies do not perform the same functions; that the antitrust regulation of the Federal Trade Commission involves different principles than, say, the price-and-entry regulation of the Civil Aeronautics Board. Lowi suggests in a later essay that political processes vary with different types of public policy outputs.[33] This marriage of political dynamics to organizational behavior represents a theoretical approach I share. Lowi's central, potent conclusion is that administrative discretion becomes a form of bargaining that favors the powerful and the organized. Regulation thus undermines the rule of law and corrupts the democratic process.

However, because in Lowi's view the broad delegation of legislative authority is the main problem, his analysis glosses over other real differences between regulatory agencies. The reasons for regulatory expansion (in the number of agencies and in their functional purviews) are left unclear, if the consequences of such are not. In the last analysis, Lowi's model best accounts for the "client" or broker-state politics typical of New Deal regulatory agencies. It does not shed enough light on how and why the social regulation of the 1960s and early 1970s came about, or why, as I will argue, such regulatory agencies as the Environmental Protection Agency and National Highway Traffic Safety Administration are *not* necessarily examples of broker-state politics.

## Conspiracy Theory

Conspiracy theory shares perverted public interest theory's assessment of the results of regulation. Regulation serves the interests and goals of the regulated industries at the expense of the public. Where conspiracy theory is different is that it denies capture. The word "capture" implies that the agency existed in a different state previously. Capture theory thus admits a public interest origin of regulatory agencies. Conspiracy theory argues radically that agencies were set up at the *behest* of industries to serve their interests. Reform and public interest rhetoric may have been bandied about, but such rhetoric functioned only to mask the *private* nature of regulation—in both genesis and operation. Conspiracy theories generally emanate from two paradoxically diverse sources, left-wing political theory and conservative free-market economic theory.

Horace Gray's seminal 1940 essay, "The Passing of the Public Utility Concept," is a major precursor to conspiracy theory. It is a nascent conspiracy theory because the position he outlines in the essay is fluid and in a sense undeveloped. Gray allows that the *concept* of public utility may have originated in public interest concerns to protect consumers against excessive charges and discriminations. The actual institution of public utility regulation, \certainly in operation if not also in genesis, however, establishes and protects monopolies. In stinging language, Gray observes that capitalists appropriated the public utility idea in order to use the state's coercive power for the construction of protected monopolies. He writes:

> Thus, between 1907 and 1938, the policy of state-created, state-protected monopoly became firmly established over a significant portion of the economy and became the keystone of modern public utility regulation. Henceforth, the public utility status was to be the haven of refuge for all aspiring monopolists who found it too difficult, too costly, or too precarious to secure and maintain monopoly by private action alone. Their future prosperity would be assured if only they could induce government to grant them monopoly power and to protect them against interlopers, provided always, of course, that government did not exact too high a price for its favors in the form of restrictive regulation.[34]

In other words, public utility status was a commodity which industries clamored after. The flaw of regulation, in Gray's view, was structural and hence inevitable. He thought it a complete delusion that private privilege could be reconciled with the public interest by means of what he termed the "alchemy" of public regulation. Worse, because of the veneer of public control, regulation legitimized monopoly, exploitation, and political corruption. The clearest solution to this was public ownership.

The most widely known example of conspiracy theory, the work of Gabriel Kolko, addresses similar themes. He writes in *The Triumph of Conservatism*, "It is business control over politics, rather than political regulation of the economy that is the significant phenomenon of the Progressive Era."[35] Reversing the standard understanding of American economic history, Kolko marshals evidence to show that the centralization and concentration of capital was far more a desire of business than a reality at the turn of the century. The merger movement was an attempt by businesses to forestall or circumvent destructive competition, an attempt which *failed*. Mergers were not more efficient, Kolko argues. In fact, they led to *more* competition. Moreover, attempts to stabilize prices and/or fix a division of markets through industrial agreement, such as the "Gary dinners" in the steel industry, failed miserably. This anarchic situation held in each of the six key industries analyzed by Kolko.

Kolko argues that it was not the existence of monopoly that caused the federal government to intervene in the economy, but the *lack* of it. The genius of big business inhered in formulating a positive theory of the state, a "political capitalism." Taking their cue from the process that had transpired earlier in railroading, industry leaders realized that only the federal government possessed the power to rationalize the (inevitably chaotic) market. Thus they championed federal regulation of business. Moreover, centralized *federal* regulation would protect businesses from the less controllable states. Hence regulation could help regularize the conditions of doing business by providing a uniform set of rules formulated in the main by business leaders themselves.

In 1887, Kolko argues, large railroaders sought government regulation and supported creation of the Interstate Commerce Act in order to suppress the destructive, internecine competition for shipping contracts. Railroads sought federal authority to guarantee their pooling arrangements and thus free them from the destructive anarchy of the market. Likewise during the Progressive Era, big bankers favored the Federal Reserve Act because it would dampen interest rate competition. Established drug firms favored food and drug legislation because it would erect entry barriers to the quacks whose practices had been undermining consumer confidence. Timber interests supported forest conservation because it would enforce preservation of the resource that yielded their profit. Meat packers favored federal quality standards and inspection because such controls would prevent smaller packers from producing and selling the low-quality products that might result in the banning of American meat from European markets. The Clayton Act and Federal Trade Commission were supported by business because they were thought to be useful tools in the suppression of competition.[36]

Kolko's analysis was joined by subsequent revisionist histories.[37] James Weinstein looked at labor (workman's compensation) and antitrust (FTC enabling mandate) legislation, along with the municipal reform movement (drawing on the work of Samuel P. Hays), and found in the National Civic Federation a class-conscious business elite capable of directing the structure and content of Progressive "reforms." In Weinstein's view, the reform impetus of the Progressive Era had lain in working-class upheavals. Nonetheless, a segment of the capitalist class saw political reform as a way of solving economic problems. These businessmen were able to coopt the reform impulse by virtue of their vast political influence and ability to articulate a new ideology of social responsibility and efficiency. Under the guise of political reforms, large corporations thus established a system where state power would supervise and rationalize private corporate activity.[38]

Again, what distinguishes conspiracy theory from capture theory is that the former argues that the purpose of regulation, in genesis and in operation, is to serve industry, to rationalize capitalism through political means. In contrast to the other theories we have looked at, conspiracy theory looks closely at the politics of regulatory creation and finds the key participation of businessmen. However, conspiracy theory generally does not delve into the actual ongoing operations of the regulatory agencies. On this point the model is deductive rather than empirical. It reads subsequent regulatory behavior and outcomes back into genesis because of the structure and centrality of capitalist power. For all the heated debate over regulatory origins, conspiracy theory does not confront the fact that agency policies are frequently dismal *failures*. How such failures serve industry is left unexplained. For example, the railroad industry's desire for legalized pooling was not secured in law until World War I. But the legalization of pooling is cited as the main reason why the industry supported the Act to Regulate Commerce in 1887.[39]

Moreover, with regard to origins, it is not enough simply to point out that some businessmen were involved in regulatory legislation. For example, other scholarship finds the impetus for national railroad regulation to be complex and multifaceted, involving various agricultural, mercantile, and railroad interests. Indeed, more than one study found that railroad men supported regulation rather reluctantly. An empirical study found that ICC rate policies before World War I responded far more to shipper than to railroad interests.[40] Other studies point out the complexity and divided nature of business support for regulation in various industries.[41]

Though overdrawn in the assessment of regulatory origin, the conspiracy model brought a systemic approach and utilized new types of information. Both Kolko and Gray argued that, contrary to conventional understanding, the conflicts surrounding regulatory origin were those of industrial instability and competition, rather than those of monopoly. Kolko's analysis correctly highlighted the new interventionist role of the state, and its effort to rationalize capitalism in a period where the market alone could not do so. Regulation historically helped to address ongoing economic and social problems as a new political institution. This is a key insight. Furthermore, conspiracy theorists highlighted the important fact that capitalists very often supported federal regulation. But these theorists largely misinterpreted that fact. The reason that capitalists generally supported federal regulation (sometimes reluctantly) was not because they necessarily believed they could control such agencies. Rather, they supported federal regulation for the Weberian-based reason that centralized federal regulation alleviated the uncertainty and irrationality of conducting business in an environment subject either to internecine, lawless competition, or to a myriad of conflicting state and local regulations.

Surprisingly, arguments similar to Kolko's began to be advanced by some economists, though without either Gray's preference for public ownership or Kolko's condemnation of "political capitalism."

## Economic Capture-Conspiracy Theory

Exponents of the "Chicago school" of free-market economics argue that regulation is a crucial mechanism by and through which many industries seek to control entry and construct artificial cartels. Regulation is a form of government-sponsored "producer protection." Most economic analyses of regulation are not explicitly theoretical with regard to the genesis of regulation. Such studies consist of empirical examinations of particular regulated industries, based largely around price theory. The economic studies conclude that price-and-entry regulation in competitive industries generates economic inefficiencies. These inefficiencies are manifested in higher prices, higher production costs, and slower technological progress than would be the case without regulation.

An early target of such studies was the domestic airline industry. Various studies claimed that domestic airline prices would be lower if there were no regulations. Using the Los Angeles-San Francisco and intra-Texas unregulated routes (unregulated, because *intrastate* air transport does not fall under Civil Aeronautics Board authority) as comparison, some economists concluded that CAB regulation significantly increased price levels and price discrimination. High-density intrastate airfares were found to be more than twice as cheap as analogous interstate airfares. The intrastate carriers were found to be more efficient operations as well. Regulation resulted in excess capacity—too many planes and too many flights for the existing demand for air travel. Though fares had been set at cartel levels by the CAB, profits had been wasted away through excess capacity. This led early economic analysts of airline regulation to the conclusion that regulation produced higher prices for the consumer, but without the industry itself benefiting from such, largely due to imperfect cartel management by the CAB.[42] Similar economic studies with similar conclusions were conducted on the regulation of gas pipelines and of surface transportation.[43]

The excess capacity argument resonated with an earlier hypothesis made by Harvey Averch and Leland L. Johnson, in a now-famous article, "Behavior of the Firm Under Regulatory Constraint." The rate-regulated firm is permitted to earn no more than some fixed proportion of the value of its capital. This constitutes the basis of the regulatory formula expressed by the phrase "fair rate of return." Averch and Johnson (and another economist, Stanislaw H. Wellisz) found that firms subject to rate of return regulation have an incentive to use inputs in proportions that differ from expected cost-minimizing input levels. That is to say, so long as regulatory pricing made plant investment the most important component in the calculation of the rate base, regulated firms would tend to overcapitalize. The rate-regulated firm would find it profitable to employ more capital relative to labor than is consistent with minimization of costs for the quantity of output produced—resulting in overall inefficiency.[44] Subsequent A-J-W school arguments found that the rate-regulated firm would seek to enter competitive markets since it could cross-subsidize any losses with the guaranteed profits of its monopoly market. The cross-subsidization of services would be profitable to the extent that it allowed the firm to expand its rate base.[45]

Implicit in these empirical investigations was the theoretical premise that regulation is a means of cartel management. Formulated explicitly and with vigor by George J. Stigler, this theory saw regulation as a highly valued political benefit actively sought by many industries. Once acquired, regulation essentially is designed by the industry and operates to that industry's benefit. All firms seek to maximize profits, and profits will be increased if competition is reduced or government subsidies are obtained. Four main mechanisms enable an industry or occupational group to be protected from competition: direct subsidy, control over entry, regulations which affect substitutes and complements, and price-fixing. Of these, argued Stigler, entry regulation is best because it uses the coercive power of the state to restrict the number of benefiting parties.[46]

Some industries, though, did not seem much affected by regulation. In a comparison of regulated and unregulated electric utilities from 1907 to 1932, Stigler and Claire Friedland found no measurable difference on the level of utility rates, on the charging of discriminatory prices, or on the market value of utility stocks.[47] In a somewhat different sense, health and safety regulations also have been accused of having no efficacy. Several econometric studies argue that regulatory efforts to improve health and safety have been statistically insignificant in achieving these goals. Whatever small improvements had occured in traffic safety, environmental pollution, and workplace safety predated the activities of the agencies.[48] And though they have little efficacy in achieving stated regulatory goals, the economists argued that such regulations *do* function to increase system-wide economic inefficiency. In this view, regulation acts as a significant sink on GNP and a drain on productivity. Murray Weidenbaum and Robert DeFina, then of the American Enterprise Institute, calculated that government regulation cost $66 billion in 1976 and up to $100 billion in 1979. And these figures are low compared to the *US News and World Report* estimate of $105–$130 billion a year.[49]

It should be noted again that most empirical accounts of producer protection/cartel management are not especially concerned with general *theories* of regulation. They are concerned with the economic results of regulation, as tested within price theory. To the extent that these accounts *are* self-reflectively theoretical, they pose explanations of regulation which employ *economic* theoretical constructions, such as supply/demand and rational actor models. These explanations float between conspiracy theory and capture theory. The extent to which they are conspiracy theories depends on how functionalist and schematic are their explanations. Stigler's model, for instance, sets up an *a priori* functionalist explanation that regulation will be supplied to those who value it most. The external influence on, or creation of, regulatory policy depends not on the number of constituents interested nor on the intrinsic social value of one policy as opposed to another, but rather on the *intensity* of interest among those concerned. The unmistakable inference is that regulation, in genesis and in operation, reflects the needs and desires of the most interested regulated parties. Actual historical matters need not be consulted.

Economic theories of *capture* (also characterized by a logical functionalism and paucity of historical presentation) utilize the "intensity of interest" argument and bring it to the regulatory process and legislative arena. The central notion underlying most economic capture theory derives from the work of Anthony Downs. Drawing from Downs, economic capture theory posits a government run by individuals who try to maximize a private, rather than public, utility function. Public officials are seen not as bureaucrats concerned with public matters, but rather as private individuals trying to maximize their own "utility" (staying in office, allocating more power to themselves, ensuring lucrative employment opportunities outside government—just in case) in much the same way a firm maximizes profits.[50] In effect, regulation (and most political action for that matter) is just another commodity which obeys the laws of the market. The needs of politicians/regulators and the needs of interested industrial parties meet in the familiar field of supply and demand, with cartel theory helping us to locate the supply and demand "curves."[51]

Richard Posner and Sam Peltzman thus argue that regulation is a device whereby politicians transfer income or power to well-organized groups if the groups will return the favor with votes and contributions. Peltzman, Fiorina, Niskanen, Weingast, and to some extent, Noll, to name the most widely known, all employ a "rational actor" model of regulatory behavior which focuses on the self-interested actions of key bureaucrats. With different emphases, they all essentially argue that the structure of Congressional politics makes for an "iron triangle" of legislators, regulatory bureaucrats, and industrial beneficiaries who work to mutual benefit.[52]

Most economic capture theorists simply assert the historical validity of capture, or implicitly dismiss genesis questions as unimportant. Either it doesn't matter who runs the agencies, because the rational forces of politics and economics produce the expected results regardless, or such forces select for industry-minded regulators. Operationality is read back into genesis. But because some versions of capture theory are predicated on *intensity* of interest, they concede that *a priori* predictions of the direction of income and power distribution are impossible to determine. Some versions of economic or rational actor theory thus remain open to the recognition of political dynamics.

Richard Posner contends that much regulation may be the product of coalitions between industry and customer groups, the former obtaining some monopoly profits as the latter obtains better service or lower prices than either would in an unregulated market. Posner looks at the interaction of interest groups in the formation of regulatory policy to find a kind of state-sanctioned redistributive politics—hence the ingenious view of regulation as a form of "taxation."[53] But this is *not* public interest theory. The interest group bargaining takes place at the expense of the unorganized. Moreover, there is no conception here of the state as a positive actor. The state is little more than the vehicle for private group compromise and the source of coercion to enforce that agreement.[54]

The economic capture theory, like capture theory generally, is based on a pluralist view of the state. Governmental agencies, essentially neutral apparatuses of coercion, can be captured—sometimes even created—by the parties with the most resources and most intense interest. Normally, that party is an industry—but not always. Indeed, such a perspective of the state underlay a newer claim by political conservatives that the advent of environmental and safety regulatory agencies in the 1960s and 1970s represented a different kind of capture. The argument is that social regulation in particular (and regulatory activism in general) was advanced by, and marked the ascendancy of, a "new class." Consisting of young upper-middle-income liberal professionals who came of age in the context of post-World War II affluence, members of the new class tended to work in nonprofit institutions such as universities, hospitals, and especially government. This class was fundamentally resentful of private enterprise. Its power base was government generally, and regulation specifically. The new class was said to create and/or capture regulatory agencies in order to increase its power and to impose its (elitist) vision on US society. The "new class" aggrandized itself by championing the expansion of the public sector.[55]

Clearly, the "new class" argument is different from the standard economic theory of regulation as producer protection. Yet it links up with one important variant of the economic theory—that regulation causes gross inefficiencies. The increase in the type and amount of regulation, and the subsequent prolongation of the timeframe for regulatory decisions (referred to as "regulatory lag") acts to slow GNP growth and causes general productivity decline.

The major advance of the economic analysis of regulation, in my view, is its concreteness. Studies look at specific regulatory policies and attempt to measure their effects against roughly comparable examples of unregulated markets. The notions of producer protection and cartel management are particularly valuable, for they capture a central feature of traditional economic regulation. However, serious problems emerge, as I see it, when economic analysis moves toward a general theory. While economic measures may permit insightful empirical comparisons, they cannot assess things which do not easily compare or which are not measurable in purely economic terms. One can plot the effects of health and safety regulations on economic efficiency, for example, but in so doing the researcher must exclude noneconomic variables from the analysis and must implicitly accept crucial, highly debatable assumptions about what constitute "effects" and "efficiency."

Conflating genesis with operationality, economic capture-conspiracy theories do not specify how industries manage to get regulatory agencies established. Even if agencies are seen as serving the general needs of regulated parties as a group, how do group needs get translated into group pressures and action? This, of course, is an argument regarding the fractured nature of "interests." At the simplest level, most regulatory agencies serve multiple regulated parties. The FCC, for example, regulates commercial and nonprofit radio and television, amateur and private point-to-point communications, international and domestic telephony and telegraphy. Surely these different industries and constituencies often have different and deeply conflicting interests. Of equal certitude is that conflicts engulf parties *within* those particular industries as well. The greater the number of regulated parties, presumably the more difficulty in conspiring to create or coopt a regulatory agency.[56] This matter of the fractured nature of industry interests affects the agency in respect to both genesis and operation. What does it mean to claim, for example, that the FCC "serves" an industry by design, or is captured by "the" industry? Logically, given the conflict of interests, for the agency to operate in the *general* interests of the regulated industries, it cannot be beholden to any one of those interests. But the economic theory does not recognize genuine independence of operation to the agency. Two more recent theoretical schools do acknowledge an autonomy to agency operations.

## Organizational Theory

To claim that there is an organizational "theory" *per se* may be overstating the case. However, there is a loosely identifiable group of studies of regulatory policy and behavior that considers the organizational imperatives of an agency to be the key variable in understanding regulatory behavior. In contrast to the "regulator as politician" perspective, the subject of the organizational model is the agency as an organization *per se*. Organization theory finds that regulatory behavior can be best understood by examining basic, organizationally-rooted imperatives of the agency.

This can mean different things. On the one hand, it means that organizations guard their autonomy, and thus are not easily influenced by *any* party. On the other hand, it may mean that agencies, buffeted by a myriad of demands and conflicts, and possessing limited resources to deal with complexity, operate with limited rationality and search for "satisfactory," as opposed to "optimal," outcomes.

One variant of the organizational perspective resonates with the politically conservative argument that regulation imposes great costs on the economy. This view finds that regulatory agencies, concerned with organizational preservation, and regulatory staffs, preoccupied with professionalism, will be *regulation-oriented* rather than industry-oriented. Regulators want to do what they are hired to do— make and enforce regulations. They are regulation-minded, that is, they act under the presumption that more and better regulations will solve the problems brought before them. The historical growth in number and size of regulatory agencies and the expansion of their jurisdictions are seen as evidence for this perspective.[57] Variations of this view are held by some former regulators. For example, John W. Snow, former transportation regulator, has written:

> Agencies like NHTSA are created largely in an open-ended way. The Congress says that there is a problem of deaths and injuries on the nation's highways. They create an agency to solve the problem, but they do not tell the administrator or the staff of the agency what the time-frame is or how much of the problem the Congress thinks can be resolved through regulation. The administrator of such an agency finds himself with a strong mandate, a mandate to achieve safety with little or no consideration for the cost. Thus, there is a built-in bias to issue more and more regulation.[58]

It remains for other theorists to argue that the plethora of regulations serve only the needs of agencies and regulators, and wreak havoc on the regulated industry. Economist Paul W. MacAvoy writes in this vein to some degree. In his early study of natural gas regulation, MacAvoy claimed that stringent regulation led to inadequate returns and "regulation-induced shortages." He expanded this thesis to other rate-regulated industries. He asserted that under the inflationary spirals and consumer activism of the late 1960s and early 1970s, coupled with the regulatory lag in making rate decisions, agency-allowed annual percentage price increases were smaller and output growth larger than in those industries not subject to price controls. With reduced profitability, annual real net investment declined, slowing the growth rate of production, and causing regulated industries to lag behind the rest of the economy by the end of the 1970s. Worse, according to MacAvoy, the investment cutback in energy and transportation industries governed by price and entry regulation would show up ten or so years hence in the form of serious and irreparable service shortfalls. With regard to health and safety regulation, because there are no price limits imposed by such regulation, MacAvoy claimed that the higher costs are passed on to consumers in higher prices, thereby reducing consumption growth and ultimately reducing economy-wide GNP growth.[59]

"Regulation-mindedness" may not be the result of such pro-regulation bureaucrats. It may result from the need of regulators and inspectors to "cover their asses" from charges of laxity by dangerous political predators. As Eugene Bardach and Robert A. Kagan argue in *Going by the Book,* there are strong political and bureaucratic incentives for regulators to apply rules "unreasonably," that is, literally.[60] This is particularly true of the "social" regulatory agencies. If OSHA inspectors exercise discretion in the application of a particular rule to a particular workplace, they are open to charges of favoritism and corruption. So, the authors claim, even when a workplace is fundamentally in compliance, OSHA inspectors often enforce rules literally.

Bardach and Kagan tie this organizational imperative of self-protection to the cost-benefit analysis of regulation found in most economic studies of social regulation. According to the authors, regulatory unreasonableness means that compliance entails costs which exceed the resulting social benefits. The sheer diversity of enterprises to be regulated under, say, an OSHA rule, makes it nearly impossible to devise a single rule that will "make sense" in scores of different workplaces and even across different industries. Bardach and Kagan argue that such regulation not only increases economic inefficiency, but generates intense frustration among businessmen—including those who generally support OSHA's objectives.[61]

The other broad type of organizational theory posits an agency characterized by rational goals and behaviors, but buffeted by conflicts, external constraints, and often the mutually exclusive demands of interest groups. The organizational imperative is to lessen such conflicts and demands. In Robert Chatov's almost psychological formulation, the regulatory agency will naturally attempt to diminish the conflicts that envelop it. The agency thus will construct, and become the focal point of, "consensus networks," within which parties will generally compromise and agree to general procedures and goals.[62] Paul Joskow's quasi-organizational view finds similarly that agencies fundamentally seek to minimize conflict and criticism. Once the agency "satisfactorily" balances the conflicting pressures from its external environment, it routinizes the organizational structures and procedures which fashioned that equilibrium. The agency then will operate in a predictable and reactive— even passive—mode, repeatedly using these established structures and procedures.[63] Hence agency organizational procedures come to reflect the balance of interest-group power.[64] So, "regulation as usual" may often be in the general interests of both the strongest regulated parties and the agency itself. This is an important point for my theory. But, Joskow claims, a disturbance in the equilibrium—usually from rapidly transformed external conditions—may push the agency into an innovative stance. This describes the case of public utility commissions in the early 1970s, when their traditional pricing structures and regulatory procedures were rendered obsolete by rapid inflation.

Two students of the FCC, employing versions of this organizational perspective, found that (contrary to Joskow's model), disturbances in the equilibrium reinforced "regulation as usual." Vincent Mosco argues that in the FCC's regulation of broadcasting, the continuous complexity and uncertainty over pursuing mutually exclusive rational goals pushed the FCC toward ongoing simple and conservative decisions. "Regulation as usual" was the organizational response to unrelenting complexity. Don R. LeDuc's study of FCC treatment of cable television from the 1950s to the early 1970s found evidence of regulatory "sabotage." The agency perceived technological innovation as a threat to its standard definitions and procedures. The FCC undermined the promise of cable television by forcing it to fit into the structure of previously established regulatory formulae and policies.[65]

This organizational perspective, then, looks at the behavior of the regulatory agency as a key variable in explaining regulatory policy. It does not have much to say about the genesis of agencies, but does have an implicit theory of the state. The state is seen not as a set of neutral apparatuses that groups may capture *per se,* or of politicians as private maximizers, but rather each apparatus has a certain organizationally based, self-regarding orientation. Though the agency may be primarily reactive, it is an actor whose actions are not reducible to the interests of external parties. However, as I will argue, regulation-as-usual tends to protect both the agency and the balance of power in the regulated industry.

## Capitalist State Theory

Recent neo-Marxist theorists on the capitalist state have not concerned themselves with the analysis of regulation *per se*. But their preoccupation with state policy-making makes their writings pertinent to this discussion. "Structurally" oriented Marxism looks at political institutions such as regulatory agencies within a larger theory of state intervention in the period of advanced capitalism. Such political institutions occupy a crucial interstice between contradictory systemic demands to safeguard capitalist accumulation on the one hand, and to secure political legitimation on the other. Neo-Marxian structuralism looks at the rise and functions of state "apparatuses" (such as regulatory agencies) abstractly, as part of the myriad demands placed on the state in the era of advanced, or "monopoly," capitalism. Regulatory agencies in a sense are an institutional response of the political system to the demands and contradictions created by the emergence of monopoly capitalism. The theory rarely looks at the actual historical events of regulatory origin; it is content to understand origin abstractly. This is a Marxist version of functionalism. Regulatory agencies arise due to the inability of the market to regulate capitalist behavior, whether in terms of intercapitalist competition or in terms of the social externalities of such behavior.

In capitalist state theory, the state is considered inherently biased toward actions which will support the capitalist system.[66] This bias is structural. Because the state is dependent upon taxes and is enjoined by the nature of capitalism and property law from engaging in production itself, the state must safeguard and enhance the private accumulation of capital. In other words, the state must act to keep the economy healthy and growing. It makes little difference who actually has their hands on state apparatuses—the structural imperative constrains the actions of all state "managers," regardless of their ideologies.

State intervention may take different forms depending on specific conditions and circumstances. In general, in the period of advanced capitalism, the state socializes more and more capital costs—giving corporations tax breaks and supplying essential services to corporations to induce investment. The capitalist state acts to provide social insurance programs, such as unemployment compensation and social security, to deal with dysfunctional externalities of a capitalist economy. The state takes on the costs of educating and training the next generation of workers. In those instances where private capital cannot or will not take the risks to invest in economically and/or socially necessary capital, the state will underwrite or subsidize such investment directly. The state socializes risk. James O'Connor argues that the state is indispensable to the expansion of private industry, particularly monopoly industries.[67] The state and monopoly sectors grow together, but the expansion of state activity and expenditure causes state budget deficits.

Industries destabilized by the anarchy of the market call forth, or create a functional need for, some mechanism of social control. Regulatory agencies—a new institution of social control—act to maintain market order on behalf of the industry as a whole. This "long-range" interest of the regulatory agency in the industry it oversees may cause it to act against specific interests within that industry. Because the state assumes the role of rationalizer of economic contradictions, the various state apparatuses *must* exercise some degree of autonomy from any specific interest. A "structurally" capitalist state thus accounts for the paradox that state apparatuses exercise autonomy in their policies and actions *and* serve the long-term needs of capital. In fact, the theory argues that only *because* the state is autonomous, yet absolutely bound by the constraints of capital accumulation, can it perform its rationalizing function.[68] This is what distinguishes capitalist state theory from the more Marxist varieties of conspiracy theory.

But if capitalist state apparatuses are not simple reflections of interest-group politics, neither are they "neutral" tools. The state is structurally biased toward capitalism. It should be noted that the structural bias of the state toward capitalism—a cardinal principle of structuralist Marxism—is not necessarily a Marxist idea *per se*. The non-Marxist political scientist Charles Lindblom argues much the same thing:

> Because public functions in the market system rest in the hands of businessmen, it follows that jobs, prices, production, growth, the standard of living, and the economic security of everyone all rest in their hands. Consequently, government officials cannot be indifferent to how well business performs its functions. Depression, inflation, or other economic distress can bring down a government. A major function of government, therefore, is to see to it that businessmen perform their tasks. . . . But take particular note of another familiar feature of these systems. Constitutional rules— especially the law of private property—specify that, although governments can forbid certain kinds of activity, they cannot command business to perform. They must induce rather than command. They must therefore offer benefits to businessmen in order to stimulate the required performance.[69]

This structural relationship accounts for the privileged position of business in capitalist democracies. It means that most of the time and as a matter of course, state policies, including regulation, will favor capital. Yet the state must and does respond to popular agitation, to demands for redistribution, to demands for fairness. In structuralist Marxism, there is a second major constraint on the state, that of legitimation. In a formally democratic polity, class and popular struggles cannot be ignored or simply repressed. A government must to some degree command the trust of the electorate in a democratic polity. In capitalist state theory, the state will respond to such struggles, but will seek to defuse and/or coopt them in ways which will not threaten continued accumulation and will be compatible with the expanded reproduction of capital. The character and intensity of legitimation demands, and the degree of economic crisis means that in certain periods the state has more leeway vis-à-vis capital.[70] The problem is that the state is unable to respond to the myriad demands of capital and popular agitation without also generating new contradictions, be these a state fiscal crisis or further legitimation problems.[71]

In a certain sense, a capitalist state theory of regulation also conflates genesis and operationality, though the conflation is at such an abstract level that it may be meaningless. The theory assumes that genesis and operationality are indeed related—at the level of the accumulation-legitimation constraints placed upon the state. The abstract nature of the theory causes it to be extremely imprecise at any empirical level of analysis. Yet, the same abstract nature allows the theory to situate regulation within the larger context of the relation of state and economy. Moreover, the theory postulates the autonomy of regulators, but locates (albeit abstractly) the factors which constrain that autonomy.

Each of the theories examined above has something to offer to the understanding of regulation. Each theory, in my view, also has its drawbacks. Public interest theories, attentive to the origin of regulatory agencies, ignore the actual practice of regulation. They misapprehend the public interest to be the consumer's interest, and are peculiarly silent on the actual consequences of regulatory practice. Regulatory failure and capture theories, attentive to the results of regulatory practice, still understand regulation in the terms established by public interest theory. Consequently, their understanding of the nature of influence is limited and reflects an inadequate pluralist view of the state. Capture theories incorrectly conceptualize the state as a neutral apparatus of coercion, infinitely malleable and capturable precisely because the state is seen as having no essential functions or internal prerogatives. Economic theories of regulation help us gain a concrete appreciation of the effects of regulation in specific circumstances. But the application of a rational actor model to regulatory agencies cannot explain their genesis, nor is the model ultimately satisfactory in understanding how regulation actually works in other than strictly economic settings. Conspiracy theories are important in that they point us in the direction of the structure of capitalism and the nature of state intervention. Regulation is a new political institution which arises to deal with particular social and economic problems. But such theories are skimpy on empirical analysis of the practice of regulation. They proceed on the *a priori* assumption of the centrality of capitalist power and assume that the participation of businessmen means that businessmen control regulation. Organizational theories restore a sense of independence and autonomy to agencies, but this is just a small piece of the regulatory picture. Capitalist state theories are helpful because they are able to situate regulatory agencies within much larger structures of power and constraint. They are of much less use when analyzing a concrete phenomenon such as a specific regulatory agency or a particular regulatory policy.

My theory accepts from structuralist Marxist theory the notion that the state is an actor within a capitalist democracy. The actions of the state and of state "managers'' are important, and are not "directed" by capitalists. However, the autonomy of such actions is subject to constraint. The state can function only within parameters constituted by the two fundamental system constraints of "accumulation" and "legitimation." The state must safeguard the conditions for continued economic growth and performance, and at the same time meet democratic demands relating to equity and due process. But for three reasons this is a selective borrowing. First, there is a problem with the abstract level of the structuralist model. As one moves into the empirical history of telecommunications regulation and deregulation, it becomes difficult to impute motives and/or interests to abstractions like "the state," which is made up of different apparatuses sometimes with conflicting agendas. Different regulatory agencies represent different constellations of political constituencies and administrative logics, and these differences are, to some degree, embedded in the functional mandate of each agency. Likewise, "capital" implies a structured unity which in large part does not exist except on a very few issues.

Second, the accumulation-legitimation dual constraint theory does not adequately recognize the interest of the state (or of a single state agency) in preserving itself. This is where organization theory is helpful. Recognition of a principle of *raison d'état* maps onto a theory of regulation not just the national security dimension usually associated with *raison d'état,* but also the desires for organizational integrity/autonomy found at many levels of state organization. In this, my analysis of regulation borrows from organization theories.

Third, structuralist neo-Marxism, like most social theory, generally does not recognize law as a "semi-autonomous" normative structure, irreducible to economic or political forces. It was Max Weber who best understood this. Indeed, the semi-autonomous nature of law helps us better understand the otherwise abstract notion of legitimation. Though legitimation demands are normally conceived as the popular demands of subordinate groups against the state, particularly with regard to matters relating to the redistribution of wealth, legitimation is also found in the expectations associated with the rule of law. This is embodied in the expectation that similarly situated persons will be treated similarly, that standards of judgment be open and rational, that due process be respected. The Weberian analysis of substantive and formal rationality is a useful tool for understanding the binds of regulation and the paradoxes of regulatory practice. If this study utilizes neo-Marxist theory to examine the origins of regulation and the institutional constraints on this mode of state intervention, it also utilizes neo-Weberian theory to analyze how regulation works in practice.

A comprehensive theory should account separately for both the genesis and the operationality of regulatory agencies. The history and analysis of actual regulatory decisions should be considered within the context of the structure of American political power and fundamental economic conditions. The problem with most theories of regulation is the same of most theories of power—they are *static*. A proper study of regulation must account not only for the real differences between agencies, but also for the differences in the temporal political coalitions whose demands underlie the establishment of particular agencies.

Each of the three waves of regulatory genesis is characterized by a general type of agency with similar functions. Each type of agency reflects a specific kind of politics and a specific administrative practice. Notwithstanding, there is no fault-free way to predict which industries will be regulated and which will not. This is not a predictive, "modeling" theory, it is a historical theory. At the same time, all agencies are situated similarly within the general institutional structure of political power and, within that context of power, are constrained by both the accumulation needs of the capitalist mode of production and the legitimation demands inherent in a democratic polity. Regulatory agencies are also limited by the difficulty of their tasks. Just because an agency is mandated to achieve a certain goal does not mean the attainment of that goal is administratively possible. Finally, because temporality and changes in political dynamics *are* factors in regulatory behavior, there is no *single* pattern to the behavior of agencies.[72]

# CHAPTER
## 3
• • •

# The "Gateway of Commerce": A Theory of Regulation

To speak of a single theory of regulation already creates problems. It implies that all regulatory agencies are manifestations of a single principle or activity called regulation. This hazards a mistaken assumption that all agencies do roughly the same things and are affected by the same problems. But the functions and goals of, say, the regulation of water pollution are far different from those of the regulation of motor carriers. Nevertheless, we commonly conceptualize the activities of such different bodies as "regulation"—a form of activity whereby a governmental authority formulates rules to mold private, usually economic, conduct. Yet this definition points to a boundary problem in the other direction as well. Why should the subject of regulation refer only to the actions of governmental bodies specifically designated as regulatory agencies? Surely other state policy-making apparatuses seek to accomplish the same or similar goals. What, indeed, is meant by regulation?

Barry Mitnick writes, "Regulation is a process consisting of the intentional restriction of a subject's choice of activity, by an entity not directly party to or involved in that activity."[1] Such a process-oriented definition is broad enough to encompass the myriad goals of regulatory activity, but the definition is so broad that it excludes very little. What is distinctive about regulation is that it employs the coercive power of the state in a new and modern way. Regulation not only restricts a subject's choice of activity, but does so by means of a political institution which consolidates legislative, executive, and judicial functions in a single apparatus. Regulatory agencies create substantive rules and policies which have the force of law, that is, they impose obligations on conduct and punish nonconformance. As they emerged in the late 19th and early 20th century, regulatory agencies constituted a new institution of political power and a new body of law—administrative law. The regulatory mode of social control was designed to be informal and flexible, a combination of case-by-case adjudication and more formal policy-making by the drafting of rules.[2]

The rise of regulatory agencies significantly reconfigured the structure of American political power. Nineteenth-century political power was divided effectively between a predominantly local, party-based legislative authority and a nationally oriented federal judiciary. Regulatory agencies established a new national, administrative political institution. The examination of the rise of regulatory agencies, then, cannot be simply a matter of analyzing interest-group politics. It is a matter of state-building as well.[3]

While the regulatory agency forms a new institution of political power, its goals tend to be very much in line with the old common law. As early as the reign of Edward I, English common law courts gave certain kinds of occupations, hence certain kinds of property, a special status which incurred privileges and obligations. Ferrymen, bakers, carriers, innkeepers, and millers, among others, were awarded local monopolies in exchange for an obligation to serve all at reasonable charges. The common law of public callings had the intention (and often the effect) of demolishing the social and political barriers to a thriving commerce. At the same time it had embedded within it a fundamental principle of social equity, bound up in the duty to serve.[4]

The modern regulatory agency in many ways constituted a new institutional form of the common law. Historically coterminous with the emergence of a truly national economy and the reign of judicial formalism, regulatory agencies came at a time of dramatic incongruity between economic and political systems. While business in the late 19th century began to operate in national as well as regional markets, the political system remained local, its authority residing theoretically in federal and state levels of government but practically in the state governments. In the most general and abstract sense, early regulatory agencies arose to create a predictable environment for *national* economic activity. A primary means of creating such a predictable environment for economic activity was through the regulation of infrastructure industries (first transportation, later communication, banking, and energy), and the oversight of their commerce-bearing function.

Regulation took over from the federal judiciary the role of defining the grounds and terms of market exchange—hence the role of guiding the course of American economic development. It is in this sense that the rise and general function of regulatory agencies represent a new stage in the role of the state. The particularly virulent socio-economic conflicts of the late 19th century (between labor and capital and between capitalists competing for market advantage) and the complexity posed by the transition from a localistic to a national, corporate economy prompted the expansion of the institutional capabilities of the state. Regulatory agencies became the modern *form* of state intervention to reconcile the expanded and complex needs of capital (accumulation) with the democratic demands for social controls of corporate activity and of fairness generally (legitimation). Regulatory agencies applied common law principles to guarantee the free and unfettered flow of commerce *and* to guarantee a fundamental fairness (within a capitalist framework, of course). Later regulatory agencies arose within the same general accumulation-legitimation framework as different sorts of problems affected economic activity (depression in the 1930s and destructive spillover effects of corporate activity in the 1960s). The differing functions of regulatory agencies correspond to the specific social, political, and economic conditions of the three distinct historical periods of regulatory creation already mentioned.

The second important feature of regulatory agencies concerns the distinctively *informal* mode of rule-making which they practice, and the relationship of regulatory power to other institutions of political power. The normal practice of an agency is to hear the various positions and grievances of parties involved in a dispute within the agency's jurisdiction. The agency assesses these positions along with the supposedly nonpartisan, scientific arguments of outside experts, and then formulates specific rules and general policies. Though the coercive power of the state lies behind it, the regulatory mode of social control is informal and flexible. Its authority has been described as "discretionary."[5] Its rules and policies are substantive, that is, they are intended to be highly concrete, molded to accommodate the specific issues and needs of a particular industry or economic function. But such discretionary authority tends to create a dynamic whereby the agency bargains with the principal contending parties. The open-ended and vague, often contradictory mandate given the agency by Congress in its enabling legislation tends to exacerbate this dynamic of discretionary bargaining over specific policies. Consequently, few clear or steadfast policies are formulated or followed.

At the same time, regulatory agencies do not so much centralize political power as create a new layer of political power to vie with older structures of power in the dispersed American political system. Commissioners are appointed by the President, subject to the approval of Congress; agency budgets are allocated by Congress on a yearly basis; agency actions are overseen by Congressional committees or the Office of Management and Budget; agency rules and policies are subject to judicial review by the federal courts. The private parties brought under the agency's jurisdiction tend to bring pressure upon the agency through all levels. The private parties challenge agency rules and jurisdiction in court continually.

The agency, under various political and judicial pressures, is situated in a web of hard constraints. It often becomes concerned with protecting its organizational integrity. Agency actions and policies tend to be conservative, bound up with formal procedures, methods, and reliance on precedent. But the formalization of regulatory agencies, though it may protect the due process rights of regulated parties and enhance organizational integrity, also hampers the agency in carrying out its primary mandated function—the formulation of substantive rules and policies. As agencies become increasingly formalized, over time, administrative rationality and economic rationality tend to diverge. Regulatory rules often make administrative, but not economic, sense.

## The Genesis of Regulatory Agencies

Any adequate theory of regulation must situate regulatory agencies in the historical context out of which they arose. The advent of regulatory agencies is concomitant with the rise of a national economy and the need for a new institution of political power to establish effective social controls on and for industry. The existing institutions of political power of the 19th century—the courts and the political parties—were not capable of dealing with the instability, class and inter-business conflicts, and complexity generated by the corporate economy.

Despite a highly localistic political structure, rapid economic development proceeded in 19th-century America under the aegis of the specific promotional actions of state legislatures and general environment created by the federal courts. In an undeveloped nation beset by a scarcity of fluid, mobile capital, individual states promoted "internal improvements" by means of monetary subsidies, the granting of exclusive corporate charters to protect the risked capital, and the limiting of legal liability for such projects. These improvements tended to be industrial projects that built up the transportation infrastructure of the states, such as bridges, turnpikes, canals, and later railroads and telegraph systems. Early corporations essentially were special development projects, chartered by legislatures to benefit the community as a whole. As such, early corporations embodied a clear public interest. State promotionalism was made possible by crucial changes in the conception of the common law, changes related to the emergence of an activist judiciary which fashioned laws favoring economic development. A primary instrument in this effort was the law of eminent domain, the taking of private property for the purpose of "public" improvement.

As the century progressed, the judiciary undermined the protection of chartered projects by refusing to recognize the exclusivity of charters. Instead, judges began to foster an environment of competition. In a key decision, the courts permitted a new bridge to be built next to an originally chartered bridge. The judicial move to foster economic competition was accomplished through the federalization of all commercial law and by denying states the right to act on economic activity (if the effects of state actions were thought to impede the flow of interstate commerce). The courts attempted to carve out a national area for the circulation of capital. In so doing, the courts unbundled the earlier link between corporations and the public interest. Corporations became legally recognized as private entities distinct from the public purpose. After mid-century, the rights of contract were expanded in the judicial effort to expand private rights and to spur capitalist economic development. Tort liability also expanded, but in a narrow fashion so as not to inhibit economic risk-taking.

But certain types of economic activity continued to seem imbued with a public purpose of some kind. Though it is difficult to discern a consistent principle behind this intuitive notion of business affected with a public purpose, it primarily involved infrastructure services and the fact of public dependence upon them. In common law, certain types of occupations have always been subject to special rights and obligations. These occupations, or "common callings," were considered to be affected with a public interest because they were absolutely pivotal for commerce and because they involved the patronage of the public generally. Notwithstanding the growing private right of contract as the 19th century wore on, states and localities continued to exercise controls over businesses perceived as affected with a public purpose. Railroads, because they so fundamentally altered the local patterns of commerce, seemed especially worthy of regulation by the states. But the exercise of local controls came into conflict with the movement toward a national economy. Early regulatory agencies arose when a federal judiciary, increasingly oriented toward the expansion of contract rights, prohibited states from regulating the local operations of national industries. Regulatory agencies constituted national administrative political institutions to deal with the massive social and economic instability caused by the corporate transformation of the economy.

## The Political Structure of the Early American Republic

The structure of political power in early America was dispersed and localistic. Indeed, the dominant constitutional model is one of dividing, separating, and checking powers so as to *contain* government.[6] The singularly important place of law and courts in American society derives from this heritage. As Samuel P. Huntington has argued, the supremacy of law in the United States was mated to the rejection of authority or supremacy in a single institution. European absolutism attempted to rationalize authority and sought to destroy older corporate orders of status so that a single authority would be the sole source of law. In contrast, the absence of a feudal class system in America, along with the colonists' experience of oppression by a distant, centralized sovereign, made the centralization of power unnecessary and unwanted. Beneath the political arguments for the separation of powers and a decentralized state system was the idea that the sovereignty of law permitted a multiplicity and diffusion of human authorities. Huntington's characterization of American government as one of "courts and parties" reflects the immense power of the judiciary in a highly *localized* political democracy, where power was diffused among many institutions which shared many of the same functions.[7]

Constitutional federalism inhibited the emergence of central power. Each state had its own institutional organization, legal code, and law enforcement apparatus. Political parties, as "constituent" parties, functioned to bind the national government to geographic locales. As such, Congressional operations essentially consisted of a log-rolling politics which could best service the states and localities. The federal government functioned in a distributive mode—it especially distributed land and also enacted certain tariffs. Those national governmental institutions which did develop consisted of basic services parceled out to localities, such as post offices, land offices, and customhouses.[8] It is true that the federal government did undertake some projects of a non-distributive nature in the early 1800s, such as the construction of post roads, but this function was undermined by state and sectional conflicts.[9]

Only Constitutional law underlay all political institutions. This put the federal judiciary in a key structural position as the only institution capable of exercising a centralizing political function. Yet, despite the rhetoric of the "rule of law," there was no written law pertaining to the early republic as a whole. The Constitution essentially was a plan for the structure of government. That law which did exist was the English common law, known primarily by means of a textbook, Blackstone's *Commentaries on the Laws of England*. In the 18th century, common law doctrines were thought to be derived from *natural* principles of justice, themselves said to derive from the perfection of reason—fixed and settled rules of conduct legitimized by immemorial usage. Judges were to "discover" common law and apply it according to strict precedent.

But this conception of common law was beginning to change by the end of the 18th century in the United States. The American colonists' hatred of things British, the change in political thought registered in the Constitution's theory of political legitimacy, and the expanding practices of the mercantile community led to a change in judges' attitude toward the nature of law.[10] This new attitude found common law to be both uncertain and unpredictable. An emerging "will" theory of law underlay jurists' contentions that they had a popular charter to mold legal doctrine according to broad conceptions of public policy. Morton J. Horwitz (no relation to this author) argues that the transformation from precedent to substantive doctrines in the early years of the 19th century was the result of conscious judicial decisions to foster techniques which would allow greater predictability of legal consequences. These techniques would, then, allow men to order their affairs with regularity. This "anti-precedent" attitude toward common law resurrected the doctrines of Blackstone's historical rival, Lord Mansfield. Mansfieldian emphasis on and sensitivity toward the actual practices of the mercantile community are in evidence in judicial decisions of the early 1800s, and his influence is directly acknowledged by, among others, Justice Joseph Story, one of the key 19th-century commercial law jurists. There is also the important example of the "Law Merchant" (from which Mansfield appropriated many principles), an international body of law which governed mercantile activities in the 15th and 16th centuries. "Law Merchant" derived from the general customs and law sense of European traders, and was enforced by the consortia of merchants rather than guaranteed by the state.[11]

The "parallel" between legal and economic rationality was noted by the sociologist and legal scholar Max Weber. Weber's work establishes that a formally rational system of economic organization—that is, a system permitting the maximum possible *calculability* of economic activity and expectations—can exist only upon a firm foundation of formally rational law which grants to private parties the empowering rights emanating from property and which guarantees the security of those rights by public authority. The connection between modern, rational law and capitalism is that the legal system provided legal arrangements that guaranteed private entrepreneurs certainty and predictability of economic consequences.[12] In early 19th-century America, the altered conception of the nature of judicial action, in conjunction with the structurally key position of the judiciary in the early American political system, meant that judges assumed the role of formulating general economic policy through a substantive transformation of the common law. The courts came to look with favor on the *productive* use of property. The change in the common law first appeared in property right doctrine in riparian, or water rights, disputes.

## Nineteenth-Century Law and Economic Development

In traditional common law, property right doctrine reflected the recreational use of land by the English landed gentry. The context of the doctrine was a predominantly agrarian economy. The common law granted a property owner absolute dominion over land, entitling an owner to undisturbed enjoyment. Such right was inherently anti-developmental, as it limited property owners to what courts regarded as the "natural" uses of land. Natural meant agrarian. "Natural use" was just one theory behind traditional common law property right. The other was "priority of development," which conferred a right to arrest a future conflicting use. This meant, for example, if a property owner wished to construct a mill on his land, his neighbor could easily block such a project because the mill would conflict with his own quiet enjoyment.

Priority and natural right normally buttressed each other, but in the first two decades of the 19th century, these theories began to take on different operational meanings in riparian (water) disputes. The advent of mills and the productive use of water power in the industrializing American northeast led to suits filed against mill owners for flood damages. As the common law was pulled into the utilitarian world of economic development, "priority" came to be argued as protecting not the recreational property owner, but rather the first developmental entrant, because of the risks the latter assumed.[13] Morton Horwitz argues that the granting of exclusionary privileges to first entrants became the dominant doctrine of property law in the early stages of American economic growth. The pattern of protection of the first economic entrant is characteristic of mercantilism.[14]

Such a mercantilist doctrine of property law enabled states and municipalities to extend incorporation and grant exclusive franchises to private concerns in the effort to stimulate economic development. Exclusive franchises served to lessen risk, hence guaranteed wary investors greater certainty and predictability of economic consequences. The most important of these guarantees was protection against competitive injury, for, in an underdeveloped society with little available capital, economic competition could squander scarce capital and cripple development.[15]

One aspect of judicially provided protection for early capitalists was the development of a narrow conception of tort liability. The 19th century saw a huge expansion of tort law, but one which was designed not to impede economic activity. As Morton Horwitz argues, tort law entailed a general limitation on legal liability for injury brought about by risk-producing (public promotional) activity. This was accomplished through the triumph of the private law principle of negligence over the older, public law principle of just compensation in nuisance action. Prior to the 1840s, common law nuisance dominated tort actions for injuries. Nuisance was a strict liability doctrine. This meant that any and every injury had to be fully compensated. Negligence inserted the element of carelessness into the picture, thus undermining the presumption of compensation. With the doctrine of negligence, injury brought about by risk-producing activity was itself no ground for imposing legal liability. The triumph of negligence over nuisance in the 1840s added to the encouragement of economic development.[16]

Similar principles pervaded the emerging law of industrial accidents. The infamous "fellow servant" rule functioned to protect the enterprise from personal injury lawsuits. Under this rule, a servant (employee) could not sue his master (employer) for injuries caused by the negligence of another employee. He could sue his employer only if the employer *personally* caused the injury through negligent misconduct—an unlikely possibility, particularly with regard to large enterprises.

An allied legal conception was the "assumption of risk." A plaintiff could not recover damages for injury if he had put himself willingly in a position of danger. Included in this category were most workmen. Finally there was the doctrine of "contributory negligence." If a plaintiff was negligent himself in the context of an injury, even slightly, he could not recover from a defendant. As Lawrence Friedman argues, these were useful methods for judges to keep tort claims from the deliberations of generally generous juries.[17] Nineteenth-century tort law thus favored economic development.

Early corporations, created by special legislation, embodied a mercantilist understanding that any incorporation was sanctioned for the common good. Many, if not most, early 19th-century corporate franchises were granted to construct and establish the infrastructure projects of bridges, roads, and canals. Later franchises and public subsidies facilitated the construction of railroads and telegraph lines. Louis Hartz's study of Pennsylvania during this period is the leading work on the relationship between the developing economy and state government. Hartz shows that Pennsylvania undertook an interventionist, pro-development role through state public works in canals and railroads, the chartering and regulation of corporations (particularly in banks and railroads), the elimination of slavery, and the regulation of factory and mine working conditions.[18] In the period before the Civil War, state governments committed some $300 million in cash or credit to internal improvements. Local governments committed more than $125 million for such projects, some of which went to entice railroad building through their towns in the middle decades of the 19th century. The federal government gave some money to states for internal improvement programs along with massive gifts of land.[19]

Overall, 70 percent of the cost of canal construction from 1815 to 1860 was provided by public investment. Until 1861, government agencies provided close to 30 percent of the entire investment in railroad building, *not* including land. The one major case of direct financial aid from the federal government was a post-Civil War loan of $65 million to the railroad companies that constructed the first transcontinental line.[20] Federal aid to telegraphy rested largely with a Congressional authorization in 1866 that permitted telegraph companies to run their lines freely along post roads and across public lands, and to fell trees for poles gratis. Seventy-six percent of all commercial telegraph pole line was located on right-of-way by 1900. Public subsidies to telegraph systems did not approach the amounts granted to railroads. Nonetheless, federal and state governments provided "seed money" at several critical junctures in telegraph history.[21]

These projects were made possible by the legal weapon of eminent domain, that is, coerced takings of private property with limited compensation. Eminent domain reflected a monumental transformation in the conception of property. Property was now something to be *used*, developed. Yet the justification of eminent domain utilized the older arguments of common law. The new doctrine of limited compensation for "takings" was tied to older arguments that all property originally had been at the sufference of the state (or that just compensation clauses were restrictions of state sovereignty).[22] Moreover, eminent domain was exercised for the public purpose. In early decisions upholding the delegation of eminent domain to transport companies, the courts frequently invoked the argument that "the opening of good and easy internal communications is one of the highest duties of government."[23] As late as 1848, in a case called *West River Bridge v. Dix,* the Supreme Court validated the eminent domain power of the states as one "paramount to all private rights vested under the government." The opinion pointed to the importance of eminent domain for economic development.

> In fact, the whole policy of the country, relative to roads, mills, bridges, and canals, rests upon this single power, under which lands have always been condemned; and without the extention of this power, not one of the improvements just mentioned could be constructed.[24]

The use of eminent domain for publicly chartered corporations to construct canals, roads, and bridges in the early 19th century constituted a new legal instrument for the accomplishment of goals traditional to common law in England. With the demise of feudalism, English common law judges typically permitted the continuance of local monopolies in certain occupations so as to facilitate commerce. The *quid pro quo* of monopoly power was the legal obligation of the monopolist to serve all comers without discrimination and at reasonable charges.[25]

However, in America the mercantilist conception of property as monopolistic and exclusionary succeeded, as it were, too well. Exclusive charters provided legal arrangements that guaranteed private investors predictability of economic consequences. But this absolute property right in the first entrant became a fetter to *continued* economic development. By the second quarter of the century, state efforts to encourage economic growth began to diverge from private efforts to preserve existing legal expectations. As Morton Horwitz argues, under continuing pressure to encourage further investment, the legal system gradually began to distinguish between public and private interests, and to sanction various uncompensated injuries to property. Out of this redefinition of property emerged a legal presumption in favor of economic competition.[26] Two Supreme Court decisions were of key importance in this transformation, *Dartmouth College v. Woodward* (1819) and *Charles River Bridge v. Warren Bridge* (1837).[27]

## The Emergence of Private Corporations and Economic Competition

In keeping with the early conception of the corporation as a public body, every grant of corporate status depended upon specific state legislation. As the economy expanded in the first quarter of the 19th century[28]—to some degree on the basis of the infrastructural services created by monopolistic improvement projects—entrepreneurs demanded access to the corporate form as an efficient way to finance and structure their business ventures. Increasingly, corporate charters were granted to private concerns not primarily involved in infrastructure improvements or their security (i.e., banks and insurance companies). In *Dartmouth College,* the Supreme Court employed the contract clause of the Constitution to recognize the contract rights of a chartered corporation against changes demanded by a state legislature. The case concerned an attempt by the New Hampshire legislature to pack the Dartmouth College board of trustees and alter its faculty in order to change the college into a public institution. The Court ruled that these changes violated Dartmouth's 1769 charter from King George III. The effect of *Dartmouth College* was that it severed the corporate form from its public project origins, and began the long judicial process of attempting to distinguish legally between public and private corporations.[29]

The *Dartmouth College* case recognized business corporations as essentially private entities. Certain political developments soon reaffirmed this distinction between public and private. Until the late 1830s, most internal improvements were either publicly owned or were to be taken over by the states after a definite period of time (often after private investors had been rewarded with a fair return). This pattern characterized some states' policies toward railroads as well. The pattern changed significantly following the economic panic of 1837–39 and the collapse of many public projects. The financial ruin of many state governments precipitated a far-reaching backlash against public works. Thereafter, the dominant pattern of state promotion moved toward subsidization of private incorporated enterprise, rather than public projects.[30]

The corporate form became sought after as a device to promote continuity and to minimize risks in the pursuit of private gain. As the press of charter legislation became heavier to cope with increasing requests for corporate status, eventually corporations were created not by legislation but by simple act of registry. Except for projects of special importance, charters became standardized until they were finally replaced, at mid-century, by general incorporation laws.[31]

*Dartmouth College* recognized the importance of *contract* for the business enterprise, in the guarantee of stability of legally constructed arrangements. But a major contradiction remained inherent in this case. If the connection between public and private interests had been breached in the recognition of corporations as private entities, such entities still retained the monopolistic protection of property afforded by that prior connection. The *Charles River Bridge* case resolved that contradiction by setting the course of economic development in favor of unbridled competition.

The Charles River Bridge was built in 1785 to connect Boston and Charlestown. By 1827, when the Massachusetts legislature authorized the construction of another Boston-Charlestown bridge, the populations of these two cities had increased several times and the original bridge often proved inadequate to handle expanded traffic. The opening of the Warren Bridge siphoned traffic (and revenues) from the Charles River Bridge, and the latter bridge's proprietors sued for damages due to competitive injury. The Massachusetts and U.S. Supreme Courts ruled against Charles River Bridge, claiming that state legislatures had the right to grant competing franchises. Behind this ruling rested conscious and direct debates among justices over the proper legal elements to ensure economic progress.[32] The victorious opinion held that monopolistic protection no longer was necessary to encourage private investment. Risk-taking was to be encouraged by allowing for competitive injury, and guaranteed by legal enforcement of the convergence of wills in contractual obligation.

## The Federalization of Commercial Law and the Beginnings of Legal Formalism

The triumph of competition as the mode of economic development after 1840 meant a corresponding expansion of private rights. In practice this meant an expansion in the "empowering right" (the term is Max Weber's) of business enterprises to enter into privately determined agreements, and the commitment of government to enforce those agreements. In other words, the middle and late decades of the 19th century saw the rise of the "pure" theory of contract. The expansion of private rights meant the emergence of a deep conflict over "vested private rights" versus the legislative prerogatives of the states. Increasingly, this took the form of a constitutional battle over the ability of state legislatures to exercise their "police powers" in enacting controls over business enterprises.

There were two main features to this long battle. The first was the question of distinguishing between private business and business "affected with a public interest." The second was the question of the proper jurisdiction over commerce. These issues were settled by an increasingly formalistic federal judiciary. In contrast to the earlier period of substantive law creation, the period from the Civil War to World War I was one in which the courts adhered to a strict conceptualism of legal reasoning, guided by the idea that the judicial function was never to legislate, but merely to declare the law that already exists.[33] These controversies and their resolution by a formalistic judiciary directly conditioned the emergence of regulatory agencies.

In addition to making changes in property and tort law, the federal judiciary also oversaw 19th-century economic development through its assertion of jurisdiction over matters of commerce. Facilitated by what Grant Gilmore calls an "expansive reading" of the Constitution, the Supreme Court granted jurisdictional powers to the federal government and federal courts. At first these powers concerned admiralty and maritime jurisdiction: the Court federalized the law relating to all waterborne transportation. Later this encompassed all interstate commerce.[34] The federalization of all waterborne transportation law included the heavily litigated field of marine insurance contracts. This development was extremely significant, since before 1815 commercial law revolved almost entirely around maritime transactions.[35] Equally important was the courts' determination that admiralty disputes would be resolved by judges alone. Juries were excluded from maritime insurance cases. Now federal judges effectively controlled the direction of commercial law.[36]

Justice Marshall's commerce caluse opinions of the 1820s had meaning largely in terms of economic public policy: national over state and local interest. In *Gibbons v. Ogden* (1824) and *Brown v. Maryland* (1827), the Court basically created a freedom of economic movement across multi-state areas, even though it was not until the second half of the century that industry could really utilize such freedom.[37] In *Gibbons v. Ogden* Justice Marshall gave the word commerce a broad definition (not the simple traffic of commodities, but "intercourse" generally) and determined that its jurisdiction was federal.[38] These decisions established the principle that the Court would declare invalid any state legislation whose effects would impair interstate commerce—even in situations where Congress had not chosen to legislate.

The doctrine established by *Gibbons* and *Brown* is labeled by some legal scholars as the "negative Commerce Clause doctrine." It sought to establish a national area of free trade, yet limited Congressional authority over commerce to the interstate level. *Gibbons* recognized the police powers of the states to regulate commerce internal to state borders. Nonetheless, the decision effectively put national trade and potential national capital under the protection of the federal judiciary. In addition, in *Swift v. Tyson* (1842) the Court (ironically, a Jacksonian, that is, a states' rights court) declared that in diversity (multi-state) cases the federal courts would exercise an independent judgment in questions of commercial law. *Swift v. Tyson* declared that the federal courts would not be bound by the law of any state, but would decide cases in light of "general principles."[39]

The course of 19th-century commercial law thus generally circumscribed the power of state courts and legislatures to intervene in the economy—at least with respect to interstate commerce. By mid-century, developments in property and tort law began to undermine state powers with regard to corporate enterprises even *within* state boundaries. The concept of vested rights as embodied in *Dartmouth College* came into conflict with the heritage of states' use of eminent domain powers. State legislatures, populated at mid-century with some anti-corporate interests in certain states, intended to use their powers of eminent domain in ways that might (further) redistribute wealth. In opposition to this came constitutional doctrines of vested rights. As Morton Horwitz argues, the concept of vested rights correlates with a rise in legal formalism and the effort to jettison the instrumental conception of law.

Legal formalism embodied a concern with legal process rather than with substantive goals. A formalized body of law gave law the appearance of being self-contained, inexorable, and apolitical. Such a formalized law had advantages for various interests. Once the substantive transformations of the law and the economy were successful, the major beneficiaries of that transformation (the bar in general, and men of commerce and industry in particular) could benefit if both the recent origins and the foundations in policy and group self-interest of all newly established legal doctrines could be disguised. The grant of constitutional status to vested rights and subsequent formulation of "objective" theories of contract and tort reflected the attempt to freeze legal doctrine and to conceive of law not as a malleable instrument of will, but as a fixed and inexorable system of logically deducible rules.[40]

The formalization of the law coincided with the challenge to the police powers of the states. Already in the 1840s some state courts began to distinguish between public and private takings by eminent domain—though the Supreme Court continued to leave states with wide condemnation powers during this period. Nonetheless, judicial actions reflect the attempt to clearly distinguish between public and private. For example, in the 1850s and 1860s courts began to impose tight restrictions on the taxing powers of local governments to use tax revenues for the subsidization of business enterprises.[41] According to Harry Scheiber, it was the ratification of the Fourteenth Amendment in 1868 which was decisive in opening the door to corporate challenges to state police power (including eminent domain) in federal courts.[42] The "due process" and "equal protection" clauses of the Fourteenth Amendment were designed to protect the legal rights of newly freed black slaves.[43] The irony was that these protections were used by corporations and conservative, laissez-faire-oriented jurists to roll back the powers of state legislatures vis-à-vis corporations.[44]

## The Granger Laws and Munn v. Illinois

The expansion of railroads inexorably altered the established, largely local, patterns of trade in various regions of the country. Railroads greatly expanded the development of inter-regional markets begun by the system of waterways and canals. Railroad transportation was fast and relatively cheap and thus hastened the expansion of trade and competition. Because railroads quickly became the chief means of commerce, their power was enormous and unprecedented. The direction of trade was determined by transportation and storage costs. This was especially true of the upper Mississippi Valley states of Illinois, Iowa, Minnesota, and Wisconsin in the period of the 1860s. As George Miller demonstrates, in the area west of the Great Lakes terminals, the success or failure of a particular merchant, a commercial center, or an entire marketing system was dependent on the structure of railroad rates. Likewise, competitive opportunities in western trade were radically distorted by arbitrary and discriminatory rate-making practices.[45]

In their effort to gain market share and increase their profits, railroads imposed different charges on different shippers for the same service, in the form of preferential rates, secret rebates, drawbacks, underweighing, and/or underclassification. Railroads cut rates for big shippers in competitive markets. Rate differentials sometimes created monopolies for favored enterprises. Standard Oil Company, for example, achieved preeminence in the oil refinery business by means of secret rebates and secret exclusive contracts with railroads. Other industries, such as beef, iron, and coal, experienced similar concentration.[46] Discrimination against localities jeopardized the economic chances of entire communities. The primary complaint against railroads (and warehouses and grain elevators) in the upper Mississippi Valley was rate discrimination: the unequal treatment of shippers and localities.

The widespread outcry against rate discrimination led to the passage of several laws to control rates in the early 1870s. These became known as "Granger laws," due to the agitation of the Grange for the control of monopolies. Notwithstanding the Granger appellation, support for and opposition to regulation was primarily sectional. As George Miller shows, in communities served by railroads, most merchants, shippers, and farmers backed political efforts to regulate. In communities not served by railroads the same interests opposed regulation because they thought such laws would discourage railroad building. Anti-monopoly Granger sentiment did suffuse the debates, but the fact that the principal political issue was rate "discrimination" rather than the farmers' cry of "extortion" indicates that commercial and community interests were at the core of the Granger laws.[47]

Despite their notoriety, the Granger laws were relatively mild and sometimes ineffectual. In Miller's interpretation, all of the important Granger innovations—the strong regulatory commission, judicial review, classification of railroads based on earnings—were concessions to railroad interests. And in the face of rapidly changing conditions in interstate railroad commerce (for one thing, a state could regulate only within its boundaries), the Granger laws were able to accomplish very little.[48] Nonetheless, the Granger laws did raise the larger question of power. The large interstate railroad systems challenged the Granger laws, looking, on the one hand, to destroy state restrictions, and on the other, to find some measure of security under *federal* jurisdiction. The Granger cases were agglomerated in *Munn v. Illinois.*[49] In *Munn* the railroad attorneys maintained that the Granger laws interfered with interstate commerce and violated certain charter rights. The railroads argued that as private enterprises, their status barred judicial supervision. Furthermore, state regulations impaired the obligations of contracts between railroads and creditors. The railroads asked the court to recognize anticipated income as a part of property right, and to eliminate the threat of legislative infringement upon these rights.

The Supreme Court rejected all of these arguments. The majority opinion maintained that the exercise of police power by Granger legislation was entirely consistent with common law. Though the opinion cited the 17th-century treatise by English Lord Chief Justice Matthew Hale, *De Portibus Maris,* the central concept of business affected with a public interest was familiar in riparian and eminent domain law, and entirely consistent with the common law principles embodied in the earlier period of chartered internal improvements.[50] *Munn* stated

> . . . that when private property is "affected with a public interest, it ceases to be *juris privati* only.". . . Property does become clothed with a public interest when used in a manner to make it of public consequence, and affect the community at large.[51]

The *Munn* decision can be read in more than one way. The Court recognized the right of states to regulate certain businesses. But the Court also restrained the states' police powers, by limiting the exercise of such power to businesses affected with a public interest. *Munn* thus placed a broad class of private rights beyond the reach of the state legislatures. Moreover, the determination as to whether or not a business was clothed with a public interest was now to be made not by state legislatures but by the courts. Though vague, *Munn* established that public control could be exercised only where there was existence of a monopoly or virtual monopoly, in the sense that the public was "compelled" to make use of the services involved. In this particular case, the Court determined that Chicago grain elevators and western railroads constituted businesses clothed with a public interest, inasmuch as they "stand in the very 'gateway of commerce, and take toll from all who pass.' "[52] The quasi-monopoly power of such businesses permitted regulation.

*Munn* raised the issue of publicly oriented business, and returned to the common law for guidance as to why certain businesses are clothed with a public interest. In common law certain occupations, or "callings," were deemed "common" or public. There were four essential charges placed on such callings: they must serve all, they must provide adequate (and safe) facilities, they must charge reasonable rates, they must not discriminate among customers.[53] Specific callings were classified as common for a variety of reasons, yet all in some way related to the issue of monopoly power and/or general dependence on service. Some callings required so much capital for their means of production, such as wharfingers, millers, and to some degree bakers, that the lord or sovereign constructed them or granted exclusive franchises to those who would. Tailors and surgeons were characterized by such scarcity that they were deemed common callings. Smiths, victualers, innkeepers, carriers, and ferrymen were common callings presumably because people had to depend on them in order to travel and trade.[54]

The close connection between carriers and commerce is of central importance. According to two 19th-century treatises on the law of bailments, carriers may have been required to meet the obligations of common callings in order to favor and encourage commerce by guarding against the carrier's collusion or coordination with thieves and robbers.[55] More recent scholarship has argued that carriers were considered a common calling and pressed with the obligation to serve as part of the effort by Edward I (1272–1307) to assert central authority against the taking of tolls by barons. This was part of an effort to demolish the political and social barriers to commerce and a central government.[56]

With the rise of a capitalist mode of production, surgeons, smiths, and tailors were dropped from common callings. This was because, with the extension of markets, the law moved from status-based obligations toward free will (contract) and fault (tort) as the basis for legal liabilities. A centralized authority could guarantee legal transactions—contracts—through legal coercion.[57] Still, the adaptation of common law to the American context saw states fixing prices of innkeepers, bakers, millers, and carriers well into the 19th century.[58] Moreover, the use of eminent domain in the period of internal improvements essentially applied the principles of common callings. Entrepreneurs were granted exclusive charters and public subsidies to construct necessary transportation infrastructures. In exchange for this exclusivity, the chartered corporations had to abide by common carrier obligations. They had to serve all persons on reasonable terms and without discrimination. In this sense, traditional common carrier obligations embodied a principle of equity, a kind of *quid pro quo* for the exercise of monopoly power. The unambiguous economic consequence of such common carrier legal arrangements was to facilitate the movement of goods and the development of the economy.[59] Whatever the original explanation, as it was employed in a developing United States, common carrier legal arrangements functioned to promote the development of the economic infrastructures of transportation and communication and to hence to subsidize the circulation of capital.

### The Triumph of Laissez-Faire and the Crisis of Social Control

*Munn* reasserted the common law principle of public interest regulatory controls, but denied state legislatures the ability to determine which businesses were clothed with a public interest. The Court determined that railroads were common carrier-like. Yet, just nine years later, in *Wabash, St. Louis and Pacific Railway Company v. Illinois* (1886), the Supreme Court took away the states' powers to exercise those controls over railroads, because of the effect of those controls on interstate commerce.[60] There are two important dimensions to *Wabash*. At the practical and political levels, the regulation of railroads by the various states proved to be chaotic for an industry which operated in interstate and increasingly in national markets. At the legal level, *Wabash* marked a critical melding of the federal judiciary's traditional protection of interstate commerce with the rising conservative embrace of vested property rights.

In the 1870s the railroad network consisted of many railroad lines. Many lines were as short as a few hundred miles in length. Fixed costs (those costs that did not vary with the amount of traffic carried) were very high, and hence the pressures to increase traffic were terrific. This was the competitive dynamic behind rate discrimination and rate-cutting. These factors of high fixed costs and rate competition convinced railroad managers that uncontrolled competition for through traffic would be ruinous. They turned to various means of interfirm cooperation to control competition, including pooling and cartel federations. Most often these efforts did not work. In their efforts to increase traffic, roads practiced secret rebating or illegal freight classification. Some pool members took traffic that was not allocated to them and often failed to return income to be redistributed by the pool. The great cartels of the late 1870s were also ineffectual against rate-cutting.

As an industry, railroading was beset by instability and too much competition. Such instability encompassed commerce generally, inasmuch as transportation rate wars discriminated against particular localities and generally disrupted the ability of merchants and shippers to predict the economic consequences of their actions. At the same time, various farmer and merchant organizations attacked the railroad cartel and pooling arrangements as attempts to maintain rates at artificially high levels. The ability of state legislatures to control rates within their borders only complicated railroad problems, especially when railroads began to attack the competition problem by building large, interstate systems in the 1880s. By 1884 the rate structure was in chaos, many roads had gone or were going bankrupt, and many railroad managers and owners pressed for state and/or national legislation to legalize pooling.[61]

Instability manifested itself in other than strictly commercial spheres. The transformation of the economy begun by the railroads generated deep hostility among the growing industrial working class and among farmers and merchants increasingly dependent upon distant corporations. It is this dependence which some social historians identify as crucial to the social unrest of the late 19th century.[62] The great and violent railroad strike of 1877 saw an alliance of a railroad working class and older communities against the railroads, a testament to the solidarity of the old community against the "alien" nature of outside capital.[63] Other uproarious labor and political upheavals (such as the Haymarket affair of 1886, the Homestead and Coeur d'Alene labor battles of 1892, the Pullman railroad boycott of 1894 to name the most famous) reflect the severe social conflicts of this period. The widespread "anti-monopoly" popular sentiment of the late 19th century (which fueled the passage of the Sherman Antitrust Act in 1890) must be seen in the context of the social instability caused by the corporate transformation of the economy. As a contemporary, James Hudson, described it in 1886:

> Power now left in the hands of the railway managers, to change their rates so as to discriminate in favor of one set of shippers and against another, or to manipulate the business of their corporations so as to affect the stock market, is a dangerous and intolerable threat to commerce, to investors, and to the whole social fabric. . . .[64]

This economic transformation and consequent social instability were facilitated by a federal judiciary which systematically struck down all local controls over corporate activity.

The advent of an activist and conservative Court was portended by Justice

Stephen Field's vigorous dissent in *Munn*. Field agreed with the arguments of the railroad lawyers at every turn and called the majority opinion "subversive of the rights of private property." He lamented that in *Munn* the Court had passed up the opportunity to define the limits of state powers and to provide rules of action relevant to the new national economy.[65] By the mid-1880s Field's views on "substantive due process" had triumphed. *Wabash* and subsequent Court decisions in the 1890s asserted federal judicial authority over the economy in order to expand contract liberty and to serve laissez-faire economic principles.[66] This is the period (beginning in the 1870s and ending with the Depression) where the Court scrutinized and invalidated economic regulations pursuant to the due process clause of the Fourteenth Amendment. Laws aimed at redistributing resources were considered by their very nature dangerous and falling outside the legislative function. Laurence Tribe describes this period of legal formalism as constitutive of a model of implied limitations on government. He writes in *American Constitutional Law*,

> By defining the spheres of private, state, and national power in terms of the essential character and hence the implied limitations of each, federal judges believed they had derived a science of rights in which congressional laws intruding upon the state domain would be invalidated just as state laws invading the private domain would be struck down.[67]

This period of the "science of rights" was characterized by maximum contractual freedom and narrowed tort liability. The law was to encourage risk-taking as part of the public good and to restrict liability for the incidentally harmful consequences of such socially useful activity. As Oliver Wendell Holmes wrote in *The Common Law* (1881), a hugely influential legal treatise, "under common law a man *acts* at his peril." He continued,

> . . . the general principle of our law is that loss from accident must lie where it falls, and this principle is not affected by the fact that a human being is the instrument of misfortune. . . . A man need not, it is true, do this or that act—the term *act* implies a choice—but he must act somehow. Furthermore, the public generally profits by individual activity. As action cannot be avoided, and tends to the public good, there is obviously no policy in throwing the hazard of what is at once desirable and inevitable upon the actor.[68]

The negative Commerce Clause doctrine, in the interest of forging a national area of trade, struck down all state and local regulations which were thought to impinge on this trading area. The laissez-faire economic theory, buttressed by judicial expansion of contract rights, asserted that each entrepreneur. acting in his own self-interest, would best satisfy the public welfare. The economy would control or regulate itself. But the events of the late 19th century revealed that without *some* controls, the economy did not work properly and, worse, threatened the very social fabric. Labor strife and community resentment against "the trusts" were rife. Furthermore, the strict formalism of the law itself became a fetter to the predictability of economic risk-taking. The new theories of contracts and torts had served to overthrow all precommercial and older anti-developmental restraints on economic activity, including, however, protection of the reliance interest in contracts and precontractual duty to bargain in good faith. As indicated earlier, a major problem with the original national industry—the railroads—was widespread corruption, secret and discriminatory rates and rebates, and too much competition, resulting in disruption in the flow of commerce. Thus, maximum contractual freedom and minimum tort liability did *not* promote rational economic development, particularly when the transportation infrastructure was subject to uncertainty.[69]

## The Rise of the Interstate Commerce Commission

The combination of class strife, often anarchic conditions in commerce, and a conservative judiciary created major social conflicts without mechanisms for their solution. In the wake of the *Wabash* decision, conflict focused on the railroads. Striking down local control of railroads, *Wabash* created a vacuum which satisfied no interest involved in the railroad disputes. Though *Wabash* rid the railroads of the variety of state regulations, the industry was incapable of controlling destructive internecine competition itself. The industry desperately required some means of quelling competition. One way to secure this goal was to attain enforcement of pooling agreements. The various merchant and shipper groups, depending on where they were situated in the railroad network, demanded different things, but most often an end to rate discrimination. Radical farmers wanted anti-pooling restrictions. No existing political institution could solve problems of this complexity.

The judiciary had moved to federalize commerce, recognizing the irrationality of a national economy being controlled at the state and local levels.[70] The Court's clear policy in economic matters was to guarantee contractual liberty. But pure contractual freedom—at least with regard to railroads—did not ensure economic rationality. The other institution of political power, the party, structurally was unable to exercise centralized control. The party system, uniquely capable of expressing *community* impulses on account of its geographically rooted structure, for the same reason was largely incapable of systematic *national* decision-making, of the type now "required" by the emergence of a national economic system.[71]

Though bills to regulate the railroads on a national level had been before Congress for many years, *Wabash* forced Congress to act. The instability surrounding the railroads produced a virtual unanimity of interests that some federal action was needed. Open to dispute, not surprisingly, was what type of federal action. The agrarian anti-monopoly forces of the west and south generally backed the proposal to create an absolute set of laws banning pooling and long-haul, short-haul rate differentials. Such laws would be overseen by the courts.[72] Pro-railroad and industry experts (horrified by the economic irrationality of the anti-monopoly position) and some important shippers argued in favor of a commission charged with general guidelines, but which would examine each railroad issue and complaint on its merits. The proposal for an administrative commission was conceived as a way to remove all politically divisive and potentially dangerous policy decisions from the legislative arena.[73] The compromise legislation which resulted in the Act to Regulate Interstate Commerce gave something to everybody—and in this respect prefigured one of the main problems in the operations of the ICC and most subsequent regulatory agencies, the problem of the vague and imprecise legislative mandate.

The commission form was adopted along with a general anti-pooling provision and an ambiguous long-haul, short-haul provision. Beyond general common carrier regulations, such as prohibition of personal discrimination, and obligation that rates be "reasonable" and clearly posted, the Commission's mandate would need clarification by the courts. Indeed, the immediate loser was the railroad industry, inasmuch as the ICC's mandate prohibited pooling. As Stephen Skowronek and others have observed, the problem with the Interstate Commerce Act was not that it served any one interest but that it ventured into inconsistency and ambiguity by failing to choose among the interests. Congress didn't transform social and economic conflicts into a coherent regulatory policy so much as shift those conflicts to a new institution.[74] Whereas the creation of the Interstate Commerce Commission did signal the genesis of a new administrative political institution to deal with the national economy, the ICC was hemmed in by the two existing institutions of political power. Hampered from the beginning by an inconsistent mandate which reflected the geographic pluralism of the legislative arena, the ICC's authority and actions would be consistently undercut by the federal judiciary.

In spite of its weak and inconsistent mandate, the early ICC evolved into an agency that attempted to promote a rational railroad system and foster further economic development. The Commission chose to ignore provisions of its enabling legislation which were economically irrational, and put its stamp on provisions of the act which were left ambiguous. However, in nearly all of these efforts, the courts rebuffed the ICC.[75] Though the Court paved the way for the ICC with *Wabash,* the dynamics of legal formalism were so strong that the Court struck down any exercise of administrative rule-making unless it was explicitly tied to the provisions of the Interstate Commerce Act. And even then the principle of contractual freedom overrode regulation. These Court actions over commission authority did not necessarily help the railroad industry. For instance, the ICC's tacit acceptance of pooling arrangements was struck down in 1897 and 1898.[76] Given its judicial emasculation, the ICC suffered from the vagueness of its legislative mandate. The agency had neither the power nor the autonomy, in the despairing words of Aldace walker, ICC Commissioner and railroad man, to "protect them (the railroads) not so much against the public as against themselves and against each other."[77] To the extent that the first venture in national regulation had any consequence whatever, it may have contributed slightly to the decline of the railroad industry.[78]

Notwithstanding its early inefficacy, the Interstate Commerce Commission marked a shift of political power. It constituted a new institution of political power. Unlike the party, which was receptive to geographically based constituent concerns and interests, the administrative agency was created to be receptive to national concerns and interests. In this sense, the administrative agency was the product of the rise of a national economy. The railroad was the first true national industry, whose operation disrupted older local economies and constructed the means by which a national economy would emerge. The instability it caused and the complexity of alleviating that instability required a new institution of social control. A formalistic judiciary helped facilitate the transformation of the economy but put forward no mechanisms of social control beyond contractual freedom and the self-regulating market. If the ICC was originally a way for a divided Congress to shirk responsibility over national railroad policy, the administrative solution (composed of an expert body in continual session) became legitimated as most appropriate to the regulation of a complex and changing industry.[79] Regulation is "administration," that is, an ongoing process of rational oversight and manipulation. A signal advantage of regulation (over the "absolute" nature of legislation and judicial opinion) is that it is substantive and continuous; such oversight is molded to concrete problems and cases on an ongoing basis. Regulatory agencies thus mark a new phase in the state's dual role of protecting capital and responding to social grievances. The early ICC sought to guide *and* control. The first genuine "phase" of regulatory creation came during the period of Progressive Era reforms.

## The Three Phases of Regulation

As I have argued, regulatory agencies constitute a new institution of political power, concomitant with the rise of a national economy. Regulatory oversight is characteristically substantive and continuous. Underlying the creation of *all* agencies is their ability to establish administrative controls on and for industry. Though all regulatory agencies reflect the need for a new institution of social control, agencies are different and fulfill different functions. The essential function of an agency is generally tied to the historical conditions within which it arises. There have been three major waves of regulatory genesis in American history, each period characterized by a particular set of problems, a particular kind of politics, and a particular type of regulatory agency.

The second section of the chapter describes the three phases and general types of regulation. The Progressive Era saw the rise of agencies to deal with the economic and social instability created by the transition to a national, corporate economy. Those agencies sought to construct general rules for business behavior. New Deal regulatory agencies sought to construct cartels for particular industries destabilized by the economic conditions of the Depression. Great Society regulatory agencies sought to expand regulation beyond purely economic concerns. These agencies were established in large part to control "externalities," the unintended social consequences of business behavior.

### The Progressive Era: The Construction of General Market Rules (1900– 1916)

Key regulatory agencies were established in the Progressive Era to formulate *general* rules for business behavior. The important agencies established in the Progressive Era were the Federal Reserve Board (1913), the Federal Trade Commission (1914), and, to a far lesser degree of importance, the United States Shipping Board (1916). Also, the Interstate Commerce Commission was endowed with more expansive powers in the Progressive Era. The politics of regulatory creation are part and parcel of the general politics of reform during the Progressive Era. The question of who initiated and who benefited from reform is the subject of a vigorous historical debate. The period saw the creation of administrative capabilities at various levels of government. Cities set up administrative authorities to oversee the provision of municipal services, such as streetcar transportation and electric power. Some states set up authorities to oversee factory safety. In addition to the *bona fide* regulatory agencies, the federal government exercised quasi-regulatory functions through other agencies as well, notably the management of natural resource use by the Forest Service (created in 1905), some oversight of food and drug adulteration consequent to the 1906 Pure Food and Drug Act, and the enforcement of the antitrust laws by the Justice Department's Antitrust Division (established in 1903).

Along with the ICC, perhaps the most important backdrop to the Progressive Era agencies was the passage of the Sherman Antitrust Act in 1890. The Sherman Act reflected the widespread feelings of dependence upon and animosity toward corporate activity. The Sherman Act took old common-law proscriptions against restraint of trade and encased them in federal legislation. These, of course, were general proscriptions. The Sherman Act refrained from spelling out distinct standards by which private economic power would be regulated. In fact, Congress' decision not to place antitrust in a regulatory agency ensured that the fleshing-out of antitrust standards would proceed on a case-by-case basis rather than by general rule.[80] The conservative Court interpreted the Sherman Act narrowly, ruling against only loose combines, not against the tight combinations of holding companies and mergers. The great era of business consolidation, the years 1897–1904, came after the Sherman Act—not before.[81]

The basic premise behind antitrust was that the unemcumbered free market did not always work to secure economic rationality. The market sometimes resulted in the concentration of economic power, and such concentration permitted the exercise of "monopoly power." The general idea was that economic concentration was possible because corporations could engage in activities specifically designed to restrain trade. Antitrust law would make those activities illegal, thus restore competition and the proper functioning of the market. But the actual execution of the Sherman Act under the machinery of the judiciary was conservative and slow. Popular antagonism to "the trusts" continued unabated throughout the first decade of the century. William Jennings Bryan's two presidential campaigns were dominated by strong attacks on the trusts as the by-products of Republican policy.[82]

Following the Supreme Court's 1911 decisions in the *Standard Oil* and *American Tobacco* cases, in which the Court asserted a difference between "reasonable" and "unreasonable" business combinations, that is, between "good" and "bad" trusts, popular and legislative action moved toward creating an antitrust regulatory commission.[83] These two cases had much the same stimulus on trade commission legislation as *Wabash* had had for railroad legislation. However, if popular antagonism toward the trusts fueled the legislative impulse, nearly all interests supported the idea of a trade commission in the aftermath of *Standard Oil* and *American Tobacco* (albeit for different reasons). Many businessmen supported the idea of a commission, expecting that it would clarify what they could and could not do. They also hoped that a commission might pass in advance upon forms of business organization and methods of business conduct. Anti-monopolists saw a manifest need for an expert, continuing, and impartial agency to ferret out violations of the law and aid in their prosecution. A third group believed that corporations engaged in interstate commerce should be licensed under federal law. The administration of such a licensing law would be carried out by a commission.[84]

The 1914 Clayton Act and Federal Trade Commission enabling act represented typical compromise legislation. They sought to define more precisely those activities that came within the purview of the antitrust laws. The Clayton Act singled out price discrimination, exclusive dealing and tying contracts, intercorporate stockholding, and interlocking directorates as actions which restrained trade.[85] The Federal Trade Commission Act established a commission to enforce the provisions of the Clayton Act and carry out investigations of unlawful trade practices. In principle, then, antitrust was an effort by the federal government to construct guidelines by which corporations could gauge their decisions regarding legal operations and mergers—in effect, rules and standards for market behavior.

In an analogous manner, the Federal Reserve Board marked the assertion of federal authority over an infrastructure whose unregulated function underlay serious economic instability. The banking system historically was punctuated by periodic bank panics that generated widespread economic effects. By the 1900s, the American economy was plagued by inelastic currency and an inadequate reserve structure. Gabriel Kolko asserts that the rise of the merger movement and the market for industrial securities sharply increased the amount of speculative activity in finance. One consequence of this was to diffuse banking power away from the large New York banks. The Panic of 1907 underscored the decline of New York banking power and the trend toward instability in finance. Plagued by an acute unavailability of money and a threatened collapse of key trust companies, the 1907 Panic required the intervention of the Treasury Department. Treasury deposited $37 million in New York banks and issued $150 million in certificates and bonds so that banks could issue currency on the bonds as collateral.[86]

In conjunction with bank crises, popular sentiment against bankers, stirred by the House subcommittee investigation of the "Money Trust" in 1912, impelled the legislative movement toward banking reform. Some bankers began to move toward some reform legislation, though there was bitter disagreement over what form this might take. In the end, banking interests fought against the bill that was to become the Federal Reserve Act.[87]

The Federal Reserve Act of 1913 created a regional system built around twelve federal reserve banks, and placed this system under the direction of a Federal Reserve Board. These were bankers' banks, created mainly to hold bank reserves. All national banks under the Act were required to become part of the Federal Reserve System and to subscribe to capital stock in the Federal Bank (equal to 6 percent of their paid-up capital stock and surplus). The Board could fix the rates for rediscounted paper in the districts, suspend and adjust reserve requirements, issue and retire Reserve notes, and exercise extensive controls over the various district banks. In short, the Board essentially was given the power to regulate the currency supply and the responsibility to see that banks secured some part of their notes.[88] Whether or not the Federal Reserve Act signified the victory of New York bankers, as Kolko asserts it did, the act clearly represents the intervention of federal administrative authority in an attempt to rationalize important aspects of the currency infrastructure. A more elastic and presumably more secure money supply would meet the needs of an expanding and increasingly complex economy.

The establishment of the U.S. Shipping Board and the grant of greater powers to the Interstate Commerce Commission are less clearly exercises of administrative authority in the service of general rules for business conduct, for they constitute the regulation of particular industries. However, the importance of railroads and ocean shipping for interstate and international commerce underscores the general, commerce-based nature of their regulation. The Mann-Elkins Act of 1910 not only gave the ICC power to suspend proposed increases in railroad rates by carriers, but expanded the ICC's jurisdiction over the telecommunications infrastructure (telegraph, telephone, and cable companies) as well.

The Shipping Act of 1916 took place amidst a crisis of ocean shipping rates during World War I. With European vessels pulled out of U.S. shipping markets due to wartime needs, ocean shipping rates jumped tenfold between 1914 and 1916. After years of failure to obtain government subsidies for American shipping, the industry faced legislation to solve exorbitant and discriminatory shipping rates. The Shipping Act in fact provided both regulation and subsidy. To alleviate the shortage of ships, the Shipping Board was allocated $50 million to purchase, lease, or construct vessels, and to sell these to private parties. In addition, the Board required all carriers to file all agreements on rates and charges. The Board was empowered to disapprove or cancel rates which were unjustly discriminatory, unfair, or injurious to commerce, and to approve the others.[89] In other words, the Board brought traditional common carrier principles to ocean shipping.

Though popular clamor against corporations did indeed galvanize the effort to create regulatory agencies during the Progressive Era, the "public interest" interpretation of reform as the unambiguous victory of the people over the trust cannot truly be sustained. (See Table 1.) In some instances, notably the creation of the FTC, there was widespread agreement—even among businessmen—that a trade commission should be established. Progressive reforms and regulatory agencies constituted the creation of administrative structures designed to construct general market rules for business activity. They were designed for "producers." To the extent that "the people" in general benefited from Progressive regulation, it was that such regulation did relieve some economic instability, and the construction of market rules did eliminate certain abuses. Even the Pure Food and Drug Act was not truly consumer protection legislation—its main purpose was to abolish unfair competition in trade. In this respect, the first phase of regulation very much reflected the common law principles from which much regulatory law was drawn. The common law of public callings was designed primarily to facilitate commerce. It was not consciously animated by a desire to advance a lot of the have-nots. Nonetheless, the have-nots benefited because nondiscrimination, the core of the state's protection of commerce, necessarily entails an equity principle.

If Progressive Era regulation formulated general rules for capitalist behavior, regulation was not very obtrusive. Agencies did not venture too far into private arrangements, and when they did, regulated parties could depend on the courts to invoke the doctrine of substantive due process to strike down the most burdensome agency decisions.[90] However, neither capture nor conspiracy theories of regulatory

TABLE 1.    Regulatory Agencies Created in the Progressive Era

| Agency | Year established | Regulatory responsibility |
|---|---|---|
| Interstate Commerce Commission | 1887 | Prices and entry in railroads (expanded to trucking and buses in 1935, and inland and coastal waterways in 1940) |
| Forest Service (in Executive Branch) | 1905 | Management of resource use |
| Federal Reserve System | 1913 | Interest rates and reserve requirements for national banks; approval of bank mergers, bank holding company acquisitions |
| Federal Trade Commission | 1914 | Business practices, advertising, consumer information |
| US Tariff Commission (now US International Trade Commission) | 1916 | Study all factors relating to US foreign trade; exclude articles from domestic entry |
| US Shipping Board | 1916 | Prices of intercoastal shipping |

Source: Congressional Quarterly, *Federal Regulatory Directory, 1983–84* (Washington, DC: Congressional Quarterly, Inc., 1985).

origin can stand. The regulatory reestablishment of order and the construction of market rules was not necessarily an abandonment of the public interest in favor of business. Rather it was an attempt to solve systemic problems of instability *within* the confines of a capitalist economy. Notwithstanding some anti-corporate rhetoric, Progressive Era reforms defined the public interest within the context of a rationally functioning capitalist system. Consumer welfare was considered enhanced through expanded, rational competition. The establishment of market rules through antitrust, the steps to rationalize the money supply, the attempts to oversee two of the major commerce-bearing transportation systems (and, to a far lesser degree, the telecommunications infrastructure) constituted the major regulatory efforts of the Progressive Era. This regulatory activity marked the expansion of federal jurisdiction to impose nationwide standards and regulations, the object of which was to facilitate free and rational commerce over a national trading area. A byproduct of the effort to facilitate commerce was the emergence of the equity principle of a duty to serve at reasonable charges.

## The New Deal: Price-and-Entry Control for the Protection of Key Industries (1930–1938)

Underlying the second phase of regulatory genesis was the Great Depression and the disintegration of the economy. New Deal agencies extended federal controls over particular industries whose market controls had collapsed. With the three main Progressive Era agencies (ICC, FTC, Federal Reserve), the federal government had sought to establish economic and social stability generally, by formulating general rules for business behavior and by safeguarding the national flow of commerce. In the New Deal, Congress created numerous agencies to rescue *particular* industries burdened by some destabilizing condition. Railroads, trucking, airlines, and bituminous coal were beset by too much competition. Telephony, electricity, and natural gas demonstrated problems and abuses associated with monopolistic holding companies. Radio broadcasting suffered from an absence of industry-wide technical and economic operating rules. The financial securities system, bereft of effective operating controls or oversight, was prone to manipulation and corruption. The collapse of the savings and loan industry and the agricultural credit system signaled deep problems in the banking industry and agriculture generally.

New Deal agencies characteristically were given jurisdiction over a single industry. And whereas some industries fought against regulatory legislation during the Progressive Era, regulation was nearly always welcomed—indeed, advocated—by the affected industries during the New Deal. The main new agencies were the Federal Communications Commission, the Securities and Exchange Commission, the Civil Aeronautics Board, and the National Labor Relations Board. In addition to new agencies, existing agencies were given new responsibilities or additional industries to regulate. The Motor Carrier Act of 1935 brought interstate trucking under the aegis of the Interstate Commerce Commission. The Transportation Act of 1940 placed jurisdiction over domestic waterways in the ICC. The Federal Power Commission was invigorated by the Federal Power Act of 1935, which permitted the FPC to oversee and regulate power holding companies. The Robinson-Patman Act of 1936 gave the Federal Trade Commission new regulatory authority in the area of price discrimination practices. The Wheeler-Lea Act of 1938 enlarged the powers of the FTC and strengthened its powers of enforcement. The agencies created during this period (see Table 2) generally received broad, yet vague mandates from Congress, along with an ability to exercise wide discretion in policy-making.

The politics of regulatory creation in the New Deal period, though not uniform, for the most part etched a discernable pattern: depression-wracked, destabilized industries looked to the federal government to help them get out from under and, ultimately, to rationalize. The politics of New Deal regulatory genesis cannot be divorced from the general politics of industrial recovery and the phenomenon of industrial code creation consequent to the National Industrial Recovery Act.[91] It is in this respect that the traditional public interest interpretation of the relation between business and government falls short, and revisionist historiography comes into its own. That standard view held that the public, through its national government, expanded its invasion of the private sector, over the strenuous objections of businessmen. On the contrary, in industry after industry in the 1930s, the principal business players advocated the use of state authority to effectuate cartelization, price stability, and production controls.

The National Industrial Recovery Act, like much New Deal policy, was riddled with contradictions. The act provided a broad economic charter, not any particular course of action. The NIRA appealed to conflicting pressure groups and reflected within its language conflicting ideologies about economic recovery and business structure. As Ellis Hawley argues, the policy struggle was a "three cornered af-

TABLE 2.   Regulatory Agencies Created in the Depression/New Deal Period

| Agency | Year established | Regulatory responsibility |
|---|---|---|
| Federal Power Commission (FPC) (though established in 1920, FPC was unsuccessful and was reorganized in 1930) | 1920/1930 | Prices for interstate power; security issues of interstate power companies; licensing of private power projects on public lands |
| Food and Drug Administration (FDA) (in Dept. of Health, Education & Welfare) | 1931 | Licenses and controls the labeling of food and drugs |
| Federal Home Loan Bank Board (FHLBB) | 1932 | Interest rates and entry into the savings and loan industry |
| Agricultural Marketing Service (AMS) (in Dept. of Agriculture) | 1932 | Prices and standards for most farm commodities |
| Commodity Credit Corporation (CCC) (in Dept. of Agriculture) | 1933 | Prices and credit for agriculture |
| Federal Deposit Insurance Corporation (FDIC) | 1933 | Supervises insured banks |
| Federal Communications Commission (FCC) | 1934 | Entry into broadcasting; prices and entry into the interstate telecommunications industry |
| Securities and Exchange Commission (SEC) | 1934 | Investor information and securities exchange transactions |
| National Labor Relations Board (NLRB) | 1935 | Labor contracts, negotiations, unfair labor practices |
| National Bituminous Coal Commission (in Interior Dept.; abolished 1939) | 1935 | Regulation of coal prices, unfair trade practices |
| United States Maritime Commission | 1936 | Prices and scheduling of trans-ocean freight carriers |
| Civil Aeronautics Board (CAB) | 1938 | Prices and entry into airline industry |

Source: Congressional Quarterly, *Federal Regulatory Directory, 1983–84* (Washington, DC: Congressional Quarterly, Inc., 1985).

fair'': a business vision of a rational, cartelized business commonwealth in which the industrialists would plan and direct the economy; a vision of a cooperative, collectivist democracy through expert governmental planning; the old competitive model of classical economics, buttressed by antitrust law. The actual act gave something to nearly everyone. Business got government authorization to draft code agreements exempt from the antitrust laws; the planners won their demand for government licensing of business; labor received the right to bargain collectively and wage/hour standards; the unemployed got a public works authorization. For the most part, however, the business vision won out in practice. Under the National Recovery Administration (NRA), industries essentially were given the go-ahead to constitute self-governing trade associations that would write their own codes of law and business behavior. Actual government coercion was minimal. This was a kind of government-sponsored cartelization.[92]

The effects of industrial self-government entailed some initial stability in specific industries, but also resulted in higher prices across the board, the circumvention of the labor provisions by company unions, and the undermining of the efforts to rescue agriculture. These consequences allowed those with competing visions to deadlock much NRA policy by 1934. In public pronouncements, if not always in actual practice, the NRA began to support the concept of the free market and echoed the old anti-monopoly antitrust tradition.[93] Moreover, by the end of 1934, the codes and controls had broken down in many industries. In May 1935, the Supreme Court put an end to the process. The Court struck down the NRA in the *Schechter* case as an improper delegation of legislative powers to the executive and an unconstitutional regulation of interstate commerce.[94]

Though the NRA failed, much of its impetus and goals—and contradictions—survived in the New Deal regulatory agencies. The New Deal price-and-entry regulatory agencies did effectively cartelize certain (infrastructure) industries (on a smaller scale) in the post-*Schechter* era. Indeed, some of this process of cartelization had begun earlier. With telephony, the immense corporate strength of the American Telephone and Telegraph Company, along with Congressional support of the idea that telephony constituted a "natural monopoly," permitted that company to dominate the telephone industry in the 1920s. When the telephone industry was brought under the regulatory jurisdiction of the Federal Communications Commission in 1934, AT&T already monopolized the industry. For years, AT&T supported the idea of federal regulation, so as to lend political legitimacy and economic stability to the monopolized telephone industry. FCC regulation did just that.

In broadcasting, the competition for scarce desirable radio frequencies and operating time slots in the mid- and late 1920s led to a breakdown of the nascent radio broadcast system. In the absence of effective governmental oversight, market controls in broadcasting ultimately resulted in chaos over the airwaves. Broadcasters transmitted on any frequency at the highest power of which they were capable, and the resulting interference meant that clear reception was impossible. Many interest groups and Congressmen had advocated the regulation of broadcasting for several years—with marginal success. With the interference problems of the mid-1920s, the beleaguered major broadcasters also turned to Congress for (limited) oversight. The resulting legislation created the Federal Radio Commission (FRC) in 1928 to function as a licensing body. The FRC was given limited jurisdiction over radio broadcasting, but did have the power to assign broadcasters to specific radio frequencies at designated power and designated times. In other words, the FRC applied administrative authority to control entry into and to set technical operating standards for radio broadcasting. These controls stabilized radio and indirectly permitted the emergence of a cartel of commercial networks. The Communications Act of 1934 moved the early principles of broadcast regulation into the Federal Communications Commission.[95]

## How the New Deal Agencies Work

In the largest sense, the New Deal agency's job was to bring rationality to the particular industry whose market controls had failed. In fulfilling the goal to stabilize these various industries, the New Deal regulatory agencies reflected the same ideological conflicts found in the National Industrial Recovery Act. The legislative mandates obliged the agencies to protect, to guide, and to police—at the same time. Typically, agencies established how many and which firms could enter into business, set general pricing levels, and formulated rules specific to the operation of an industry, such as which routes a certain trucking firm would service or which radio frequency a licensee would occupy. In practice, this most often meant cartelization. The New Deal regulatory agencies created structures of mutual benefit—cartels— among the major interests (often including organized labor) in the industries placed under regulatory oversight. Industries and markets were saved precisely by not permitting marketplace controls to function freely. Regulation substituted administrative rationality and informal political decision-making for market rationality. Hence, the major functions of New Deal agencies were the setting of prices and the control of entry.

The ICC's oversight of trucking is typical. Fierce competition in trucking during the 1930s was believed to drive prices well below costs. This dynamic threatened to culminate either in monopolization or the destruction of the industry entirely. With the Depression's drastic drop in demand and a consequent internecine struggle for markets, large trucking firms began to support some system of regulation that would establish minimum rates and wages and eliminate "irresponsible" (that is, rate-cutting) operators. Moreover, competition from trucking severely affected the fortunes of the railroads. The railroads (which, in terms of national investment, was outranked only by agriculture in the 1930s) strongly urged that trucking be regulated. Though truckers did not want to be regulated by an agency, particularly the railroad-identified Interstate Commerce Commission, with the collapse of the NRA the industry vigorously supported legislation that would give the ICC oversight over trucking.[96] The Roosevelt Administration supported the extension of the ICC's jurisdiction to trucking, believing that eliminating or moderating competition would stabilize the industry and help end the Depression. Similar logic pertained to the other transportation industries and to energy-related industries.

In a process highly reminiscent of the NRA, transportation carriers brought under regulation were deemed exempt from the antitrust laws. The ICC delegated rate-making power to "rate bureaus," which were associations of private carriers operating under a grant of antitrust immunity provided by the Reed-Bulwinkle Act. Carriers were expected to meet and collectively set the rates and terms of service on particular routes. The ICC periodically would review the rates for reasonableness. Regulation also controlled entry into the industry, in effect cartelizing it. The ICC controlled entry into the trucking business through a complex licensing system. The agency constructed myriad rules concerning the types of cargo and routes for particular truck licenses, and authorized acquisitions and mergers of trucking firms. An applicant for a new common carrier truck route, for example, would have to meet the difficult test of proving that the new route was "required by the present or future public convenience and necessity.'' The primary test for approval of new entrants was whether the new operation or service would serve a useful public purpose without endangering the operations of existing carriers. Historically, the ICC interpreted the statute to mean in part that an applicant for new service must show that the area could not be served as well by existing carriers. The burden of proof was on new applicants.[97] The regulatory discouragement of new entrants meant that the cartel-determined price would hold. In so doing, the ICC constructed regulatory-enforced cartels that stabilized the trucking industry through the protection of existing trucking firms from competition.[98]

These essential characteristics of ICC regulation of trucking hold for many of the other regulatory policies of this period. The CAB employed its powers of rate fixing and entry restriction to bring stability and effective cartelization to commercial airlines. The FPC brought order to interstate power companies through fixing rates and overseeing the business organization of interstate power companies. The FCC provided oversight and rate regulation over telecommunications, and set technical and licensing standards for broadcasting. The SEC established strict rules over securities trading and the operation of exchanges.[99] The FHLBB and FDIC brought order to banking by setting interest rate ceilings and extending government backing to some notes. The CCC and AMS began the complex involvement of the federal government to stabilize agriculture, by extending credit and setting prices of certain farm commodities.

This should not mislead the reader that such regulatory intervention fulfilled all of its goals, or always operated logically or consistently. It did not, for reasons which will be discussed. Nor should the reader be misled into thinking that New Deal regulatory interventions substantially altered the pre-existing institutional structures of specific industries. The FCC, for example, did nothing to change the advertising-based, privately operated, commercial radio system. Except in highly specific instances (such as interstate power companies), New Deal regulatory interventions accepted pre-existing institutional structures and applied controls that would stabilize the structures of those industries under their jurisdictions. And for the most part the regulatory agencies were successful in this fundamental endeavor.

Again, for the most part New Deal regulatory agencies engaged in a complex form of protection. It is in this vein that scholars who view New Deal regulation as a form of ''broker statism'' are descriptively on the mark.[100] But, again, the New Deal regulatory agencies also reflected some of the ideological conflicts and contradictions found in the NIRA. The regulatory stabilization of these industries thus embodied a familiar *quid pro quo:* the expansion of service by the imposition of common carrier-type obligations. This fact highlights the overriding *commerce* function of much of New Deal regulation. Regulation was to stabilize an industry *and* foster its development at least partly by requiring that suppliers fulfill expanded service obligations. Industries under regulation had to provide adequate and nondiscriminatory service, even in unprofitable markets. Regardless of profit potential, regulated buses, trucks, and airlines had to serve out-of-the-way areas; local telephone service was made relatively cheap and universally available; television licenses would be reserved for geographic communities, and broadcasters were obliged to act as ''public trustees'' of the airwaves.

In order to facilitate this commerce function, regulatory agencies formulated complex rate structures to cross-subsidize certain types of routes and services.[101] The common carrier obligations which guaranteed (often cheap) service thus had the effect of bringing consumers into the regulatory system of mutual benefits and compromises. And the protections provided to regulated businesses also had the effect of bringing labor into the system of mutual benefits and compromises. The stabilization of those industries, along with the establishment of the other crucial New Deal agency, the National Labor Relations Board, facilitated the broad unionization of regulated industries. Thus, New Deal regulation defined the public interest as the government oversight of rationally functioning, privately owned businesses that provided services universally, relatively cheaply, and in nondiscriminatory fashion. The economic consequence of this was to stabilize and universalize the infrastructure for commerce.

It would be mistaken to try to reduce the plentitude of New Deal regulation to a single principle. A Federal Trade Commission acting under the antitrust-oriented Robinson-Patman Act embraces different ideological principles than do the cartelized trucking rate bureaus acting under the imprimatur of a protectionist ICC. The New Deal consisted of several conflicting ideologies. Nonetheless, when looking at the main regulatory agencies, the infrastructure-commerce principle stands out. The industries to which federal regulation was extended in this period were transportation, telecommunications, energy, financial exchanges, and some "sick" industries such as coal and agriculture. The first four constitute infrastructural services for economic growth. The stabilization of these, and the imposition of common law obligations to extend transportation, energy, and telecommunications service, served the state's goal of facilitating commerce in an era of economic collapse.

Of course, the New Dealers did seek to expand regulatory controls to other than infrastructure industries. The NRA's attempt to institute government-fostered price and production controls in 1933 was a bold effort to cartelize some 450 industries. Also, state legislatures passed laws which placed regulatory controls over industries not belonging to the judicially recognized select circle of businesses sufficiently clothed with a public interest.[102] Again, however, the infrastructure-commerce rationale stands out. Until the Supreme Court's decision in *Nebbia v. New York,* the Court struck down the extension of regulation to the manufacture of food, clothing, and fuels, and the operations of theater ticket brokers, employment agencies, gasoline service stations, and ice manufacturing plants.[103] The Court determined that these businesses were essentially private in nature—that is, not clothed with a public interest—and thus beyond the reach of regulation. *Nebbia,* which upheld New York's right to fix a minimum price for milk, threw out the old constitutional standard of businesses clothed with a public interest. *Nebbia* essentially approved any government regulation for the public welfare, so long as such regulation is not unreasonable, arbitrary, or capricious.[104]

Notwithstanding the important constitutional change marked by *Nebbia,* New Deal regulation for the most part remained ensconced within the infrastructure-commerce mode. This is illustrated by the logic of the key judicial decisions of the period. In the famous *Schechter* case, the Supreme Court ruled that the NRA was an improper delegation of legislative powers to the executive and an unconstitutional

regulation of interstate commerce. The Court struck down the entire statutory delegation as unduly broad.[105] And in *Baldwin v. Seelig* the Court unanimously struck
down the New York regulations upheld in *Nebbia* insofar as they applied to milk
purchased outside the state—precisely because these regulations disrupted interstate
commerce.[106] Thus, if the facilitation of commerce permitted extensive government
intervention by means of federal and state regulatory agencies during the New Deal,
commerce also constituted the *limit* to such intervention.

With this in mind, it should not be surprising that the National Labor Relations
Board, one of two important New Deal agencies which don't seem to fit my
categories very well (the NLRB and the Food and Drug Administration in many
respects are more like the social regulatory agencies created during the Great Society), passed judicial scrutiny precisely on the basis of its *commerce* function. The
NLRB was not an agency which regulated an industry at all. What the NLRB did
was to institutionalize in a federal agency the newly achieved power of organized
labor and to establish labor as "countervailing force" in the American economy.
However, for our purposes what is interesting is the Court's logic in upholding the
constitutionality of the National Labor Relations Act. In *NLRB v. Jones and Laughlin Steel Corp.*, the Court upheld the National Labor Relations Act because it would
protect commerce from the evils of industrial labor strife. Similar logic upheld the
legitimacy of minimum wage and maximum working hours standards in *United
States v. Darby*.[107] In this regard, the NLRB does fit into the basic infrastructure-
commerce characteristics of New Deal regulatory agencies.

### The Great Society: "Externalities" and the Triumph of Consumer Values (1965–1977)

Though Progressive Era and New Deal regulatory agencies often represented themselves as defending the "consumer's interest," in fact the orientation of these
agencies was toward the *producers*. These regulatory agencies defined the public
interest within the context of a rationally functioning capitalist economy. The construction of general operating rules and specific industrial cartels constituted governmental intervention into the problems of competition among producers. With the
third phase of regulatory origin, the orientation of regulatory activity changed. The
agencies created during the 1965–1977 period regulated the social consequences of
business behavior. The "social" regulatory agencies reflected the values of activist
non-producer groups (usually categorized as "consumer," "environmentalist," or
"public interest" groups).

The social regulatory phase began in the mid-1960s as a partial outgrowth of the
Johnson Administration's Great Society programs. As David Vogel has argued, the
Great Society programs sought to utilize the incentives of the profit system to
ameliorate the urban crisis. With the rise of liberal and left-oriented social movements, a limited reform effort grew into an explicit challenge to corporate prerogatives. The political agenda expanded between 1968 and 1977 to take up issues
that were previously assumed to be the legitimate province of capital. These included the distribution of wealth, the political control of capital allocation, the
ownership of natural resources—as manifested in the debates over tax reform, the

proposal for a federal energy corporation, and the debate over national economic planning.[108] Notwithstanding the structural bias of the state toward capital, clearly this was a period where the political agenda was defined by those hostile to capital.

With the opening of the political agenda by the Civil Rights movement and later by New Left, consumer, and environmental activism, pressures for increased social responsibility were transformed into demands for greater corporate accountability. The demands of these various groups—more often than not allied with those of labor—were pursued in the political arena under the aegis of an amalgam of committed and effective groups popularly referred to as the "public interest" movement. The demands for greater corporate accountability culminated with the passage of a remarkable amount of regulatory legislation and the creation of many new regulatory agencies. Though the process began with the concern for civil rights and the establishment in 1965 of the Equal Employment Opportunity Commission (EEOC), the major orientation of newly created agencies was in the areas of environmental, occupational, and consumer protection.

Like Progressive Era agencies, Great Society agencies were created amidst popular uproar over corporate activity. Unlike those earlier agencies, however, the new legislation and new agencies defined the public interest outside of the context of industry needs. "Externalities" is the term economists ascribe to the unintended consequences and costs attendant to private decisions, such as air and water pollution and unsafe and/or unhealthful commodities and workplaces. To a large degree, Great Society agencies entailed an effort to force corporations to take responsibility for the externalities caused by their business decisions. The social regulatory agencies became the expression of, and forum wherein, the public interest movement and elements of organized labor challenged the purposes and prerogatives of the modern corporation. Not surprisingly, most social regulatory agencies were created over the opposition of capital.

Twenty of the nation's 55 major regulatory agencies were established between 1964 and 1977. Of these a majority was established directly to protect either consumers, employees, or the general public from physical harm due to corporate activities. Sixty-two new laws were enacted between 1964 and 1979 to restrict corporate social conduct in the broad area of consumer safety and health.[109] Many of these laws constrained business actions and caused business compliance costs. The jurisdiction of these agencies most often cut across industry lines, affecting nearly the entire business community (see Table 3).

The regulatory activism of the phase-three period was fueled in part by new muckrakers. The thalidomide shock of the early 1960s and Rachel Carson's *Silent Spring* (1962) resonated with a larger public fear over the industrial use of chemicals. Jessica Mitford's *The American Way of Death* (1963), which exposed abuses in funeral practices, indirectly led to an FTC investigation of the industry. Ralph Nader's *Unsafe at Any Speed* (1965) evoked a widespread response over auto safety and corporate misconduct, and galvanized Congress to consider automobile safety.[110] It is difficult to overestimate the role of Nader. As Michael Pertschuk relates in *Revolt Against Regulation*, Nader's role as muckraker was augmented by his extraordinary skill and effectiveness as an advocate *within* the legislative and regulatory processes. Nader also spawned specific organizations—the non-profit pub-

TABLE 3.  Regulatory Agencies Created in the Great Society Period

| Agency | Year established | Regulatory responsibility |
|--------|------------------|---------------------------|
| Equal Employment Opportunity Commission (independent) | 1965 | Administer Title VII of 1964 Civil Rights Act which prohibits discrimination in hiring |
| Federal Highway Administration (in Transportation Dept.) | 1966 | Safety standards for construction, design and maintenance of highways; interstate truck and bus operator safety |
| Federal Railroad Administration (in Transportation Dept.) | 1966 | Safety of interstate rail transportation |
| Council on Environmental Quality (independent executive) | 1969 | Pollution oversight |
| Environmental Protection Agency (independent executive) | 1970 | Air and water quality standards; emission standards for pollutants; pesticide classification and safety |
| Cost Accounting Standards Board (legislative agency) | 1970 | Standards for cost accounting methods used by federal defense contractors and subcontractors |
| National Credit Union Administration (independent executive) | 1970 | Approve or disapprove application for federal credit union charters |
| National Highway Traffic and Safety Administration (in Transportation Dept.) | 1970 | Safety standards for automobiles; establish fuel use limits; tire standards |
| Securities Investors Protection Commission | 1970 | Investor information and securities exchange transactions |
| National Oceanic and Atmospheric Administration (in Commerce Dept.) | 1970 | Management of marine resources; protection of marine mammals |
| Farm Credit Administration (independent) | 1971 | Supervising, regulating, examining the Farm Credit System |
| Consumer Product Safety Commission (independent) | 1972 | Establish mandatory safety standards governing the design, construction, contents, performance, and labeling of consumer products |
| Domestic and International Administration (now the Industry and Trade Administration in Commerce Dept.) | 1972 | Research, analysis, development of policy initiatives in areas of trade, finance, and investment; import quotas (formerly Bureau of Manufactures) |
| Occupational Safety and Health Administration (in Dept. of Labor) | 1973 | Develop and enforce mandatory job safety and health standards; reporting and recordkeeping of same |
| Drug Enforcement Administration (in Justice Dept.) | 1973 | Combating trade in narcotics |
| Federal Energy Administration (became Economy Regulatory Administration in Energy Dept.) | 1973 | Set prices for petroleum; coal conversion programs; temperature limits for buildings; energy standards for new buildings |

TABLE 3   *Cont.*

| Agency | Year established | Regulatory responsibility |
|---|---|---|
| Mining Enforcement and Safety Administration (in Interior Dept.; now Mine Safety and Health Administration in Labor Dept.) | 1973 | Develop mandatory safety and health standards for mines |
| Council on Wage and Price Stability (executive agency) | 1974 | Investigate wage and price increases to determine their effect on inflation |
| Foreign Agricultural US Service (in Agriculture Dept.) | 1974 | Information for marketing of farm products abroad |
| Federal Election Commission (independent) | 1975 | Supervision of electoral campaign financing and contributions |
| National Transportation Safety Board (independent) | 1975 | Investigate all transportation accidents |
| Commodity Futures Trading Commission (independent) | 1975 | Sets terms and conditions for futures contracts and the exchanges trading such contracts |
| Materials Transporation Bureau (in Transportation Dept.) | 1975 | Equipment and operating safety for transportation of all materials by pipeline and all hazardous materials by any mode |
| Nuclear Regulatory Commission (independent, reorganized from Atomic Energy Commission) | 1975 | Licensing of nuclear reactors; plant safety and design |
| Copyright Royalty Tribunal | 1976 | Sets fees and charges on copyright materials |
| Federal Grain Inspection Service (in Agriculture Dept.) | 1976 | Standards for grain; weighing |
| Office of Consumer Affairs and Regulatory Functions (in Housing and Urban Development Dept.) | 1977 | Ensuring participation by voluntary and non-governmental organizations in development of urban and regional areas; enforcing laws regarding real estate; mobile home safety standards |
| Office of Surface Mining Reclamation and Enforcement (in Interior Dept.) | 1977 | Environmental effects of surface (strip) mining |
| Federal Energy Regulatory Commission (in Energy Dept.) (took over old Federal Power Commission functions) | 1977 | Prices and transportation of natural gas; construction of interstate gas pipelines; stock issues and mergers of electric utilities; prices of oil transported by pipeline |

Source: Congressional Quarterly, *Federal Regulatory Directory, 1983–84* (Washington, DC: Congressional Quarterly, 1985).

lic interest groups—to extend investigations and consumer advocacy to many areas of corporate activity and their governmental oversight.[111]

There was also an element of Congressional "entrepreneurism" behind the growth of regulatory agencies during the period of 1965–1977. In the New Deal, President Roosevelt secured the electoral fealty of the mobilizing labor and poor people's movements by means of the Wagner and Social Security acts. In a similar way, activist liberal professionals in and out of Congress advocated legislation and the establishment of various regulatory mechanisms to represent the new public interest group constituencies. This specifically brought into the regulatory process those mobilized social actors who had been excluded from politics—first blacks, to some degree nonunionized workers, and later various classes of citizens organized as "consumers."[112] These activists both tapped into and gave form to generalized health and environmental fears and inchoate anti-corporate sentiment.[113] The success of these moral entrepreneurs underlay the emergence of "new class" theories of regulation (which often seemed designed to discredit the public interest activists and the regulations they fostered).

Though the creation of new consumer, environmental, and worker protection agencies was the hallmark of the Great Society period, the "democratic distemper" affected older agencies as well. The Nader-sponsored studies took on the older economic regulatory agencies from a consumer perspective and produced several exposés asserting that the public interest had been subverted by the traditional regulatory process. The older agencies came under attack for their cartelizing and rate-setting functions, which were claimed to coddle already fat corporate interests. The "standardless" exercise of discretionary authority was denounced as a mechanism of graft and corruption.[114] Older agencies were pushed into more activist stances, particularly when the public interest groups gained the standing to argue before regulatory agencies and to file suits on behalf of public interests.[115]

The expansion of standing rights not only constituted a key (albeit indirect) factor in the growth of new agencies, it underlay a transformation in the nature of administrative law. The traditional model of administrative law constructed a system of judicial review to limit agency actions to those clearly authorized by legislative directives. The traditional model is an essentially negative instrument for checking governmental power. Judicial oversight of agency discretion was to protect the private autonomy of those subject to regulation. The original test of standing in the federal courts was whether the interest asserted by the plaintiff amounted to a "legal right" entitled to the protection of the common law. Essentially this meant that standing was accorded to those parties possessing a property interest potentially affected by agency action. Those parties without property right were thought to be protected by the regulatory agency itself and had no legal standing.

During the Great Society the traditional model of judicial review changed. The courts essentially accepted the argument that regulatory agencies had been captured by regulated industries. The expansion of standing would permit other than industry groups to articulate interests and policies before regulatory agencies. The courts now conceived regulatory agencies not as embodiments of the public interest, but rather as quasi legislative forums for interest representation. The expansion of standing combined with new, active judicial oversight of substantive agency policies. The Court of Appeals, District of Columbia Circuit played the leading role in this transformation. The effect of the transformation was to ensure the fair representation of a wide range of affected interests in the process of administrative decision.[116]

The public interest movement's attack on the practices of the older agencies (in conjunction with older government critiques of the independent regulatory commissions—the Hoover, Landis, and Ash reports) effected alterations in the structure of the newly created agencies. First, the regulatory agencies created in the Great Society for the most part were housed in the executive branch of government as either "independent executive" agencies under a single strong administrator (such as the EPA or EEOC), or as bureaus in cabinet departments (such as OSHA, which is part of the Department of Labor). Some traditional independent regulatory commissions were broken up and their responsibilities handed to new agencies located in the executive. The old Federal Power Commission was moved into the executive Department of Energy. The new agencies were (and are) funded under the authority of the Office of Management and Budget. Executive agencies thus were more answerable to the President, a proposal rejected by the Congress during the New Deal for fear of further expanding the power of the President.[117] Indeed, the President may request the resignation of executive agency officials at any time.

Second, in reaction to the criticism that the older agencies suffered from vague legislative mandates, the health and safety agencies tended to be charged with more precise mandates. In some instances they were charged with detailed specifications as to what, how, and when certain regulatory objectives were to be accomplished.[118] The EPA, for example, must meet specific deadlines in achieving clean air and water, both of which are defined in specific terms. This expanded Congress' role in regulatory policy-making. Last, unlike the New Deal agencies' concern for a single industry, the social regulatory agencies oversaw broad processes which affected nearly all industries. These latter two characteristics tied the social regulatory agencies more closely to their original mandates and made them less "capturable" by industry interests.

In important respects, then, the Great Society regulatory agencies were different from the agencies established in the previous two phases of regulatory creation. They were distinctive in the subject area of activities they regulated and in the socioeconomic aims underlying regulatory action. They generally were given more precise legislative mandates, sometimes with timetables of expected action. They were incorporated into the executive branch as "line" agencies rather than established as "independent regulatory commissions." Finally, they were established in the context of a larger political audience, due to the liberalized court interpretations of standing. To some degree, these factors established a different regulatory tradition and different set of operating principles.

The social regulatory agencies, true to their mandates, entered into battle with industry interests and imposed rules and regulations to the great dismay of many industries. The consequence of this was that businesses counterattacked. This also was a new feature. True, some industries bridled at regulation in earlier periods. The financial community rose up vehemently against the nascent Securities and Exchange Commission in the late 1930s.[119] But generally, businesses and industries went along with, and sometimes applauded, regulation during the Progressive Era and New Deal.

In contrast, by 1974, having been politically quiescent for a decade and having considered themselves politically impotent, businessmen began to mobilize against the public interest movement and the left agenda generally. More than any other factor, it was the growth of regulation which prompted the business political counterattack. Individual businesses and trade associations increased their Washington presence enormously in the early 1970s. A new and powerful organization—the Business Roundtable—was formed in 1972 to elucidate business' political goals. Older, largely neglected organizations such as the Chamber of Commerce became more aggressive.

Business' political goals concentrated on countering regulatory agency rules and on halting the creation of new agencies. Moreover, corporations sponsored studies of regulation, commissioned analyses of the "new class" which supposedly created regulation, and bought space in newspapers for advocacy essays. With their new lobbying power, business was able to prevent passage of the proposed Consumer Protection Agency in 1977.[120] This effectively marked the end of the period of the creation of social regulatory agencies and the beginning of the deregulation movement. Deregulation was bound up with the transformation of political culture, from a critical commitment to the regulatory process to a denunciation of that process.

## Operationality: How Regulatory Agencies Work

I have asserted that regulatory agencies constitute a new institution of political power, originally concomitant with the rise of a complex, national economy and the reign of judicial formalism. Thereafter, regulatory decision-making became the political institution of choice to deal with ongoing economic and social problems. Administrative decision-making was broadly perceived as more appropriate to ongoing problems of complexity than either legislative statutes or judicial rulings. Three historical periods of regulatory origin created agencies of three respective general types. Progressive Era agencies were to solve economic and social instability by constructing general rules for business behavior and by rationalizing specific industries that provided key infrastructural services. Depression era/New Deal agencies were established to reestablish order to specific (usually commerce-related) industries whose market controls had collapsed during the Depression. Great Society agencies, reflecting the interests of consumers and to some extent the disenfranchised generally, were created to control the social effects of business decisions.

Regulation marks the displacement of private law by a reduction of the scope of the freedom of contract. Yet, in operation, regulation is largely conservative, often protective of the industries under regulatory jurisdiction. This, of course, is most characteristic of the single-industry agencies primarily established in the New Deal. For these agencies were established with the expressed purpose of protecting their respective industries. The operation of regulatory agencies is conditioned by the historically determined function of the particular agency. Nonetheless, conservatism—in the sense not only of industry protection, but also of agency dependence on set rules, formulae, and precedents, and openness to *ex parte* influence—characterizes the actual operation of most regulatory agencies. This is because the structural context of regulatory power and the conflicting sets of pressures placed on agencies are fairly constant, and affect all agencies. This conservatism highlights the inadequacy of the regulatory agency to act *either* as a harsh taskmaster *against* industry or as a rationalizing planner *for* industry. Here we discuss the actual operations of regulatory agencies. The key theme is the nature of regulatory power, or, the problem of "discretion." Regulatory conservatism is an outgrowth of the problem of discretion and its solution.

## The Context of Regulatory Power

### The Vague Congressional Mandate

Notwithstanding the fact that regulatory agencies are a new institution of political power, they are situated within a terrain of power in which they are just one player. Moreover, regulatory agencies are often in a structurally weak position within this terrain of power. The other institutions are Congress, the courts, the executive branch, and the corporations brought under regulation. Each historical period which saw a burst of agency genesis was characterized by some atmosphere of crisis. The crisis galvanized political action, and thus political dynamics must be recognized as playing an important role in the creation (and sometimes in the revitalization) of agencies. Nonetheless, the Congressional legislation which created regulatory agencies usually was the end-product of pitched battles between opposing interests and ideologies.

The Congressional mandate, reflecting these battles, is itself conflicted. The Communications Act of 1934, for example, called for an agency to promote and to police, to set technical and operating standards and to prevent monopolization. At first glance these responsibilities seem clear enough. In practice, these general goals sometimes proved mutually exclusive. Yet, until the Great Society phase, agencies were given few clear guidelines to direct the choice between mutually exclusive goals beyond such vague and general proscriptions as the directive to regulate "in the public interest, convenience, and necessity." In fact, these "public interest" proscriptions served to gloss over the conflicts and contradictions with the language of democratic legitimacy, which in reality were but vague and rather empty slogans.

It is not surprising that legislative mandates to regulatory agencies are general and vague. After all, the stated purpose of the generic regulatory agency is to formulate the kinds of substantive rules which a legislative body has neither the time nor expertise to make. With some recent exceptions (such as certain EPA guidelines), agencies have been delegated broad authority to deal with the industries or problems over which they have jurisdiction. Agencies can exercise wide latitude of discretionary authority.

### The Problem of Discretion and the Solution of Judicial Review

In a polity based on legal norms and the rule of law (especially a contractual theory of politics that official intrusions into private liberty or property must be sanctioned by popular consent), regulation demanded some form of review. After all, regulation is the passing of judgment on private persons by unelected officials (and the concern over due process is a major aspect of legitimation demands in general). The courts constituted the check on the exercise of regulatory discretion through judicial review. The traditional model of administrative law evolved from statutory enactments and judicial decisions in the wake of regulations made by the Interstate Commerce Commission. This model was designed to control government intrusions into private liberty and property interests by relying on the judiciary to limit agency powers to those granted by the legislature. These were essentially *procedural* safeguards which had important consequences for regulatory jurisdiction and the exercise of discretionary authority. The traditional model of administrative law had four essential elements.[121]

First, the imposition of administratively determined sanctions on private persons must be authorized by the legislature through rules which control agency action. In other words, the type and degree of authority exercised by an agency must be clearly defined within its legislative mandate.

Second, the decision-making procedures utilized by the agency must tend to ensure agency compliance with authorizing legislative directives. To ensure even-handed justice, agency procedures must be accurate, impartial, and rational. This has meant trial-type hearings at which parties affected by regulation are entitled to present evidence and challenge the agency's legal and factual basis to act.

Third, judicial review must be available to ensure agency utilization of accurate and impartial decision-making procedures and agency compliance with legislative directives.

Fourth, agency decisional processes must facilitate the exercise of such judicial review. In practice this has meant that agencies must keep an orderly record of the factual findings and legal conclusions which form the basis for agency actions.

The traditional model of administrative law was an exacting review of regulatory power. Late 19th-century liberal theory rejected administrative law, which is to say, rejected a notion of a public interest over private interests. Disputes between government and the individual were to be treated like other legal disputes—as private law matters where the judge would treat both parties as equal. Consequently, in the first decades of the 20th century, the courts usually struck down ICC and FTC decisions. Regulated parties challenged agency rulings in court, and the courts reviewed agency decisions as to whether the agency had the power to so act and whether the agency's record supported any particular action. In line with the doctrine of constitutional limitations and the famous nondelegation doctrine, courts ruled that administrative sanctions on private individuals must be authorized by legislatures.[122]

Though the Court's hostility to regulatory authority relaxed with the Depression, the traditional model of administrative law set up the ongoing procedural norms which establish the essential relation between regulatory agencies and the courts. If the traditional model was designed to protect the due process rights of parties subject to regulation, it also created a dynamic toward formalism within the agencies. Under constant threat of judicial review and reversal, agencies tended to develop trial-like procedures, evidentiary recordkeeping, and a reliance on precedent to justify decisions.

The Administrative Procedure Act of 1946 (APA) made this tendency mandatory. That act represented a compromise between an alliance of corporations and ideological critics of the New Deal and the supporters of regulatory action. The APA systematized many procedural safeguards. It required that most agency rules and regulations be published in the Federal Register, that most agency documents be made available to public scrutiny, and that most agency meetings be open to the public. The APA also required that agencies provide opportunity for interested parties to submit written or oral comments on proposed rules, and mandated modified trial-type hearing procedures in rulemaking. Some procedural safeguards resulted in the further bureaucratization of regulatory agencies, particularly the insistence on a structural separation between policy-making and adjudication functions within agencies. In instances where the agency adjudicates, there must be opportunity for a trial-type hearing before independent "hearing examiners," followed by an appeal procedure to the head of the agency. Finally, the APA made clear that reviewing courts not only must determine whether administrators complied with relevant statutes, but also must examine whether the agency's action was "arbitrary, capricious, or an abuse of discretion." The act required courts to determine whether the agency's fact-findings were supported by "substantial evidence" in the record as a whole.[123]

## The Politics of Regulation and the Practice of "Bargaining"

If judicial review generally and the Administrative Procedure Act in particular push agencies to be more judicial-like and hence circumspect, other aspects of the regulatory process push agencies in an opposite direction. Regulatory agencies have incentives to "bargain" with regulated parties, that is, to decide conflicts not on the basis of rules but rather by what is expedient and achievable by compromise. There are two aspects to bargaining. In theory, the benefit of the regulatory process is that it is informal and substantive. A law is too hard and fast a remedy for problems that change rapidly. A court ruling takes far too long, and often applies to a narrow set of facts only. In contrast, the flexibility of informal rulemaking by regulation takes into account all of the complexities of a particular industry or social problem and permits the construction of policies molded to those complexities.[124] The problem is that even regulatory rules are too steadfast; they vitiate regulatory flexibility. For this reason, agencies often tend to formulate general (often vague) policies rather than strictly formal rules. The policies then guide the agency in substantive decisions and negotiations, and permit great flexibility. In practice, formal rules have the added disagreeable feature (from the agency's standpoint) of requiring the agency to take a clear position on a potentially conflict-laden issue.

But the agency seeks to avoid conflict, for conflict threatens the autonomy of an organization situated amidst a sea of pressures and challenges to its authority. The regulatory agency is in an inherently weak position. The pressures of a vague, often internally contradictory mandate and of judicial review have already been noted. Less important, but nonetheless significant are conflicting pressures from Congress and the executive branch. Congressional oversight committees and Presidential investigatory commissions may berate a regulatory agency for its failure to formulate consistent rules, even as Congressmen or executive branch officials make *ex parte* contacts with agency commissioners on behalf of constituent industry groups. Regulatory agencies are dependent on these political institutions for their operating budgets and to some degree their effective political legitimacy.

Finally there is the pressure from the industry. The process of regulation transfers intra-industry struggles onto the agency itself. The power of the industry and the conservatism of the regulating agency in large part derive from the crucial fact that agency actions proceed within an *already constituted industrial framework*. The general economic and institutional structures of an industry are there prior to the onset of regulatory controls. Regulated firms retain primary control over their affairs; their own degree of discretion *after* regulation is generally very large. In contrast, the agency's power is essentially a negative power. Any regulatory actions must confront existing firms, practices, and institutional arrangements which facilitate the provision of important economic and social services. Even if these pre-existing practices and regulations are not entirely rational, the agency must consider the possibility that any particular rule could impair or disrupt service.

Here, again, agencies are hemmed in by mutually exclusive mandated responsibilities and the prospect of hostile judicial review. To give but a minor example, in 1945 the FCC constructed rules to prevent concentration of ownership in the relatively new and small service of FM radio. Yet the Commission did not apply these rules to AM radio—where concentration really mattered—because it could not countenance the potential diminution of service that might follow divestment.[125] The consequence of such factors is that regulatory agencies have a tendency not just to act conservatively, but to avoid rulemaking. According to Kenneth Culp Davis, a leading student of administrative law,

> . . . probably about ninety percent of all administrative action involves a combination of (1) informal action, that is action taken without trial procedure, (2) discretionary determinations that are mostly or altogether uncontrolled or unguided by announced rules or principles, and (3) lack of judicial review in fact, whether or not the action is theoretically reviewable.[126]

At the very least, agencies tend to avoid formulating clear and consistent policies.[127]

Instead, they bargain. Though the tendency to bargain is present in all regulatory agencies, it is particularly strong in the Depression/New Deal price-and-entry agencies which have jurisdiction over a single industry. They bargain on the construction of rules and on the application of the rules. When there is to be a genuine rule, the agency acts not as a policy-maker, but as an arbitrator or facilitator among the principal interested parties. This practice has been widely criticized as the "broker state" phenomenon. The practice is partly due to the fact that limited agency resources ultimately require the agency to depend on the regulated firms for information and policy development. But it also is related to the type of agency and its general function.

Particularly in price-and-entry agencies, regulatory power becomes a commodity for parties with standing (until recently, the factions of an industry only) to manipulate in their internecine struggles for grants of authority or certificates of need or approval of rates. The price-and-entry agencies were established to bring some order to these industries, literally to save them from themselves. The agencies reestablished order and rational economic functioning by setting basic non-market ground rules and then by granting a high degree of autonomy to the private interests, including participation in rulemaking. Regulatory agencies essentially provided a forum for parties with standing to work out conflicts through informal negotiations. The compromises reached would have the force of law.[128]

The conservatism of bargaining on the rules can be seen in two ways. First, bargaining is conducted only with parties with legal standing. Second, once the rule is determined, it represents a fundamental compromise which the agency is generally loath to disturb. Thus basic regulatory formulas, whether rules or policies or methods, achieve a kind of settledness; they become like political constitutions which structure all rules and policies thereafter.[129] For similar reasons, agencies also bargain on adjudication. Typical agency practice is to formulate a ruling designed to eliminate a problem *and* to "grandfather" in all arrangements which called forth the need for the new rule in the first place. Blanket application of a wide-ranging new rule could undermine the basic formulas which represent settled compromises. Also, the courts have essentially ruled that blanket application of new rules denies the due process rights of parties that had acted legally and with reliance on the law prior to any new rule.[130] Thus, though formalism and bargaining are opposite tendencies, in another sense they feed on each other. Both contribute to agency conservatism.[131]

## The Road to Deregulation

In Progressive Era and New Deal regulatory agencies, the public interest was defined within the context of the rational functioning of capitalist economic institutions. The nature of legal standing was such that only those parties with a property interest subject to regulatory controls had access to the regulatory process. These regulatory agencies essentially constructed political institutions receptive to specific organized *functional* (as opposed to geographic) interests. If political parties were structurally receptive to geographic interests, regulatory agencies were structurally attuned to functional, or industry, interests.[132] The public, possessing no independent standing before such agencies, was considered protected by the supposedly nonpartisan and objective science of public administration.[133]

During the Great Society period, the ideology of expertise embedded in Progressive and New Deal regulatory agencies became recognized as a politics hiding under the guise of scientism. Judicial decisions acknowledged the (essentially left-based) criticism of regulatory agencies, and moved toward a conception that the public interest was not "a monolith," rather, it "involves a balance of many interests."[134] Once the Court recognized regulation as a system of interest representation, it expanded standing to allow other interests into the process and reviewed agency decisions with an eye to protecting those usually unrepresented interests.

But the expansion of standing rights in the traditional agencies (not to mention the hostility of the new social regulatory agencies toward certain business practices) could only disrupt the balance of formalism and bargaining historically receptive to industry interests. As the regulatory process became more open, more democratic, and hence *more politicized* in the Great Society period, industry found regulation increasingly burdensome, time-consuming, and contentious. The increase of participation led generally to an increase of formalism, each party taking full advantage of procedural safeguards and judicial review.[135] An underground rule of thumb of public interest groups (and indeed of *any* regulated party) was that if they couldn't defeat an industry proposal in the regulatory forum on the merits, they might win by imposing accumulated costs through requests for reconsideration of rules and through appeals for judicial review. The increase in formalism resulted in time delay and, most important, a reduction in industry's ability to calculate the future consequences of its economic decisions. In addition, the new social regulations imposed considerable compliance costs.

As corporations began to organize themselves against regulation in the 1970s, they were increasingly successful in ideologically tying the troubling phenomenon of falling national productivity rates to "over-regulation." The liberal criticism of regulation, which had at its core principles of equity and political participation, began to be displaced by a pro-business, often right-wing criticism of regulation, which had economic efficiency as its basic principle. The move toward deregulation had begun.

Regulatory agencies are political institutions whose origins, operations, successes, and failings are reflective of the two fundamental constraints on the state in a democratic capitalist society—accumulation and legitimation. Agencies regulate in the effort to rationalize dysfunctional aspects of the capitalist system. This is esespecially true as regulation relates to the maintainance of infrastructure services for economic growth and the free flow of commerce. In this regard, regulatory agencies in the 20th century have taken on the 19th-century role of the federal judiciary in acting to carve out a national area of free and rational commerce. In the context of safeguarding, even expanding, the circulation of capital, regulation resurrected common law principles of common carriers and embedded them as "public interest" obligations. These include nondiscrimination, universal and relatively low-cost service, and cross-subsidy arrangements to facilitate such service. Democratic demands *do* often result in the creation of regulatory agencies, and the public interest—in the form of service-based entitlements—was encoded in basic regulatory formulas. But up until the Great Society period, only those with property rights were accorded legal standing before regulatory agencies. Notwithstanding the service-based entitlements, Progressive and New Deal regulatory agencies constituted essentially private forums within which economic interests could settle conflicts and set basic industry rules.

But regulatory agencies do not centralize political power. They are situated within a system of checks and balances in which they are often the weakest player. The pressure of judicial review, understandably there to protect the due process rights of regulated parties, leads to a tendency for the regulatory agency to become more formalistic. Pressure from the regulated industry combined with the regulatory agency's efforts to preserve its organizational integrity tends to encourage regulation in the form of bargaining. Until the Great Society period, formalism and bargaining struck a kind of balance, the effect of which was to favor conservative action (or inaction) on the part of the regulatory agency. Such conservative regulation, though often opposed by *particular* industry interests, was largely conducive to *general* industry interests. Regulation set basic ground rules and stabilized (even cartelized) various (particularly commerce-bearing) industries.

Great Society regulatory activism and a corresponding transformation in the judicial concept of the public interest undermined the balance between formalism and bargaining. Health and safety regulations imposed considerable costs on businesses, and regulatory activism generally caused businesses unacceptable foreclosure of economic predictability. Regulatory agencies, opened up to more democratic participation, became less able to bargain and more bound to procedural norms. Administrative rationality and economic rationality diverged, and by the mid-1970s business engaged in a wholesale revolt against regulation.

CHAPTER
4

• • •

# The Evolution of the American Telecommunications System and the Origins of Communication Regulation

The previous chapter held that the prior structure of an industry had great bearing on the functions of a regulatory agency and on the agency's effective parameters of discretion. This chapter fleshes out that theoretical assertion with an empirical examination of the structure of the telecommunications industry prior to the era of regulation. It will chronicle the development of telegraphy, telephony, and broadcasting up to the creation of the FCC. The state has always had an important hand in the establishment of various telecommunications services. The state helped establish a privately owned and operated communications infrastructure, by way of promotion, subsidy, and direct intervention. Notwithstanding the fact of their private ownership (indeed, partly *because* of it) these services came to require state intervention in the form of regulation—but only *after* the telecommunications system was already established. Regulatory formulae directly reflected those preestablished industry structures.

The endpoint of this chapter is the examination of the Federal Communications Commission, the key player in the regulation of telecommunications in the United States. A New Deal price-and-entry control regulatory agency, the FCC was given charge over communication by wire and communications over the air in 1934. The FCC came to regulate industries whose basic institutional and economic structures (and to some extent their nascent regulatory treatment) had been defined previously. Those structures evolved within the general confines of the usual pattern of government promotion of private industry. The telegraph, telephone, and radio industries developed as private businesses, protected by patent law and enjoying the benefits of direct and indirect government subsidies. Telegraphy and telephony tended toward an institutional arrangement where numerous small companies were interconnected by one giant, dominant company. As these industries became monopolized, common carrier obligations were imposed by law. In the case of radio, government-facilitated patent pools permitted the industry to emerge during and just after the First World War.

Like most New Deal regulatory agencies, the FCC's legislative mandate was broad and in certain respects internally contradictory. Notwithstanding the fact that the Communications Act was passed at the height of the New Deal, the legislation reflected a profoundly conservative intent. With regard to broadcasting, the Communications Act left unmolested the private, commercial nature of the broadcast system. While such a system did safeguard freedom of speech for private entrepreneurs who earlier had entered the business of broadcasting, regulation did little to structure a truly free marketplace of ideas. A major reason for this was that at the outset federal regulation misconstrued the economic structure of broadcasting. The act created the FCC primarily as a licensing agent for individual stations; it gave the FCC no jurisdiction over network organizations. This would have great consequences for the establishment and maintenance of a network broadcasting cartel. With respect to telephony, the FCC was entrusted more or less to watch over the AT&T monopoly which had been sanctioned by earlier legislation. The FCC ministered to the needs of AT&T through rate regulation.

Basic regulatory formulas reflected industrial compromises fashioned earlier among the principal competing corporations. These included the recognition of natural monopoly in wired carriers, and the institutional separation of voice from record carriers (that is, of AT&T from Western Union). An important division between broadcasters and common carriers—hence the separation between ''content'' and ''conduit''—reflected an intercorporate agreement fashioned between AT&T and RCA. One consequence of early regulation was to stabilize the broadcast and telephone industries in their previous commercial forms. Like other New Deal agencies, the FCC embedded certain public interest obligations within the basic regulatory formulas. Telephone service was to be universal and non-discriminatory; the electromagnetic spectrum was deemed a public resource, and broadcast service in theory was to be distributed equitably to all areas of the nation.

## Telegraph

''Invention'' and ''inventor'' are words which beg misunderstanding of the scientific/technologic enterprise. They conjure up isolated, eccentric tinkers who, by force of genius and/or good fortune, happen upon a momentous discovery. While no doubt there have been incidents of this kind throughout history, the technologic enterprise is generally more communal, and certainly more derivative, than the popular impression of invention. For example, Samuel F. B. Morse, known for the Morse code and usually credited with the invention of the telegraph, built upon earlier experiments that employed electricity and magnetism in the transmission of signals over wire. In the early 1800s Ampere, Oersted, and Faraday theorized about the principles that would underlie telegraphy.

But the misperception engendered by the term invention does underscore an important point. "Invention" is usually ascribed to the form of device which first finds a niche in the world of practice. "Invention" is credited to the first successful practical implementation of a device (which is to say, in a capitalist economy, the mode of implementation which generates a business profit). "Inventor" status is usually credited to the individual responsible for finding that niche. In the 19th-century world of productive capitalism, those technologists became entrepreneurs. It is for this reason that this discussion of telegraphy, telephony, and radio slights the history of their invention and concentrates on the history and conditions of their implementation.

Following government support of his experimental telegraph line, in 1845 Samuel F. B. Morse offered his telegraph patent to the US government. The unprofitability of early telegraphy, and the reluctance of the government to engage in one more business enterprise (particularly considering the hostility during this time to new internal improvements), underlay the government's decision not to purchase Morse's patent. By default, telegraphy became a private, commercial venture. The reluctance of the government to engage in communications service beyond the postal system would be repeated for all subsequent communication technologies in the 19th and 20th centuries.

Given the uncertainty of potential demand for telegraph service and the difficulty of raising capital in this period, the four Morse patent holders pursued a strategy of licensing small, geographically delimited companies, while holding out the option of selling the entire enterprise to the government. Profitable initial operation indicated that there was adequate demand. Rapid advances in technology and a dispute with a licensee sparked an expansion of telegraph building. But the original patent holders did not purchase alternative inventions, and thus could not construct a technological barrier to entry. By 1849 there were three competitive lines on Boston-Washington and New York-Buffalo routes.[1]

Notwithstanding some direct and indirect public subsidy, it was extraordinary business demand that spurred the growth of telegraphy after 1846. After all, telegraphy revolutionized business communications. In tandem with the railroads, the telegraph forged extra-local links among merchants, shippers, bankers, and brokers, and thus facilitated regional (as opposed to local) commerce. The telegraph industry was itself characterized by brisk competition. The first decade saw the rise of numerous poorly capitalized small telegraph companies which often constructed duplicate lines. The industry was plagued by wildcat speculation, insecure investments, bankruptcies, and sometimes ruinous internecine competition.[2] Unlike railroads, however, the unstable, competitive era in telegraphy was short-lived.

As Richard DuBoff argues, the telegraph simultaneously promoted both competition *and* monopoly in the economy at large. The telegraph was instrumental in the rise of the large corporation. Instantaneous communication greatly lowered information and transaction costs for many firms, enabling them to widen their markets. This had the effect of increasing their size and scale. Lowered transaction costs underlay the opening-up of hitherto insulated, local markets to extra-local firms increasingly national in scope. The opening of seven major commodity exchanges between 1845 and 1854 coincided with the growth of telegraphic communications. The speed and secrecy of intelligence transmitted by telegraph was a key element in the growth of large-scale bureaucratic business organization. Geographically dispersed operations and agents could be brought under centralized supervision. Organizational economies developed by the nascent large corporation rested in part on the new modes of information-processing ushered in by the telegraph.[3]

The increases in scale promoted by the telegraph among its customer firms affected the telegraph industry itself. The growth of telegraphy and the concentration of ownership were very rapid. In 1852, six years after the technology's start as a private enterprise, over 23,000 miles of wire were in operation. By 1866 the Western Union company monopolized telegraphy with over 75,000 miles of wire and 37,000 miles of line.[4] The reason for this swift expansion and centralization was that in telegraphy what was important was long-distance "through" traffic, not intra-urban communication. The stages of competition, cooperation, and consolidation were compressed into a much shorter time frame than happened in the railroads. In the mid-1850s, telegraph companies cooperated to send messages across competing wires. Though pooling efforts in telegraphy failed, acquisition and merger succeeded. In 1866 the two other major telegraph companies merged with Western Union, creating a corporation with a combined capitalization of $41 million. This made it the largest firm in American history up to that point, and the first industrial monopoly. System-building came so quickly that the telegraph companies never looked to government intervention to support cartel arrangements.[5] More than this, the successful and rapid concentration of the telegraph industry made industry leaders hostile to government intervention.

With the great consolidations that produced the Western Union monopoly, the basic structure of the telegraph industry was set. A privately operated system (after the British nationalization of telegraphy in 1868, only the United States and Canada had private systems), the American telegraph industry consisted of numerous small companies which serviced selected local areas and an enormous corporation which monopolized through traffic.[6] Message rate structures were high compared with European telegraph rates. Rates were largely discriminatory, with some local telegrams costing more than long-distance messages. Rate making itself bore no uniform relation to underlying cost.[7]

Although the telegraph grew up in the period of hostility to internal improvements, it benefited from critical infusions of government support. The principal mode of public subsidy was indirect support through right-of-way. This was augmented by various direct subsidies from state governments and occasionally by the federal government.[8] The telegraph industry, and Western Union in particular, also benefited from the Civil War. The war increased demand dramatically. Because Western Union's network was concentrated in the North, it did not suffer from split lines between the Union and the Confederacy as did its competitors. During the Civil War the Union government constructed 15,000 miles of wire as part of the United States Military Telegraph. After the war, much of this was turned over to

Western Union as compensation for losses suffered by the company during the war. The war also generated technological spinoffs, especially in construction methods and in wiretapping.[9]

Government treatment of the telegraph industry replicated the classic pattern typical of government-business relations in the second half of the 19th century. Apart from subsidy and promotion, government kept its hands off the industry. However, following the emergence of the Western Union monopoly and an exclusive contract fashioned in 1867 between Western Union and Associated Press (AP), a popular movement for telegraph reform arose. The provisions of the agreement between the telegraph giant and the dominant wire service were that New York AP and Western AP pledged not to use the wires of companies other than Western Union and promised to oppose new telegraph companies. Western Union agreed not to enter the news gathering field and offered special discount rates to the two press associations. The dual news service and telegraph monopoly was attacked in the press and in Congress for the next twenty years, but no real reform legislation was passed.[10]

The many proposals for telegraph reform rested on the complaint that rates were too high and that this was caused by monopoly. Early reform proposals focused on instituting a government-sponsored telegraph system to compete with Western Union. A proposal to nationalize telegraphy under the Post Office was introduced in Congress in 1870. Variations of these proposals surfaced for the next two decades, but were effectively blocked by the telegraph industry.[11] Western Union's Washington lobby mobilized ideological arguments against government intervention, and the company granted telegraph franking privileges to Congressmen sympathetic to its cause. The industry used various laws to fight off both the nationalization proposal and the efforts of individual states to control telegraphy. In legislative debates Western Union invoked state incorporation statutes to challenge any federal right to intervene in the telegraph business. The company also tapped into the rising judicial formalism of the period. When the state of Florida attempted to control the telegraph industry within its borders by franchising a Florida company and excluding Western Union, the corporation's arguments convinced the Supreme Court to overturn the right of state governments to regulate firms engaged in interstate commerce.[12]

The only major legislative bill affecting telegraphy was passed in 1866. Though essentially an exercise in the promotion of the industry, the legislation also was intended as a prelude to the establishment of a government-run "postal telegraph." The bill granted any state-chartered company the right to construct and operate telegraphs along the nation's post roads and through public lands. It permitted the companies to fell trees for poles without charge. The government guaranteed for itself priority to use the lines of firms taking advantage of the act. Rates for government use would be fixed by the Postmaster General. Companies accepting the bill's privileges were prohibited from selling their lines to other companies. Significantly, they also had to provide service like a common carrier, to all comers, without discrimination. The government retained the option to purchase the companies which had accepted the privileges of the act, five years after the bill's passage. The act thus gave tentative legislative approval to nationalize that part of the industry when the five years were up in 1871.[13] This option was not exercised, but the privilege of building on post roads and public lands entailed the imposition of common carrier obligations on the telegraph companies.

Thus, the imposition of common carrier requirements was a middle-of-the-road response to Western Union's monopoly abuses, a secondary consequence of the effort to nationalize telegraphy.[14] Because they exercised the power of eminent domain and usually operated under a franchise from the state or municipality, telegraph operations fell rather easily into the category of businesses cloaked with a public interest. Yet this did not coalesce as a national policy until the 1890s.

Though early on telegraph service was held by many state courts to be a public calling, its common carrier obligations were limited and often unenforced. Telegraph service was frequently discriminatory, a consequence of the relatively limited carrying capacity of the wires and the fact that, as an entrepreneurial venture, the telegraph followed established routes of trade. Telegraphy first linked the great trade centers of New York, Philadelphia, Boston, Washington, New Orleans, and St. Louis. Users in small towns often found that the lines were tied up by heavy volumes of messages traveling between and within major cities. Waiting time for any telegraph station depended on the number of messages being transmitted by the "higher order" stations ahead of it, an advantage which the busier stations automatically passed on to their best customers. This situation apparently did not much change even after telegraph technology improved in the 1870s.[15] The exclusive agreement between Western Union and Associated Press constituted perhaps the most egregious case of discrimination. This particular discrimination was responsible not only for restraining the creation of new news services, but also for tampering with information. A Senate investigation conducted in 1874 documented instances in which Western Union had cut off transmission of news reports to papers that criticized the telegraph company or the content of AP dispatches.[16]

Unlike physical carriers, who were liable for all damage and loss of goods during the carriage (except in the instance of an act of God), telegraph companies were often freed from the liability of an erroneous telegram. The judicial record in these matters is mixed.[17] The reasons for this limited liability were varied, but hinged on the intangible nature of information and the technically bound exigencies of passing messages by electrical means. Carriers had actual possession of the goods entrusted them; telegraph companies did not. In relaying a message, the company might make an error, but nothing was stolen or lost. Also, unlike physical carriers, no direct relationship existed between costs of transmission and the value of the message. In an influential 1867 Michigan case, the state supreme court reasoned that it would be unjust to hold telegraph companies absolutely liable, considering the small amount of consideration for sending a message.[18] In *Primrose v. Western Union Telegraph Company* (1893), the case which clearly established the common carrier obligations of telegraph companies, the Supreme Court upheld the limited liability doctrine for mistakes in unrepeated telegrams. The opinion in *Primrose* stated:

> Telegraph companies resemble railroad companies and other common carriers, in that they are instruments of commerce; and in that they exercise a public employment, and

are therefore bound to serve all customers alike, without discrimination. They have, doubtless, a duty to the public, to receive, to the extent of their capacity, all messages clearly and intelligibly written, and to transmit them upon reasonable terms. But they are not common carriers; their duties are different, and are performed in different ways; and they are not subject to the same liabilities.[19]

The telegraph clearly was considered an agent of commerce, and was treated accordingly. Common carrier obligations, as they became enforced in the early 20th century, meant that telegraph companies had to serve all without discrimination. They could not refuse to take a particular telegram that would be unprofitable under the circumstances.[20] They could not refuse to forward a telegraphic message to connecting lines, even if those lines were operated by competitors.[21] This last created a legal mandate for wire interconnection. Telegraph companies generally were enjoined from discriminating against senders on the basis of the content of the message, but this protection of "speech" was contained within the umbrella of the protection of commerce. For instance, a telegraph operator could not refuse to take a message complaining of his own conduct, for not only would such a refusal be discriminatory, but it might bring the operator private advantage.[22] Moreover, with regard to message content, the telegraph operator was *obliged* to censor messages whose transmission furthered illegal commerce. A telegraph company should refuse to send libelous or obscene messages, or those which clearly indicate the furtherance of an illegal act (such as a message sending for prostitutes), or the perpetration of some crime.[23] The upshot of these obligations was the maintenance of a wired telegraph network to facilitate the movement of commerce. Between monopoly controls and common carrier obligations, telegraphy served business communication needs.

By the 1890s Western Union had to deal with a competitor. The Commercial Cable Company, which laid a competitive transatlantic cable in 1884, bought a small telegraph company called Postal Telegraph in order to expand domestically. Commercial Cable merged several small companies and built new lines. Though it never seriously challenged Western Union's domestic business, Commercial Cable did constrain Western's pricing freedom.[24] Telegraph rates came under the jurisdiction of the Interstate Commerce Commission in 1910.

## Telephone

The telephone began as an experiment to increase the carrying capacity of the telegraph line. A telegraph line carried a single message by coded electrical signal. Alexander Graham Bell, a speech physiologist by training, experimented on a multiplex telegraph that would distinguish between musical notes and thus make possible the transmission of several messages simultaneously on a single wire. Bell filed a patent on February 14, 1876, for his improvements in telegraph transmission, some hours before Elisha Gray, an electrician employed by Western Union, applied for a patent on a similar invention. Rather than a true multiplex telegraph, Bell's device permitted the electrical transmission of vocal sounds. His financial backers were skeptical of the practical implementation of the device, and encouraged Bell to orient his tinkering toward the multiplex telegraph. In fact, one of Bell's backers, Gardiner Hubbard, offered all rights to the telephone to Western Union for $100,000 in the winter of 1877. Western Union declined the offer. Bell filed a second basic patent in January 1877 covering the combined receiver-transmitter instrument and its various mechanical features. The Bell Telephone Company was formed July 9, 1877.[25]

By the fall of 1877 Western Union had a change of heart and challenged Bell patents on the basis of its ownership of Elisha Gray's work and that of another inventor, Amos Dolbear. Western Union set up a telephone subsidiary, the American Speaking Telephone Company, and hired Thomas Edison to put his inventive talents to work in the effort to crush Bell. Both the Bell and Western Union companies aggressively expanded telephone development during 1878. It became quickly evident that the best utilization of the technology could be derived by connecting each local phone to a switching center. Without a central switch, each telephone subscriber would have to be connected to other subscribers by separate, individual wires. Such switching exchanges required extensive capital, and the underfinanced Bell Company went the route of franchising local operating companies. Bell also obtained new financing from Boston capitalists.

## The First Division of Industry: Voice and Record Communications

A lengthy patent suit ensued between Western Union and the Bell Telephone Company, which appeared to favor Bell. Around the same time period, Western Union came under assault from financier Jay Gould. Gould's predations disrupted Western Union's telephone plans. In the late 1870s Jay Gould engineered a series of mergers of smaller telegraph companies to establish nationwide connections, and cut prices by 40 percent. Gould sought to drive down Western Union's stock price and attempt a buy out. Gould also bought into some of the Bell operating companies, pushing at Western Union from the telephone direction as well.[26] Western Union concluded an out-of-court settlement with the fledgling National Bell Company in 1879, which effectively constructed a division in the electrical communications industry. Western Union agreed to surrender all of its patents, claims, and facilities in the telephone business, including its network of 56,000 phones in 55 cities, in exchange for $325,000 and 20 percent of Bell telephone rental receipts over the 17-year life of the Bell patents. Western Union agreed that during the life of the contract it would confine its message-transmitting activities to the telegraph field. For its end of the bargain, Bell agreed to stay out of telegraphy. The settlement headed off Gould's challenge to Western Union's monopoly, and eliminated an uncertain and costly battle between Bell and Western Union. Lastly, the division of industry reduced the risk of additional entrants in *both* fields.[27]

The agreement with Western Union gave Bell, reconstituted in 1880 with Boston capital as the American Bell Company, a virtual monopoly of telephony. The telephone industry in the United States has been characterized by alternating periods of monopoly and competition.[28] The 17-year span of patent protection established the American Bell Company as *the* telephone company from 1876 until 1894. By 1885 the company succeeded in integrating vertically. Bell entered into permanent relationships with the operating companies licensed under its patents, established a manufacturing arm, and began construction of a long-distance system.

Bell's early strategy was to license numerous operating companies as territorial monopolies in desirable metropolitan locations. Bell provided them with equipment and insisted upon certain contractual guidelines. The licensed companies could construct long-distance lines within their territories, but they were prohibited from connecting their exchanges with those of another operating company—this was the preserve of the parent. A long-distance network that tied together all the local Bell exchanges would have the effect of keeping control over the local operating companies and would give Bell an enormous advantage over potential competitors. Licensed Bell companies were prohibited from connecting with potential independent telephone companies, and they agreed to use only instruments licensed by the parent. In 1882 Bell bought a controlling interest in the Western Electric Company, an equipment supply arm for Western Union. Western Electric became the principal manufacturer of Bell telephone apparatus. In 1885 Bell created a subsidiary, the American Telephone and Telegraph Company, to operate its nascent long-distance system (to be known as AT&T Long Lines). After 1900 Bell began to purchase majority interest in its local operating licensees.[29]

The company vigorously litigated patent infringements. In the decade of the 1880s, Bell won all 600-plus lawsuits over its patents. The monopoly period was very profitable for Bell. Its growth was stupendous. By 1895 Bell's revenue was 98 percent that of Western Union's.[30] With the expiration of Bell's two basic patents in 1893–94, a spate of independent telephone companies sprouted up. The second phase of telephone history was characterized by direct intra-industry competition. Bell had built its system in metropolitan centers only. Demand in small towns and rural areas induced new entrants. More than 4000 independent telephone systems were established by 1902, servicing 44 percent of all telephones. The Bell system reacted to competition in several ways. In areas where Bell-licensed companies were confronted with direct competition, the Bell companies cut telephone rates. Bell greatly expanded its operating plants and established new exchanges, often resulting in head-to-head competition with independents in various cities. The company sought to expand its long-distance service in order to press its *system* advantage over isolated competitors.

In conjunction with its own expansion, the company also exercised its political influence and financial power to curb the growth of independents and to sabotage an attempt to establish an independent long-distance company.[31] Bell attempted to take over competing equipment manufacturers, but ultimately was rebuffed by the antitrust laws. Bell companies refused to interconnect independent telephone companies into the long-distance or local networks except in particular instances where Bell could benefit from such interconnection, and prohibited Western Electric from supplying independents. Though Bell clearly remained the dominant firm with tremendous competitive advantage, for the most part its tactics were unsuccessful. In their heyday of 1907, independents controlled about 50 percent of all telephones.[32]

The financial burden of expansion effectively pushed the company into the orbit of the Morgan banking interests.[33] Under Morgan, Theodore Vail was brought in to be president of AT&T in 1907. Thereafter, the company's tactics changed. Bell began an aggressive campaign to buy out many independent systems. Selective offers of interconnection to the Bell System of independents at strategically located exchanges effectively made those independents sublicensees of AT&T. By the early 1910s, these actions began to quell competition. In 1912, for example, 65 percent of all independent telephones were connected with the Bell System.[34] Bell also sought to increase its advantage in the long-distance market by seeking to merge with a telegraph company. Bell began merger efforts with the Postal Telegraph-Cable System because of its international cable business. These efforts came to naught, and in 1909, in a great irony of business history, AT&T purchased a controlling share of the Western Union Telegraph Company. At the same time, Vail began to speak favorably of government regulation, arguing that such policy, if enlightened and uncorrupt, could be a beneficial and stabilizing force for telephony.

## Natural Monopoly and Government Policy

Under the leadership of Theodore Vail, AT&T maintained that telephony constituted a natural monopoly. "One policy, one system, and universal service" was Vail's oft-repeated slogan.[35] Two general arguments were advanced to support the natural monopoly contention. One was an economic argument. Vail claimed that competing telephone systems squandered resources and duplicated services, and that the value of telephone service increased with the number of subscribers. The second argument was technical in nature. A single entity could best provide technically integrated, end-to-end service. Enlightened government regulation, argued Vail, could see to the proper development of a telephone monopoly.[36]

Though it seems on its face that non-interconnected, competing telephone service would impose burdens (duplication of plant, subscribers requiring more than one telephone) which support the contention that telephony is a natural monopoly, the period of 1894 to 1913 indicates that competition brought certain benefits. The competitive era was chaotic and many of the independents provided poor and unreliable service. Nonetheless, it was the competitive pressure from the independents which forced Bell to vastly expand its services and which extended telephone service to more people. Competition served to transform the Bell corporate philosophy from one that viewed telephony as a limited and expensive service to a perspective that viewed telephony as a relatively cheap, potentially universal service.[37] Competition also brought down the price of telephone service and spurred technical innovation in telephony.[38]

Early legal treatment of the telephone generally placed it in the telegraph mold. Many early cases involved the refusal of telephone companies to serve all applicants, and the companies almost always lost in state courts. The logic was that telephony was the functional equivalent of telegraph, and thus shared the duty to grant open access without discrimination. Even though telephone companies in this era had no *legal* monopoly, state courts invoked the common law to impose common carrier obligations on them. Telephony was considered a public calling, but like telegraphy, one with limited liability. State courts consistently removed telephone companies from various kinds of customer damage suits.[39]

One important legal difference between telephony and telegraphy was established in a 1899 Supreme Court decision called *Richmond v. Southern Bell Tel. & Tel. Co.* In this case the Court held that the 1866 Post Roads Act allowing telegraph companies right-of-way and free timber on public lands and post roads did not apply to the telephone.[40] Thus federal subsidy was denied to the early telephone industry. With regard to the interconnection between telephone companies, mandated interconnection could not be insisted upon at common law, but legislation specifically compelling such connections was held constitutional by the first decade of the 20th century.[41]

The 1910 Mann-Elkins Act, whose primary purpose was to expand the power of the Interstate Commerce Commission over the railroads, also formally brought the communications industry under the ICC's regulatory ambit. Congress gave the ICC jurisdiction over interstate rates charged by telegraph, telephone, and cable companies. The extension of ICC jurisdiction over communications was the subject of little controversy or debate.[42] Notwithstanding its new powers, the ICC, preoccupied with railroad problems, exercised very little regulatory oversight of the telephone industry beyond instituting an accounting system for the industry. For the most part, there was little regulation of the telephone until the establishment of the Federal Communications Commission in 1934.

This is not to say that there was no governmental *policy* toward the telephone before 1934, but such policy was caught up in the conflict over the limits of regulation by states. Most states had commissions that regulated telephone rates and practices. Initially railroad commissions, the jurisdictions of these bodies widened to encompass telephony. They began as advisory bodies to legislatures, and eventually became adjudicatory agencies with power to oversee local rates. The problem of competition between telephone companies in the same locale led some states to require that telephone companies obtain certificates of convenience from the public utilities commissions. Some states refused such certificates to companies wishing to compete.[43] However, under the *Pensacola* telegraph predecent, which forbade state intrusion in interstate commerce in telegraphy, the courts could control the actions of state public utilities commissions. Federal judicial oversight generally frustrated state efforts at rate-setting.[44]

## *The Kingsbury Commitment and the Failure of "Postalization"*

At the federal level, Bell's actions against independents, as well as complaints against AT&T from the Commercial Cable/Postal Telegraph concern, prompted the Wilson Administration to propose antitrust action (and even public ownership) in telephony. It is likely that AT&T became concerned about antitrust in the aftermath of the Supreme Court's decisions in the 1911 *Standard Oil* and *American Tobacco* cases. Indeed, the government moved against Bell in 1913, charging that the Northwestern Bell Telephone Company's buy outs of independents in Oregon violated the Sherman Act.[45] More disturbing to AT&T, various voices in the early Wilson Administration called for the nationalization (or, in the argot of the day, "postalization") of the telephone and telegraph under the Post Office.[46] These threats led to an agreement in 1913 between AT&T and the Justice Department, known as the

"Kingsbury Commitment." With the Kingsbury Commitment, AT&T agreed to dispose of its holdings in Western Union and purchase no more independent telephone companies without prior approval by the ICC. Bell was permitted to purchase only noncompeting independents.[47]

Most important, AT&T agreed to allow independents to interconnect into the Bell system. In exchange, the Justice Department relaxed its pressure on AT&T. The Kingsbury Commitment marked the beginning of the reemergence of Bell dominance. The agreement prevented the *complete* takeover of the industry by AT&T, but, by reducing competition between Bell and the independents, the Commitment also established a presumption of telephony as a local monopoly. With mandated interconnection, the independents gained a stake in the Bell system, and became less averse to AT&T takeovers. The Kingsbury Commitment also meant the recognition by law of the 1879 division of fields between voice and record communications.[48]

With World War I, the advocates of postalization achieved what would turn out to be a Pyrrhic victory. The nation's railroads had been placed under government operation in December 1917, and calls for a similar wartime nationalization of communications led to Congressional hearings in July 1918.[49] A joint resolution was passed by Congress, and control of wire communications devolved to the Post Office on August 1, 1918. The record is murky how AT&T responded to the war emergency measure, but it is abundantly clear that the corporation did well by the contract that covered the conditions of government operation and compensation. Very likely AT&T also got a taste of the benefits of conservative federal oversight.

The government signed a contract with terms highly favorable to AT&T, in effect assuming responsibility for the Bell System's obligations while guaranteeing the payment of its dividends. AT&T kept operational control over the now nominally nationalized telephone system. The government, as would have been expected, agreed to keep up standards and repairs. Yet it also agreed to set aside a very generous 5.72 percent of book value each year for depreciation. The traditional 4.5 percent license fee that AT&T charged its local operating companies—long the subject of heated rate disputes, as we shall see *infra*—was paid by the government. AT&T's dividend (about $8 a share) also would be paid by the government. In other words, the government agreed to a compensation plan that fixed and legitimated numbers about which there had long been huge controversy. As Noobar Danielian argues, the various Bell subsidiaries happily pointed to the federal compensation contract in subsequent local rate cases, as evidence of the fairness of telephone company policies with respect to license fee and depreciation rates.[50]

Moreover, to meet its obligations to AT&T and to guarantee expanded wartime service, the Postmaster General found himself forced to raise telephone rates. Postmaster Burleson ordered the imposition of a "service connection charge" in August 1918. This was a charge ($3.50) Bell had been trying to institute for years without success, because of opposition from state public utility commissions. In December 1918, the Postmaster General ordered a 20 percent long-distance rate hike. And in March 1919, Burleson gave blanket approval for an increase in Bell local operating company rates. These rate hikes and service charges amounted to approximately $42 million a year for AT&T.[51] Resistance by local authorities to federally mandated rate hikes was beaten back by the Supreme Court. The Court ruled in *Dakota Central Telephone Co. v. State of South Dakota ex rel. Payne, Attorney General,* that under the joint resolution, the Postmaster General had the power to set telephone rates.[52] Though Postmaster General Burleson (and AT&T) argued that the rate increases were caused by higher materiel prices and higher wages, others claimed the cause was the onerous terms of the compensation contract. Regardless, the public furor over government-mandated rate hikes doomed any prospect for continued government ownership of telephony. The wires were returned to private ownership on August 1, 1919.[53] At the same time, the postalization episode convinced AT&T that federal oversight could play a strategic role in the company's grand designs. Postalization may have been perceived by most as a failure, but its positive lessons were not lost on AT&T.

The 1921 Willis-Graham Act furthered Bell's aims and put legislative seal on early federal telephone policy. That act, which gave the ICC powers to approve or disapprove consolidations and mergers of telegraph and telephone companies, permitted AT&T to purchase competing independent telephone companies.[54] The Congressional debates indicate that a strong push in support of Willis-Graham came from the competing independent telephone companies. Their financial fortunes had declined and many wished to be bought out by Bell. The prevailing Congressional view was that telephony clearly constituted a natural monopoly, and that governmental policy should not prevent monopolization.[55] Following the Kingsbury Commitment's mandate of interconnection, Willis-Graham provided antitrust immunity to AT&T.

Thus governmental policy was instrumental in structuring the telephone industry. The combination of market forces, the Kingsbury Commitment, the "failure" of postalization, and the Willis-Graham Act produced an industrial structure that favored geographical monopoly and system-wide interconnection. Inasmuch as AT&T controlled the most lucrative local operating companies and the only long-distance system capable of linking all telephone companies into a single network, the industrial structure which coalesced after 1913 had the effect of consolidating AT&T's control over the telephone business. AT&T clearly dominated the telephone industry. By 1932 AT&T's market share reached 79 percent, with control of the major local operating companies, the major equipment manufacturing apparatus, and the long-distance network.[56] AT&T's dominance had the consequence of establishing a coherent, technically rational telephone industry.

With the industrial structure essentially set, actual regulatory control was minimal. As a practical matter, the ICC did not increase regulatory oversight over telephony after 1921.[57] And state public utilities commissions were stymied by judicial decisions. Telephone companies consistently appealed state-determined rates to federal district courts. The courts would discard the record and conclusions of the state commissions, and begin the long process of determining rates themselves. Because of such judicial review, there was a tendency for state regulatory commissions to avoid rate cases altogether, especially telephone cases.[58] The system of competing federal and state regulation, together with the complex Bell structure, prevented real regulatory control while providing the protection and legitimacy of a regulated utility. Regulation substituted a guaranteed return on capital and management freedom for the uncertainties of the marketplace.[59] This was precisely the kind of regulation Vail had sought.

## Rate-Making

One final pre-FCC structure requires some discussion: that of telephone rate making. Unlike other utilities, telephony provided a service, not a distinct and measurable product. The value of telephone communication to any one subscriber essentially depended upon the number of people connected into the network. The costs to connect a single subscriber thus were common costs. The interdependence of demand for telephone service led to the early conclusion that telephone rates should be based primarily on value of service criteria. Thus, very early on an interrelation of rate making and basic socio-political goals of telephone development became apparent. Rates should be based on value of service, and telephone service should be extended to as many subscribers as possible.[60]

How to facilitate the goal of extension of service through rates was another matter. Since *Munn v. Illinois,* the law had insisted that the owner of property clothed with a public interest was entitled to a "reasonable compensation for its use." The primary issue in rate making was the valuation of the property of the utility. This was the subject of major judicial controversy, not to mention practical difficulty. In *Smythe v. Ames* (1898), the Supreme Court specified its criteria of reasonableness in determining the rates of utilities as the "fair value" of the property.[61] But, as Alfred Kahn has argued, in practice this meant endless controversy over the proper valuation of sunk capital. There is no objective, unequivocal method of ascertaining the cost of capital, even for a particular regulated company at a particular time and place.[62] In the telephone industry, the valuation controversy was entangled with a jurisdictional controversy over the relation between the property, including rates, of the local operating companies (intrastate), and the property of the parent company (interstate).

In the aftermath of the Kingsbury Commitment, all telephone companies were permitted to connect into AT&T's long-distance system. As a practical matter, telephone services share much of the same plant. After all, for long distance to function, it must begin and end in local facilities. Nevertheless, early judicial rulings called for the complete disaggregation, or separation, of long-distance and local rates. In the Minnesota Rate Cases (1913), the Court established the so-called "board-to-board" principle, which essentially held that all the costs of providing local service should be recovered from local charges.[63] Under the board-to-board philosophy, a long-distance call was viewed as having just one cost element, that is, from the switchboard of the originating exchange to the switchboard in the completing exchange. This also made some sense given the jurisdictional complexities; long distance was interstate commerce, presumably out of bounds to state regulatory commissions.

But AT&T was a system—actually a powerful holding company—which largely defied the legal jurisdictions. Besides the long distance-local rate separations issue, the other key problem in this regard centered around the license fee that Bell charged its local operating companies. The license fee, comprising a hefty 4.5 percent of the local operating company's revenues, supposedly represented payment for services provided to the operating companies by the AT&T parent. Generally speaking, AT&T's control enabled it to shift costs and services between jurisdictions. For example, AT&T was able to require the local operating companies to route toll calls over the facilities of AT&T Long Lines even in instances where the operating companies had parallel facilities.[64] Thus, between the jurisdictional confusion and vacuum of control at the national level, AT&T in effect was able to pull revenue out of the local operating companies into the parent company. All through the 1920s AT&T was profitable and paid consistently high dividends, while the financial situation of the local operating companies was far less rosy.[65] Efforts of state regulatory commissions to alter this balance were rebuffed by the courts. In an important 1923 decision, the Supreme Court refused to permit the Public Service Commission of Missouri to disallow certain payments by the local Bell company to AT&T.[66]

The role of the federal courts in thwarting effective state regulation, combined with the jurisdictional problem over the regulation of commerce, led to speculation that national regulation was needed.[67] This was not just a problem of telephony; it had to do with a conservative judiciary and the ability of holding companies in general to circumvent effective controls.[68] And so it was the Depression, whose cause was often laid at the door of holding company pyramiding schemes, which sparked a change in the judiciary's attitude toward regulation.

In *Smith v. Illinois Bell Telephone Company* (1930), the Court ruled that AT&T charges to the local operating companies must be justified in terms of the costs to AT&T of performing the services. *Smith* also effectively mandated a "station-to-station" theory of separations, whereby long distance would have to pay some percentage of the joint costs of the local exchange. *Smith* thus strengthened state regulation, permitting the public utilities commissions to check on the payments by their various Bell companies for Western Electric equipment and supplies. The commissions were no longer bound to accept the reasonableness of the division of toll revenues prescribed by the license contracts. But *Smith* also clearly ruled that interstate toll rates were beyond the authority of the state commissions.[69] The need for a governmental body with the appropriate jurisdiction to deal with interstate toll rates would be one reason behind the emergence of the FCC.

Between market forces and the federal policy inaugurated by the Kingsbury Commitment, the telegraph and telephone industries in the pre-regulation era evolved into monopolies. Basic common law secured the crucial common carrier goal of nondiscrimination, and the Willis-Graham Act mandated interconnection. The Kingsbury Commitment guaranteed the institutional and technological separation between voice and record carriers. AT&T, successfully arguing the case for telephony as a natural monopoly, welcomed the government intervention which served to secure its control over the industry. Apart from the Kingsbury Commitment, however. there was no effective regulation of AT&T during this era. AT&T obtained the benefit of a *de facto* sanctioned monopoly without the *quid pro quo* of regulatory oversight.

## Radio

The origins of radio, or "wireless," rest in 19th-century developments in theoretical physics. James Clerk Maxwell, following earlier hypotheses of Faraday and Newton, conjectured that energy travels through a medium in waves—periodic disturbances—which correspond to the speed and level at which the energy oscillates. In the late 1880s Heinrich Hertz was able to confirm Maxwell's electromagnetic wave theory. Hertz demonstrated that electricity moves in waves through a particular medium, the electromagnetic spectrum. The spectrum is the natural resource through which radio waves propagate and which makes broadcast communication possible. Guglielmo Marconi looked for uses of wireless communication in wireless telegraphy in the late 1890s. He patented his experiments, received financial backing from British capitalists, and formed the Marconi Wireless Telegraph Company.

Just as telephony began in the context of the search to augment an existing communications technology, so too did wireless. Early radio was conceived as a point-to-point communications device. Its early users were sea-going ships. The United Fruit Company used wireless to direct its vessels laden with fruit to particular ports. The Marconi Company planned to install wireless equipment on lighthouses and ships along the English coast for ship-shore safety. In this context, Marconi secured two important contracts, one with Lloyd's (the insurer) and another with the British Admiralty.

The United States Navy also used wireless to keep in contact with ships and coordinate naval maneuvers. As early as 1904 the Navy was given authority over coastal stations. This began the Navy's long relationship with radio; it put much money and research into radio installations, and contracted out for wireless equipment from foreign suppliers and among the several small American inventor-entrepreneurs. The Navy later became interested in the possibility of using radio signals to guide torpedoes.[70] Navy control over coastal stations effectively made it the key governmental player in wireless communications, notwithstanding the 1912 Radio Act's vestment in the Commerce Department the authority to dispense radio licenses to civilians.

Conceived as a point-to-point technology, a major problem with early radio was its lack of secrecy—the inability to exclude others from hearing the communication. Radio was also beset by a problem of "syntony," where transmitting and receiving instruments had to be accurately tuned so that the latter would respond only to vibrations of the frequency emitted by the former. Radio's lack of secrecy enhanced its appeal for some. Amateurs, or "hams," got involved with the technology very early, becoming a politically active interest group as well as a market for electronics equipment.[71]

Marconi's American subsidiary quickly established dominance in the wireless field, though international competitors began to challenge the company. In the early 1900s small companies associated with inventors Reginald Fessenden and Lee de Forest emerged in the United States. They received some government contracts to build experimental wireless sets and stations. A great boost was provided by the sinking of the ocean vessels *Republic* in 1909 and *Titanic* in 1912, because these disasters prompted the passage of laws requiring all ships above a certain size to carry wireless equipment. Nevertheless, the early American wireless industry recapitulated the stock watering, circus boosterism, and patent infringement problems that had occurred in the early history of the telegraph. There was no American equivalent of the Marconi Company. Indeed, Marconi's hold on wireless patents caused the bankruptcy of the United Wireless Company in 1912. American Marconi acquired its assets, giving it roughly 90 percent of American ship-shore business between 1912 and World War I.[72]

## The Vacuum Tube and the Threat to AT&T

By 1910 both Fessenden and de Forest transmitted speech and music by wireless. In the categories of the day this was wireless *telephony,* and AT&T soon perceived wireless as a potential direct competitive threat. Of key importance was de Forest's three-element vacuum tube, the triode, which the inventor developed in 1906. The vacuum tube was the most important of three devices (the others being the oscillating arc and the radiofrequency alternator) that could transform radio technology from the relatively crude "spark" transmitting system to a symmetric, or continuous wave, transmitting system.[73] Continuous wave transmission enabled a far more accurate use of the spectrum, and could carry voice as well as telegraph signal. As a technological device, the vacuum tube also allowed efficient and accurate amplification of electrical current.

This made it important for long-distance telephony as well. As discussed previously, in many ways the long-distance system was a key to AT&T's success in establishing dominance in telephony. Long-distance constituted the means of interconnection of local exchanges, and provided legitimacy to the claim of one interdependent wired system under AT&T's tutelage. A major problem for AT&T rested in the vast costs and dubious reliability of its long-distance network. Voice signals over long distances of wire had the tendency to attenuate. In order to compensate for signal fade, wire had to be very thick. Before 1900, long-distance lines demanded wire about ⅛ inch thick. One-fourth of all capital invested in the telephone system before 1900 was spent on copper wire. With the Pupin loading coil, developed around 1900, the diameter of the wire could be halved. "Pupinized" lines extended the limits of long-distance service to about 1500 miles. But without some means of repeating or amplifying the signal, greater distances were not possible.[74]

For AT&T, de Forest's vacuum tube represented both a benefit and a threat. Used as a signal repeater, the vacuum tube augured additional savings and as much technical promise as the Pupin coil in establishing truly transcontinental long-distance telephony. It could help secure AT&T's long-distance network as the linchpin of the telephone system, and thus cement AT&T's dominance of the industry. But the vacuum tube, by permitting the possibility of *wireless* telephony, also posed a dire threat to AT&T's dominance. This threat induced the corporation to expand its research capabilities between 1909 and 1915. Indeed, the search for a repeater led to the establishment of the Research Branch of the Western Electric Engineering Department, the precursor to the renowned Bell Telephone Laboratories. Nonetheless, the corporation could not come up with an in-house repeater, and hence purchased de Forest's patent for the triode vacuum tube in 1913. AT&T undertook successful transatlantic radiotelephone experiments in 1915, but played down their importance, lest they encourage radio-based competitors to the wired telephone system. To protect its wired flank, AT&T began to take out patents on any device potentially useful in the development of radio. This included the 1917 purchase of an exclusive license to all the remaining rights on de Forest's inventions. AT&T moved to achieve control of what it believed to be the key vacuum tube patents.[75]

Notwithstanding the importance of the vacuum tube, its capabilities as an amplification device were dependent on another invention, the negative feedback circuit, which was patented by Edwin Armstrong in 1911. Armstrong sold his rights to the device to the Westinghouse Electric and Manufacturing Company. Thus, a pattern emerged in the pre-World War I period where several key devices were owned by individual inventors, who then sold the patents to rival corporations. Without some patent consolidation, no successful amplifier could be constructed. Corporations and inventors engaged in a sort of multiple courtship, and all became embroiled in bitter patent litigation battles.

## The Formation of Radio Corporation of America

Technological developments in electronics quickened in the years preceding World War I, but progress in wireless in the United States was impeded by the competing proprietary patent claims and accompanying litigation. Though its initial patent position was weak with regard to vacuum tubes, the General Electric Company (GE) conducted experiments with the device and engineered some modifications of it. GE also exercised patent control over the Alexanderson alternator, at the time among the most promising technologies for the production of high-powered, continuous waves. Westinghouse owned the Armstrong feedback circuit patents which allowed the production of high-frequency waves with a vacuum tube. From 1912 to 1926, GE and AT&T had no less than 20 important patent conflicts between them.[76]

The flurry of electronic patent litigation in the years preceding World War I nearly brought manufacturing of radio apparatus in the US to a halt. In theory, patent law's protection of the proprietary rights of individual inventors was intended (in part) to establish an environment hospitable to technological advance and commercial development. Paradoxically, patent protection worked too well with regard to wireless. As inventor Edwin Armstrong testified before the Federal Trade Commission in a 1923 investigation of the radio industry, "It was absolutely impossible to manufacture any kind of workable apparatus without using practically all the inventions which were then known."[77] The dispersion of electronic patent holdings not only prevented the emergence of any American corporation from securing dominance, it stymied the American industry as a whole. There was no American company to challenge the hegemony of the American Marconi Company.

But with the entry of the United States into World War I, wireless was needed for military purposes. Under its wartime powers, the government authorized manufacturers to use one another's patents. This served to break the complex patent logjam over inventions and facilitated the mass production of wireless equipment for military use. Under the Navy Department's guiding organizational hand, and benefiting from its tremendous wartime user-pull, the electronics industry left the era of the individual inventor/tinkerer and entered into the arena of large-scale corporate capitalism. The need for vacuum tubes brought the two great lamp-bulb manufacturers. General Electric and Westinghouse, directly into the radio industry. The Navy assumed operating control of radio stations for the duration of the war, and built high-power transmission stations. During the war the US achieved direct contact with its forces in Europe via wireless. The Committee on Public Information (better known as the ''Creel Committee,'' after its chairman, George Creel), whose mission was to disseminate American wartime propaganda, successfully used radio for this purpose in Europe.

After the war, the Navy made a bid to continue its control of radio. Having lost the struggle to postalize the wire communications system, proponents of nationalization made alliance with the Navy to argue for government ownership of wireless. Though the Navy operated all stations, it did not own all of them. Besides the Navy stations, there were four privately owned wireless systems operating on American soil: the Federal Telegraph Company, Tropical Radio (a subsidiary of United Fruit Company), Atlantic Communications Company (a subsidiary of the German firm, Telefunken), and American Marconi. Of these American Marconi was by far the most powerful and extensive. The Wilson Administration generally supported government ownership of wireless, seeing in the technology a means of establishing a firm US presence in post-war international commercial and military arrangements.[78] Among the primary reasons for this policy was the desire to challenge British control of international communications.

The British held a near-monopoly of the supply of the natural rubberlike insulator known as ''gutta-percha,'' which was essential for the insulation of undersea cables. This control, combined with the historic supremacy of the British Navy, meant that Britain possessed a virtual monopoly of the financing and construction of the cable systems of the world. The world cable network had been laid out in such a pattern as to give Britain and her territorial possessions the status of nodal points in the system. Key landing and relay points in the network were under British control. Indeed, the pattern of undersea cables was a factor in the long British domination of international news. From 1870 until World War I, Reuters, the British news agency based at the hub of the world cable system in London, dominated the world flow of news.[79] The control of information was not merely a neutral consequence of the structure of undersea cable layout. The pattern of landing and relay points could and sometimes did permit the British to intercept, delay, and/or distort messages. During World War I such control (along with the cutting of German cables) meant the cut-off of the Central Powers from their international communication links.[80]

The British control of cable facilitated a blockade of German long-distance communications. This blockade and interception was not just of diplomatic messages, but of commercial ones as well. The disruption of German cables meant that it lost access to the New York money market, hence to the ability to sell securities to raise foreign currency for its war effort. The lesson was not lost on Britain's soon-to-be-ally, the United States. Indeed, the Senate Interstate Commerce Committee held hearings in 1921 on undersea cables during which it was asserted that Britain had intercepted a great deal of commercial cable traffic during the war for the benefit of its private national companies.[81] The United States came to believe that undersea cable was not a neutral carrier.

Long-distance wireless held promise as a technological means to break the British dominance of international communication. The advantage of wireless for military purposes, of course, was that communication could not be physically cut. Moreover, the technological advances in wireless—particularly the advances in continuous wave technology—were centered in the United States. But the British-owned American Marconi Company was by far the most powerful wireless company operating in the United States. Marconi's industrial and patent strength aroused fears within the US Navy that the British might not only acquire a monopoly of world wireless communications, but also compromise a new tool of national defense. Though Marconi was a capitalist firm with no overt connection to the British government, the company was perceived by the Navy as advancing British political interests. A major factor, then, behind the Navy effort to maintain control over American radio was to establish a *national* wireless communications system for military and strategic purposes.

However, in keeping with the traditional American relation between state and economy, the national wireless system was to be privately owned and operated, notwithstanding the crucial role the government would play in its formation. The Navy bid to retain the wartime command system over communication electronics was permanently tabled by the 1918 Congress.[82] Both commercial and amateur interests vigorously opposed the Navy's efforts. Nonetheless, the most likely factor for the defeat of the nationalization proposal was that control of Congress had passed to the Republicans with the 1918 election. Republicans strongly opposed government ownership of industry and strongly advocated the doctrine of laissez-faire. Such ideological predispositions had wide appeal, particularly in the aftermath of the federal government's poor wartime performance in managing the temporarily nationalized telegraph and telephone systems. Those few in Congress who actually understood radio, such as Maine Republican congressman Wallace H. White, Jr., began drafting bills to keep control over radio with the Secretary of Commerce.

The rejection of a government monopoly of wireless, however, did not prevent the federal government from assisting in the creation of a structure for a national radio system. If government ownership of wireless could not garner sufficient political support, the prospect of American communications being controlled by a foreign company was not acceptable to lawmakers either.[83] But there existed no American company to challenge Marconi.

Wartime governmental control of all wireless coastal stations put the Navy in a position to stymie American Marconi. Marconi needed to convert its wireless system from spark to continuous wave. In early 1918 the company approached the premier manufacturer of arc technology, the longtime Navy supplier Federal Telegraph, for the rights to Federal's patents. The Navy, getting wind of the deal, quickly outbid Marconi. In May 1918 the Navy purchased Federal's operating stations and patents to prevent Marconi from obtaining continuous-wave technology.[84] Around the same time, the Navy moved to prevent Marconi from gaining access to the other system of generating continuous waves, the Alexanderson alternator.

General Electric, the holder of the alternator patent, had been negotiating intermittently with Marconi since 1915. By 1918, when Ernst Alexanderson finally installed an impressive alternator in Marconi's New Brunswick station, GE and Marconi expressed readiness to cut a deal. GE had invested heavily in research and Marconi was the only market for the alternator. Nonetheless, GE had wide differences with Marconi over the question of exclusive control of the device and the amount of royalties to be paid to GE. Negotiations dragged on through April 1919, whereupon GE terminated them. The precipitating cause of the breakdown in GE-Marconi negotiations was the entrance of the US Navy. The Navy intervened with a proposal that promised both a market for the alternators and freedom from the Marconi insistence on exclusive control.

On April 19, 1919, a conference was held between GE executives (the key figure was Owen D. Young, then head of GE's legal department, later to become chairman of the board) and Navy representatives. Appealing to their patriotism, Navy representatives Admiral William H. G. Bullard and Commander Stanley C. Hooper pleaded with the GE executives not to sell the Alexanderson alternator to Marconi.[85] Such appeals found fertile soil in GE executives, but GE was also concerned for its considerable investment in the alternator (estimated at $550,000). After all, Marconi was the only visible buyer of the device. The Navy thus floated a proposition which proved satisfactory to both parties. If GE would create an American-controlled radio company, the Navy would try to secure for the company a commercial monopoly of long-distance radio communications. The Navy talked about a "partnership" between government and GE, promising, among other things, that any Navy-held patents useful in long-distance wireless would be turned over to GE. The Navy also gave GE vague assurances that the new radio company would be allocated the lion's-share of scarce frequencies.[86]

Such were the origins of the Radio Corporation of America (RCA). As Hugh Aitken claims, though the galvanizing issue had been the transfer of alternator technology to the British, the real import of the Navy-GE negotiations was the creation of an American radio corporation. (Indeed, alternator technology was sold both to British Marconi and to other foreign wireless concerns shortly after the establishment of RCA.) GE used the Navy's antipathy toward foreign wireless concerns to pressure British Marconi into selling its interest in its American Marconi subsidiary. GE then bought out the holdings of American stockholders of American Marconi. Thereafter, the Navy turned over the former American Marconi stations it had seized during the war. In December 1919, RCA opened its doors for business, with former American Marconi executives Edward J. Nally and David Sarnoff at its helm and Admiral Bullard on its board of directors. Notwithstanding earlier Navy assurances, RCA would have neither exclusive privileges nor a legal monopoly.[87] Nonetheless, the nascent RCA company moved quickly into international wireless communications. Some of RCA's earliest moves as a corporate entity were to set up a radiotelegraph consortium in Latin America.

One serious problem loomed large on the wireless horizon. The end of World

War I also ended the Navy's rationalization of the patent logjam. A crucial aspect of the formation of RCA was that it merged the patents held exclusively by GE and American Marconi, and made them available to RCA. However, some patent reciprocation with AT&T was necessary if radio was to proceed. The post-war situation in telegraphy, sound recording, electrical circuit arrangements, photoelectric cells, telephoto, and television was characterized by overlapping and conflictual patents. Each major manufacturer pushed its research as far as possible only to encounter a part, circuit, or arrangement that was already patented by another.[88] The vacuum tube was the technology most in demand and most in contention. In July 1920, GE and AT&T entered into a patent cross-licensing agreement which authorized the pooling of patents for delineated activities. The agreement expanded in 1921 when Wireless Specialty Apparatus Company, United Fruit, and Westinghouse were brought into the patent pool.

A patent pool could solve certain problems in a rapidly developing, highly technological industry. If any one company could not gain market advantage by means of patent control, the group of patent-holding companies could pool their patents, and apportion market control by assigning pool members to specific parts of the industry. In effect, the cross-licensing agreements of 1920 and 1921 amounted to an intricate division of industry of the field of communications.

The "Radio Group," consisting of RCA, GE, Westinghouse, United Fruit, Tropical Radio Telegraph Company, and Wireless Specialty Apparatus Company, received rights in areas of wireless telegraphy. Of the major Radio Group players, GE and Westinghouse were granted a nonexclusive right to manufacture wireless receiving sets and to establish and maintain wireless transmitting stations. RCA was allotted the exclusive right to sell those receiving sets. The "Telephone Group" (AT&T and Western Electric) received rights in the fields of wire telegraphy and wire telephony, and the right to make, use, and sell wireless telephone (radio) apparatus connected to or operated as part of a public service telephone system. AT&T's victory in maintaining total control over telephonic communication was ensured by an additional right to the manufacture and sale or lease of transmitters. General Electric and Westinghouse could use the pooled patents to make transmitters for themselves but not for sale to others. Both groups granted to each other nonexclusive licenses in wireless apparatus for experimental purposes. Finally, the main corporations purchased interests in RCA.

Each corporation entered into the license agreement to expand its opportunities and to protect those opportunities from further entry. GE could now operate its new wireless business with outside patents and without fear of entry from AT&T. For AT&T, the agreement precluded the possible development of a competitive wire plant for telephone communication. Because the agreement gave AT&T exclusive rights to develop radio-telephones as a public network, it allowed the company to exploit radio technology in its established business. The pooling of patents was indispensable to the firms belonging to the pool, and erected an insurmountable obstacle to those corporations wishing to enter the business who were not party to the agreements.[89]

At the time of these agreements, radio broadcasting was not contemplated. The dominant market for radio at the time was wireless *telegraphy*. It was only after the unforeseen success of the first broadcast station, Westinghouse's KDKA, that new economic opportunities made problematic the general language and stipulations of the cross-licensing agreements, and conflicts among the patent pool members came to the fore. It was perhaps not so much an issue of the "generality" of the cross-licensing language as it was that new economic opportunities created situations which made the previous contractual agreements ambiguous. That ambiguity created a sort of behavioral no-man's land for the corporations involved.

## The Rise of Broadcasting

Broadcasting—the dissemination of electrical messages through the airwaves to an undifferentiated audience—may not have been contemplated, but it was inherent in the technology of radio. The ability to tune in to any and every wireless communication was the attraction for the radio amateurs. The amateurs typically competed to pick up distant signals (a practice called "d-xing"), and many sent transmissions themselves. Radio interference from amateurs was one reason behind the passage of the Radio Act of 1912. While a major function of the 1912 act was to elucidate the requirement that ships carry wireless, it also was designed to protect military and ship-shore communications from radio interference. The act allocated certain frequencies for the use of the government and forbade the operation of a civilian radio station without a license from the Secretary of Commerce.[90]

Along with amateurs, wireless had an association with commercial boosterism, if not commercialism *per se*. In 1910 the John Wanamaker Company struck a contract with American Marconi for experimental point-to-point wireless stations to be installed in its New York and Philadelphia department stores. Wireless gave Wanamaker both inter-store telegraphic communication and publicity.[91] The Bamberger Department store (and 39 other less well-known retail outlets) also found that a radio station on its premises served to draw in business.[92]

The real impetus to broadcasting came in 1920, when Westinghouse escalated an amateur station of one of its Pittsburgh employees into a full-scale broadcast station. The amateur broadcasts had sparked the sale of crystal sets in Pittsburgh, and Westinghouse gambled that a more powerful and regularized broadcast transmission would spur sales of its new radio sets. By all accounts, Westinghouse station KDKA caused a sensation. Radio broadcasting mushroomed soon thereafter. The boom came in 1922. By May, 218 licenses had been issued. By early 1923 the number of licenses was well over 500.[93] Nascent broadcasters early on programmed what has become standard radio fare: orchestral music, drama, political addresses, church services, sports events. The popularity of broadcasting precipitated a demand for factory-produced receivers.[94]

The Radio Act of 1912 had failed to set aside particular frequencies for broadcast use. The Secretary of Commerce selected 360 meters (or 833 kilocycles) and licensed all stations to operate at this frequency. Stations were left to work out among themselves operating time and transmission power arrangements. Not surprisingly, interference quickly became a problem. The corporations involved in broadcasting lost money on it; broadcasting was a sideline activity to the main business of manufacturing and selling receivers. Until the mid-1920s, radio was a popular, and for set manufacturers lucrative, but still primarily an amateur pastime. Most of those early stations were small-time operations. The amateur "hams" still dominated transmission and reception, and constituted an active lobby in radio circles. The Radio Group, with much more money and more powerful transmitting equipment, operated five stations. Stations not backed by adequate financing, particularly educational stations, often went off the air.[95]

But because broadcasting created a demand for receivers, it disrupted the industrial boundaries constituted by the 1920/1921 license agreements. Radio broadcasting, after all, was the projection of the human voice through the airwaves, that is to say, wireless *telephony*. AT&T regarded this as part of its natural domain, and decided that radio broadcasting, as an adjunct to telephony, should be controlled by the company. AT&T began to establish its own radio stations interconnected with telephone wires to form a network. AT&T asserted that the Radio Group had no right to engage in broadcasting. This was but one source of controversy. Another conflict emerged over whether AT&T could sell radio receivers. This hung on the definition of "amateur purposes," a phrase contained within the 1920 agreement between AT&T and GE which granted to GE "an exclusive license to make, use, lease, and sell all wireless telephone apparatus for amateur purposes." Did "amateur purposes" apply to the ordinary radio listener or did it apply only to those persons experimenting with wireless as a scientific pursuit? If interpreted to apply only to the latter, AT&T might gain entrance to the very important field of manufacture of radio receiving sets. AT&T access to the exploding radio set market probably was the largest threat to the Radio Group and the most bitter controversy of the early 1920s.[96]

Still another controversy, that over "remote pickups," presaged a future difficult problem of carriage of radio broadcasts. Pickup wires were required when a station aired an event which took place outside the station. Rather than string new wires, telephone wires could be utilized for this connection. Up to early 1922, it was AT&T's policy to refuse the use of Bell telephone wires—necessary for remote pickups or for linking up distant stations—to radio broadcast stations not owned by Bell. A liberalized private line leasing policy in 1922 specifically excluded AT&T's main rivals. RCA, GE, and Westinghouse were forced to use telegraph wires for remote pickups and interconnection of their broadcast stations.[97] In general, controversies arose over the precise rights of the Radio and Telephone groups. AT&T saw broadcasting and the manufacture of wireless equipment as extensions of its telephone industry, and sought to gain competitive advantage in radio. Noobar Danielian advances the plausible claim that AT&T, in its corporate decisions regarding radio, not only sought to protect its telephone flank from possible competition, but actually intended to monopolize broadcasting.[98]

The question of how to finance broadcasting emerged within the context of such intercorporate rivalries. Advertising on the air was considered an anathema in the early 1920s. The first issue of *Radio Broadcast* magazine (May 1922) contained several suggestions for financing the new medium, including endowment by wealthy individuals (along the model of the benefactor of a library) and local financing through tax revenues, but no mention was made of advertising. David Sarnoff's earliest plan for a proto-national broadcasting company called for a percentage of RCA's radio manufacturing revenues to defray the programming and administrative costs of a broadcast company which was to be nonprofit.[99] Sarnoff was a proponent of the "public service" model of broadcasting, conceived as an activity to be kept free of the taint of money-making. Secretary of Commerce Herbert Hoover, while frowning upon the idea of advertising ("I believe the quickest way to kill broadcasting would be to use it for direct advertising," he declared to the National Radio Conference of 1924), offered no lead in solving the very real problem of how to finance the activity.[100] Financial problems prompted the return of more than half of the broadcast licenses issued by the Commerce Department between 1921 and 1926.[101]

AT&T established its WEAF flagship station in 1922. In keeping with the idea of wireless telephony, AT&T intended to operate its radio stations as if they were part of the telephone system. As such, the phone company instituted a practice it called "toll broadcasting." This was an arrangement whereby broadcast facilities would be open (for an appropriate fee) to individuals to send out their messages to the general public. The facilities were called, metaphorically, "phone booths of the air."[102] The strategic importance of establishing broadcasting as "radio telephony" rested in the fact that under the cross-licensing agreements, public service telephony on a commercial basis was the exclusive province of AT&T. AT&T's effort to establish radio broadcasting as an adjunct to telephony served to make the connection of broadcasting to commercial boosterism direct. In August 1922 AT&T's WEAF station attracted its first customer, a real-estate firm which paid for broadcast time to praise its new housing development. Initially slow in attracting customers, WEAF gradually gained sponsors and originated the practice of "institutional sponsorship" by corporations of quality entertainment programming.

The entrance of WEAF into the broadcast scene spawned both a technical and a programming competition between Radio Group stations and WEAF. As early as the fall of 1922, WEAF began to experiment with long-distance interconnection of stations. In March 1924, spectacular transatlantic and transcontinental broadcast experiments were undertaken by Westinghouse's WJZ. Rebroadcasts of these programs constituted the first efforts in networking, labeled "chain broadcasting." The interest in the 1924 Republican and Democratic conventions gave great impetus to the growth of radio networks. AT&T set up a 22-station hookup for a Calvin Coolidge speech in October 1924. By December 1925, AT&T's regular network had grown to 26 stations and had gross revenues of $750,000 from the sale of air time.[103] Thus, though networking soon would become a built-in structural feature of an advertising-based broadcasting system, networking as a practice occurred well before the advertising structure was in place. That AT&T set up the first network is not surprising, given both its control of the wires which facilitated the linkage and its ability to finance such experiments with toll revenue. The Radio Group's inability to use AT&T lines for interconnection and remote pickups prompted experimentation with carriage by shortwave radio frequencies and by Western Union telegraph lines (both of which were technically inferior to AT&T's interconnection apparatus).

Networking emerged as a corollary to the nature of the mass communicative event as *spectacle,* and the new technical ability to reproduce that otherwise unitary event without geographic limitation. What made radio exciting to the early amateurs was the new combination of immediacy and distance it created. The idea of national radio broadcasting predated either its technical solution in networking or its financial solution in advertising.[104] Secretary of Commerce Hoover consistently praised technical efforts to provide nationwide broadcasting.

The content of early radio was primarily entertainment. Early American radio was the classic era for live pop music. Radio's adoption of the Tin Pan Alley tradition was structured to some degree by the pressure of newspaper interests (some of which owned radio stations as a means of collecting news and for publicity in the manner of the department stores) to keep radio out of the two key preserves of news and advertising.[105] The financial ability of some stations and not others to tap into the "star" system, to attract and program "talent," was reinforced by a Department of Commerce ruling issued to ease congestion in the spring of 1922. At that time, 400 meters (or 750 kilocycles) was made available for broadcasting, but under certain provisions. A new classification of station, termed class "B," was authorized to operate at 400 meters, but would have to transmit at a high-powered 500-1000 watts and would not be allowed to use phonograph records. Stations unable to meet such qualifications would have to remain at the heavily populated 360-meter spot. The rule tended to create an aristocracy of well-financed stations at 400 and a congested aggregation of amateurs at 360. This type of ruling underscored the fact that the Department of Commerce relied primarily on the advice of the electronics manufacturers in technical matters, and favored their broadcasting interests over amateurs'. Hoover's explicit championing of interconnection could but mean strong support for national programming, and thus for those entities capable of delivering it.[106]

Evidence of a changed atmosphere with regard to the financing of broadcasting can be found in RCA preparations for its new "super-power" New York flagship station in the summer of 1923. RCA planned to permit advertisers the use of the facilities of the stations, allowing them free time on the air but requiring them to pay the cost of programs of high quality. Nonetheless, a *New York Times* article on the financing of broadcasting in the summer of 1924 indicates that among leaders of American broadcasting, only H.B. Thayer of AT&T advocated and defended toll broadcasting.[107] But by 1925 advertising seemed inevitable. Only AT&T and the stations brought into its network had managed to solve the problem of how to finance broadcast programming.[108] And even these stations did not garner sufficient advertising revenue to meet annual expenses. In fact, no radio station had met its operating expenses with advertising revenue at the time the Federal Radio Commission was created in March 1927. The death rate among all stations in 1924 was over 50 percent.[109]

By the mid-1920s the options for a structure for the financing of broadcasting grew less distinct and less satisfactory to the radio community. Whereas at the 1924 National Radio Conference Secretary of Commerce Hoover saw the problem as whether or not advertising had a place on radio at all, at the 1925 Conference he urged the radio industry to distinguish between "unobtrusive publicity" and "advertising in the intrusive sense."[110] The problem of how to finance the burgeoning radio industry was becoming part of the conflicted anti-"government interference" sentiment within the industry. The 1925 Conference found that though direct and mixed advertising "were objectionable to the listening public," the problem rested in the *manner* in which the broadcaster employed advertising. The conference resolved that the "problems of radio publicity should be solved by the industry itself, and not by Government compulsion or by legislation."[111]

This spirit of self-regulation was endorsed heartily by the federal government, represented at the conference by Secretary Hoover. The radio conferences were part of the 1920s relationship between business and government that Ellis Hawley has labeled "Hooverian associationalism." Hoover did not envision government as a regulator. Rather, the government was to function as an aide to the private sector in formulating mechanisms for continued social and economic progress.[112] What this meant was that the market, not the government or public, should decide the usage of the airwaves. At this point, the transition to commercial broadcasting proceeded quickly. In 1925, 235 stations—43 percent of the total—engaged in commercial broadcasting.[113]

In a March 1925 memorandum on establishing a national broadcasting company, David Sarnoff appeared to have given up his desire for a system of endowed broadcasting. Instead he turned to commercialization. If the Radio Group stations were ever to compete with the AT&T network, the logic went, they would have to merge into one entity of national broadcast capability.[114] However, as late as 1925 it remained unclear whether the original 1920 license agreement gave the Radio Group an unchallenged right to sell time on the air. This and other issues remained to be resolved. AT&T announced that it planned to manufacture receiving sets in 1926 when some RCA-controlled patents were to expire. Efforts at arbitrating differences between the Radio Group and the Telephone Group were difficult, long, and unavailing.

## A New Corporate Division of Industry

Throughout 1925 and the first half of 1926 negotiations ensued between the Radio Group and AT&T to resolve the industrial controversy. RCA had won an inconclusive victory in a 1924 arbitration over the disagreements as to respective rights to use radio patents according to the 1920 license agreement. The two groups settled the disputes in a set of three contracts entered into on July 1, 1926, designed to reconfigure the industrial boundaries in light of the developments since 1920. This was accomplished by having each party give the other exclusive licenses to use the patents in particular fields of activity reserved to it. Most important, the agreements took AT&T out of broadcasting entirely for the price of keeping the Radio Group not only out of wire telephony, but out of the *carriage* of radio program transmission as well.

Though AT&T couched the decision to withdraw from radio in the context that its involvement had taken the company far afield from its primary business, this explanation must be greeted with some skepticism. Barred from using AT&T lines for the interconnection of its radio stations, Radio Group members had begun experimenting with interconnection by other means. Westinghouse successfully used shortwave transmissions to interconnect its radio stations. This, of course, approximated a radiotelephone, and undoubtedly caused AT&T consternation. Even worse, RCA considered constructing its own wire system to interconnect its stations. Such a wire system would have constituted a technologically advanced competitor to AT&T's wire system.

The solution to the intra-industry battles was to strike a new division of the industry and create new exclusive boundaries of operation. AT&T sold its WEAF station (the finest station in the United States at that time) to RCA for $1 million. The Radio Group gained exclusive rights to broadcasting and would purchase carriage facilities from AT&T exclusively. In addition, the Radio Group obtained the right to use the patents in radio receiving sets and the right to sell transmission equipment. The agreement monopolized both domestic and international radiotelephony as a Bell System service, and freed AT&T from the threat of a competing wireless phone system. AT&T received exclusive licenses from the Radio Group to use their patents in wire telegraphy on land. In return, it yielded domestic and international wireless telegraph service to RCA.

Of lesser significance at the time, AT&T was granted exclusive licenses under the patents of the Radio Group for use in electrical sound-recording apparatus, electrical phonographs, and sound-picture equipment when these were used in relation to, or connected with, the field of wire telephony. This retained for AT&T the right of using patents of both parties in wire transmission of television. The Radio Group could employ all patents for use in sound-recording and the like where these were related to, or connected with, the fields of one-way wireless telephone reception and transmission.[115] The significance of the 1926 agreements cannot be overestimated. This corporate division of labor would come to define the legal parameters of the regulation of telecommunications and constitute the basic regulatory formulas. Following the agreement of 1926, RCA formed a broadcasting subsidiary, the National Broadcasting Company.

## Government Regulation: The Radio Act of 1927

By 1927 over 700 stations were operating. Radio interference was becoming an intractable problem, especially after a 1926 district court decision ruled that under the Radio Act of 1912 the Commerce Secretary had no authority to refuse licenses or to compel licensees to comply with rules regarding frequency, power limits, or hours of operation.[116] Until that decision, Commerce Secretary Hoover had had some success persuading, and occasionally compelling stations to agree to time-sharing and power limitation agreements. However, following the *Zenith* case, stations jumped frequencies, boosted transmission power, and changed operating hours at will. The resulting interference led to a drop in radio sales.[117] Broadcasters, through the national radio conferences, had been calling for more regulation for years—though they envisioned regulation in the Hooverian spirit, that is, regulation to help the industry iron out its problems, not regulation *over* the industry. This vision was underscored by the 1925 Radio Conference's insistence that the problem of advertising was an industry, not a governmental, matter. More than fifteen bills to regulate radio were introduced in Congress between 1921 and 1927. They died in committees, most often without hearings.[118]

The fourth Radio Conference called for a limitation on broadcast time and power. The recommendations of that conference were embodied in a bill (H.R. 5589) which eventually became the Radio Act of 1927. Thus, federal control was asserted only after the *technical* consequences of broadcast expansion had become chaotic. The Radio Act of 1927 established a commission to license stations, assign frequency bands and station wavelengths, fix operating times and power levels, and stabilize the usage of the airwaves generally in the "public convenience, interest, or necessity." Radio service was to be distributed equitably, so as to give "fair, efficient, and equitable radio service" to the different states. The act, while denying licensees any property rights in the electromagnetic spectrum, permitted broadcasters to exercise editorial discretion in all matters concerning broadcast programming. Inasmuch as the Radio Act was adopted whole into the 1934 Communications Act, the basic provisions of the 1927 act were crucial to the structure of radio in the United States.

The debates surrounding the Radio Act reflected a divided Congress. Conservative legislators (largely representing the concerns of broadcasters) inveighed against the idea of a regulatory commission, preferring to vest licensing control in the Secretary of Commerce. They feared that the commission form would politicize broadcasting. As part of this fear, they advocated autonomy for broadcasters along the lines of that enjoyed by newspapers.[119] These legislators, supported by their broadcast allies, succeeded in defeating nearly every amendment that sought to strengthen the provisions of the act relating to issues of corporate control and monopoly.[120] On the other side, those who were anxious about the propaganda power of broadcasting advocated a strong commission, strong anti-monopoly provisions, and, significantly, a public utility-common carrier status for radio stations.

The original Senate bill reported out of committee imposed clear-cut common carrier obligations on broadcasters with regard to the discussion of public issues and the use of broadcast facilities during political campaigns. The common carrier provision read:

> If any licensee shall permit a broadcasting station to be used as aforesaid, or by a candidate or candidates for any public office, or for the discussion of any question affecting the public, he shall make no discrimination as to the use of such broadcasting station, and with respect to said matters the licensee shall be deemed a common carrier in interstate commerce.[121]

The bill's sponsor, Senator Clarence Dill, struck this language and substituted a far weaker amendment. The amendment dropped common carrier provisions with regard to public issues and reimposed it for advertising. A station could not discriminate in its advertising rates. Candidates for political office remained protected; if a radio station gave an candidate air time, the station was obliged to offer time to all other candidates. Senator Dill's decision to repeal the common carrier provision seemed to be based on two reasons. First, broadcasters themselves vehemently opposed the provision. Dill said, "The broadcasters were so opposed to having themselves designated as common carriers we thought it unwise at this stage of the development of the art to do it." Second, he seemed concerned about the vagueness of the phrase "any question affecting the public."[122]

The anti-monopolists in Congress succeeded in inserting general anti-monopoly provisions into the act. In Sections 13 and 15 the licensing authority was directed to refuse a license to (or revoke a license from) any entity found guilty in federal court of attempting to monopolize radio communications. Section 17 prohibited any entity with broadcast holdings from having any financial interest in wired communications.[123] This encoded into law the division of the industry hammered out between AT&T and RCA in 1926. These general anti-monopoly provisions kept AT&T from getting into broadcasting, but did little to confront monopoly in radio. Indeed, Congressman Edwin L. Davis and others charged that the strong anti-monopoly provisions had been sabotaged by the effective lobbying of the great radio interests. Because the authorized anti-monopoly stipulations were to become effective only after passage of the act, Davis charged that this provision was to circumvent a then pending complaint of the Federal Trade Commission charging that certain radio companies were violating the antitrust laws.[124]

Significantly, the act barely mentioned two of the more important developments in radio: advertising and chain broadcasting. Section 4(h) merely stated that the commission had "authority to make special regulations applicable to radio stations engaged in chain broadcasting." Section 19 obliged stations to announce if any particular program was sponsored and to identify the sponsor. The act's default on these two key issues guaranteed that the evolution of the broadcast industry would follow the dictates of the market.

## The Rights of Broadcasters: First Amendment Protection Modified by Public Trustee Status

The 1927 Radio Act accomplished several things. It asserted a public interest in broadcasting and stabilized the use of the airwaves. By licensing a private party to control the programming of a particular radio frequency for a three-year period, the act constructed a new legal category—the broadcaster—possessed of certain privileges and responsibilities. Though the holder of a broadcast license was accorded near-complete rights of editorial discretion, the law did not consider the broadcaster equivalent to a newspaper publisher. A broadcast was not treated as a newpaper. The broadcaster was accorded the civil freedoms rooted in the basic legal orientation to the market, but the degree of those civil freedoms was constrained by technological factors. Unlike the newspaper or book publisher, the broadcaster not only had to be licensed, but in theory had to operate in the public interest. This included, ultimately, the necessity of airing a broad mix of programming and of covering issues of community concern in a balanced fashion.

The standard reasons for the lesser degree of First Amendment protection accorded broadcasters have to do with the peculiar technological nature of the broadcast medium. The electromagnetic spectrum—the airwaves—was considered *public domain,* a natural resource held in common by the people and government of the United States. Moreover, the spectrum was a "scarce" resource. It could not accommodate all those who wished to exercise their speech rights in the broadcast medium. Indeed, for the medium to function, the government had to impose operating rules and limit the number of entities actually using the airwaves. Because of this technologically rooted limitation, and the necessity of having government "choose" who could use the airwaves, licensed broadcasters could not enjoy "absolute" free speech. In theory, they had to accommodate the views, tastes, and concerns of those *excluded* from the airwaves. Broadcast licensees were entrusted with a piece of public domain, and were to act as fiduciaries on behalf of the public, as proxies for those who did not have access to the airwaves.

But neither was the broadcaster a common carrier *per se*. Broadcast regulation essentially represented an uneasy compromise between formal First Amendment protections and a narrow form of common carrier obligations. The broadcaster had to provide equal opportunity of air time to candidates for political office and was generally obliged to present balanced programming. (This general obligation was later codified into the FCC's fairness doctrine.) In this sense public trustee status embodied a narrow form of the common carrier concept. At the same time, the act enjoined the regulatory agencies from any act of censorship.

Yet, this standard legitimation of broadcasting's modified First Amendment status in many ways is an explanation developed *post hoc* in judicial opinions, most notably in *National Broadcasting Company v. United States* (1943) and *Red Lion Broadcasting Co. v. Federal Communications Commission* (1969).[125] In the 1920s, radio, like motion pictures, was not really considered part of the press. In three associated cases in 1915, the Supreme Court upheld the right of states to engage in censorship of motion pictures. The Court's logic was that motion pictures were entertainment, and that entertainment is not really protected by the First Amendment. Similar logic applied to early radio broadcasting.[126] At the time of the Radio Act, the issue was that existing commercial broadcasters were unable to establish workable arrangements for market behavior. They appealed to the government to establish a policeman of the air.

For legislators, an important reason for broadcasting's limited, or modified, First Amendment status was fear of the power of the new means of communication if it were used for propagandistic purposes. During World War I, newspapers and posters had played a significant role in portraying the enemy as immoral and brutal.[127] The immediacy and drama of radio convinced many that the new medium possessed a frightening ability to mold the opinions and behaviors of the masses. Indeed, the guiding perspective on the effects of mass communication during the 1920s was the "hypodermic" theory, which saw media effects as powerful, uniform, and direct.[128] Though the hypodermic theory of media effects emerged as the accompaniment to middle-class fears over the influence of motion pictures, the theoretical perspective applied to radio as well. Radio, like motion pictures, was thought capable of "injecting" essentially passive and uncritical masses with information, perspective, emotion, and, potentially, untruths.[129] The fear of radio's power permeated the Congressional debates about the proper legal framework for the technology. But the fear had varied origins, rooted in opposite political philosophies. Those who feared government use of radio for propaganda advocated absolute First Amendment rights for private broadcasters. Those who feared that capital would use the medium to "colonize" ideas and behavior advocated strong governmental oversight.

Thus the Radio Act—hence broadcasting's legal status—constituted an interesting compromise. It granted free speech rights to occupiers of particular frequencies, but, because of its licensing function, government retained an ability to exercise indirect control over the potential "abuse" of the new medium. The Federal Radio Commission constituted "weak" government oversight. And to guard against potential partisanship and/or unfairness in the political process, Congress mandated that political candidates be treated equitably by broadcasters. But this compromise would be inherently unstable. On the one hand, there is a built-in tension between choosing licensees in the public interest and the prohibition against censorship. On the other hand, freedom for broadcasters does not necessarily translate into a free marketplace of ideas. These tensions would become major problems for the FRC and its successor agency, the FCC.

Because of the inherent connection between freedom of speech and the decisions of private entrepreneurs in the (broadcast) marketplace, the Radio Act sanctioned the commercial basis of broadcasting. And because the act only peripherally addressed the phenomenon of chain broadcasting, it left the structure of broadcasting to develop without benefit of government policy. This is why Erik Barnouw, *the* historian of American broadcasting, has asserted that the 1927 Radio Act was obsolete when passed.[130] Though the practice of networking began prior to the commercialization of broadcasting, and one reason for networks rested in the relative scarcity of talent, once broadcasting became advertiser-based, advertising and networking reinforced each other. A broadcaster increased his advertising revenue to the extent he could enlarge the station's potential circulation, accomplished by increasing the transmitting power, by linking the station with others in a chain or network, or by programming "name" entertainment.

Chain broadcasting allowed nationally popular figures to be heard on big-city and outlying stations otherwise unable to afford or attract such entertainment. Local station dependence on national programming networks occurred almost at the outset. As early as 1929 the less than 20 percent of all stations with network affiliation claimed 72 percent of the $27 million spent on broadcast advertising.[131] The error of the 1927 Radio Act was to assume that each local station would engage in its own programming. Instead, the local stations increasingly surrendered programming and prime air time to the emerging national broadcast entities. The FRC's stabilization of the airwaves served to untether the economic forces of commercialization, hitherto bound by technical and market conflicts.

The importance of the Federal Radio Act was that it established market and technical stability in broadcasting, an event which coincided with the emergence of permanent national networks and a system financed through direct, over-the-air advertising. RCA formed a broadcasting subsidiary, the National Broadcasting Company (NBC) in 1926. NBC operated two national networks, the "Red" and "Blue" networks, initially comprised of 23 and 18 stations respectively. The Columbia Broadcasting System (CBS) began broadcasting in earnest in 1929. The Mutual Broadcasting System (MBS) came into being in 1934.

The Federal Radio Commission's authority had to be renewed annually by Congress from 1927 to 1930. Its mandated task to stabilize the airwaves was thought to be relatively simple and temporally delimited. The annual reauthorization made it a relatively timid agency, sensitive to Congressional criticisms and appeals.[132] The original distribution of radio licenses turned out to be mainly a first-come, first-served process—a demand system. The FRC was to have no planned program for assigning stations to communities, nor would there be controls on the interconnection of stations into networks. Predictably, since stations were free to develop anywhere there was available spectrum space, they tended to concentrate in areas of high population density where advertising revenues would be greatest. As a result, many rural communities had no radio service at all.[133] In metropolitan areas radio interference was horrendous. The FRC's authority over stations was limited, politically speaking. Despite several early legislative and regulatory attempts to formulate some general policy for the geographical apportionment of facilities and service of AM radio broadcasting, regulatory redistribution was countered success-fully by claims of "squatter sovereignty" and heavy political pressure. A configu-ration of 80 to 100 major (and profitable) stations and 500 minor operations became an immutable reality within a year after the FRC began its supervisory role.[134]

## The Communications Act of 1934

The administrative deficiencies both of ICC oversight of wired communications and of FRC oversight of radio saw legislative proposals as early as 1929 to consolidate federal authority over communications in one agency. In 1932 President Roosevelt proposed the creation of a federal commission that would consolidate the existing dispersed authority over communications. This particular proposal was just part of a broad plan to reorganize the executive branch of government.[135] A Congressional study (the Splawn Report) also came to the conclusion that consolidation in commu-nications regulation was necessary. The Communications Act of 1934 was drafted and was passed quickly, with very little debate. The act essentially was seen as an administrative consolidation. Its House sponsor, Sam Rayburn, pointedly said the House bill did not change existing law.[136] What debate did ensue focused upon broadcasting.

The contrast between the legislative environment in 1926 and that of 1934 is noteworthy. In 1926 a chaotic radio industry turned to Congress to stabilize market and operating conditions. FRC regulation succeeded in stabilizing the airwaves and in so doing permitted the rise of strong commercial network organizations. By 1934 the broadcast lobby was quite powerful. There were two areas of controversy over the proposed Communications Act; in both areas the broadcast lobby emerged victorious. The original Senate bill (S.2910) called for the repeal of the Radio Act of 1927. The National Association of Broadcasters, the industry trade association, worked hard against this, because repeal of the essentially favorable 1927 act might reopen debate over the basic regulatory framework. The second controversial item was the Wagner-Hatfield amendment. This amendment called for the complete reassignment of all broadcast frequencies in order to reserve and allocate 25 percent of such frequencies to educational, religious, agricultural, labor, cooperative, and similar non-profit-making associations.[137] According to *Variety*, the NAB wrote to all senators asking them "not to destroy the whole structure of American broadcast-ing."[138] Such lobbying had effect. The amendment was defeated and the commer-cial nature of radio safeguarded.

To the extent that the Federal Radio Commission had direct effect on the 1934 Communications Act, it may have lent weight to the "inevitability" of maintaining the existing structure of radio broadcasting. In response to a 1932 Senate Resolution which asked the FRC to study the extent of commercial advertising in radio and to postulate alternatives to such, the FRC issued a report entitled "Commercial Radio Advertising." The report underscored the investment of many millions of dollars in equipment and tangible property, and portrayed the radio industry as a healthy one wherein commercial advertising played a positive role. The report argued that broadcasters were in a singularly favorable position to learn audience needs and desires. Advertising revenue assisted them in the effort to provide good broadcast service. A flat restriction placed upon the amount of advertising time would likely work inequitable results among the different classes of stations. Lastly, the report asserted that

> . . . limitations upon the use of time for commercial advertising, if too severe, would result in a loss of revenue to stations which, in all probability, would be reflected in a reduction in the quantity and quality of programs available to the public.[139]

Appended to the report were over two score statements of advertising executives who argued that it would neither be practicable nor satisfactory to restrict advertising on radio.

The Communications Act did not alter the structure of American communications, though it did introduce a few provisions not contained in previous legislation. It proclaimed a fundamental goal of making available "a rapid, efficient, Nationwide, and world-wide wire and radio communication service with adequate facilities at reasonable charges."[140] While it explicitly elucidated this and other general legislative goals, such as a mandate to study new uses for radio, the act clearly left specific policies and implementation up to the new seven-person commission.[141] The act clarified the commission's powers vis-à-vis broadcasters and common carriers, and spelled out the obligations of broadcasters and common carriers. Broadcasters were to allowed to use the public airwaves so long as they used them in the public interest. Common carriers were charged with a duty to furnish nondiscriminatory service, to interconnect, to file rates, and to obtain certificates of public convenience.

In other words, the Communications Act essentially reproduced the existing law of wire and wireless communications. In so doing, the act built upon the pre-existing institutional structures of each industry, and froze into law the industrial boundaries which had been cast by the 1913 Kingsbury Commitment and the 1926 agreement between RCA and AT&T. The structure of the common carrier system was determined first of all by the practical ability of Western Union and AT&T to establish dominance over their respective industries. Following the *fact* of effective monopolization was the public policy assumption that telephone and telegraph service each constituted *natural* monopolies (though there was some controversy about whether *all* forms of competition in wire communications were wasteful[142]). Competition between monopolized services would be maintained by regulation and the antitrust laws. The regulation of communications common carriage was required to oversee and protect the monopoly carriers. This would be accomplished through the control over entry and oversight of rates. An overwhelmingly dominant AT&T supervised an integrated national telephone system comprised of that company and a hundred or so small, independent telephone companies.

The place of broadcasting in the overall telecommunications system was defined by the division of industry consequent to the 1926 agreement between AT&T and RCA. Broadcasters would control the content of communication over the airwaves, and would require licenses to gain access to the means of communication (a frequency). Regulation was needed to bring technical order to the industry.

The structure of broadcasting itself ultimately was determined by the radio manufacturing institutions (with crucial initial assistance from the Navy), both directly, through the sale of sets, and indirectly, through the supply of advertising money. Almost from the beginning the broadcasting *public* was effectively the competitive broadcasting *market*. Individual radio stations sold time to advertisers in order to finance programming. Inasmuch as early regulation dealt with neither commercialization nor networking, the broadcast industry quickly became dominated by two national commercial network organizations. The two national networks supplied programming to affiliate stations, connected by AT&T lines. The FCC controlled entry into broadcasting by means of a licensing system. Though they did not possess "absolute" free speech rights, for all intents and purposes broadcasters had near-complete discretion over programming. The FCC instituted the classic kind or market, or commerce-based, regulatory controls into which were inserted, with great difficulty and controversy, notions of a nonmarket public interest.[143] The regulation of broadcasting thus exhibited the paradox of liberal state intervention. Regulation facilitated the construction of an electronic public sphere, but could not guarantee that a real marketplace of ideas would actually prevail.

In terms of the overall regulation of telecommunications, however, the commerce-based principle of separating telecommunications media by technology did indirectly serve democratic-based First Amendment interests. The traditional law of communications came to consist of three main frameworks which were embedded in distinct and historically defined technologies: print, wired electrical communications, and broadcast communications. Each "system" of communication, ultimately defined according to its means of delivery, was governed by logic deemed appropriate to its fundamental technological characteristics and consonant with prior legal principles.

By the mid-1920s, the three basic technological distinctions among communications services had become clear. Moreover, the corporations which engaged in the provision of communication services, for the most part, provided just one service. AT&T provided telephone-based common carriage, the New York Times published a newspaper, RCA broadcast radio programs over the air. Some of this separation was simply the result of early patterns of the economic/industrial development of each technology. Some was the outcome of agreements reached between the major industrial players to divide up the services. Such industrial "turf" agreements underlay, for instance, the early separation between news dissemination and the transmission of that news. That separation paradoxically was fashioned by the mutually self-serving agreement between Associated Press and Western Union to create an associative, double-barreled monopoly in the 1860s. Turf agreements also underlay the division between telephone and telegraph, established by the understanding worked out between AT&T and Western Union in 1879. The division constructed between telephone and broadcasting was the result of the 1926 settlement between feuding rivals, AT&T and RCA.

Subsequent antitrust and regulatory law recapitulated these previously determined industrial boundaries. The imposition of common carrier status on telegraphy in 1893, among many other things, effectively reiterated the "messenger-only" function of telegraphy and established the principle of the separation between content and conduit. The 1913 "Kingsbury Commitment" between AT&T and the Wilson Administration resurrected the line between telephony and telegraphy. That action compelled AT&T to divest itself of Western Union and forgo any interests in telegraphy. This separation of wire-delivered print from wire-delivered voice proceeded in spite of the fact that, technically, AT&T copper wires could carry both services easily. In a recognition of the 1926 intercorporate agreement between RCA and AT&T, the Communications Act barred common carriers from exercising any control or from having an interest in the content transmitted over their lines. The act stipulated that a broadcaster could not also be considered a common carrier as well. A general governmental policy arose to keep telecommunications services *separated,* and telecommunications corporations in a single field of operation. Governmental policy sought to maintain the one-to-one relationship that was thought to exist between a medium and its use.[144]

# CHAPTER

## 5

### • • •

# "One Policy, One System, and Universal Service"

This chapter examines the actions and policies of the Federal Communications Commission in the area of common carriers. Because that field is so thoroughly dominated by the American Telephone and Telegraph Company, the chapter for the most part explores the interrelation between the history of the AT&T monopoly and government regulation of it. We discover a long period of normalcy in regulation, from the inception of the FCC stretching to the early 1970s. Regulatory normalcy was characterized by the acceptance of a policy of natural monopoly. The practical consequence was the regulatory protection of AT&T.

The Federal Communications Commission's mandate was vague and general, sometimes internally contradictory. Its broadest charge was to secure a rapid, efficient, nationwide wire and radio communications service at reasonable rates. The Commission was to oversee the operation of corporations engaged in the business of communications carriage, ensure these carriers provided good service at reasonable rates, and see to it that they were financially and operationally sound. In addition, the FCC had to apportion the electromagnetic spectrum among various services and applicants, ensuring the most efficient and equitable use of the public natural resource. This included choosing the most appropriate license applicants for the use of the broadcast portion of the spectrum.

Though the Commission was thought to possess wide discretion, the actual extent of its powers was untested. Charged with the goal of securing efficient nationwide communication service, the Commission faced already existing economic institutions and already functioning technical arrangements. Without a clear mandate to do otherwise, the FCC provided for efficient nationwide communication service by stabilizing and (to some extent) reforming the existing institutional arrangements in broadcasting and common carrier communications. To the extent that basic regulatory formulae, procedures, and policies were consistent over the years, the FCC constructed a system of regulation that favored pre-existing institutions and services. In this sense FCC actions were largely "conservative." But contrary to capture theory, the agency was not so much captured by industry lobbyists as by institutional arrangements which represented the distillation of initial decisions and inherited structures.

The FCC accepted the institutional structures of the industries it was charged with overseeing, and with slight changes adopted them as the foundation of its *regulatory* structure. Regulation entailed the insertion of genuine, though limited, public interest principles into arrangements beneficial to the established interests of the telecommunications industries.

In telegraphy and telephony, regulatory policy meant acceptance of monopoly. Western Union ultimately was encouraged to assert monopoly control over record (that is, signals culminating in a written message) telecommunications. Likewise, AT&T was permitted to exercise monopoly control over long-distance voice telecommunications and to operate local monopoly telephone operating companies. In return for not interfering with the industries' monopoly status, the FCC could enforce common carrier legal obligations. It could command mandatory interconnection of carriers and charge carriers with a duty to serve all who requested service. The agency could manipulate rates to expand service. And by guaranteeing a fair rate of return, the agency could stabilize the costs of doing business. Stabilization would safeguard and promote a crucial infrastructure.

Having inherited a commercial broadcast system, the FCC adopted rules to make sure that system worked. The Commission policed the airwaves and constructed a licensing system. Commercial broadcasters were licensed to monopolize the programming of a designated radio frequency for a renewable three-year period with the vague proviso that they broadcast in the "public interest, convenience, or necessity." Nonetheless, because the spectrum was deemed a scarce public resource, broadcasters were not granted property rights in the electromagnetic spectrum.

Such arrangements did facilitate the expansion of communication services as mandated by Section 1 of the Communications Act. The FCC therefore considered its basic regulatory policies manifest of the public interest. After all, such policies took advantage of the creative, enterprising dynamic of capitalism while ostensibly subjecting that dynamic to some public controls. In the sphere of wired communications, regulation avoided the perceived political evils and economic inefficiencies characteristic of state-run enterprises, while (in theory) serving the social interest of fairness. In broadcast, regulation vitiated against the political evil of government propaganda. At the same time, regulation harnessed the dynamism of private enterprise under the aegis of a system of government oversight.

Once established, the fundamental regulatory structures conditioned all subsequent industry controversies and even technical developments. Given the difficulties of accommodating conflicting industry demands and operating within a system

of institutional constraints and limited resources, once basic policies were established they were difficult to change. Regulatory policies represented fundamental
industry compromises. Even if sometimes disputed by specific parties, the basic
policies were rational for the industry as a whole because the ground rules they
established provided relative certainty to business decisions. At the same time, they
were seen as accomplishing public interest goals. Consequently, regulatory and
industrial structures in telecommunications together constituted an edifice able to
withstand challenges for forty years.

The solidity of basic regulatory structures paradoxically was buttressed by pressures challenging the organizational integrity of the Commission. Demands to
change the basic policies could re-open basic industry conflicts, and even threaten
the continued provision of communications service to the public. Not only would
this make business decisions less certain, but it would make regulatory decisions
less certain. If there were a bottom line to communications regulation, it would be
that the FCC acted to safeguard the continuous provision of service to the public.
The regulation of telecommunications was essentially protective because, despite
problems, the system *worked*. The FCC's reluctance to challenge the industry was
understandable. After all, AT&T was one of the world's largest, most successful
enterprises. It provided a technically sophisticated service rather well. Who was the
FCC—an agency composed of lawyers, former broadcasters, and a few techni-
cians—to barge in and perhaps muck up the nationwide telephone service?

This bottom line had conservative outcomes. The intensely close interrelationship between the basic goals of telecommunications regulation and the existence of the Bell monopoly meant that the FCC was loath to disrupt the integrated
structure of the Bell monopoly or to challenge AT&T rate determinations. The FCC
never had the ability or the means to effectively monitor AT&T's rates and charges.
Rather than regulate in a manner which could threaten the ongoing, reliable functioning of telephone service, the FCC consistently deferred to AT&T's judgment.

Nonetheless, there were serious antitrust problems raised by the Bell System's
vertical monopoly. AT&T not only offered the only long-distance service and
controlled local telephone service in most major metropolises, but the firm provided
for all its equipment needs through its own equipment manufacturer, Western
Electric. This vertical monopoly structure allegedly enabled AT&T to shift costs
internally and hence boost its rate base artificially. Consequently, the question was
raised whether AT&T should remain a vertically integrated corporation, and
whether regulation was capable of guaranteeing the public interest. The political
challenges to the Bell System during this period, with one early exception, were
undertaken by the Justice Department—not by the FCC. Moreover, there is good
evidence that the FCC, with help from the Defense Department and Atomic Energy
Commission, acted as AT&T's advocate when the corporation ran afoul of the
antitrust laws. These agencies helped prevent a break-up of the Bell System in
1956.

In broadcasting, the powerful broadcast lobby, combined with the threat of
judicial review, and the complexities posed by the First Amendment, left the Commission leery of either making large structural changes or setting hard and fast
criteria that would clearly define programming "in the public interest." Confronted

with pressures from several fronts, and faced with rapid changes in both technology and demands for entry, the FCC clung to the clear, if increasingly outmoded regulatory arrangements upon which it could continue to exercise a modicum of rational control.[1]

From 1934 to the 1970s, the regulation of both common carriers and broadcasting was characterized by a central dilemma: did the safeguarding of communication service to the public require the protection of companies that provided service? Generally speaking, during this period the answer was affirmative. The regulatory dilemma in common carriage was how to maintain the universal, technically proficient, and relatively cheap service provided by a monopoly, while insuring that the company would continue to innovate and could not abuse its monopoly power. That the FCC favored the structure of monopoly is shown by its early championing of the consolidation of telegraphy under the aegis of Western Union. That the FCC had no good solution to the problem of monopoly power is evident in its deferential treatment of AT&T. Notwithstanding evidence of monopoly-generated abuses and service shortfalls, the FCC chose to ignore the problem side of the AT&T monopoly.

The FCC protected AT&T in two important ways. One was to protect AT&T from the danger of competitive entry. This involved the regulatory policy toward new telecommunications services and new technologies. Until the late 1950s, the Commission required that all new telecommunications services and technologies be placed under common carrier regulations. This effectively meant that new services and technologies would be under AT&T's control. The second means of protection rested in the informal method of rate determination known as "continuing surveillance." This describes the normal FCC practice of watching AT&T earnings and informally suggesting rate adjustments, rather than convening formal evidentiary hearings on rates. The upshot of such informal procedure was that AT&T was able to control the process, largely because it alone possessed the salient information.

The Commission chose to fight monopoly power by erecting operating barriers between telecommunications services. Voice common carriers could not also be record carriers. Western Union, as the domestic record monopoly carrier, could have no interest in international telegraphy. Common carriers could not also be broadcasters, and vice-versa. This barrier had First Amendment as well as antitrust ramifications, for it ensured that the entity which transmitted the message could not affect the content of the message. With technological developments, new institutional barriers were erected, such as those between voice and data and between telecommunications and computing.

In broadcasting the regulatory dilemma had two aspects. First, the Commission never could reconcile its policy of localism (that each station should control its own programming) with the actual networking structure of the industry. To truly uphold localism would have inevitably undermined how the industry actually functioned. The solution to this basic contradiction was to preach the desirability of localism while constructing no supports for the policy in regulatory practice. The Commission balked at formulating explicit, substantive public interest criteria for programming, facing at the outset loud broadcaster outcry, the economic reality of networking and, later, the inherent conflict with First Amendment guarantees. Second, and in seeming contradiction, adherence to a weak localism standard legitimated FCC decisions that effectively undermined broadcast technologies and services potentially competitive to standard broadcasting. The outcome of the "reluctant" regulation of broadcasting was to secure the position of the entrenched networks and to sabotage new uses of the broadcast medium.

## *"Natural Monopoly," Competition, and the Public Interest: The Merger of Postal Telegraph and Western Union*

The Communications Act of 1934 essentially empowered a modern agency to carry out the traditional provisions of the common law of public callings. The FCC controlled entry into and exit from the telecommunications industry, required and set just and reasonable rates, ensured nondiscriminatory access, and mandated interconnection between carriers. These empowerments permitted the state to oversee and regularize an important infrastructure for the movement of commerce. The Commission interpreted its regulatory responsibilities in common carriage as a mandate to rationalize the industry. More than anything else, this meant a regulatory policy that viewed separate, monopolized services as best implementing the public interest in communications carriage.

Early regulatory actions toward telegraphy reveal Commission policy. While the telephone system presented the FCC with a *fait accompli* monopoly, a similar situation did not exist in telegraphy. Postal Telegraph Company, which had emerged in the 1890s as a competitor to Western Union, was by the 1930s in severe financial trouble. In the late 1930s the firm went into receivership. Western Union itself began to show substantial losses around this time. Meanwhile, the FCC determined that the effective outcome of competition between Postal Telegraph and Western Union had been to prevent the development of telegraphy as a truly national service. As early as 1935 the FCC asked Congress to amend the Communications Act so as to give the Commission the power to authorize the consolidation of telegraph companies.[2] The agency argued that competition in domestic telegraphy developed in those cities where most of the business originated and where it was profitable. Competition did not result in the expansion of telegraph service to communities that lacked it. Competition created inefficient duplication of plant and equipment, useless paralleling of facilities, and wasteful expenditures of resources and manpower.

When communications was viewed as a whole, reasoned the FCC, telegraphy was a service in competition with air mail and long-distance telephony. The telegraph industry did not gain by internal competition. "Telegraph companies," the FCC argued, "are engaged in fruitless strife with each other, while other means of communication are taking away what has heretofore been telegraph business."[3] The Commission argued for the absorption of Postal Telegraph by Western Union, and the creation of a true telegraph monopoly. This would be done by legally compelling the consolidated company to extend service and to prevent abandonments of service. Drawing from the example of AT&T, the FCC argued that greater technical improvements should follow industrial consolidation. And if, following merger, management did not pursue technical innovation, the Commission could license new radiotelegraph companies and new telegraph lines.

The proposal sat dormant for several years, but was taken up and passed by Congress in 1943. In the intervening years, $6 million was pumped into Postal Telegraph through New Deal Reconstruction Finance Corporation loans, but Postal Telegraph still languished. In the early 1940s, the military lent its weight to the forces asking for consolidation. In a letter to the Senate Committee on Interstate Commerce, the Defense Communications Board wrote:

> There is a real prospect that unless merger is promptly accomplished, the company [Postal Telegraph] will be forced to take action which will produce substantial disloca-tion in the telegraph facilities available to the country and its military establishments.[4]

This argument underscored the defense establishment's long support of monopoly in telecommunications networks. Similar arguments would be advanced on behalf of the AT&T monopoly.

In the 1942 Senate hearings, the executive branch, via Secretary of Commerce Jesse Jones, also lent support to consolidation. Jones argued that "the telegraph business is as much a natural monopoly as is the telephone business or, you might say, the Post Office."[5] Congress amended the Communications Act (adding section 222) in 1943. In the proceeding which authorized the merger, the FCC embraced this notion of telegraphy as a "natural monopoly":

> . . . telegraph service appears to fall within the field of "natural monopolies," such as the telephone, power and gas distribution utilities, where it has usually been found by experience that one company adequately regulated can be expected to render a superior service at lower cost than that provided by competing companies.[6]

The alternative to merger, according to the Commission, could not be tolerated if the interests of the public were to be protected. Without government support, Postal would cease functioning, resulting in junking a plant of 31,345 pole line miles and 396,650 wire miles, the closing of 6,799 offices serving all regions of the country, and in depriving the more than 9,000 Postal Telegraph workers of em-ployment. In conclusion, the FCC argued,

> This alternative would result in an indefensible loss of manpower essential to a critical industry and would produce a disastrous disruption of telegraph service which might disorganize the effective functioning of the Nation's war economy.[7]

This is a classic statement of the traditional principles of regulatory policy in common carrier communications. In order to create a nationwide, efficient, and rational telegraph service for commerce and the national defense, the government would encourage a monopoly, so long as regulatory oversight compelled the exten-sion of service, prevented the abandonment of service, guaranteed fair rates, and guaranteed the consolidated company a fair rate of return. In the effort to safeguard an industry in decline, the FCC approved substantial rate increases and reductions in hours of service throughout the 1950s. The public interest was maintained by the creation of a monopoly *internal* to a communications service, but with competition between *separated* services. Indeed, the Congressional mandate in the passage of the Communications Act amendments not only barred Western Union from any interest in international telegraphy, but also called for the company "to consolidate or merge with all or any part of the domestic telegraph operations or any carrier which is not primarily a telegraph carrier."[8] This was intended to impel the sale of AT&T's switched teletype service (TWX)—a record service which Bell had begun in 1931—to Western Union.[9]

## AT&T, the Public Interest, and FCC Accommodation

The policy calling for a monopoly in domestic telegraphy applied in a similar, if more complicated fashion, to the telephone industry. One of the complicating factors was the historical division between intrastate and interstate jurisdictions. The FCC (formally restricted to the regulation of *interstate* wire and radio communications only) and state regulatory agencies fashioned a cooperative system of telephone oversight. In fact, the cooperative relations between the FCC and the association of state regulatory commissioners (National Association of Railroad [later Regulatory] and Utility Commissioners which went by its acronym, NARUC) were in marked contrast to the historically contentious relations between the Interstate Commerce Commission and NARUC.

Regulation granted local telephone monopoly franchises and secured the stabilization of business risk. State regulatory commissions erected barriers to competitive entry into local exchange service. Though no explicit FCC rule granted AT&T a monopoly in long distance, the Commission regulated in a manner which secured *de facto* monopoly. The stabilization of business risk was accomplished through a guaranteed fair rate of return and a policy of long-term capitalization. In return, regulation was able to "extract" from telephone companies the public interest obligation of service to all—"universal service." Universal service meant that telephone service must be made available to and be generally affordable by everyone. The policy of long amortization of plant and equipment was inherent in the principle of universal service. Because telephony was characterized by large capital investment in a comparatively simple technology, a long amortization schedule would have the effect of spreading service as broadly as possible and of keeping operating costs down. Universal service served the socio-political goal of increasing the utility of the network, since the utility of the network increased exponentially the more subscribers were hooked in.

This regulatory scheme seemed to presuppose the monopoly provision of services, for universal service could be accomplished best through a complex amalgam of value-of-service pricing and general rate averaging. Value-of-service pricing theoretically takes advantage of different demand curves in order to expand the telephone network. Users willing to pay more for a given service are charged more, even though it may actually cost less to service them than to service those least willing to pay. This meant generally that urban residents paid more than rural subscribers for telephone services, and businesses paid more than residential subscribers. Rate averaging is the policy of charging equally for interstate calls of the same distance, regardless of whether there were different actual costs due to different routing.[10] Rate averaging presumably fulfilled the mandated prohibition against discrimination.

The FCC and the state public utilities commissions developed a system of ratemaking. "Separations" was the name of the procedures by which regulators divided assets and costs between the interstate and intrastate jurisdictions. "Settlements" was the term for similar averaging procedures worked out between AT&T and independent telephone systems. "Separations and settlements" constituted procedures by which the AT&T parent company paid local telephone operating companies for handling the local-exchange ends of long-distance traffic.

The complicated ratemaking procedures were necessary for technical and jurisdictional reasons. Technically, every long-distance call must begin and end in a local exchange. A call originating, say, from a residence in Minneapolis to a business in San Diego first goes to the local exchange central switching center in Minneapolis. The signal is then switched onto AT&T long-distance lines where it is routed to the San Diego local exchange central switching center. Finally, the signal is delivered to the San Diego business. Local exchange facilities thus are used both to connect callers within the exchange and to begin and end long distance calls. These different services share equipment and plant. Jurisdictionally, local telephone exchanges are regulated both by state public utilities commissions and by the FCC. Long-distance traffic may be intrastate (such as telephone traffic between Los Angeles and San Francisco) and hence under public utilities commission authority, or interstate (traffic between Boston and Hartford), under the jurisdiction of the FCC.

Separations and settlements policies would have the effect of bringing unified control to the national network, even though that network was owned by many different entities. AT&T monitored the construction programs of the independent telephone companies, preventing waste and duplication. Beginning in the 1950s, separations procedures theoretically were utilized to secure an internal cross-subsidy which shifted costs indirectly to business users and directly to long-distance in order to support local (and especially rural) telephone service.

The actual development of this system of regulatory oversight was somewhat rocky. In the 1930 case of *Smith v. Illinois Bell Telephone Company*, the Supreme Court endorsed what was known as the "station-to-station" theory of separations. Station-to-station meant that long-distance (AT&T) must pay some percentage of the joint costs shared between it and the local exchange. Prior to this, long-distance did not have to pay local exchanges for joint costs—a policy dear to AT&T. Though the *Smith* decision called for station to-station separations procedures, the case actually concerned the legal issue of confiscation, and did not fully resolve the separations controversy. A 1934 case, *Lindheimer v. Illinois Bell Telephone Company*, in fact undermined the rate-making implications of *Smith*.[11] State public utilities commissions employed widely different rate-making theories and procedures, and AT&T fought against station-to-station separations in the courts until 1943.

The controversy over separations procedures was the dominant regulatory issue in the late 1930s and early 1940s.[12] Part of the problem here was the old problem of jurisdiction: the states had no authority over interstate rate making, even though telephony constituted an integrated system. Moreover, it was becoming increasingly clear that the economics of the industry were changing. Economies of scale and the growth of demand meant that, already in the late 1930s and early 1940s, long-distance service (and revenues) began to outpace the local operating exchanges. The newly created FCC did possess jurisdiction over interstate telephony, of course, but had no policy guide. The Communications Act did not address the issue of rate making beyond the stipulation that communication services be "reasonable."

After the FCC negotiated a series of interstate rate reductions with AT&T between 1935 and 1937, it found itself in the midst of the rate-making quandary.[13] The FCC dealt with the separations issues by proclaiming in 1939 the principle of nationwide rate averaging (the policy of charging equally for interstate calls of the same distance, regardless of the actual costs of routing). Rate averaging could serve two important functions. First, such a practice fulfilled the Commission's mandated responsibility to prevent rate discrimination. Second, it greatly simplified the separations problem because it required only the determination of *aggregate* interstate costs.[14] A determination of actual, individual interstate costs was far beyond the FCC's competence.

The separations issue illustrates the kind of regulatory control the FCC exercised over telephony. The FCC preferred to deal with AT&T rates by *negotiation* rather than by holding formal hearings on separations procedures and valuation of the company's property. Regulation by negotiation was called, euphemistically, "continuing surveillance." As Bernard Strassburg, chief of the FCC Common Carrier Bureau from 1964 to 1973, explained the process, the FCC would watch AT&T reported earnings and then ask for a rate adjustment. There were no clearly defined standards or procedures upon which to assess the information given.[15] This method of regulation did provide certain benefits. As distinct from the formal hearing, negotiation had the effect of keeping pace with the quickly changing economic dynamics of the telephone industry. But regulation by negotiation also had the effect of never determining actual policy. By the 1940s it became clear that a policy had to be set. In 1942 the FCC convened a formal rule-making proceeding on separations. In 1943 the FCC and AT&T negotiated a $50 million reduction in interstate toll rates, and AT&T agreed both to establish interstate rates according the station-to-station principle and to increase the percentage of toll revenues going to the local exchanges.[16] Though the FCC finally did establish a policy on separations, the process of regulation by negotiation proceeded as before.

Other problems were intrinsic to separations negotiations. Though separations and settlements were reputed to be effected on a cost basis (on the basis of actual costs associated with the provision of any given telephone service), this is open to question. It is argued that the association of services, costs, and charges was and is so complex that any attempt to do so is fundamentally arbitrary.[17] Administratively, cost-averaging is infinitely simpler than determining the fairest way to allocate the *joint costs* between urban local, rural local, and intrastate and interstate long-distance services. These services share much of the same equipment and plant, but in proportions which are exceedingly difficult to determine. Some costs are calculable on the basis of the type and amount of telephone traffic. However, with respect to large portions of shared equipment, costs simply are not calculable. This portion of the equipment is referred to as "non-traffic-sensitive" costs, that is, those costs which do not vary with the extent to which the facilities are used. The basic cost of installing and maintaining a local exchange remains the same whether the customer uses the exchange to make one call or hundreds, or whether those calls are local or long-distance. Thus the rate-setting process historically has been a process half acknowledged as one of *political* accommodation between telephone providers, various regulatory bodies, and (more recently) consumers. Why the process is only *half* acknowledged as political is because all the players must rely on the figures, statistics, and analyses provided by the Bell System before they deal.

Notwithstanding separations, the subsidy of local telephone rates by long-distance rates did not amount to much until the 1950s and 1960s, at which time developments in microwave transmission and direct distance dialing resulted in cheaper long-distance costs. And notwithstanding the intent of the cost-averaging and separations policies, service to all cannot be attributed wholly to the implementation of these procedures. At least as important in the expansion of telephone service, particularly to rural areas, was the post-World War II economic boom and the explicit government subsidies provided through the Rural Electrification Administration and the Rural Telephone Bank.[18] Indeed, most of the unattractive rural telephone markets were served by non-Bell independents. But given the general regulatory arrangement, it is not difficult to see that the protection of the public interest in telephony for the most part became equated with the successful operation of the Bell System.

## The Question of the "Subsidy"

The question of the long-distance subsidy of local rates is at the heart of controversies over telephone regulation. In the aftermath of the FCC's 1943 policy on separations, it is a commonplace that local telephone rates are subsidized by long-distance. According to an AT&T source, in the early 1980s local service (intrastate) accounted for 92 percent of usage of the common facilities. Long-distance (interstate) accounted for 8 percent. Yet, under 1982 FCC rules the share of joint costs allocated to interstate long distance was over 26 percent.[19] This ostensibly amounted to a yearly subsidy of approximately $7 billion to local operating companies. But there has never been a comprehensive study which establishes the amount of that cross-subsidy. For the very reasons that the joint uses and costs were already difficult to calculate during the 1930s, some AT&T critics have questioned the figures provided on the cross-subsidy.

Several arguments undermine, or at least complicate, the subsidy claim. One involves the pricing of "private line" services. A private line consists basically of an open line between two fixed points, and is used primarily by corporations to interconnect distant offices, by news wire services to newspapers, or by television networks to transmit signals to distant affiliate stations. "Foreign exchange" (FX) is one form of specialized private line service, which consists of a private line connected to the local exchange at one end. The FCC historically did not require users of private line services to contribute, as ordinary long-distance callers do, to local plant costs allocated to the interstate jurisdiction.[20] Now, it is efficient to purchase AT&T private line and foreign exchange facilities only if one uses the facilities a great deal. Consequently, the purchasers of these special facilities historically have been large corporations. Thus the largest users of the telephone system were exempted from contributing toward the support of the local telephone plant. To the extent that private line users utilize local telephone exchanges, it is these users and these services which have benefited from a subsidy.

Another argument which calls into question the existence and amount of the traditionally alleged subsidy harkens back to the first antitrust investigation of AT&T. The Bell Operating Companies bought equipment and services from AT&T, at prices which may have been inflated. At the very least, it seems likely that the BOCs purchased more equipment and services than was cost-effective. This follows the Averch-Johnson-Wellisz hypothesis that the firm under rate-of-return regulatory constraint will tend to invest more capital than necessary as a means of increasing its rate base.[21] The overbuilding or "goldplating" of local telephone plant would constitute a capital flow back to AT&T through equipment purchases as well as through the boosting of the overall rate base.

These claims, of course, are not settled issues. But even if the BOCs' capital investments cannot be characterized as overbuilding, such investments usually were legitimized as being necessary to meet "peak demand." Yet peak demand generally meant the upgrading of local plant to accommodate the local exchange needs of long-distance and business users during the business day. The added costs of such investment would be charged to the local operating company, though the principal beneficiaries were long-distance and business users. Lastly, other subsidies flow to AT&T from the local operating companies. The "license contract fee," it will be remembered, was a percentage of local telephone operating company revenues paid to the AT&T central organization in exchange for services provided to the BOCs. The cost of these services was arbitrarily determined by AT&T, and long had been the subject of regulatory disputes.

"Subsidy," then, must be seen as part of the politics of representation. Another way of looking at the subsidy is that without the local connections, there could be no long distance. The above arguments highlight the fact that it is not the numbers and statistics *per se* which are subject to dispute in matters of telephone costs and prices, but rather the fundamental assumptions upon which the numbers are based. Again, I do not claim that the traditionally construed "subsidy" does not exist. Rather, given the absence of definitive studies on the subject, the entire area is highly problematic. Any simple assertion of the subsidy of local service by long distance must be treated skeptically, because of the complexity of *other* subsidy arrangements. Further research indicates that some states in effect subsidized others; urban users subsidized those in affluent suburbs as well as the residents of poor rural areas. In light of the above arguments, the "subsidy" claim (and matters of telephone costs generally) might be seen as a sort of shell game that AT&T has played with regulators.

The underlying reason why the subsidy issues were only a matter of conjecture and not easily settled was that AT&T priced its various services as a "bundle," that is, without direct reference to their individual costs. A useful management tool (it enabled the telephone company to stimulate demand for a new service by underpricing it, or to respond to political exigencies on residential rates), bundling preserved AT&T's monopoly on information. The FCC's and state public utilities commissions' historic lack of information easily pushed them into a conservative regulatory posture which relied upon AT&T's representation of the public interest in telephony. This dynamic became clear even as the Commission discovered, in its investigation of the telephone industry during the late 1930s, that AT&T's representation of the public interest was problematic.

## The Telephone Investigation

Some of the basic issues that underlie the questionable nature of the "subsidy" first surfaced in a 1935 FCC investigation of AT&T. With support from NARUC, Congress specially allocated $750,000 in 1935 to fund such an investigation. Prior to this study, there was little public information on interstate telephone operations. Known colloquially as the "Walker Report," after the chief investigator, FCC Commissioner Paul A. Walker, the investigation looked into the capital structure of the Bell System, inter-company contracts, accounting and depreciation procedures, and telephone costs and prices.

Although the Walker Report found no scandal in telephony to compare with that in electric utility holding companies, it claimed, among other things, that AT&T's equipment subsidiary, the Western Electric Company, charged unreasonably high prices for equipment to AT&T and the Bell Operating Companies. Because Western Electric was the sole equipment supplier to the Bell System, these pricing practices created an internal subsidy which functioned to inflate the rate base from which telephone rates were derived. Remember, the Bell System was a vertical monopoly, consisting of 23 Bell Operating Companies (which provided local telephone exchange service), Long Lines (the long-distance company), and Western Electric (the sole equipment supplier to the System). The Walker Report charged that Western Electric overcharges cost telephone subscribers approximately $51 million per year.

Part of the explanation of Western Electric's pricing had to do with an inadequate cost accounting system, but most of the problem rested in the fact that telephone equipment simply was not a natural monopoly. Without competition or *direct* regulation (the FCC could regulate Western Electric only indirectly and inadequately, by the adjustment of AT&T's overall rate of return), Western Electric's prices could be entirely arbitrary. Unable to obtain the appropriate data from AT&T (notwithstanding mountains of documents provided by the company), the investigators studied Western's internal methods of cost determination and also attempted to compare Western's costs with those of the small number of independent telephone equipment manufacturers. The report concluded that "the evidence indicates that Western's prices bear no reasonable relation to the indicated cost of manufacture."[22] Moreover, the report continued, "the prices paid by associated companies for Western products apparently do not have any logical relation to costs as determined by Western."[23] In other words, the very vertical monopoly which permitted technical integrity and universal service in telephony was also responsible for AT&T's ability to inflate its rate base by means of exhorbitant internal equipment costs. The Walker Report estimated that Western could cut prices 37 percent and still earn an adequate 6 percent return on its capital.[24]

The Walker Report also charged that AT&T's depreciation accounting practices from their inception in 1913 had been variable and erratic, the result of which was to maintain a higher rate base. High depreciation allowances, amounting to approximately 28 percent of Bell physical properties, were added to operating expenses (and hence to rates), but only "observable" depreciation, ranging from 5 to 10 percent, was deducted in determining the rate base. AT&T thus received a return on property for which the consumer had already paid—a large sum, inasmuch as depreciation charges amount to almost one-fifth of operating expenses.[25] Walker argued in favor of a statutory definition for the basis upon which to value the property of interstate telephone companies.[26]

Finally, the report found that the license fee paid by the associated companies to AT&T was arbitrary because the costs of services rendered by the parent company were undocumented and unknown. The Walker Report's conclusions offered three ways to secure the public interest in telephony: effective competition, government ownership, or effective regulation. It acknowledged that competition was impossible as a practical matter, and was not desirable because the nation required a single, national, unified wire communications system. The option of government ownership, though not ruled out, was not studied because it seemed more desirable to accomplish the necessary objectives under regulation. The report did assert, however, that in the event of the failure of regulation, "government ownership would be almost the only means remaining for attainment of telephone service at low cost."[27]

The Walker Report thus recommended that the FCC be given direct authority to review and approve or disapprove the central policies of the Bell System (including depreciation calculations, plant expenditures, and intercompany contracts) *before*, rather than after such policies were implemented. To protect Bell System financial resources against the risk inherent in participation in competitive enterprises, the report recommended that Bell be enjoined from engaging in activities outside the communications field. With regard to the telephone equipment field, the report indicated two options. One was to mandate competition, by requiring the local operating companies to purchase equipment through competitive bidding between Western and other manufacturers. The other option was the regulation of Western Electric as a public utility, which would entail, among other things, direct determination of Western's prices.[28]

AT&T orchestrated an extensive campaign to undermine the report's recommendations. In the fall of 1938 AT&T issued a "Brief on the Proposed Report" which attempted to refute the Walker Report point by point, and which criticized the *ex parte* nature of many of the proceedings held under the investigation.[29] The campaign was successful in moderating the FCC's Final Report, though it is difficult to know how crucial a role AT&T's public relations actions played. The Final Report accepted the Walker Report's factual data and substituted a drastically more conservative set of recommendations. Probably the major determinant of FCC's scuttling of the Walker Report's recommendations lay in the nature of the organization of the telephone system. Because of the complex interrelation between the perception of the public interest in telephony, the maintenance of the telephone system as a system, and the *integrated* structure of AT&T, most of the Walker Report's recommendations were dropped in the FCC Final Report. The Final Report's recommendations were a remarkable combination of self-serving generalities and a very few actual specific remedies. The FCC simply asserted the necessity of the regulation of telephony, claimed that the process of the telephone investigation itself had produced some $30 million in savings for consumers, and authorized the Commission to prescribe basic cost-accounting methods for Western Electric.[30]

## *The Informal Process of Ratemaking: Protection by Means of Bargaining*

One effect of the telephone investigation was that it provided the FCC with enough information to enable the process of "continuing surveillance" to actually function. In addition to the interstate rate reductions it got Bell to agree to in the 1930s and '40s, the FCC used its influence to cause the Bell Operating Companies to restate their plant accounts and revise depreciation rates in the early 1950s.[31] But it is simply impossible to assess the real effect of these moves, because the Commission acted without anything approaching complete information. As the 1962 Booz-Allen & Hamilton analysis of the FCC put it:

> . . . it is clear that the important functions of surveillance and regulation of common carrier rates and rate base have not been adequately undertaken. These functions do not seem to have been accorded an appropriately high priority by the Commission in the allocation of resources and direction of attention. While the staff has sought to establish essential criteria for judging rates of return, the Commission, in fact, has established no firm criteria governing such rates of return and does not demonstrate that the reductions negotiated actually bring the overall rate of return down to reasonable limits.[32]

In its entire history, the FCC held a full-blown, formal, evidentiary rate hearing only *once*. Even then, the Commission attempted to stop that hearing before it was complete on the ground that it was impossibly beyond FCC resources. Only Congressional pressure and a special appropriation caused the Commission to resume the rate hearing.[33]

Indeed, the informal process of rate negotiation generally served AT&T quite will. Bell System representatives would present the facts and figures before public utilities commissions and the FCC, and request rate alterations accordingly. The commissions, generally understaffed and usually without the kinds of resources to independently check Bell's presentation, would negotiate a rate change in closed session with Bell representatives. The advantage of the informal process of "continuing surveillance" for AT&T was twofold. First, it permitted the corporation to put its stamp on the representation of facts and salient issues. And second, the process of informal negotiation allowed very quick decisions on rate changes.

With regard to the presentation of facts, the issue is not simply that AT&T may or may not have been consciously duplicitous. The issue is that the crucial matters involving the calculation of the rate base, the terms of depreciation, and the costs of service not only are immensely complicated, but are also subject to interpretation at the most basic levels. Without independent investigation of the matters, the regulatory agencies were dependent on Bell for cost and profit data. And the acceptance of such data meant acceptance of the underlying principles upon which these were calculated. For similar reasons, formal hearings on rate requests are so complex and subject to fundamental differences, that they tend to drag on interminably. A New York Telephone Company rate case begun in 1920 was resolved only in 1930. An Ohio Bell case dragged on from 1924 to 1937. The formal hearing begun by the FCC in 1965 dragged on through 1976. These drawn-out hearings make AT&T's financial environment subject to uncertainty, and place enormous stresses on the regulatory agency's resources.

Consequently, the tendency to bargain serves both parties, and yet underscores how tenuous is the actual relation between the facts and the negotiated outcome. Drawing conclusions from an FCC-approved negotiated rate hike in 1953, Joseph Goulden writes, quite accurately, of the mutual benefits of compromise and the accompanying arbitrariness of settlement by negotiation:

> The [FCC] staff's warning is a revealing commentary of FCC ratemaking policies. [The staff counseled against forcing AT&T into a public hearing.] It demonstrates the strong bargaining power that AT&T wields in a negotiation type of regulation: "Give me this amount, and I'll be satisfied; make me work for an increase, and I'll work for more." It shows that both sides are prone to compromise rather than risk total defeat in a formal hearing. And it shows the lack of an objective base for determining what is a justifiable rate of return and that reasonableness in actuality is no more than a mixture of educated guess, corporate aspiration, and regulatory permissiveness.[34]

The negotiated compromises tended to remain in place so long as they benefited AT&T. For instance, following that 1953 decision to boost AT&T earnings to 6.5 percent, the corporation filed a new interstate long-distance rate schedule to bring in the additional revenues. Notwithstanding the higher long-distance rates, long-distance traffic expanded between 1954 and 1961. The additional revenue boosted AT&T's rate of return well over the 6.5 percent negotiated in 1953. Yet the FCC never mandated a new rate schedule to rectify the disparity.[35]

Informal negotiation and continuing surveillance constituted a conservative mode of regulatory behavior which benefited both AT&T and the FCC. In informal negotiation AT&T generally could use its control of the pertinent data, and put to work its vast array of economists, engineers, and attorneys to get what it wanted. Continuing surveillance permitted the FCC to keep a hand in rate making without having to expend enormous budget and political resources. The FCC changed its normal regulatory practices only after a *state* hearing on local Bell rates.

The California Public Utilities Commission's (PUC) treatment of Pacific Telephone and Telegraph's (PT&T) rate hike requests essentially mirrored that of the FCC. However, having agreed with most rate hike requests between 1948 and 1954, the California PUC ordered public hearings in 1962 over a request for a hefty rate increase. In the context of PUC investigation and public hearings, PT&T could not prove its case. Indeed, the PUC found that PT&T had overcharged California subscribers and consequently ordered cuts in phone bills. The California PUC filed suit in federal court asking that the FCC be required to reopen a recently announced negotiated reduction in interstate rates and that it be compelled to determine whether AT&T's rates were justifiable and reasonable.[36] The FCC, put in a politically difficult situation, declined to reopen that particular negotiation, but did announce its intention to convene a formal hearing on AT&T rates. This was the origin of the 1965 formal hearing on rates. And this hearing began to open up the Pandora's box of rate determination. We will discern some of the consequences of this in chapter 8.

### The Resurrection of Antitrust Actions and the 1956 Consent Decree

Notwithstanding the occasional appearance of regulatory activism, after the FCC scuttled its own Walker Report, the agency essentially safeguarded the public interest in telephony by ministering to the needs of AT&T. The FCC, however, was not the only federal agency involved in telephone policy. Notwithstanding the FCC's final position in the Telephone Investigation Final Report, the antitrust issue embedded in the Western Electric controversy could not go away. It was resurrected in January 1949, when the Justice Department filed suit against Western Electric and AT&T for violations of the Sherman Act in the manufacture and sale of telephone equipment and supplies. State public utilities commissions had complained to the Justice Department that they were unable to determine the reasonableness of Western Electric's charges.[37] AT&T's control of the market for telephone equipment, together with Western Electric's position as exclusive supplier for the system, in the words of Attorney General Tom Clark, "permits these two concerns to control both plant investments and operating expenses, factors upon which the federal and state regulatory authorities must fix rates to be charged subscribers for local and long distance telephone calls."[38] The suit also alleged that AT&T's monopoly of basic patents in the area of wire telephony had led to the suppression of improvements.

The suit sought to separate the provision of monopoly-regulated services from an unregulated equipment supply market. The Justice Department recommended that Western Electric be split into three companies and require that AT&T and the Bell Operating Companies buy telephone equipment only under competitive bidding. Justice asked for an end to all restrictive agreements between AT&T, Western Electric, and the BOCs. Lastly, Justice asked that Western Electric and AT&T be required to license their patents to all applicants on a nondiscriminatory and reasonable royalty basis.

The 1949 antitrust suit was settled in 1956 by a consent decree. The Consent Decree did not truly address the monopoly issue. The settlement placed most of its emphasis on patents, owing largely to AT&T's historic hold on telephone patents and the perceived importance of the newly invented transistor. The transistor was a small, semiconducting electrical device developed at Bell Labs which could replace the vacuum tube. The settlement formalized an already existing policy to allow any applicant the use of some 8600 existing AT&T patents, without having to pay royalties to AT&T. The rationale for this was based in part on the recognition that

AT&T research and development were publicly subsidized. In a bow to AT&T, however, companies which applied to use AT&T patents had to share their own patents with AT&T. The Consent Decree thus constituted a combination of minimal AT&T concessions and the construction of new regulatory barriers. It called for Western Electric to institute uniform cost accounting procedures and enjoined Western Electric from paying any patent royalties to AT&T (which could inflate the rate base). Most significant for future developments, AT&T agreed to the creation of a new operating barrier. Bell agreed not to engage in any activities external to those of a regulated communications common carrier (except, importantly, for military work). In exchange, the Consent Decree legally sanctified AT&T as a vertically integrated monopoly.[39]

The Consent Decree later was discovered to be marred by improprieties. According to a 1958 report of the Antitrust Subcommittee of the House Judiciary Committee, Eisenhower's Attorney General, Herbert Brownell, improperly suggested to AT&T's general counsel that the company examine its operations and tell the Justice Department what practices might be enjoined without subjecting the corporation to any real injury.[40] The House Report concluded, "Upon all the evidence adduced in the committee's investigation, the consent decree entered in the AT&T case stands revealed devoid of merit and ineffective as an instrument to accomplish the purpose of the antitrust laws."[41] In addition, there is ample evidence that the Defense Department and Atomic Energy Commission exercised considerable influence to maintain the integrated nature of AT&T. The July 10, 1953, letter from the Secretary of Defense, C.E. Wilson, to Attorney General Brownell reveals intense pressure to dismiss the suit.

> The Department of Defense wishes to express its serious concern regarding the further prosecution of the antitrust case now pending against Western Electric Co. and AT&T Co. in which it is asked that Western Electric be completely severed from the Bell System. . . . The pending antitrust case seriously threatens the continuation of the important work which the Bell System is now carrying forward in the interests of national defense. This is for the reason that the severance of Western Electric from the system would effectively disintegrate the coordinated organization which is fundamental to the successful carrying forward of these critical defense projects, and it appears could virtually destroy its usefulness for the future. This result would, in the judgment of this Department, be contrary to the vital interests of the Nation. . . . That work [electronics and atomic energy] is still underway on an expanded scale and new responsibilities in these and other critical areas have been assumed by the Bell System organization. It is now clear that no terminal date can be placed upon the special usefulness of that organization. Its importance to the national defense will increase as the race for supremacy in the application of advancing technology to military uses continues, as we must assume that it will for the indefinite future. For these reasons, it is now evident that a mere postponement of the prosecution of this case does not adequately protect the vital interests involved. It is therefore respectfully urged that the Department of Justice review this situation with a view of making suggestions as to how this potential hazard to national security can be removed or alleviated.[42]

Many letters attesting to the crucial integrated nature of the Bell System are extant in the Antitrust Subcommittee files. These reflected the role of the Bell

System as virtually a "quasi-state apparatus" with regard to its relations with the Defense Department. After all, in 1949 Bell was asked to manage and operate the Defense Department's high-tech weapons installation known as Sandia Laboratory. Western Electric's original five-year contract was renewed in 1954, in 1959, and throughout the 1960s. In 1950 the US Army chose Western Electric as prime contractor for the Nike Ajax guided aircraft missle; in 1954 AT&T became a key player in the vast project to extend the Distant Early Warning air defense radar system.[43]

Not all of the testimony rested on the importance of AT&T as a prime defense contractor. AT&T consistently claimed that the integrated nature of the Bell System served to keep costs *down*. Certain evidence convinced some Justice Department attorneys that divestiture of Western Electric would increase the cost of telephone communications equipment. This belief that divestiture would *increase* equipment costs likely was part of the general improprieties surrounding the case, and again points to the largely protectionist role of the FCC. Bernard Strassburg (at the time an FCC telephone expert and later chief of the FCC's Common Carrier Bureau) wrote a highly equivocal response to a Justice query as to whether the FCC could regulate the vertically integrated AT&T in the public interest. The original letter was edited and seriously distorted by FCC commissioners.[44] Because of the FCC's unambiguous assertion of its competency in overseeing AT&T, according to the account of one commentator, some of the attorneys believed that the government would lose if the case went to trial. According to Bernard Strassburg, the FCC was set up as a patsy to back a settlement. Once Justice dropped its insistence on divestiture, a settlement could ensue.[45]

## Why Would AT&T Agree to Stay Out of Computers?

At the time, the Consent Decree seemed a clear victory for AT&T. The fly in the ointment was that AT&T was able to remain "whole" at the expense of forgoing entry into computers and data processing at the dawn of the computer age. The Consent Decree fashioned an operating boundary for AT&T, but did so in a manner which relied upon a technological distinction soon to become obsolete. The murkiness of the technological distinction between telecommunications and data processing, and the corresponding economic boundary between common carrier and non-common carrier activities, becomes crucial in later years.

The company's desire for an out-of-court settlement is understandable. After all, by settling with the government AT&T avoided the uncertainty posed by a possible negative court judgment. Along with that possibility came the specter of numerous private antitrust suits, which would use a court judgment as *prima facie* evidence of antitrust violations. A judgment entered by consent cannot be used as *prima facie* evidence of violation of the antitrust laws in subsequent civil action.

That the maintenance of AT&T's monopoly was a victory for the corporation is unquestionable. And it is consistent with AT&T's long tradition of advocacy of end-to-end service and monopoly in telephony. What is perplexing about the Consent Decree is the company's concession to limit its legal operating arena to communications common carriage. Given the rise in computers and data processing—

beginning contemporaneous with the period of the Consent Decree—why would AT&T forgo the possibility of getting into the computer field at the dawn of the computer age? After all, the most critical technological component of the second generation of computers, the transistor, was invented by research scientists at Bell Labs in 1947. The 1954 and 1955 Annual Reports to its shareholders indicate that AT&T had a fairly good idea of the possibilities of the transistor's applications. In the 1954 Annual Report, the corporation claimed that the computer was fast becoming an important business technology, and that AT&T would begin to move in ways to "service" these developments.[46]

In fact, the corporation was involved in more than just service to the emerging computer industry. AT&T had been experimenting with computers since the late 1930s. The firm built the first all-transistor computer, named TRADIC, for the Defense Department in 1954. (In contrast, IBM did not market an all-transistor computer until 1959, when it introduced its 7090 series.) AT&T even flirted with the idea of designing a machine to handle all of its own data processing, but dropped the idea in 1958 when IBM came out with a better model.[47] Nonetheless, AT&T did subsequently build computers for telephone switching. The renowned UNIX computer operating system came out of AT&T's computer research. Lastly, military contracts for continuing transistor-based military hardware were forthcoming throughout the 1950s.[48]

Thus the constriction of AT&T business operations posed by the 1956 Consent Decree is puzzling. In an address before the Spring Joint Computer Conference in Atlantic City, April 30, 1968, AT&T Chairman H.I. Romnes offered this explanation of AT&T's actions:

> We did in fact—using relays—build the very first electrically operated digital computer (in 1939) and up to 1950 had produced more than half of all the large ones made. With that kind of head start, and considering also our position in transistors and solid-state technology generally, what might have been a surprise was that we took ourselves completely out of the business of providing computer services. The reason was simply that we wanted to concentrate on communications.[49]

This explanation is insufficient. After all, it was the threat of antitrust action which precipitated the Kingsbury Commitment and AT&T's spinning off of Western Union in 1913. It took RCA's threat to construct its own radio network interconnect system to finally push AT&T to negotiate the corporate division of industry in 1926 and get out of radio broadcasting. And it took the threat of antitrust action to get AT&T out of the business of motion picture projection equipment in 1935. It was unlike the corporation to withdraw from a market in which it promised to be a heavy hitter. The claim that a company under regulatory constraints becomes risk-averse, especially in this case where AT&T would have to face IBM in head-to-head competition, does seem compelling. But this must be taken in a highly specific context. AT&T's decision to agree to stay out of computers and data processing may have been very intelligent, indeed—at least for the short run.

The 1956 Consent Decree specifically suspended the boundary between regulated common carriage and unregulated markets if the customer of such AT&T

provided services was any agency of the federal government or other communications carriers. In the mid-1950s the market for computers was growing, but the scope and extent of growth was very uncertain. In a 1980 advertisement IBM claimed, perhaps disingenuously, that in the early 1950s it had estimated its market for computers to be about fifty machines.[50] One aspect which was very clear, however, was that the federal government (particularly the Department of Defense) would be a major, if not *the* major customer of computers and data processing for the foreseeable future. Computer industry historians generally agree that the first electronic computers were built for the federal government, and ever since then, the federal government has been a major (in some decades the largest) purchaser and lessor of computers.[51] AT&T's experience with computers and its obvious expertise with interconnection presumably would keep the company in excellent bidding position for federal contracts. Given the fact that the federal government was the effective market for such services in the 1950s, the terms of the Consent Decree allowed AT&T access to the best customer without running the considerable risks of entering the public marketplace. This arrangement also underscores the tendency of the government to integrate AT&T as a quasi-state apparatus.

This risk management factor joins another important economic factor. The intense post-war boom in telephone demand taxed AT&T's capacity to meet this demand. Despite staggering increases in investment and manpower, for several years through the mid-1950s AT&T could not meet telephone demand.[52] The new business of television interconnection revealed other AT&T service shortfalls. In the early 1950s, AT&T could not service the four fledgling television networks with as much signal carriage as they requested. Notwithstanding its experience with computers, AT&T could not have easily entered another equipment market, especially an intensely competitive one. Lastly, AT&T reasonably could have expected to gain peripherally from a strong computer market, because the company would expect to carry computer-generated data via its telephone lines. This presumably would generate some multiplier effects in the equipment area as well. For example, until 1969, only AT&T-manufactured modems could be used to interface computers to the telephone network. Modem devices manufactured by others, including IBM, were considered illegal "foreign attachments."

The 1949 antitrust suit was initiated against a backdrop of complaints against AT&T by state public utilities commissions and was filed in the context of the last hurrahs of the New Deal "trustbusters." Though the 1956 Consent Decree did confine AT&T to the provision of common carriage telecommunications services only, it largely repeated the scenario of the Walker Report by permitting AT&T to retain its vertical monopoly. The basic structures of the industry and its regulation remained intact. The public interest in telephony still was seen to inhere in the leadership and dominance of a vertically integrated Bell System. As before, the FCC was expected to regulate AT&T in the public interest. But because the Consent Decree removed patent control from AT&T's arsenal in the company's unceasing effort to protect its monopoly, AT&T was forced to rely more heavily on FCC regulation to control entry and safeguard its monopoly. For the most part, early Commission actions lived up to Bell's expectations.

*Natural Monopoly and Regulatory Protectionism: The Television Interconnection Challenge*

A clear instance of FCC identification of the public interest in telecommunications with the maintenance of the AT&T monopoly was revealed in the early issues surrounding television interconnection. The massive amounts of research underwritten by the Defense Department during World War II had significant spillover effects in the post-war electronics industry. In contrast to the pre-war years, AT&T no longer was the exclusive source of research and development in telecommunications. One important development from wartime radar research was microwave technology. Microwaves are radio waves of some three thousand times higher frequency than that of AM radio. Such waves tend to travel in straight lines and can be focused as narrow beams, requiring line-of-sight relay stations every thirty or so miles. Microwave technology thus became one means of providing interconnection for the nascent post-war television network system.

Television signals contain a tremendous amount of information. Hence the relay of television programming from network production centers to affiliate stations required great carrying capacity. Standard telephone wires were insufficient to carry television signals. The relatively small carrying capacity of standard telephone wire make it a "narrowband" technology. Television signals require "broadband" carriage technology. AT&T intended to provide television interconnection service via coaxial cable, a technology it developed in the 1930s. But microwave technology was another matter. Because so much of microwave technology was developed under the auspices of the US Signal Corps, there was no proprietary patent situation. Consequently, any number of companies, including Western Union, Philco, and DuMont Laboratories (a television equipment manufacturer and broadcaster) were poised to provide television interconnection services. IBM and General Electric planned a joint venture for the transmission of business data by microwave. Raytheon Corporation proposed an ambitious venture to construct a transcontinental relay system for television and business uses.[53]

Because microwave did not entail the physical stringing of wires, the nascent microwave providers did not face major right-of-way problems. Microwave thus posed a clear threat not just to AT&T's plans to interconnect television stations, but to its long-distance monopoly in telephony. However, microwave technology did utilize the electromagnetic spectrum, and the prospective companies had to receive permission from the FCC to use particular frequencies. The crucial regulatory question was whether the provision of broadband television carriage would be considered adjunct to the wire public telephone network, or whether broadband microwave service would be classified as a new, largely competitive service.

AT&T's interest, of course, was to secure broadband carriage as a service to be provided by legitimate common carriers only. Its strategy was to work against the potential microwave companies in their efforts to obtain frequency authorization. AT&T made strong arguments which drew upon its enormous reputation in the provision of integrated networks, and which couched themselves in the terms of the Communications Act. AT&T claimed that the public interest goals which underlay regulatory arrangements in standard telephony applied to television carriage as well.

Investment of the scale required for an integrated nationwide broadband delivery system would be reasonable only if it were protected from competition, the company argued. One entity could best coordinate a highly technical system, and an exclusive franchise would result in the most efficient use of scarce radio frequencies for video interconnection. Lastly, AT&T argued that such an arrangement was necessary in the interest of uniform and reasonable rates, because in contrast with the common carriers' obligation to serve all, competitive carriers would provide service only in the most lucrative markets.[54]

These arguments had their effect with the FCC. Though the Commission declined to rule that intercity video carriage be supplied on a monopoly basis, in 1948 the FCC adopted a rule that reserved permanent use of the microwave frequencies to common, as opposed to private, carriers.[55] In conjunction with this, the Commission agreed (at the request of Western Union) to restrict the experimental licenses of the private microwave companies to purely experimental activities. The ruling denied the private companies the opportunity to use their frequencies commercially.[56]

Faced with the need to facilitate the development of a new broadband carriage network, the FCC opted to go with the tried and tested (monopoly) common carrier approach. After all, the system worked with regard to telephony. Moreover, AT&T's arguments could not be ignored. The Commission partially legitimated its decision on the better use that common carriers make of scarce radio spectrum.[57] The effect of these rulings, of course, was to freeze the microwave companies out of television and data carriage. Without any reasonable expectation that they would be permitted to engage in business, the private microwave companies dropped their plans because construction costs were too high and the risks too great. AT&T cemented its success in the effort to monopolize television carriage when it refused to interconnect any television signal which used any other than AT&T carriage facilities. Philco's legal efforts against the AT&T interconnect prohibition proved unsuccessful.[58]

The FCC did not *explicitly* rule that intercity video carriage was to be a monopoly service. Nonetheless, the Commission's policy that such service should be provided by common carriers only, without a mandatory interconnection requirement, had the clear effect of giving AT&T such a monopoly. Philco, GE, IBM, Raytheon, and DuMont dropped their microwave plans by 1950. Without interconnection arrangements, Western Union was contained to the New York-Philadelphia-Pittsburgh route. The *de facto* monopoly was obvious. As the two dissenting Commissioners wrote in the 1952 decision which ruled that AT&T could decline to interconnect,

> The decision of the majority, while it states in its conclusions that "it is not intended to support any claim which the Bell System may have made to a monopoly in the field of intercity video transmission," effectively does grant such a monopoly to Bell. Moreover, this *de facto* monopoly is granted without specific recognition by the Commission of such effect and without a finding that such a result would be in the public interest.[59]

AT&T's lobbying might and its record as a successful provider of telecommunications services, plus the general acceptance that the electromagnetic spectrum was limited and scarce, when combined with the Commission's conservatism and historical proclivity toward monopoly, meant the equivalence of the public interest with the desires of AT&T. On the other hand, Commission conservatism does not explain the refusal of the FCC to require interconnection among the common carriers of video signals. Inasmuch as interconnection had been a general policy since the Kingsbury Commitment, and a fundamental principle which facilitated the free flow of commerce, it can only be concluded that the FCC's decision reflected the majority's desire to protect AT&T against possible competition from the only other legitimate carrier, Western Union.[60]

AT&T had been able to win this battle even when it did not have the capacity to meet the demand for television carriage. AT&T's lack of capacity, combined with frantic television broadcasters arguing in favor of a private carriage system, convinced the FCC to allow private (broadcaster-operated) systems on an interim basis. Though the Commission believed that the insufficient availability of carriage facilities in 1948 was only a temporary problem, the FCC authorized the operation by broadcasters of private microwave relaying facilities on an interim basis, pending the availability of common carrier facilities.[61]

This bow to broadcasters meant very little. AT&T effectively monopolized intercity video delivery with implicit FCC approval. But the bow to broadcasters is instructive because it highlights the process through which regulation as producer protection gradually began to unravel. The inability or slowness of AT&T to service new types of telecommunications needs gave new providers and users an opening to urge regulatory authorization for the provision of "specialized" telecommunications services by private companies. Without any real change in the protectionist regulatory paradigm, the FCC would permit small liberalizations of entry in the areas of private lines and terminal equipment in the 1960s. These liberalizations would have crucial unforeseen consequences by the 1970s, especially with regard to the traditional policy of service monopolies.

## Court-Ordered Protectionism: The Case of Federal Communications Commission v. RCA Communications, Inc.

Even in the unusual circumstance where the FCC ruled against the policy of monopoly, the Commission was pushed back toward that policy. In the early 1950s the MacKay Radio and Telegraph Company successfully petitioned the FCC for a license permitting the company to open two new radiotelegraph circuits to Portugal and the Netherlands. Radiotelegraph links to these countries were already established by RCA circuits. RCA opposed the authorization, arguing it would unnecessarily duplicate facilities. The Commission determined that competition would not impair the ability of the existing radio carrier to render adequate service. Nonetheless, RCA's existing circuits already were more than adequate to handle the present and expected volume of telegraph traffic. And the Commission conceded that MacKay's proposed service would not result in speedier or more comprehensive service or lower rates than RCA's service. The FCC justified the license grant because of "the national policy in favor of competition." From this policy, the

Commission said, it follows that competition is in the public interest where it is "reasonably feasible."[62]

The Supreme Court heard the case and reversed, arguing that the record of the case could not support the Commission's interpretation of the public interest standard. The Court determined that the FCC made its authorization only on the basis of an interpretation of national policy, rather than having based its decision on matters within its own special competency. Indeed, the Court cast doubt on the existence of a national policy of competition.

> That there is a national policy favoring competition cannot be maintained today without careful qualification. It is only in a blunt, undiscriminating sense that we speak of competition as an ultimate good. Certainly, even in those areas of economic activity where the play of private forces has been subjected only to the negative prohibitions of the Sherman Law, this Court has not held that competition is an absolute. . . . To do so would disregard not only those areas of economic activity so long committed to government monopoly as no longer to be thought open to competition, such as the post office . . . and those areas, loosely spoken of as natural monopolies or—more broadly—public utilities, in which active regulation has been found necessary to compensate for the inability of competition to provide adequate regulation.[63]

This was a strong judicial reiteration of the regulatory function, especially in public utilities. The Court did not declare that competition could *not* be considered a factor in determining the public interest, but did demand that the FCC show how competition would serve some beneficial purpose. "Merely to assume that competition is bound to be of advantage, in an industry so regulated and so largely closed as is this one, is not enough."[64] *FCC v. RCA* indicates that the status quo in common carrier telecommunications was as strong in the judicial arena as it usually was in the regulatory arena. Maintenance of the public interest essentially meant a presumption against competitive entry.

## The Case of COMSAT: Protectionism, but Incomplete

Like the technologies of radio and microwaves, AT&T discerned in the possibility of space satellites a grave threat to its telecommunications monopoly. Just as in the 1920s AT&T pulled radio into its orbit by representing the service as a "phonebooth of the air," so it sought to represent satellites as a sort of new telephone pole. AT&T intended to dominate satellites as a means both to expand its operations (and rate base) and to eliminate the considerable danger posed by the new technology to its land line system. Bell Labs and Western Electric began research and experimentation on satellites in the 1950s, but the main player was the Defense Department. In the turbulent wake of the Soviet launch of Sputnik in October 1957, the US commenced upon a crash program in space technology. Congress established the National Aeronautics and Space Administration (NASA) in October 1958 as the agency responsible for the American space effort. NASA centralized various aeronautics projects previously dispersed under the jurisdictions of the branches of the armed services.

In late 1959 AT&T proposed to NASA that the agency give AT&T title to the entire satellite communications field. AT&T's logic essentially mirrored the logic displayed in the television interconnection matter. Space satellites would be used for communications, and AT&T was the premier communications corporation, best able to provide an efficient, technically integrated service.[65] But NASA was not the FCC. Not only was NASA not a *regulatory* agency, but it had not yet established set ways of doing things. NASA had no system to protect and no commitment to things like common carrier arrangements. Furthermore, AT&T was not the only large corporation to have NASA's ear. NASA, with its extensive contacts with aerospace firms, did not buy AT&T's pitch that satellites were solely telecommunications technologies. NASA refused AT&T's offer, and continued the practice of requiring competitive bids on projects. Thereafter, AT&T utilized the FCC and the Commission's historic pattern of protectionism to pursue its ends in the satellite field.

Because much of the early space efforts *would* go toward the launching of communications satellites, in 1959 President Eisenhower ordered NASA to cooperate with the FCC.[66] In February 1961 NASA and the FCC signed a memorandum of understanding which divided up jurisdiction over the satellite field. NASA was given charge of the technological phase of space communication development. The FCC was to determine the structure and utilization of space communications. This meant that the FCC would determine who would own the satellite system and how the system would function. The following month, the Commission opened a formal inquiry addressing the questions of ownership and operation of the new venture.[67]

The Commission's position at the end of this inquiry essentially was that espoused by AT&T. Notwithstanding the opposition of such heavy hitters as General Telephone and Electric, Hughes Aircraft, Lockheed, and General Electric, the FCC concluded that satellites were a "supplementary" communications service and should be integrated into the existing telecommunications system. Notwithstanding the sunk *public* investment of some $20–25 billion in satellite experimentation, the FCC recommended that the system be privately owned. Further, the Commission resolved that ownership should be restricted to *bona fide* international carriers only.

This position clearly resonated with that of AT&T. The Commission's report determined that satellites should be used for *international* communications only. The report did not even mention the use of satellites for domestic purposes. Also, the FCC saw nothing good coming from allowing ownership participation by the aerospace and communications equipment industries. Indeed, the Commission claimed that such participation

> . . . may well result in encumbering the system with complicated and costly corporate relationships, disrupting operational patterns that have been established in the international common carrier industry, and impeding effective regulation of the rates and services of the industry.[68]

In the aftermath of this inquiry, the FCC established an *Ad Hoc* Carrier Committee composed of the international carriers to formulate a structure for the new satellite corporation.[69]

It should be recognized that the FCC's position served both AT&T's ends and its own organizational needs as well. Of the four major international carriers that might participate in owning the satellite system, AT&T was the most powerful by far. It could expect to dominate in such an ownership arrangement.[70] And by setting up a traditional common carrier system in satellites, the FCC would be on familiar regulatory ground. Given organizational conservatism, it is not surprising that the FCC would balk at allowing unregulated aerospace firms to complicate the ownership and operation of the system. Kennedy liberals, such as FCC Chairman Newton N. Minow, rejected both the option of broader private ownership and the option of government ownership of the satellite system. The common carrier structure, in Minow's words, was the "more manageable solution of the problem. After all, I recognize that we as a Commission look at it purely in regulatory narrow terms."[71]

The Department of Justice opposed the FCC's position, claiming that such a structure would not be consistent with antitrust laws. Like the FCC, Justice advocated a private enterprise system. But Justice also argued in support of a competitive system, open to all interested communication carriers and equipment manufacturers. At least part of Justice's concern rested in the historic problems with AT&T and the manufacturing exclusivity of Western Electric. Implicit in these worries was that an AT&T-dominated satellite system, regulated under the traditional terms of common carrier regulation, would manifest the same problems of internal cross-subsidization as were alleged in the 1949 antitrust case against AT&T. Justice Department representatives argued that AT&T dominance likely would mean slower development of satellites, because the corporation would be reluctant to jeopardize its investment in cable facilities.[72]

Department of Justice reticence and the vociferous objections of liberal Congressmen convinced President Kennedy to move the satellite ownership matter from the regulatory arena to Congress.[73] The debates in Congress were strangely reminiscent of the old debate over the telegraph. Liberals, citing statistics of public investment in satellite experimentation to the tune of $20–25 billion, advocated a Post Office-type structure. Most Congressmen, however, favored a private enterprise approach. The FCC backed AT&T. The aerospace and communication corporations fought over the terms of the private enterprise structure.

The executive-backed compromise which became the Communications Satellite Act of 1962 established a private enterprise satellite system, superficially akin to the 1919 creation of RCA in radio. Just as RCA was created with the intention of becoming America's flagship entity in international radio, the Communications Satellite Act created COMSAT as a chosen instrument with exclusive right to operate the US segment of an international satellite communication system. There would be no monopoly, though the common carriers would automatically own 50 percent of the satellite corporation. The other 50 percent would be available as a public stock offering. This supposedly would allow electronics manufacturers and aerospace companies to own part of the system, and would protect the public's past investment by way of giving the public an investment opportunity. The State Department would have the power to intervene in international telecommunications negotiations. The FCC was mandated to insure effective competition and was given the power to license the operation of ground stations.[74]

In the short term, the Communications Satellite Act maintained the traditional structures in telecommunications. The rates, profits, and areas of activity of space communications became regulated just like other regulated communication services. To protect the existing structure of American international carriers, COMSAT was not to provide services to end users. Rather, COMSAT became a carrier's carrier for international telecommunications traffic, and thus did not compete with existing carriers.

AT&T was able to get into a major new communications field while protecting its ocean cables. The arrangement transferred any antitrust complications of AT&T's satellite involvement to the new COMSAT entity. The initial technology of weak satellite signal and massive terrestrial dishes meant that the ground links (in the lingo, "gateways") were expensive and few in number. Most of the rate charge to users of international telephone via satellite was for the *terrestrial* leg—controlled by AT&T in the US and by a Post, Telegraph, and Telephone (PTT) monopoly on the other end in Europe.[75] AT&T thus benefited peripherally from its role as the domestic terrestrial link to the international satellite communications system. And the possiblity of using satellites for domestic traffic was not addressed by the act, at least partly due to AT&T's insistence as to the impossibility of geosynchronous satellites.[76]

At the same time, the structure of COMSAT essentially denied AT&T control of the satellite system. Notwithstanding that AT&T owned about a quarter of COMSAT, Bell moved ahead with its transoceanic telephone cables (known as "TAT" cables), and by the mid-1960s petitioned the FCC for its own domestic satellites. Indeed, when the issue of domestic satellites arose in the mid-1960s, COMSAT, along with other corporate entities, represented a potential competitor to AT&T. In the long run, the new telecommunication technology and the institution which structured it helped undermine the traditional pattern in telecommunications.

In the period prior to FCC regulation, AT&T was able to dispatch its predators largely through its control of patents. When the corporation could not keep potential competitors out by this means, it usually negotiated a momentous division of the electronics industry, the result of which was to secure its monopoly of voice telecommunications carriage. FCC regulation brought the principle of monopoly into the very structures of regulation. The FCC saw telecommunications carriage as a set of natural monopolies. It moved to establish that monopoly in telegraphy, and acted to safeguard it in telephony. Monopoly brought with it many benefits. It permitted carriers to establish end-to-end, technically integrated service, taking advantage of economies of scale and eliminating wasteful duplication of facilities. As a regulated service, a monopoly presented the regulatory agency with a relatively easy object with which both to maintain a crucial infrastructure service and to effect certain public interest goals.

The FCC guaranteed AT&T a fair rate of return, and at the same time charged the company with the obligation to serve. Together, AT&T and the FCC manipulated rates so that service might be extended universally. The FCC saw the public interest in telecommunications and the vertically integrated Bell System as one and the same. And as long as telecommunications services were kept institutionally separated, monopoly problems would be averted. The FCC protected the Bell

System in two main ways: by extending AT&T's corporate reach into new services and technologies and by deferring to AT&T on rates through the informal process of "continuing surveillance." AT&T was able to extend its reach because the Commission had developed a commitment to the natural monopoly, common carrier regulatory formula. Any new service or technology was seen as a supplement to the existing system, and should not be permitted to disrupt that system. Moreover, the FCC was on familiar ground with this type of structure and this type of regulation. The informal process of negotiation on rates enabled AT&T to set the agenda and control the representation of prices, rates, and costs. At the same time, informal negotiation permitted an agency without the money, staff, or expertise to adequately regulate the mammoth Bell System the ability to exercise a modicum of (perhaps illusory) oversight. Each of these policies both served AT&T's ends and functioned to safeguard the organizational integrity of the FCC.

Two factors began to undermine the long period of regulatory protection— antitrust problems and AT&T's inability to meet demand. Certain antitrust matters, concerning the nature of the Bell System as a vertically integrated regulated monopoly, continually called into question the rationality of the regulatory arrangement. The antitrust matters took policy-making on telecommunications matters out of the arena of just the FCC. So, while Bell was able to retain its monopoly with the 1956 Consent Decree, the *quid pro quo* was the erection of another operating barrier. This would become important later, with the advent of computers and data processing. The antitrust issues also helped push the determination of satellite policy out of the realm of the FCC. Though the Communications Satellite Act protected AT&T in the short run, it did not permit the corporation to monopolize satellites. Lastly, AT&T's inability to meet demonstrated demand, as glimpsed in the television interconnection matter, would form the basis of small regulatory liberalizations later. These liberalizations would have important consequences. Together with new technologies and new demands, they would help unravel the long-perceived connection between the vertically integrated Bell monopoly and the public interest in telecommunications.

# "Congress Intended to Leave Competition in the Business of Broadcasting Where It Found It"

This chapter presents a thematic analysis of regulatory actions in the broadcast area from early rulings of the Federal Radio Commission, founded in 1928, up to the late 1960s. In so doing, it also presents a condensed history of the evolution of American broadcasting, particularly the beginnings of television.

The regulation of broadcasting came about as a way to alleviate technical chaos and market instability. The licensing system and technical oversight provided by the actions of the Federal Radio Commission accomplished these two basic tasks. The FRC was not created to alter substantially the structure of (commercial) broadcasting—and the Commission was true to its mission. By the time Congress passed the Communications Act in 1934, broadcasting had evolved into a highly profitable commercial industry. With the commercial and network structure of broadcasting in place and operating relatively well, the FCC was confronted with two major regulatory problems. First, at the micro level, the Commission had to formulate substantive guidelines for what was to constitute broadcasting in the public interest. This was important, for the Commission would have to have some reflective criteria upon which to grant and renew broadcast licenses, to determine the appropriate response to complaints about a specific broadcaster, and to deal with charges of media monopoly.

Second, at the macro level, the Commission had to develop guidelines for the utilization of the electromagnetic spectrum. The spectrum is the natural resource through which radio waves propagate and makes broadcast communication possible. The spectrum is divided into frequencies, and one of the tasks of the FCC was to allocate specific parts of the spectrum to different communication services. Different communication uses require more or less spectrum space, or bandwidth, depending on how much information is carried by the signal. For instance, a television signal demands a bandwidth 600 times wider than that of an AM radio broadcast. The FCC was quickly confronted with sometimes conflicting requests for spectrum space allocation. After all, in the 1930s radio frequencies were used not just by commercial broadcasters, but also by various branches of the federal government, by local police and fire-fighting services, by amateurs, by ships and airplanes, by the press, and for experimentation. Even a casual glance at the early dockets on spectrum allocation reveals a difficult regulatory dilemma at reconciling the desires of competing interest groups amidst a confusing thicket of technical constraints. The biggest constraint, of course, was that the electromagnetic spectrum was thought to be finite in its usability. The Commission had to accommodate or deny requests for spectrum space and had to have some rationale for such decisions. Some of the most portentous of these decisions concerned spectrum allocation requests for technical innovations which would compete with existing broadcast services.

The identification of these two major regulatory problems is the product of historical hindsight. At the time of its creation the FCC did not identify these as areas for which it needed to formulate clear-cut policies. In fact, the Commission *never* formulated clear-cut policies or rules with regard to licensee behavior, the awarding of broadcast licenses, or network-affiliate relations (including station ownership limits). Conversely, where the FCC did enact formal rules—in spectrum allocation—the Commission stuck steadfastly to a fundamentally flawed and inadequate plan. The history of FCC regulatory activity in the area of broadcasting illuminates the two basic, dialectically interrelated problems of regulation: bargaining in *ad hoc* adjudication proceedings and inflexibility of formal rule making.

License-related controversies came to the young FCC early and never let up. (For the purposes of simplicity, the Federal Radio Commission and Federal Communications Commission are considered the same agency here). The Commission essentially dealt with them on a continuing *ad hoc,* case-by-case basis, often bargaining with the involved parties. Though there was an identifiable, if often ambiguous policy goal underlying many Commission decisions—namely, localism (the principle that each broadcast station should serve the needs of the community in which it operated)—the essential regulatory dynamic was that *ad hoc* decisions generated a kind of mushy policy foundation to which subsequent decisions, conflicts, and controversies had to adapt. Paradoxically, the Commission often ignored its previous determinations at the individual case level precisely because there were no definitive, formal rules.

The allocation of the spectrum presented a task of a different order. The lack of an allocation plan for AM radio meant that the service evolved on a case-by-case consideration of individual applications. Radio developed on a demand basis, and the FCC had to consider each license application without the benefit of guidance from a master plan. The problems incurred by such an adjudicatory mode of decision-making convinced the Commission to allocate spectrum for television and FM radio by formal rule making. Case-by-case allocations also had left broadcast entrepreneurs somewhat uncertain about their investments and the risks of doing business. Indeed, before the allocation rules, services such as FM radio were shifted in the spectrum, and some of the early corporate battles in television took place precisely over the issue of specific spectrum spaces. By the early 1940s, the FCC saw a need to establish a unified, formal policy in the area of spectrum allocation. This the Commission did. However, once the FCC established an allocation policy, it acted to protect that plan—even after the plan generated severe problems. FCC spectrum allocation policy resulted in an artificial scarcity of good television outlets in major markets. More than any other factor, spectrum allocation policy limited commercial television to three networks only.

The conservatism of the Commission affected both its *ad hoc* orientation to licensee matters and its inflexibility on spectrum matters. This conservatism was based in a fundamental reluctance to implement regulations which might "impair" broadcast service to the public. Protecting broadcast service to the public had the effect of protecting not only the original commercial structure the FCC inherited, but also existing broadcasters, existing broadcast services, and existing business arrangements. The FCC's decision to protect the broadcast system resulted in the *de facto* protection of existing broadcasters and broadcast services from the possibility of competitive injury. This meant that innovations were squeezed into existing regulatory molds and treated as ancillary to standard broadcasting. Such treatment effectively "sabotaged" the communication technologies of FM radio, UHF television, and cable television (CATV) as potential competitors or as potential new uses of the medium.

With regard to licensee behavior, regulatory conservatism meant the presumption of license renewal, the favoring of the tried and true (or, at least, the previously licensed) broadcaster, and a reluctance or inability to stipulate substantive performance criteria other than technical. The Commission instead sought to influence licensee behavior and programming decisions by broad, ultimately unenforceable policy statements and by means of indirect, subtle threats that it intended to rule in this or that manner. The latter dynamic has been called "regulation by raised eyebrow."[1] Commission conservatism was strongly reinforced by pressures from the industry, Congress, and the courts. Also, because the post-Depression judicial philosophy was to give regulatory agencies relatively free rein, the courts gave inadvertent approval to Commission conservatism.[2]

In those few instances when the Commission did eventually act to rectify structural problems—such as the UHF television debacle—it was a matter of too little, too late. Likewise, in the few instances where the FCC attempted to formulate clear-cut policy guidelines—for example, criteria to guide the Commission in comparative license renewal decisions, such guidelines were vigorously challenged in the courts and in Congress. The upshot was the creation and maintenance of a commercial network oligopoly in broadcasting, where broadcast licensees exercised *de facto* property rights in the spectrum.

This chapter will look at agency actions and policies in the context of three interrelated areas: licensee behavior, network-affiliate relations, and spectrum allocation. The key issue in all of these is the basic commercial network-affiliate structure of the industry and the Commission's unwillingness either to alter that structure or somehow harness it to establish a competitive, diverse broadcast system. Indeed, it often seemed the Commission did not really understand the structure of broadcasting—hence its occasional activist efforts to regulate in the public interest were doomed to failure.

## The Network-Affiliate Commercial Structure of Broadcasting and the FCC's Dilemma on Licensee Behavior

The FCC was given charge of a commercial radio system that aired primarily entertainment programming that was financed and produced in large part by advertisers. Given an advertising-based system, networking seems to have been inevitable, since the high costs of producing and distributing a program are unaffected by the number of listeners who listen to it. Because there are economies of scale that extend across programs, networks—which offered an extensive array of pre-packaged programs—made economic sense. By affiliating with a network, a local radio licensee could gain access to nationally popular figures and entertainers whom it had little chance to attract to its studio. By affiliating, an individual station alleviated much of the need to produce expensive programming or to seek out and strike individually fashioned contracts with program suppliers. Network affiliation relieved the local station from some of the burden of attracting advertisers, since the network centralized this task. From the advertiser's perspective, the existence of a network allowed advertisers to purchase time on a large number of stations in a single transaction, knowing that the ad would appear at the same time in each market. The network form thus permitted otherwise numerous individual transactions, negotiations, and uncertainties to be resolved in a few bold (and substantially cheaper) strokes. This is even more the case with television, where production costs are many times greater than in radio.[3]

Notwithstanding the centrality of the network form to the business of broadcasting, the Commission was created primarily as the licensing body of *individual stations*. The Commission was mandated to extend radio service in an equitable fashion to all the people of the United States. It was to accomplish this by licensing stations. Though nationwide programming was encouraged even before the advent of the Federal Radio Commission, the option of a few national superpower stations was dropped in favor of a structure consisting of many local broadcast outlets operating at lower power. The responsibility of the broadcaster is to render the best practicable service to the local community served.

Localism, then, as a fundamental regulatory principle, was a logical outgrowth of the Commission's essential licensing function and the "public trustee" status of the broadcaster. The FCC saw the local broadcaster as the bedrock of the broadcast system. The local broadcast outlet was assumed to provide its local community with local service, to present programs of interest and concern to that community, to serve as an outlet for local expression. The Commission had no explicit authority over network organizations. Localism, as regulatory intent, has been one of the very few unwavering Commission policies throughout its existence, and has substantially affected FCC policies on licensee behavior, spectrum allocation, and ownership limits. As we shall see, however, in concrete policy matters localism was often a profoundly ambiguous concept.

In the matter of licensing, the FRC interpreted the public interest obligations of the broadcast licensee as early as 1929 to be such "that the tastes, needs, and desires of all substantial groups among the listening public should be met, in some fair proportion, by a well-rounded program. . . ." All licensees were obliged to air "public service" programs such as news, religious programs, weather, and other types of local productions.[4] In the same statement, however, the FRC acknowledged that, though licensees were to so serve their communities,

> there are differences between communities as to the need for one type [of program service] as against another. The commission does not propose to erect a rigid schedule specifying the hours or minutes that may be devoted to one kind of program or another.[5]

Thus, one can discern in the earliest policy statement concerning licensing and the public interest a pattern which would characterize the Commission's continuing approach in these matters. The Commission set out very broad and general goals while refraining from identifying—much less imposing—substantive criteria that might secure those broad public interest goals.

While the Commission refrained from dictating what was "acceptable" behavior beyond broad generalities, it found itself faced with "unacceptable" broadcasters in the early days. One of these broadcasters was the infamous Dr. John R. Brinkley. Brinkley's very popular station featured the doctor's "Medical Question Box" program, on which Brinkley dispensed dubious medical information (including surgical procedures) and prescribed his own prescription drugs. Brinkley's medical speciality was a "goat gland" operation in the scrota of men seeking sexual rejuvenation. Arguing that the public interest standard was not unconstitutionally indefinite, the FRC refused to renew Brinkley's license. The FRC legitimated its action on the basis that Brinkley used the station for *personal*, as opposed to *public*, purposes, and that his medical information was inimical to the public health and safety. The Court of Appeals upheld the FRC's right to consider a station's past programming when deciding whether or not renewal would serve the public interest. According to the court, such consideration did not constitute censorship.[6] In another early case, the FRC refused to renew the license of Reverend Robert Shuler on the basis that he had used the airwaves to wage personal attacks on persons and groups which opposed him and to vilify racial or religious minorities. The court upheld the FRC, arguing that broadcasts "without facts to sustain or to justify them" may be found to lie outside the penumbra of the public interest.[7]

Notwithstanding judicial backing, the Commission realized it had wandered into the treacherous territory of dictating "acceptable" and "unacceptable" programming, and its ambiguous statements and decisions on licensee behavior reflect this. The essential contradiction, of course, was that despite the prohibition of censorship stipulated by the Communications Act and the First Amendment generally, the Commission's basic job was to choose among competing applicants for limited broadcast frequencies. Because broadcasters were legally obligated to serve the public interest, there had to be *some* substantive criteria underlying the Commission's choices. Given this contradiction, it is not surprising that the Commission's solution was to assert its *ability* to use past programming as a basis for license renewal decisions (and competitive license grants), but to invoke that power only rarely—and only on a case-by-case basis, not by rule. Instead, the FCC sought to rely on more program- or speech-neutral criteria to grant licenses or renewals— even if these criteria sometimes functioned as a smokescreen for Commission concerns over speech.

Early on such speech-neutral criteria included the applicant's financial status and evidence of commercial support, whether or not the applicant had previous broadcast experience, or, if a license renewal, an assessment of the licensee's past technical performance. Criteria which might count against an license applicant included misrepresentations made to the Commission, the dubious "character" of an applicant, and in renewal cases, evidence that a licensee had aired programs containing "obscene" language. In the aftermath of the Brinkley episode, the Commission did not look kindly on "advice" programs with monetary donation tie-ins, fraudulent advertising, or broadcasts concerning lotteries. Nonetheless, though programming was a factor, what was of more concern to the Commission in granting a license was whether an applicant would have the financial and technical wherewithal to deliver radio service. This was legitimated by the pragmatic fact that, inasmuch as the spectrum was a scarce resource, the Commission wanted to be sure that an assigned frequency would, indeed, be utilized.[8]

With regard to "unacceptable" programming—and, hence, the matter of license renewal—so long as a licensee did not venture into the pale of advocacy, personal attacks, or misleading advertising, renewal could be reasonably assured. Indeed, the fear of licensee advocacy led to the Mayflower Doctrine in 1941. With this doctrine, the Commission enacted a policy which strongly discouraged the use of the airwaves for editorializing or advocacy. But this soon was found to be unworkable. Better the overt editorialist than the covert propagandist. In a policy reversal in 1949, the FCC returned to its "balanced program" view. The Commission encouraged, indeed, required, broadcasters to editorialize, so long as they were balanced in the coverage of public or controversial issues. This was the basis of the Commission's famous Fairness Doctrine.

The Fairness Doctrine emerged as a seemingly neutral way for the Commission to ensure that a scarce frequency be used for "public," rather than private purposes, without the Commission itself dictating the content of programming. The Fairness Doctrine declared a paramount right of the public to be informed and thus required the broadcaster to present a "balanced" treatment of controversial issues of public importance. But the doctrine left the choice of time and subjects of such treatment to the discretion of the broadcast licensee. The doctrine mandated a reasonable opportunity for opposing viewpoints, but entrusted the presentation of such with the licensee as a matter of editorial discretion. Thus, the Fairness Doctrine mandated an abstract obligation on the broadcaster, without stipulating specific speech or requiring access.[9]

The *presumption* of license renewal, on the ground that past service had been "acceptable" and was likely to continue, was established in the Commission's first year of operation and was validated in judicial review.[10] Even in the 1930s, a period when the Commission revoked more licenses than in subsequent decades, it did so very rarely, and usually on the basis of non-speech-related violations. Notwithstanding that, at the time, broadcasting's First Amendment status was ambiguous, the FCC was leery of engaging in censorship via license revocation. In those rare instances where the FCC rules against an incumbent licensee in a renewal case (even in the 1970s, another period of comparatively more license revocations), the rationale for non-renewal usually was *not* program related.[11]

However, this did not and has not prevented the FCC from engaging in censorship when morals and particularly obscenity are involved. Over the years the FCC regularly upbraided and penalized broadcasters who had offended the Commissioners' sense of propriety and good taste. In a 1970 decision, for instance, the Commission reduced the license renewal term of an outstanding listener-supported radio station because of a single objectionable program. The FCC issued a notice in 1971 aiming to pressure radio broadcasters to eliminate from their playlists songs that glorified drug use.[12] The left-wing Pacifica Foundation, the licensee of several listener-supported radio stations, incurred the FCC's wrath throughout the 1960s and 1970s for airing programs ruled "indecent" and/or "obscene."[13] Even in 1987, at a time when the FCC was busy throwing out regulations left and right, and trumpeting the full First Amendment rights of broadcasters, the Commission cracked down on "indecent" radio programming.[14] The duplicity of this heated regulatory action on obscenity and morals is that the Commission exhibits extreme reticence and utmost deference to First Amendment implications when dealing with the far more important issue of a licensee's overall public interest programming obligations. For example, though thousands of Fairness Doctrine violation complaints are filed each year, the Commission only once unambiguously refused to renew a license due to gross Fairness Doctrine violations.[15] During the Civil Rights period, the FCC had to be reversed twice in a case where it had routinely renewed the license of a blatantly racist and discriminatory broadcaster.[16]

The area of license grants and renewals is one which underscores the problem of agency discretion and the fine line between free speech and the public interest. How could the Commission ensure that broadcast licensees fulfill their public interest obligations as trustees of the airwaves, and at the same time not take the first step down the slippery slope where government dictated what speech was or was not acceptable? The elucidation of general and somewhat vague criteria was one rational way out of this dilemma, albeit a way out which normally maintained the status quo.[17]

It is ironic that, though the criterion of public over private interest legitimated the removal of the most egregious broadcasters from the airwaves and helped the FCC mask one of the major dilemmas of its mandate (the public interest vs. censorship problem), one effect was to exacerbate the "homogenized" character of radio. The problem of broadcasting as a scarce and powerful soapbox was solved by restricting the soapbox to the sale of (legitimate) soap. And within this context of sanctioning broadly inoffensive entertainment programming, the Commission's reluctance to formulate substantive public interest programming guidelines meant that the market alone would determine programming. As it was, broadcasters aired very little news, public affairs, educational, or minority-oriented programming. They sold consumer products and, implicitly, the system that created those products.

## Content Regulations

The Commission addressed the fact that it was the market which determined programming in a document called *Public Service Responsibility of Broadcast Licensees* (colloquially known as the "Blue Book"), released in 1946. The "Blue Book" claimed that, while much of American radio was good, it could be far better, and that the Commission's responsibility was to see that licensees fulfill their public interest obligations. The report complained that stations shirked their responsibilities as local outlets by the extensive use of network programs, transcriptions (recorded music), and wire programs. Some stations had become, in the report's phrasing, "mere common carriers of program material piped in from outside the community."[18] Research suggested that local stations made little use of available local talent, nor did stations provide ample time for the discussion of public issues. To remedy these failures, the document proposed that in issuing and in renewing licenses the Commission would consider four program service factors relevant to the public interest:

(1) the carrying of sustaining programs, including network sustaining programs [unsponsored, broadcaster-produced shows], with particular reference to the retention by licensees of a proper discretion and responsibility for maintaining a well-balanced program structure; (2) the carrying of local live programs; (3) the carrying of programs devoted to the discussion of public issues, and (4) the elimination of advertising excesses.[19]

The document argued that purely commercial considerations had the effect of limiting program choice. The economics of sponsorship and its interrelation with the network-affiliate structure of broadcasting meant that programming oriented toward minority tastes (including broadly "educational" programming) was rarely aired. Consequently, the Commission would encourage the airing of unsponsored sustaining shows, live local programming, and discussion-type programming because they "broadened" broadcasting. Such regulatory encouragement would induce licensees to provide air time for programs serving particular minority tastes and interests, for nonprofit organizations, and for experimental and artistic self-expression. Applicants for new stations would be required to show their proposed program plans. Applicants for license renewals would be required to demonstrate a sample week under their previous license. With the "Blue Book," the Commission appeared committed to using its licensing power to compel *diversity* in broadcasting.

However, the "Blue Book" was not released as a body of rules. It merely reflected the "thinking" of some at the FCC during this period of time. Given its critical and activist tenor, the "Blue Book" represented the work of one faction of the Commission staff.[20] But its publication as a general policy without status as a body of rules meant that the "Blue Book" had no actual significance in the real world of regulation. The storm of protest from broadcasters, their trade association (the National Association of Broadcasters), and their trade publication, *Broadcasting,* made certain that the document would be merely a disembodied statement of principles. Broadcasters raised the specter of censorship and decried the violation of the First Amendment.[21]

It is probably true that the document generated some indirect ripple effects, as it gave broadcasters a sense of what the Commission expected of licensees. Applicants for licenses and renewals thereafter would couch their applications in some of the language and arguments presented in the "Blue Book." The NAB strengthened its voluntary radio "Code of Practices" in response to the "Blue Book." In other words, after the storm of protest, the "Blue Book" was coopted by the promise of industry "self regulation." The principles of the "Blue Book" were never directly brought into Commission proceedings on the behavior of broadcast licensees.[22]

Another ill-fated, indirect attempt to affect licensee behavior can be seen in the rulings on station trafficking. Because they were a scarce commodity, licenses had a cash value on the market. Corporations took advantage of the low capital gains tax on the sale of stations to facilitate an active business of buying and selling stations. This not only contravened the spirit of the Communications Act that licenses do not represent ownership of a frequency, but also undermined the Commission's theory that in awarding a license to a given applicant, that applicant would engage in broadcasting. By 1945 more than 50 percent of the existing licensees at that time had been selected not by the Commission but by transferors.

To remedy this, the Commission's "Avco Rule" of 1945 declared that in any future transfer of broadcast stations, there would be an opportunity for others to apply for the channel being vacated. In comparative hearing, the FCC would then designate the transferee according to public interest criteria.[23] Between the broadcasting industry's outcry and trotting out of the First Amendment and the NAB's formulation of its much-heralded but little-followed Code, the FCC rescinded most of the provisions of its Avco ruling in 1949. In 1952 Congress passed a series of amendments to the Communications Act which formally forbade the FCC to call for competitive bids in transfer cases.[24]

One important conclusion to be drawn here is that at various times in its history, the FCC *did* attempt to formulate *some* substantive criteria regarding the public interest in broadcast programming. The "Blue Book," Avco Rule, and en Banc Programming Inquiry describe the some of the more formal Commission efforts in the area of licensee programming. There were other efforts over the years—which also failed—to affect the content of broadcast programming. One of these was a 1963 FCC inquiry to determine whether it should set a regulatory limit on the amount of advertising on stations. In a close vote, the Commission proposed rules that would require all broadcast stations to observe the limitations on advertising time set by the NAB Code. Intense opposition not only from broadcasters but from the House Commerce Committee (and later from the full House itself) undermined the Commission's proposal.[25]

Because the FCC's occasional efforts at formal rulemaking on licensee behavior generally were thwarted, the Commission often turned to more informal stategies, seeking to fashion agreements among the three networks to secure specific types of programming. For example, following the television quiz show scandals of the late 1950s and consequent Congressional unhappiness with the broadcast industry, FCC Chairman John Doerfer devised a plan that would rotate the airing of public affiairs programming among the three networks during prime time (8 pm to 11 pm). The ascension of regulatory activist Newton Minow to the chairmanship in 1960 saw several attempts to affect programming. In 1961, for instance, Minow proposed a daily "children's hour," where each network would air educational fare for children in the late afternoon for one hour twice weekly. Neither the Doerfer Plan nor Minow's children's hour materialized. The Doerfer Plan fell apart after he was accused of flagrant *ex parte* contacts with Storer Broadcasting. The political and industrial coalition collapsed under the evidence of additional scandal. Minow's children's hour proposal could not secure the support of ABC.[26]

Under Minow, another informal strategy gained favor. The FCC broadcast staff (under the stewardship of Minow appointee Kenneth Cox) scrutinized the gaps between a licensee's public service programming pledges on its license application and the actual programming aired. Occasionally the FCC staff would recommend the revocation of a license, but, more frequently, it would delay acting on the license, thereby using the regulatory lag to impose costs and indicate displeasure to the regulated party. Such Commission practices constituted the basis of "regulation by raised eyebrow." Through the informal vehicles of speeches, published articles, a letter to a station, or contacts between the FCC staff and a station, Commissioners could indicate "concern" over the practices of a specific broadcaster. The message was: Clean house, or we may have to take formal action.[27]

Yet, the ultimate effect of raised eyebrow regulation (for all of its denunciation by legal scholars and others) was largely insignificant, because the Commission very rarely revoked licenses. As former FCC Chief Counsel Henry Geller has argued, despite clear evidence that large numbers of licensees were unwilling to commit even a small portion of their air time to news or public affairs programming, the Commission in its entire history has not denied renewal of a broadcast license on the ground that the applicant failed to minimally serve as a local or informational outlet.[28]

There were two reasons for the Commission's reticence to revoke licenses. First, despite the Communications Act's claim that a broadcast license was not a property right, most Commissioners practically regarded it as such. Revocation of a license was seen as the gravest penalty, a step to be avoided if at all possible.[29] Moreover, revocation might impair broadcast service to the public. Most Commissioners considered "raised eyebrow" regulation as a way to warn an aberrant broadcaster, hoping such a warning would induce changes. Second, some Commissioners were genuinely leery of the First Amendment ramifications of either formal content controls or informal warnings on program content.

Indeed, there was good political reason for the Commission to be conservative on the issue of license revocation. The courts had ruled early on that while a broadcast license did not confer a property right, it did confer certain rights or equities to the station owner.[30] With the 1952 McFarland amendments, Congress passed legislation that narrowed the scope of FCC discretion and further broadened the due process rights of regulated parties. The McFarland amendments weakened the Commission's ability to resist perfunctory renewal of licenses, and essentially dismantled the antimonopoly provisions of the Communications Act. The amendments added several new categories where judicial appeal could be brought, greatly broadened the rights of any "party in interest" to obtain a hearing before the Commission, and deleted language which empowered the Commission to refuse a license to anyone adjudged guilty of unlawfully monopolizing radio communications. The McFarland amendments clearly trimmed the discretionary authority of the FCC in favor of the interests of the broadcast industry.[31]

By shrinking the discretionary authority of the FCC, the McFarland amendments augmented the earlier Administrative Procedure Act (1946). The APA had created several separations of functions within regulatory agencies. Agency staffs were insulated from other parts of the agency during adjudicatory matters. The APA, attempting to construct a dichotomy between adjudication and rule-making functions, removed hearing officers from their former position as agents of the agencies, and gave them the status of judicial officers. Hearing officers were barred from consulting with commissioners, even over basic policy matters. The Administrative Procedure Act also obliged regulatory agencies to provide notice of potential rule changes and invite comment from interested parties. The McFarland amendments set up another bureaucratic layer in the form of a review staff to prosecute cases before the hearing examiners. Both laws greatly expanded the ability of any aggrieved party (with a property interest) to attain a hearing before the Commission and judicial review in the federal courts. For example, the amendments required the Commission to conduct hearings upon the insistence of any party seeking a license. At the same time, the amendments curtailed the standing of third parties without proprietary interest in a license.[32]

Such due process rules increased the time factor in Commission proceedings enormously and fragmented Commission functions and operations. They are at least partially responsible for the oft-criticized failure of the FCC to see "the big picture" in broadcasting. Yet such rules and time delays indirectly served the designs of the established entities in the industry, if only because delay perpetuated the status quo.

The Administrative Procedure Act was sponsored by the American Bar Association, and generally backed by regulated industries in context of the late-1940s reaction to the New Deal. The McFarland amendments to the Communications Act were strongly supported by broadcasters. These Congressional curtailments of agency authority stand in marked contrast to the fate of an earlier attempt to redefine the FCC's authority. Like the APA and McFarland amendments, the 1947 White-Wolverton bill (S. 1333) also was proposed to rein in the FCC's discretionary authority.[33] But *this* reining-in was far more ambiguous politically. The bill clarified what the Congress felt the "public interest" was in specific circumstances, such as policy in license transfer cases, in the broadcaster's handling of news and public issues, and in chain broadcasting. As such, White-Wolverton constituted an political hodgepodge. For example, it would prohibit the Commission from exercising any "discrimination" in the granting of licenses. This presumably progressive provision also had the effect of preventing the Commission from ruling against the award of broadcast licenses to newspapers—even though such cross-ownership might create a local news monopoly.

For the broadcast industry the real problem with White-Wolverton was that the bill adopted certain principles from the "Blue Book" and would give the Commission explicit power to examine the overall operation of a station. In other words, broadcasters shrank in terror from the bill's determination of *specificity* to the FCC's mandate. The broadcast industry's intense and successful opposition to White-Wolverton underscores its quest to keep the FCC's mandate general and *vague*. This political dynamic is wonderfully captured by an early dissertation on broadcast regulation by Robert Sears McMahon.

> As long as the Commission's powers were not clearly defined in the law—the industry would have free room to argue that it did not in actual fact possess many powers that it claimed to have, and the Commission could not assert otherwise without a bitter struggle of the kind it was usually anxious to avoid. Once these powers were to be more clearly defined however, then there could be no denial of their existence. The industry much preferred to deal with a Commission that possessed the kind of "unlimited authority" and "well-nigh unfettered discretion" that it was reluctant to employ.[34]

The White-Wolverton bill never came to a vote in either the Senate or the House.

## Licensing

Given evidence of the Commission's efforts to establish substantive public interest criteria in broadcast programming (if only occasional and overwhelmingly unsuccessful), the "capture" thesis seems untenable. A more appropriate interpretation of broadcast regulation would find the FCC a relatively weak agency as much constrained by the prerogatives of other branches of government as pressured by the broadcast industry. Such pressures likely reinforced the agency's own conservative understanding of its legislative mandate. The resulting regulatory inefficacy, however, *did* serve the established interests of the broadcast industry because it maintained the status quo.

On the other hand, individual licensing matters do provide some evidence of corruption (if not "capture") on the part of some Commissioners. At the very least, licensing matters at times reveal the FCC to be deferential to power and open to influence—whether that influence came from industry "heavy hitters" or from individual Congressmen. On a more theoretical level, individual licensing matters point to the problem of discretionary authority free of formal rules.

Licensing matters (particularly in the 1950s but not confined to the Eisenhower FCC) reveal instance after instance of wildly inconsistent, often contradictory findings and decisions. Television provides a good example, because most TV license applications required a comparative hearing, given the scarcity of outlets.[35] Though the criteria for the selection of one applicant over another nowhere were formally stated, they were often acknowledged in the testimony of FCC Commissioners before Congressional hearings. In one acute analysis made in 1958 and reported as a confidential memorandum to the House Subcommittee on Legislative Oversight in its investigation of the FCC, Dr. Bernard Schwartz, then Chief Counsel to the FCC, identified the determinative criteria in comparative license applications as:[36]

1. local ownership;
2. integration of ownership and management;
3. past performance;
4. broadcast experience;
5. proposed programming and policies; and
6. diversification of control of the media of mass communications.

The Legislative Oversight Subcommittee staff examined the outcome of some sixty comparative television cases. Its conclusion illuminates the *ad hoc,* often arbitrary nature of the licensing process. The staff found, according to Schwartz,

> A most disturbing inconsistency on the part of the Commission in its application of the standards developed by it in particular cases. Such inconsistency has, in effect, enabled the Commissioners to act in individual cases on the basis more of whim and caprice than that of the applications of settled law to the facts of the case. At times, in truth, the Commission appears to have made decisions which are diametrically opposed both to the standards which it itself has developed and to its own decisions in other contemporaneous cases.
>
> In addition, there has been observed a tendency in the Federal Communications Commission in recent years to modify the weight given to the different criteria developed by it. Such modification has been in the direction of diminishing the importance of criteria such as local ownership, integration of ownership and management, and diversification of control of the media of mass communications (all of which tend to favor the small newcomer, without established broadcasting interests) and magnifying the weight given to the criterion of broadcast experience (which tends to favor the large established company, with extensive broadcast interests), In a number of recent cases, indeed, the experience factor has tended to be all but conclusive. The result has been a growing number of decisions which increase the already pronounced tendency toward concentration of ownership in the broadcast field. Even more disquieting, perhaps, than the trend toward modification by the Commission just noted is the fact that the Commission has not been consistent in its application of the modified criteria. Thus, alongside the decisions just noted, which appear unduly to favor the large applicant with extensive broadcast interests, there are other cases in recent years where the Commission has continued to give a preponderant weight to those standards, such as local ownership, integration of ownership and management, and diversification, which favor the small local applicant without extensive interests in radio and television. Such inconsistency by the Commission may enable it to reach the result in a given case toward which it is predisposed, even though such result is contrary to its decisions in other similar cases.[37]

It is at the licensing level of regulatory discretion that political favoritism and *ex parte* contacts operate. At this level "regulatory capture" can be real. The disclosures at these hearings that Commissioners had engaged in compromising *ex parte* contacts and had accepted broadcast industry gifts prompted one resignation from the Commission.[38] Over the years, other Commissioners left the agency with less than stellar records in the area of *ex parte* contacts.

The Commission's inconsistent, sometimes suspect actions in license grants illuminate some of the problems of discretion without guidance by rule. Whether a consequence of administrative overload, the influence of industry and Congressional lobbying, the avoidance of judicial challenge, outright graft on the part of individual Commissioners, or a melange of all of these, the effect of license grants over the years was clear. First, because the FRC wanted to ensure that scarce frequencies actually were utilized, the original licensing of radio stations tended to reflect the fortunes of financially sound stations. This, not surprisingly, favored the commercial stations and those associated with networks. The same rationale carried over into television licensing, where spectrum scarcity was more stringent and station operational costs were far greater. Second, given the bias toward already existing broadcasters in the licensing of *new* radio and television stations, the expansion of broadcasting tended to further concentrate the power of existing station owners and further restrict entry to those with past broadcast experience. Third, with regard to license *renewal,* the fundamental presumption in favor of renewing the license of the existing, average broadcaster could but strengthen the power of existing broadcasters. Together these trends tended to reinforce existing ownership patterns as well as a lack of diversity in programming, because they rewarded the average broadcaster. This dynamic would be disrupted in a small way only when the Great Society period of consumer activism affected FCC actions in the late 1960s.[39]

It is not easy to evaluate FCC actions in the area of content regulations with a broad summary judgment. The composition of the Commission and its political outlook changed over time, and these have had some bearing on the agency's actions and policies at various points in its history. The Commission of the Newton Minow era embraced different methods and saw the industry in far different terms than the Commission under, say, John Doerfer. However, the final regulatory outcomes were essentially the same, regardless of the political proclivities of different temporal Commissions. The explanation for this rests in the structure of power within which the regulatory agency is situated, and in the constraints which limit the available regulatory options. In the area of content regulation, the Commission was constrained by several factors, not the least being the commercial structure of the broadcast industry and the economic tendencies which flowed therefrom. Congress, though often publicly critical of FCC inaction, more often hemmed in the agency's activism. Broadcasters may have been revoltingly self-serving when they trotted out the First Amendment to protect their economically based programming decisions, but content regulations did implicate free speech problems. As a result, although broadcasters did not enjoy the breadth of First Amendment protection as did publishers, they nonetheless enjoyed enormous discretion and flexibility in what they could program.

## The Problem of Monopolization

If clear-cut rules on individual licensee behavior and program content were politically impossible to enact and also raised First Amendment questions, there were other proposed remedies to the problems of American broadcasting. The proposal with the most currency in the 1940s was to restructure the economic basis of the industry. Reformers looked for a remedy which would force the industry to become more competitive. This would be accomplished by disrupting the relationship between networks and affiliates. The commonly accepted theory was that the networks exercised a strangle-hold over affiliates, sucking up profits and preventing the local stations from exercising proper, localistic control over programming. The early efforts at enacting *structural* rules over broadcasting thus were part of the New Deal discourse on "monopolization."

There were always vociferous critics of the commercial network-affiliate structure of broadcasting, and these critics were not mollified by the creation of federal regulatory oversight. Throughout the New Deal, resolutions and bills were introduced in Congress which sought to diminish the power of large broadcasters, colloquially referred to as the "Radio Trust." Unable to secure legislation, these anti-monopoly Congressmen sought to initiate investigations of the FCC as a way to achieve their aims. These efforts also came to nothing, though they did put pressure on the Commission to address the issue of the corporate control of radio.[40]

Congressional pressure, and, more direct, a complaint from the smallest of the major radio networks, the Mutual Broadcasting System, led in 1938 to a Commission investigation of "chain broadcasting." Mutual alleged that it had encountered difficulty in obtaining station affiliations in its attempt to expand into a national radio network. Like the earlier investigation of the telephone industry, the investigation of the chain monopoly was far-reaching and critical of the institutional practices of the broadcast industry. The FCC found that NBC and CBS exerted enormous control over the broadcast industry. Of the 660 commercial stations on the air in 1938, 161 were affiliated with NBC, 113 with CBS, and 107 with Mutual. (Mutual's numbers are deceptive, because its affiliates were small, mostly rural stations.) These stations represented almost 98 percent of the total wattage of radio transmitted power. NBC and CBS controlled more than 86 percent of total wattage. They controlled all but two of the 50 clear channel stations and most of the full-time regional stations. (Clear channels were frequencies kept free of local signals at night. High-powered transmissions could travel great distances at night, utilizing the propagation technique known as "skywave.") Forty four percent of the "net time sales" (advertising) for the industry represented NBC and CBS network time sales. The 23 stations owned and operated by NBC and CBS, most of which were located in well-populated and lucrative markets, had net time sales for non-network programs amounting to 7 percent of the total net time sales of the entire industry.[41]

The chain monopoly investigation found that through contractual arrangements, the networks exercised considerable control over the practices and earnings of their affiliates. These contractual practices (primarily those known as "exclusive affiliation" and "option time") served not only to discourage stations from airing local programming, but also functioned to prevent the formation of competitive networks. Exclusive affiliation bound a station to its network. It prohibited a station from offering its facilities to any other network. The terms of the affiliation contract by 1936 were to bind stations to networks for 5 years, but the network could cancel on 12 months' notice. Option time was a contract specifying the number of hours per day an affiliate had to clear for network programs, these hours at network prerogative. For a certain number of hours all proceeds went to the network. After this minimum was reached, the local station was given a proportional share of the total proceeds, the proportion increasing as more network program hours were aired.

Option time was at the heart of the affiliation contract, because it permitted the network to set up a certain block of stations for advertisers. The practice produced strong pressures for local stations to clear all or most of their prime-time schedules to the networks. NBC's so-called "liquidated damage" policy obliged the affiliate station to pay over to the network any additional revenue it received above the network rate if the affiliate substituted for a network program. A related contractual clause tied the affiliate to use of network "live" programming by preventing the station from reducing its "spot" advertising rate below the network rate. This would discourage a station from programming recorded material. The practices resulted in a grossly inequitable relation between the networks and their outlet stations to the advantage of the networks. The networks' control of the music recording business (called, at the time, "transcriptions") and of the talent supply also tended to restrict competition.[42]

Completed in June 1940, the original *Report on Chain Broadcasting* consisted of the investigation and the conclusions and recommendations of the three Commissioners who signed it. In many ways the conclusions constituted a sharp, critical analysis of the organization of American broadcasting, and one of the few clear instances in which the Commission drew connections between the structure of the industry and the *values* that underlie the First Amendment.

> The inescapable conclusion is that National and Columbia, directed by a few men, hold a powerful influence over the public domain of the air and measurably control radio communication to the people of the United States. If freedom of communication is one of the precious possessions of the American people, such a condition is not thought by the committee to be in the public interest and presents inherent dangers to the welfare of a country where democratic processes prevail . . . . To the extent that the ownership of and control of radio-broadcast stations falls into fewer and fewer hands, whether they be network organizations or other private interests, the free dissemination of ideas and information, upon which our democracy depends, is threatened.[43]

The investigators called for the elimination of various network-affiliate practices. They also recommended a reevaluation of the clear channel policy, in order to encourage more local use of channels used by high-powered stations. The advisability of a single corporate entity operating two network operations (namely, NBC, which operated "Red" and "Blue" networks) was severely questioned. The investigators then directed the Commission to certain key "problems suggested by the report":

1. The necessity and advisability of requiring networks to be licensed by the Commission.
2. The ownership of stations by networks.
3. The ownership of more than one station by an individual or corporation.
4. The control of talent by networks.

5. The dominant position of National [NBC] in the transcription field.
6. The difficulties involved in supervising the transfer of control of corporate licensees because of their stock being listed on stock exchanges.[44]

The tone, context, and wording of the conclusions indicate that the investigators wanted their colleagues to rule decisively on these matters. This, however, was not to be. In response to the *Report on Chain Broadcasting* the Commission issued its "Chain Rules" on May 2, 1941. The rules addressed the problems of broadcasting by issuing rules on network-affiliate contractual relations only. The "Chain Rules" loosened the practices of exclusive affiliation and option time. Two rules affecting station ownership were designed to eliminate the operation of two stations within the same market by a single owner and, indirectly, to eliminate the operation of two networks by a single firm.[45]

But the rules did not address the key question of whether a network should be allowed to own broadcast stations at all. The *Report* suggested that network ownership of stations "bottled up" the best facilities from competition, had a discouraging effect upon the creation and growth of new networks, and created a conflict of interest between station and network. Even so, the *Report* itself hedged, claiming it "inadvisable to compel these networks to divest themselves of all of their stations."[46] Also not addressed was whether it made sense to establish a ceiling on the number of stations that could be owned by one entity. The choke-hold that the networks held on transcriptions and talent was not addressed. In short, the "Chain Rules," perhaps the most invasive action in the history of the Commission with regard to the structure of the broadcast industry, dealt with barely a part of the identified problems of American broadcasting.

Notwithstanding the enormous discrepancies between the *Chain Report*'s diagnosis and the Commission's remedy, NBC, CBS, and large broadcasters fulminated against the "Chain Rules." They forecast dire consequences for the broadcast system and brought legal action against the rules. The Senate convened a hearing in 1941 to hold up implementation of the "Chain Rules" pending investigation of whether the FCC had exceeded its authority. Even acknowledging the great pressure brought to bear on the Commission by the broadcast lobby and by various Congressmen, perhaps the fundamental reason for the essential conservatism of the "Chain Rules" was that more radical rules might threaten the structure of the broadcast system. And altering the structure of the system likely would impair broadcast service to the public. As FCC Chairman James L. Fly, who was vilified in the broadcasting trade press and by various Congressmen as a demagogue and a Communist, testified before the 1941 Senate investigation of the FCC,

> I just do not think, by any stretch of the imagination, that we ought to talk about these chains going out of business. They are not going out of business. *For that matter, I think it ought to be part of the Commission's job to see that they do not go out of business, because no one could contemplate with equanimity a substantial impairment of the Nation-wide network service.*[47]

Yet, even as it acknowledged the broadcasting system as a network system, the Commission declined to regulate the system in a way that really recognized its operational system as network-based. The minority report to the *Chain Report* was actually more consistent, in that it identified the broadcasting system as a network system, and sought to strengthen it. The dissenting Commissioners asserted:

> There is a temptation to over-emphasize local interest to the detriment of national interest, and vice-versa. The real goal should be efficiency of service from a national standpoint rather than a vague objective which fosters a conglomeration of local units uncoordinated for rendering a truly national service.[48]

Given the strictures placed upon chain broadcasting by the "Chain Rules," and the vague commitment to localism, the minority report forecast disaster.

> It is, therefore, no exaggeration to predict that the decision of the majority instead of resulting in "free competition," would more likely create "anarchy" or a kind of business chaos in which the service to the public would suffer.[49]

In actuality the minority's conclusions were wrong. The "Chain Rules" had relatively little effect on radio broadcasting. But the minority report was correct in identifying the broadcast system as nationally oriented and network-based. The majority, in trying to find some middle ground between acceptance of the network system (as it was then constituted) and the promotion of local broadcasting, directly contributed to a situation which impeded competitive network entry and thus forestalled the creation of a more competitive (albeit commercial) nationwide radio service.[50] The most important consequence of the "Chain Rules" was that NBC's second network acquired a new owner. NBC Blue became the American Broadcasting Company in 1945. On the other side of the coin, this middle ground merely paid lip service to local broadcasting while providing no institutional supports for it.[51]

Some compromise between networking and localism was necessary. The economics (and benefits) of networking are clear and forceful. The policy of localism was based on a vision of democratic communication. But the middle ground constructed by the "Chain Rules" and subsequent ownership decisions did not constitute a compromise based upon a theoretically consistent set of goals. They constituted instead a middle ground based on pragmatic and organizational expediency. In contrast, the *Chain Report*'s original recommendations did rest on a theoretically consistent basis. Those recommendations—asking for the divestment of stations from networks, for the severe limitation of group ownership of stations, for the freeing up the networks' hold on the supply of talent and transcriptions—hoped to transform networking into a competitive business of program purveyance. Freed from the contractual pressures imposed by network affiliation, the hope was that local stations would have incentives to engage in local programming, and, at the very least, would have a far greater number of programming choices available for purchase and airing.

Because the Commission's theoretical understanding of the nature of the broadcast system was unresolved at best and deluded at worst, a kind of pall of inconsequentiality clouded most of the post-"Chain Rules" decisions concerning ownership. The Commission never developed any coherent theory or consistent set of guidelines concerning ownership questions. Instead, the "middle ground" between networking and localism found the Commission formulating policies in response to political pressures and to the failure of other FCC policies.

For instance, following the *Report on Chain Broadcasting,* no explicit rule established an upper limit on the number of AM radio stations a single entity could own.[52] Ownership questions were handled on a case-by-case, adjudicatory basis. Nonetheless, after the "Chain Rules" an "understanding" existed between the FCC and broadcasters that the upper limit was seven. (This number was set by rule in 1953. The FCC established formal ownership limits on the new services of FM radio—six—and television—five—at the outset of these services.) Yet, there was never any explanation or rationale as to why seven became the limit. Most likely the number pragmatically reflected the actual ownership patterns in AM radio after NBC sold the Blue network.

A rule on multiple ownership made sense given the FCC's stated goal to promote diversification of ownership, but the Commissioners never could agree on a comprehensive set of formal rules governing the whole area of media concentration. The problems with the Commission's ownership ceiling were manifold. At one level, *any* ceiling reflected an acceptance of the principle of multiple ownership of stations, despite the fact that studies strongly suggested that such practice eroded the local ownership and diversity of ownership doctrines.[53] Related to this was acceptance of the multiple ownership of stations by the three networks, despite the warnings that network ownership bottled up the best stations. A more practical problem was that the ownership limit treated all stations as equivalent, whether they reached an audience of two thousand or ten million. Clearly, all stations were not created equal.

The basic issue was that an ownership ceiling (set arbitrarily at seven) was established without benefit of any theory of networking or any theory of the effect that multiple ownership might have on the creation of new networks. This was because the whole area of the relationship between networking, good local programming, and ownership was unresolved. The Commission explicitly wanted local stations to program in the public interest. At the same time, the Commission implicitly recognized that networks not only provided most programming, but most of the *good* programming. As such, the panoply of Commission actions on multiple ownership constituted another pragmatic middle-ground decision which facilitated not the diversification of ownership, the promotion of local broadcasting, nor the establishment of new networks.

Changes in the ownership rules reflected failures in other aspects of regulation. For example, the original ceiling for the ownership of television stations was five. In 1954 this was changed to seven stations—5 VHF and 2 UHF. (VHF refers to a portion of the spectrum designated as the "very high frequencies," an arbitrarily designated portion of the spectrum from 54 to 216 megacycles. UHF refers to "ultra high frequencies," the portion of the spectrum from 470 to 890 megacycles. Television was initially authorized to begin service in the VHF, though there was not very much spectrum space. By the time the FCC authorized television to use the UHF as well, VHF was established as the standard. The early network organizations had already established VHF affiliates and put their energies and investments in that band of the spectrum. UHF, both technically inferior and economically undesirable, was a hobbling ancillary service.[54]) The major impetus behind this ownership rule was to promote network backing of the failing UHF television service. In this decision the Commission acknowledged that, given the commercial structure and the enormous costs of television production, the new service (UHF) required centralized networks to provide programming. Based on the fact that, in the early days of television, all the nascent television networks had scrambled to acquire many stations, the FCC came to the unproven conclusion that multiple ownership facilitated the formation of networks.[55] Thus the Commission raised the ownership ceiling to seven stations. (Of course, because of its commitment to the principle of localism, the Commission still proclaimed its vigilance against monopolization in television.)

As television evolved into a two-and-a-half-network oligopoly in the VHF (ABC ran an extremely poor third to NBC and CBS for many years) and a failure in the UHF, the Commission formulated the "Top 50 Market" policy in 1965. This policy limited ownership to three stations in the top 50 markets, only two of which could be VHF.[56] Yet, typical FCC policy was to admit, or "grandfather," all arrangements prior to the enactment of a new rule. Such a conservative course had several consequences. It relieved the FCC from the onerous necessity of ordering existing broadcasters to divest some of their presently held broadcast properties. This softened the industry's opposition to the rule, and probably obviated otherwise certain litigation. Yet it also had the effect of stabilizing the very condition for which the rule was thought necessary. Moreover, the Top 50 rule was unenforced. The large group owners not only attacked it, they commissioned an independent study of group ownership that challenged the Commission's logic in the "Top 50" rule. The report of United Research, Inc., concluded that the program activities of group-owned stations were closer to the FCC's goals of program diversity than were the similar activities of single-station owners. The report deemed groups as a procompetitive, not an anti-competitive force in television broadcasting. In the years after adoption of the rule, the Commission granted waivers in each of the eight cases where the "Top 50" rule should have dictated a rejection of the application.[57]

The gutting of the "Top 50" policy was, in large part, the result of a theoretical agreement between large group owners and the Commission that too restrictive a rule might curtail the chances for another network.[58] Seeing in group owners the abstract potential for networking, the Commission again found itself caught between its localism standard and its unsubstantiated hope that these owners would do what they never had done before—move from the trafficking and operation of stations to the provision of *bona fide* network programming. Not surprisingly, the Commission opted for the latter course, especially if the implementation of the "Top 50" policy would require divestiture. But it was never clear what factors would prompt the establishment of additional networks. The group owners seemed content to "trade up" for more lucrative stations in major markets and to air the programming of the three established networks.

The whole area of media ownership highlighted basic issues about diversity which the Commission never could resolve. The Commission was always implicitly hopeful that a diversity of owners of broadcast properties would translate into a diversity of programming. The logic was that different owners, with different viewpoints, would program differently and provide a genuine marketplace of ideas. But, in the economic world of commercial broadcasting, program diversity simply does not follow diversity of ownership. The same economic opportunities and pitfalls confront any owner, and induce that owner to air programs which will attract the largest possible audience. Programming, therefore, tends to be imitative and seeks to be inoffensive.[59] That the Commission did recognize this economic reality is evidenced in part by its reluctance to compel diversification to such a degree that the action would preclude the emergence of another network. In short, the Commission's policies on ownership, unguided either by a clear understanding of the structure of broadcasting or by clear policy intentions, constituted an *ad hoc* melange which, if it had any efficacy at all, served mainly to protect existing networks and large owners.

## The "Sabotage" of New Technologies and New Broadcast Services

By now it should be apparent how interconnected and interdependent were the various aspects of broadcast regulation. It also should be apparent that the underlying policy of the FCC with regard to broadcasting—localism—could not succeed in the face of actual commercial broadcast economics unless the Commission acted radically. This conservative reliance on the policy of localism joined with other factors to sabotage the potentially competitive broadcast services and technologies of FM radio, UHF television, and cable television. (Cable television was a method of delivering television signals through wire rather than over the air.) Where the FCC might have helped these services alleviate some of the endemic problems of conventional broadcasting, the Commission regulated them as troublesome, ancillary adjuncts to the existing system. Much of this sabotage took place within the context of industry struggles over spectrum space. The Commission's 1952 allocation plan for television, legitimated by localism, constructed a regulatory-imposed scarcity of television frequencies that culminated in a three-network oligopoly. Localism represented a surprisingly conscious policy which aimed at nurturing a geographically and economically decentralized, even democratic broadcast system—within the bounds of commercial ownership, of course. The paradox is that such a policy, in the absence of clear analysis of the economics of broadcasting, functioned to protect existing broadcasters and existing technologies.

### FM Radio

Among the drawbacks of AM radio was its susceptibility to static interference. AM stands for "amplitude modulation." The early accepted means of overcoming static was to increase transmitting power. In the early 1930s another method, FM, "frequency modulation," was developed by Edwin Armstrong, a radio engineer who had a close relationship with RCA. RCA played an important role in Armstrong's FM experimentation. Armstrong patented his experiments on FM in the early 1930s, but he ran afoul of RCA because he conceived of FM not as a means of solving static problems in AM radio, but as a total replacement for the AM system. As a separate radio service, FM promised not only significant technical advantages over existing AM radio, but also provided policy options for the broadcast system as a whole. After all, FM not only could deliver a static-free signal with greater frequency range than AM, it also had the ability to exist quite close to other FM stations on the same frequency (known as "co-channels") without the mutual interference experienced on the AM band.

Because of these qualities, FM presented an opportunity for a significant increase in broadcast competition through the licensing of large numbers of new stations in a new frequency band. This perhaps could present a challenge to network control of programming through the diversification of broadcast services.[60] Moreover, FM conceivably could help alleviate the problem of the large rural service gap. But as a separate broadcast service, FM threatened RCA's investment in AM radio. This threat precipitated the break between Armstrong and RCA. In 1935 RCA decided to ignore FM radio (and thus ignore a means of improving an existing technical system) and put its investment capital into the development of television.[61]

Though the prestigious Institute of Radio Engineers showered accolades upon Armstrong for FM's technical brilliance as early as 1935, the FCC took little notice of the innovation until late in the decade. It was then that commercial interests began constructing experimental FM stations and clamoring for permanent spectrum space. With the strong backing of FCC Chairman Fly, in May 1940 the FCC allocated 35 channels for commercial FM use at 44-50 kHz and reserved 42-43 kHz for educational use. But the Commission's understanding of the role and place of FM in the broadcasting system is of crucial importance. In granting this spectrum allocation, the Commission stated that this ". . . new and additional service would not supplant the service of standard broadcast stations generally, and that, therefore, this service will not make obsolete the receivers now in use."[62] The 1940 FCC *Annual Report* reveals that the Commission sought to avoid the monopoly problem in FM that it felt hindered program diversity in AM. The Commission ruled:

> To obviate possible monopoly, and to encourage local initiative, no person or group is permitted to control more than one FM station in the same area, and not more than six in the Nation as a whole.[63]

In contrast, as we have seen, the "Chain Broadcasting Rules" a year later would decline to set any formal limit on the ownership of AM stations.

Ownership was not the only limit the Commission imposed on FM. In a 1945 decision the FCC set upward limits on FM station transmitting power. The "single market plan" set maximum limits on the power of FM transmission (20 kilowatts) and on antenna heights (500 feet). Justified by localism, the "single market plan" was designed to prevent monopoly concentration and to maximize the number of local FM outlets.[64] With the intent of localism thwarted by the AM network system, the FCC sought to foster it with the new FM service. There was explicit recognition by the Commission that FM represented a way "to correct numerous defects and inequalities now existing in the standard broadcast band."[65] The allocation of 20 FM channels for educational use was part of the recognition of AM's failure. But, as Vincent Mosco observes so incisively, by supporting competition *within* the FM industry (and not without for radio as a whole), the FCC lost the opportunity to use the new service in a manner that would provide a competitive challenge to the AM system. Rather than use FM as a corrective to the problems discussed at such length in the *Report on Chain Broadcasting,* the Commission sought to ensure that the innovative service would not develop similar problems. Reduced coverage and ownership limits acted to hamper the development of networks which could then compete with AM radio. A fledgling FM radio network known as the Yankee Network, for example, was forced to cut back its coverage by more than 40 percent.[66]

Non-regulatory factors also contributed to the stunted growth of FM radio. FM's development was legally halted in 1942 with the entry of the United States into World War II. Electronic materials were needed for the war effort. But it was regulatory action which finally sabotaged FM as a possible competitor to AM. Military experimentation during World War II greatly expanded the usable spectrum. However, the military took a vast portion of the spectrum for its own needs. After the war, a scramble over scarce civilian spectrum space pit FM interests against a powerful amalgam of forces wishing to begin commercial television broadcasting in the part of the spectrum occupied by FM.

The controversy over FM's spectrum space in the FCC's 1944–45 allocation hearings formed just a part of complex battles within the broadcast industry over the technical standards and spectrum allocations of post-war broadcasting. For those allocation proceedings, the FCC asked broadcasters to coordinate their views concerning frequency allocations through the establishment of a technical body tied to the trade association, the Radio Manufacturers Association (RMA). This new body was called the Radio Technical Planning Board (RTPB).[67] In the face of contrary opinion by a substantial majority of propagation experts of the RTPB, the Commission decided to move FM up the spectrum, from 42-50 kHz to 88-108 kHz. The technical case against low-frequency FM rested largely on the flawed and classified testimony of Kenneth A. Norton of the Signal Corps, former FCC Assistant Chief Engineer. Norton believed that ''sporadic E and F2 layer'' interference would plague FM at its then present spectrum position as increased sunspot activity approached.[68] Though FM's new spectrum allocation gave it 100 channels, as compared with 40 channels under its previous allocation, the move upstairs severely damaged its economic prospects. Erik Barnouw estimates that it cost station owners $75 million to convert transmitters to the new spectrum area. The move rendered obsolete all 47 operating FM stations and half a million receivers.[69]

The FCC's treatment of FM is difficult to understand. The vacated Channel 1 (44-50 kHz) was reallocated first to television, later to police services. Yet the Commission did not consider that the same interference would pose a problem for these services. In view of the fact that television is generally more prone to interference than FM, and considering the emergency nature of police and fire service transmissions, the Commission's subsequent nonconsideration of interference is baffling.[70] It seems significant that RCA opposed the FM shift, because the corporation feared that such action might set a precedent for shifting television out of the VHF band; CBS supported the shift for the same reasons.[71] Thus the Commission's

FM actions cannot be ascribed to industry pressure *per se* because the industry was fundamentally divided. The most plausible explanation is that the Commission conceived FM as ancillary to the standard broadcast system and thus did not see any special need to foster it. The protective concern that the FCC exercised with regard to AM stations and the public investment in AM receivers did not apply to a service considered supplementary to standard broadcasting.

As FM service began to falter in the 1950s, the Commission encouraged AM owners to take over FM operations and to duplicate their programming on these stations. Any relevant "Chain Rules" were suspended, including option time. As the FCC dropped a requirement for two hours of independent programming on FM, AM owners came to use FM as a complete duplication source which would protect AM against the risks of technical development and competition. FM became a hobbling, ancillary service, gradually taken over by AM interests.[72]

## Television

The history of television regulation highlights the failures of the FCC and again illuminates the constraints on regulatory action, once a technical and institutional structure is established. Yet television represents a different case than earlier communication services. With radio and telephony, the FCC was given charge of industries whose basic structures were already established. In the face of working radio and telephone institutions, the Commission's regulatory leeway was not very great and its conservatism was partly a function of this. Television, on the other hand, presented the Commission with a new medium unencumbered by previous operating arrangements and institutional structures, commitment to particular technical systems, or substantial public investment. And yet, the outcome of a "freer" regulatory situation eventuated in a regulation-imposed inadequate commercial television system. A three-network commercial television oligopoly was a direct result of early FCC television policy.

The Commission not only succumbed to the pressures of the industry to permit the commercialization of television, it constructed a technical system with an inadequate number of television channels for that commercial service to be truly competitive. In effect, the Commission tied its own hands in the early spectrum allocation for television. Hoping to launch television rapidly in the post-war period, the FCC established a functional, but quickly revealed inadequate structure for post-war television. Once that structure was set up the Commission found it both extremely difficult to alter and yet necessary to protect. The ongoing regulatory debacle consigned "non-standard" television technologies, such as UHF and cable television, to the economic hinterlands. The key to understanding much of American television is in the early spectrum allocation hearings.

## The Early Experimental Period in TV

The notion that it might be possible to "see by electricity" circulated among inventors after the light-sensitive properties of selenium were discovered in the 1870s. By 1925 American and British inventors succeeded in sending electrical transmissions of moving images from one place to another. In April 1927 the Bell System orchestrated two spectacular demonstrations which transmitted images over its wire facilities and over the airwaves. Soon thereafter several corporate entities began experimental television broadcasts over the airwaves, including RCA, CBS, General Electric, a company formed by the most prominent American television researcher, C. Francis Jenkins, as well as a few independent radio stations. By 1930 television was publicized as being just around the corner.[73]

Television's early history thus was pre-structured by the fact that commercial radio broadcasting and related electronics manufacturing industries (with their established technical facilities and knowledge of the radio business, relevant patent holdings, and financial capabilities) were the entities developing the technology. Moreover, at television's technical birth there existed a radio-proven economic framework for the commercial development of the new technology. Electronics manufacturers and advertisers, watching the meteoric rise of radio broadcasting and the accompanying sale of radio sets in the late 1920s, reasoned that television would prove even more popular (and more profitable). As with earlier communications technologies, the promoters waxed visionary with proclamations about the potential of television to extend human senses and broaden cultural understanding. As RCA chairman David Sarnoff declared in a 1931 speech,

> When television has fulfilled its ultimate destiny, man's sense of physical limitation will be swept away and his boundaries of sight and hearing will be the limits of the earth itself. With this may come a new horizon, a new philosophy, a new sense of freedom, and greatest of all, perhaps, a finer and broader understanding between all the peoples of the world.[74]

RCA's actions were crucial because this company became the largest, most powerful backer of television from 1935 on, when it announced a grandiose commitment to the development of the technology.[75] Prior to this announcement, RCA had put considerable energy toward convincing advertisers that television was a marvelous medium.[76] In testimony before 1940 Senate hearings on television, Sarnoff argued strongly in favor of private financing for the television industry, and against the British model of a noncommercial public corporation.[77] Given all this, the establishment of television as a *commercial* medium was nearly a forgone conclusion. Indeed, the promoters of television had petitioned the FRC to commercialize television as early as 1928. Promoters claimed even then that "a large potential audience in the (medium-wave) broadcast band is already at hand."[78] The question seems to have been not *whether* television would be commercial, but *when* it would happen.

In the early years, the Commission dodged the pressure from commercial promoters, asserting that service to the public was not yet of acceptable quality.[79] The Commission assigned television to "experimental" status, which meant that the innovation was noncommercial and without uniform standards. Experimental television broadcasting was placed primarily in the higher frequencies of the spectrum we now call the VHF. This placement was due to interference problems in lower frequencies and because there was ample room only in these higher frequencies.[80]

Though the Commission was vigilant against the commercial sponsorship of experimental television broadcasts throughout the 1930s, the language of the Commission on television matters supports a conclusion that commercialization was expected—the only real question was *when* this would be permitted. The FCC *Annual Report* of 1937 is typical. The Commission stated,

> Considerable development has taken place in both television and facsimile broadcasting during the fiscal year. Yet it is still generally conceded that neither has reached the stage of development that will permit standardization and commercialized operation.[81]

It seems noteworthy that in legitimating its decision to keep television experimental—a policy which remained constant over a 12-year period—the FCC did not voice much of a concern about commercialization *per se*. Rather, the Commission consistently defended its policy on the bases of a perceived danger of equipment obsolescence and a reticence to freeze the technology's technical development at a low level.[82] There were some who voiced dismay about the possible commercialization of television, but they were few and far between.[83]

The FCC refused to consider commercialization only until there was industry-wide agreement on technical standards. As the technology improved by the late 1930s, the pressures from the established manufacturers for commercialization became fierce.[84] Just as in the earlier history of radio, there was a pressing need to establish some stream of revenue to finance television's technical progress and program development. Commercialization represented the easiest course. Not only was commercialism a successful pattern already established by radio, it was the course supported by the developers of television.

However, the nascent television industry was riven by internal conflicts over technical standards. The newcomers to television manufacturing, including CBS, Philco, and DuMont, challenged the established manufacturers' standards. The newcomers argued that television not be frozen at the low level of standards sought by RCA and Farnsworth. Though all the industry players wanted commercialization, the newcomers fought early commercialization because such a move would freeze standards at the RCA level (and thus freeze the newcomers out because of RCA's manufacturing and patent strength). The FCC, caught amidst vituperative industry squabbling and pressure, formulated a compromise ruling which undid the historical tie between standards and commercialization.

The Commission enunciated a policy allowing "limited commercial service" on February 29, 1940, ostensibly to allow operators to recoup some of their outlays on television experiments and thus with the intention of improving the quality of programming. In so doing, the FCC chose to accept a distinction between commercialization and standardization. It would leave technical decisions to the industry. In many ways, this represented a typical FCC compromise policy. Commercialization satisfied RCA and Farnsworth, while no standards was an attempt to mollify DuMont, Philco, CBS, and Zenith. But the decision only worsened the intra-industry battles. RCA immediately initiated a widespread promotional campaign to sell receiving sets with the intention of achieving a *fait accompli* with regard to technical standards and spectrum position. If RCA could quickly capture the television set market, it would effectively present the Commission with a situation where it would be impossible to deny *de facto* recognition of RCA standards. A furious

FCC vacated its limited commercial service order and returned to the original policy of requiring the industry to agree on standards before authorizing commercial operation.[85]

Following the rebuff of RCA, the Commission acted to promote a television system having industry-wide support. With FCC prodding, a National Television Systems Committee (NTSC) was formed under the auspices of the Radio Manufacturers Association (RMA) to achieve a consensus on technical matters.[86] On April 30, 1941, the Commission promulgated rules incorporating NTSC recommendations for technical standards and spectrum allocation for television. Television was to be placed in the VHF band, with space for 18 channels, 6 megacycles wide, between 50 and 294 megacycles. There would be a 525-line picture at 30 frames per second; the audio portion of TV transmission would be FM. Again, television was situated in the higher frequencies not so much on the basis of their inherent suitability (about which little was known) but because they were the only frequencies abundantly available for television broadcasting. With the standards problem solved, commercialization could begin.[87]

The Commission's announcement of technical standards and spectrum allocation quickly was put in abeyance, as World War II put all electronic materials to military use. It must be noted, however, that the NTSC recommendations bore the heavy stamp of RCA. The now-permanent technical standards were but a slight improvement of those that RCA had attempted to secure by promotional *fait accompli* a year earlier.

## The Establishment of an Inadequate Structure for Post-War Television

There were four major, interrelated, and contentious intra-industry battles during the 1944–1948 period of the shaping of the post-war broadcast system. These included standards and spectrum allocation for post-war television, station assignment, FM radio allocation, and standards for color television. In 1944 the FCC held a long set of hearings on post-war spectrum allocation. These hearings were sparked by a jurisdictional clash between the FCC and the Interdepartmental Radio Advisory Committee (IRAC).[88] IRAC completed a spectrum allocation plan for post-war use of the spectrum, but had not formally consulted the FCC in this plan. Incensed, the FCC convened its own hearings on the post-war spectrum. It was at these hearings that the battles over post-war television were waged, and the inadequate structure of American television was established.

The old question of standards was re-run. An RCA-led coalition of manufacturers representing the heaviest investment and longest research experience (RCA, GE, Philco, and Farnsworth, this time joined by Dumont and the Don Lee Broadcasting System) argued that post-war television should be allowed to proceed with the use of pre-war standards and frequencies. Standardization, they claimed, would be the best method to obtain orderly progress, and would allow a clamoring public to enjoy the fruits of technology. The opposition, led by CBS and including Westinghouse, Zenith, Federal Telephone and Radio Corporation, and the Yankee Network, asserted that the public would be irreparably disillusioned if large numbers of receivers with the inherently low-quality standards were sold. Inferior standardization, CBS argued, would hamper practical progress. The question of standards encompassed the questions of spectrum allocation and color as well. Without impugning the stances of these corporations too severely, it is not difficult to discern that the "public" and its "interest" were brought centrally into the legitimation of policies which, in reality, stood for the particular industrial capabilities and strategies of these corporate groups at the time.

CBS set the stage for the hearing, proposing the relocation of television to the ultra high frequencies (UHF). In large part, this proposal was due to CBS's sponsorship of a high-definition mechanical color television system whose bandwidth requirements of 16 megacycles could be met only in the then uncrowded UHF portion of the spectrum. If higher quality standards were ever to be developed, CBS asserted, the time would be before post-war television commenced. The public investment of $2 million in some 7000 to 10,000 TV receivers prior to 1944 was miniscule compared to the estimated $200 million which would be spent on a million receivers within two years after the war. CBS pointed to military wartime research on UHF that would enable the company to demonstrate the new, higher-standard television system within a year.

In conjunction with the argument about technical standards, CBS criticized the placement of television in the limited VHF band. The CBS proposal asserted that if television remained in the VHF portion of the spectrum, there would not be an adequate number of channel assignments to accommodate a competitive system. CBS called for at least *30* channels in UHF.[89]

Opposing the CBS proposals was a formidable alliance of manufacturers led by RCA, which desired to start up some sort of television system immediately. The RCA alliance disputed CBS's engineering claims on mechanical color and the use of UHF. RCA's vehement support of the status quo maintained that any disruption in television's spectrum allocation or any change in technical standards would make present systems obsolete, at great harm to the public and the post-war economy. The introduction of new standards would require extensive retooling, and the delay might mean that producers of black and white television would miss out on the profits to be made from the expected post-war surge of consumer buying. Supporters of the RCA position testified that the public's enthusiasm should be exploited as soon as possible, and that television would promote employment and spur the national economy.[90]

The vehement disputation over technical matters made things difficult for the FCC. Technical matters, of course, are supposed to be objective. Luckily for the Commission, the industry's influential Radio Technical Planning Board issued a spectrum allocation report which was extremely damaging to CBS's case and supported the basic contentions of RCA and its allies. The RTPB television panel did not believe that the CBS color system was viable and saw no reason to delay commercial television. The panel recommended that television maintain present (RCA) standards, but in recognition of CBS's other argument, recommended that "every effort should be made to provide a continuous frequency spectrum of thirty channels for immediate post-war commercial monochrome television broadcast." This would include the existing channels.[91] The RTPB final report modified this somewhat, calling for 26 noncontinuous television channels in the VHF portion of the spectrum. These recommendations were legitimated by the fact that they would require a minimum of shifting of existing services, they would provide a reasonable approximation to the ideal of 30 continuous channels, and they permitted television service to begin quickly.[92] Though the RTPB also recommended experimental use of the UHF for color and/or high-definition television, the recommendations essentially reflected the RCA logic that existing standards were good and that there was no reason to delay commercial television—even if the service might find its eventual "home" higher in the spectrum.

The Commission's 1945 report on the hearings accepted much of the logic of the RTPB recommendations, but implemented only some of them because of tremendous demand for spectrum space. The FCC authorized the development of commercial television using the pre-war standards, but the Commission reduced television allocation to 13 noncontinuous VHF channels, 12 of which were to be shared with the fixed and mobile services (police and fire).[93] Also allocated was a portion of the UHF band for experimental purposes, because the Commission observed that the 12 VHF channels were inadequate for nationwide service. In a prescient statement regarding spectrum space, the Commission noted:

> The Commission is still of the opinion that there is insufficient spectrum space available below 300 megacycles to make possible a truly nation-wide and competitive television system. Such a system, if it is to be developed, must find its lodging higher up in the spectrum where more space exists and where color pictures and superior monochrome pictures can be developed through the use of wider channels.[94]

The FCC strongly intimated that television ultimately should be located entirely in the UHF band, because everyone agreed that 12 or 13 channels were not enough to foster a nationwide, competitive television service.[95] Though the Commission acknowledged the inadequacy of its spectrum allocation for television, expediency induced it to act conservatively. The Commission wanted to establish post-war commercial television quickly. It followed the report of the industry Radio Technical Planning Board that moving television out of the VHF portion of the spectrum and into the UHF was unwarranted and would unduly delay commercial television. Such a decision represented a bow toward the expedient, short-term, away from the ultimate, long-term solution, even though that short-term expediency sabotaged any possibility to implement a better long-term plan. The drawbacks of the 1945 decisions were quickly revealed. Despite its very large share of the desirable portion of the spectrum, television was faced with a potential dearth of channels in any one geographic area after the 13 channels (soon reduced to 12) were apportioned to avoid mutual interference between stations.

## The Television Freeze and the Sixth Report and Order

Commercial television did grow quickly, but soon ran into difficulties. By the end of 1948 some thirty stations were bringing television broadcast service to 17 metropolitan districts. Another 80 or so applicants had received construction permits to build stations.[96] Several companies announced plans to establish television networks. However, in the fall of 1948 the FCC faced two serious technical problems.

First, its 1945 allocation plan demonstrated grossly inadequate spacing between channels and was the source of considerable technical interference. Interference problems were exacerbated by Commission actions because, as entrepreneurs made requests for television assignments, the FCC repeatedly narrowed the mileage separations on co- and adjacent channels.[97] Second, the technical standards for color television remained unresolved. The Commission called for an engineering conference to consider revisions of its rules and standards. Pending the outcome of the conference, there would be a freeze on the processing of applications for new television stations. The famous "freeze," envisaged to last only a few months, began September 30, 1948, and extended until July 1, 1952.

The television freeze supposedly gave the Commission the opportunity to study interference and assignment problems without the pressure of continued industry growth. The situation facing the Commission from 1948–1952 was uncannily similar to the one which faced the FRC in 1927 with radio. In each period the Commission was faced with the problem of fashioning a regulatory design for an evolving and internally conflicted industry. And in each case, the industries were not yet profitable, at least partly because operating standards were not determined and because interference problems were not yet solved. The Commission's task during the television freeze was to determine a system of frequency assignments that would solve the interference problem. But other choices were imbricated in this solution, to wit, how many assignments to make and on what basis to designate such assignments. One peculiar version of *localism* constituted the conceptual basis of the assignment system.

## Localism and "Intermixture"

In a departure from the 1945 market-based plan for television assignments, the Commission issued a rulemaking in July 1949 based on *ideological* objectives. Television would be a planned, local broadcast service, to be distributed equitably among the nation's communities. The Commission envisioned a single class of TV stations (different from radio's clear channel, regional, local classifications) with coverages as uniform as power and antenna-height adjustments would allow. Each channel would be assigned directly to a specific community and reserved until an applicant appeared who was willing to use the channel to serve that community.[98] In so doing, the FCC claimed compliance with section 307 (b) of the Communications Act by providing

> . . . television service, as far as possible, to all people of the United States and to provide a fair, efficient and equitable distribution of television broadcast stations to the several states and communities.[99]

The *Sixth Report and Order,* which lifted the television freeze order, established a nation-wide, city-by-city table of television channel assignments amendable by rule making only.[100] These assignments were based on five priorities:

Priority 1: To provide at least one television service to all parts of the United States.

Priority 2: To provide each community with at least one television broadcast station.

Priority 3: To provide a choice of at least two television services to all parts of the United States.

Priority 4: To provide each community with at least two television broadcast stations.

Priority 5: Any channels which remain unassigned under the foregoing priorities will be assigned to the various communities depending on the size of the population of each community, the geographical location of such community, and the number of television services available to such community from television services located in other communities.[101]

The *Sixth Report* established that commercial television would remain principally in the VHF part of the spectrum, though it also authorized the use of UHF channels to increase the number of stations available for assignment. (This meant, of course, that, while there would be more channels for television, the UHF would no longer be reserved for a higher quality system.)

The table of assignments established by the *Sixth Report and Order* reflected incompatible policy objectives and represented another instance of the Commission's middle ground between networking and the individual station. The most glaring contradiction was that between political ideal and economic reality. Wedded to the ideal of an equitable, locally based, national television system, the *Sixth Report* reserved television assignments for communities whose population (and hence advertising base) was not large enough to support a commercial television station. At first glance, this seems a reasonable and progressive policy, for it would protect the future communications needs of small communities and prevent television from becoming purely a demand system. A closer look finds, however, that this vision of local television was a chimera at the outset, for it misunderstood the network basis of television program production and ignored simple television economics. As Edward Bowles put it,

> The off-the-cuff pronouncement that every community large enough to support a newspaper should have its local television station may be captivating, but is rational only if some interest other than the Government is willing to pay the bills. The greatest contributing factor to the growth of community television is a prosperous national enterprise in the larger markets, which will generate programs otherwise out of reach and incentive to the industry at large to cut costs. No amount of legislation, unless it be government subsidy, no mere assignment of channels to small communities, will engender local outlets. Economic support is the product of enterprise, including risk, not of regulatory fiat.[102]

As argued previously, a network offers local stations the economies of scale associated with the production of programs and the obtaining of commercial sponsorship. Conversely, the local television station provides the network with a distribution outlet. The most salient economic factor in successful commercial station operation is population density. Advertising revenues are calculated on the numbers of people watching the station's program offerings. There simply must be a mini-mum potential audience base to recoup operation costs.[103] On the network end, successful network operation requires that there be a large number of station outlets in major markets. Because of the costs of production, television was destined to become a network-based medium comprised of affiliates in major markets. The upshot of the FCC's assignment policy was a regulation-induced shortage of com-petitive television assignments in major markets.

Two factors underlay the shortage of television outlets. One was the reservation of TV frequencies to communities which could not support them (without some kind of governmental subsidy or support). Reserving frequencies meant that televi-sion channels were saved, for example, for communities in Wyoming which offered an audience of 3600. There was no possibility of such a community supporting a television station. And such reservations meant that far fewer television slots were available for the major markets which *could* support additional stations.[104] The second factor was the technical constraint of avoiding interference on co- and adjacent channels. Following the freeze, the Commission dealt with the interference problem by increasing the mileage separation between stations. This meant a fewer number of stations in the VHF band. The upshot of these two factors meant that, of the top 100 television markets, there were just 51 where the *Sixth Report* permitted more than three commercial television assignments.[105] However, even this is a deceiving statistic, because of a third factor, the policy of *intermixture*.

Intermixture meant the "mixing" of VHF and UHF services in the same broad-cast market. The intermixing of the new and as yet undeveloped UHF service with the established and operating VHF service put UHF at an immediate and continuing economic and technical competitive disadvantage. Indeed, many television manu-facturers testified that intermixture would create such a severe economic handicap for UHF that the policy would deter the construction of UHF stations. CBS took a stand against intermixture as early as 1949, noting that "UHF stations would be required to operate at a serious competitive disadvantage with the VHF sta-tions."[106] DuMont, the weakest of the nascent networks, argued powerfully against intermixture. DuMont's objections were to prove remarkably accurate. DuMont argued that UHF transmitting equipment was inferior to available VHF equipment in power and efficiency. Large, established VHF audiences would be withheld from UHF stations because of the need to install receiver adapters (hard to come by and relatively expensive) and to erect special UHF receiving antennas. The UHF signal was not received as well as the VHF signal, particularly in built-up or rough-terrain areas. In metropolitan markets, advertisers would prefer VHF stations with estab-lished audiences and would prefer networks with VHF affiliates.[107] In other words, UHF, hobbled by economic and technological handicaps, would be undermined by intermixture.

When intermixture and the UHF handicap are added to the television assignment equation, a new picture is revealed. Of those 51 markets with 3 or more assign-ments, only seven received more than three VHF assignments. Three nonintermixed UHF markets (that is, UHF only) received more than 3 television assignments. The rest were intermixed, with the UHF's unlikely to be competitively viable. This means that under the FCC's 1952 plan, there were only 10 markets in which it was technically and economically *feasible* to form and operate more than three commercial networks.[108]

Between the grandfathering of the pre-freeze VHFs, the holding of assignments for communities with small populations, and the intermixture of UHF and VHF, the *Sixth Report and Order* thus virtually assured that only two strong networks (NBC and CBS) could emerge quickly. The third network "spot" would be a fight between the less powerful emerging network organizations. Indeed, the freeze consolidated the power of NBC and CBS because most pre-freeze VHF assignments went to interests already affiliated by radio to NBC or CBS.[109] DuMont and ABC were left to fight it out over the third network position. In 1955 DuMont abandoned its national network operations, and the three-network oligopoly assumed its shape.

## Exploring the Reasons for FCC Television Policies

Intermixture and the reservation of television assignments to low-population communities resulted in an inadequate, poorly competitive, barely national television system. The reason for intermixture was the "grandfathering" of the 108 pre-freeze VHF stations *as* VHFs. In his comprehensive 1958 analysis of television allocations for the Senate Interstate and Foreign Commerce Committee, Edward L. Bowles concluded that intermixture was made *inevitable* by the *prior* decision of the FCC to maintain the 108 pre-freeze stations in their VHF slots.[110]

The Commission's dual commitment to intermixture and to reserving television frequencies to some 1200 communities underlay its rejection of two alternative assignment plans, both put forward by DuMont. The first DuMont plan provided a minimum of four equivalent channels per city in most of the 140 metropolitan districts of the nation, and reserved many UHF slots for "latecomer" broadcasters wishing to serve small communities. When it became clear the Commission supported intermixture, DuMont submitted a second assignment plan. The second DuMont plan assigned four or more VHF channels to as many of the major markets as possible. This plan centered on network competition and the number of people receiving television *service*.[111] The FCC rejected this plan primarily on the basis of localism, but also threw in a bit of technological determinism for good measure.[112] Ironically, then, it was localism combined with Commission conservatism (revealed most baldly in the reluctance to move the pre-freeze VHFs) which guaranteed a three-network oligopoly in television.

The policy of localism constitutes a lovely set of paradoxes that goes to the heart of the contradiction of mass communication in a capitalist democracy. A vague, progressive, almost Jeffersonian vision of a democratically communicating local community, localism naively assumed that local broadcast entrepreneurs would operate television stations that would "serve" the local community in the manner envisaged by the "Blue Book." In the same spirit, the Commission righteously saved television slots for communities which could not possibly support a television station. This is because in the concept of localism, the Commission held on to an older, geographically based notion of community, defining it the same for sparsely populated, geographically dispersed rural regions as for densely populated metropolises. Because the FCC's understanding of localism was not population-based, there could be no relation between television assignment policy and actual broadcast economics. Assignment policy thus again reflected that misunderstood middle ground between the chimeric hopes for the local broadcaster and the unacknowledged network-based economics of broadcasting.

## The Sabotage of UHF

Technical disadvantages, intermixture, and basic broadcast economics undermined UHF television at the outset. Television sets were not equipped to receive the UHF signal, so audiences were miniscule. UHF transmission standards at the time were inherently worse than those of VHF, and the technology generally was at least ten years behind VHF. Consequently, UHF stations had great difficulty obtaining network programming. CBS and NBC acquired VHF affiliates in most major markets. In many cases, there were *just* two VHF outlets in major markets. ABC and DuMont (with far sparser program schedules than CBS or NBC) often settled for secondary affiliation with VHFs rather than primary affiliation with UHFs. Without network affiliation it was virtually impossible to obtain any national advertising. And without national advertising no television station was able to operate at a profit. Broadcast entrepreneurs generally did not pick up UHF assignments, and those that did often went bust quickly. UHF began to fail already in the mid-1950s. By 1961, its prospects were dismal. About 100 UHF stations had gone off the air, leaving 39 operating—most at a loss. Ninety-four percent of television sets could not even receive UHF signals at this time.[113]

In the early 1950s UHF operators asked the FCC to ''deintermix'' certain markets. These operators argued that UHF-only markets might foster the successful development of UHF. The Commission routinely dismissed such petitions with little more than a reiteration of the premises of the *Sixth Report and Order*. Again, the Commission intended that its television allocations policy be a rule and difficult to amend. By the mid-1950s, however, the FCC acknowledged that the hopes of the *Sixth Report* for UHF, for a nationwide, competitive television system, had not materialized. Numerous proposals for rectifying the UHF problem were proposed by various parties throughout the 1950s. These included proposals for an expanded all-VHF system, an all-UHF system, complete or partial deintermixture, directional antennas, and various drop-in stations with shortened mileage separations. For example, ABC, struggling to gain affiliates in major markets, pressed the FCC to ''drop in'' several new VHFs, reassign unused educational reservations, and deintermix certain markets. Struggling UHFs sought complete deintermixture.[114]

The FCC entertained deintermixture in its Second Report on Deintermixture, issued in June 1956. In this report, the Commission came to the surprising conclusion that a complete shift of television to the UHF band would be the best long-range solution to the television allocation problem. In a sense, this was another of those broad policy pronouncements which likely had no real practical import. Indeed, just a year before, the FCC dismissed going to an all-UHF system as a ''drastic remedy,'' possible only if Congress itself determined such a move to be in the long-run social good. The Commission's conclusion here was very much in keeping with its traditional conception of the public interest, inasmuch as the allocation change "would involve tremendous dislocation of existing operations and have [such] a severe impact on millions of viewers."[115] Not surprisingly, then, the Commission would not entertain such a bold move in 1956 without additional research and a transition period. Notwithstanding the bold pronouncement in the Second Report on Deintermixture, the FCC set no specific future date for the conversion. (This was a serious error, for setting a date for spectrum conversion might have stimulated demand for all-channel receivers—whether or not any actual conversion would ever be carried out.) As an interim solution, the Commission declared that it would undertake a policy of selective deintermixture in certain markets.[116]

Notwithstanding widespread agreement as to the UHF debacle and the industry's problem of noncompetitiveness, the only remedies that saw light of day were an ineffectual, case-by-case FCC deintermixture policy and an unobtrusive piece of Congressional legislation that required television manufacturers to make sets capable of receiving VHF and UHF.[117] Selective deintermixture affected so few markets, so late, that the policy had virtually no effect.[118] The 1962 All-Channel Receiver Act supposedly reflected a deal between Congress, broadcast industry leaders, and the FCC. Congress would give the Commission the authority to require that all television sets sold in interstate commerce be capable of receiving UHF signals, if the FCC dropped the idea of deintermixture.[119] Such a solution would cause no costly conversion of existing stations. Moreover, the legislation could have a (indirect) positive effect on the fortunes of UHF (and, thus, greater competition in the industry as a whole) only after an entire generation of television sets was retired. It was a solution that entrenched broadcasters could live with.

With the *Sixth Report,* the FCC established a basic structure which it found nearly impossible to alter. In a very real sense, the die was cast by the *Sixth Report.* Investments were made, expectations were raised, influence blocs were established, television service was rendered. Every proposal to alleviate the UHF problem had crucial secondary drawbacks, and consequently generated opponents within and without the Commission. As such, and given the FCC's conservative understanding of its public interest mandate—to maintain and protect communications service to the public—the solution to the UHF problem was virtually a non-solution. The FCC once again was in the position of trying to secure the public interest in the context of zero-sum choices it had itself helped fabricate. True to the basic pattern, existing service would be safeguarded over any broad solution that might threaten existing service in the short run. For instance, at the same time that the Commission worried about the fate of UHF and entertained ways to save the service, it refused to stay grants of VHF construction permits in hitherto all-UHF areas, and also granted some VHF "drop-ins."[120] The effect of additional VHFs could only further damage UHF's prospects. The drop-in policy was legitimated on the pragmatic basis that some communities were not getting adequate television service. And VHF had proven its ability to provide the public with television service.

Paradoxically, the casualty of the flawed structure of broadcasting would also become part of the protected structure. Though the Commission was unwilling and/or unable to alter the existing structure of broadcasting so as to rescue UHF, it directly handicapped an emerging cable television industry in the name of UHF.

## The Sabotage of Community Antenna Television (CATV)

The UHF debacle might have induced the Commission to seek solutions to the lack of nationwide television service elsewhere. Certainly poor television service prompted the development of other options among the populace. Community antenna television (CATV, re-christened "cable TV" in the late 1960s) utilized an older technology (wire-fed communications) to retransmit local television signals in areas with poor or no over-the-air reception. CATV might have provided the Commission with new regulatory possibilities for enhancing television service. This route, however, was not taken. Originally neglected by the FCC in the 1950s, CATV was brought under restrictive regulations in the 1960s which treated the service as a bothersome supplement to conventional broadcast television. Such conservative regulatory treatment not only hampered CATV's development, it also effectively undermined any innovative use of the service to rectify some of the structural deficiencies of television broadcasting. The principal stated reason for restricting CATV was the protection of the actual and potential local (most often, UHF) broadcaster.

CATV was established originally as a service to retransmit television signals for communities generally just beyond the effective coverages of over-the-air television signals. A large antenna situated on a nearby mountain or tall building would receive two or three of the closest television stations, amplify their signals, and then feed those signals to home subscribers via coaxial cable. An alternative but somewhat similar system in rural areas of the west used a "booster" or repeater (instead of wire) to retransmit those distant signals to homes. Booster systems, however, caused interference to the originating station.

CATV thus began as but one of several industry and populist responses to the limitations caused by the *Sixth Report*. In the 1950s these and other audience-extension facilities appeared to deliver service to the approximately 20 percent of homes which could not receive television by means of normal, over-the-air delivery. CATV grew slowly but gradually, serving about 650,000 homes via 640 systems by 1960s.[121]

As retransmitters of local signals, early CATV systems were often welcomed by broadcasters because CATV expanded the local broadcast audience and enhanced potential ad revenue. This relationship changed when CATV operators began the practice of pulling in *distant* television signals through the use of microwave relay systems. The reader may recall that microwave relay is a system of broadband carriage of electronic communication by high-frequency radio waves rather than through wire. The practice of using microwave systems, approved by the FCC in 1954, permitted CATV operators more geographic mobility.[122] Previously, CATV systems mainly operated just outside the reception areas of cities. With microwave relay, CATV could move into sparsely populated areas as well. The addition of more (distant) signals elicited negative reaction from small, local broadcasters, who feared that more signals would fragment their local audiences and reduce their ad revenues. The Senate Commerce Committee's "Television Inquiry" hearings of the late 1950s served as a platform for small-market western broadcasters to launch attacks on CATV systems. The common theme was that CATV would fragment markets that were already marginal.[123] Broadcasters asked the FCC to place CATV and other "auxiliary" broadcast services under its jurisdiction.

Notwithstanding the UHF problem, the Commission viewed CATV and auxiliary services as temporary aberrations, destined to disappear as the broadcast system became more rationalized and coverage expanded. The FCC held an inquiry into the effect of auxiliary services on television broadcasting in 1959 and concluded that auxiliary services benefited the public. Such services would be permitted so long as they did not so adversely injure local stations as to jeopardize the very *existence* of the local station.[124] The Commission also indicated some reluctance to extend its regulatory jurisdiction over CATV. The FCC sought to avoid ruling on CATV in general, partly because Commissioners wanted no additional administrative duties, and partly because CATV escaped the existing regulatory "boxes" of broadcast or common carrier.[125] The Commission did, however, state its intention to ask Congress to amend the Communications Act such that it would require CATV systems to obtain the consent of broadcasters to retransmit their signals.[126]

## The Restriction of CATV in Favor of the Local Broadcaster

The 1959 Community Antenna Systems Inquiry indicated that the Commission did not wish to regulate CATV—for a variety of reasons. Not long afterward, however, the FCC reversed this policy of benign neglect. In a 1962 decision, the Commission denied the request of a microwave relay company to deliver a distant signal to a cable system on the ground that the distant signal would economically harm a local television station.[127] With *Carter Mountain,* the FCC in effect began to regulate cable indirectly, through its common carrier regulatory authority. The Commission, whose composition had changed with the Kennedy appointments, now had doubts neither about the threat that CATV posed to local broadcasters nor about its own ability to exercise controls over CATV.[128]

The Commission had two largely incompatible judicial standards by which to abide in these matters, and its shift in *Carter Mountain* reflected these. One was the *Sanders Brothers* precedent of 1940. The other was a 1958 appellate court decision in *Carroll Broadcasting Co. v. FCC.* Both of these cases dealt with the issue of competitive injury in broadcast license grants. Was the public interest best served by a large number of competing broadcast outlets operating perhaps at the margins of financial health, or was it the FCC's responsibility to make sure, given the scarcity of the spectrum, that existing stations were economically secure? The Supreme Court's decision in *Sanders Brothers* was equivocal and engendered varied interpretations for many years. The decision did hold, however, that economic injury was not an appropriate element to be taken into consideration by the FCC in determining whether to grant or withhold a license when taken as "a separate and independent element."[129] Following *Sanders Brothers,* the FCC moved toward a more pro-competitive stance vis-à-vis license grants—which may in part explain the Commission's relative neglect of CATV in the 1950s.

However, in *Carroll,* the D.C. Circuit Court of Appeals rejected this logic. The court said,

Economic injury to an existing station, while not in and of itself a matter of moment, becomes important when on the facts it spells diminution or destruction of service. At that point the element of injury ceases to be a matter of purely private concern.[130]

The Commission's logic in *Carter Mountain* reflected the reasoning enunciated in *Carroll*. The potential adverse effects of CATV on the fortunes of small broadcasters led the Commission to codify its CATV rules in 1965. At this time the Commission announced that it would treat CATV as a supplementary service, adjunct to standard television broadcast service. The FCC determined that CATV posed a threat to the local broadcaster because it competed with broadcasters in an unfair manner. To rectify this, the Commission imposed two conditions on CATV systems. One was that the CATV system must carry all local broadcast signals. The second rule was that a CATV system could not carry the programs of a distant station when these programs duplicated those of local stations during a period of fifteen days before or after the local broadcast.[131] It was the *local* nature of the conventional over-the-air broadcaster—and all the unfulfilled, but hoped-for expectations of the broadcast station as a medium of local self-expression—which the Commission thought threatened by CATV. The FCC wrote:

[If] CATV operations should drive out television broadcasting service, the public as a whole would lose far more—in free service, in service to outlying areas, in local service with local control and selection of programs—than it would gain.[132]

With the Second Report and Order in 1966, the Commission erected very restrictive regulations around CATV—this time in major markets. "Must carry" and "nonduplication" rules were extended to all CATV systems (though the length of nonduplication protection was reduced to a single day). Most important, the 1966 rules blocked further CATV development in the top 100 markets. The new rules did not permit the carriage of a distant broadcast signal into any of the top 100 markets,

. . . except upon showing made in an evidentiary hearing that such operations would be consistent with the public interest and particularly the establishment and healthy maintenance of UHF television broadcast service.[133]

This was a nearly impossible burden, for the CATV operator would have to demonstrate that distant signal importation would not harm the *potential* development of a UHF station. Thus the main reason behind this regulatory-imposed freeze on CATV development was the protection of the *potential* development of UHF.[134] UHF's best prospects were thought to lie in the major markets and the FCC did not want CATV to jeopardize this hoped-for solution to the UHF problem. The awful irony of the restrictive CATV rules is that there was no clear evidence of threat to the local broadcaster—particularly in the major markets. The FCC's own study on the effects of CATV, the Seiden Report, presented to the Commission in 1965, argued to the contrary that CATV could help, rather than hurt, UHF. CATV carriage would equalize signal reception, thereby allowing UHF to compete technically with VHF for the first time. Further, the Seiden study found no positive correlation between declining local advertising revenues and CATV competition.[135] Nevertheless, in the judgment of the Commission, the perceived threat to UHF justified, even necessitated the restrictions on CATV.[136]

The FCC continued to hamstring CATV during this time by extending the rules that had been applied to over-the-air subscription television to CATV. Pay television had always been a logical possibility, particularly for struggling UHFs searching for hard-to-find programming, audiences, and ad revenue. The FCC avoided ruling on subscription television (STV) for years, seeing it as an unknown entity—a possibly beneficial supplement to conventional television or a possibly detrimental *siphon* of quality programming from conventional or "free" television. For the most part, the latter argument won out, especially given the united opposition to STV from movie theater owners and television networks. In 1968 the Commission agreed to license subscription systems for commercial operation, but only under extremely restrictive market and anti-siphoning conditions.[137] The same anti-siphoning restrictions were applied to CATV in 1970.[138]

Given CATV's freedom from the space constraints of the broadcast spectrum (the equipment for twelve-channel capacity CATV systems was developed in the early 1960s), freedom from interference problems (and corresponding ability to provide crystal-clear reception for any signal carried on the cable), and an ability to pull in distant signals, the service posed both a potential threat and a promise to the conventional system of broadcasting. Intuitively, CATV did pose a threat to the small market broadcaster, though the empirical evidence of the magnitude of this threat was equivocal. On the other hand, it was clear that CATV benefited viewers—particularly those left out of the system established by the FCC's *Sixth Report and Order*.

Nonetheless, the Commission saw in CATV only danger to the established structure of television broadcasting. This may have been more a matter of organizational commitment to prior and traditionally conceived definitions than simply due to the pressure of the broadcast industry. Of course, industry pressure, Congressional inaction, and judicial precedent likely would buttress the traditional regulatory definitions and assumptions held by the Commission.

Organizational conservatism, then, was the key to the FCC's treatment of CATV. By declaring the service a troublesome adjunct to conventional television, the FCC was able to cling to the concept of localism and the fiction of the local broadcaster. These principles, as we have seen, underlay the entire panoply of broadcast regulations. Don Le Duc argues powerfully that in avoiding a serious look at CATV, the FCC also avoided reevaluation of such fundamental assumptions as "public interest" or "local service."[139] Such conservatism also had the effect of circumventing any revamp of the *Sixth Report and Order* and, even further, any reconsideration of the basic regulatory "boxes" of broadcast and common carrier. CATV obviously straddled such designations.

Instead, when the FCC did assume jurisdiction over CATV, it did so with the presumption that broadcasters should be protected at all costs. The fiction of the local broadcaster and the accompanying desire to promote the failing UHF service (within the established structure of the *Sixth Report*) were responsible for the regulatory restriction of CATV. Thus, the Commission missed an opportunity to harness the unique attributes of each competing technique (broadcast and CATV) in a single electronic delivery system of maximum benefit to the public. Such a goal may have been impossible, as Don Le Duc concedes, but lacking a basic understanding of the competitive elements of either service, and committed to accepted formulas and definitions, the Commission was unable even to make the attempt.[140]

The FCC's actions in the broadcast area reveal it to be a relatively weak agency with a broad, but vague mandate. That kind of mandate was typical of the single-industry regulatory agencies established during the New Deal. The mandate embodied a Congressional hope in the flexibility of the administrative process and reflected the inability of normal legislative bodies such as Congress to deal with complex, changing infrastructure industries like communications. The supposed advantage of the regulatory agency was that it sat continuously, accumulated expertise, and could exercise wise oversight over an industry by way of a unique combination of case-by-case discretionary adjudication and formal rule.

But without concretely mandated goals and responsibilities, the FCC interpreted its abstract public interest mandate pragmatically and conservatively. (Of course, it was precisely *because* Congress was ignorant of communications and created the FCC to deal with the infrastructure that it formulated no *concrete* goals in the Commission's enabling legislation.) The FCC saw its main role as the protector of communications service to the public, and enacted regulations accordingly. The agency avoided regulations whose effect might jeopardize existing communication service, and promulgated policies that took advantage of tried and true forms. In this highly constrained sense, one could say that the FCC did function in the "public interest."

This pragmatic and conservative regulatory philosophy may have been the conscious policy of some FCC Commissioners. But more likely, the approach reflected the institutional situation within which the agency operated. It represented an organizational adaptation to the many constraints the agency continually faced. The Commission operated with a limited lexicon of regulatory possibilities, given the pressures from other institutions of political power and the weight of existing, functioning systems of communication. The combination of a vague mandate and strong institutional constraints affected the FCC's case-by-case adjudication decisions in that such decisions often had no guidance by rule. Discretionary adjudication usually reflected short-run, pragmatic aims, and hence were often inconsistent. The same factors also made formal rule making difficult and time-consuming. Formal rules and policies often constituted a crystallization of difficult compromises, the result of long and complex bargaining with antagonistic regulated parties. As a result, once a formal rule was established, it generated a fixity, because it alleviated both business and regulatory uncertainty. The FCC clung to familiar definitions and formulas long after their adequacy had become ambiguous.

It is crucial to acknowledge the weight of existing communication structures in understanding Commission conservatism. With telephony and radio the FCC was given charge of commercial services, technologies, and business practices which were already in place and which worked—more or less. These services just needed some coercive state apparatus to provide a rationalizing authority over anarchic market conditions. The FCC's leeway in exercising this rationalizing function was small. As the Court argued in the *Sanders Brothers* decision, Congress basically intended "to leave competition in the business of broadcasting where it found it." Television grew up within the structures established by radio.

This is not to argue that regulation in broadcasting was either useless or represented a purely symbolic politics. The FCC may have been a relatively weak agency, but it did construct rules and structures for broadcasting, and provided a forum for industry conflicts to be worked out. In that regard, regulations, even if sometimes ill-thought-out, possessed the force of law, and therefore imposed rules onto unstable or unknown situations and provided channels for the adjudication of conflicts. They thus rendered more predictable the consequences of action in general, and economic risk-taking in particular. However, the regulatory rules and the administrative forum were rooted in, and hence facilitated, the pre-established commercial structure of the industry. As a rationalizing force, then, the FCC's overall performance is equivocal. Broadcast service was extended throughout the nation, but in a distinctly haphazard and limited fashion. Publicly the industry may have complained bitterly and constantly of regulatory interference, delay, stupidity, or cupidity. But privately the industry found that any rules were often better than none, especially since the rules were nearly always circumspect of industry discretion and profit-making.

Neither is it to argue that various Commissions did not sometimes attempt to regulate broadcasting with a genuinely broader vision of the public interest. On several occasions the FCC searched for ways to get broadcasters to provide more than just money-making programs. But the occasional attempts at regulation in the broader public interest could rarely succeed given the institutional weakness of the agency and the actual, yet unacknowledged, economics of broadcasting.

Here the Commission's policy of localism is important. The policy underscored the FCC's vague commitment to democratic communication. At the same time, localism undermined that very goal because it so misconstrued the nature of a capitalist communications system. The Commission's image of the broadcaster in the mythic haze of the small-town Jeffersonian public sphere served only to veil the actual practices and consequences of a commercially organized, national system of network broadcasting. In so doing, the FCC may have robbed itself of the available means to make broadcasting better and more diverse. As it was, the combination of the Commission's conservatism and its commitment to a chimeric localism meant that many of its well-intentioned policies either had little effect on the industry, or reinforced the power of the major broadcast players and the services they provided.

The Commission's version of the public interest was one which protected broadcasters, and which mistakenly assumed that privately operated broadcast stations would foster a genuinely free and open marketplace of ideas. Conservative regulation for the most part did avoid the evil of government censorship, but in so doing only facilitated the commerce interests of the broadcast industry and the viewpoints of station owners.

The relation between commerce-based regulation and free speech in the United States is inherently paradoxical. The commerce-based regulation of telecommunication common carriers indirectly served free speech interests, by requiring non-discriminatory access to the means of communication. Such common carrier controls also served free speech by constructing a separation between the means of communication and the content of the information which passed through the lines. Conversely, the protection provided to broadcasters under the Communications Act directly served broadcasters' commerce interests. Though subject to some (largely unenforced) FCC obligations, broadcasters were free to follow the opportunities of the commercial broadcast market. And the regulatory protection of broadcasters was thought the best means to secure public interest programming. Together, commerce-based regulation and First Amendment constraints did facilitate a marketplace of ideas, but a distinctly flawed one. The "benefits" of such regulation, combined with powerful institutional constraints, maintained a 40-year period of regulatory conservatism.

# CHAPTER
## 7
### • • •

# The Road to Regulatory Reform

The preceding chapters reveal that telecommunications, a crucial infrastructure industry for both commerce and defense, historically has been the recipient of state solicitousness, whether by way of promotion, subsidy, or regulatory oversight. The state watched over the establishment of the telegraph, providing subsidies and right-of-way privileges. The state did less for the telephone in its early years (beyond the protection afforded by patent law), but more than made up for this later in *de facto* sanction of legal monopoly and in awarding tremendously lucrative defense contracts. Radio required the command authority of the state to establish a patent pool and engineer the emergence of a private American radio company, RCA. Thereafter, the regulatory system of licensing and technical oversight helped create and maintain a three commercial-network oligopoly in television broadcasting.

We found that regulation was a conservative mode of state activity, largely protective of the established corporate interests and traditional services of the telecommunications industry. This was due in part to the legislative mandate and in part to the regulatory agency's lack of power vis-à-vis the industry, the Congress, and the courts. In the context of its institutional weakness and its vague legislative mandate to promote greater use of telecommunications, the FCC saw its role as one of safeguarding and facilitating nation-wide broadcast and telephone service. The Commission thus sought to rationalize existing communication services. Consequently, regulatory structures essentially reflected preexisting industry structures. Basic regulatory structures and formulae generally assumed a known, tried and true fixity which not only maintained communications service to the public and protected established corporate interests, but also tended to guard the organizational integrity of the Commission itself.

196

All of this notwithstanding, such regulation secured many benefits. The American telecommunications system developed in a universal manner, constantly expanding service to more people and more geographic areas and generally improving technologically at the same time. In sum, the system of regulation helped secure a well-functioning telecommunications infrastructure for commerce and defense. This general characterization largely applied to all the infrastructure industries brought under price-and-entry regulation.

The unique combination of equity and commerce-serving principles that underlay regulation produced national systems in transportation, communication, and, to a lesser degree, energy and banking, which were universal, nondiscriminatory, reliable, and largely rational. Particularly in the context of the Depression, regulation provided the stability necessary for such infrastructure industries to function. The command authority of administrative rule-making quelled "destructive" competition. The *quid pro quo* of economic stabilization was the equity-based obligation to serve and complex cross-subsidy arrangements. These were absolutely essential in the establishment of universal service.

Commercial air transport, for example, suffered from excessive competition and a scandal over Postal Service airmail subsidies in the 1930s. By establishing a cartel and requiring that all air carriers flying a certain route charge the same rates for the same class of customer, the Civil Aeronautics Board could structure airline rates to achieve both stability and larger social goals. The CAB restricted entry into the industry and essentially apportioned market shares. As part of this arrangement, the CAB subsidized short-haul flights by long-haul flight profits because short hauls were judged elastic. Short-haul flights were susceptible to destabilizing competition from other modes of transportation. CAB regulation depressed short-haul prices below their average cost in order to expand markets and ensure air transport to small communities.

The Interstate Commerce Commission pursued a similar logic with railroads and trucks. Plagued by excess capacity, corruption, and discriminatory rates, the instability of the railroad system disrupted the flow of commerce in the late 19th century. Regulation was designed to rationalize the railroad system. In the 1930s, the trucking industry was judged anarchic due to excess competition. In general, the ICC sought to stabilize those industries by cartelizing them, restricting entry, and permitting a collective setting of rates under ICC imprimatur. The ICC set rates above costs in high density lines in order to subsidize light density feeder service to shippers in small communities.

Likewise, in telephony, regulation encouraged AT&T's incorporation of competing telephone companies into one integrated network. The FCC approved the cross-subsidy of local, residential telephone rates so as to induce more and more people to connect into the nationwide telephone system. In a more skewed, but to some degree similar way, one could consider the FCC's regulatory demands ("nudges" might be the more appropriate verb) that broadcasters program in the broader, but unremunerative, public interest as the *quid pro quo* for the regulatory establishment of technical stability and the protection of traditional broadcast services.

Finally, the New Deal banking laws and oversight of the securities trade by the

Securities and Exchange Commission sought to bring stability to a financial industry whose anarchic practices were considered in part to have caused the Depression. Regulations divided financial services from areas of banking operation, and stipulated which financial institutions could engage in each. Banks agreed to limits on their operations in return for certain privileges, among which were a legal ceiling on bank interest, protection of deposits by the newly established Federal Deposit Insurance Company (FDIC), and limited entry into banking.

In other words, New Deal price-and-entry regulation stabilized infrastructure industries and greatly reduced the level of business uncertainty—both within the industries themselves and for the users who relied on their services. Regulation expanded and subsidized the growth of service markets. Thus, regulation produced real system-wide and customer group benefits. Not only were infrastructural systems universalized, but the firms that provided service were shielded from the anarchy of the marketplace. Such protection presumably freed these firms to concentrate on providing excellent service to the public. Workers in those firms were unionized and received comparatively high wages and benefits. Customers received good service relatively cheaply. Indeed, cheap service was the key to the social goal of expanding service. Yet, by the end of the 1970s, most of these systems were being dismantled through deregulation. How and why could this occur?

To the extent that we can discern a pattern to deregulation, we find that the phenomenon occurred in price-and-entry regulated infrastructure industries *only*, and for similar reasons. The reasons are, as usual, a complex mosaic of regulatory, political, economic, legal, and ideological factors. In telecommunications and banking they include technological changes as well. But rather than hide behind a multiplicity of factors theory, I suggest that deregulation is at bottom a *political* phenomenon. Deregulation is basically a story of political movement from regulatory activism to regulatory "reform."

Nonetheless, deregulation *could not have occurred* without these supporting, underlying factors. Changes in the legal conceptualization of the public interest greatly abetted the rise of regulatory activism. The same transformation of legal theory later underlay a reluctance of the courts to sanction regulation-enforced cartels and producer protection. Economic factors, particularly the inflation and productivity decline of the 1970s, are absolutely crucial as material forces behind political choices. Inflation caused the prices of regulated services to rise. In the now-politicized regulatory arena, public interest groups were often able to protect the rates of basic services at the expense of effectively increasing the internal cross-subsidies paid by large users. These factors greatly increased the incentives for large service users to bypass the regulated systems, and at the same time set in motion a new round of regulatory protectionism to prevent bypass. Inflation also accentuated the costs of business compliance to new social regulations, and the predictability of business decisions was reduced by drawn-out contentious battles over particular regulatory policies. As a consequence, by the mid-1970s regulation came to be held responsible for the fall of American economic productivity. That ideological shift was surprisingly important, especially because it underlay the changing terms in which various political elites conceptualized regulation.

Technological factors played an important role, particularly in telecommunications. New technologies enabled new business entrants to push at regulation-enforced boundaries and constituted the means by which large users could bypass the regulated system. Moreover, new communication technologies permitted financial service companies to exploit gaps in banking regulations and offer bank-like services. And, of course, regulation is at the heart of all of these changes, because it was through and in and against the traditional price-and-entry regulatory structures that these changes took shape. This chapter constructs the mosaic of the evolving political dynamic that eventuated in the general deregulation phenomenon. The piecing together begins with the regulatory activism of the Great Society period.

## Regulatory Activism: Democracy Hits the Agencies

The Great Society period was characterized by the political ascendance of groups which in many ways turned out to be hostile to capital. The decade of 1965 to 1975 was a period of extraordinary grassroots political activism, sparked by the violent unrest in the nation's cities in the early 1960s and fanned by widespread opposition to American military involvement in Vietnam as the decade wore on. Johnson Administration efforts to increase political participation and obtain public benefits for disadvantaged constituencies—particularly urban blacks—came on the heels of the Civil Rights movement and provided additional impetus to the creation of numerous grassroots political organizations.[1] Grassroots community action and minority rights organizations proliferated in the mid-1960s, joined later by New Left student protest and consumer and environmental activist groups. These generally liberal-left organizations succeeded in transforming the nation's basic political agenda. Against a backdrop of poverty and racism, decaying, polluted cities, and foreign military involvement, they brought the issues of power and the distribution of wealth directly into the political arena.[2]

These issues could not but bring into question the political power of corporations. The early Civil Rights movement targeted both corporate and governmental policies. The sit-ins and business boycotts of the early 1960s, though not directed at corporate power *per se,* aimed at alleviating some of the horrific economic conditions endured by black Americans. It may be that challenging the discriminatory practices of corporations provided one of the few avenues of political participation for groups largely cut out of the political process. Thus the sit-ins, boycotts, and shareholders' actions were as much efforts to transform the *political* agenda as they were actions to secure concrete economic gains. And they did help change the political agenda. The political activism of this period resulted in cultural and intellectual ferment, in an expansion of the welfare state, in the passage of some momentous civil rights legislation such as the Voting Rights Act and Civil Rights Act.

Under the enormous shadow of American presence in Vietnam, by the latter part of the 1960s grassroots actions against corporations often became anti-corporate *per se.* The Students for a Democratic Society spoke of an ineluctable link between American imperialism and the corporate economy. Corporations were considered as much responsible for the direction of US foreign policy as was the US government.

Throughout the 1960s and early 1970s radical groups attacked high-profile weapons producers such as Dow Chemical and Honeywell, and the banking institutions that financed the war effort, such as the Bank of America. New Left antiwar groups challenged corporate recruiters at college campuses and disrupted corporate share-holders' meetings. These protests not only attacked corporations for complicity in the war machine, but directly challenged the legitimacy of the corporate decision-making process.[3]

New Left activism helped spawn other, less overtly radical organizations that focused on different aspects of perceived corporate malfeasance. Consumer and environmental activist groups (which came to be known under the moniker, "the public interest movement") came to criticize the central role of capital in manufac-turing shoddy, often dangerous products, and in polluting the environment. The public interest groups tended to work, in the parlance of the day, "within the system." As Michael Pertschuk argues, the consumer movement consisted of mutu-ally reinforcing "political entrepreneurs" who gave voice to the changing political agenda on consumer products and corporate responsibility.[4]

Consumer and environmental activist groups aimed to pass legislation to control corporate prerogatives. Notwithstanding the left-liberal distrust of the state over Vietnam, the logic of the public interest movement was that only a strong state could serve as an effective counterweight to big business. Indeed, one aspect of the anti-big-corporation ethos of the period was an upsurge of efforts in the antitrust area. The liberal Congressmen allied with the public interest movement engineered legislation that broadened the investigative powers of the Justice Department's Antitrust division, and attempted to make large mergers more difficult. Senator Philip D. Hart, consumer advocate and self-conceived heir to the classic trust-busters, drafted sweeping legislation in 1973 (the Industrial Reorganization Act) designed to restructure some of the nation's largest industries.

In the eyes of capital, the main visible thrust of the entire period of political activism was the passage of consumer-oriented legislation and the creation of large numbers of regulatory agencies to implement that legislation. Twenty of the na-tion's 55 major regulatory agencies were established between 1964 and 1977, with the main years of activity crowded between 1967 and 1973. Unlike most previous regulatory agencies, the new agencies were trans-industrial; they had jurisdiction over all industries. Most of these new agencies were mandated to protect consumers or workers from harm consequent to corporate decisions and actions. For these reasons they are often referred to as "social" regulatory agencies.

## The "Alliance" Between Activist Groups and the Courts

Ideology, as reflected in the reigning critique of regulation, was a significant factor in this period (as it would be in the later reaction *against* regulatory activism). The public interest movement subscribed to the regulatory failure theory of regulation. In the public interest movement's eyes, traditional regulatory agencies served the needs of those they regulated. The movement proposed to remedy this situation with greater participation in the proceedings of traditional agencies and by working for the creation of new agencies legislatively designed to represent the general needs and concerns of citizens (as opposed to the narrow desires of particular industries). Increased citizen participation and vigilance, public ridicule, and media exposés might make older agencies more responsive to citizens. The public interest organizations and their leaders (Ralph Nader in particular) were masters of these tactics. The news copy they generated and the popular exposés they published on instances of regulatory and corporate malfeasance likely had more effect on the public awareness of regulatory and business behavior than any other source. Public opinion polls indicated that respect for business plummeted during the period of regulatory activism. Until the mid-1970s, business was distrusted by the public and it was on the defensive.[5]

The liberal political agenda was reflected in, and subsequently boosted by, a transformation in the judicial conception of the public interest. The expansion of "standing" before administrative agencies by two mid-1960s appellate court decisions essentially reconceptualized the "public interest" as a sort of interest representation. With the decisions in *Office of the United Church of Christ v. Federal Communications Commission* and *Scenic Hudson Preservation Conference v. Federal Power Commission*, the courts opened up regulatory proceedings to more than those parties with an economic interest.[6] No longer did the court consider parties without property interest as represented by the regulatory agency itself.[7] The conception of the regulatory agency as itself the *embodiment* of the public interest gave way to a conception of the regulatory agency as a political, quasi-legislative forum wherein competing interests would vie to define the public interest. The expansion of standing vastly enhanced the ability of the nascent public interest movement to intervene in regulatory proceedings.

The judicial transformation on the matter of regulatory standing reflected the widespread critique of the 1950s and '60s—that regulatory agencies had been captured by the industries they regulated. The judicial reconceptualization of the public interest did not simply permit regulatory participation by citizen intervenors; the reconceptualization sparked a change in the character of judicial review itself. In the aftermath of the New Deal, appellate court review of regulatory decisions for the most part had been deferential toward the administrative agencies. Adhering to the New Deal notion of the regulator as professional, expert, and objective assessor of the public interest, the reviewing courts held to a "arbitrary and capricious" model of review. This meant that so long as administrative procedures had been according to form and the policy met a minimum test of rationality, the appellate court would generally uphold the agency's decisions. Judicial review was to protect the autonomy of regulated parties (with standing) by requiring agencies to act with fidelity to congressional purpose and in accordance with the procedural norms outlined by the Administrative Procedure Act.

But given the new conception of the regulatory arena as a forum for interest representation, judicial review (particularly the District of Columbia Court of Appeals under the leadership of Judge David Bazelon) increasingly tended to consider whether regulatory decisions had accorded "adequate consideration" to all interests involved in a regulatory controversy.[8] Though the scope of judicial review was still primarily procedural, the new standard pushed the court to indirectly consider the substantive facts of regulatory decisions. In other words, in this new era of regulatory activism, not only did regulatory agencies have to listen to public interest groups, but the courts would remand regulatory decisions if those decisions did not reflect that adequate scrutiny had been accorded the new intervenors' concerns.

The structure of the newly created social regulatory agencies also reflected the earlier criticisms of regulation. The new agencies for the most part were not independent regulatory commissions. They were "line" agencies of the executive branch, led by one strong administrator, appointed or fired at the pleasure of the President, often housed in a Cabinet department. Like the independent regulatory commissions, line agencies were given the usual broad mandate (to protect the health and safety of all American workers, for example), but were also often charged with quite specific tasks, complete with timetables for their accomplishment. In theory this structure would streamline the agency and reduce the now-disparaged discretionary authority of agency administrators. Concrete mandates and "sunset" laws (where Congress set a future date to formally review an agency's enabling legislation) were enacted to tie the agency more closely to the will of the legislature. Housing the agency in the executive was designed to force the agency to be better coordinated with the actions of other agencies and be more attuned to presidential policy in general.

It should be understood, then, that the regulatory activism of the Great Society period embodied a political logic of democratic participation and political fairness—in other words, of legitimation. The new social regulatory agencies represented the concerns and values of political groups left outside of most of the regulatory politics of agencies created in earlier periods. These were the concerns— indeed, alleged *rights*—of consumers, of workers, of those citizens who experienced racial discrimination in employment and housing, of citizens who breathed air and drank water.[9]

Procedurally, the regulatory process was made more democratic and more open to public scrutiny. In addition to the crucial expansion of legal standing to citizen parties, the courts required that all information in agency files or consultants' reports be disclosed to all participants for comment, that agency decision-makers refrain from *ex parte* contacts and from communicating in secret with particular parties. Moreover, some effort was made to authorize regulatory agencies to pay the attorneys' fees and costs of rule-making participation to any group representing an interest that would not otherwise be represented in such a proceeding.[10]

The expansion of procedural fairness was in one sense the result of the courts responding to socio-political change and social activism. But in another sense, procedural fairness had been built into the regulatory process through earlier "reforms," the most important of which was the 1946 Administrative Procedure Act. Those procedural reforms, readers may recall, had been won by businesses *against* the regulatory agencies so as to rein in the discretionary authority of agency commissioners and ensure that the agencies acted in accordance with the due process rights of regulated parties. Politically, the Administrative Procedure Act was in many respects a successful effort by business to scale back the New Deal. Unable to secure *substantive* relief from New Deal policies, business gained relief through a revamp of *procedure*. In a later time period, now galvanized by citizen activism, those same due process assurances were "logically" extended to additional (citizen) parties.

## The Effects of Regulatory Activism on Rate-of-Return Regulated Firms: The "Regulatory Lag"

Public interest groups entered as vociferous participants and intervenors in numerous regulatory arenas, from broadcast license renewals to the establishment of cotton dust standards to the determination of electricity rates. Citizen intervention in areas of traditional economic regulation had significant effects, particularly because such regulatory activism coincided with important macroeconomic changes, namely, sustained high inflation.

Traditional rate regulation was rarely a matter of formal rate determination. Though AT&T may have been the extreme case, the tendency to raise or lower rates by means of informal adjustments was a pattern typical of many if not most rate-setting public utilities commissions. And because the decision-making process in formal determinations was lengthy and complex, commissions tended to institute rate changes infrequently. However, the infrequency of rate readjustment didn't much matter in the post-World War II period, because this was a time characterized by decreasing input costs, owing largely to the realization of economies of scale and technological improvements. In energy-related industries the relatively stable costs for fuel were an additional factor. If anything, the infrequency of rate adjustments until the mid-1960s favored the regulated industries, because rate adjustments were often downwards. Though this literally describes electric utilities, the essential pattern holds true for most rate-regulated industries.[11]

With airlines, for instance, the introduction of jet aircraft in the late 1950s and early 1960s greatly reduced the costs of air travel. Nonetheless, the Civil Aeronautics Board's price adjustments were very minor and clearly benefited the airlines. In this case, however, the regulated airlines did not actually pocket large profits (labeled in the economics literature, "monopoly rents") because they engaged in extensive nonprice service competition, particularly the scheduling of large numbers of additional flights. This lowered the load factor, that is, it created more flights with high percentages of empty seats. Hence the airline industry was characterized by high prices, low efficiency (with regard to load factor), excess capacity, and profits uncharacteristic of a cartel.[12]

By the late 1960s these economic factors had changed radically. This was primarily due to inflation and rising nominal interest rates. Increased capital costs and rising labor costs produced a cost-price skew, and regulated firms found they had to raise prices.[13] This triggered formal regulatory reviews. But the "technology" of rate regulation (borrowing Paul Joskow's nice term)[14] could not cope with the ever-burgeoning number of demands for rate increases. The inflationary spiral meant that firms could not be satisfied with a single rate increase, but quickly went back to the commission with another request. This situation was compounded by the price shocks consequent to the OPEC oil embargo of 1973.

Rate increase requests sparked the intervention of consumer advocates, who invoked their newly won participation rights to jump into the formerly tranquil rate-making arena. They generated a good deal of political heat and pressure on regulators to keep rates down.

Environmental activists also intervened, inasmuch as utility decisions generated a myriad of environmental externalities. Indeed, criticisms raised by public interest intervenors went to the heart of rate regulation. They effectively criticized the regulatory agencies for establishing price structures that encouraged inefficient demand growth and laxity in the evaluation of generating and transmission site alternatives.[15] Environmentalist intervenors—sometimes joined by academic economists—forced public utilities commissions to consider the concept of marginal cost in the structure of pricing outputs. The irony of the attacks on the traditional price structures was that these were the very structures which in a different economic period of time had stimulated demand and the expansion of service. In a period of rapid inflation the traditional price structures were seen to engender unwanted and inefficient demand.

The upshot of this combination of inflation, repeated requests for rate increases, and regulatory activism was a sharp increase in the time it took regulatory agencies to issue decisions. This became known as the "regulatory lag." In a period of rapid inflation, in which regulated industries lost money as they awaited regulatory decisions, firms increasingly came to consider the regulatory lag burdensome. The CAB, for instance, took four and a half years to complete its general passenger fare rate investigation in the late 1960s—years after the regulated airline industry requested rate hikes.[16] Under political pressure from public interest groups, some commissions typically granted only part of the increases requested by regulated firms. Without the ability to adjust to rapidly changing economic conditions through normal market mechanisms, rate-regulated industries experienced financial difficulties. The airline industry, for example, hit by the massive jump in fuel prices and economic recession after 1973, was in trouble. The returns on investment in airlines, trucking, railroads, and telecommunications were substantially lower in the early 1970s than they were in the early 1960s.[17]

Notwithstanding these troubles, rate-regulated industries did *not* call for the end of regulatory controls. They merely wanted the regulatory arena to be less contentious. They wanted regulators to look at their plight with more sympathy and deference. They likely wanted public interest groups banished from the regulatory arena. They wanted to resurrect the relation between regulator and regulated industry that had prevailed prior to the period of regulatory activism. This was made abundantly clear, as we will see, by the vociferous opposition most regulated firms showed to proposals for deregulation.[18] In some cases, these industries got what they wanted. The 1973 recession induced the ICC and particularly the CAB to pursue highly protectionist policies.[19] So, we find the interesting phenomenon that, though they began to suffer under regulatory constraints in the late 1960s, for the most part, firms under rate-of-return regulation did not rebel against regulation *per se*. This reaction was markedly different from that of business in general, which by the early 1970s had shed its defensive, quiescent pose. What caused capital in general to rear its head and howl mightily was "social" regulation.

## The Rise of a Corporate Counterattack

The regulatory lag affected far more than the financial fortunes of rate-regulated industries. It clung to the implementation of rules and regulations imposed by the new, social regulatory agencies as well. Parties affected by new rules—or with an interest in them, to wit, the public interest groups—would often appeal agency decisions, adding considerable delay to the time when a rule finally would go into effect. Though such delays might satisfy any number of parties in the short run, one longer range consequence was that the regulatory lag magnified entrepreneurial uncertainty. A mining firm, weighing the possibility of opening a new pit, for example, needed to know whether its plan might violate Environmental Protection Agency standards. That firm would also need to be able to calculate how much it might have to spend on OSHA-mandated safety equipment. The Mine Enforcement and Safety Administration might also have something to say. If the determination of standards were thrust back and forth between the various agencies and courts in a continuous ping-pong process of litigation and remand, the mining firm's ability to calculate costs and risks (the bottom line for business decisions) would be reduced considerably. Moreover, entrepreneurial calculability is more difficult in a period of inflation, for a presumably wise investment decision made in 1971 might be questionable by 1974 because of markedly increased costs. Partly because of this, the manipulation of the regulatory lag became a new and innovative means of imposing costs on a competitor or opponent.

In addition to increasing entrepreneurial uncertainty, regulations themselves began to entail general compliance costs on business. This, not surprisingly, was particularly true of rules issued by the new social regulatory agencies, whose jurisdictions were *trans*-industrial and whose regulations logically affected a great number of varied industries. After all, the new agencies were established to accomplish specific, concrete tasks, and they acted accordingly. In so doing, the new agencies imposed both compliance costs and new paperwork obligations on many firms. It was also the case that older trans-industrial regulatory agencies—primarily the Federal Trade Commission—were envigorated during the period of regulatory activism. The Magnuson-Moss Act of 1975 empowered the FTC with new authority, including industry-wide rule-making powers and the ability to impose civil penalties for rule violations. The FTC moved vigorously to investigate many areas of business practice. Michael Pertschuk asserts that by the mid-1970s the FTC had 30 to 40 major investigations or rule-making proceedings underway, each potentially significant for major segments of industry and each posing a threat to "crucial market strategies."[20]

Social regulation had begun to affect the degree of risk calculability. Further, businessmen began to see regulation as a kind of "creeping socialism." In their eyes, regulation was affecting the balance of power within the economic system. Business experienced regulatory-imposed paperwork obligations as onerous and authoritarian. In effect, businessmen began to see regulation as a *class* issue, where government robbed them of private prerogative and autonomy.[21] In response, they launched a counterattack.

The business counterattack against regulation consisted of several elements, the most effective of which was the reorganizing of trade associations into political lobbying organizations. Taking their cues from the public interest movement, in the early 1970s businesses increased their Washington presence and organized themselves into viable lobbying groups. Individual firms constructed *ad hoc* political alliances with other firms to lobby Congress, to file lawsuits to influence the implementation of regulatory policy, to formulate strategies to garner favorable media coverage, and to organize citizens at the grassroots level. Business Roundtable was among the most visible of the new organizations. The child of a 1972 merger of three *ad hoc* business committees, the Roundtable was established by chief executive officers of major economic institutions because it was felt that lobbying through specific trade associations was narrow and unproductive. The organization met to study selected policy issues and to develop positions and strategies. Its recommendations were then paraded in the public arena, with high-profile distribution to policy-makers and the media. Business Roundtable was described by *Business Week* in 1976 as "business' most powerful lobby in Washington."[22]

Older trade organizations breathed new life. The Chamber of Commerce took on a new gloss with a much increased membership, new leadership, and substantial budget. Former FTC Chairman Pertschuk documents the ability of organizations such as the Chamber to mobilize groups of local businessmen to write letters of complaint, or better, to visit their Congressmen. Invariably the theme was "over-regulation," and, according to Pertschuk, the complaints had a clear effect on the political agenda as perceived by legislators.[23]

Business' lobbying power, paradoxically, was enhanced by federal election campaign financing reforms of the early 1970s. Though at the time the ability to establish Political Action Committees (PACs) was a legislative victory for organized labor, by 1974 business discovered the form and thereafter business PACs abounded. The business PACs became one more weapon in the counterattack against regulation, inasmuch as they constituted a new locus for businesses to organize themselves to pursue political goals. PACs began to transform the nature of Congressional election campaigns and the amount of money made available to them.[24]

## The "Alliance" Between Corporations and Academic Economists

If the alliance between grassroots political activism and the courts fueled the public interest movement and the growth of regulation, a new alliance forged between business political activism and academic economists underlay the transformation of the political agenda *against* regulation. As early as the early 1960s some academic economists had conducted empirical studies of regulations in specific industries. Assessing the consequences of regulation within the analytical matrix of price theory, they concluded that regulation was sometimes irrational, and often was used as a means of cartel management. Two academic journals were particularly important in this scholarly movement: the *Journal of Law and Economics* (commencing publication in 1958) and the *Bell Journal of Economics and Management Science*, now the *Rand Journal of Economics and Management Science* (commencing publication in 1970). These economists had been criticizing regulation for years, but now they had an audience in business. Academic studies became part of business strategy to transform the political agenda on government regulation.

One of the ways business moved to transform the political agenda was by directly intervening in the academic realm. Conservative and right-wing think tanks such as the American Enterprise Institute for Public Policy Research and the Hoover Institution received massive corporate gifts beginning in the mid-1970s. Conservative foundations, such as the John M. Olin Foundation, directed its largesse in support of ''scholarship in the philosophy of a free society and the economics of the free market.''[25] Business money established new conservative think tanks, such as the Institute for Contemporary Studies in San Francisco in 1974 and the International Institute for Economic Research in Los Angeles in 1975. Murray Weidenbaum's pro-business Center for the Study of American Business was established with corporate donations, as were other private enterprise-oriented schools within universities. Between 30 and 40 endowed chairs for free enterprise were established in the 1970s.[26]

Corporate money funded a large number of scholarly projects that were critical of regulation. Whereas the early economic studies had concentrated on the irrationalities of rate-of-return regulation, by the mid-1970s the American Enterprise Institute (among others) was sponsoring a myriad of studies on social regulation.[27] The new studies invariably concluded that health and safety regulations countenanced the worst of both worlds—they were both ineffective and extremely costly.[28] Subsequent macroeconomic studies tried to calculate the costs of regulation to the economy. The most celebrated figure claimed that regulation cost $100 billion per year.[29] Notwithstanding the questionable underlying assumptions and the necessarily conjectural nature of such estimates (after all, the number and complexity of variables involved in such an estimate are staggering and therefore ooze with arbitrariness), these widely publicized numbers had great impact among policymakers. The studies critical of social regulation enabled business to link ''overregulation'' to the demise of the US economy. The blame for the dismal economic performance of the 1970s—high inflation, low productivity, and slow growth—was laid at regulation's door.[30] Evidence that the ideology of ''overregulation'' had begun to transform the political agenda can be seen in the early efforts at ''regulatory reform.'' In effect, the alliance between business groups which had mobilized against regulation and academic economists who lauded the benefits of free enterprise succeeded in altering the reigning political discourse on regulation.

## Regulatory Reform

In the 1960s ''regulatory reform'' meant the end of regulatory capture. In the early 1970s, ''regulatory reform'' meant reining in social regulation. Businesses, worried about social regulation generally, and particularly alarmed at the potential costs of environmental regulation, communicated their anxiety to the Nixon Commerce Department. In response, the White House instituted a review process over line agencies in 1971. Termed the ''Quality of Life Review,'' this process required interagency review of environmental, consumer protection, and other health and safety regulations prior to their publication as final rules. The review was to be carried out by the Office of Management and Budget (OMB). OMB asserted its right to review and clear regulations. In so doing, OMB raised the hackles both of agency administrators (whose authority and integrity were threatened) and of health and safety advocates (who howled that the reviews simply constituted an effort to undermine health and safety rule making). For the most part, the political heat rendered the Quality of Life Review impotent.[31]

The attempt to bring regulation under executive control was begun anew in the Ford Administration, particularly as the economy continued to deteriorate. With inflation running at about 11 percent, President Ford issued an executive order in late 1974 whose underlying logic reflected a linkage between regulation and inflation. The order required that

> . . . major proposals for legislation and for the promulgation of rules by any executive branch agency must be accompanied by a statement which certifies that the inflationary impact of the proposal has been evaluated.[32]

The Council on Wage and Price Stability (CWPS) reviewed inflation impact statements. The Council was an executive body created earlier in 1974 and staffed primarily by economists, a number of whom had published tracts critical of regulation in the academic journals. CWPS filed formal analyses of the possible economic consequences of important proposed regulations. That executive body did not repeat the high-handed tactics of Nixon's Office of Management and Budget (OMB) and thus CWPS's filings were accepted by the line agencies and Congress as a legitimate part of the entire regulatory process.

Reflecting the changing political discourse on regulation, in April 1975, Ford lambasted "unnecessary and ineffective government regulations" before the White House Conference on Domestic Inflation and Economic Affairs. He assessed the price of regulation to be on the order of $2000 per family per year.[33] That same year Ford called for the initiation of a major effort aimed at regulatory reform. He established a Domestic Council Review Group (DCRG) on Regulatory Reform (also staffed in large part by economists, notably including Paul MacAvoy). DCRG convened weekly meetings in the White House, bringing together regulatory reform proponents from the Department of Justice, Council of Economic Advisers, Office of Management and Budget, Department of Transportation, and Council on Wage and Price Stability. The Domestic Council Review Group undertook studies and set in motion agency and department initiatives on regulatory reform.[34]

Yet, I do not wish to imply that the regulatory reformers who had gained important posts in the Ford Administration were "lackeys" of business. Inflation *was* very high, and regulation seemed to play a significant role in it. Moreover, the economic critique of regulation had some validity. Clearly, as we have seen, regulation often functioned as a mode of industry protection. Indeed, by the mid- to late 1970s, the combination of inflation and the business counterattack on regulation succeeded in altering the political discourse on regulation. The Business Roundtable's *Cost of Government Regulation Study* could quote unabashed Congressional liberals, conservative economists, union presidents, and former regulators all saying that a new intelligence and pragmatism were needed in regulation.

For instance, the Business Roundtable study quoted Robert A. Georgine, president of the Building and Construction Trades Department, AFL-CIO, as saying, "Government intervention in all forms—but particularly the growing dictatorship of regulators—is one of the most serious threats faced by the American economy today." Senator Edward M. Kennedy was also quoted:

> A new pragmatism in regulation is needed. We must change the government mentality that sees regulation as the natural order of the universe, that equates the Federal Register with Holy Writ, and that believes that anything the marketplace can do, the government can do better.

Yale economist Paul MacAvoy commented on regulation's effect on the economy:

> The shift of investment from productive projects to programs mandated by regulation has cut the growth of the US gross national product by one quarter to one half of a point every year since the early 1970s.

And former FCC Commissioner Lee Loevinger was quoted on regulation and freedom:

> What the nation cannot afford, and must find ways to avoid, are the social costs of the impact of regulation on productivity, innovation, prices, and ultimately, personal freedom and democracy itself.[35]

The main efforts at regulatory reform began during the Ford Administration. President Ford's efforts, though they partook of and added fuel to the business-inspired revolt against regulation, were crucially different from those advocated by business. Underscoring the ironies of regulatory reform during the Ford Administration (Ford's occasional rhetoric aside) was the fact that the main area singled out for regulatory reform was *not* social regulation, but rather traditional, price-and-entry economic regulation.

In fact, the business counterattack against regulation achieved and continues to achieve only partial success. It managed to halt the proliferation of new agencies. In 1977 various business lobbies put together a coalition of more than 450 separate organizations and institutions to defeat a bill that would create a Consumer Protection Agency. In 1978 a similar coalition helped defeat the proposed labor law reform bill. In 1980 intense business pressure underlay a successful effort to decrease the Federal Trade Commission's authority.[36] Finally, the transformation of the political agenda on regulation meant that the principle of cost-benefit trade-off became ensconced into the consideration of new regulations. Even under President Jimmy Carter, a Democrat who expressed strong support for health and safety regulation, cost-benefit analysis became part of the review of new regulations which was centralized under his Regulatory Analysis Review Group (RARG).[37]

But business did not really succeed in rolling back social regulation. This is true even under the Reagan Administration, which came into office fairly chortling of its intention to liberate the economy from the chokehold of (social) regulation. While the Reagan Administration has cut back social regulation some, it has been able to do so only indirectly, through agency budget cuts, by the appointment of administrators hostile to regulation, and through nonenforcement. To be sure, the Reagan

Administration initiated important structural changes through which it hoped to institutionalize a rollback of social regulation. Through Executive Order No. 12291, issued February 19, 1981, Reagan centralized the review process of line agencies through the Office of Management and Budget (OMB). The line agencies are those directly under the authority of the President. The order not only required that agencies conduct cost-benefit analyses of new regulations, but gave OMB authority to interpret and review those cost-benefit analyses. This gave OMB pre-publication review of all new regulations. This, evidently, was not enough. Executive Order No. 12498 amended the earlier order to permit OMB to conduct *pre-proposal* review of regulatory activities. The standard of OMB review was not just cost-benefit, but whether any new rule was consistent with the Administration's regulatory priorities. In addition, the Reagan-sponsored Paperwork Reduction Act of 1980 reduces the recordkeeping and reporting obligations of regulated firms, thereby making the enforcement of rules more difficult.[38]

However, these actions backfired to a degree. Witness the scandal in the early 1980s over the running of the Environmental Protection Agency by Reagan appointee, Anne Gorsuch. Though it is true that the Reagan Administration has undermined *effective* social regulation through deliberate delay and inaction at the agencies (a Machinists Union official told me, for example, that the union now "expects nothing from OSHA"[39]), it must be acknowledged that all social regulatory agencies remain statutorily intact. The Reagan Administration has simply been unable to win substantive reforms. The importance of this should not be underestimated. Under a different Administration, the social regulatory agencies could quickly gear back up and pursue their mandated responsibilities. Even the Reagan Administration's efforts to secure *procedural* reforms have come to nothing. For example, proposed legislation in 1983 to streamline Nuclear Regulatory Commission procedures—which would reduce the need for trial-like procedures and eliminate the necessity for two hearings for the licensing of nuclear power plants—foundered in Congress.[40]

Beyond the matter of intact statutes, there is a reasonably clear pattern of judicial rejection of agency policy reversals and nonenforcement actions. Agency-initiated deregulation has not easily passed judicial muster. The courts have struck down much administrative deregulation of the social agencies as inconsistent with their legislative mandates and the procedural norms established by the Administrative Procedure Act. For example, in an early deregulation case called *Natural Resources Defense Council, Inc. v. EPA,* the court remanded the Environmental Protection Agency's indefinite postponement of the effective date of final amendments to certain regulations dealing with the discharge of toxic pollutants into publicly owned treatment works. The court ruled that President Reagan's executive order which prompted the postponement of the amendments did not constitute good cause to dispense with Administrative Procedure Act requirements. The court ordered EPA to reinstate all amendments. Since then the courts have rejected many more agency deregulatory actions along similar lines of reasoning. In a 1987 case, *Farmworker Justice Fund, Inc. v. Brock,* an angry Court of Appeals ordered the Secretary of Labor to issue field sanitation standards providing access to drinking water and toilets for agricultural workers. The court ruled that OSHA's long failure to issue such standards was beyond the scope of the Secretary's discretion and was unreasonable. In another 1987 case, *Union of Concerned Scientists v. Nuclear Regulatory Commission,* the court overturned a NRC regulation that required an analysis of costs as opposed to benefits in determining whether and how existing nuclear power plants should be refitted to meet the standard of adequate protection for health and safety. The court said it was illegal to apply cost factors in safety matters, according to the mandate found in the agency's enabling statute. There are many more examples of judicial rejection of agency deregulations.[41]

The court rulings underscore the historical irony of procedural reforms. If the Administrative Procedure Act wound conservatizing webs around New Deal agencies by virtue of myriad procedures, these very procedures—notably the notice and comment procedures—also have inhibited the Reagan social agencies' rollback of rules. Such procedural issues were precisely those at stake in *Natural Resources Defense Council, Inc. v. EPA,* in which the court ruled that the EPA's delays violated the Administrative Procedure Act.[42] The Supreme Court ruled in 1982 that an agency's failure to implement or enforce a clearly delineated statutory scheme is arbitrary and capricious.[43] Indeed, in one case the Court of Appeals directly acknowledged the conflict between the court's scope of review and Presidential policy:

> We recognize that a new administration may try to effectuate new philosophies that have been implicitly endorsed by the democratic process. Nonetheless, it is axiomatic that the leaders of every administration are required to adhere to the dictates of statutes that are also products of democratic decisionmaking. Unless officials of the Executive Branch can convince Congress to change the statutes they find objectionable, their duty is to implement the statutory mandates in a rational manner.[44]

The courts also have remanded deregulation actions of New Deal agencies when those actions were exercised without "reasoned decision-making." For example, in a stinging rebuke to the hell-bent, free-market orientation of the FCC, the Court of Appeals vacated the Commission's decision to abandon its commercial guidelines for children's television, arguing that the Commission offered neither facts nor analysis to defend its decision.[45]

Again, this is not to argue that passive deregulation has not occurred. Clearly it has. The Reagan Administration, particularly via its OMB review process, has achieved some success in freezing and rolling back social regulation.[46] Many agency actions of delay and nonenforcement never reach the judicial arena. And even judicial remand cannot easily compel recalcitrant agencies to enforce rules, much less issue new ones. However, between the intact nature of social agencies' statutes and the often watchful eye of reviewing courts, far less deregulation has occurred than one would expect—particularly in the area of social regulation. The social agencies are in eclipse but they have not disappeared.

Changes in the standard of judicial review make the Reagan Administration's inability to secure statutory deregulation of the social agencies important for the future. By the late 1970s, the Supreme Court began moving away from the participatory, "adequate consideration" model of regulation and returned to the model of the regulatory agency as expert arbiter of the public interest.[47] The agency once again has a high degree of discretionary authority. However, the Court also insists on greater agency deference to its legislative mandate.

In a 1984 case called *Chevron v. Natural Resources Defense Council,* the Court developed a clear-cut, two-step process for analyzing the validity of an agency's interpretation of a regulatory statute. If Congress' intent is clear, the agency has no choice but to implement it. But if the statute is silent or ambiguous, a reviewing court has a duty to respect the policy choices of the agency.[48] The effect of this new standard is to tie the social agencies even closer to the power of the President. In the short run, this may permit a conservative Reagan Administration to undertake effective deregulation by nonenforcement and "reasoned" policy reversals. In the long run, however, it means that an incoming Administration can more easily mold social regulatory policies to fit that Administration's perceived political mandate. Assuming that liberal candidates will capture the White House sometime in the near future, the fact that the Reagan Administration was unable to secure statutory deregulation will come back to haunt conservatives.

## The Deregulation of Rate-Regulated Industries

The irony which looms large in the first chapter of this book can finally be confronted. While social regulation remains statutorily intact, traditional economic regulation of infrastructure services has been substantially dismantled. How did it come to pass that with all the rhetoric about overregulation and getting the government off industry's back, the industries which came to be deregulated were those which traditionally did quite well by regulation? A related paradox confronts us. I have underscored the overall benefits of infrastructure regulation to general capitalist development, as well as how ingrained were the protectionist regulatory structures. How could these structures be dismantled? Is the institution of regulation for some reason no longer useful in addressing certain socio-economic problems?

The complex movement toward deregulation reflected changed economic and regulatory conditions and an odd coalescence of two different political logics. One was simply free market economics. The reasons for the reinvigoration of this traditional ideology lie beyond the scope of this book, as they implicate deep cultural, as well as political-economic forces.[49] Nonetheless, free market ideology appears to be a reaction intimately connected to the rise of social regulation. The ideology pervades the alliance between business, with its rhetoric about regulation's dire effect on the economy, and scholarly critics of regulation.

Yet, that alliance, although successful in transforming the political agenda on regulation, was more precarious than it seemed at first glance. Notwithstanding the broad rhetoric of "overregulation," the real preoccupation of business was social regulation. Business, generally speaking, is pragmatic, and economic regulation was mostly useful to business. In contrast, the academic economists were often ideologically committed to free enterprise—not to business pragmatism. "Regulatory reform" meant one thing to business and something different to the economists.[50]

The second political logic was the regulatory activism rooted in the leftist ideology of participatory democracy. Regulatory activism did not wilt under the business counterattack; it continued to play itself out alongside the newly ascendant political ideology of free enterprise. The lovely paradox of deregulation is that left-liberal regulatory activists and conservative free enterprisers both went after price-and-entry regulation consistent with their respective ideological frameworks. Historically pro-regulation Congressional liberals, prodded and buttressed by the public interest groups, attacked the price-and-entry regulatory agencies as prime examples of regulatory capture. The free market economists who had gained key posts in the Ford Administration, bent on regulatory reform, attacked the same agencies as examples of inept regulatory protectionism where the market was far more appropriate.

This odd concatenation of ordinarily opposed political logics underlay the wholly unexpected ability of political actors to prevail over entrenched interests in the passage of deregulation legislation. The fact that these political logics and actors clashed over *social* regulation meant that deregulation could occur only in traditional economic regulation. By the mid-1970s, the discourse of "regulatory reform," which meant different things to different people, achieved a stable definition when applied to price-and-entry regulatory agencies. It came to mean pro-competition. In other words, the transformation of the political agenda which eventuated in deregulation was *not* one which accepted business ideology hook, line, and sinker. The political agenda did register a change from an orientation toward democratic due process to one obsessed with economic efficiency and competition. But two things made this transformation paradoxical. First, rhetoric notwithstanding, competition is not necessarily what business wants. Business as a whole agitated for a rollback of social regulation, but it got the dismantling of economic regulation instead. Second, in the context of price-and-entry regulated firms in the mid-1970s, democratic due process and efficiency/competition were not necessarily opposed logics. Despite surface appearances, the deregulation juggernaut is far more ambiguous that it appears.

## Economic and Regulatory Contradictions and "Regulatory Reform"

In their fine book on deregulation, Martha Derthick and Paul J. Quirk argue convincingly that deregulation cannot be accounted for in terms of economics or an economic-based political theory. The economic theory of politics would argue that new economic conditions induce regulated parties (those with the most intense interest and power) to turn away from regulation. But, as has been indicated, with some notable exceptions (such as railroad firms and large money-center banks) it was precisely those regulated firms which fought vigorously *against* dereglation. Rather, Derthick and Quirk argue that deregulation can best be understood as a distinctly *political* phenomenon.[51] What they mean by this is that conscious political actors, armed with ideas and operating in the open political arena, were responsible for a new public policy. Not only can deregulation not be reduced to interest theories, the phenomenon directly contradicts capture theory.

While I agree with these assertions, I believe that the authors slight the fundamental economic and regulatory changes which underlay the politics of deregulation and which permitted what I have termed the concatenation of two political logics. If deregulation is a distinctly political phenomenon, it was set up by changes which exacerbated the contradictions between economic rationality and administrative rationality. The politics of deregulation, to put it crudely, had clear "material" underpinnings.

The underlying economic changes were relatively simple, if obscure. The long reign of protective regulation of infrastructure industries had worked to stabilize and universalize them. The universalization of service could be accomplished with value-of-service pricing and cross-subsidies, particularly in the context of the long period of sustained economic growth and rising incomes characteristic of the post-World War II American economy. Yet the very factors which were responsible for universalizing these services also made them expensive and inflexible to large and "specialized" users. This was particularly true in telecommunications, where large corporate users with new and sophisticated communication needs felt constrained by AT&T's offerings. It was also true in other price-and-entry regulated industries such as trucking, where large shippers found it increasingly economic to move their goods through their own truck fleets rather than via regulated truckers.

Because there was little direct relation between prices and costs in regulated services, there were built-in economic incentives for large users to bypass the regulated services with self-supply. This tendency was made worse by the consequences of regulatory activism during the period of inflation. Public interest group intervention often successfully kept the rate increases of *basic* services from rising as fast as inflation. In a fair rate of return system, where the slack had to be taken up somewhere, the cross-subsidy burden of large (generally business) users tended to increase. Again, this was most clearly true in telephone, where monthly residential service rates were kept relatively low, and the slack was taken up by increases in long-distance rates. In 1972 the methodology for determining telephone separations and settlements was revised such that long distance paid an increasingly higher percentage of local telephone plant costs.[52]

The same cross-subsidy arrangements created incentives for prospective competitors to try to enter the regulated business with a type of service designed to undercut the high prices caused by regulation and cross-subsidy arrangements. In airlines this was illustrated by the rise of charter airlines, which partially escaped the regulated system. Charters, claiming they were a completely different category of air carrier than the regulated carriers, offered air service to charter "members" under constrained conditions but at prices significantly lower than those determined by the CAB. Later, with slight liberalizations in CAB controls, the bypass incentive could be seen in the clamoring of airlines to offer cheap, minimal service or "no-frills" fares on high density coast-to-coast flights. In banking, high inflation and the low legal ceiling on interest rates produced enormous incentives for nonbank financial institutions to find a way to offer higher than legal interest rates on accounts. A fortuitous combination of new communication technologies and gaps in the banking regulatory structure permitted nonbanks to offer higher interest rates—precisely because they were not official banking institutions and could bypass existing banking regulations.

Traditionally, the regulatory agency acted to scotch any economic incentives to bypass the regulated system through protectionistic rules. The FCC was a case in point. The FCC permitted the common carriers to pull new technologies and services (such as microwave and television carriage) into the traditional regulatory formulas, and, hence, practically speaking, into the ambit of AT&T. This process held for most price-and-entry regulatory agencies. The process entailed the proliferation of regulations which made good administrative sense (in the sense of constructing a consistent set of rules which might safeguard the regulated industry structure as a whole, and which at the same time reaffirmed the basic regulatory formulas of the agency) but made questionable immediate economic sense. Trucking provides a good example of this growing contradiction between administrative and economic rationality.

About 20 percent of all intercity trucking (measured in ton-miles) is accounted for by for-hire carriers exempt from ICC regulation. These include trucks carrying agricultural products, carrying goods within special commercial zones around cities, and carrying goods intrastate. Many of these carriers are small, one-man operations. To guard against additional bypass of the regulated system, over the years the ICC enacted several highly protectionist rules. One of these was the so-called "poisoned vehicle" doctrine, which held that if a vehicle was ever used to transport nonexempt goods, it automatically lost the benefit of the exemption. Another set of rules rested in restrictive interpretations of exempted commodities. Agricultural goods which had gone through a manufacturing process, such as nuts that had been shelled or poultry that had been dressed, were adjudged by the ICC as nonexempt commodities.[53]

Most of these regulations eventually were struck down by the courts. But similar administratively rational, economically irrational rules characterized trucking, such as the so-called "backhaul" problem. Under ICC regulations, trucks were given specific licenses to carry certain types of freight only. A truck might dump its load but return home empty (a phenomenon called "deadheading") because it lacked the proper license to haul the available freight. This economically irrational practice elicited additional opprobrium during the OPEC oil embargo because of its energy-related inefficiencies. Practices such as deadheading contributed to bypass incentives. As fuel became an increasingly expensive factor in shipping by truck (wholesale fuel prices increased 160 percent during 1973–1976[54]), large companies experienced additional incentives to provide their own truck fleets. Such private fleets would be unencumbered by ICC licensing rules and presumably could realize fuel economies.[55]

In airlines, the problems of overcapacity and load factor inefficiency led the CAB to formulate additional protectionist policies in 1971. These included attempts to quash charter airlines. Between 1971 and 1975 the CAB encouraged airlines to make agreements to limit the number of flights that each would provide on particular routes. The object was to increase airline profits by limiting service competition. The CAB readily approved these "capacity-reduction agreements." The effects of the OPEC price hikes on airline fortunes found the CAB renaming these agreements "fuel-saving agreements" in 1973. This policy (and an earlier, related policy that imposed a general route moratorium) were instituted without prior hearings. The CAB's procedural improprieties would prove significant in helping galvanize Congressional interest in the CAB's substantive policies.[56]

In other words, the problems that inflation posed for rate-regulated industries during the period of regulatory activism engendered inconsistent responses from the agencies. On the one hand, the regulatory agencies often reacted by establishing additional protectionist rules with regard to entry matters. On the other hand, the politics of regulatory activism (coupled with the "regulatory lag") often pushed the agencies to allow only part of the rate increases requested by the regulated industries. The allowed rate increases sometimes magnified the traditional cross-subsidy and thus shifted a larger percentage of costs onto large users. Such users (and prospective firms which wished to service them) had even greater incentive to get outside the regulated system. This combination made rate regulation appear both protectionist *and* inefficient.

Expanded protectionism worked against economic efficiency. This had political ramifications particularly in a time of perceived decline of American economic prowess. Academic economists pounced on the contradiction. By now, the stream of academic criticism of rate regulation had grown into a river. And with the expansion of protectionist regulation, critics had a remarkably clear and salient *measure* of inefficient protectionism. In airlines, for example, the CAB's fuel-saving arrangements had indeed boosted airline profits. Because of jurisdictional rules under the Constitution, *intrastate* air travel was not subject to regulation by the CAB. The experience of non-CAB-regulated intrastate air transport in California and Texas provided a real-world counterfactual example (as opposed to an abstract economic theorem) to CAB regulation. High-density intrastate airfares in 1974 were more than twice as cheap as analogous interstate airfares. The intrastate carriers had a more efficient load factor as well. For example, the January 1975 fare for PSA's Los Angeles-San Francisco run of 338 miles was $18.75. The roughly equivalent 399 miles on the CAB-regulated run between Boston and Washington cost a passenger $41.67.[57] A less precise, but roughly similar comparison could be constructed in trucking. In the 1950s the courts added poultry to the set of commodities exempted from the requirement that carriage be via regulated trucks. As a result, prices declined for the carriage of fresh poultry on an average of 33 percent.[58]

In fact, such measures existed well *before* the regulatory-economic contradictions caused any political heat. The difference was that in the mid-1970s these contradictions awakened regulatory reformers in both the progressive and the free enterprise camps.[59]

## Congressional Hearings and Court Rulings Push the Agencies to Experiment

As Derthick and Quirk tell it, in 1974 Senator Edward Kennedy was fishing for an issue to kindle his nascent presidential bid. An aide—presumably Stephen Breyer—convinced him that the reform of airline regulation was that issue.[60] Kennedy held highly publicized, incisive, carefully formatted hearings on the drawbacks of airline regulation in his Subcommittee on Administrative Practice and Procedure. The Kennedy hearings highlighted the economic irrationalities of airline regulation, but, significantly, did so *within* the public interest movement's analytical framework of regulatory capture. Kennedy highlighted the CAB's violations of accepted norms of administrative behavior, the extensive *ex parte* contacts between commissioners and industry representatives, the fact that commissioners had been treated to "freebies" by the airlines. The hearings were used to dramatic effect, raising questions as to why the CAB's only defender was the airline industry and why the executive agencies in the Ford Administration were uniformly critical of the CAB. The Kennedy hearings effectively established that CAB regulation led to high prices and injured the public. In other words, the effective "capture" of the CAB by the industry hurt *consumers*.

Kennedy's opening statement set the tone of the hearings and framed the problem of airline regulation in a general capture theory.

> Federal regulation of transportation began in the 1880's with two objectives: First, to protect the consumer from concentrations of economic power, and second, to guarantee that essential transportation would be available to all Americans. But regulation has gone astray. What may have been good for the last quarter of the 19th century is a disaster for the last quarter of the 20th century. Either because they have become captives of regulated industries or captains of outmoded administrative agencies, regulators all too often encourage or approve unreasonably high prices, inadequate service, and anticompetitive behavior. The cost of this regulation is always passed on to the consumer. And that cost is astronomical.[61]

Kennedy also harped on a traditional aspect of liberal displeasure with regulatory agencies, and one which fit well with the "capture" frame, namely, the *ex parte* contacts between agency commissioners and regulated parties.

Notwithstanding Kennedy's consumer-oriented frame, support for regulatory reform in airlines came from many different quarters, each armed with its own ideology of regulatory reform. From the liberal left came the Nader-affiliated Aviation Consumer Action Project, whose analysts (including Nader) testified at the Kennedy hearings against CAB regulation. From the liberal center came the Consumers Union. From the right came the American Conservative Union. From business came the National Association of Manufacturers, the American Farm Bureau Federation, the National Federation of Independent Business, and Sears Roebuck. Economists from all institutional settings testified in favor of regulatory reform. On the other side, the airline industry (with the single exception of United Airlines) and its associated unions strongly opposed the movement toward deregulation.[62]

Kennedy's subcommittee had no real jurisdiction over airline regulation, but his hearings kicked the political process of deregulation into motion. The Subcommittee on Communications of the House Interstate and Foreign Commerce Committee began considering changes in the regulatory oversight of telecommunications in 1975. Similar hearings were held on banking and railroads. In 1977 the Senate Commerce Committee under Chairman Howard Cannon took up hearings on airline regulation. At the end of 1977 Kennedy, inspired by his success with airlines, directed his Subcommittee on Antitrust and Monopoly to hold hearings on trucking. Kennedy's trucking hearings pushed the Senate Commerce Committee to hold hearings in 1979.

One important consequence of the reform ferment in the legislative arena was that Congressional agitation induced the regulatory agencies to move in experimental ways. This was abetted immeasurably by implicit Presidential support of regulatory reform, demonstrated through Presidential appointments to the agencies.

For instance, after the appointment of reform-minded commissioners to the CAB (John Robson by President Ford, and economists Alfred Kahn and Elizabeth Bailey by President Carter), the Board itself acted to inject experimental doses of competition. Under Robson, the CAB relaxed its restrictions on charter operations in 1976. When Kahn took control in 1977, the CAB permitted experimental fare discounts and began to permit carriers to enter or exit a route without CAB intervention. Pursued within the bounds of existing legislation, the experiments proved successful (they resulted in cheaper airfares and did not destabilize the industry) and thus constituted an important "market test" for Congress.

Moreover, regulatory experimentation undertaken by the agencies had the consequence of undercutting effective industry opposition. As the CAB continued to pursue deregulatory policies, the airline industry's anti-reform bloc eroded, in large part because its opposition served only to prolong uncertainty about the actual terms of deregulation. By the spring of 1978, nearly all the airlines endorsed the principle of substituting market forces for regulatory controls.[63] In April 1978 the Airline Deregulation Act passed both houses by overwhelming majorities.[64]

Where the ferment in Congress gave reform-minded commissioners some leeway to experiment with competition, the courts began to play an important role in compelling parallel changes in regulatory decision-making. Again, one of the more fascinating aspects of the implicit judicial support for deregulation (or, at least, for regulatory reform) lay in the transformation of the judicial conception of the public interest—a transformation in many respects rooted in the "regulatory capture" theory. The 1970 case of *Moss v. CAB* provides a glimpse into this.

On the surface, *Moss v. CAB* is simply another case of abuse of regulatory discretion. The CAB had instituted a general fare hike in 1969 without calling it such, thus avoiding formal hearings and opportunities for comment. The District of Columbia Circuit Court of Appeals remanded the case, ruling that the CAB did not comply with public notice and hearing requirements. What is interesting for our purposes is the discursive frame constructed by Judge J. Skelly Wright:

> This appeal presents the recurring question which has plagued public regulation of industry: whether the regulatory agency is unduly oriented toward the interests of the industry it is designed to regulate, rather than the public interest it is designed to protect. Petitioners, some 32 congressmen, alleged that the Civil Aeronautics Board, in considering the lawfulness of increases in domestic passenger fares filed by all the major air lines, excluded the public from *ex parte* meetings with representatives of the air line industry and then held a *pro forma* hearing limited to oral argument, as a result of which changes in the fare structure resulting in a six per cent rise in domestic fares were unlawfully approved . . . . We hold that the procedure used by the Board is contrary to the statutory rate-making plan in that it fences the public out of the rate-making process and tends to frustrate judicial review.[65]

Note the connection drawn between public participation in regulatory proceedings and the public interest. Without that participation, regulation is a form of industry protection which is not consistent with the public interest. The decision also asserted:

While we recognize that under the statute the Board has an obligation to afford the carriers sufficient revenues, that obligation cannot become a *carte blanche* allowing the Board to deal only with the carriers and disregard the other factors, such as the traveling public's interest in the lowest possible fares and high standards of service, which are also enumerated in the Act as rate-making criteria.[66]

In *Moss v. CAB* the court merely asserted the public's interest in low fares and reminded the CAB about the manifold character of its legislative mandate. Five years later, in another case before the District of Columbia Circuit Court of Appeals, *Continential Airlines v. CAB*, the court drew an explicit link between the public's interest in low fares and economic competition. The court wrote that the Federal Aviation Act required the Board "to foster competition as a means of enhancing the development and improvement of air transportation service on routes generating sufficient traffic to support competing carriers."[67]

This ruling and others like it had an effect on the price-and-entry regulatory commissions. The Interstate Commerce Commission, which underwent a process of deregulation similar to that of the CAB, was significantly affected by an appellate court ruling in 1977. In *P.C. White Truck Line v. ICC*, the District of Columbia Circuit Court of Appeals ruled that the ICC could not deny an applicant for operating rights solely on the ground that the applicant had failed to prove the inadequacy of existing service. Rather, the ICC was required to weigh the possible benefit to the public of increased competition.[68] Following that ruling, the ICC began to ease entry procedures, to the deep chagrin of the American Trucking Association and the Teamsters.

Thus, the judicial transformation that began with the expansion of standing to public interest groups moved toward a view of the public interest which demanded that regulatory agencies consider all policy alternatives—including the benefits of competition. The "adequate consideration" model of regulatory decision-making required agencies to look closely at all alternatives. This was the court's way of ensuring that the concerns of public interest groups would be properly addressed. Ironically, the very model also provided the opening for other industry groups to challenge the regulatory status quo. This judicial evolution constituted but another piece in the changed political culture vis-à-vis economic regulation. The traditional structures of price-and-entry regulation, so appropriate and rational for decades, by the mid-1970s came under attack from ideologically diverse quarters as politically undemocratic and economically inefficient.

The basis for the attack on the traditional regulatory structures inhered in the disjuncture between administrative rationality and economic rationality consequent to regulatory activism and high inflation. To guard against bypass of the regulated system, the regulatory agencies erected ever-more-protectionist rules. Greater protectionism raised the hackles of liberal-left activists as evidence of regulatory capture. Protectionism also raised the hackles of conservative free enterprisers as evidence of government-induced economic inefficiency. The concatenation of these usually opposed political logics gave legislators and regulators the "political capital" to oppose the entrenched interests of regulated firms and their unions. And notwithstanding the business rhetoric of getting (social) regulation off the public's back—a rhetoric that was crucial in altering the prevailing political discourse—deregulation occurred in industries not targeted by such rhetoric.

The decline of the judicial conception of the regulatory agency as embodiment of the public interest may have been more than the public interest movement bargained for. By the 1980s, the courts began to rule that in some instances marketplace competition *was* the public interest, so long as the regulatory agency could defend and substantiate such a policy.[69] But before entering into that discussion, the particular story of telecommunications deregulation needs to be told.

# CHAPTER
## 8
• • •

# The Deregulation of Telecommunications

The dynamics of deregulation in telecommunications generally approximated the pattern sketched out in the previous chapter. Common carrier telecommunication was a price-and-entry regulated industry, and the economic conditions that affected the rate-regulated infrastructure industries affected telecommunications similarly. The concatenation of regulatory activism and inflation produced incentives both for large users to get outside the regulated system and for new competitors to provide new services that often escaped regulatory control. As a licensing system, the regulation of broadcasting controlled the conditions of entry. Regulatory protectionism of traditional broadcasters created incentives for prospective competitors. The overall political environment around regulation—from democratic, participatory activism to corporate counterattack to "regulatory reform"—played an important role in the ultimate deregulation of telecommunications, as it did all industries under economic regulation.

But the process of deregulation in telecommunications is unique—in four ways. First, technological innovation introduced an important factor not found in the deregulation of other industries. New technologies exacerbated the user demands to bypass the basic regulated system in the common carrier sphere. They were a crucial part of the train of events which liberalized entry into broadcasting. Indeed, new technologies in part underlay a change in the policy-oriented *discourse* about regulation. The heterodox political coalition calling for regulatory reform appeared earlier in telecommunications than in other industries.

Second, unlike trucking, railroads, banking, or airlines, the actual deregulation process in telecommunications was centered largely in the regulatory agency, not in Congress. Because of the entrepreneurial opportunities created by new technologies, the regulatory arena became an early and ongoing battleground for aspiring entrepreneurs and large users looking for better options. Early decisions in the regulatory arena permitted the entry of new entrepreneurs and, in so doing, induced AT&T to take actions which correspondingly generated serious antitrust concerns later on. Cable television long pecked at the system of regulatory protectionism in broadcasting.

Third, because of antitrust problems, the judicial system came to play a much earlier, more central role than it played in that of other industries. As a result, the deregulation of telecommunications took place in a different arena than did the deregulation of the other industries. Indeed, the ultimate arbiters in the most consequential piece of telecommunications deregulation—the breakup of AT&T—were the Justice Department and a Federal District Court judge.

Fourth, because the telecommunication infrastructure implicates not just concerns about commerce and consumer equity, but about free speech as well, the consequences of deregulation in telecommunications are perhaps more complicated and ambiguous than those in the other price-and-entry industries. This is especially true with regard to the deregulation of broadcasting. I should hasten to add that, though they share many features, common carrier deregulation and broadcast deregulation are characterized also by different forces, factors, and events. The regulatory protection of AT&T began to erode far earlier than did that of conventional broadcasters. Hence common carrier and broadcast are presented separately here, with an eye toward explaining their interrelation late in the chapter.

## The Breakup of AT&T

*Preconditions: "Here Comes Mysteryland!"* [1]

We noted in the preceding chapter that the cross-subsidized rate structures of price-and-entry regulated industries tended to create incentives for large users to bypass the regulated system. In common carrier telecommunications this incentive worked as follows. Readers will recall that value-of-service pricing and cost-averaging served two ends. They helped spread the overall cost of service and hence induced more people to hook into the network. They also alleviated the daunting regulatory task of determining a cost breakdown for individual services that often shared facilities and plant. Consequently, long-distance telephone rates were based on a nationwide charge per circuit for a given mileage. No volume discounts were available. A large user on a high-density route paid the same rate per circuit mile as did a small business in a lightly populated area. These pricing strategies combined with the historically long depreciation schedules to the benefit of AT&T and to the detriment of large users.

Rates were based on average costs of installed equipment rather than current costs of the most efficient equipment. This formula, too, was consonant with traditional telephone policy inasmuch as it helped to spread costs over time. After World War II, as Gerald Brock explains, rapid technological progress in long distance, combined with AT&T's slow depreciation of installed equipment caused

AT&T's book cost of circuit miles to be well above the level of minimum cost technology. In a competitive market, the old equipment would have suffered a capital loss as cheaper equipment became available, but in the monopoly market the old equipment could still be carried at original book values as if technological progress had not taken place.[2] This created a real economic inducement for large users to find a way out of the Bell System.

These longstanding bypass incentives were magnified by the consequences of regulatory activism of the late 1960s and early 1970s. Under pressure from consumer groups to keep residential telephone rates low, state public utilities commissioners won changes in the procedures for separations and settlements. After 1971, long distance would have to pay a greater share of non-traffic-sensitive joint costs. Because large corporations made the lion's share of long-distance calls, their telecommunication costs effectively went up—as did their incentives to bypass the Bell System.

The rate structure incentives were augmented by AT&T's inability to meet new user demands in the late 1950s. Large and new telecommunication users were generating demands for new and increased services. These demands taxed AT&T's ability to provide service. AT&T's insufficient capacity, along with the lobbying of large telecommunications users, pushed the FCC to permit the entry of new providers of "specialized" telecommunications services. The policy of liberalized entry for special service providers began completely *within* the dominant protectionist regulatory paradigm. Specialized providers were thought by the FCC to have no adverse impact on AT&T. And the FCC believed that liberalized entry might be of some indirect assistance in the ongoing, difficult problem of rate determination. But the policy of partially liberalized entry, with time, did have an impact on AT&T, inasmuch as it created small competitive markets at the borders of the AT&T monopoly. The evolving logic of regulatory liberalization and the unexpected *versatility* of technological apparatuses set in motion a process of competitors snapping at the edges of the Bell monopoly and AT&T countermeasures that rekindled the old antitrust embers.

## New Players, New Technologies

The long process of liberalized entry began with seemingly innocuous rulings on television signal carriage. As we have seen, AT&T facilities were not sufficient to meet network demands to transmit television signals to their affiliates. The FCC disallowed competitive entry in the developing market for the transmission of television signals, but because of AT&T's insufficient capacity, the Commission declined to address AT&T's argument that video interconnection should be supplied on a *monopoly* basis. The FCC authorized the operation by broadcasters of private microwave relaying facilities (the high-frequency, large-bandwidth focusable radio signals) on an interim basis, pending the availability of common carrier facilities.[3]

Television interconnection set the stage for another controversy over private line carriage. The advent of computers and the rise of digital data transfer highlighted both the shortage of AT&T (and Western Union) carriage facilities and, more crucially, the inappropriateness of terminal devices and carriage networks geared to analog voice communications for the transmission of digital data. "Analog" and "digital" refer to the mode in which information is encoded for electrical transmission. Analog-encoded information is transmitted as changes in voltage. In analog mode, like broadcasting or traditional telephony, the output signal bears a continuous relationship to the input signal. There is a continuous relation between transmission and reception. In contrast, digitally encoded information breaks information into a code of binary numbers. This code can be expressed as electrical pulses—hence the power of the computer. The operation is discontinuous; it requires no continuous relationship between transmission and reception, but it does require large bandwidth.

High-speed, error-free business data transmission was a digital and "broadband" service, that is, it required much larger carriage capacity than the telephone network normally provided for "narrowband" telephone service. Most important, data processing required unfailingly high transmission quality, because uncompensated interruptions can mean the loss of network synchronization and the garbling of signals. "Noise" creates errors. The small bandwidth and relatively noisy analog AT&T phone lines presented a problem to firms wishing to transfer large amounts of computer-generated data.

Strictly technological issues were hardly the only issues in the private line controversy. In many respects the technological issues were secondary, a smokescreen for issues of control over telecommunications prerogatives. New technologies and new economic players emerged together. Independent electronics and computer manufacturers wanted access to the lucrative new field of computer communications. New suppliers could emerge because, in contrast to the earlier years, AT&T no longer was the exclusive source of research and development in telecommunications. The massive amounts of research underwritten by the government during World War II had significant spillover effects in the post-war electronics industry. The development of microwave technology (from wartime radar research) permitted radio equipment firms to enter the telecommunications market.[4]

It is crucial to understand that the emergence of new technologies and new entrants in telecommunications was intimately tied to the World War II-established pattern of state subsidization of research and development in defense-related industries. Because the research on microwave technology was conducted under the auspices of the armed forces, there was no proprietary patent situation. The upshot of this was that AT&T no longer would be the only entity to develop and introduce communication technologies. Indeed, the microwave pattern played itself out in later important technologies. The development of satellite technology under the direction of the Department of Defense and NASA enabled large aerospace contractors to enter a now broadened telecommunications equipment market in the 1960s. Satellites were feasible only with the development of tiny, lightweight electronics components that cut down on the size and weight of the space-based relay apparatuses. Microelectronics, beginning with the transistor, was an industry that required massive government subsidies to move it through the so-called "learning curve" of technological development. That technology (or, better, complex of technologies) later became compatible with, even supplementary to, telecommunications.

In the case at hand—private line telecommunications in the late 1950s—more important than nascent entrants were the potential *users* of private line telecommunications systems. These were large corporations which sought to break the external hold AT&T held on management telecommunications prerogatives. As Dan Schiller has persuasively argued, new telecommunications needs must be seen as arising within a larger context of the pattern of post-World War II capitalist expansion. Large multi-unit and nascent transnational corporations, needing to communicate quickly with their geographically dispersed operations, experienced the slow, analog, narrowband (and, for data transmission, somewhat error-prone) Bell System as a hindrance.[5] With the 1959 *Above 890* case, the technological and economic power issues came to a head.

## Above 890 *and Interest-Group Liberalism: The Opening of Private Line Entry*

The case was formally called *In the Matter of Allocation of Microwave Frequencies in the Band Above 890 Mc.* In it the FCC established a presumption in favor of the authorization of new communication services, permitting the establishment of private transmission facilities for all private line services, including video delivery, irrespective of the availability of common carrier services. In this case, an alliance of prospective private users and manufacturers (including the Automobile Manufacturers Association, the National Retail and Dry Goods Association, the American Newspaper Publishers Association, the National Association of Manufacturers, and the Central Committee on Radio Facilities of the American Petroleum Institute) asked the FCC for permission to use the frequencies above 890 megacycles in the spectrum for special, non-common carrier microwave service. The Electronic Industries Association, representing microwave manufacturers, presented an extensive engineering study which showed that microwave service could be accommodated within spectrum constraints without generating interference problems.

AT&T, leading the opposition by the common carriers, pulled out its heavy artillery. The company asserted that the licensing of private systems would cause irreparable harm to universal service and would increase the cost of communication service to individuals, to small businessmen, and to the economy generally. Finally, AT&T warned the FCC that private systems would jeopardize common carrier readiness "in times of national emergency." According to AT&T, private microwave systems might jeopardize national security.[6]

Whether because of the lobbying power of the microwave applicants or the logic of the arguments and evidence, this time the FCC did not go along with AT&T. *Above 890* was more a victory for AT&T's opponents than a theoretical ruling on the virtues of competition. The FCC noted that the common carriers that opposed the liberalization of entry had failed to substantiate their claim that the indiscriminate authorization of private facilities would cause them substantial financial injury. Contradistinct to the Commission's usual policy in the broadcast area, the Commission declared in *Above 890* that "a finding on adverse economic effects cannot be based upon a speculative possibility of future adverse effects."[7] On the other hand, the Commission left open the possibility that future competition could be curtailed to alleviate possible economic harm to existing carriers.

Beyond the economic harm issue, the most telling reason for entry liberalization was AT&T's incapacity. The Commission noted that AT&T simply had not met the demand for private point-to-point systems. And, within this context, the FCC implicitly addressed aspects of the old Western Electric antitrust problem as well. Asserting that "the expanded eligibility will afford a competitive spur in the manufacturing of equipment and in the development of the communications art," the Commission implicitly acknowledged the problem that, as a regulated monopoly, AT&T was in the position to slow down the pace of technical innovation. The FCC noted that competition would promote innovation in both technology and services.[8]

*Above 890* revealed the two power blocs behind the liberalization of common carrier entry regulations. These were the heaviest corporate users of telecommunications and the potential competitors to AT&T in servicing those users. The efforts of these two blocs continued unabated for twenty-five years. It is they who, in the last battle, most wanted divestiture.

*Above 890* essentially permitted in one special segment of the telecommunications industry what the ICC had allowed in trucking generally—users could construct systems for their own use. The decision had little direct effect on the industry, but it had two very important indirect effects, each of which engendered a chain of unforeseen consequences. First, the delimited liberalization of entry established in *Above 890* set the stage for subsequent decisions that would open entry much more widely to other specialized telecommunications services. Second, AT&T's response to *Above 890* was to engage in practices that reawakened the old antitrust fears.

The threat of its major corporate customers building their own private systems led AT&T to institute a bulk private line discount service called "TELPAK." Spurred by charges from Western Union and Motorola (both potential suppliers of microwave equipment) that AT&T priced TELPAK rates artificially low, the FCC initiated a series of proceedings on AT&T's tariffs. The FCC did not have enough data to determine whether or not TELPAK rates covered the costs of providing the service. However, the TELPAK rate controversy was joined to a general inquiry on AT&T rate determination. Recall that in 1965, in response to pressure from the California Public Utilities Commission (and to the tremendous pique of AT&T), the FCC instituted the first formal inquiry into AT&T rates and rate base calculation procedures. These ongoing investigations later were consolidated into a proceeding known as "Docket 18128." Though in the short run the interminable FCC proceedings deterred entry and prevented antitrust challenges to TELPAK, in the long run they opened up AT&T's rates to scrutiny. In 1976 the FCC ruled that the TELPAK rates and de-averaged private line tariffs were unlawful.[9]

## Competition at the Margins: The Liberalization of Entry in Specialized Services

*Above 890* did not create a *market* for private lines; rather the decision gave corporations the possibility of creating their own internal communication systems. In fact, *Above 890* forbade joint usage of private facilities and avoided ruling on the question of interconnection between private systems and common carriers. The 1969

*MCI* decision did create a market for private lines, for it authorized the Microwave Communications, Inc. to be a specialized service provider.

In 1963 MCI, a fledgling, underfinanced company, applied for a permit to construct a microwave link between Chicago and St. Louis to meet the interoffice and interplant communications needs of small businesses. The private systems permitted by *Above 890* effectively could be built by very large users only. The MCI private line system was ostensibly more technically sophisticated, flexible, and cheaper than AT&T offerings, and, importantly, the system permitted use by small businesses because of channel sharing arrangements. The proposed MCI private line system would not connect subscribers into the telephone system local loop.

It took the FCC until 1969 to come to a decision, because of both the potential ramifications of the case and the heavy lobbying of the Bell System to deny the MCI proposal. In a 4-3 vote, the Commission approved the MCI application largely because it felt MCI could capture a latent market. In addition, the Commission had been receiving complaints from computer service companies about inadequate communications carriage. The *MCI* decision reflected those complaints. The Commission came to the conclusion that MCI offered a new service that would benefit a "segment of the population which presently can not avail itself to such a service."[10]

In some respects, the decision also reflected the influence of the environment of regulatory activism. As in the first decade of the century, AT&T's size and corporate tactics had begun to generate popular antipathy toward the corporation. It seems no accident that two popularistic, highly critical histories of the corporation, Joseph C. Goulden's *Monopoly,* and John Patrick's *Ma Bell's Millions,* emerged during this period.[11] These books and kindred articles reflected the ubiquity of the capture theory of regulation. Economic regulation generally was thought to be captured by the regulated industries. Telecommunication was no exception. MCI capitalized on this anti-big-corporation ethos, presenting itself as a tiny player under assault from the largest company in the world.[12] Nicholas Johnson, probably the most outspoken liberal on the FCC since Lawrence Fly, supported the MCI application in part out of his antipathy toward AT&T and in part due to a growing distaste for regulatory protectionism. In his concurring statement Johnson wrote:

> No one has ever suggested that Government regulation is a panacea for men's ills. It is a last resort; a patchwork remedy for the failings and special cases of the marketplace . . . . I am not satisfied with the job the FCC has been doing. And I am still looking, at this juncture, for ways to add a little salt and pepper of competition to the rather tasteless stew of regulatory protection that this Commission and Bell have cooked up.[13]

With this decision, the Commission essentially created MCI and established a competitor to the Bell System.

In the aftermath of the *MCI* decision, the FCC was inundated with requests to construct private line systems for hire. In *Specialized Common Carrier,* the FCC sought to formulate general policy. This policy favored new entry into the specialized communications (primarily data carriage) field. The FCC's logic was twofold. The primary argument continued the logic first elucidated in *Above 890,* that entrants would provide new services to customers with needs that had not been met by the established carriers. The Commission advanced a secondary, important new argument as well. The Commission declared that liberalization of entry might provide a standard of comparison to help it in the determination of rate tariffs. The decision declared:

> In an industry of the size and growing complexity of the communications common carrier industry, the entry of new carriers could provide a useful regulatory tool which would assist in achieving the statutory objective of adequate and efficient services at reasonable charges. Competition could afford some standard for comparing the performance of one carrier with another. Moreover, competitive pressure may encourage beneficial changes in AT&T's services and charges in the specialized field and stimulate counter innovation or the more rapid introduction of new technology.[14]

In other words, though the FCC did not sanction competition *per se,* by the time of *Specialized Common Carrier* the Commission availed itself of the benefits that delimited competition could provide with regard to the determination of rates.

*Specialized Common Carrier* ruled that AT&T would have to make its local telephone exchanges accessible to the new firms under reasonable terms. AT&T denied interconnection, arguing that local telephone companies were intrastate services, not subject to FCC jurisdiction. However, the FCC's position was strengthened in 1974 when the courts held that AT&T had to provide its private line service competitors with the same types of facilities that it provided to its own private line operations. AT&T responded by initiating long negotiations and permitting interconnection but imposing restrictions and tariffs on the specialized carrier companies.[15] The difficulties experienced by MCI in obtaining interconnection into the Bell System became the source of its lawsuit filed against AT&T in March 1974.

To complete the liberalization of entry in specialized services, the Commission, in a series of decisions in the mid-1970s, permitted the entry of what are known as "value-added" carriers. These were companies which proposed to lease channels from existing common carriers and attach computers and software in order to transmit data with more efficiency and less error.[16] In sum, in these decisions the FCC required AT&T to lease lines to companies that provided new services. The irony is that, ultimately, some of these services would compete with AT&T while using AT&T basic services to do so.

Though the corporate proponents of these liberalizations legitimated their policy positions on the basis of the *general* beneficence of "competition," in reality this meant freedom of choice for the very largest corporate telecommunications users.[17] And though the FCC did not authorize such liberalizations of entry on the basis of direct competition with traditional carriers, clearly this general policy was in response to heavy corporate demands for efficient computer communications. Without impugning the motives of the FCC, the Commission did not (perhaps could not) foresee the consequences of the liberalization of private line services. After all, at the time of *Specialized Common Carrier* in 1971, private line services accounted for only about 4 percent of Bell's total revenues.[18] Nonetheless, the liberalized entry into specialized telecommunication services would have significant consequences, particularly as technological developments made the distinction between "specialized" and basic services untenable.

## Domestic Satellites

In some ways, the rationale for the liberalization of private line entry underlay the so-called "Open Skies" policy for domestic satellite communications in 1972. The satellite policy, strongly advocated by the Nixon Administration, ruled that essentially any company was free to establish a satellite communications network. Like the private line liberalizations, the domestic satellite policy was both a victory for large telecommunications users *and* a regulatory reaction to some of the problems engendered by monopoly common carriage. On the one hand, the creation of a privately owned and operated satellite system amounted to a stupendous give-away to capital of the benefits of over $20 billion in publicly subsidized research and development in the space program. On the other hand, the "Open Skies" policy permitted the creation of a significant new telecommunications service largely outside the control of AT&T. AT&T was permitted to lease satellite circuits, but not to own a satellite for several years. Nor was AT&T allowed to lease satellite facilities for its commercial private line services until 1979. The FCC believed that precluding AT&T from engaging in satellite-delivered services was necessary to assure that AT&T did not foreclose entry by other firms. The FCC voiced worries that if AT&T were permitted full access to the satellite business, the company's great strength might permit it to engage in cross-subsidization and to forestall innovation.[19]

If the creation of a new telecommunications service outside of AT&T's control was the most significant consequence of the Open Skies policy, perhaps the most telling aspect of how the policy favored large telecommunications users was how it doomed a radically innovative proposal to fund the public television system. In 1965 the struggling American Broadcasting Company (in concert with Hughes Aircraft) proposed to the FCC a scheme that would allow the network to carry its own programs by means of a domestic satellite. The proposal requested authorization for a private satellite system rather than one operated by traditional common carriers. The cost of radio and television network carriage via AT&T's Long Lines was $65 million in 1965. It was estimated that a satellite could do the job for $25-30 million.[20] It is no surprise that the proposal was opposed by AT&T, Comsat, and other common carriers.

The Ford Foundation (whose largest grant recipient at the time was National Educational Television) submitted a proposal that called for a new and innovative structure for domestic satellites. Under the guidance of former CBS news executive Fred Friendly, the Ford Foundation proposed that a satellite system be operated by a non-profit organization, and the profits of satellite carriage go toward founding a *bona fide,* financially assured educational network.[21] Faced with opposition from the common carriers and prospective satellite companies, and with hesitant support from the broadcast networks, the FCC sat on the Ford proposal and put aside all of the satellite proposals "for study." The Commission returned the ABC application to the company "without prejudice." When the Nixon Administration came into office, the FCC went along with the private, open-entry approach to the satellite system.

Thus, by the early 1970s, the tenor of FCC policy had changed to some extent. Open entry in satellites was a sharp departure from traditional FCC policy. In the past, the FCC brought new telecommunication services under traditional regulatory formulas, and hence under the ambit of AT&T. This time, the Commission seemed to have bought the logic of prospective satellite service providers and the large telecommunications users that satellite services be *competitive* and that AT&T be restricted with regard to the technology. As in the case of microwave private line service, a new technology outside of Bell's control brought in new entrants, or, better put, new technologies and new entrants emerged together. In the case of satellites, the free enterprise ideology of the Nixon Administration played a crucial role in buttressing the open-entry demands of new entrepreneurs.

Clearly, the FCC no longer thought of specialized services as "peripheral" to common carrier telecommunications. Yet, regulatory protectionism did not disappear. The FCC's protection of AT&T and the common carrier system continued alongside the new policy of liberalized entry in specialized services. Indeed, the general tone of the *DOMSAT* decision was one that saw AT&T as potential predator, not as a company in danger of being hurt by a potential challenge to its monopoly. *DOMSAT* reveals an FCC promoting competition in specialized services on the one hand, and expecting to protect AT&T's traditional monopoly turf on the other.

## The "Hush-a-Phone" Precedent

What *Above 890* was to private lines, *Hush-a-Phone* was to "foreign attachments" or "terminal equipment." These are the names for the devices that terminate a telephone wire on the customer's premises. The standard telephone set is the most common terminal device. The *Hush-a-Phone* case concerned a mechanical device which could be attached to a telephone receiver. The device enabled more private conversations in crowded office conditions. AT&T had a complete prohibition against non-Bell attachments, on the ground that foreign attachments posed a threat to the technical integrity of the phone system. AT&T argued that malfunctioning foreign devices could harm the network. Bell notified distributors and users of the Hush-a-Phone device that the device violated AT&T tariffs. Whether or not this "threat" was genuine, the blanket prohibition served Bell's economic interests well. Because there was no longer any significant patent control in basic telephone equipment—particularly after the licensing provisions of the 1956 Consent Decree—the barriers to entry in the manufacture of telephone equipment were low. However, Bell was able to establish an insurmountable barrier by way of its prohibition on foreign attachments.

The Hush-a-Phone Corporation appealed the prohibition to the FCC. After a six-year delay, the FCC upheld Bell's invocation of restrictions against the device. After all, reasoned the FCC, who knew better than Bell if a device posed harm to the network? It is difficult to imagine a plastic cup-like device harming the telephone system, however, and Hush-a-Phone Corporation promptly took the case to court. The Court of Appeals reversed the FCC, finding that there was no evidence to show that the Hush-a-Phone device harmed the public telephone system. In remanding the case to the FCC, the Court of Appeals also raised the antitrust specter, seeing an inherent danger in tariff restrictions that put control over a potential competitor's business in the hands of a regulated manufacturer.[22]

*Hush-a-Phone* did little to alter the terminal equipment market, largely because AT&T's response was to allow mechanical attachments but restrict electrical ones, again on the basis of preserving the technical integrity of the telephone system. However, the *Hush-a-Phone* precedent put pressure on the FCC to rule against AT&T's restrictive tariffs on electrical attachments in the much more consequential 1968 *Carterfone* decision. The Carterfone device connected the national telephone land line system with two-way mobile radios to provide radio telephony to oil drillers located too far away from local networks. Though the *Carterfone* decision was decided on the narrow grounds that there was no showing of harm to the telephone system, the FCC also found that the device satisfied an unmet demand. Again, large users backed the liberalization of entry, including the American Petroleum Institute and the National Retail Merchants Association. Bell simply was not putting out the sophisticated terminal devices increasingly demanded by large businesses.

Lest it be thought that in *Carterfone* the FCC simply reflected the demands of the increasingly powerful organizations of large users, hard constraints pushed the Commission to liberalize entry in terminal equipment. The factually parallel *Hush-a-Phone* precedent loomed large, and the Justice Department made it known to the Commission that AT&T's tariff provisions against foreign attachments were contrary to the antitrust laws. As part of the *Carterfone* decision, the FCC ordered the common carriers to submit recommendations which would protect the telephone system against technically harmful devices, but which otherwise would allow the customer to provide his/her own terminal equipment.[23] *Carterfone* served to open the telephone attachment market generally, notwithstanding AT&T's attempt to restrict competition.

AT&T, in a move ostensibly designed to protect the integrity of the telephone system, required that all "foreign attachments" first connect to "protective coupling" devices manufactured and sold (no surprise here) only by AT&T. AT&T's actions in restricting the terminal equipment market and attaching tariffs to would-be competitors prompted those smaller companies to sue AT&T. Those AT&T actions also would constitute evidence in the Justice Department's antitrust suit. These actions seriously hurt AT&T politically as well. The company's intransigence on terminal equipment competition was based on dire, though vague technical threats. But no non-Bell manufactured device ever disrupted the network. AT&T's credibility suffered accordingly. Notwithstanding legitimate technical fears over foreign attachments, the protective coupling gambit appeared to most observers as a bald anticompetitive move by a monopoly struggling to retain total control.

## Entry Liberalization: Causes

In private lines, the FCC's rationale for liberalizing entry was tied to the idea of responding to unmet service demands from large and specialized corporate users. In foreign attachments, a combination of service demands and judicial constraints pushed the Commission in a parallel liberalizing direction. With *Hush-a-Phone,* the FCC was bound by judicial thinking which took seriously the *public utility* rationale embodied within common carrier regulation. *Hush-a-Phone* asserted "the telephone subscriber's right to reasonably use his telephone in ways which are privately beneficial without being publicly detrimental."[24] This logic seemed to resurrect a strict common law conception of common carriage, by which the carrier could have no control over how the lines would be used by patrons. Under the law that had evolved for railroads, carriers may not ask their customers to waive their rights, for these rights arise from common or statute law and not from the contract for service.[25] In this case, the separation between medium and use effectively created a market for emerging microelectronics manufacturers and equipment suppliers.[26]

In the matter of domestic satellites, open entry was the consequence of several interrelated factors, including the fear of AT&T's ability to stifle the new service and the ever-present interests of prospective entrants and large communication users. Equally important in the open-entry policy for satellites was the ideology of free enterprise manifested in a new, direct executive role in telecommunications policy. President Lyndon Johnson's Task Force on Communications Policy had called for a stronger executive role in telecommunications. This 1968 study, under the direction of Eugene Rostow, highlighted the importance of telecommunications for industry and government and called for a strengthening of policy-making capability in the Presidency.[27] Among other things, the Rostow report recommended that the FCC authorize the quasi-public satellite corporation, Comsat, to manage a pilot program for the development of a domestic satellite system. With the election of Richard Nixon in 1968 and his appointment of Dean Burch to head the FCC in 1969, the traditional common carrier approach to satellites was scrapped. Nixon's newly created Office of Telecommunications Policy (centralizing executive policy-making, as per the Rostow report) engineered the free-enterprise Open Skies policy, and, with the appointment of two more Republicans to the Commission in 1971, open entry became policy.[28]

It is essential to see that the liberalizations of private line and terminal equipment regulations—and even the open-entry policy in satellites—were undertaken *not* on the basis of a theoretical rationale which advocated head-to-head competition with AT&T. Rather, given AT&T's inability or slowness in meeting specific demands, and faced with heavy lobbying from major corporations, the FCC reasoned that new entry would mean new services which were unlikely to have any significant adverse effects on AT&T. Specialized common carriers were thought to provide *new* services and markets (primarily for large corporate users), and would tap latent but undeveloped markets for existing services. The FCC believed this would thus expand the size of the total communications market rather than take business away from AT&T. With regard to the liberalization of the terminal equipment market, the FCC was bound by judicial constraints deriving from strict interpretation of common carrier and antitrust law.

On the other hand, the FCC did promote competition *indirectly* in ways which harken back to the antitrust complaints against Western Electric. As the new ancillary products and services came into being, the FCC hoped that these could create an environment where the established carriers would be pressured to provide their specialized services at rates wholly related to costs. In other words, faced with the herculean problems of rate tariff determination in common carriage generally (problems owing to the fact that service tariff requests were largely unrelated to actual costs), the FCC saw in new service providers a possible tool for comparison.

In a very real sense, the new service providers provided too good a tool for comparison. Liberalized entry set in motion disputes over rates and the methodologies of their determination. Because some marginal telecommunication services were competitive, AT&T's non-cost-related rate determination in these markets would be the subject of increased regulatory scrutiny and competitor-initiated judicial action. Moreover, the public interest groups entered this battle, often allied for tactical purposes with the new corporate competitors. Both the public interest groups and new corporate competitors attacked AT&T's formulas and FCC complicity in the matter of basic AT&T rates.[29] In the context of disputing AT&T rate formulas, the public interest groups put heat on state public utilities commissions to deny local telephone rate increases.

## Entry Liberalization: Consequences

The consequences of these developments are tremendously complex. The regulatory decisions which liberalized entry in private lines and terminal equipment could not effectively *contain* those services. This became especially true as technological innovation blurred service lines and as the courts, moving toward a competition model of the public interest, often *widened* the scope of FCC decisions. For instance, genuine competition in the long-distance telephone market was created when the Court of Appeals reversed the FCC in the 1977 *Execunet* case. The case pivoted around MCI.

## *Judicial Activism and* Execunet

MCI offered a service in 1975 (''Execunet'') which effectively duplicated AT&T's regular message toll service, and the FCC hastily ordered MCI to eliminate the Execunet service.[30] The FCC ruled that MCI had been authorized to offer private line services only. The Court of Appeals reversed. The court ruled that once the FCC licensed a firm to provide *any* service, it could provide *every* service (with the same equipment) unless the FCC specifically focused upon, and denied it, the right to do so. The FCC had not so stipulated, and thus MCI was allowed to offer the service. The Court's reasoning is significant. The Court conceded that the FCC

> . . . did not perhaps intend to open the field of common carrier communcations generally, but its constant stress on the fact that specialized carriers would provide

new, innovative, and hitherto unheard-of communications services clearly indicates
that it had no very clear idea of precisely how far or to what services the field should be
opened.[31]

Moreover, the Court explicitly raised the question of the legitimacy of AT&T's
monopoly. The decision concluded:

> The question whether AT&T should be granted a *de jure* monopoly was not among
> those proposed to be decided in *Specialized Common Carriers,* and nowhere in that
> decision can justification be found for continuing or propagating a monopoly that,
> according to the staff, had theretofore just grown like Topsy. Of course, there may be
> very good reasons for according AT&T *de jure* freedom from competition in certain
> fields; however, one such reason is not simply that AT&T got there first.[32]

Evidence on how far the court had moved toward a new conception of the public
interest can be seen in its shift away from the 1953 decision in *FCC v. RCA
Communications.* In that case, the reader will recall, the FCC's decision to grant a
license for new trans-Atlantic radiotelephone circuits was reversed by the court. The
court rebuked the FCC for its assumption that there was a national policy in favor of
competition. In contrast, the closing sentences of the *Execunet* case state that:

> . . . the Commission must be ever mindful that, just as it is not free to create competi-
> tion for competition's sake [the reference to *FCC v. RCA*], it is not free to propogate
> monopoly for monopoly's sake. The ultimate test of industry structure in the commu-
> nications common carrier field must be the public interest, not the private financial
> interests of those who have until now enjoyed the fruits of *de facto* monopoly.[33]

The consequences of the *Execunet* decision were manifold. Microwave private
lines, computer-based terminal equipment, and domestic satellite delivery created
not only new services, but also new ways of delivering older services which had
been the sole province of the traditional common carriers. Though for years the
FCC had allowed entry into *specialized* markets, the Commission had sought to
contain entry to those markets only.[34] It was the courts which permitted head-to-
head competition in what hitherto had been regulated monopoly services. At the
same time it is worth noting the change in the regulatory environment by the time of
the *Execunet* decision. The FCC, now under the chairmanship of Carter appointee
Charles Ferris, chose not to appeal the ruling.

The opening of long distance to competition could serve only to make even
more ambiguous the boundary between regulated and competitive markets in telecommunication services. This ambiguity generated two serious interconnected consequences: competition posed a threat to AT&T's rate structure on the one hand,
and it created incentives for AT&T to engage in antitrust behavior on the other.
AT&T would try to keep competitors out of specialized telecommunications services by hindering the competitors' access to AT&T common carrier lines and by
underpricing its own offerings in these services.

As the line between computer and communications technologies became less
clear (and as these technologies became increasingly compatible, interchangeable,
and mutually supplementary), alternative delivery systems became available for
myriad uses. After all, a basic computer network essentially replicates a commu-

nications system. Computer technology replaced electromechanical devices in one of the primary areas of telephone technology, namely, switches. Sophisticated telecommunications can process data. The versatility of computer-related technology made it possible for large users to consider opting out of the Bell system partially or completely. Large users could use their private line systems for many telecommunications uses. This became officially known as the "bypass" problem. Although estimates differed as to its immediate economic impact, bypass potentially could place AT&T's internal-subsidy, average-pricing rate structure in danger. Moreover, because new carriage competitors did not have to include any of the local plant costs that AT&T had to allocate to its interstate rate base, the competitors could always undercut AT&T rates. AT&T vigorously opposed this iniquity, labeling it "cream-skimming."

## Regulatory Activism and the Ozark Plan

If *Execunet* and the versatility of technology made bypass increasingly possible, the economic incentives to get outside of the Bell System had been boosted by a 1971 change in the cost allocation methodology to determine separations and settlements. Here, again, the politics of regulatory activism spawned unforeseen consequences. State public utility commissioners (with support from public interest groups) successfully negotiated a new plan for separations and settlements in 1970. Known as the Ozark Plan, the new cost allocation methodology changed existing practices by shifting more of the recovery of non-traffic-sensitive costs from local to toll rates.[35] In other words, regulatory activism secured lower local telephone rates by increasing the percentage of monies paid to the local telephone operating companies by AT&T long distance. But private line systems and later the competing long-distance carriers did not have to include local telephone plant costs in their rates (in part because the latters' connections into the local telephone company were inferior to those of AT&T). The price differential increased the incentives for large users to opt out of AT&T's long-distance system.

Because AT&T now was just one (albeit the largest by far) of several players in a few competitive markets, it could use the guaranteed fair rate of return profits of its monopoly switched telephone service to practice "predatory pricing," or, more accurately, pricing without regard to cost, because no one knew AT&T costs. In order to prevent what it believed was destructive cream-skimming, AT&T underpriced its offerings in competitive markets. This practice, along with others designed to make difficult competitors' connection into the Bell System, led to a popular inversion of AT&T's ad jingle, "Reach out, reach out and touch someone," to "Reach out, reach out and crush someone."

## The Problem of Boundaries

These developments raised significant issues of public policy regarding the appropriate boundary between *regulated* monopoly communications activities and *unregulated* competitive data processing services. The 1956 Consent Decree constructed this boundary and declared that AT&T could be in the business of providing regulated common carrier telecommunications services only. However, this boundary was undermined by the interaction of new technologies and regulatory liberalizations. The FCC attempted to deal with this situation in the first of two "Computer Inquiries," opened in 1966. Under heavy pressure from large users, the Commission sought to segregate data processing, which was presumed to lie outside FCC jurisdiction, from regulated telecommunications.[36] But the intrinsic versatility of computerization defied regulatory compartmentalization. After all, time-sharing use of a central computer via scattered locations creates a communications system. By the time of the Second Computer Inquiry, opened in 1976, the Commission abandoned the notion of a well-defined, fixed domain of regulated monopoly service.[37]

The FCC, in the meanwhile, faced the problem of determining AT&T rate charges in a situation where, historically, charges were not cost-based. But now AT&T no longer had monopoly control over telecommunication services. Readers may recall that it was the monopoly provision of services which permitted the relatively easy non-cost-related determination of tariffs and political accommodations between carriers, regulators, and customers. The long accepted procedures of value-of-service pricing, cost-averaging, and separations and settlements depended on AT&T's monopoly provision of services.

These developments served to make the cost, price, and shared equipment problem of AT&T even more complicated and difficult to resolve. The presence of competitors forced the FCC to face the issue of cost allocation, which it did in the 1976–78 Docket 18128 proceeding. By this time, the FCC and all parties agreed that the actual costs of providing service should be the dominant criterion in rate-setting. Thus the FCC moved toward a fully distributed cost approach to the pricing of both AT&T's monopoly and competitive services. The problem was which methodology to employ in such rate determination. The methodology would determine whether, for instance, AT&T could offer private line services priced equivalent to, or even below, competitors. And the issue this raised was whether AT&T would then use its regulated monopoly profits in basic telephone to cross-subsidize its operations in competitive markets. The Commission determined that the returns from AT&T's private line services *were* in fact being cross-subsidized by its monopoly services. AT&T was ordered to file tariff rate revisions for all services in order to yield rate levels in accordance with the costing guidelines and methodologies established in its decision.[38] The problem, of course, went again to the difficulty of figuring what was what within the Bell System. As economist Leland Johnson has written, evaluating Bell's underlying costs to determine whether it is competing "fairly" was a monumental task.[39]

Such anti-competitive practices constituted the bulk of the Justice Department's suit against AT&T, filed late in November 1974, just seven months after MCI filed its private antitrust suit against AT&T. The Justice Department's suit charged AT&T with illegal methods of keeping out competitors mainly in the area of services provided to business, but also in long-distance and customer equipment. It charged that AT&T tried to thwart competition in intercity communication by refusing interconnection with the local exchanges and by engaging in predatory pricing. In fact, Justice charged that AT&T had used the regulatory process to impose costs on entrants and to give itself time to develop competitive offerings.

The 1974 suit again addressed the longstanding issue of Western Electric being the sole equipment provider to the local telephone operating companies. The suit asked for the divestiture of Western Electric and all the local operating companies.

The decision by the Department of Justice to go after AT&T in 1974 in some ways reflected the same anti-big-corporation ethos that also fed regulatory activism. After all, some of the initial soundings against AT&T had surfaced in hearings in Senator Philip Hart's Subcommittee on Antitrust and Monopoly in 1973. Hart, a liberal antitruster and consumer advocate with close ties to the Justice Department's Antitrust Division professionals, had introduced legislation in 1973 (the Industrial Reorganization Act) designed to restructure some of the nation's largest industries. Antitrust actions against large corporations fit well with the concerns of the liberal consumer movement. At the same time, Justice's lawsuit against AT&T also may have reflected internal professional desires within the Department to exorcise the scandal that had tainted it with the 1956 Consent Decree. A secret 1973 internal Antitrust Division reappraisal of the Western Electric problem lends some credence to this.[40]

Together, entry liberalizations and boundary ambiguities had significant consequences for AT&T. By the 1970s, the company faced what it considered an untenable state of affairs. The most lucrative fields of the telecommunications business—terminal equipment, private lines, data communications—were becoming increasingly competitive. The 1956 Consent Decree prevented AT&T from entering the growing field of data processing. At the same time, the politics of regulatory activism of the early 1970s meant that Bell Operating Companies were receiving only part of the rate increases requested for local switched telephone service. And because the percentage of long-distance subsidy to local service increased with the Ozark Plan, and emerging long-distance competitors could undercut AT&T rates, AT&T could only foresee gradual loss of long-distance customers. The boundary issue primarily and the rate structure issue begged for a dramatic solution, especially as they increasingly called into question the relevance of the regulatory formulae which defined the life of AT&T. The major corporate users also were quite concerned with the boundary issue, as they feared that the regulatory quagmire could bring specialized services and data processing under greater regulatory supervision. At the same time, major corporate users were concerned over the possible degradation of the basic switched network system.[41]

But if these factors "forced" a restructuring of common carrier telecommunications, they did not determine the *actual* restructuring. That determination is found in the policy arena. In a sense, the long process of regulatory change constituted the preconditions necessary for the emergence of a new forum for policy-making in telecommunications.

## The Politics of Divestiture

The FCC, having inadvertently set in motion a process of liberalized entry at the margins of the AT&T monopoly, saw the process escape its control and recognized that the "margins" had become central. Liberalized entry allowed the large users and new competitors an opening through which service demands attained a coherence outside of AT&T-controlled options. Together, large users and new competitors began to affect the Commission's historic protection of AT&T. To some extent with the 1972 domestic satellite policy, and certainly by the mid-1970s, the FCC adapted itself (hesitantly and sometimes inconsistently) to the movement toward change in common carrier communications. When, in 1973, AT&T Chairman John deButts called upon the FCC to institute "a moratorium" on what he termed "further experiments in economics," the Commission flatly refused.[42] In 1976, when AT&T made a bid for legislation that would restore monopoly to common carrier communications, the FCC publicly opposed the legislation.[43]

Just as Civil Aeronautics Board regulatory experiments in competition in airlines performed a market test for Congress, so FCC entry liberalizations posed such a test for the executive. The Carter Administration National Telecommunications and Information Administration, under Henry Geller, argued publicly for wide-open entry. In 1977 President Carter appointed a reform-minded chairman to the FCC. Charles Ferris, like Alfred Kahn at the CAB, expanded the role of economists in FCC policy-making.[44] Perhaps the crowning piece of anti-protectionist FCC policy was the Second Computer Inquiry. Begun in 1976, that policy pointedly retreated from traditional public utility regulation and moved toward pro-competitive deregulation. Indeed, in 1979 both Chairman Ferris and Common Carrier Bureau Chief Verveer suggested publicly that AT&T should be broken up.[45] The liberal agenda against regulatory protectionism—ensconced within its own political logic—by the late 1970s coalesced with the agenda of new entrepreneurial entrants and large users of telecommunications services.

Finding itself losing battles with the FCC and with the Court of Appeals in the matter of safeguarding its monopoly, by the mid-1970s AT&T turned to Congress to preserve as much of its dominance in telecommunications common carriage as possible. This was embodied in a 1976 bill called the Consumer Communications Reform Act, which was so pro-AT&T that it came to be known as the "Bell Bill." This bill was the last hurrah of the traditionally constituted Bill *System,* and fittingly was directed by traditionalist AT&T Chairman John deButts. DeButts stridently defended the traditional monopoly and the common carrier principle. The Consumer Communications Reform Act would have restored to AT&T both the long-distance monopoly and a monopoly of telephone equipment markets.[46]

However, the move toward Congress backfired, and the bill failed. AT&T's ferocious lobbying antagonized many Congressmen.[47] The emerging "culture" of deregulation caused many to question AT&T's representation of the issues. This questioning was encouraged by the fact that large corporations, noted economists, citizens groups such as Congress Watch and the Consumer Federation of America, and often the FCC argued against AT&T.[48] In many instances Bell data and projections could not be justified. Moreover, the bid to restore a monopoly in telephone equipment was ludicrous. That market was already effectively competitive, and Bell's insistence on monopolizing it looked very bad. Again, like airlines and trucking, the coalition which opposed AT&T was strikingly heterogeneous politically. And again, true to the general pattern of the politics of deregulation, the only major entity to support the traditional status quo was the regulated industry itself. On the other hand, the issues in telecommunications were so complex, the stakes so high, and AT&T's power so sufficient, that, unlike deregulation in other areas, Congressional legislation to deregulate telecommunications was stymied.

The issues first posed in the Consumer Communications Reform Act were taken up in subsequent Congressional attempts to rewrite the Communications Act—in ways not always to AT&T's liking. The first version of the rewrite would have forced AT&T to divest itself of Western Electric in exchange for permission to enter the computer and data processing fields. By the late 1970s, many other players possessing conflicting agendas, and large numbers of experts armed with competing testimony, were part of the relatively open Congressional policy-making arena.

By 1977 the Congressional deregulatory environment that had upended the treatment of airlines and trucking began to affect telecommunications as well. In April 1977 the House Communications Subcommittee released a document called *The Options Papers*. The *Options Papers* covered the whole range of telecommunications issues, from broadcasting to common carriers to cable, and outlined policy options for each. The status quo was treated as just one option among several reasonable alternatives.[49] The importance of the *Options Papers,* among other things, was that they indicated that telecommunications policy was in flux at all levels of policy-making. Notwithstanding its enormous lobbying power, the legislative arena could not be stage-managed by AT&T. Indeed, in a time of deregulatory fever, the relatively open legislative arena posed real dangers to AT&T.

The 1974 antitrust suit, passed on to the Reagan Administration Department of Justice, eventually became the one policy arena where AT&T could exercise its voice and be heard. In fact, the forum established by the lawsuit had been used twice to explore the terms of a possible settlement between the Department of Justice and AT&T, once in the fall of 1979 and another in late 1980. The terms of these settlement explorations required AT&T to divest itself of three Bell Operating Companies, to spin off some 40 percent of Western Electric assets, and to establish a framework for equal interconnection of competing long-distance carriers into the local exchanges. AT&T agreed to these basic provisions, but both settlement efforts fell through.[50]

The Reagan Administration did not want divestiture. Indeed, during the 1980 campaign candidate Reagan had said the government's suit was a mistake. For Reagan's people, the suit against AT&T constituted another grievous instance of big government riding roughshod over business. The new Administration convened a working group on telecommunications composed of the Departments of Agriculture, Defense, Commerce, and Energy, and the Federal Energy Management Agency to deal with the AT&T antitrust suit. This working group cared far less about the merits of the case than the perceived national interest in telecommunications. As Secretary of Commerce Malcolm Baldrige later testified to the Senate Judiciary Committee:

> We found in this task force that the state of the art in the [telecommunications] industry had leapfrogged itself so many times that it was imperative to deregulate and make this competitive if we were not going to relinquish leadership to other countries in the future.[51]

But the commerce interest in international competition had to be balanced against the longstanding defense interest in safeguarding the integrated nature of the telecommunications network. As Department of Defense General Counsel William H. Taft IV testified at the Senate Judiciary Committee hearings,

> . . . court-ordered divestiture could cause substantial harm to our national defense and security, and emergency preparedness telecommunication capacities. . . . From a national defense and security and emergency preparedness standpoint, the telecommunications network cannot properly be artifically divided between the inter-city and local exchange functions. . . . Artificial division of the Bell System between local exchange and intercity functions ignores the physical and functional operation of the telecommunications network, will reduce or eliminate the incentives for the Bell Operating Companies to participate in joint network planning and management, and will eventually result in fragmentation of the nationwide telecommunications network.[52]

After all, all national defense circuitry, Strategic Air Command (SAC) circuitry, Presidential support circuitry, warning circuitry, and North American Radar Air Defense (NORAD) circuitry is provided by the common carrier system. The Defense establishment worried that the dismantling of AT&T would jeopardize this system and would destroy standards in telecommunications as well.[53]

Commerce and Defense came to a consensus and the task force recommended to President Reagan that he order the Justice Department to dismiss the suit. However, vociferous opposition by the Justice Department (that is, Antitrust chief William F. Baxter) and questions about the negative political fallout consequent to a dismissal order derailed the task force's recommendation.[54]

Rather than order the suit dismissed, the Reagan Administration tied the fate of the lawsuit to pending telecommunications legislation, the Telecommunications Deregulation and Competition Act of 1981 (S.898). Whereas the relief sought by the original antitrust suit entailed the divestment of Western Electric and some or all BOCs, S.898 advocated the much less radical solution (already approved by the FCC in its Second Computer Inquiry) of creating fully separate subsidiaries to be overseen by the FCC. (This action, of course, would create new responsibilities for the FCC to allocate costs in order to ensure that these subsidiaries did not receive cross-subsidies—functions which the Commission already could not do effectively.) In July 1981, the Justice Department, joined by AT&T, requested that the Federal District Court grant an approximate one-year continuance in the antitrust case. The Administration's argument was that the AT&T case was just part of the larger issue of reformulating telecommunications policy. Congress, it was argued, was the proper arena for this rather than the ''much narrower'' judicial forum, but Congress could not go ahead without a pause in the judicial proceeding.

But the Congressional arena was stalemated, particularly in the House of Representatives, where Representative Tim Wirth, Chairman of the Telecommunications Subcommittee, drafted a bill far tougher on AT&T than was S.898. More important, presiding Federal District Court Judge Harold Greene denied the request for a continuance. In contrast to the usual course of large antitrust matters, Judge Greene all along intended to bring the suit to trial in relatively quick fashion. He denied all requests for postponements. Greene's power lay in his being positioned as the key mediating player between adversaries whose options had narrowed. Judge Greene's

*Opinions* on AT&T's motion for dismissal and on the settlement proposal gave clear indication that he would have found AT&T in violation of the Sherman Act.[55]

But if it was clear that Judge Greene would have found AT&T guilty, it is not so clear what he would do vis-à-vis relief. If Greene had the *chutzpah* to order so consequential a move as divestiture, it was not clear what would be divested. The type of divestiture was crucial to all parties. Though the relief sought at the time of the filing of the case centered on separating Western Electric from AT&T, by the time of the trial Justice was far more interested in divesting the local operating companies from AT&T. AT&T itself had come to share Justice's thinking (for different reasons) on the terms of any divestiture, notwithstanding the company's public posture against any divestiture. The Reagan Administration's intense regard for the international commerce capabilities of AT&T depended on the integrated nature of AT&T's manufacturing and long-distance units. However, the indications were that Judge Greene was most interested in the Western Electric issue.[56] However, speculation regarding Greene's opinion is largely irrelevant. Regardless of the court's decision, it is extremely likely the case would have been appealed by some party (if not by AT&T), and would have dragged on for another decade.

In contrast, the negotiating forum between AT&T and the Justice Department could keep out all other players. Though they were "adversaries" of a sort, AT&T and Justice nonetheless had many interests in common. A settlement offered many potential advantages to the principal players. It would benefit the various state interests in telecommunications and information technology. Unlike a judicial ruling, a settlement forum would allow the conflicting national security and commerce interests to be ironed out in negotiation. For AT&T, a settlement would preclude the use of the government's antitrust case as *prima facie* evidence in private antitrust actions against the company. Most important, unlike a judicial ruling (whose appeal, and hence further delays, was likely), a settlement presumably would end the uncertainty of action for AT&T. The company needed to move quickly into the "information age."

On January 8, 1982, the Department of Justice and AT&T jointly announced that they had reached a settlement in the case. The broadest terms of the divestiture were these: the 22 Bell Operating Companies were to be divested from their AT&T parent and consolidated into seven separate and independent regional telephone monopolies. These companies would be subject to traditional rate-of-return regulatory oversight, and would not be allowed into competitive markets of long distance, equipment manufacture, or data processing. AT&T would remain a vertically integrated company consisting of Long Lines, Western Electric, and Bell Labs (some of which have since been reorganized and given new names.) AT&T no longer would be in the business of providing basic local switched telephone service, but was given free entry into any and all domestic and international competitive markets (with the exception of domestic "electronic publishing" for a period of seven years). AT&T was officially released from the strictures of the 1956 Consent Decree.

Not surprisingly, the settlement is one which protects the state's commerce interest, for it preserves, even enhances, the international business capabilities of AT&T in the burgeoning field of information technology. It was no accident that the

Reagan Administration settled on the same day the AT&T case and an equally longstanding antitrust suit against IBM. The statements of Assistant Attorney General William F. Baxter are telling in this regard. Baxter testified to the Senate Judiciary Committee, in its oversight hearings on the *U.S. v. AT&T* case:

> A great deal more than the enforcement of the antitrust law is involved in this situation. The telecommunications industry arguably is our most important industry even at the present time. The boundary lines between telecommunication and data processing and word processing are rapidly becoming blurred beyond recognition. I think there is almost no doubt that it will be our most important industry by a wide margin over the next quarter of a century . . . . In some respects, I thought the most effective relief I could find in the IBM case was freeing AT&T from the 1956 Consent Decree, and in some respects the most appropriate relief in the AT&T case was freeing IBM from further harassment in that litigation.[57]

At the same time, the settlement represents a near-total realization of the historic agenda of the large telecommunications users. The large users are able to utilize the competition-generated spate of new technologies and services. And the settlement does minimally safeguard the financial and technical viability of the basic switched telephone network, upon which the new technologies depend.

For the Department of Defense, the settlement is a reasonable "second best" solution. Though the Defense Department's comments on the Modified Final Judgment retain the flavor of opposition to the divestiture, in fact the Modified Final Judgment goes a fair distance to meeting Department of Defense objections. The national security provision reads:

> Notwithstanding separation of ownership, the BOCs may support and share the costs of a centralized organization for the provision of engineering, administrative and other services which can most efficiently be provided on a centralized basis. The BOCs shall provide, through a centralized organization, a single point of contact for coordination of BOCs to meet the requirements of national security and emergency preparedness.[58]

The settlement thus safeguards the national security interests of the Defense Department through the back door. Lastly, the settlement reflects AT&T's need to finally move decisively into the information technology field. It resolves most of the technological and business contradictions discussed above, *and* leaves intact the vertically integrated nature of AT&T. Though this was not what AT&T wanted— up to the end, AT&T publicly sought to preserve the system—it was a very good second best for AT&T.[59]

Yet it may be that AT&T was somewhat disingenuous in its public pronouncements. The transition in chairmanship from John deButts to Charles L. Brown in 1979 reflected a change in corporate philosophy from the traditional "universal service in the public interest" to a plea to be rid of the barriers to diversification.[60] The form divestiture took met the new needs of AT&T in two crucial ways. *Without* divestiture, AT&T would have faced intolerable regulatory and antitrust pressures—due to the continuing boundary problem between regulated and unregulated spheres. Even had the company created a wholly independent subsidiary to enter competitive markets, it is likely that AT&T's competitors would continue to have hounded AT&T in regulatory and legal arenas. Second, there is that matter of the company's size. It is an open question how quickly the company would have been able to introduce new services or new products with a hugely capitalized, regulated monopoly dragging it down. Moreover, regulated local exchange telephony was considered the slow-growth, low-profit end of the telecommunications business. The settlement offered AT&T a clean break, permitting it to slough off regulated local service and move into the high-profile, high-profit business of information technology.[61]

The traditional structure of American common carrier telecommunications constituted a precarious balance between the benefits and drawbacks of regulated monopoly. So long as the technology and uses of telephony were relatively simple, regulators and policy makers ("assisted" by the existing structure of the industry and AT&T's massive lobbying power) found the benefit side of monopoly to outweigh its problems. Value-of-service pricing and cost-averaging served to universalize telephone service. The structure of common carrier telecommunications worked well enough, notwithstanding the inability and/or unwillingness of the FCC to oversee the industry adequately.

However, the peculiar inefficiencies of the monopoly firm under regulatory constraint—to wit, slow innovation, limited service options, and relatively high prices for heavy users—created economic and technical incentives for large users to get out from under the Bell monopoly and for new providers to service those corporate customers. These incentives later were magnified by the results of citizen action to keep basic telephone rates low in a period of high inflation.

The rise in large corporate telecommunications use and the inability of AT&T to accommodate demand pushed the FCC to liberalize entry in special services. *Above 890* and *MCI* (and in certain ways the *DOMSAT* decision) can be interpreted as little more than large corporate users and prospective providers prevailing in the regulatory arena over AT&T in the face of new technological needs and the demonstrated incapacity of AT&T to provide for them. They constitute clear examples of interest group liberalism—abetted by technological change—at work in the regulatory arena. Nevertheless, the early liberalizations of entry were of marginal importance at the time. They in no way altered the dominant protectionist mode of FCC regulation and did little to affect AT&T's fortunes.

*Hush-a-Phone* and court-ordered decisions such as *Execunet* constitute a separate level of constraint and determination, beyond interest politics *per se*. The law does not stand "outside" socioeconomic life, and it would be foolish to assert its complete autonomy. It is the conflict between economic players which allows the courts to play a role at all. Nonetheless, socioeconomic factors influence law only indirectly most of the time. Law is affected as much by its own independent history, language, and logic. The essential characteristic of modern rational law, as a body of rules and procedures, is to apply logical criteria with reference to standards of universality and equity. Legal rationality and precedent, as in *Hush-a-Phone* and *Execunet,* constitute another dimension of determination, for these judicial decisions exploded the FCC's belief that small entry liberalizations were "containable." The ramifications of FCC and court-ordered entry liberalizations, then, engendered a further spiral of legal constraint. AT&T's actions to circumvent the effects of entry liberalization put the corporation in direct conflict with the antitrust laws.

The advent of digital technology (perhaps the key factor in the versatility of communication-related technology) made such liberalizations unexpectedly consequential. Liberalized entry created competitive markets which, in turn, confused boundaries between regulated and nonregulated realms and jeopardized AT&T's averaged rate structure. AT&T's actions in meeting competition reawakened the old specter of antitrust and the problem side of the telephone monopoly. The problem side of monopoly had been bracketed, but not solved by the 1956 Consent Decree. Indeed, the construction of technologically determined operating boundaries made future problems nearly inevitable. Liberalized entry, new players, and, crucially, a deregulatory environment that affected all branches of government, made it impossible for AT&T to recapture its monopoly. The 1974 antitrust suit constructed a new policy forum in which the major players could hammer out a compromise and reconfigure common carrier telecommunications.

Though divestiture and deregulation are not necessarily the same political phenomenon, they are enough linked that divestiture is being used to expand the program of the deregulation of telecommunications. Nonetheless, it would be incorrect to conclude that common carrier telecommunications is deregulated *per se.* Indeed, the transition period away from regulated monopoly may be characterized by an *ad hoc* form of "regulated competition." The divestiture of AT&T, though it resolves many regulatory and economic contradictions, serves to undermine many of the traditional principles of American telecommunications policy. Moreover, this post-divestiture *ad hoc* regime of regulated competition, under an *ad hoc* jurisdiction balanced between the FCC and Judge Greene, seems poised at recreating many of the structural problems of pre-divestiture telecommunications. I will discuss these contemporary issues in the final chapter.

## The Deregulation of Broadcast Communications

Like the deregulation of common carrier telecommunications, broadcast deregulation is partial and still in process. Quite unlike railroads, trucking, airlines, or banking, there have been no omnibus bills that directly dismantle regulation in broadcasting. The Cable Communications Policy Act of 1984—the only piece of legislation remotely like the bills that deregulated airlines, railroads, and trucking— reduced and reconfigured the scope of regulation of the cable television industry, but did not go further. The FCC still allocates spectrum space, grants broadcast licenses and renewals, and oversees broadcast content in the most general way. However, notwithstanding the absence of deregulatory legislation, broadcasting has undergone extensive direct and *de facto* deregulation at the hands of the FCC itself. Indeed, the very theoretical underpinnings of the Communications Act have come under strong attack.

Broadcast deregulation has taken two forms. First, the orientation of the FCC has changed from one that protected conventional broadcasters and conventional broadcast technologies to an orientation which *encourages* the entry of new broadcast services and technologies (though the Reagan Administration FCC is ambivalent with regard to new services). Second, the FCC has moved away from exercising indirect controls over program content and direct controls over the structure of the broadcast industry. These two forms of deregulation constitute separate, but interlinked moments.

Entry liberalization came in the latter part of the 1970s, generally evolving along the lines established by other entry-controlled infrastructure industries. Like airlines and trucking, liberalization of entry in broadcasting was a policy hinted at during the Ford Administration and consummated by the Carter Administration. In the mid-1970s, contradictions between regulations designed to protect conventional broadcasters combined with the opportunities afforded by new technologies to inadvertently set in motion small relaxations of entry rules. By 1977, FCC Chairman Charles D. Ferris, a Carter appointee, talked openly about the FCC's "historical tilt" in favor of broadcasters, and of removing that tilt. During Ferris' tenure as chairman from 1977 to 1981, the Commission effectively deregulated cable television and seriously initiated efforts to bring into being *new* broadcast services, including direct broadcast satellites, multi-point distribution service, and low-power television. Under Ferris the FCC proposed increasing the number of AM radio stations by reducing the frequency spacing between assignments.

In general, the Ferris-led FCC rejected protectionism and pursued an expansion of broadcast technologies and services. Low-power television, a television service whose transmission power is so low that it was thought not to cause interference on co- and adjacent channel frequencies, was a bold ploy in this regard. The service originally was thought to accommodate three to four thousand new television outlets. Again, as in the pattern of deregulation in airlines and trucking, a surprisingly heterodox coalition of groups, interests, and ideologies strongly backed entry liberalization. Only the entrenched industry grouping—conventional broadcasters—opposed entry liberalization. And as in those other cases, the entrenched industry grouping failed in its bid to maintain the regulatory status quo.

The policies to remove structural and content rules generally came later, reaching a peak with the Reagan Administration's appointment to the FCC of self-identified free-market ideologues. This type of deregulation was and is far more politically contentious than entry liberalization. Nevertheless, the dismantling of structural and content regulations proceeded rapidly. Indeed, one might argue that it is in broadcasting—more than any other industry—where the right-wing cries against regulation have been heard and successfully acted upon. In marked contrast to its posture toward entry liberalization, the broadcast industry loudly applauds the dismantling of structural and content regulations.

The underlying rationale for the deregulation of structural and content controls is that broadcasting is a *business,* pure and simple. Under FCC Chairman Mark Fowler, a Reagan appointee, the Commission moved to explode the traditional notion of the broadcaster as public trustee. As Fowler put it, "Television is just another appliance. It's a toaster with pictures."[62]

Since 1981 the FCC has acted to remove most content-based regulations. Among other things, the FCC greatly loosened guidelines that required nonentertainment programming and coverage of community issues. Broadcasters no longer have to provide minimum amounts of news and public affairs programs. The Commission relaxed rules requiring licenses to air "informative" children's programming, and rejected restrictions on cartoon shows based on toys. Annual financial reports are no longer required by the FCC, and the Commission has endeavored to do the same with station programming logs. The Commission authorized broadcasters to sponsor political debates without being subject to equal time requests, and, in that vein, the FCC voted in 1987 to rescind the Fairness Doctrine.

Under Chairman Fowler, the FCC has sought to let the market prevail in broadcasting. Thus the Commission eliminated time and frequency limits on TV commercials, allowing more commercials per hour and program-length ads. The FCC moved to eliminate various structural rules. It enhanced station trafficking by rescinding the rules that prohibited a station buyer from reselling a station until three years after purchase. It eliminated the regional concentration rule (which had prohibited ownership of three broadcast stations when two were located within 100 miles of the third), and terminated a proposed rule that aimed at creating multiple ownership rules for cable television. Finally, after hard lobbying, the Commission won Congressional approval to raise the limit on group ownership of broadcast properties from seven television, AM, and FM radio stations to twelve of each. The term of license tenure, previously set at 3 three years, has been increased to 5 years for a television license and 7 years for a radio license.

While the differences between entry liberalization and the removal of structural/content controls are real, the difference between the Ferris-led FCC and the Fowler-led FCC is one of degree, not of kind. Indeed, the entry liberalization pursued under Ferris made possible structural/content deregulation, because the increase in effective broadcast outlets could not but bring into question the traditional scarcity rationale for the regulation of broadcasting. In fact, the far-ranging proposals for rule changes to remove content controls on radio were instituted in *1979*, by the Ferris-led FCC. The logic behind the radio deregulation proposals was that commercial radio, with nearly 9,000 local outlets, no longer could be said to be characterized by technical scarcity.

Technology, then, was central to the deregulation of broadcasting—both at the tangible level of new services and new delivery options provided by satellites and microwaves *and* at the ideological level of undermining the traditional rationale for regulation. Indeed, what made the process of broadcast deregulation different from deregulation in other industries was in part the role of technology and the policy *discourse* around technology. Sparked by the regulatory activism of the "broadcast reform movement," by the early 1970s an oddly heterodox political coalition— including public interest groups, free market economists, and Presidential task forces—demanded the relaxation of FCC regulatory controls, particularly around cable television. The change in the political discourse had indirect effects within the FCC itself. Contradictions between protectionist regulations permitted the FCC to relax various minor cable rules. Against the backdrop of the regulatory and technical developments in common carrier telecommunications, these small liberalizations resulted in the inadvertent emergence of new broadcast services.

Though their histories are largely separate, it seems unlikely that the regulatory changes in the broadcast area would have occurred in the absence of the transformation of common carrier telecommunications. At the very least, it was the new delivery technology of satellites which permitted cable television to carve out a new and important niche in the broadcast market. The new services constituted a market test of competition, in effect providing the FCC with a concrete example by which to reassess its traditional policy of broadcast protectionism.

Though cable was the most visible galvanizing agent in the dismantling of the traditional protectionist role of the FCC in the broadcast area, many other factors— including court decisions—were part of this movement. Again, I liken the deregulatory process to a complicated mosaic of political, economic, regulatory, judicial, and technological forces. The process began with the regulatory activism of the late 1960s and early 1970s.

## The Broadcast Reform Movement

Though "listener groups" existed in the time of radio, it was the citizen activism of the 1960s which was responsible for the rise of the broadcast reform movement. The watershed in this development was the court decision in the *United Church of Christ* case in 1966.[63] *UCC v. FCC,* as we have seen, constituted one of the two cases which expanded legal standing in general. And because it was a broadcast case, *UCC v. FCC* stimulated a proliferation of groups concerned with the lack of minority-oriented programming, with the amount of television violence, with the wretched state of television for children. Various national groups such as the Citizens Communication Center, National Citizens Committee for Broadcasting, Action for Children's Television, American Council for Better Broadcasts, and the Office of Communications of the United Church of Christ, as well as *ad hoc* local groups, mobilized to challenge broadcasters within the regulatory forum.

The "broadcast reform movement," as the very loose confederation of public interest groups came to be known, engaged in three identifiably separate struggles in the effort to improve broadcasting in the United States. These were: (1) the fight to improve broadcast programming through intervention in the broadcast license renewal regulatory process; (2) the legal fight for citizen access to broadcast facilities; and (3) the effort to expand service alternatives to traditional broadcasting. The first two strategies occasionally merged, when groups filed petitions to deny license renewal based on Fairness Doctrine violations. The latter involved the successful effort to create a public broadcasting network and the championing of cable television as a technology that could potentially "democratize" American broadcasting.[64]

## "Petitions to Deny" License Renewal

The most direct strategy of the various public interest broadcast groups lay in the matter of licensing. Citizens groups challenged the propriety of FCC grants of license renewal to existing broadcasters. As we have seen, license renewal was one of those difficult areas for the Commission, and so it tended to automatically renew all but the most egregiously offensive broadcasters. In the aftermath of *UCC v. FCC,* citizens groups filed "petitions to deny" the license renewal applications of existing broadcasters. The public interest groups argued that the licensees had not lived up to various aspects of their public interest obligations. They also filed challenges to license transfers (sales), arguing that in many cases, the license transfer would concentrate media holdings, and hence reduce potential broadcast diversity.

Broadcast reform groups entered into the licensing arena armed with the language of the Communications Act and demanded that the FCC hold broadcast licensees to their public interest obligations. As in the case of public interest interventions in regulatory proceedings before other agencies, these license challenges did not often succeed directly. However, the expansion of democratic participation in FCC regulatory proceedings doomed the traditionally *pro forma* character of broadcast licensing determinations and greatly increased the time and money broadcasters were forced to spend in order to secure renewal or justify license transfers. Again, parallel to the experience of other agencies, the number of broadcast renewal and transfer challenges created a case backlog at the FCC and a corresponding regulatory "lag."[65] Licensees were granted temporary renewals, but broadcasters had to keep their lawyers on retainer until the matter could be taken up by the Commission.

In addition to the time and expense the petitions to deny imposed upon broadcasters, renewal challenges also raised the remote but harrowing specter that a challenged licensee could ultimately be stripped of its license. The horror with which the broadcast industry viewed the 1969 FCC decision to strip WHDH-TV Boston of its television license convinced broadcasters that they had to reckon with a new situation.[66] The industry moved in two directions simultaneously. One the one hand, broadcasters under citizen challenge entered into negotiations with the public interest groups and agreed to meet some of the demands in return for a dropping of the petition challenge. The FCC honored such negotiations and made the terms binding. Moreover, in some cases, the challenged stations agreed to pay some of the participation expenses of the citizen group petitioners.[67] In specific instances then, the broadcast reform movement won concessions on matters of minority hiring, locally oriented programming, etc. On the other hand, the broadcast industry concentrated its considerable lobbying powers toward Congress in an effort to secure license renewal relief. The move toward Congress added to the rising sense that all telecommunications policy was in need of reevaluation.

Broadcasters were also troubled by parallel regulatory changes. The strength and weakness of the broadcast reform movement was that it could rely on one (often dormant) strain of FCC policy: that the local broadcast station was licensed to serve the local community. For instance, pressure from the citizens groups underlay the Commission's 1971 "community ascertainment" policy.[68] That policy outlined concrete requirements a broadcast license was obliged to fulfill vis-à-vis local community concerns and the general nature of programming. The licensee was to go out into the community, determine its economic, ethnic, and social composition, and ascertain what specific issues were pertinent and of interest to the community in which it broadcast. Broadcasters ultimately were instructed to go out into the community and interview some 19 specified "institutions and elements commonly found in a community,'' and write a formal report on the results. Again, it is unlikely the ascertainment requirements had much impact on what broadcasters actually aired. However, such requirements, along with the petitions to deny license renewals, did impose additional expenses and paperwork burdens on broadcasters.[69] Ascertainment requirements also legitimated the public trustee model of broadcasting in a concrete way.

## Access to Broadcasting

The second area marked out for reform was over the question of citizen access to the airwaves. The bottom-line legal rationale for the regulation of broadcasting is the scarcity of the electromagnetic spectrum. Almost all broadcast regulation flows from this fact. Because of this scarcity, a broadcast licensee may not use a frequency to promote solely his own views. The frequency, because it is scarce and part of the public domain, is operated in the public trust. This has meant that the licensee must air programs of interest and controversy to the local community, and be balanced in such programming.

This essentially describes the Fairness Doctrine. The constitutionality of the Fairness Doctrine and its related provisions of section 315 of the Communications Act were unanimously upheld in the strongly worded 1969 Supreme Court decision, *Red Lion Broadcasting Co. v. FCC*.[70] Public interest groups and labor unions, emboldened by the *Red Lion* decision, employed the doctrine in a gambit to gain access to the airwaves. The most effective strategy was found in the filing of Fairness Doctrine challenges to stations for their carriage of commercial advertisements said to invite controversy. Cigarette advertising was among the first targets. The Commission reluctantly agreed that here was an issue of interest and controversy on which broadcasters had aired only one side. The FCC apprised broadcast licensees of their obligation to air anti-smoking programming. Although the licensee could decide how to meet the requirement to present programming on the dangers of smoking, most broadcasters aired materials that had been prepared by outside groups. Indeed, some broadcasters permitted anti-smoking groups to air ''counter'' commercials.[71]

The FCC attempted to treat cigarettes as a unique case. When public interest groups began filing Fairness Doctrine challenges on other issues, such as ads that promoted high-powered automobiles, the FCC blanched and retreated, realizing that it may have opened a Pandora's Box. Friends of the Earth, an environmental group, demanded that the FCC require that broadcast licensees present contrasting views on the value of such automobiles. The Commission refused, but the Court of Appeals ruled that because it could not distinguish between the cigarette case and the high-powered car case, the FCC had to be consistent.[72] Thereafter, the FCC constructed a pragmatic (but theoretically dubious) distinction between commercials that simply sold commodities and those which advocated a point of view on a controversial issue of public importance. The Commission determined that the Fairness Doctrine was not a proper way to respond to purely commercial advertising. The Court of Appeals upheld the FCC.[73]

A related access challenge came in the form of a call for a limited, but mandatory right to purchase airtime for advocacy programs and spots. One of the primary movers behind this was a law professor, Jerome A. Barron. In a 1967 *Harvard Law Review* article Barron wrote an incisive, provocative critique of what he termed the "romantic" theory of free speech. He argued that the marketplace of ideas model of free speech was an antiquated notion in this age of powerful, centralized media. Free speech could not occur in print or broadcast so long as there was not a mandatory right of reply or citizen access to the media. Publishers and broadcasters, as gatekeepers with strong economic interests, would always operate to ensure the greatest possible audience. In Barron's view, this meant that many newspapers and nearly all broadcasters would print copy or air programs whose most salient characteristic was blandness, inoffensiveness.

But, Barron argued, the discussion of important and controversial public issues is bound to offend some, perhaps many, viewers and readers. Without a citizens right of access, media owners stifle speech. Broadcasting's Fairness Doctrine posed little help in this regard, in Barron's view. In fact, the doctrine thwarted access claims and free speech because it allowed the broadcaster to remain the absolute gatekeeper. (This complaint, though clearly different in the source of its motivation, echoed similar complaints from broadcasters and conservatives about the efficacy of the Fairness Doctrine.) In short, a model of free speech which fails to acknowledge the centralized power of modern media gives media owners the very censorship role which had been denied the government by the First Amendment.[74]

At the very minimum, Barron suggested, were two remedies: a non-discriminatory right to purchase editorial advertisements in daily newspapers and broadcast media, and a right of reply for public figures and public officers defamed in the press. Surprisingly, the parties to test this access theory in broadcasting were the Democratic National Committee (DNC) and a group of liberal businessmen. The DNC sought to purchase time on CBS to air a fundraising program. The Business Executives' Move for Vietnam Peace wished to buy time from the Washington, DC, radio outlet to air an advocacy spot against Nixon Administration policy in Vietnam. The broadcasters refused to sell airtime and both groups sued. The cases were joined, and, in a 1973 decision, the Supreme Court dashed the access strategy. The Court majority rejected any mandatory right of access to the airwaves. The decision argued that the Fairness Doctrine worked adequately; that a right of access would destroy editorial autonomy and discretion, and risked an unacceptable enlargement of government control over broadcast speech. A year later, a unanimous Supreme Court rejected a right of reply statute for newspapers. Rejecting all notions of public interest, fairness, or balance, the Court claimed that press freedom is imperiled as soon as government tries to compel what is to go into a newspaper.[75]

However, *CBS v. DNC* did not dash access completely. The ruling held out a hope for access in cable television, a medium as yet unencumbered with a long history of case law.[76] This brings us to the broadcast reform movement's third strategy to improve American broadcasting, the championing of new technologies—cable television in particular.

## The Embrace of New Technologies

While most of the broadcast reform movement's efforts went toward pressuring individual local broadcasters, some in the movement concentrated on larger, systemic concerns. Despairing of the likelihood of successfully pressuring local commercial broadcasters to act against their economic interests, those disenchanted with commercial television sought to create alternatives to the conventional commercial system. The Public Broadcasting Act represented the first fruit of this effort. Broadcast reformers of all political allegiances, including some within the FCC, allied with educators, the Carnegie Commission, and, ultimately, President Lyndon Johnson, successfully advanced legislation in 1967 that established a modest public broadcast network from the scattered, isolated, underfunded educational stations.[77]

In the late 1960s a similar, but more politically heterodox confederation of groups, including broadcast citizens groups, think tanks, and the White House (in the form of a Presidential Task Force on Communications Policy) turned to cable television as an alternative to the standard commercial broadcast system. Though CATV, which retransmitted broadcast television signals by wire, was a relatively old technology by communications standards, in the late 1960s it began to be hailed along with satellites as one of the "new technologies" that promised a revolution in communications. In fact, the replacement of the name, "community antenna television," or "CATV," with the new term, "cable television," signaled a transformation of the discourse around the technology.[78]

It was the championing of "new technologies" which ultimately had the most direct impact on the deregulation of broadcasting. This was because the new discourse became allied with an ongoing material factor—the growth of cable systems. Moreover, the "new technologies" discourse became an important factor in the FCC's policy change vis-à-vis cable. The broadcast reform movement saw in cable television the end of the commercial chokehold on American television. Cable's capacity to carry enormous amounts of information and potential for two-way broadcast communication were cited as "revolutionary," not only because the television of abundance could accommodate new voices, but because two-way cable altered the nature of broadcast communication itself. With so many channels and two-way capability, broadcast communication could be participatory and democratic. Cable appeared to offer the opportunity for direct access to television to those left out by conventional television: seniors, minorities, nonprofit organizations, local arts groups. Local government and community meetings could be carried live. Schools and hospitals would be interconnected for teaching purposes. In short, the embrace of cable as a potentially participatory medium reflected the participatory utopianism of the grassroots citizens movement itself.[79]

But the public interest movement did not have a corner on the "new technologies" rhetoric. President Johnson's Task Force on Communications Policy dealt up a report in 1968 which highlighted the profusion of new communication technologies and advocated a much greater governmental role in their coordination. Cable television, according to the report, was one such promising technology. Echoing some of the broadcast reform arguments, the report saw cable TV as a solution to the problems of conventional commercial broadcasting. The report went so far as to suggest that the access to cable television by minorities and disaffected groups might help solve some of the social unrest of the 1960s.[80] The Nixon Administration, picking up on the Task Force Report, formed a Cabinet Committee on Cable Communications in 1971 to study the options for the technology. The Ford Administration's Domestic Council Review Group on Regulatory Reform (DCRG) followed suit in 1975. That study *started* from the premise that most cable rules should be eliminated.[81]

A third source of new technologies rhetoric came attached to scholarly free market economic analyses of FCC regulations. As was the case with airlines, trucking, and railroads, academic criticism of communications regulation existed in the economics literature for some years. By the early 1970s that criticism reached a crescendo, focusing on the FCC's role in obstructing technological innovation. The Rand Corporation published several reports in the early 1970s that explored cable's technical promise and harshly criticized the FCC regulations that had long disabled the technology. These studies argued that the problem with American broadcasting was simply a lack of competition—a situation which flowed straight from regulatory protectionism.[82] An influential Sloan Commission report on cable released 1971 contained more ballyhoo on cable's potential than the dry economic reports, but came to similar conclusions.[83]

In cable policy, then, various interests and constituencies coalesced in a loosely united and vague, but definite opposition to FCC rules. As was the case in airlines, each group opposed the regulatory restriction of cable for different reasons, consonant with the basic premises of its unique ideological framework. Liberals and broadcast reformers saw the problem of commercial broadcasting as a problem of citizen access, thus champoined cable TV as an abundant wellspring for such access. Free market economists saw the problem of commercial broadcasting as an artificially produced paucity of competition, thus advocated the end of regulatory restrictions on cable TV as a way to let the broadcast market function "naturally."[84] The quasi-technocratic report of the President's Task Force championed cable TV as part of its proposed program for the government to enhance new telecommunications technologies generally. The "new technologies" discourse was not *the* reason for the FCC's cautious policy change for cable in 1972, but it was an important factor.[85]

## The Change in the Regulatory Environment

By the early 1970s cable television's fortunes began to change. An important reason was the increasingly loud denunciation from many quarters of the Commission's restrictive cable rules. But there were clear material reasons as well. The cable industry sustained modest but steady growth throughout the 1960s.[86] At the same time, an increasing concentration of cable ownership during 1967–1973 began to transform the cable industry from a confederation of "mom and pop" operations to one of increasingly large corporations which owned several cable systems (in the lingo, "multiple system operators" or MSOs).[87] Between growth and concentration, cable interests began acquiring wider representation and lobbying power. The industry's economic success permitted a viable cable lobby to arise and enter into the regulatory fray.

Cable entrepreneurs, not surprisingly, were quite happy about all the public commotion about the potential of the technology. That discourse assisted in their effort to establish cable as a major independent player rather than as a technology adjunct to conventional broadcasting. Another ownership factor had bearing on this, as well. By the early 1970s broadcasters owned well over 30 percent of all cable systems (38 percent in 1972). Because of this ownership, broadcasters' interests became less clear regarding cable regulatory policy.[88]

The growth of cable, the new strength of the cable lobby, and the emergence of a new discourse around cable helped to generate internal changes in FCC bureaucratic structure. In 1970 the Commission created a separate Cable Bureau within its staff to attend to cable matters. Previously, the Broadcast Bureau had been responsible for cable issues. The creation of a separate Cable Bureau was due in part to the increasing numbers of cable matters to which the Commission had to attend. But it also represented a recognition within the FCC that cable had been sabotaged by regulation. According to former FCC Commissioner Glen O. Robinson,

> . . . The point of giving a separate bureau status to cable in 1970 was not merely to enhance the status and prerequisites of cable staff personnel (though this clearly was an important element in the dynamics of the cable bureau's evolution); it was to give added status to cable television as an industry, as a technology and as a service. Many critics (myself included) believe that the development of cable television is still being unreasonably restrained to protect the interests of broadcasting and past Commission policies centered on broadcast service. A merger of the cable and broadcast bureaus would, if anything, reinforce the Commission's protectionist instincts.[89]

The creation of a separate Cable Bureau led, in classical organizational fashion, to the development of in-house cable advocates. The new Cable Bureau fostered a staff freed from the broadcast system mindset (thus permitting the entertainment of more theoretical possibilities for cable and its regulation) and also initiated a competition over regulatory turf with the Broadcast Bureau. As former Commissioner Nicholas Johnson put it, "The FCC's Cable Bureau is the cable industry's most vociferous advocate."[90] If the creation of the Cable Bureau was a blossom of the "new technologies" discourse, the Bureau also constituted the humus in which the discourse grew at the Commission.

## The 1972 Cable Rules

Historically, the FCC restricted cable in order to protect conventional broadcasting. One problem the Commission had with cable was the "unfair advantage" cable secured by its ability to retransmit broadcast signals without incurring copyright liability.[91] Following the Supreme Court's ruling in the *Fortnightly* case, Congress began serious consideration of rewriting the Copyright Act of 1909. In light of pending Congressional action on copyright, the FCC proposed to revise its regulation of cable television in 1971.[92] A year later the FCC adopted an agreement, supervised by the White House through the Office of Telecommunications Policy, between cable, programming, and broadcast interests. It is at this point where the changed environment altered cable's fortunes.[93]

For the most part, the 1972 cable rules represented a complex compromise between cable and broadcast industries. (See Table 4.) The rules permitted a degree of liberalization: now cable was allowed to expand into major markets. But by no means did the rules eliminate the protection of conventional broadcasters. The 1972 cable rules placed strict controls on the number and type of signals a cable system could import. Other rules restricted the timing of cable programming. At the same time, the fact that the new rules required that all new cable systems carry a mini-

TABLE 4.   Summary of 1972 Cable Rules

| | Markets 1–50 | Markets 51–200 | Smaller Markets | Outside All Markets |
|---|---|---|---|---|
| Must carry | All local signals | All local signals | All local signals | All local signals* |
| Minimum service | 3 network stations<br>3 independents | 3 network stations<br>2 independents | 3 network stations<br>1 independent | |
| Additional service | 2 independents** | 2 independents** | None | Any other signals |
| Leapfrogging | If either or both of the first two independents is from among the top 25 markets they must be from one or both of the two closest such markets. | | | None |
| Exclusivity | No carriage of a syndicated program during a period one year after the program is sold anywhere in the US<br>During run of exclusive contract to a local station | During run of exclusive contract to a local station | None | None |
| Channel capacity | Minimum of 20 channels | | No requirement | |
| Program origination | Required of all systems with 3500 or more subscribers. | | | |
| Access | Free public educational and government access channels (one each); leased access required for all unused channels. | | | |
| Expansion of capacity | Whenever all channels are in use 80 percent of weekdays for 80 percent of the time during any 3-hour period for 6 weeks running, an additional channel must be added. | | | |

*The definition of local signals is slightly less stringent for stations outside a television market.
**Can be carried only to the extent they were not employed to meet the minimum service standard.
Source: Stanley M. Besen and Robert W. Crandall, "The Deregulation of Cable Television," *Law and Contemporary Problems* 44/1 (Winter 1981), 77–124.

mum of 20 channels (and that existing systems be upgraded to 20 channels), some of which would be allocated to public access, reveals the 1972 rules to bear the stamp of the "new technologies" discourse. Though the 1972 rules still restricted cable, they also established it as a technology no longer conceptualized by the FCC as simply ancillary to conventional broadcasting.

The 1972 rules eased entry for cable, even as the FCC sought to maintain protection for conventional broadcasters. It was a situation not unlike that of common carrier regulation, where the Commission liberalized entry in specialized telecommunication services while expecting to protect AT&T's monopoly turf. The irony in broadcast is that the very terms of continued broadcast protection inadvertently formed the avenue for expanded liberalization. This was because the protectionist rules were mutually contradictory in certain instances, and forced the FCC to make rule adjustments. In the context of the deregulatory environment and the efforts of cable proponents within the Commission, those regulatory adjustments went in the direction of relaxation of rules.

"Leapfrogging" and "syndicated exclusivity" were the rules designed to protect broadcasters which inadvertently relaxed that protection. Leapfrogging rules were intended to restrict distant signal importation by cable systems. The FCC reasoned that distant signal importation posed a threat to the entire *local* system of frequency allocations. In an attempt both to tie the cable operator to his/her local community and to protect local broadcast signals, imported signals were required to be the geographically closest signals or the closest within the same state.[94] As part of the same logic, cable systems serving more than 3500 subscribers were required to originate programming.[95]

Syndicated exclusivity rules required cable operators to black out programs on their imported distant signals if these duplicated that day's programming offered by local broadcast stations. Rather than compel the cable channel to be blacked out when this occurred, the FCC relaxed the leapfrogging rules, allowing the cable system operator to import programming to fill this channel from any station in the country.[96] In 1974 the Commission allowed unlimited distant signal importation after all local "must carry" stations had signed off the air. The Commission justified this liberalization, in keeping with its historically protectionist concerns, by asserting that "importation . . . would have no adverse impact on stations that were already off the air."[97] More than that, the Commission hoped this policy would encourage local broadcasters to program on a 24-hour basis to prevent late night signal importation on cable systems.[98]

But broadcasters did not take this cue from the Commission. In fact, when the FCC eliminated the leapfrogging requirements, in Henry Geller's words, "it was a big yawn to broadcasters."[99] What happened instead was that this ruling paved the way for the creation of a new broadcast service. The space these regulatory contradictions opened for cable operator discretion allowed operators to utilize the new technology of satellite delivery. The ultimate upshot of these developments was the "superstation," an independent broadcast station whose signals could be carried via satellite to cable systems nationwide. The superstation became the same sort of market test of competition in broadcasting that Alfred Kahn's early competitive experiments had played in the regulated airline industry. Ted Turner, owner of a failing Atlanta UHF station (WTCG), used his partial ownership of Atlanta professional sports teams to offer attractive videotaped major sports events for late-night distant signal importation on cable systems. A few other stations began to be used for late-night cable carriage. At the time, all importation was delivered on terrestrial microwave and only a very few cable systems imported these signals. A combination of the satellite and liberalizations in the common carrier arena changed this.

## The Rise of the Superstation

The small liberalizations in leapfrogging and distant signal importation were more than a logical Commission response to regulatory contradictions. They also represented the influence within the FCC of the general political environment toward deregulation. The Commission instituted a "Reregulation Task Force" for cable television in 1974 to reexamine its 1972 rules. That name was a calculated misnomer, designed by FCC Chairman Richard Wiley not to raise the hackles of Congressional and broadcast industry proponents of regulation. As Wiley tells it, the "Reregulation Task Force" was in fact an exploration into deregulation.[100]

By 1976 the Commission abandoned nearly all leapfrogging restrictions, offering several reasons for such action. First, leapfrogging rules had resulted in irrational importation patterns. They sometimes required cable operators to import signals from markets with very few cultural or economic ties to the cable system market (e.g., upstate New York cable systems were required to import signals from Boston or Hartford rather than from New York City). Second, the Commission noted that leapfrogging rules often added burdensome costs, requiring the importation of signals along two or three microwave routes. Finally, the Commission felt the threat of the development of superstations was overstated, largely because microwave costs and the geographic dispersion of possible advertising benefits would cause cable operators to choose the closest signal regardless.[101]

But technological developments and liberalizations in the common carrier area undermined the Commission's reasoning. As we saw, the policy of liberalized entry in specialized telecommunications service logically extended to the authorization of resale carriers.[102] A resale carrier is a firm that purchases facilities from a common carrier and offers services directly to the public for profit. This included satellite delivery. In a 1976 decision the Commission authorized a common carrier to use satellite rather than terrestrial microwave facilities for the delivery of a distant signal (Turner's WTCG) to cable systems.[103] Continuing the general policy to prevent barriers to the realization of cost savings made possible by interconnection advances in new, specialized technologies, the Commission authorized the construction of 4.5-meter receive-only satellite earth stations.[104]

With leapfrogging restrictions gone, the carrier decisions made it easier for cable operators to base distant signal importation choices on programming rather than on importation costs. Due to the nature of satellite interconnection, a uniform price for nationwide delivery of a broadcast signal beamed up to the satellite could be set, usually cheaper than the cost of importing signals via terrestrial facilities.[105] The late-night major sports programming of superstations such as Turner's WTCG proved to be very attractive in this respect.

If the development of superstations was not the upshot of a conscious or planned FCC policy, the lessons learned were not lost on the Commission. As Stanley Besen and Robert Crandall put it, each relaxation of cable rules moved the Commission away from its presumption that the whole panoply of regulations it adopted in 1972 was necessary for the protection of broadcasters. In each case, the Commission invited broadcasters to demonstrate injury from the prospective liberalization, and when they could not so demonstrate, the Commission further relaxed the regulations.[106] In other words, the largely inadvertent rise of superstations created a "real world" instance with which to gauge the effect and efficacy of Commission cable rules and entry policies in general.

By 1977, amidst the deregulation debates over airlines, trucking, and common carrier telecommunications, the FCC began to shift the burden of proof from cable systems to broadcasters. The new FCC Chairman, Carter appointee Charles Ferris, talked about removing the historical tilt of regulation toward broadcasters.[107] With the fairly clear intention of removing all distant signal carriage and syndicated exclusivity rules, in 1977 the Commission announced an economic inquiry into the relationship between cable television and conventional broadcasting.[108] That inquiry, undertaken by the Commission's Cable Bureau and a group of academic economists, concluded that the removal of these rules benefited the public more than they harmed the television industry.[109]

In a sense, the final rule making to drop the cable regulations was after the fact. By 1978 the Commission had dropped many of the limitations on cable imposed by the 1972 rules, and the courts forced abandonment of others. In a 1977 case involving a Washington, DC, cable system's imported signals, the Commission substantially reduced the burden on a cable system in seeking relief from FCC rules. In reconsideration, the FCC effectively shifted the burden of proof of injury from cable operators to the complaining broadcasters. Thereafter, broadcasters would have to provide data showing that cable carriage would endanger their ability to provide local broadcast service. The Commission suggested that they "would anticipate that *prima facie* showings of little or no impact [of cable on broadcasters] could be made in the larger markets."[110]

## Court Challenge to Protectionism

The courts played an important role in the liberalization of entry in broadcasting and even expanded the FCC's agenda in this area. The reader will recall how related were the rise of citizen activism and the new "interest representation" standard of judicial review. The liberalization of standing permitted far more participation in regulatory policy. Regulatory agencies now were viewed as quasi-legislative arenas wherein competing social interests would define the public interest. To ensure that all interests were indeed represented within the regulatory forum, reviewing courts often would discern whether "adequate consideration" had been accorded all reasonable interests and policy alternatives. As the doctrine developed, by the latter 1970s the courts demanded increasingly detailed explanations of an agency's factual support and rationale in reaching a decision. The courts began to take what came to be known as a "hard look" at procedural and substantive aspects of agency decisions.[111] This more rigorous review had significant impact on some of the FCC's most basic protectionist policies.

In the long effort to protect conventional broadcasting, the Commission made the existence of a "pay" version of television nearly impossible. FCC rules barred subscription television from showing any sports that were regularly carried on conventional television and restricted the showing of feature films that were more than three but less than ten years old. Commercials were barred and no more than 90 percent of the programming could be sports and movies. If we put the most benign face on what were known as "anti-siphoning" rules, we find that the FCC acted consonant with its traditional view of the public interest in broadcasting. Anti-siphoning rules were designed to prevent the transfer of popular programs and revenue away from conventional television. Such a transfer presumably would impair the local station's financial ability to air the unremunerative public interest programs sought by the Commission. With the rise of cable and a subscription service in cable, the Commission promulgated similar restrictions for pay cable.

In *Home Box Office v. FCC,* the District of Columbia Court of Appeals struck down such protectionism in a strong decision along three major lines of reasoning. First the court found that the FCC had not established justifiable jurisdiction: the case did not involve the scarce spectrum. Because the presentation of feature films via cable television did not use the electromagnetic spectrum for initial transmission and did not involve the retransmission of broadcast programs, the Commission had erred in adopting program content restrictions. The upshot of this reasoning was that cable was *not,* as the Commission asserted, "just like television." The court reasoned that cable television systems were more akin to newspapers.[112]

Second, the court denied FCC jurisdiction on the merits. The anti-siphoning rules were not supported by evidence that indicated they were necessary to promote any legitimate goal within FCC regulatory authority. The Commission had failed to conduct actual experiments and inquiries—according to the court its rules were based on speculation. Furthermore, the FCC had failed to respond to significant public comments, particularly those that asserted cable's potential in serving cultural and minority-group tastes. The court would not acknowledge Commission jurisdiction in the absence of evidence which convincingly elucidated the threat pay television posed to nationwide television service. In other words, the Court dismissed the theory of presumptive harm.

Third, the court disputed the FCC's implicit claim that cable should be a supplement to broadcast television. The anti-siphoning rules maintained that certain programs must be available to free-television viewers, yet the Commission specifically declined to require conventional broadcasters actually to air these, citing First Amendment concerns.[113] Following this decision, the FCC abandoned its anti-siphoning rules.

The other major court decision that contributed significantly to deregulation was the 1979 case, *United States v. Midwest Video Corp.* The FCC adopted a mandatory program origination requirement for cable systems in 1969. The Commission, ever worried about cable television's impact on the theory of localism, reasoned that mandatory "cablecasting" pushed cable systems toward a local broadcast model. Inasmuch as cable operators had positioned themselves within the system of television broadcasting, the FCC could require them to engage in an approximation of local broadcasting. The local origination requirement was challenged by Midwest Video Corporation, but in a close decision, the Supreme Court ruled that mandatory origination was "reasonably ancillary" to the FCC's obligations to regulate over-the-air television.[114]

Because of the burden the origination requirement placed on cable operators, the FCC rescinded it in 1975, and replaced it with an order for cable systems to provide channels for educational, governmental, and public access.[115] Channels and studio equipment were to be made available on a nondiscriminatory, first-come, first-served basis, at charges controlled by the Commission. Midwest Video Corporation sued again, and this time the Court agreed with its complaint. The Court ruled that the FCC access rules violated the Communications Act, inasmuch as the Commission's access rules effectively imposed common carrier status on cable operators. But the Commission had already treated cable as a broadcaster. This, the Court declared, directly violated the Communications Act, because an entity engaged in broadcasting cannot also be deemed a common carrier. The Court ruled that authority to compel cable operators to provide common carriage of public-originated transmissions must come specifically from Congress.[116] In the aftermath of this decision, regulatory policy on cable did shift to Congress, which passed the Cable Communications Policy Act in 1984.[117]

## From Entry Liberalization to Deregulation

In the aftermath of *HBO, Midwest Video,* and the Commission's policy to rescind signal carriage and exclusivity rules, the cable industry began to flourish. The FCC, now self-conscious of its protectionist past, moved to make amends by increasing competition in the delivery of program service.[118] Under Chairman Charles Ferris, the FCC hastened to create more broadcast outlets. Removing the "historical tilt" of regulation meant authorizing new VHF television drop-ins and beginning a rulemaking that would create scores of new AM radio stations (by reducing the separation between existing frequencies). Exorcising the ghosts of the protectionist past entailed nurturing new broadcast services such as direct broadcast satellites, multi-point distribution service, and low-power television.[119]

The liberalization of entry under the Ferris Commission retained some commitment to the liberal agenda of the broadcast reform movement. The broadcast industry's unyielding opposition to entry liberalization lent to the FCC the same veneer of reform that had cloaked Civil Aeronautics Board and Interstate Commerce Commission deregulatory actions. The FCC imposed stricter regulation in the cause of equal employment opportunity alongside its pursuance of entry liberalization. And some of the new broadcast services, low-power television in particular, were intended in part to encourage television station ownership by minority groups and nonprofit organizations.[120]

At the same time, the liberalization of entry proceeded under the ideological rubric of the free market. In Ferris' words:

Remove the Commission from the marketplace. Force it to justify the need for regulation. Get it out of the way of industry driven by new technology. If a company has the money to invest in a telecommunications service, let it, and leave it to the public to determine whether the service will survive.[121]

The clear inference was that those areas of the industry where the market was thought to "work" did not justify a need for regulation. Thus it was the Ferris-led FCC which in 1979 instituted the rule-making changes to deregulate commercial radio. The Commission identified as its goal the "potential reduction or elimination of regulations no longer appropriate to certain marketplace conditions."[122]

The Commission reasoned that whereas radio constituted the sole source of broadcast entertainment and information at the time of the Communications Act in 1934, the medium was distinctly secondary to television in this regard by 1979. Moreover, the existence of some 8,654 stations indicated that radio was an industry characterized by healthy competition. There effectively was no salient scarcity issue in commercial radio. Because of these factors, the Commission argued that competitive forces were far more responsive to the wants and needs of the listening audience than government regulators could be.

The Commission did not advocate a strict market approach, but did propose a substantial relaxation of content-based regulations, including:

1. eliminating quantitative guidelines for nonentertainment programming and retaining a modified and more limited obligation to provide such programming;
2. eliminating formal ascertainment procedures;
3. eliminating quantitative guidelines for commercial time; and
4. eliminating program logs requirements.

In a 1983 decision, the District of Columbia Court of Appeals upheld the bulk of radio deregulation as consistent with the Commission's statutory obligations.[123]

Under Reagan appointee Mark Fowler, the FCC took the logic of the radio deregulation inquiry and applied it as gospel to content and structural rules across the board. The Fowler-led FCC sought to eliminate the public trustee status of broadcasters and replace regulation with a marketplace approach. In Fowler's words:

> The theory is "free the businessman; let the businessman react in the marketplace; let the consumer, in other words, be sovereign." The old philosophy was that we had to have big government dictating program content, big government dictating all kinds of standards, big government dictating business conduct in areas that were far afield from the relevant requirements of the Communications Act. All of these things substituted bureaucratic determinations for consumer or marketplace determinations. I think our philosophy is more consistent with a free and democratic society, that we're letting the consumer make those choices.[124]

In September 1981 the FCC issued a package of proposals for Congressional legislation, highlighted by the endorsement of the marketplace-over-regulation policy, the elimination of the equal time and Fairness Doctrines, elimination of the reasonable access and equitable distribution provisions of the 1934 Act, deletion of the comparative license renewal process, and codification of radio deregulation.[125]

The Commission proposed to raise the ownership cap from seven to twelve for an interim period, and then eliminate it altogether in 1990. Though many of these proposed changes have not yet passed Congressional muster, they set the stage for scores of less headline-grabbing, but still highly significant deregulatory actions.

For instance, in the area of broadcast industry structure, there has been a marked move to eliminate ownership ceilings. Congress agreed to raise the station ownership limit to twelve (with the provision that the combined potential audience of the twelve TV stations not exceed 25 percent of US television households). License terms—now renewable by postcard—were extended to 5 years for television and 7 years for radio.[126] In early 1987 the Commission released a notice of inquiry to consider abolition of the long-standing rules against a single entity owning radio stations and television stations in the same city (a key section of the cross-ownership rules).[127]

The content area has also seen crucial changes, particularly with respect to the public trustee model of broadcasting. In 1984 the Commission extended to television the deregulation previously accorded radio. Television content deregulation removed the already minimal quantitative requirements that a licensee should devote to informational, nonentertainment, and locally produced programming.[128] This and the abolition of the ascertainment and log-keeping requirements made license renewal completely *pro forma,* because there would exist no record of a station's programming on which to base a renewal challenge. The Commission essentially eliminated the opportunities of citizens groups to petition to deny a license renewal. For this reason, the Court of Appeals again vacated and remanded the FCC's rules on recordkeeping.[129]

The deregulation of program content and structure of the broadcast industry are intimately linked by a narrow reading of the First Amendment and a belief in the beneficence of the market. We earlier noted the rule changes regarding children's television programming and station trafficking. There are no longer any restrictions on the trading of broadcast stations. Licensees no longer have to air "informative" children's programming, and there are no restrictions on cartoon shows based on toys. The children's television issues reveal how drastically the FCC has changed course under the chairmanship of Mark Fowler. Throughout the 1970s the broadcast reform movement goaded the Commission to rectify the dearth of programs aimed at children. In 1979 the Commission noted that children's programming per station had not increased in the five years since the previous study, and proposed several possible steps, including quotas. True to form, in 1984 the Fowler Commission rejected any mandatory steps, asserting that the marketplace would fill the programming gap, and that, regardless, any such quotas violated broadcasters' First Amendment rights.[130]

Likewise, the FCC's elimination in 1982 of time and frequency limits on commercials and rescission of anti-trafficking rules were enacted to allow the broadcast marketplace to operate free of government interference.[131] Finally, Congress approved the FCC's plan to use a lottery system in awarding low-power television and other kinds of licenses. This was a prelude to the Fowler Commission's effort not to weigh suitability factors in awarding licenses, including the effect a license award would have on diversity, on media concentration, or in implementing the goal of promoting minority ownership. Equal opportunity provisions for ethnic minorities and women were cut back where politically feasible.[132]

It is no wonder that Mark Fowler was the darling of the broadcast industry. The Commission under his chairmanship relentlessly pursued an agenda which mirrored the fifty-year-old demands of the broadcast industry—neutral technical oversight over a broadcast system which is otherwise completely private and market-driven. Indeed, the deregulation of content and structural controls lies behind the highly speculative and volatile trade in broadcast properties in the mid-1980s, including the takeover of ABC by Capital Cities Communications, of RCA by General Electric, and of Metromedia by press baron Rupert Murdoch. Under Fowler, the FCC's policy of "unregulation" was so pro-industry that the Commission scotched certain efforts to extend the entry liberalization begun under Charles Ferris. This was most apparent in its decision not to create additional AM radio stations, but also can be seen in the Commission's refusal to consider new VHF TV stations and its hampering of AM stereo standards.

The process of deregulation in broadcasting—at least with respect to the liberalization of entry—fit much of the pattern of the politics of deregulation we traced out in chapter 7. An oddly heterodox political coalition emerged by the early 1970s to challenge regulatory protectionism. The politically multifaceted championing of cable television assisted in that technology's movement from out of the shadow of conventional broadcasting. For one thing, the new policy discourse on cable television induced the FCC to create a Cable Bureau within the Commission. The Cable Bureau and other proponents of cable (including the Office of Telecommunications Policy) helped fashion the 1972 compromise cable rules that, with time, altered cable's regulatory environment.

Technological factors were crucial in the train of events which eventuated in entry liberalization. In broadcasting, technologically based options created the incentives for prospective entrepreneurs to challenge regulatory orthodoxy. Opportunities created by technological options (in part due to earlier entry liberalizations in the common carrier area) led to contradictions between regulations and eventually caused them to be relaxed. Though undertaken entirely within the traditional protectionist paradigm, these rule relaxations generated inadvertent consequences. The resulting experiments in new services, combined with the emerging "culture" of deregulation, led the Commission to reverse the burden of proof in its long-held competitive harm doctrine. By the late 1970s the FCC itself had come to view its past actions as protectionist and partly responsible for network dominance in television.

Finally, trends in First Amendment law pushed the FCC away from continued emphasis on content controls and toward expanding the structure of broadcasting. *Red Lion* was a highwater mark from which the Court retreated. If that decision's assertion of the rights of listeners and viewers came to the edge of content control, subsequent decisions, most notably, *CBS v. DNC,* developed a concept of editorial autonomy which strongly denied any expansion of content controls or access rights. *HBO,* in addition to undermining the Commission's presumptive harm doctrine, denied the FCC the ability to impose content controls on other media which it declined to impose on conventional broadcasters. Finally, an ongoing debate over the efficacy of the Fairness Doctrine also pushed the FCC in the direction of expanding the number of media outlets. The hope was that this expansion would expand the opportunities for speech generally. Indeed, in the Ferris years, there were some policy-makers who considered the effort to expand the number of media outlets as a better way to realize the historic goals of the broadcast reform movement.

The deregulation of broadcast content and structural rules is different from the pattern of entry liberalization in economically regulated industries. In many ways the Fowler FCC's deregulation efforts seem the only (or most sustained) instance where the attack on social regulation has succeeded. The public trusteeship concept of broadcasting—now under erosion—was in some sense an early form of social regulation. Public trusteeship imposed (however poorly in execution) positive obligations of fairness on broadcast licensees and diversity for the broadcast system as a whole. However, it was a form of social regulation built directly upon an economic and technical edifice. Hence the dismantling of the public trusteeship concept—along with the content and structural rules that implemented it—follows logically from the liberalization of entry. That, of course, is because the legal basis for the regulation of broadcasting hinges fundamentally on the notion of a technical scarcity of the airwaves.[133] The liberalization of entry and success of new media sources are said to make moot the notion of technical scarcity. As Mark Fowler has asserted, let the regulators step aside and let the market decide.

# Conclusion: From Deregulation to Reregulation?

The Reagan Administration came to power in 1980 on a program of reducing the size of government and getting government out of the economy. The dismantling of regulation—particularly *social* regulation—loomed large in these plans. In the eyes of the Reaganites, such regulation not only stoked the fires of inflation, debilitated industrial productivity, and undermined the competitiveness of US commodities in the international marketplace but, perhaps most significant, compromised freedom itself. Nonetheless, after all the rhetoric and all the efforts to roll back social regulation, those agencies have not been dismantled. Their statutes remain intact, and legislative campaigns to weaken specific mandates (such as the Clean Air Act) have failed. An effort to deregulate the social agencies internally through a conscious pattern of slow-down, policy reversal, and nonenforcement has had some, but as the record of judicial review shows, also limited success. A central irony of the deregulation phenomenon is that only those industries whose principal players generally desired continued regulatory oversight were deregulated. Deregulation has affected only the traditional New Deal economic regulatory agencies which exercised price-and-entry controls over infrastructure industries. Furthermore, the dissolution of economic regulation took place largely *before* Reagan came to power.

How was it that the state came to dismantle a part of itself, particularly given the weight of entrenched regulated interests and, for the most part, an admirable, 40-plus-year record of regulatory success? After all, price-and-entry regulation did establish stability in infrastructure industries and succeeded in achieving universal, nondiscriminatory service. The short answer is that deregulation was a *political* process, whereby politicians and regulators changed their minds about the benefits of regulation and defeated the entrenched industry interests that wanted maintenance of the regulatory status quo.

However, the short answer *per se* is somewhat deceptive. Certain features of this political dynamic must be noted. First, following the period of regulatory activism of the Great Society period, corporate political reaction prompted a change in the political agenda such that regulation (in general) became perceived as an institution much in need of "reform." Second, certain preconditions were crucial to the reform dynamic, preconditions which reveal why only industries under *economic* regulation could be deregulated. Those preconditions included (a) regulation-enforced cross-subsidy arrangements that universalized service by shifting the rate burden to large service users; (b) high, sustained inflation which exacerbated the already strong incentives for large service users to bypass the regulated system and for new entrepreneurial entrants to service those users; and (c) attempts by the regulatory agency (or in common carrier telecommunications, by AT&T itself) to frustrate any bypass of the regulated system. In tandem, these intertwined economic and regulatory forces laid the foundation for the emergence of a highly diverse, vocal coalition of businesses and public interest groups opposed to status quo regulation of industries under price-and-entry controls. Moreover, the efforts by regulators to safeguard the traditional regulatory structures and formulas created a growing, bald contradiction between administrative and economic rationality which regulatory reformers of all persuasions found galling.

Hence, third, the regulatory reform movement consisted of a surprisingly heterogeneous political coalition, one which included historically pro-regulation Congressional liberals, free market economists, various corporate lobbies and individual businesses, and public interest groups. Joined within that coalition were two political logics usually diametrically opposed to each other—conservative free market economic theory and a left-liberal theory of political participation. Each "logic" attacked regulation from the standpoint of its own theoretical position. Liberals and public interest groups, embodying the logic of participatory democracy and seeing in traditional regulatory agencies evidence of "capture," came to advocate deregulation as a solution to entrenched corporate power. Conservatives and free market economists, rooted in laissez-faire ideology and seeing in regulatory agencies vast bureaucracies whose arbitrariness engendered economic inefficiency and artificial protectionism, championed deregulation as the avatar of economic efficiency. In various price-and-entry controlled industries, the empirical example of an unregulated service provided the ideologically diverse reform coalition with a powerful model that legitimated competition as a practice which fulfilled the values of both efficiency and equity. In broadcasting, the critical economic conditions discussed above did not apply, of course, but the ideological battles were essentially the same and were central. In broadcasting, cable television constituted the same sort of empirical example of a service not completely covered by regulation, and which could be used to challenge regulatory protectionism.

These conditions were there for airlines, trucking, railroads, telecommunications, banking, and, in slightly different form, broadcasting. They were not there for social regulation. Political conservatives and liberals clashed deeply and fundamentally over social regulation. Because there was no consensus over social regulation, the status quo remained and those agencies could not be dismantled statutorily. The attempts to legislate the deregulation of the social agencies have come to nothing.

Finally, a transformation in the standards for judicial review favored the political dynamic for both the deregulation of economic controls *and* the continued support of social regulation. With the liberalization of standing before regulatory agencies came a new standard for judicial review. Regulatory agencies not only had to meet the traditional "arbitrary and capricious" test in judicial review, but now had to show that regulatory decisions had accorded "adequate consideration" to all interests involved in a regulatory controversy. If "adequate consideration" assisted public interest groups in the period of regulatory activism, by the mid-1970s that standard of review also helped would-be entrepreneurial competitors in their efforts to offer new (sometimes unregulated) services. By forcing regulatory agencies to accord consideration to the claims of would-be entrants and new service offerings, and by compelling the agencies to offer genuine evidence for a policy (rather than just tradition), the courts sometimes directly challenged regulatory protectionism. Meanwhile, the same adequate consideration standard limited the corporate and conservative effort to derail social regulation. Reagan-appointed agency administrators, though somewhat successful in pursuing deregulation through nonenforcement and policy-reversal, had to contend with a barrage of lawsuits from labor unions and public interest groups. In a significant number of these cases, the regulatory agency was and continues to be reversed.[1]

These politics of deregulation raise larger theoretical concerns. The very fact of deregulation tends to invalidate capture and conspiracy theories of regulation, and to restore a measure of autonomy to state action. Most directly affected corporations did not want deregulation and lobbied hard against it. The fact that deregulation is specific to a certain type of agency and a certain type of industry indicates that regulation and deregulation cannot be discussed in the abstract, but require historical and empirical elucidation. The accumulation-legitimation model of the state, tied to an organizational view of regulatory constraints and behavior, seems most appropriate in this regard.

The accumulation-legitimation model, though too general and abstract to permit prediction, is broad enough to show that regulation is ensconced within a balance of constraints which *usually* make regulation conservative. The New Deal price-and-entry regulatory agencies were set up to reestablish stability to industries essential to commerce and the economy generally. The structures of those infrastructure industries—including, crucially, their private natures—were already set. Regulation helped permit them to function, expand, and be profitable. In short, regulation guaranteed infrastructures by protecting the private corporations which delivered those infrastructural services. To the extent that such regulation served a "public interest," it was a public interest achieved within a pre-determined capitalist universe. The public interest largely entailed the facilitation of the free flow of commerce. Conservatism characterized agency actions on the day-to-day level as well. Situated as perhaps the weakest player in the terrain of power, regulatory agencies usually opted for decisions which proved organizationally the easiest, self-preserving, and protective of the difficult decisions and compromises fashioned previously.

Yet regulation does respond to shifts in the political agenda, to "legitimation" demands. Regulatory agencies do possess some degree of "autonomy." Both the Great Society period of regulatory activism and the succeeding period of regulatory reform illuminate this. The demands of left-liberal publics underlay the extraordinary creation of new regulatory agencies and the striking level of increased participation in the proceedings of older regulatory agencies in the late 1960s to early 1970s. Likewise, corporate complaints and demands in the succeeding period of regulatory reform induced changes in the nature of regulation. Indeed, against the wishes of the principal industrial players, regulators themselves sometimes pursued experiments in competition during this period.

Another theoretical concern must be addressed. The economic regulation of infrastructure industries was a marvelous example of the balance between accumulation and legitimation imperatives in a capitalist society. Drawing from the common law of public callings, New Deal regulatory agencies exercised command controls in order to promote the free flow of commerce. They achieved this via the fundamental common law principle of nondiscrimination. Through the control of entry and the stifling of market mechanisms, regulation established stability in industries deemed particularly essential to economic development and growth. At the same time—again reaching back to common law—regulation established social equity through imposition of a duty to serve all, and at reasonable rates. What is this if not rationalization of capitalism by the state within the dual imperatives/constraints of accumulation and legitimation? It was, in today's political lingo, a successful "industrial policy." If this is so, how do we understand the dissolution of this arrangement? By way of answering this final question, we must examine empirically what deregulation has wrought. It is here we discern a second irony of deregulation.

Historically pro-regulation, liberals reversed their traditional predilections and championed deregulation by the end of the 1970s. They advocated deregulation because of the supposed capture of the economic agencies by regulated industries. Deregulation, they hoped, would deconstruct the almost feudal tie that had developed between regulated industries and their client agencies. With the destruction of that unholy relationship, liberals expected that open entry and competition would thereby facilitate efficiency *and* equity. As we shall see below, however, deregulation appears to betray liberal hopes. Deregulation may untie the connection between regulated industry and agency, but, in so doing, it unleashes the very forces which called forth regulatory controls in the first place. Open entry and competition make for short-run efficiencies and long-run economic uncertainties. By distributing risks and benefits in a decidedly differential fashion, deregulation undermines the traditional principle of equity.

## The Ambiguous Consequences of Deregulation

In all industries, deregulation has deconstructed the cartels established by regulation, and the affected economic players quickly have adpated to open entry. Just as similar structural features of these industries made them ripe for deregulation, so these have eventuated in roughly similar trends in deregulation's aftermath.

## Airlines

Because airlines have the longest history of deregulation, post-regulation developments in that industry present almost an ideal type. Gaps in service caused by the initial retreat of major airline carriers from low-density markets to known profitable routes initiated the emergence of small local and regional air carriers. According to CAB statistics, while 30 airlines provided scheduled interstate service in 1978, after deregulation the number increased to 37 airlines in 1984. This figure understates the growth of new carriers. Former intrastate airlines expanded into neighboring states, while new commuter airlines moved into the less-traveled, short-haul markets. The market share of the dominant "trunk" airlines (now classified as "majors") decreased slightly but constantly since deregulation to 1984.[2]

Faced with increasing competition from local-service airlines with well-developed feeder operations, the trunks realigned their routes to adopt the "hub and spoke" pattern. Rather than schedule innumerable separate flights directly between cities, the major airlines set up regional airport distribution centers into which all flights go and from which flights are redirected to final destinations. For instance, nearly all TWA flights are routed through TWA's hub in St. Louis. The hub and spoke structure is reputed to provide greater overall efficiency and a better integrated service network. One early study (1982) held that total factor productivity growth (the ratio of all airline outputs, in terms of passenger miles and ton-miles of freight, to all airline inputs, including labor, aircraft, fuel, terminal equipment, advertising, etc.) of US airlines during the first five years after deregulation was 80 percent greater than the final six years prior to deregulation.[3] Airlines offer more price/service options than they did under regulation, and, according to the CAB, airlines also offer flights to more markets than they did under regulation. Route changes and new service increased the number of markets with through-plane competitive service by 55 percent by 1984. Competition has created incentives for some carriers to improve their productivity through the purchase of more cost-efficient jets.[4]

Consequently, airline fares, adjusted for inflation, declined some 13 percent between 1978 (when deregulation began) and 1986. A 1988 Federal Trade Commission report claimed that fares have dropped about 25 percent.[5] A 1986 Brookings Institution study concluded that airline deregulation saves Americans $6 billion a year through lower fares and better service. In 1988 Brookings recalculated that figure to $12 billion. For a variety of reasons, including lower fares, air traffic nearly doubled between 1979 and 1987.[6] Fare competition on high-density routes was brisk through 1985. Though fares rose in 1986, Continental Airlines set off a new airfare war with announced fare reductions in November of that year.[7] This would indicate that on *contested* high-density routes, fare competition is likely to continue.

On the other hand, without the obligation to serve and the continued subsidy of low-density routes, some 114 small and medium-sized communities, formerly served by some air carrier, were abandoned by October 1984. There no longer was commercial air service to or from these communities.[8] The reductions in airfares and gains in airline productivity were and continue to be spread in a highly differential, some might say discriminatory, fashion. Passengers on competitive, high-density routes receive substantial discounts; passengers on low-density, generally noncompetitive, routes see fares go up—sometimes substantially. Low-density runs also tend to experience unexpected shifts in operating schedules. Hence some cities have lost commerce due to unpredictable (or a lack of) air service.

Productivity gains have been posted partly from adoption of the hub and spoke structure, but also because of significant concessions wrested from airline unions. Competition from the small nonunion airline entrants creates pressures on the large carriers to cut costs. The most variable cost, of course, is labor. The destabilizing effects of straight-out competition underlie, and were used to legitimate, the union-busting strategies of Continental Airlines, the exaction of worker give-backs at Eastern Airlines, and the change in pay scales and work rules at several airlines in the aftermath of deregulation.[9]

Competitive pressures may be a factor in declining air safety records. While capital-rich major carriers such as American can afford to purchase new jets to improve their productivity, most new airline entrants buy older aircraft, some as old as 16 years. Cost-cutting efforts have meant the deferring of maintenance. The Federal Aviation Authority has cited major carriers both for violating record-keeping regulations and for using improper or nonstandard parts. According to the International Association of Machinists, there are approximately 12 to 15 percent fewer mechanics in the industry today than before deregulation, even though airlines are now flying one-third more aircraft. In addition, the congestion caused by the hub and spoke system may be partially responsible for the significant increase in air disasters in the last couple of years. The FAA has fewer inspectors to cope with a greater number of aircraft. Nineteen eighty-five was the worst year for fatalities in commercial aviation history.[10]

The resurrection of marketplace discipline has been a success—perhaps too great of a success. The issues of stability and concentration are perhaps the most crucial in any assessment of deregulation. To no one's surprise, financial problems have accompanied the transition to deregulation. However, after a brief period of promise, recent evidence indicates that the new airline entrants are struggling to maintain the small inroads they have made. Several new airlines and some older ones have declared bnakruptcy.[11] Frightened by the large number of failures of new carriers, investors have become leery of backing new airlines. In sharp counter-point, the declining market share of the major airlines reversed abruptly in 1984. By the end of 1986, the six largest carriers controlled an estimated 84 percent of the market, as opposed to 73 percent in 1978 (the last year under regulation). As of September 1987, statistics indicated that the eight largest carriers controlled 94 percent of domestic air travel.[12]

Nineteen eighty-four seems to be the year when competition was transformed from a force that bore new entrants and impelled productivity gains to a juggernaut that brought forth industrial instability and takeover activity. Competitive pressures and financial instability underlie a ferocious merger and buy-out movement in the airline industry. The concentration of ownership in airlines reached epic proportions in 1986, with the purchase of Frontier by People Express; of New York Air, Eastern, and People Express by Texas Air; of Ozark by TWA; of Republic by

Northwest; of National and Ransome by Pan Am; of Western by Delta; of AirCal by American; of PSA by US Air. United Airlines bought Pan Am's Pacific routes. Texas Air Corporation, now the largest domestic airline holding company, continued its relentless growth in 1987, purchasing the gates and airport facilities of Presidential Airways (a small east-coast carrier) in January. In January 1987, rumors circulated about a merger between American Airlines and the troubled Pan Am. Many industry analysts predict that the wave of consolidation will culminate in half a dozen major airlines supported by twenty to thirty smaller regional carriers. The oligopolistic structure will allow *de facto* price-setting.[13]

The danger of concentration is not alleviated by open entry. This is because entry into the airline business is affected by other factors which lessen the "contestability" of markets. The most important of these factors lies in the bottlenecks of landing slots and terminal facilities at airports. The number of landing slots and terminals are limited and inelastic. There is a brisk market for access to these among the various carriers. New entrants can be frozen out of routes and hubs simply because of their inability to secure landing slots. When United Airlines negotiated with People Express for the purchase of Frontier Airlines in July 1986, what United was really after was Frontier's landing slots. These would augment and consolidate United's Denver hub. Indeed, some research argues that the hub and spoke networks themselves erect barriers to competition. Some markets, such as Minneapolis, Memphis, Pittsburgh, Detroit, and St. Louis, have become so dominated by one major carrier that the market will largely be immune to competition, and fares could rise considerably.[14]

Another factor which dampens entry is the impact of computerized reservation systems. Deregulation resulted in a dramatic increase in the number of fares, which in turn contributed to a growing reliance on travel agents as marketers of airline tickets. Together, these sparked a growing importance of computerized reservation systems (CRS). The CRSs operated by United and American Airlines together accounted for 70 percent of the domestic revenues booked by travel agents nationwide, according to a 1986 study by the US General Accounting Office. Small carriers cannot afford to establish their own CRSs, and they must pay high rates to participate in the existing systems. Moreover, biased computerized reservation screens were found to have diverted customers to the CRS-owning carriers, because they had listed those carriers' flights first.[15]

A final problem consequent to deregulation must be considered. If it is true that deregulation-fueled competition has lowered airfares, the same competitive dynamic underlies airport congestion, substantial delay and increasing customer frustration, and safety problems. Competition means competition over scheduling. Airlines tend to declare schedules which they cannot actually meet. The hub-and-spoke system, reputed to be more efficient, also means that margins of error in scheduling are very slim. Consequently, the number of missed airline connections is enormous. The economic effects of, say, missed business conferences due to airline delays, are rarely counted into figures touting the economic benefits of airline deregulation. Deregulation has brought competition and short-run economic efficiencies in airlines along with the loss of service to some, discriminatorily spread benefits, and long-run uncertainties about concentration and stability. This general situation describes trucking, railroads, banking, and telecommunications as well.

## Trucking, Intercity Buses, and Railroads

Trucking has seen the proliferation of entry and a fair amount of rate discounting since deregulation. In the market for whole truckload shipments, for example, prices fell by 25 percent during the first three years of deregulation.[16] Competition among interstate truckers has been fierce, with some 17,000 new entrants and 6,470 failures by 1986. The trade association figures indicate that 25 to 30 percent of all truckers were in the red between 1983 and 1985.[17] The mostly open entry has virtually eliminated some of the energy inefficient regulations that plagued the old regulatory arrangements. In the estimation of most transportation analysts, the industry is more efficient now.[18]

But the competition has come in the full truckload part of the industry; there has been little change in the less-than-truckload (LTL) business, which requires a terminal to sort shipments. Indeed, there has been no entry into the LTL market from companies not formerly in trucking. The competition in LTL has been a modest expansion by companies previously in particular regions to new regions.[19] Again, evidence suggests that the terminal network (trucking's version of the airline hub and spoke system) erects a tremendous barrier to entry. According to the GAO, the limited data available indicate that concentration has generally increased in each region since deregulation in 1980. The big three national LTL carriers—Yellow Freight System, Roadway Services, and Consolidated Freightways—now control more than 25 percent of the LTL market, up 10 points in the past five years.[20]

Prices have gone down with deregulation, but, like airlines, the benefits are distributed differentially. In LTL shipments, the widespread practice of discounting is based on volume. Hence, large shippers have gained most (K-Mart reportedly sometimes gets 50 percent discounts) while small shippers receive small (on the order of 10–15 percent) or no discounts, and often have to pay high minimum charges. This raises the question of whether small shippers are in effect subsidizing competition for contracts from big shippers. And national LTL truckers, expanding into regional markets, reportedly are using profits from less competitive long-haul routes to subsidize discounts on short-hauls. This may drive out small regional carriers.[21]

Like airlines, there is some evidence that the competitive pressures untethered by deregulation have contributed to a rise in accidents and safety violations involving trucks. Nationwide, the number of accidents involving interstate trucks rose 23.4 percent in 1985, to 39,030, from 31,628 in 1983, according to a report by the Senate Committee on Commerce, Science and Transportation.[22]

In trucking, the abandonment of the obligation to serve may not have had any consequences whatever, in large part because the obligation was a myth to begin with. The hearings on trucking regulafion established that in the case of certificated motor carriers to small towns, there was no evidence whatever of its cross-subsidization. The ICC had no record of what carriers were serving which towns. It had never refused a carrier's request to be permitted to drop such service. The most important service to small communities was provided by exempt carriers, who presumably did so because it was profitable. In Alfred Kahn's words, "The widely asserted benefits of regulation in insuring service to small communities, proved, upon examination, to be a complete fraud."[23]

The same cannot be said, however, of intercity bus service, which was partially deregulated in 1982. The Bus Regulatory Reform Act, among other things, made it much easier for bus companies to abandon unprofitable routes. As a consequence, many rural communities and small towns whose only public transportation was intercity bus service have seen that service disappear. By the end of 1986, some 3,763 communities lost bus service and 751 other cities suffered a reduction of service, according to the ICC.[24] The competitive shakeout came quickly. In June 1987, Greyhound Lines, Inc., the nation's largest interstate bus company, announced that it would buy the bus routes and other assets of its last remaining nationwide competitor, Trailways Corporation.[25]

Railroads, in decline for decades, began to recapture shipping contracts from trucking companies in the early aftermath of the Staggers Rail Act of 1980. The act created a regulation-free zone of rate change within which carriers could raise or lower rates. The law streamlined procedures for abandonment of service and looked more favorably on railroad mergers. As a result, railroad revenues and profits went up—the return on investment for the twelve months ending October 1985 was 4.6 percent. *Forbes* magazine called railroad deregulation "one of the great success stories of US business."[26]

Yet, a series of mergers has reduced the number of large rail-freight carriers from 13 in 1978 to 6 huge regional systems by 1986. These carry 86 percent of the rail freight and earn 93 percent of the profits, according to *Business Week*. The merged lines have consolidated operations and sold off thousands of miles of unprofitable branches. Entry has been confined to nonunion "short lines" which feed traffic to the major railroad lines. Shippers who have no realistic alternative to a single railroad, such as Montana wheat growers, have charged that without rate regulation, they are captives to monopoly power.[27]

## Banking

Concentration, instability, and differentially distributed benefits also characterize the partially deregulated banking system, set loose with the Depository Institutions Deregulation and Monetary Control Act of 1980. The financial services industry has become competitive with the elimination of federal limits on interest rates and the relaxation of barriers that divided financial services from areas of banking operation. Some claim that banking deregulation has increased the nation's economic efficiency. Competition has forced traditional providers of financial services to analyze their costs and streamline their operations. Competition for high-balance depositors has resulted in higher rates of interest for all savers. And with more institutions making loans, riskier entrepreneurial ventures are more likely to get credit.[28]

But that very competitive dynamic means that banks make bad loans. In 1985, commercial banks charged off $13 billion in bad loans. By comparison, in 1968 they charged off just $300 million. The figure in 1986 was higher than that registered in 1985. The failure of small banks and savings and loan institutions must be seen as a major consequence of banking deregulation. Forty-eight banks failed in 1983—by far the greatest number since the Depression. The number of bank failures in 1984 was over 80. By 1985, 120 banks either failed or required financial assistance from the FDIC. In 1986 the number exceeded 135. The Federal Home Loan Bank Board expects to have to rescue at least 216 savings and loan institutions in the next three years, at a cost that could reach $25 billion. A third of the nation's 3,147 savings and loan associations lost money in 1987. The auditing arm of Congress estimates that hundreds of other banks are weak. These bank failures cannot be attributed to deregulation alone, but, with some exceptions, a large number were small savings and loan institutions that folded because high interest rates siphoned money out of them. Some were larger, entrepreneurial banks which made a series of bad loans.[29]

Because of bank instability, the competitive process augurs many more mergers with powerful commercial banks. A 1984 Booz-Allen & Hamilton study predicted that, of the current 14,000 US banks, as many as two-thirds will no longer exist independently by the end of the decade.[30] Technological changes favor the large commercial banks over smaller institutions. Through ~lectronic funds transfers (EFT), large financial institutions can move money out of demand deposits into "near-money" assets such as treasury bills and commerical paper extremely rapidly. Such computerized cash management services tend to concentrate funds in the hands of fewer banks in the money-center cities.[31] At the same time, competition seems to proceed at the expense of small depositors. Since the poor and small depositors supposedly impose higher transaction costs on banks, banking institutions have instituted significant charges for services that had been free or cheap prior to decontrol.[32]

The special characteristic of the banking business is that it can so quickly affect the stability of the national economy. Hence, in the case of banking, there is no true discipline of the market—particularly for large banks. The near collapse of Continental Illinois in May 1984 underscores this in a spectacular way. Continental Illinois National Bank and Trust Company is the nation's eighth largest bank. Its collapse could shake not only the foundations of US banking, but international financial institutions as well. Thus the Federal Reserve and FDIC guaranteed that no depositor, no matter how large, would lose any amount of its deposits with Continental Illinois. In late June 1984, the federal government also announced a $4.5 billion financial aid package to keep Continental Illinois in business. In effect nationalizing the bank, the government acted to protect all depositors and creditors by taking over a huge portfolio of bad loans and supplying the institution with new cash. As Representative Fernand J. St. Germain, chairman of the House Banking Committee, said, "The truth is, large banking institutions, despite all the talk about free enterrpise, marketplaces and deregulation, do not fail under our system of government protection."[33] Bank deregulation makes it more difficult for the

Federal Reserve to exercise macroeconomic controls, if only because market-determined interest rates now quickly adapt to Fed moves to inflate or shrink the money supply.

## Carrier Communications

The breakup of AT&T and corresponding deregulation of common carrier communications sets up a competitive dynamic in telecommunications. In both telecommunications and broadcasting, there has been a profusion of service options and technological innovations as competitors carve out new market niches and try to capture larger market shares in established services. Quite possibly, the most hoped-for and potentially most important result of telecommunications deregulation—competition in the burgeoning field of information technology—will eventuate in economy-wide productivity gains. That, however, is a long-term question and is complicated by the larger changes which accompany the transformation of the economy from goods production to services and "information." For it is clear that the same telecommunications technologies which may raise productivity also make possible the continuing export abroad of domestic jobs and capital.[34]

Notwithstanding the differences in telecommunications on account of its technological revolution, the consequences of deregulation in telecommunications mirror those of other infrastructure industries. With some notable exceptions, such as telephone instruments, the options and innovations triggered by divestiture and deregulation come largely to specialized information users—primarily businesses—while basic telephone users, for example, pay higher rates and may look forward to a decline in the quality of service. Bereft of their traditional internal subsidies and required to upgrade their facilities to permit access by any long-distance company, the local telephone companies have asked for hefty raise increases from public utility commissions and have instituted "zone usage measurement" for local service in many areas. All telephone users now pay FCC-imposed "end-user access fees," now set (for residential users) at $2 per month and slated to rise. Local telephone rates have gone up about 40 percent since 1984.[35]

Local telephone monopolies still have an obligation to serve all who request service, but installation fees no longer are absorbed by the system as a whole. This affects prospective rural and poor telephone users dramatically. For example, according to statistics compiled by the Public Utility Law Project of New York, less than 75 percent of low-income households in New York Telephone Company territory have phones. This compares with a national telephone penetration rate of 92 to 93 percent. The major factor in the absence of telephones in low-income households is the high installation rate (about $60 to $120 in New York Telephone territory).[36] Installation fees in rural areas are far more expensive. Extending a new line to a farmhouse in a sparsely populated area may cost several thousand dollars.

In contrast, long-distance rates have dropped nearly 30 percent during that same period. Yet, according to AT&T figures compiled in 1984, just 10 percent of residential users make over $25 worth of long-distance calls per month; just 14 percent of business users make over $50 worth of long-distance calls per month.[37] It is *these* users who benefit from deregulation. Any assessment of the divestiture which claims that the increase in local telephone rates will be balanced by a corresponding decrease in long-distance rates fails to recognize the vast difference in user classes.

Because the bypass of the regulated local telephone system by business looms as a continuing and major threat, the local monopolies have offered large users rate reductions in order to keep them in the system.[38] The incentives to bypass have a technological as well as an economic component. Broadband data and video carriage are hindered by the small bit capacity of the so-called "local loop," the telephone wire that goes into the residence or business (also known in the argot as the "last mile"). Companies with big data needs may find interconnection into the local loop a burden—slow and error-prone. Hence, some local telephone monopolies have moved to upgrade their facilities to accommodate large business users, even entire financial districts.[39] These considerable costs are then added to the ratebase, ultimately paid in disproportionate measure by the basic residential telephone user. In other words, large, sohpisticated users have the ability and incentive to drop out of the public system. In order to keep those heavy users in the system, telephone companies offer what are in effect below-market rates. Hence, the new environment of competitive/regulated telecommunications in effect reverses the traditionally alleged direction of cross-subsidy. The new, market-driven cross-subsidy goes from basic and local users to sophisticated and business users.

Higher costs for local service can only get worse as bypass technologies get better and large corporate users drop out of the public network. At the time of the divestiture, most studies were inconclusive about bypass. Many, including many Public Utilities Commissions, believed that the local telephone companies in effect "cried wolf" over bypass in order to justify exorbitant rate hike requests.[40] However, a GAO study on bypass published in 1986 found that 16 to 29 percent of large volume telephone users were currently bypassing. Another 19 to 53 percent indicated plans to initiate or increase bypass (though it must be said that corporate plans shift constantly, hence a statistic on intentions may not mean very much). The BOCs estimate that the loss of 1 percent of business institutional locations could represent 14 to 48 percent (dèpending on the state) of their total long-distance revenues.[41]

The telecommunications equipment market is competitive and relatively well balanced among several firms. Deregulation spawned hundreds of new businesses. However, even in the equipment market a shakeout looks likely as oversupply sets in and profit margins erode. Already, 70 percent of the market for private branch exchanges (PBX), those computerized devices that act as mini-switchboards for large offices, is divided among Northern Telecom, AT&T, Rolm, and Mitel.[42]

The long-distance market is not competitive. Initial competition in long-distance was largely the result of the early stages of regulated competition and the fact that AT&T competitors had inferior connections into the local loop. Because of those inferior connections, new long-distance vendors were charged less to obtain access to the local loop. The vendors could then offer consumers long-distance rates markedly cheaper to those of AT&T. As the local telephone companies upgrade their facilities to permit equitable, high-quality access to any and all long-distance carriers, however, the new companies have to pay the same access charges as does

AT&T. Hence, the price difference between AT&T and its competitors lessens. AT&T, however, remains under rate-of-return regulation on its long-distance service. And because AT&T's profits are high (due to several factors, including recent declines in interest rates, lower access charges into local telephone companies generally, and labor force reductions at AT&T), the FCC has continued to order AT&T to make rate reductions to stay within the 12.2 percent authorized rate of return. These rate reductions have the effect of further closing the rate differential with its competitors.

Following the "equal access" balloting in 1986, where consumers were obliged to choose a primary long-distance telephone company, AT&T emerged with over 80 percent of the market. The major competitors such as US Sprint (a merger of GTE Corporation and United Telecommunications Inc.) and MCI (now backed by IBM, which has a 17 percent stake in the company) have had to keep their rates low to gain any market share in their competition with AT&T. At the same time, MCI and Sprint are in the midst of expensive efforts to construct their own advanced fiber optic networks (to replace older microwave and cable networks).[43] This capital drain diminishes the ability of these competitors to discount their rates much further. The consequence of low rates and high expenditures to upgrade networks, not surprisingly, is mounting losses. MCI lost $448 million in 1986. Sprint posted a $1.1 billion loss in 1987.[44] These economic forces have dramatically reduced the number of competitors in the field. From the dozens of major competitors offering long-distance service in the year after the divestiture, effectively only three remain: AT&T, MCI, and Sprint. In August 1987 the FCC announced a proposal to cease regulating AT&T's long-distance rates on a rate-of-return basis. The plan would set a cap on the prices AT&T may charge, but not on its profits. According to the FCC, the cap plan would protect consumers while providing AT&T incentives to become more efficient. Overall, this may save competition between the three remaining long-distance companies, but only with the almost certain consequence of a steady, long-term rise in long-distance rates.[45]

Regulatory palliatives to AT&T's continuing power in long distance threaten to resurrect some of the very problems the divestiture was supposed to rectify. In February 1987 the Justice Department filed a detailed recommendation with Judge Greene that would permit the seven Regional Holding Companies (or, in the current argot, RBOCs, the acronym for Regional Bell Operating Company) to enter the competitive long-distance market in areas outside their geographic telephone monopoly service. That filing also asked that the RBOCs be allowed to manufacture telephone equipment, to expand into new businesses without prior court approval, and to sell electronic information services (such as message services, automated listings to classified advertising, and services that permit computer protocol conversion).[46] In other words, the Justice Department filing asked Judge Greene to drop all of the major structural restrictions that had been placed on the divested Bell Operating Companies consequent to the break-up.

The Justice Department's deregulatory recommendations and the theory that underlay them were based on a massive report entitled "The Geodesic Network." The report, written under the supervision of lawyer, economist, and mechanical engineer Peter Huber, strongly advocated continued deregulation in telecommunications in the name of national and international "competitiveness." Backed by the RBOCs, the Justice Department recommendations went so far as to suggest a possible end to monopoly service in the local loop. The filing recommended that in the future the prohibition on "in region" long-distance service be lifted only in those areas where the states remove the regulatory protection that guarantees the local Bell company a monopoly franchise for local telephone service.[47] Justice insisted that because of new FCC rules (the Third Computer Inquiry), the removal of the consent decree restrictions on the RBOCs would not leave those companies free to practice anticompetitive discrimination in equipment manufacture or information services.[48] The irony in all this, of course, is that just five years earlier, the Justice Department insisted that structural problems in telephony required the break-up of AT&T. The same structural problems apply to the RBOCs, yet now the Justice Department argued that they should be released from restrictions because there is no real potential for anticompetitive abuse.

In September 1987 Judge Greene issued his ruling on the Justice Department's filing. Declaring that the structural incentives to engage in anticompetitive behavior remain unchanged, the judge refused to lift the core restrictions that prohibit the RBOCs from providing long-distance service and from making telephone equipment. Greene did rule that the RBOCs could use their telephone networks to transmit electronic information services such as electronic mail and voice messaging. However, he upheld the restriction that bans them from providing the actual service, citing the danger of the monopoly conduit provider being also in the business of generating information content.[49] The barrage of criticism from diverse quarters that greeted Judge Greene's ruling indicates that the issues will not disappear.[50] More important, because of the global dynamic introduced by American deregulation, telecommunication offerings now constitute a key factor in international comparative economic advantage. For example, several trans-national corporations have moved all or part of their communications centers to Great Britain from West Germany, citing as reasons lower telephone-line charges and less burdensome regulations. The user demands of transnational corporations, along with the pleas of domestic information technology firms to service them free of regulatory constraints, will continue to exert enormous pressures for further deregulation.

The Justice Department recommendation hints at the other side of deregulation in telecommunications carriage, and underscores the fact that the same problems that existed prior to divestiture have taken on new forms. Just as there is now (some) competition in long-distance (or "interexchange") communications, deregulatory actions have begun to open the door to competition in local distribution (or "intraexchange"). Cable television, though overwhelmingly dedicated to the provision of video entertainment at present, nonetheless has the technical capability to challenge the local telephone company for many communications services. After all, cable is simply another wire (and one with incredibly larger bandwidth) into homes and businesses. Indeed, in many cities cable television has an option to become an unregulated competitor of the telephone company for private line, enhanced data, access bypass, and other specialized telecommunciations services. New York City, for example, uses Manhattan Cable for some of its voice and data communications needs. Boston does the same.[51] The FCC has authorized other services capable of local distribution service. Among these are Digital Termination Services (DTS), Multipoint Distribution Services (MDS), and cellular radio.[52] None of these alternatives to local distribution would be used for residential telephony, of course. They would be used for business (and government) voice and data—in other words, a form of bypass and creamskimming.

Deregulation thus raises questions about the telecommunications system itself. Continuing problems of competition and monopoly seem to require judicial or regulatory rulings that themselves create new conflicts and contradictions. In the long run, deregulation may eventually translate into economy-wide efficiency gains as the telecommunications infrastructure becomes transformed by new and sophisticated information technologies. In the short to middle run, however, given the many players and service resellers and equipment suppliers, each with different technical standards and tariffs, deregulation may mean innovation in specific parts of the system, but neglect of other parts, and a fair degree of anarchy for the system as a whole.

Admittedly, there is a certain amount of "Chicken Little" syndrome in the fears over future of the telephone system. After all, other complex services such as electricity work well without ever having had near the degree of system integration as did the Bell System. However, it is certainly true that research and development in telecommunications no longer will be undertaken with *systemwide* improvement in mind. As Bell Labs reorients its activities toward the market, its unique role in the overall construction and maintenance of the telephone system will disappear. The divested Bell Operating Companies, champing at the bit to diversify into more lucrative business ventures, may allow their guaranteed fair rate of return telephone monopolies to take the back seat. The BOCs moved quickly into competitive businesses where they are not subject to rate-of-return restrictions, including ventures in real estate, international telecommunications consulting, computer retailing, and equipment leasing.[53] Indeed, some analysts foresee large problems ahead due to generally poorer standards and a deterioration in the physical plant of local telephone companies.[54]

## Broadcast Communications

The deregulation of broadcasting and cable has brought about a situation where, for the most part, the FCC no longer acts as the primary barrier to entry. As regulatory-imposed barriers withered away, alternative broadcast technologies and video services began to flourish. By 1984, 83 percent of US households received nine or more television and cable channels combined. The median cable subscriber in 1984 had a choice of about 28 channels. By 1987 approximately 50 percent of American households received cable. There are more than 50 national satellite-delivered cable program services, and a score of regional program services.[55]

Broadcasting (conceived in the broad sense of conventional broadcast, cable, and other video technologies) is becoming competitive. The traditional three-network television oligopoly gradually, but inexorably, has been losing audience market share (down 14 percent between 1975 and 1985, to about 73 percent of the viewing audience) to other broadcast services, notably cable but also to fast-growing independent broadcast stations.[56] Notwithstanding traditional broadcasters' declining audience share, the initial consequences of deregulation were an overall expansion of broadcasting. Advertising revenues for traditional broadcasters were strong in 1984, despite their lower audience shares. However, competition has led to a shakeout. Whereas the networks commonly saw advertising revenues grow on the order of 13 percent a year, those revenues fell to 2.8 percent in 1986.[57] Fear of further audience fragmentation has resulted in widespread cost-cutting campaigns at the networks, and greater concern for the bottom line. This has included the cutback of the traditionally unprofitable public service program enterprises such as documentaries, and a trimming of all the network news divisions.[58] In December 1986, ABC indicated that it would cut network compensation payments to its program-carrying affiliates because of hefty financial losses. CBS was expected to follow suit.[59]

Though historically there was always a fair amount of station trafficking, deregulation (along with new tools of financing, to wit, high-risk, high-yielding "junk bonds") has unleashed a tremendous takeover frenzy in broadcasting. This dynamic was abetted, of course, by the raising of the ownership limit of stations from seven to twelve. In keeping with its view that broadcasting is a business like any other, the Fowler FCC got out of the way of station trafficking. Where historically the Commission dampened takeovers by requiring approval of a potential buyer's "fitness" to be a broadcaster, the Fowler FCC reduced the concept of fitness to financial terms only. The explosive increase in broadcast station trading since 1981 has been accomplished by a steady increase in dollar values assigned to station properties.[60] The expected long-term outcome of the merger movement in broadcast communications is a consolidation of ownership. By the end of 1986, the boom in independent television stations softened, and industry watchers were talking about a general shakeout. The winners will be the networks, other capital-rich communications corporations such as Gannett and Time, Inc., and the strong traditional group owners, such as Metromedia and Westinghouse. The uncertain short-run economic climate for the networks, combined with the general volatile merger movement of the mid-1980s put all three networks on the takeover/merger block in 1985–1986. Each is now controlled by a new owner: General Electric acquired NBC's parent company, RCA; Capital Cities bought ABC, and Laurence A. Tisch became the controlling shareholder and acting chief executive at CBS.[61]

A similar takeover movement in cable is expected to concentrate that industry. As Jeremy Tunstall relates, by 1985 it was widely expected that the top ten multiple system operators (MSOs), which already controlled half the total cable business, would control some 80 percent. Cable began a brisk period of system transaction and merger in 1987.[62] At the level of cable program suppliers, concentration is evident as well. Many of the strongest programs are owned by the same large corporations, some of which also are powerful MSOs. According to a *Channels* compilation, the concentration trend in the field of electronic media is illuminated by the fact that the top 25 players now include: (a) owners of the three television networks and the Fox Broadcasting Company network; (b) nine of the ten television station groups with the greatest potential audience; (c) seven of the ten most extensive cable system holdings, serving more than one-third of cable subscribers; (d) eleven of the 15 top syndicators of television programming; and (e) seven of the ten top ten publishers of pre-recorded videocassettes, with some two-thirds of sales.[63]

Though deregulation has opened up entry, the effect on programming is more difficult to judge. Clearly, there is more on the tube. It is harder to say whether more is better, or even whether more is more diverse. This is an extraordinarily murky area, and cannot be discussed extensively, much less settled, here. Nonetheless, some things can be said. In radio, which was already quite competitive, the elimination of structural and content regulations has meant additional impetus toward the utilization by stations of syndicated packages of automated, pre-recorded and pre-constructed shows. These packages usually consist of a standardized music format with very short inserts (usually between 1 and 3 minutes) for news, weather, and chit-chat. In the typical market, the average FM station runs three and a half minutes of news per hour.[64] And notwithstanding an average of 25 to 30 radio stations in a reasonably sized market, there is a great deal of format duplication. Because the market share commanded by a duplicated format often exceeds a new or different format's market share, format duplication tends to be widespread, as much as 40 percent.[65]

The same can be said for the "new" television. A thriving cable industry and newly invigorated independent television syndication market give viewers more— more sports, more old and new Hollywood movies, more reruns. To many viewers, more *is* better; deregulated television does provide more choices. Nonetheless, more is not more diverse. In the words of one student of broadcast deregulation, more programming means more *variety*, not more diversity.[66] Variety refers to more choices within a relatively narrow set of market-determined formats. Diversity is a more philosophically based concept than simply a market-based notion of consumer choice. Diversity is ensconced within the values which underlie the freedom of speech, values which demand divergent points of view both because they nurture an informed, self-governing citizenry and because they promote cultural pluralism. As the Court wrote in *Associated Press v. United States,* the First Amendment "rests on the assumption that the widest possible dissemination of information from diverse and antagonistic sources is essential to the welfare of the public."[67] This affirmative reading of the First Amendment underlay the decade-long effort of the District of Columbia Circuit Court of Appeals to force the FCC to consider whether radio format changes were in the public interest.[68]

It may be too early to tell whether open entry in broadcasting will engender diversity. To the extent that one of the major reasons for the lack of diversity on traditional television was the artificial scarcity of broadcast outlets, open entry rectifies that problem. The early results, however, are deeply disappointing. As the networks adapt to competition, the low-rated, "cross-subsidized" (after a fashion) public service programs, such as documentaries, get replaced by more popular, glitzy, so-called "news magazines," such as CBS's "West 57th." Childrens' programming is abandoned because it cannot bring in adequate ad revenue. Open cable channels get utilized for ludicrously inane home shopping bazaars.

At the local level, programming won by citizen pressure, such as weekend public affairs shows geared to minority audiences, have been cut back dramatically because such shows do not attract large enough audiences. With more stations fighting for advertising dollars, and more choices for television viewers threatening additional audience fragmentation, station managers cite competitive pressures as the reason for dropping what FCC Chairman Fowler derisively calls "Dudley Do-Good" programming. As a *Wall Street Journal* article reported, one television station replaced five hours of public affairs programming with an interview show, cartoons, a general newscast, and a beauty-contest show.[69] With deregulation, citizens groups cannot use the fear of FCC intervention to force station managers to air better shows. The new video services, with some exceptions, carve out their market share from known and profitable formats. Apart from the growth of religious networks, the widely anticipated phenomenon of "narrowcasting"—where the new television economics would induce station managers to cater to small, interested audiences—never happened. The broadcast reform movement's hoped-for "television of abundance" is simply more television—without any greater degree of access or programming to minority tastes.

This, perhaps, is the harder-edged point with respect to the often nebulous debate over program diversity. Given the economics of the broadcast industry and how those monies translate into production values, it seems doubtful that the "television of abundance" could ever have worked. After all, when a full-power UFH television station in a major market such as San Diego (KTTY channel 69) is able to charge only $350 for a thirty-second advertising spot during prime time, there is little expectation that the station can purchase, much less produce, new programming of any quality. In comparison, the local CBS affiliate KFMB channel 8, charges $3000 for a thirty-second spot during prime time.[70] Given the commercial structure of American broadcasting, after a certain point the fragmentation of audience logically must mean a diminution of broadcast "standards."

And without the public trustee underpinnings, the market does not seem to provide for the kind of programming envisioned by the FCC in the "Blue Book," for the very reasons of economy elucidated by that report in 1946. Greater diversity does not (or, at least, has not yet) accompany more competition. The monopoly rent conditions—which allowed the FCC on occasion to pressure the networks to air public service programming—have eroded. With free market ideologues running the show at the FCC, even low-power television licenses—a sort of informal *quid pro quo* to minority and citizens groups in exchange for deregulation—have been awarded to established corporate interests. Open entry, in conjunction with the deregulation of content and structural rules, essentially grants complete property rights in a resource that hitherto had been considered public.

In short, without some principle of access or without affirmative regulatory obligations, the expanded broadcast system does not fulfill the values which underlie the First Amendment. The broadcast system merely (and admittedly, this is a complex "merely") follows the dictates of the market, that is, the entrepreneurial interests of media owners. Deregulated broadcasting simply recapitulates the traditional tension between liberalism and democracy in the speech "marketplace," in which a formalistic First Amendment theory legitimates complete freedom for those wealthy enough to own media outlets. But with media concentration and a modern society increasingly dependent upon information and communications, a formalistic First Amendment theory can only legitimate existing power. Jerome Barron had it right: large private media interests act as private censors. Wealth buys media access and communication power, and the marketplace of ideas is overwhelmed by the wealthy. The First Amendment right of most citizens is a right to listen and watch. The free and open debate necessary to a democracy goes unfulfilled.[71]

The final twist, of course, is that the expansion of the broadcast system undermines the legal legitimacy for regulation. The scarcity rationale for the regulation of broadcasting has come under increasing fire.[72] After threatening for several years, in August 1987 the FCC voted to abolish the Fairness Doctrine. The Court of Appeals had ruled in 1986 that the Fairness Doctrine was an administrative construction, not a binding statutory directive.[73] Citing doctrine's chilling effect on broadcast speech and pointing to the multiplicity of broadcast voices now available to the public, the FCC declared the doctrine harmful to the marketplace of ideas.[74] The traditional justification for the regulation of broadcasting rested upon a technical rationale. That rationale clearly has eroded, but there has appeared no widely accepted argument—apart from tradition itself—to counter the free market/formalistic First Amendment theory and justify the continued regulation of broadcasting.

## Deregulation and Labor

Although the impact of deregulation on particular industries has been mixed and ambiguous, the effect on labor is far less equivocal. A consequence of deregulation in most industries has been a marked weakening of unions. In trucking, since 1980 sixty-nine unionized general freight carriers with 103,000 workers under the Teamsters' National Master Freight Agreement have ended operations, and 30,000 to 40,000 Teamster jobs have been lost permanently. According to the Labor Research Association, over 100,000 Teamsters remain on layoff—that is, some 30 percent of all Teamster trucking industry workers.[75]

By 1983, job losses in commercial airlines were around 30,000.[76] And, though that figure is no longer accurate—the airline industry has expanded since then—new hires are predominantly nonunion or are hired under the two-tier system, at substantially lower wages.[77] Between 1982 and 1984 the Communications Workers of America's telephone industry membership fell by 64,000.[78] Since divestiture, AT&T has eliminated 80,000 jobs—a fifth of its work force.[79] The subsidiaries set up by the divested Regional Bell Operating Companies are nonunion. The information industry, with which the old telecommunications industry now competes, is only about 15 percent organized. Hence the pressures on telecommunications unions will increase.

More than inducing layoffs, deregulation has been used to abrogate labor contracts. In 1983, Greyhound, the largest intercity bus carrier, forced deep concessions in wages and work rules from its workers, claiming that deregulation had so radically altered the structure of its operating climate that the company required such concessions in order to remain competitive. Trailways Bus Lines soon followed suit. Indeed, in late December 1986 the owners of Greyhound sold the company principally because they could not wrest further concessions from the members of the Amalgamated Transit Union. Greyhound's new owners contend that they are under no obligation to honor union contracts or to keep the current work force of 8500.[80]

Likewise, Continental Airlines justified its 1983 union-busting bankruptcy maneuver by the cutthroat competition deregulation had created. At American Airlines, key concessions won from unions in 1983 included hiring new employees at much lower wages than senior workers and the ability of management to cross-utilize workers. The 1985 Pan American flight attendants' contracts resulted in permanently reduced new hire rates and concessions on overtime and staffing levels. Eastern Airlines' 1986 contract with its 4200 pilots included a 20 percent wage cut, a two-tier wage plan, and concessions in workrules, increased flight hours, and reduced benefits.[81] The Regional Bell Operating Companies, notwithstanding their continued monopoly power and impressive post-divestiture earnings, contend that CWA operators and clerical workers are overpaid some 30 percent.

Thus, deregulation has become a tool in a new era of labor-capital relations. The flexibility of new capitalists in deregulated industries comes in part from the freedom they have from union contracts. New unions don't grow with the new little companies in trucking, busing, telecommunications, or airlines. In the short run, at least, deregulation does increase competition, which creates pressures and opportunities for companies to make themselves competitive on the backs of their labor unions. As for entrants into the newly competitive arenas, their low-profit margins often force early bankruptcies. Deregulation has undermined the national character of much labor-contract negotiation. The national bargaining system in trucking, the Master Freight Agreement, built by labor leaders, management, and the ICC since the 1950s, is in jeopardy. In airlines, collective bargaining has been conducted on a company-by-company, rather than industry-wide basis since 1978. Under the AT&T monopoly, labor contracts were the product of one-stop negotiations. Since divestiture, the CWA must negotiate separately with all telephone companies.

The use of deregulation as a legitimation for union-busting indicates a problem in American unionization, especially the crisis of the post-World War II agreement between monopoly-sector unions and the effectively cartelized industries with which they bargain. Under such disparate sources of pressure as increased competition, inflation, and deregulation, these older cartels have begun to dissolve, and the economic and social conditions that favored the exchange of decent wages for labor peace also disappear. The competitive domestic and international economic environment underscores labor's increasingly diminished power. Labor's power is local and politically rooted. Capital's power is economic and increasingly international in scope. When the nation-state does not support the conditions that favor labor interests, labor unions are undermined.

The deregulation of price-and-entry-controlled infrastructure industries appeared to make sense to various political actors in the context of high inflation, regulatory protectionism, and, in telecommunications, technological ferment. With universal service accomplished, and with regulatory barriers seemingly blocking progress and innovation in infrastructure industries, the traditional combination of industry protection, nondiscrimination, and reasonable rates seemed outmoded to reformers of many ideological stripes. Broadcasting, though characterized by somewhat different issues than price-and-entry-controlled industries, was seen to exhibit similar problems of protectionism. Reformers came to believe that the protection of conventional broadcasters undermined structural possibilities for change. Given the economic and political context, regulatory protectionism appeared to abridge both efficiency and equity.

In all the affected industries, deregulation has begun to deconstruct the cartels established by regulation. Deregulation has brought competition and short-run economic efficiencies along with long-run uncertainties about stability, concentration, and discrimination. The deconstruction of the cartels has meant the decline of the labor unions that grew up with cartelization. And equally important, deregulation dismantles the system of internal cross-subsidies that historically secured the expansion of service. (In broadcasting, a version of this cross-subsidy, loosely speaking, secured unremunerative, "public interest" programming.) The end of cross-subsidy arrangements pushes the deregulated industries to move toward a cost-based system of service pricing.

Deregulation, therefore, undermines the service-based entitlements that went along with traditional regulation, entitlements which may have been inefficient in a strict economic reckoning, but which we have come to consider the public interest. In telecommunications, deregulation and technological change together undermined the public interest principles that long had been attached to concrete technologies. In telephone this meant universal, reliable service at relatively cheap prices. In broadcasting, this meant acknowledgment that licensees must serve as local outlets for information and community discussion. Thus, deregulation may mean breaking down producer protection, but it dertainly does not mean a democratization of industry. Indeed, if we accept that the government is representative of the public (as poor and contradictory a mediation as that may be), government's retreat from regulation constitutes a retreat from democratic process.

Overall, deregulation may alleviate protectionism, regulatory ineptitude, and bureaucratic formalism. But, in time, it may also decrease established standards of operation and jeopardize the overall stability of infrastructure industries. The short-run, deregulation-induced efficiencies may be of a type that undermine the "system character" of infrastructure services. Ultimately, deregulation also limits democratic access to the policy-making process. These tendencies may induce a reemergence of the economic and social demands that historically called forth many regulatory controls. Indeed, partial moves toward reregulation have begun in the airline industry.[82] The long-run problems of concentration and instability in infrastructure industries can only cause accumulation problems. The discriminatory effects of market-based prices on the poor and on outlying areas likely will engender legitimation problems. The fact that most of the evils for which the New Deal regulatory agencies were created to correct have begun to reappear, indicates that regulation itself likely will reappear in some new form.

# Notes

## Chapter 1. Telecommunications and Their Deregulation: An Introduction

1. United States Constitution, Article I, Section 8 [3].

2. Max Weber, *On Law in Economy and Society,* Max Rheinstein (ed.) (New York: Simon & Schuster, 1954), 98–198.

3. Jürgen Habermas, *Strukturwandel der Offentlichkeit* (Neuwied: Luchterhand, 1962); idem, "The Public Sphere: An Encyclopedia Article," *New German Critique* 1/3 (Fall 1974), 49–55. Also, on the peculiar relation between capitalism and democracy, see Charles E. Lindblom, *Politics and Markets: The World's Political-Economic Systems* (New York: Basic Books, 1977), 161–233.

4. See, of course, John Stuart Mill, *On Liberty,* Currin V. Shields (ed.) (Indianapolis: Bobbs-Merrill Co., 1956). Also see Justice Louis Brandeis' classic opinion in Whitney v. California, 274 U.S. 357 (1927), and Judge Learned Hand's opinion in United States v. Associated Press, 52 F. Supp. 362 (S.D.N.Y. 1943), *aff'd* 326 U.S. 1 (1944).

5. This is a sketchy description of the Federal Communications Commission's Fairness Doctrine and Equal Opportunities Doctrine.

## Chapter 2. Theories of Regulation

1. Thomas K. McCraw, "Regulation in America: A Review Article," *Business History Review* 49/2 (Summer 1975), 159–183.

2. Barry M. Mitnick, *The Political Economy of Regulation* (New York: Columbia University Press, 1980); Barry R. Weingast, "Congress, Regulation, and the Decline of Nuclear Power," *Public Policy* 28/2 (Spring 1980), 231–255.

3. Charles Francis Adams, Jr., "Boston I," *North American Review* CVI (January 1868), 18, 25; idem, "Railroad Inflation," *North American Review* CVIII (January 1869), 158, 163–164. Cited in McCraw, "Regulation in America," 161.

4. George H. Miller, *Railroads and Granger Laws* (Madison: University of Wisconsin Press, 1971).

5. Solon Justus Buck, *The Granger Movement: A Study of Agricultural Organization and Its Political, Economic and Social Manifestations, 1870–1880* (Cambridge: Harvard University Press, 1913); Robert H. Wiebe, *The Search For Order, 1877–1920* (New York: Hill and Wang, 1967).

6. Samuel Haber, *Efficiency and Uplift: Scientific Management in the Progressive Era, 1890–1920* (Chicago: University of Chicago Press, 1964); Samuel P. Hays, *Conservation and the Gospel of Efficiency* (Cambridge: Harvard University Press, 1959).

7. See John B. Clark and John M. Clark, *The Control of Trusts* (New York: Macmillan, 1912).

8. Walter S. Weyl, *The New Democracy* (New York: Macmillan, 1912); Herbert Croly, *The Promise of American Life* (New York: Macmillan, 1909); Walter Lippmann, *Drift and Mastery* (New York: M. Kennerley, 1914); Richard Hofstadter (ed.), *The Progressive Movement, 1900–1915* (Englewood Cliffs: Prentice-Hall, 1963); David W. Noble, *The Paradox of Progressive Thought* (Minneapolis: University of Minnesota Press, 1958).

9. Benjamin Parke De Witt, *The Progressive Movement* (New York: Macmillan, 1915); William Allen White, *The Old Order Changeth* (New York, Macmillan, 1910); Charles Beard and Mary Beard, *The Rise of American Civilization* (New York: Macmillan, 1933); Vernon L. Parrington, *Main Currents of American Thought* (New York: Harcourt, Brace, 1927); I. Leo Sharfman, *The Interstate Commerce Commission* (New York: The Commonwealth Fund, 1931); Arthur M. Schlesinger, Jr., *The Age of Roosevelt*, Vol. I, *The Crisis of the Old Order: 1919–1933* (Boston: Houghton Mifflin, 1957), Vol. II, *The Coming of the New Deal* (Boston: Houghton Mifflin, 1959), Vol. III, *The Politics of Upheaval* (Boston: Houghton Mifflin, 1960); David M. Kennedy (ed.), *Progressivism: The Critical Issues* (Boston: Little, Brown, 1971).

10. This is not to say that the Granger version of public interest theory disappeared. The Granger vision implicitly informed much of the muckraking journalism of the early Progressive Era. Perhaps the most visible and effective heir to the Granger version of public interest theory was attorney and later Supreme Court Justice, Louis Brandeis. Brandeis was a tireless advocate for the small producer. His and others' hatred of large corporations and faith in the efficacy of strong antitrust laws clashed with the Progressive public interest theory during the New Deal. See Thomas K. McCraw's compelling portrait of Brandeis in *Prophets of Regulation* (Cambridge: Harvard University Press, 1984), 80–142. On the clash of Granger and Progressive versions of the public interest theory during the New Deal, see Ellis W. Hawley, *The New Deal and the Problem of Monopoly* (Princeton: Princeton University Press, 1966).

11. Joseph B. Eastman, address before the American Life Convention, Chicago, October 10, 1934. Cited in Marver H. Bernstein, *Regulating Business by Independent Commission* (Princeton: Princeton University Press, 1955), 60.

12. James M. Landis' thoughts on the Securities and Exchange Commission are apt here: "As in the case of the Interstate Commerce Commission, it was not long before it became evident that the mere proscription of abuses was insufficient to effect the realization of broad objectives that lay behind the movement for securities regulation. The primary emphasis of administrative activity had to center upon the guidance and supervision of the industry as a whole." James M. Landis, *The Administrative Process* (New Haven: Yale University Press, 1938), 15.

See also J. C. Bonbright, *Principles of Public Utility Rates* (New York: Columbia University Press, 1961); Kenneth Culp Davis, *Administrative Law Treatise* (St. Paul: West Publishing Co., 1958); Harold U. Faulkner, *The Decline of Laissez-Faire, 1897–1917* (New York: Rinehart, 1951); Merle Fainsod and Lincoln Gordon, *Government and the American Economy*, 3rd ed. (New York: Norton, 1941).

The term "countervailing power" is, of course, Galbraith's. John Kenneth Galbraith, *American Capitalism: The Concept of Countervailing Power* (Boston: Houghton-Mifflin, 1956). On the Progressive faith in science and expertise, see the references cited in note 6 and Grant McConnell, *Private Power and American Democracy* (New York: Vintage Books, 1966).

13. See, for example, the work of Merle Fainsod, particularly the essay, "Some Reflections on the Nature of the Regulatory Process," *Public Policy*, C. J. Friedrich and Edward S. Mason (eds.) (Cambridge: Harvard University Press, 1940), 297–323. Stressing the importance of "political dynamics," Fainsod asserts that regulation comes about in two distinct ways, generally in two chronologically different periods of business history. In the first, economically weak parties invoke political power in an effort to secure a more satisfactory adjustment of relationships within the industry. If the industry is in a phase of expansion, "control groups" within the industry (including labor if it has succeeded in bargaining in the profitable industry) will resist any move toward regulation. The weak industrial parties and consumers constitute the impetus toward regulation; in the late 19th century by small businessmen and farmers, in the Theodore Roosevelt era by the progressive middle class, in the Wilson period and New Deal these above were joined by labor. The dissatisfactions which produced the beginnings of regulation in expanding industries in the United States have been, in Fainsod's scheme, chiefly consumer in origin. He sees this type of regulation as essentially "negative," that is, it is reactive, designed only to curb the abuse of economic power.

The second instance of regulation occurs in contracting or depressed industries. An industry in decline finds all parties seeking to shift the burden of readjustments to other interests. In partial response to threats of this type from other parties, each party (particularly labor) may then seek help from the government through protective regulation, subsidies, or the control of economic competitors (e.g., railroads urged the extension of ICC regulation to trucking). The regulation of declining industries in Fainsod's view is "positive," it seeks to salvage and to guide.

14. Lawrence W. Lichty, "The Impact of FRC and FCC Commissioners' Backgrounds on the Regulation of Broadcasting," *Journal of Broadcasting* 6/2 (Spring 1962), 97–110; idem, "Members of the Federal Radio Commission and Federal Communications Commission, 1927–61," *Journal of Broadcasting* 6/1 (Winter 1961–62), 23–34; James R. Michael (ed.), *Working on the System: A Comprehensive Manual for Citizen Access to Federal Agencies* (New York: Basic Books, 1974); Robert C. Fellmeth, *The Interstate Commerce Omission: The Public Interest and the ICC* (New York: Grossman, 1970); James Turner, *The Chemical Feast* (New York: Grossman, 1970); Mark J. Green (ed.), *The Monopoly Makers* (New York: Grossman, 1973); Common Cause, *Serving Two Masters: A Common Cause Study of Conflicts of Interest in the Executive Branch* (Washington, DC: author, 1976).

15. G. William Domhoff, *The Powers That Be: Processes of Ruling Class Domination in America* (New York: Vintage Press, 1978).

16. Studies of FCC commissioners, for instance, have shown that a large number take jobs in the communications industry after leaving the FCC. See Michael (ed.), *Working on the System* (New York: Basic Books, 1972), 262; Lichty, "Members of the Federal Radio Commission and Federal Communications Commission," 31–34; Robert G. Noll, Merton J. Peck, and John J. McGowan, *Economic Aspects of Television Regulation* (Washington, DC: The Brookings Institution, 1973), 123–124.

17. Walter Emery, *Broadcasting and the Government: Responsibilities and Regulation* (East Lansing: Michigan State University Press, 1971); Roger Noll and Morris Fiorina, "Majority Rule Models and Legislative Elections," *Journal of Politics* 41/4 (November 1979), 1081–1104; Louis M. Kohlmeier, Jr., *The Regulators: Watchdog Agencies and the Public Interest* (New York: Harper and Row, 1969).

18. Barry Cole and Mal Oettinger, *Reluctant Regulators: The FCC and the Broadcast Audience* (Reading, Mass: Addison-Wesley, 1978).

19. Roger G. Noll, *Reforming Regulation: An Evaluation of the Ash Council Proposals* (Washington, DC: Brookings Institution, 1971); Jeremy Tunstall, *Communications Deregulation: The Unleashing of America's Communications Industry* (London: Basil Blackwell, 1986).

20. Louis Lessing, "The Television Freeze," *Fortune* XXXX (November 1949); Henry Geller, "A Modest Proposal for Modest Reform of the Federal Communications Commission," *Georgetown Law Journal*, 63/3 (February 1975), 705–724; John M. Kittross, *Television Frequency Allocation Policy in the United States* (New York: Arno Press, 1979); Don R. Le Duc, *Cable Television and the FCC: A Crisis in Media Control* (Philadelphia: Temple University Press, 1973).

21. United States, *Report of the President's Committee on Administrative Management* (Washington, DC: Government Printing Office, 1937); United States, Report of the Commission on the Organization of the Executive Branch of the Government [the first Hoover Commission Report] (Washington, D.C.: Government Printing Office, 1949); United States, Report of the Commission on the Organization of the Executive Branch of the Government [the second Hoover Commission Report] (Washington, D.C.: Government Printing Office, 1955); James M. Landis, *Report on Regulatory Agencies to the President-Elect* (Washington, D.C.: Government Printing Office, 1960); Booz-Allen & Hamilton, Inc., *Organization and Management Survey of the Federal Communications Commission for the Bureau of the Budget* (Chicago: Booz-Allen & Hamilton, 1962); The President's Advisory Council on Executive Organization, *A New Regulatory Framework: Report on Selected Independent Regulatory Agencies* [The Ash Council Report] (Washington, DC: Government Printing Office, 1971).

22. Some government reports do find that regulatory agencies serve the regulated industries. The 1960 Landis Report stated, "Irrespective of the absence of social contacts and the acceptance of undue hospitality, it is the daily machine gun-like impact on both agency and its staff of industry representation that makes for industry orientation on the part of many honest and capable agency members as well as agency staffers." Landis Report, 71.

23. Booz-Allen & Hamilton, *Organization and Management Survey of the FCC;* United States, Commission on Organization of the Executive Branch of the Government (Washington, DC: Government Printing Office, 1949).

24. For example, both the Landis Report and former SEC Commissioner, William L. Cary, criticize the undue influence that Congressmen exercise over the FCC. William L. Cary, *Politics and the Regulatory Agencies* (New York: McGraw-Hill, 1967). Other critics of the FCC warn against presidential interference with the independence of the FCC via the executive Office of Telecommunications Policy. Edwin B. Spievack, "Presidential Assault on Telecommunications," *Federal Communications Bar Journal* 23/3 (1969), 155–181; and Thomas Whiteside, "Annals of Television (The Nixon Administration and Television)," *The New Yorker*, March 17, 1975, 41–91. Conversely, the *Ash Council Report* found that regulatory agencies suffered from their "remoteness" from the other constitutional branches of government. The report recommended that most regulatory agencies be moved into the Executive branch. *Ash Council Report*, 4.

25. A structural regulatory failure theory which does not rest on the behavior of regulators is that of Stephen Breyer. Breyer's explanation for the rise of regulatory agencies is in line with traditional public interest theory. He attributes the rise of regulation to market problems, though he finds regulatory mechanisms likely to create more problems than they solve. His empirically based analysis of regulatory failure rests on a theory of "mismatches" between the particular situation and structure of a regulated industry and the regulatory

instruments applied. Breyer claims that the market problems of transportation and energy industries are compounded by the regulatory "tool" of price and entry controls. He argues, for example, that the legitimate goal of transferring windfall profits from producers to consumers in the natural gas industry cannot be achieved rationally with a classical cost-of-service rate-making regulatory regime. There is a fundamental mismatch between social goal and regulatory instrument, because rate regulation so skews underlying market forces in this industry. Far better to use a taxing scheme to effect income transfers. He asserts that the more that regulatory solutions deviate from the principle of competition, the less successful those solutions will be. Such regulation will create inefficiencies and welfare losses which are in contradiction to the original rationale for regulation. Stephen Breyer, *Regulation and Its Reform* (Cambridge: Harvard University Press, 1982).

26. Marver Bernstein, *Regulating Business by Independent Commission* (Princeton: Princeton University Press, 1955). Bernstein confined himself to the analysis of the independent regulatory commissions only. Harvard Law School professor Louis Jaffe, an astute critic of the regulatory process, also put much credence on the age of an agency and the degree of its accommodation with the regulated industry. He called it "arteriosclerosis theory." Jaffe, however, did not subscribe to the capture theory. Louis L. Jaffe, "The Effective Limits of the Administrative Process: A Reevaluation," *Harvard Law Review* 67/7 (May 1954), 1105–1135.

27. John Kenneth Galbraith, *The Great Crash* (New York: Houghton-Mifflin, 1955); Cary, *Politics and the Regulatory Agencies*. Also, Jaffe, "The Effective Limits of the Administrative Process."

28. G. Cullom Davis, "The Transformation of the Federal Trade Commission, 1914–1929," *Mississippi Valley History Review* XLIV (December 1962), 437–455; Samuel P. Huntington, "The Marasmus of the ICC: The Commission, the Railroads, and the Public Interest," *Yale Law Journal* 61/4 (April 1952), 467–509.

Davis describes the process by which the FTC, born of Progressive activism in 1914, became captured by conservative pro-business forces in 1925. The FTC changed for the simple reason that Presidents Coolidge and Harding replaced Wilsonian Progressive commissioners with pro-business conservatives. Under the reign of the pro-business forces, the FTC curtailed its own powers of publicity and investigation, began settling cases by informal, confidential agreement rather than by formal Commission order, and encouraged the use of Commission-sanctioned, industry-wide meetings so that businesses could formulate their own rules of behavior. Davis describes an agency initially hostile to business transformed into an agency serving business interests and needs.

Huntington's study of the ICC poses a combination political and organizational behavior model of regulatory capture. He claims that the ICC was created by the agitation of farmers and commercial shippers, and that up until World War I it was responsible to that constituency. As the political power of farmers and shippers declined, the ICC was forced to adapt to its new political environment, and thus shifted its responsiveness to the railroad industry. Davis and Huntington describe the transformation of particular agencies during particular time frames.

29. Olney's letter read, in part: "My impression would be that looking at the matter from a railroad point of view exclusively it [abolition of the ICC] would not be a wise thing to undertake . . . . The attempt would not be likely to succeed; if it did not succeed, and were made on the grounds of the inefficiency and uselessness of the Commission, the result would very probably be giving it the power it now lacks. The Commission, as its functions have not been limited by the courts, is, or can be made of great use to the railroads. It satisfies the popular clamor for a government supervision of railroads, at the same time that the supervision of railroads is almost entirely nominal. Further, the older such a commission gets to be,

the more inclined it will be found to take the business and railroad view of things. It thus becomes a sort of barrier between the railroad corporations and the people and a sort of protection against hasty and crude legislation hostile to railroad interests. . . . The part of wisdom is not to destroy the Commission but to utilize it." Letter of Richard Olney to Charles E. Perkins, cited in Matthew Josephson, *The Politicos, 1865–1896* (New York: Harcourt Brace & Co., 1938), 526.

30. Indeed, some regulatory agencies, such as the CAB and FCC, were *meant* to function as "managers" rather than "policemen." This distinction was made early on by James M. Landis, *The Administrative Process,* and elaborated by Louis L. Jaffe, "The Independent Agency—A New Scapegoat" [Review of Bernstein's *Regulating Business by Independent Commission*], *Yale Law Journal* 65/7 (June 1956), 1068–1076.

31. For Bernstein, age is a key variable, yet one empirical study found the age of an agency *not* to be a causative factor in regulatory behavior. Kenneth J. Meier and John Plumlee, "Regulatory Administration and Organizational Rigidity," *The Western Political Quarterly* XXXI/1 (March 1978), 80–95. See also Robert Chatov, "Government Regulation: Process and Substantive Impacts," *Research in Corporate Social Performance and Policy,* Lee E. Preston (ed.), Vol. 1 (Greenwich: JAI Press Inc, 1978), 223–254; Mitnick, *The Political Economy of Regulation,* 44–50.

32. Theodore J. Lowi, *The End of Liberalism: Ideology, Policy, and the Crisis of Public Authority* (New York: Norton, 1969); idem, *The End of Liberalism: The Second Republic of the United States* (2d. ed. 1979). An earlier formulation of the mal-effects of expansive discretionary authority is Henry Friendly, *The Federal Administrative Agencies: The Need for Better Definition of Standards* (Cambridge: Harvard University Press, 1962). Another analysis of the "broker state" is McConnell, *Private Power and American Democracy.*

33. Theodore J. Lowi, "Four Systems of Policy, Politics and Choice," *Public Administration Review* 32/4 (July/August 1972), 298–310.

34. Horace M. Gray, "The Passing of the Public Utility Concept," *Journal of Land and Public Utility Economics* 16/1 (February 1940), 1–20, at 9.

35. Gabriel Kolko, *The Triumph of Conservatism: A Reinterpretation of American History, 1900–1916* (New York: Free Press, 1963), 3.

36. Gabriel Kolko, *Railroads and Regulation, 1877–1916* (Princeton: Princeton University Press, 1965); also see George W. Hilton, "The Consistency of the Interstate Commerce Act," *Journal of Law and Economics* 9 (October 1966), 87–113.

37. Charles O. Jackson, *Food and Drug Legislation in the New Deal* (Princeton: Princeton University Press, 1970); Norman Nordhauser, "Origins of Federal Oil Regulation in the 1920s," *Business History Review* XLVII (Spring 1973), 54–71.

38. James Weinstein, *The Corporate Ideal in the Liberal State, 1900–1918* (Boston: Beacon Press, 1968); Samuel P. Hays, "The Politics of Reform in Municipal Government in the Progressive Era," *Pacific Northwest Quarterly* 55/4 (October 1964), 157–169.

39. Kolko, *Railroads and Regulation.*

40. Lee Benson argued that the single most important group behind the passage of the Interstate Commerce Act was New York merchants in his book, *Merchants, Farmers, and Railroads: Railroad Regulation and New York Politics, 1850–1887* (Cambridge: Harvard University Press, 1955). Thomas C. Cochran found that railroad men gave only reluctant support to regulation in his study, *Railroad Leaders, 1845–1890: The Business Mind in Action* (Cambridge: Harvard University Press, 1953). Gerald D. Nash attributed the regulatory impetus to various interests, but especially to Pennsylvania independent oil producers and refiners in his essay, "Origins of the Interstate Commerce Act of 1887," *Pennsylvania History* XXIV (July 1957), 181–190.

Criticisms of the Kolko thesis can be found in Otis L. Graham (ed.), *From Roosevelt to*

*Roosevelt: American Politics and Diplomacy, 1901–1941* (New York: Appleton-Century-Crofts, 1971), 69–109; Morton Keller, "The Pluralist State: American Economic Regulation in Comparative Perspective, 1900–1930," in *Regulation in Perspective*, Thomas K. McCraw (ed.), 56–94; Robert W. Harbeson, "Railroads and Regulation, 1877–1916: Conspiracy or Public Interest?," *Journal of Economic History* 27/2 (June 1967), 230–242.

41. Robert H. Wiebe, *The Search For Order;* Richard H. K. Vietor, "Businessmen and the Political Economy: The Railroad Rate Controversy of 1905," *Journal of American History* LXIV/1 (June 1977), 47–66.

42. Richard E. Caves, *Air Transport and Its Regulators* (Cambridge: Harvard University Press, 1962); Michael E. Levine, "Is Regulation Necessary? California Air Transportation and National Regulatory Policy," *Yale Law Journal* 74/8 (July 1965), 1416–1447; William A. Jordan, *Airline Regulation in America* (Baltimore: Johns Hopkins Press, 1970); George W. Douglas and James C. Miller III, *Economic Regulation of Domestic Air Transport* (Washington, DC: Brookings Institution, 1974); Lawrence J. White, "Quality Variation When Prices Are Regulated," *Bell Journal of Economics and Management Science* 3/2 (Autumn 1972), 425–436; Theodore E. Keeler, "Airline Regulation and Market Performance," *Bell Journal of Economics and Management Science* 3/2 (Autumn 1972), 399–424; C. Vincent Olson and John Trapani III, "Who Has Benefitted From Regulation of the Airline Industry?," *Journal of Law and Economics* 24/1 (April 1981), 75–93.

43. Paul W. MacAvoy and Roger G. Noll, "Relative Prices on Regulated Transactions of the Natural Gas Pipelines," *Bell Journal of Economics and Management Science* 4/1 (Spring 1973), 212–234; Richard Spann and Edward W. Erickson, "The Economics of Railroading: The Beginning of Cartelization and Regulation," *Bell Journal of Economics and Management Science* 1/2 (Autumn 1970), 227–244.

44. Harvey Averch and Leland L. Johnson, "Behavior of the Firm Under Regulatory Constraint," *American Economic Review* 52/5 (December 1962), 1052–1069; Stanislaw H. Wellisz, "Regulation of Natural Gas Pipeline Companies: An Economic Analysis," *Journal of Political Economy* 71/1 (February 1963). 30–43. The Wellisz model dealt with the same sort of regulated firm as the A-J thesis, but it was concerned primarily with the effect of regulation on peak-load pricing rather than on input usage.

45. William J. Baumol and Alvin K. Klevorick, "Input Choices and Rate-of-Return Regulation: An Overview of the Discussion," *Bell Journal of Economics and Management Science* 1/2 (Autumn 1970), 162–190.

46. George J. Stigler, "The Theory of Economic Regulation," *Bell Journal of Economics and Management Science* 2/1 (Spring 1971), 3–21.

47. George J. Stigler and Claire Friedland, "What Can Regulators Regulate? The Case of Electricity," *Journal of Law and Economics* 5 (October 1962), 1–16.

At least with regard to so-called "natural" monopolies, then, regulation would seem to do nothing. The differences between these varied findings of producer protection/cartel management, regulatory inefficacy, and regulation-induced inefficiency might be reconciled by looking at market structures. William A. Jordan found that the absence of regulatory efficacy occurred only in those industries with a prior market structure of natural monopoly. Natural monopolies appear largely unaffected by regulation. In oligopolistic and competitive industries such as transportation carriers, however, regulation registers significant increases in price levels, price discrimination, rates of return–all of which result in general producer protection. Inefficiencies, particularly excess capacity, occur partially due to incomplete regulatory control. Because, for example, the CAB cannot assign specific market shares and firms cannot compete on price to obtain larger market shares, firms compete over service quality. The continual purchase of newer equipment in airlines led to chronic overcapacity. William A. Jordan, "Producer Protection, Prior Market Structure and the Effects of Government Regulation,'' *Journal of Law and Economics* 15/1 (April 1972), 151–76. See generally the work of Ronald Coase, who is sometimes credited with having constructed the paradigm of the economic analysis of regulation. Ronald H. Coase, ''The Problem of Social Cost,'' *Journal of Law and Economics* 3/1 (October 1960), 1–44.

48. See, among others, Paul E. Sands, ''How Effective Is Safety Legislation?,'' *Journal of Law and Economics* 11/1 (April 1968), 165–179; Robert Stewart, *The Occupational Safety and Health Act* (Washington, DC: American Enterprise Institute for Public Policy Research, 1976); Aldon DiPietro, ''An Analysis of the OSHA Inspection Program in Manufacturing Industries, 1972–73,'' Draft Technical Analysis Paper, U.S. Department of Labor (Washington, DC: Government Printing Office, August 1976); A. L. Nichols and Richard Zeckhauser, ''Government Comes to the Workplace: An Assessment of OSHA,'' *The Public Interest* 49 (Fall 1977), 39–69; Sam Peltzman, *Regulation of Automobile Safety* (Washington, DC: American Enterprise Institute, 1975); H. G. Manne and R. M. Miller (Eds.), *Auto Safety Regulation: The Cure or the Problem?* (Glen Ridge, NJ: Thomas Horton, 1976).

A summary of several such studies of OSHA is found in Lester B. Lave, *The Strategy of Social Regulation* (Washington, DC: Brookings Institution, 1981). A summary of the studies on the EPA is found in Robert W. Crandall, *Controlling Industrial Pollution: The Economics and Politics of Clean Air* (Washington, DC: Brookings Institution, 1983).

These studies were highly controversial and generated virulent counter-studies which attacked the economists' assumptions and sought to show that the benefits of regulation exceeded costs. See, for instance, U.S. House of Representatives, 94th Congress, 2d Session, Hearings Before a Subcommittee of the Committee on Appropriations, *Department of Transportation and Related Agencies Appropriations for 1977,* March 1, 1976, Part 2 (Washington, DC: Government Printing Office, 1976), 369–382; National Commission on Air Quality, *To Breathe Clean Air* (Washington, DC: Government Printing Office, 1981).

49. Murray Weidenbaum and Robert DeFina, *The Costs of Federal Regulation of Economic Activity* (Washington, DC: American Enterprise Institute, Reprint No. 88, May, 1978); '' 'The Regulators,' They Cost You $130 Billion a Year,'' *US News and World Report,* June 30, 1975, 24–28. It is not surprising that the criteria upon which such numbers are arrived at are subject to wide dispute. Moreover, the meaning of such estimates is unclear. As George C. Eads and Michael Fix argue in *Relief or Reform? Reagan's Regulatory Dilemma,* notwithstanding the high costs of regulation, at worst such costs only marginally affected either the decline in US productivity rates and or the rise in inflation. (Washington, DC: The Urban Institute Press, 1984), 17–44.

50. Anthony Downs, *An Economic Theory of Democracy* (New York: Harper and Row, 1957); idem, *Inside Bureaucracy* (Boston, Little, Brown, 1967). James Buchanan, awarded a Nobel Prize for economics in 1986, is another major figure in the economic theory of politics. James M. Buchanan, *The Demand and Supply of Public Goods* (Chicago: Rand McNally, 1968); idem and Gordon Tullock, *The Calculus of Consent: Logical Foundations of Constitutional Democracy* (Ann Arbor: University of Michigan Press, 1962).

51. Richard A. Posner, ''Theories of Economic Regulation,'' *Bell Journal of Economics and Management Science* 5/2 (Autumn 1974), 335–358.

52. Sam Peltzman, ''Toward a More General Theory of Regulation,'' *Journal of Law and Economics* 19/2 (August 1976), 211–240; Morris P. Fiorina, *Congress: Keystone of the Washington Establishment* (New Haven: Yale University Press, 1977); idem and Roger G. Noll, ''Voters, Bureaucrats and Legislators,'' *Journal of Public Economics* 9/2 (April 1978), 239–254; Roger G. Noll, ''The Behavior of Regulatory Agencies,'' *Review of Social Economy* 29/9 (March 1971), 15–19; William Niskanen, ''Bureaucrats and Politicians,'' *Journal of Law and Economics* 18/3 (December 1975), 617–643; idem, *Bureaucracy and Representative Government* (Chicago: Aldine-Atherton, 1971); Barry R. Weingast, ''Regulation,

Reregulation, and Deregulation: The Political Foundations of Agency-Clientele Relationships," *Law and Contemporary Problems* 44/1 (Winter 1981), 147–178.

Weingast's elucidation of this triangle is typical of this approach. He writes: "Interest groups seek the benefits of legislation and policy-making. Congressmen seek reelection and career advancement. This implies that they bend with the wind of political opinion in general, and further the interests of attentive and politically active interest groups in particular. . . . Often agencies are the vehicle for this endeavor. Agency heads and commission members, anxious to further their careers and goals of power and prestige (including large budgets) as well as completing their own pet projects and policy initiatives, depend upon service to interest groups and key committee members for their success. In a real sense, the goals of these three sets of players are compatible. Congressmen, seeking reelection and national prominence, further the interests of new and established groups. Agencies aid powerful politicians—generally congressmen on relevant committees, though presidents are important at times—by implementing policies beneficial to constituent groups relevant for a particular policy area. Finally, the interest groups reward politicians through aiding reelection. This advances Congressional careers and helps the potential success of policy initiatives, a key to national prominence." Weingast, "Regulation, Reregulation, and Deregulation," 150–151.

53. Richard A. Posner, "Taxation by Regulation," *Bell Journal of Economics and Management Science* 2/1 (Spring 1971), 22–50.

54. A similar sort of economic group interaction model informs the theoretical work of James Q. Wilson. He constructs a comprehensive typology of expected regulatory origin and behavior, based on a broad cost-benefit analysis. When both costs and benefits of regulation are widely distributed, he argues, we can expect "majoritarian" politics, where most of society benefits and most of society expects to pay. Examples of this are the Sherman Act, Social Security Act, the Federal Trade Commission. When both costs and benefits are narrowly concentrated between competing groups, we can expect "interest" politics, where each interest works against other interests and the regulatory agency acts as an arbitrator. The public is not much part of this process. Examples include the ICC and much labor legislation. When benefits are concentrated and costs diffuse, "client" politics ensue, where the agency serves the interests of that small group. The classic example here is the Civil Aeronautics Board. Lastly, general benefits at costs borne by small segments of the population yield "entrepreneurial" politics, where skilled political operatives are able to mobilize latent public sentiment in favor of "reform" legislation. This is exemplified by such regulatory agencies as the Environmental Protection Agency or Food and Drug Administration.

Wilson's economic model of group interaction is quite helpful in conceptualizing the relation between interest intensity, the type of benefits secured, and the expected structure of regulation. Indeed, Wilson's notion of "entrepreneurial politics" is one of the few rational actor models to try to account for the rapid rise of "social" regulation in the late 1960s and early 1970s. James Q. Wilson, "The Politics of Regulation," in *The Politics of Regulation*, James Q. Wilson (ed.) (New York: Basic Books, 1980), 357–394.

55. Irving Kristol, "A Regulated Society?," *Regulation* 1/1 (July/August 1977), 12–13; William Lilley and James C. Miller III, "The New 'Social Regulation,'" *The Public Interest* 47 (Spring 1977), 49–61; B. Bruce Briggs (ed.), *The New Class* (New Brunswick: Transaction Books, 1979); Michael Novak, *The American Vision* (Washington, DC: American Enterprise Institute, 1978).

Like most conservative political sociology, this analysis derives from the elite theory of Pareto and Mosca that "producers" constitute a class versus "unproductive" types.

56. Chatov, "Government Regulation: Process and Substantive Impacts"; Mancur Olson, Jr., *The Logic of Collective Action: Public Goods and the Theory of Groups* (New York: Harvard University Press and Schocken Books, 1965).

57. James Q. Wilson, "The Dead Hand of Regulation," *The Public Interest* 25 (Fall 1971), 39–58; Louis L. Jaffe, "The Effective Limits of the Administrative Process."

58. John W. Snow, Deputy Undersecretary, Department of Transportation, 1975–76, and Administrator, National Highway Traffic and Safety Administration, 1976–77. Cited in *Unsettled Questions on Regulatory Reform,* Paul W. MacAvoy (ed.) (Washington, DC: American Enterprise Institute, 1977), 16.

59. Paul W. MacAvoy, "The Regulation-Induced Shortage of Natural Gas," *Journal of Law and Economics* XIV (April 1971), 167–199; idem, *The Regulated Industries and the Economy* (New York: Norton, 1979). See a roughly similar analysis of the early railroad industry, Albro Martin, *Enterprise Denied: Origins of the Decline of American Railroads, 1887–1917* (New York: Columbia University Press, 1971).

60. Eugene Bardach and Robert A. Kagan, *Going by the Book: The Problem of Regulatory Unreasonableness* (Philadelphia: Temple University Press, 1982). This argument resonates with the reflections of former agency head John W. Snow, cited above at note 58. Snow states, "During my time in office, the agency was criticized for slowing down the pace at which regulations were issued, and we were called before congressional committees and asked to explain why we were not advancing the cause of highway safety by issuing more regulations." *Unsettled Questions on Regulatory Reform,* 17.

61. Eugene Bardach and Robert A. Kagan, *Social Regulation: Strategies for Reform* (San Francisco: Institute for Contemporary Studies, 1982), 12–14.

62. Chatov, "Government Regulation: Process and Substantive Impacts."

63. Paul L. Joskow, "Inflation and Environmental Concern: Structural Change in the Process of Public Utility Price Regulation," *Journal of Law and Economics* 17/2 (October 1974), 291–327; idem, "Pricing Decisions of Regulated Firms: A Behavioral Approach," *Bell Journal of Economics and Management Science* 4/1 (Spring 1973), 118–140.

64. This point is made by David P. McCaffrey, *OSHA and the Politics of Health Regulation* (New York and London: Plenum Press, 1982), 137.

65. Vincent Mosco, *Broadcasting in the United States: Innovative Challenge and Organizational Control* (Norwood, NJ: Ablex, 1979); Don R. Le Duc, *Cable Television and the FCC: A Crisis in Media Control.* See also, Nicholas Johnson and John Jay Dystel, "A Day in the Life: The Federal Communications Commission," *Yale Law Journal* 82/8 (July 1973), 1575–1634.

66. Claus Offe, "Structural Problems of the Capitalist State," in *German Political Studies,* I, Klaus von Beyme (ed.) (Beverly Hills: Sage Publishing Co., 1974); 31–57; idem, "The Theory of the Capitalist State and the Problem of Policy Formation," in *Stress and Contradiction in Modern Capitalism,* Leon Lindberg et al. (eds.) (Lexington: D.C. Heath, 1975), 125–144; idem, "Crises of 'Crisis Management': Elements of a Political Crisis Theory," *International Journal of Politics* 6 (1976), 29–67; James O'Connor, *The Fiscal Crisis of the State* (New York: St. Martin's Press, 1973); Jürgen Habermas, *Legitimation Crisis* (Boston, Beacon Press, 1975); Alan Wolfe, *The Limits of Legitimacy: Political Contradictions of Contemporary Capitalism* (New York: Free Press, 1977); Fred Block, "The Ruling Class Does Not Rule: Notes on the Marxist Theory of the State," *Socialist Revolution* 7/3 (May–June 1977), 6–28; Nicos Poulantzas, *State, Power, Socialism* (London: New Left Books, 1978).

67. James O'Connor, *The Fiscal Crisis of the State.*

68. Claus Offe, "Structural Problems of the Capitalist State."

69. Charles E. Lindblom, *Politics and Markets: The World's Political-Economic Systems* (New York: Basic Books, 1977), 172–173.

70. Fred Block looks at the scope of government action during the New Deal and Great Society periods in this vein.

71. See Habermas' description of the liberal-capitalist "crisis cycle." *Legitimation Crisis*, 24–32, 130–142.

72. When I try to conceptualize what is required of a theory of regulation, or for that matter, the theoretical accounting of any long and complex historical phenomenon which involves the interaction of people and structures over time, I think of Walter Benjamin's haunting metaphor of the "angel of history." Benjamin writes: "A Klee painting named 'Agelus Novus' shows an angel looking as though he is about to move away from something he is fixedly contemplating. His eyes are staring, his mouth is open, his wings are spread. This is how one pictures the angel of history. His face is turned toward the past. Where we perceive a chain of events, he sees one single catastrophe which keeps piling wreckage upon wreckage and hurls it in front of his feet. The angel would like to stay, awaken the dead, and make whole what has been smashed. But a storm is blowing from Paradise; it has got caught in his wings with such violence that the angel can no longer close them. This storm irresistibly propels him into the future to which his back is turned, while the pile of debris before him grows skyward. This storm is what we call progress." Walter Benjamin, "Theses on the Philosophy of History," in *Illuminations*, Hannah Arendt (ed.) (New York: Schocken Books, 1969), 257–258.

## Chapter 3. The "Gateway of Commerce": A Theory of Regulation

1. Barry Mitnick, *The Political Economy of Regulation* (New York: Columbia University Press, 1980), 9.

2. On the ambiguous distinction between regulation and non-regulation, see Theodore J. Lowi, "The State in Politics: The Relation Between Policy and Administration," in *Regulatory Policy and the Social Sciences*, Roger G. Noll (ed.) (Berkeley: University of California Press, 1985), 67–105; also James W. McKie, "Regulation and the Free Market: The Problem of Boundaries," *Bell Journal of Economics and Management Science* 1/1 (Spring 1970), 6–26.

3. See Stephen Skowronek, *Building a New American State: The Expansion of National Administrative Capacities, 1877–1920* (Cambridge: Cambridge University Press, 1982).

4. See Charles M. Haar and Daniel William Fessler, *The Wrong Side of the Tracks* (New York: Simon & Schuster, 1986).

5. Kenneth Culp Davis, *Discretionary Justice: A Preliminary Inquiry* (Urbana: University of Illinois Press, 1977). Davis has heralded the concept of informal rule making as "one of the greatest inventions of modern government." Letter to the U.S. Senate, 96th Congress, 2nd Session, Judiciary Committee, Senate Report 96-1018 part 2, Joint Report of the Senate Committee on Governmental Affairs and the Committee on the Judiciary, *Reform of Federal Regulation* (Washington, DC: Government Printing Office, 1980), 51.

6. See Laurence H. Tribe, *American Constitutional Law* (Mineola: The Foundation Press, 1978), 1–19.

7. Samuel P. Huntington, *Political Order in Changing Societies* (New Haven: Yale University Press, 1968), 96–99; Louis Hartz, *The Liberal Tradition in America: An Interpretation of American Political Thought Since the Revolution* (New York: Harcourt, Brace & Jovanovich, 1955), 5–6, 43.

8. Skowronek, *Building a New American State*, 21–23; Samuel Beer, "The Modernization of American Federalism," *Publius* 3/2 (Fall 1973), 49–95; Lawrence M. Friedman, *A History of American Law* (New York: Simon and Schuster, 1973), 202–204. Claus Offe makes a similar point in a more theoretically oriented essay. "The Theory of the Capitalist State and the Problem of Policy Formation," in *Stress and Contradiction in Modern Capitalism*, Leon N. Lindberg et al. (eds.) (Lexington, Massachusetts: Lexington Books, 1975), 125–144.

9. Carter Goodrich, *Government Promotion of American Canals and Railroads, 1800–1890* (New York: Columbia University Press, 1960), 45–48.

10. Morton J. Horwitz, *The Transformation of American Law, 1780–1860* (Cambridge: Harvard University Press, 1977), 7, 17; Grant Gilmore, *The Ages of American Law* (New Haven: Yale University Press, 1977), 21–23; Haar & Fessler, *The Wrong Side of the Tracks*, 110–112.

11. Horwitz, *The Transformation of American Law*, 1–30; Gilmore, *The Ages of American Law*, 24; Friedman, *A History of American Law*, 23–24.

12. Max Weber, *On Law in Economy and Society*, Max Rheinstein (ed.) (New York: Simon and Schuster, 1954).

13. Horwitz, *The Transformation of American Law*, 31–33; also Karl Polanyi, *The Great Transformation* (Boston: Beacon Press, 1944), 181–182.

14. Horwitz, *The Transformation of American Law*, 110; also, Louis Hartz, *Economic Policy and Democratic Thought* (Cambridge: Harvard University Press, 1948); James Willard Hurst, *Law and the Conditions of Freedom in the Nineteenth Century United States* (Madison: University of Wisconsin Press, 1964). On mercantilism see Polanyi, *The Great Transformation*, and Eli F. Heckscher, *Mercantilism* (New York: Macmillan, 1935).

15. This is one of Hurst's main contentions in *Law and the Conditions of Freedom in the Nineteenth Century United States*.

16. Horwitz, *The Transformation of American Law*, 97, 99.

17. Friedman, *A History of American Law*, 262–264, 410–414; also Lawrence M. Friedman and Jack Ladinsky, "Social Change and the Law of Industrial Accidents," *Columbia Law Review* 67/1 (January 1967), 50–82.

18. Hartz, *Economic Policy and Democratic Thought*.

19. Goodrich, *Government Promotion of American Canals and Railroads*, 268.

20. *Ibid.*, 269–271.

21. Samuel F. B. Morse's experimental line between Washington and Baltimore was financed by a $30,000 Congressional appropriation in 1843. The transcontinental line to California was provided assistance through the Pacific Telegraph Act, passed by Congress in 1860. The act provided for a ten-year subsidy of $40,000 annually. Through special acts of incorporation, securing right-of-way arrangements with railroads, and sometimes subscribing to stock, southern state governments helped expand telegraphy through to New Orleans. Similar assistance characterized California's role in telegraph development. See Richard B. Du Boff, "The Rise of Communications Regulation: The Telegraph Industry, 1844–1880," *Journal of Communication* (Summer 1984), 52–66; also Ithiel de Sola Pool, *Technologies of Freedom* (Cambridge: Harvard University Press, 1983), 95.

22. Horwitz, *The Transformation of American Law*, 63–70.

23. Bonaparte v. Camden and Amboy Railroad, 3 F. Cas. 821 (Case No. 1617) (C.C.D.N.J. 1830), at 829.

24. West River Bridge v. Dix, 6 How. 507 (1848), at 531–532. Cited in Harry N. Scheiber, "The Road to *Munn:* Eminent Domain and the Concept of Public Purpose in the State Courts," *Perspectives in American History* 5 (1971), 329–404, at 380.

25. Haar & Fessler, *The Wrong Side of the Tracks*, 68–108.

26. Horwitz, *The Transformation of American Law*, 111.

27. Dartmouth College v. Woodward, 17 U.S. (4 Wheat.) 518 (1819); Charles River Bridge v. Warren Bridge, 24 Mass. (7 Pick.) 344 (1829), *aff'd* 36 U.S. (11 Pet.) 420 (1837).

28. See Stanley L. Engerman and Robert E. Gallman, "U.S. Economic Growth, 1763–1860," *Research in Economic History*, Vol. 8 (1983), 1–46.

29. Scheiber, "The Road to *Munn;*" Friedman, *A History of American Law*, 174.

Article I, paragraph 10 of the Constitution commands that "No State shall. . . pass any . . . Law impairing the Obligation of Contracts. . . ."

30. George H. Miller, *Railroads and the Granger Laws* (Madison: University of Wisconsin Press, 1971), 42–44; Carter Goodrich, "The Revulsion Against Internal Improvements," *Journal of Economic History* 10 (November 1950), 145–169.

The "public" nature of public projects can be overemphasized. Goodrich argues that public projects only occurred when private capital was insufficient. Throughout the history of internal improvements, projects that offered clear prospects of early financial return were almost universally left by common consent to private enterprise. Goodrich, *Government Promotion of American Canals and Railroads*, 279.

31. Oscar Handlin, "The Development of the Corporation," in *The Corporation: A Theological Inquiry*, Michael Novak and John W. Cooper (eds.) (Washington, DC: American Enterprise Institute for Public Policy Research, 1981), 1–16; Friedman, *A History of American Law*, 167.

32. See evidence in assembled in Horwitz, *The Transformation of American Law*, 134–139.

33. Grant Gilmore, *The Death of Contract* (Columbus: Ohio State University Press, 1974); Arnold M. Paul, *Conservative Crisis and the Rule of Law: Attitudes of Bar and Bench, 1887–1895* (Gloucester: Peter Smith, 1976).

34. Gilmore, *Ages of American Law*, 29–30.

35. Horwitz, *The Transformation of American Law*, 250–251.

36. *Ibid.*, 141–143, 228.

37. Hurst, *Law and the Conditions of Freedom in the Nineteenth Century United States*, 44–45; Gibbons v. Ogden, 22 U.S. (9 Wheat.) 1 (1824); Brown v. Maryland, 25 U.S. (12 Wheat.) 419 (1827). In *Gibbons*, a New York grant of a steamboat monopoly affecting navigation between New York and New Jersey conflicted with a federal statute licensing such interstate commerce and was therefore held void under the supremacy clause. In *Brown*, the Court held that the commerce clause prevented Maryland from requiring a foreign importer to be licensed by the state prior to selling imported goods.

38. *Gibbons v. Ogden*, at 193.

39. Swift v. Tyson, 41 U.S. (16 Pet.) 1 (1842). For one version of the "negative Commerce Clause" thesis, see Edmund W. Kitch, "Regulation and the American Common Market," in *Regulation, Federalism, and Interstate Commerce*, A. Dan Tarlock (ed.) (Cambridge: Oelgeschlager, Gunn & Hain, Publishers, 1981), 7–56. Kitch argues that *Swift v. Tyson* and the like-minded decision in Bank of Augusta v. Earle, 38 U.S. (13 Pet.) 517 (1839) were creative responses to a need for a national payments system. In these two cases, the Court honored the demands for state control that had figured so importantly in the debates over the Bank of the United States, and at the same time offered the states a common system of law by which to govern commercial transactions. Kitch's general thesis, contrary to the argument presented in this chapter, is that the Supreme Court's role as guardian of a national market is largely a myth.

40. Gilmore, *Ages of American Law*, 44–45; Horwitz, *The Transformation of American Law*, 252–266.

41. Miller, *Railroads and the Granger Laws*, 177–178; Scheiber, "The Road to *Munn*," 388–392.

42. Scheiber, "The Road to *Munn*," 381–383.

43. The relevant text of the Fourteenth Amendment reads: "All persons born or naturalized in the United States, and subject to the jurisdiction thereof, are citizens of the United States and of the State wherein they reside. No State shall make or enforce any law which

shall abridge the privileges or immunities of citizens of the United States; nor shall any State deprive any person of life, liberty, or property, without due process of law; nor deny to any person within its jurisdiction the equal protection of the laws.''

44. Chief among these conservative jurists were: Thomas Cooley, Chief Justice of the Michigan Supreme Court and author of the highly influential work, *Treatise on Constitutional Limitations* (1868); Justice John F. Dillon of the Iowa Supreme Court and US Circuit Court, author of *Treatise on Municipal Corporations* (1872); Christopher G. Tiedeman, author of *A Treatise on the Limitations of the Police Power in the United States* (1886); and Supreme Court Justice Stephen Field. See Clyde E. Jacobs, *Law Writers and the Courts: The Influence of Thomas M. Cooley, Christopher G. Tiedeman, and John F. Dillon Upon American Constitutional Law* (Berkeley, University of California Press, 1954); Paul, *Conservative Crisis and the Rule of Law.*

45. Miller, *Railroads and the Granger Laws,* 3–16.

46. See U.S. Senate, 49th Congress, 1st Session, Committee on Interstate Commerce, *Report of the Select Committee on Interstate Commerce* [known as the Cullom Committee Report], S. Rep. No. 46 (Washington, DC: Government Printing Office, 1886); William Larrabee, *The Railroad Question* (Chicago: The Schulte Publishing Co., 1893), 120, 160–162; Lewis A. Haney, *A Congressional History of Railways in the United States* (Madison, Wis.: University of Wisconsin Press, 1908; reprinted New York: Augustus M. Kelley, 1968), 285–288.

47. Miller, *Railroads and the Granger Laws,* 58–70, 91; also Haney, *A Congressional History of Railways,* 240–259.

48. Miller, *Railroads and the Granger Laws,* 168, 94, 115–116.

49. Munn v. Illinois, 94 U.S. 113 (1877).

50. Scheiber, ''The Road to *Munn,*'' 398–402.

51. *Munn v. Illinois,* at 126.

52. *Munn v. Illinois,* at 132.

53. Bruce Wyman, *The Special Law Governing Public Service Corporations and All Others Engaged in Public Employment* (New York: Baker, Voorhis & Co., 1911), Vol. I, xi.

54. Wyman, *The Special Law,* I, 6–13.

55. Sir William Jones, *An Essay on the Law of Bailments,* 4th English Edition (London: S. Sweet, 1833); Justice Joseph Story, *Commentaries on the Law of Bailments, With Illustrations from the Civil and Foreign Law,* 4th Edition (1846). Cited in Joseph K. Angell, *A Treatise on the Law of Carriers,* 5th Edition (Boston: Little, Brown, 1877), 60.

The exact reasons behind the classification of particular occupations as common callings are uncertain enough that some legal historians dispute the ''monopoly power'' argument. Irwin S. Rosenbaum (drawing upon the work of Nathan Isaacs) argues for a legalistic, even accidental interpretation of common callings. In the transition from status to contract, the only classes which survived this shift were the common carrier and the common innkeeper. The reason for this survival rested in ancient legal practice. Tradesmen carried on business in two ways, either with a pre-arranged price or without express agreement as to price. In the first case they had an ''assumpsit'' (an action for breach of an agreement) remedy at law to enforce the contract price; in the second, they had no legal remedy and could merely hold the goods as hostage for a ''fair'' price.

The carrier, innkeeper, and smith were the three classes which, because of transitory relations with their customers and because of their methods of serving, relied on their lien. They thus retained their status as common (meaning habitual or regular), rather than contractual, or special, businesses. Smiths finally dropped out of this class because of change of travel from horseback to stagecoach, and the innkeeper underwent many changes. According to Rosenbaum, modern considerations based on monopoly, dependence of society, and state functioning are afterthoughts. Irwin S. Rosenbaum, "The Common Carrier-Public Utility Concept: A Legal-Industrial View," *The Journal of Land and Public Utility Economics* 7/2 (May 1931), 155–168.

Notwithstanding this thesis, the connection between the common nature of carriers and the social desire to protect commerce can be discerned in the legal preoccupation in determining the liability of carriers. A common carrier is regarded by the law as an insurer of the property entrusted to him. He is legally responsible for acts against which he could not provide, the only exceptions being acts of God and the public enemy. Angell, *A Treatise on the Law of Carriers*, 59, 137–209. This unusual degree of liability would have the effect of ensuring that the goods carried be delivered in good condition. By the mid-19th century, however, this *absolute* liability eroded under the influence of contract theory and its laissez-faire underpinnings. A 1848 case allowed carriers to limit liability by contract. New Jersey Steam Navigation Co. v. Merchants Bank, 47 U.S. (6 How.) 344 (1848).

56. The attempts by the king to seize the processes of baronial law were in essence financially driven and were underpinned by a notion that all land and the prerogatives attached were the king's by right of conquest. The eventual emergence of national markets thus was not the result of some natural unfolding of the logic of capitalism, but clearly the result of deliberate political interventions of the Crown. Haar & Fessler, *The Wrong Side of the Tracks*, 57; also Polanyi, *The Great Transformation*, 63–67.

57. See Weber, *On Law in Economy and Society*, 98–121.

58. Miller, *Railroads and the Granger Laws*, 27.

59. Economic historians have argued that among the many factors which accounted for the growth of the American economy between 1840 and 1900, the revolutions in surface transportation (railroad) and electric communication (telegraphy) are paramount. See Alfred D. Chandler, Jr., *The Visible Hand: The Managerial Revolution in American Business* (Cambridge: Harvard University Press, 1977); P. Glenn Porter, *The Rise of Big Business, 1860–1910* (New York: 1973); Richard B. DuBoff, "Business Demand and the Development of the Telegraph in the United States," *Business History Review* 54/4 (Winter 1980), 459–479; idem, "The Telegraph and the Structure of Markets in the United States, 1845–1890," *Reasearch in Economic History* 8 (1983), 253–277; idem, "The Telegraph in Nineteenth-Century America: Technology and Monopoly," *Comparative Studies in Society and History* 26/4 (October 1984), 571–586.

60. Wabash, St. Louis and Pacific Railway Company v. Illinois, 118 U.S. 557 (1886). *Munn* was not the first case to find railroads to be common carriers. Angell cites the case of Thomas v. Boston & Providence Railroad, 10 Met. 472; also Messenger v. Pennsylvania Railroad Co., 37 N.J.L. 531 (1874). *Munn* was, of course, a Supreme Court case.

61. Chandler, *The Visible Hand*, 134–142; Gabriel Kolko, *Railroads and Regulation, 1877–1916* (Princeton: Princeton University Press, 1965), 7–29.

62. Samuel P. Hays, *The Response to Industrialism, 1885–1914* (Chicago: University of Chicago Press, 1957), 24–93; Robert H. Wiebe, *The Search for Order, 1877–1920* (New York: Hill and Wang, 1967), 44–75.

63. Melvyn Dubofsky, *Industrialism and the American Worker, 1865–1920* (Arlington Heights: AHM Publishing Co., 1975); Herbert G. Gutman, *Work, Culture and Society in Industrializing America: Essays in American Working-Class and Social History* (New York: Vintage Books, 1977).

64. James Hudson, *Railways and the Republic* (New York: Harper & Brothers, 1886), 23.

65. *Munn v. Illinois*, 184–86.

66. The case which perhaps marked the turning point in the use of the Fourteenth Amendment in the defense of property was *Barbier v. Connolly*. The Court upheld a San

Francisco ordinance prohibiting the operation of laundries at night, but warned that the due process clause protected the freedom to contract and prevented arbitrary deprivations of common-law liberty—deprivations which *by definition* could not amount to exercises of the police power, whose mission was the protection of common-law rights. 113 U.S. 27 (1885).

It was the 1905 *Lochner* decision which best typified this legal formalism in the service of contract. In *Lochner* the Court invalidated a New York law that set a 60-hour limit on a bakery employee's work week. New York claimed that the law was directly related to the promotion of employee health. The Court saw such legislation as intended to benefit bakers at their employers' expense and, moreover, determined that the law interfered with the formal contractual freedom of both employees and employers. Lochner v. New York, 198 U.S. 45 (1905).

67. Tribe, *American Constitutional Law,* 427–442; quote at 6.

68. Oliver Wendell Holmes, *The Common Law* (Boston: Little, Brown, 1951), 94–95.

69. The inability of a purely self-regulating economic system to function without undermining the social fabric is the central point of Karl Polanyi's monumental study, *The Great Transformation.*

70. *Wabash* declared: "Of the justice or propriety of the principle which lies at the foundation of the Illinois statute it is not the province of this court to speak. As restricted to a transportation which begins and ends within the limits of the State it may be very just a equitable, and it certainly is the province of the State legislature to determine that question. But when it is attempted to apply to transportation through an entire series of States a principle of this kind, and each one of the States shall attempt to establish its own rates of transportation, its own methods to prevent discrimination in rates, or to permit it, the deleterious influence upon the freedom of commerce among the States and upon the transit of goods through those States cannot be overestimated. That this species of regulation is one which must be, if established at all, of a general and national character, and cannot be safely and wisely remitted to local rules and local regulations, we think is clear from what has already been said. And if it be a regulation of commerce, as we think we have demonstrated it is, and as the Illinois court concedes it to be, it must be of that national character, and the regulation can only appropriately exist by general rules and principles, which demand that it should be done by the Congress of the United States under the commerce clause of the Constitution" (at 577).

71. William Graebner, "Federalism in the Progressive Era: A Structural Interpretation of Reform," *Journal of American History* 44/2 (September 1977), 331–357; Samuel P. Hays, "Political Parties and the Community-Society Continuum," in *The American Party Systems: Stages of Political Development,* William Nisbet Chambers and Walter Dean Burnham (eds.) (New York: Oxford University Press, 1967), 169–177.

72. As Stephen Skowronek explains, the anti-monopoly position was self-contradictory. To prohibit pooling was to try to enforce competition in the railroad industry, whereas to prohibit long- and short-haul discrimination was to destroy the essence of competition among existing railroads. The type of competition encouraged likely would result in underutilization of capacities and artificially high rates. Skowronek, *Building a New American State,* 141–142.

73. Skowronek, *Building a New American State,* citing statements of Senator Shelby Cullom, sponsor of the commission proposal, 145.

74. *Ibid.,* 149.

75. Ironically, the movement of the ICC to assert administrative authority proceeded under the guiding hand of Commission Chairman, Thomas Cooley, former exponent of constitutional limitations. In decisions in 1896–1897 the Supreme Court ruled that it was not bound by the conclusions of the Commission, that it could admit additional evidence, and that it could set aside the Commission's findings altogether. Cincinnati, New Orleans and

Texas Pacific Railway Co. v. ICC, 162 U.S. 184 (1896); ICC v. Alabama Midland Railway Co., 168 U.S. 144 (1897). The Court rejected the ICC's interpretation of an "unjust discrimination" in 1896, thus rejecting the Commission's first major attempt at setting a national policy. Texas and Pacific Railway Co. v. ICC, 162 U.S. 197 (1896).

76. In ICC v. Cincinnati, New Orleans and Texas Pacific Railway Co., 167 U.S. 479 (1897) the Court denied the ICC the power to set new rates to correct existing rates it judged unreasonable. In United States v. Trans-Missouri Freight Association, 166 U.S. 290 (1897), and United States v. Joint Traffic Association, 171 U.S. 505 (1898), the Court forbade the railroads from making agreements through traffic associations to set rates. The ICC had accepted these private arrangements as part of its plan to stabilize the railroads.

77. Aldace F. Walker, "Has the Interstate Commerce Law Been Beneficial?," *Forum* xvii (April 1894), 215, cited in Kolko, *Railroads and Regulation*, 77.

78. The tentative nature of this statement is intentional. Contrary to Kolko's general argument, regulation did not rescue the railroad industry. According to Paul W. MacAvoy's study of the early ICC, the ICC's willful blind eye to some pooling arrangements between 1887 and 1894 did result in higher long-distance grain rates. Nonetheless, the building of large, regional railroad systems did as much to relieve instability in the railroad industry as did regulation in the last decade of the 19th century. Stability aside, the industry began to go into decline in the early 20th century. However, the bold conclusion of Albro Martin's *Enterprise Denied*, that the ICC was responsible for the decline of the railroads, is also largely untenable. It is true that when the ICC finally emerged from the Court's shadow in the second decade of the 20th century, the Commission systematically denied rate increases and thus hastened railroad troubles. Yet, laying the blame at the ICC's door neglects the strong role of Congress in constraining the ICC. Ultimately, however, more consequential than regulation to the fortunes of railroading was the rise of auto transport. Both Kolko and Martin exaggerate the efficacy of ICC actions. Albro Martin, *Enterprise Denied: Origins of the Decline of American Railroads, 1897–1917* (Columbia University Press, 1971); Paul W. MacAvoy, *The Economic Effects of Regulation: The Trunk Line Railroad Cartels and the Interstate Commerce Commission Before 1900* (Cambridge: Harvard University Press, 1965); see also Chandler, *The Visible Hand*, 145–187; McCraw, "Regulation in America."

79. As Judge Brewer wrote as early as 1888 in *Chicago and N. W. Railway Co. v. Dey*, in a statement both lauding the commission form and worried about its powers, "The reasonableness of a rate changes with the changed condition of circumstances. That which would be fair and reasonable to-day, six months or a year hence may be either too high or too low. The legislature convenes only at stated periods; in this State once in two years. Justice will be more likely done if this power of fixing rates is vested in a body of continual session than if left with one meeting only at stated and long intervals. Such a power can change rates at any time, and thus meet the changing conditions of circumstances. While, of course, the argument from inconvenience cannot be pushed too far, yet is certainly a matter of inquiry whether in the increasing complexity of our civilization and our social and business relations, the power of the legislature to give increased extent to administrative functions must not be recognized." 35 Fed. 866 (1888), at 875.

80. Suzanne Weaver, "Antitrust Division of the Department of Justice," in *The Politics of Regulation*, James Q. Wilson, (ed.) (New York: Basic Books, 1980), 123–151.

81. Ellis W. Hawley, *The New Deal and the Problem of Monopoly* (Princeton: Princeton University Press, 1966), 6.

82. William Letwin, "Congress and the Sherman Antitrust Law," *The University of Chicago Law Review* 23/1 (Autumn 1955), 221–256; Weibe, *The Search for Order*.

83. United States v. American Tobacco Company, 221 U.S. 106 (1911); Standard Oil Company of New Jersey et al. v. United States, 221 U.S. 1 (1911).

The battle over good and bad trusts reflected the disputes regarding the nature of the early

20th-century economy. See the discussion of Granger vs. Progressive public interest theory in chapter 2 *supra*.

84. Robert E. Cushman, *The Independent Regulatory Commissions* (New York: Octagon Books, 1972), 178–181.

85. Morton Keller, "The Pluralist State: American Economic Regulation in Comparative Perspective, 1900–1930," in *Regulation in Perspective*, Thomas K. McCraw (ed.), 56–94.

86. Gabriel Kolko, *The Triumph of Conservatism: A Reinterpretation of American History, 1900–1916* (New York: The Free Press, 1963), 144–156.

87. Cushman, *The Independent Regulatory Commissions*, 146–150.

88. Kolko, *The Triumph of Conservatism*, 244–246; Cushman, *The Independent Regulatory Commissions*, 151–152.

89. Cushman, *The Independent Regulatory Commissions*, 228–240; Edward Mansfield, "Federal Maritime Commission," in *The Politics of Regulation*, James Q. Wilson (ed.), 42–74.

90. Thomas O. McGarity, "Regulatory Reform and the Positive State: An Historical Overview," *Administrative Law Review* 38/4 (Fall 1986), 399–425; Martin Shapiro, "On Predicting the Future of Administrative Law," *Regulation* (May/June 1982), 18–25.

91. The National Industrial Recovery Act, passed by Congress early in Franklin Roosevelt's first Administration (June 16, 1933), was a piece of legislation with comprehensive scope, designed to rescue industries destabilized by the Depression.

92. Hawley, *The New Deal and the Problem of Monopoly*, 19–71. Also, William E. Leuchtenberg, *Franklin D. Roosevelt and the New Deal, 1932–1940* (New York: Harper & Row, 1963), 41–62.

93. Hawley, *The New Deal and the Problem of Monopoly*, 91–129.

94. A.L.A. Schechter Poultry Corp. v. United States, 295 U.S. 495 (1935).

95. Where the politics of broadcast regulation diverge from the general New Deal pattern is over the issue of free speech. The creation of regulatory agencies in the New Deal was prompted by issues of industrial instability and threats to commerce. Broadcast regulation clearly was about this—indeed, it was the failure of market controls which induced broadcasters to clamor for a "policeman of the ether." But once the process was set in motion, the politics of regulatory controls in broadcasting also implicated other concerns, namely a dual fear of both censorship and propaganda. This topic will be taken up in succeeding chapters.

96. William R. Childs, *Trucking and the Public Interest: The Emergence of Federal Regulation, 1914–1940* (Knoxville: University of Tennessee Press, 1985). 79 Congressional Record, 74th Congress, 1st Session, 11813, 12196–12200, 12204–34 (1935).

97. See the ICC's interpretation of the statute in Pan American Bus Lines Operations, 1 I.C.C. 190 (1936), at 203.

98. See Childs, *Trucking and the Public Interest*.

99. Although the functions of the Securities and Exchange Commission are perfectly in keeping with the New Deal pattern, the politics of the agency's creation diverge from the pattern. For the most part, the financial community bitterly opposed the establishment of a regulatory agency. See Michael E. Parrish, *Securities Regulation and the New Deal* (New Haven: Yale University Press, 1970).

100. See, of course, Theodore J. Lowi, *The End of Liberalism: Ideology, Policy, and the Crisis of Public Authority* (New York: Norton, 1969). Also in this context of monopoly benefits and customer groups, Richard A. Posner, "Taxation by Regulation," *Bell Journal of Economics and Management Science* 2/1 (Spring 1971), 22–50.

101. Where conditions were such that capital failed to provide infrastructure institutions, the federal government intervened directly. The Rural Electrification Administration (1935)

subsidized the building of electricity plants in poor, rural areas. The Tennessee Valley Authority (1933) and Bonneville Power Administration did the same for entire geographic regions. The Public Works Administration (1933) and Works Projects Administration (1935) not only put unemployed people to work, but built and repaired roads and bridges.

102. Recognized as businesses clothed with a public interest were grain elevators and railroads in *Munn v. Illinois;* banks in Noble State Bank v. Haskell, 219 U.S. 113 (1911); fire insurance companies in German Alliance Insurance Company v. Lewis, Superintendent of Insurance of the State of Kansas, 233 U.S. 389 (1913); and insurance agents in O'Gorman & Young, Inc. v. Hartford Fire Insurance Co., 282 U.S. 251 (1931). The Court also recognized the right of legislatures to regulate the companies which operated under government franchises to provide services such as gas, electricity, water, and transport.

103. Rejected as businesses clothed with a public interests were the manufacture of food, clothing, and fuels in Chas. Wolff Packing Co. v. Court of Industrial Relations of the State of Kansas, 262 U.S. 522 (1923); the operations of theater ticket brokers in Tyson & Brother— United Theatre Ticket Officers v. Banton, District Attorney, 273 U.S. 418 (1927); employment agencies in Ribnik v. McBride, Commissioner of Labor of the State of New Jersey, 277 U.S. 350 (1928); gasoline service stations in Williams, Commissioner of Finance et al. v. Standard Oil Co. of Louisiana, 278 U.S. 235 (1929); ice manufacturing plants in New State Ice Co. v. Liebmann, 285 U.S. 262 (1932).

104. Nebbia v. New York, 291 U.S. 502 (1934).

105. A.L.A. Schechter Poultry Corp. v. United States, 295 U.S. 495 (1935); also Panama Refining Co. v. Ryan, 293 U.S. 388 (1935), which struck down the NRA codes regulating interstate shipment of oil because there was no standard or rule; and Carter v. Carter Coal Co, 298 U.S. 238 (1936), which struck down the labor provisions and price-fixing provisions of the National Bituminous Coal Conservation Act of 1935. The Court ruled that the mining of coal was a local issue with only indirect commerce effects.

106. Baldwin v. Seelig, 294 U.S. 511 (1935).

107. NLRB v. Jones and Laughlin Steel Corp., 301 U.S. 1 (1937); United States v. Darby, 312 U.S. 100 (1941). *NLRB v. Jones & Laughlin Steel* essentially reversed the Court's nondelegation doctrine espoused two years earlier in *Schechter.*

108. David Vogel, "The 'New' Social Regulation in Historical and Comparative Perspective," in *Regulation in Perspective,* Thomas K. McCraw (ed.), 155–185; idem, *Lobbying the Corporation: Citizen Challenges to Business Authority* (New York: Basic Books, 1979).

109. Vogel, "The 'New' Social Regulation," 161–162; Ronald Penoyer, (compiler), *Directory of Federal Regulatory Agencies,* 3rd Edition (St. Louis: Center for the Study of American Business, 1981); Congressional Quarterly, *Federal Regulatory Directory, 1983– 84* (Washington, DC: Congressional Quarterly, Inc., 1984).

110. Rachel Carson, *Silent Spring* (New York: Fawcett Crest, 1962); Jessica Mitford, *The American Way of Death* (New York: Simon & Schuster, 1963); Ralph Nader, *Unsafe at Any Speed: The Designed-in Dangers of the American Automobile* (New York: Grossman, 1965).

111. Michael Pertschuk, *Revolt Against Regulation: The Rise and Pause of the Consumer Movement* (Berkeley: University of California Press, 1982), 30–33.

112. Perstshuk, *Revolt Against Regulation,* 20–33; Shefter, Martin, "Party, Bureaucracy, and Political Change in the United States," Department of Politics, Cornell University, unpublished manuscript. The term, "entrepreneurialism," comes from James Q. Wilson.

This general analysis can also be discerned with regard to the welfare rights movement during the same time period in Francis Fox Piven and Richard A. Cloward, *Regulating the*

*Poor: The Functions of Public Welfare* (New York: Pantheon Books, 1971).The deeper cultural question of why the concern for health, safety, and environmental protection and fear of risks arose at this time cannot be addressed here. One interesting (though, I believe, flawed) anthropological interpretation is found in Mary Douglas and Aaron Wildavsky, *Risk and Culture* (Berkeley: University of California Press, 1982).

113. As for anti-corporate sentiment, the Harris poll reported that 55 percent of the public in 1966 expressed "a great deal of confidence" in the heads of large corporations. This figure fell to 29 percent by 1973, to 21 percent in 1974, and 15 percent in 1975. The Yankelovich survey reported that the proportion of the public that thought "business strikes a fair balance between profits and the public interest" dropped from 70 percent in 1968 to 20 percent in 1974. Cited in Leonard Silk and David Vogel, *Ethics and Profits: The Crisis of Confidence in American Business* (New York: Simon & Schuster, 1976), 21.

114. James R. Michael (ed.), *Working on the System: A Comprehensive Manual for Citizen Access to Federal Agencies* (New York: Basic Books, 1974); Robert C. Fellmeth, *The Interstate Commerce Omission: The Public Interest and the ICC* (New York: Grossman, 1970); Mark Green and Ralph Nader, "Economic Regulation vs. Competition: Uncle Sam the Monopoly Man," *Yale Law Journal* 82/5 (April 1973), 871–889.

The irony of the left-oriented criticism of regulatory agencies in the 1960s and 1970s is that the "problem of bureaucracy" had been a *conservative* complaint about the New Deal. The original conservative critique of regulatory agencies was not that they disrupted the market or had created monopolies, but that they constituted a "headless, fourth branch of government." See James Q. Wilson, "The Bureaucracy Problem," *The Public Interest* 6 (Winter 1967), 3–9.

Another strand of criticism of regulatory agencies was rooted in free market economics. An increasing number of books and articles criticized regulation for its clumsy, costly, and inappropriate actions. The more radical of these criticisms claimed that regulation-created cartels totally disrupted the market and served no public interest whatever. See chapter 2 *supra*. By the late 1970s, this conservative, market-oriented criticism supplanted the liberal criticism of regulation. See chapter 7 *infra*.

115. Scenic Hudson Preservation Conference v. FPC, 354 F.2d 608 (2d Cir. 1965), *cert. denied*, 384 U.S. 941 (1966); Office of Communication of the United Church of Christ v. Federal Communications Commission, 359 F.2d 994 (D.C. Cir. 1966).

116. See Richard B. Stewart, "The Reformation of American Administrative Law," *Harvard Law Review* 88/5 (June 1975), 1669–1813. The consequences of the expansion of standing and the changed standards of judicial review will be covered in greater detail in chapter 7.

117. See Richard Polenberg, *Reorganizing Roosevelt's Government: The Controversy Over Executive Reorganization, 1936–1939* (Cambridge: Harvard University Press, 1966).

118. Congressional Quarterly, *Federal Regulatory Directory, 1979–80* (Washington, DC: Congressional Quarterly Inc., 1979), 1–77.

119. See Parrish, *Securities Regulation and the New Deal*.

120. Vogel, "The 'New' Social Regulation," 175–179; idem, "How Business Responds to Opposition: Corporate Political Strategies During the 1970s," paper delivered to the 1979 Annual Meeting of the American Political Science Association, August 31–September 3, 1979; Pertschuk, *Revolt Against Regulation*, 47–68.

121. This discription is drawn directly from Stephen G. Breyer and Richard B. Stewart, *Administrative Law and Regulatory Policy* (Boston: Little, Brown & Co., 1979), 23–26, and Stewart, "The Reformation of American Administrative Law," 1671–1676.

122. Shapiro, "On Predicting the Future of Administrative Law."

123. Federal Administrative Procedure Act, 5 U.S.C. § 551 et seq.

124. See James M. Landis, *The Administrative Process* (New Haven: Yale University Press, 1938), 10–16, 46–50; Kenneth Culp Davis, *Discretionary Justice: A Preliminary Inquiry* (Urbana: University of Illinois Press, 1971).

125. Or, as James L. Fly, Chairman of the FCC during its most reform-minded phase, testified to the Senate Commerce Committee in 1941, "I think it ought to be part of the Commission's job to see that they [the radio networks] do not go out of business, because no one could contemplate with equanimity a substantial impairment of the nationwide service." U.S. Senate, 77th Congress, 1st Session, Committee on Interstate Commerce, Hearings on S. Res. 113, *A Resolution Directing a Study of Certain Rules and Regulations Promulgated by the Federal Communications Commission,* June 2–20, 1941, Testimony of James Lawrence Fly (Washington, DC: Government Printing Office, 1941), 95.

126. Kenneth Culp Davis, *Administrative Law Treatise,* Vol. 2, § 8:1, at 158 (2nd ed. 1979), cited in Carl McGowan, "A Reply to *Judicialization,*" *Duke Law Journal* 1986/2 (April 1986), at 227.

127. Lowi, *The End of Liberalism* (second edition); Henry Friendly, *The Federal Regulatory Agencies: The Need for Better Definition of Standards* (Cambridge: Harvard University Press, 1962); Louis Hector, "Problems of the CAB and the Independent Regulatory Commissions," *Yale Law Journal* 69/6 (May 1960), 931–964.

128. Theodore Lowi provides particularly good descriptions of the bargaining process. *The End of Liberalism,* 92–94, 107–113.

129. I owe this construction to Langdon Winner, "Do Artifacts Have Politics?," *Daedalus* 109 (Winter 1980), 121–136. Winner's discussion is of technologies, but the point holds for basic regulatory formulas as well.

130. See the Court's decision in SEC v. Chenery Corp., 332 U.S. 194 (1947), which intimated that retroactivity goes against elemental notions of fair play.

131. Of course, there are important exceptions to these general tendencies. Throughout the 1960s, the Federal Power Commission, supported by public opinion and judicial review, regulated natural gas field prices to control excess producer rents. The FPC consistently ruled against gas producers, and regulation ultimately discouraged new exploration. By the mid-1970s there was a potentially serious shortage of natural gas. Stephen Breyer, *Regulation and Its Reform* (Cambridge: Harvard University Press, 1982), 240–260. This example also underscores the potential effects of public opinion and political dynamics in altering the normal conservative tendencies of a regulatory agency.

132. This point is made by Samuel P. Hays in various of his essays. See, especially, "Political Choice in Regulatory Administration," in *Regulation in Perspective,* Thomas K. McCraw (ed.), 124–154.

133. Landis, *The Administrative Process,* 123; *President's Committee on Administrative Management, Report With Special Studies,* (1937), 324. Stewart cites the Court's decision in ICC v. Chicago, Rock Island and Pacific Railway Co., 218 U.S. 88 (1909), which states that the ICC's powers "are expected to be exercised in the coldest neutrality. . . . And the training that is required, the comprehensive knowledge which is possessed, guards or tends to guard against the accidental abuse of its powers. . . ." at 102. Stewart, "The Reformation of American Administrative Law," 1678.

134. This quotation is from Justice Frankfurter's dissent in *FPC v. Hope Natural Gas Co.,* which prefigured the view of the public interest that emerged in the Great Society period. 320 U.S. 591 (1944), at 627. For the judicial transformation in the conception of the public interest, see Stewart, "The Reformation of American Administrative Law."

135. See, for instance, Bruce M. Owen and Ronald Braeutigam, *The Regulation Game* (Cambridge: Ballinger Publishing Co., 1978).

## Chapter 4. The Evolution of the American Telecommunications System

1. Gerald W. Brock, *The Telecommunications Industry: The Dynamics of Market Structure* (Cambridge: Harvard University Press, 1981), 62–72.

2. Richard B. DuBoff, "Business Demand and the Development of the Telegraph in the United States," *Business History Review* 54/4 (Winter 1980), 459–479.

3. Alfred D. Chandler, Jr., *The Visible Hand: The Managerial Revolution in American Business* (Cambridge: Harvard University Press, 1977).

4. Richard B. DuBoff, "The Telegraph in Nineteenth-Century America: Technology and Monopoly," *Comparative Studies in Society and History* 26/4 (October 1984), 571–586; idem, "Business Demand and the Development of the Telegraph in the United States," 463; Robert Luther Thompson, *Wiring a Continent: The History of the Telegraph Industry in the United States, 1832–1866* (Princeton: Princeton University Press, 1947), 241–242, 426.

This statistic does not provide the entire picture. As mammoth as Western Union was, there were many small telegraph companies which serviced local areas. Thus the amount of operating telegraph wire was even larger.

5. Chandler, *The Visible Hand*, 197–200; Thompson, *Wiring a Continent*, 426.

6. The 1880 Census indicated that there were 58 commercial telegraph companies apart from Western Union, of which 18 were owned by railroad companies. The Western Union system embraced 77.35 percent of the total miles of line, 80.19 percent of the miles of wire, and 72.56 percent of the total number of stations or offices. It carried 92.15 percent of the telegraph messages sent during that year and received 88.81 percent of the gross revenues from messages. James M. Herring and Gerald C. Gross, *Telecommunications: Economics and Regulation* (New York: McGraw-Hill, 1936; reprinted, Arno Press, 1974), 3.

7. The Washburn Committee of the House of Representatives declared in 1870 that telegraph rates in Europe averaged less than one-half those in the United States. In England they were less than one-third, in France less than one-fourth of American rates, mile for mile. These figures were disputed however, because of difficulties in directly comparing the systems. As far as rate discrimination went, in 1873, for example, a ten-word telegram went from Washington to Boston for 55 cents. The same telegram sent to Waltham, some ten miles to the west of Boston, cost $1.75. From Washington to Chicago the rate was $1.75, but to Geneva, forty miles from Chicago, it was $3.00. Alvin F. Harlow, *Old Wires and New Waves: The History of the Telegraph, Telephone, and Wireless* (New York: D. Appleton-Century Company, 1936), 331, 334; Lester G. Lindley, *The Constitution Faces Technology: The Relationship of the National Government to the Telegraph, 1866–1884* (New York: Arno Press, 1975), 119.

8. Richard B. DuBoff, "The Rise of Communications Regulation: The Telegraph Industry, 1844–1880," *Journal of Communication* 34/3 (Summer 1984), 52–66.

9. Thompson, *Wiring a Continent*, 393–396; Harlow, *Old Wires and New Waves*, 282–286; Brock, *The Telecommunications Industry*, 81–82.

10. Daniel J. Czitrom, *Media and the American Mind: From Morse to McLuhan* (Chapel Hill: University of North Carolina Press, 1982), 25–28.

11. Lindley, *The Constitution Faces Technology*, 43–76.

12. DuBoff, "The Rise of Communications Regulation," 62, 64; idem, "The Telegraph in Nineteenth-Century America," 585; Lindley, *The Constitution Faces Technology*, 84–125; Pensacola Telegraph Company v. Western Union Telegraph Company, 96 U.S. 1 (1877). This case, similar to *Wabash, St. Louis and Pacific Railway Company v. Illinois*, predated it by nine years.

13. Act of July 24, 1866, ch. 230, 14 Stat. 221.

14. This is how Ithiel de Sola Pool puts it in *Technologies of Freedom* (Cambridge: Harvard University Press, 1983), 96.

15. DuBoff, "The Telegraph in Nineteenth-Century America," 580–581.

16. U.S. Senate, 43rd Congress, 1st session, Committee on Post Offices and Post Roads, *Postal Telegraph,* S. Rept. 242, at 1, 3. Cited in Czitrom, *Media and the American Mind,* 26.

17. See Bruce Wyman, *The Special Law Governing Public Service Corporations and All Others Engaged in Public Employment* (New York: Baker, Voorhis & Co., 1911), Vol. II, section 1014.

18. Western Union Telegraph Co. v. Carew, 15 Michigan 525 (1867).

19. Primrose v. Western Union Telegraph Co., 154 U.S. 1 (1893), at 14.

20. Western Union Tel. Co. v. Matthews, 24 Ky. Law Rep. 3 (1902).

21. Western Union Tel. Co. v. Simmons, (Tex. Civ. App.), 93 S. W. 686 (1906).

22. Western Union Tel. Co. v. Lillard, 86 Ark. 208 (1908).

23. See Wyman, *The Special Law,* sections 604–607; Gray v. Western Union Tel. Co., 87 Ga. 350 (1891); Western Union Tel. Co v. Totten, 141 Fed. 533, 72 C. C. A. 591 (1905); Godwin v. Carolina Tel. & Tel. Co., 136 N. C. 258, 48 S. E. 636 (1904).

24. Brock, *The Telecommunications Industry,* 108–109.

25. This early history draws from several sources, including N. R. Danielian, *AT&T: The Story of Industrial Conquest* (New York: Vanguard Press, 1939); John Brooks, *Telephone: The First Hundred Years* (New York: Harper & Row, 1975); Sidney H. Aronson, "Bell's Electrical Toy: What's the Use? The Sociology of Early Telephone Usage," *Social Impact of the Telephone,* Ithiel de Sola Pool (ed.) (Cambridge: MIT Press, 1977), 15–39.

Western Union's reasons for declining to purchase the Bell patents are uncertain. The traditional explanation, that Western Union president Orton dismissed the telephone as a toy, may be true but incorrectly infers that Orton was a fool. In fact, the early telephone could operate at a maximum distance of twenty miles. This would hardly be seen as a technology directly threatening to telegraphy, whose range spanned continents. Also, as Brock explains, many prior inventions related to the telegraph had turned out to be insignificant and Western Union would have found it unprofitable to purchase every invention offered to it to avoid potential competition. It is possible that Western Union believed its ownership of the Gray patent obviated the need to purchase Bell's. Lastly, the Bell Company was partly run by Gardiner Hubbard, who for years had been agitating for governmental intervention in the telegraph industry. Orton likely distrusted Hubbard and would not wish to enrich him unnecessarily. Brock, *The Telecommunications Industry,* 92; Ithiel de Sola Pool, *Forecasting the Telephone: A Retrospective Technology Assessment of the Telephone* (Norwood: Ablex Publishing Co., 1983), 106–107.

26. Chandler, *The Visible Hand,* 199–201; Brock, *The Telecommunications Industry,* 85–86.

27. J. Warren Stehman, *The Financial History of the American Telephone and Telegraph Company* (Boston: Houghton Mifflin Co., 1925; reprinted, Augustus M. Kelley, 1967), 15–16; Robert Bornholz and David S. Evans, "The Early History of Competition in the Telephone Industry," in *Breaking Up Bell: Essays on Industrial Organization and Regulation,* David S. Evans (ed.) (New York: North-Holland, 1983), 7–40.

28. Richard Gabel, "The Early Competitive Era in Telephone Communication, 1893–1920," *Law and Contemporary Problems* 34/2 (Spring 1969), 340–359.

29. Stehman, *The Financial History of AT&T,* 25–26; Bornholz & Evans, "The Early History of Competition in the Telephone Industry," 10–11; Brock, *The Telecommunications Industry,* 96–97.

30. Herring & Gross, *Telecommunications: Economics and Regulation,* 47; Brock, *The Telecommunications Industry,* 108.

31. The independents' attempt to create a long-distance system fell apart when one of the

prime financial backers, Peter Widener, withdrew his support. Gabel argues that J. P. Morgan worked out a deal with Widener to ensure the collapse of the competing long-distance initiative. Gabel, "The Early Competitive Era in Telephone Communication," 350.

32. Federal Communications Commission, *Telephone Investigation: Proposed Report* (Pursuant to Public Resolution No. 8, 74th Congress) (Washington, DC: Government Printing Office, 1938), 143–145. This massive report was undertaken by FCC staff under the supervision of Commissioner Paul Walker. The *Proposed Report* (which was revised and given a quite different conclusion by the entire FCC in its 1939 *Final Report*) often is referred to as the "Walker Report."

33. Danielian, *AT&T,* 46–69.

34. FCC, *Telephone Investigation,* Table 32, 143.

35. Cited in Pool, *Forecasting the Telephone,* 22.

36. As Vail argued, "The value of any exchange system is measured by the number of members of any community that are connected with it. If there are two systems, neither of them serving all, important users must be connected with both systems. . . . Given the same management, the public must pay double rates for service, to meet double charges, on double capital, double operating expenses and double maintenance." *AT&T Annual Report,* 1907, 18. Vail saw government regulation as a means to the creation of a single unified system.

37. Stehman, *The Financial History of AT&T,* 44–50, 260.

38. The automatic exchange and the combined receiver/transmitter telephone handset were innovations of Bell competitors. Because of this, Bell was very slow to adopt these improvements. Harry M. Trebing, "Common Carrier Regulation—The Silent Crisis," *Law and Contemporary Problems* 34/2 (Spring 1969), 302–309; Bornholz & Evans, "The Early History of Competition in the Telephone Industry," 14–22.

The question whether or not telephony is a natural monopoly resurfaces in contemporary debates. The issue, then and now, is not simply an economic one, however. The competition vs. (regulated) monopoly issue is a political policy issue, for each regimen secures different outcomes. Competition seems to advance rapid expansion and innovative service, whereas regulated monopoly seems to advance relatively cheap service to all.

39. See, for instance, State ex rel. Webster v. Nebraska Telephone Co., 17 Neb. 126 (1885); Ithiel de Sola Pool, *Technologies of Freedom* (Cambridge: Harvard University Press, 1983), 101.

40. Richmond v. Southern Bell Tel. & Tel. Co., 174 U.S. 761 (1899).

41. See Wyman, *The Special Law,* sections 525–526, 700; compare Matter of Baldwinsville Telephone Co., 24 N.Y. Misc. 221, 53 N.Y. Supp. 574 (1898) and Billings Mutual Telephone Co. v. Rocky Mtn. Bell Telephone Co., 155 Fed. 207 (1907).

42. The discussion of the Mann-Elkins and Willis-Graham Acts draws on G. Hamilton Loeb, "The Communications Act Policy Toward Competition: A Failure to Communicate," *Duke Law Journal* 1978/1 (March 1978), 1–56.

Whereas the statements of various Congressmen with regard to the extension of ICC authority over communications reflected some anti-corporate sentiment, the main impression one gets from the debates is that Congress saw ICC oversight of communications as appropriate to the overall regulation of interstate commerce. Representative Underwood's remarks were typical. He stated, "[We] cannot afford to turn our backs on [the amendment] and refuse to bring the great telegraph and telephone lines in this country within the terms of the interstate commerce act, so that they may be properly and fairly regulated in the interest of the great commercial life of the Nation." 45 Congressional Record 5536 (1910).

A letter inserted into the Senate debate from the National Independent Telephone Association indicated that the independents supported Mann-Elkins. Id., 6973–6974. Though there is no record, Theodore Vail's general positive comments toward regulation voiced as early as 1907 indicate that AT&T may have supported the extension of ICC oversight over telephony.

43. Pool, *Technologies of Freedom,* 102–103.

44. As seen in Chapter 3, the pre-New Deal judiciary in many respects rejected administrative law. Following the doctrine of constitutional limitations and the famous nondelegation doctrine, courts ruled that administrative sanctions on private individuals must be authorized by legislatures. This model of review meant that agency discretion would be firmly contained by the courts requiring specifically delegated legislative directives. During this early period, the courts essentially reprivatized this new public law by seizing judicial review power over rate setting and other agency actions, and then treating the rights of private parties seeking review as constitutionally superior to the interests of government. See Martin Shapiro, "On Predicting the Future of Administrative Law," *Regulation* (May/June 1982), 18–25; also, James W. Sichter, *Separations Procedures in the Telephone Industry: The Historical Origins of a Public Policy* (Cambridge: Program on Information Resources Policy, 1977), 9–62.

45. This case, the only instance of formal antitrust action against the Bell System in this period, was settled by agreement. "Government Sues Telephone Trust," *The New York Times,* July 25, 1913, 1.

46. The legacy of populist struggle for the nationalization of telegraphy lived on, now embracing telephony, particularly as AT&T grew. Within the Wilson Administration, Postmaster General Albert S. Burleson and Secretary of the Navy Josephus Daniels long advocated the "postalization" of wire carriers. During World War I they were joined by Secretary of War Newton D. Baker. In 1913 a Burleson-appointed committee to look into the subject of postalization recommended the consolidation of telegraph and telephone systems under Post Office control. U.S. Senate, 63rd Congress, 2d Session, Senate Document 399, *Government Ownership of Electrical Means of Communication,* Letter from the Postmaster General (Washington, DC: Government Printing Office, 1914). Also see Danielian, AT&T, 243–270; Horace Coon, *American Tel & Tel: The Story of a Great Monopoly* (New York: Longmans, Green & Co., 1939), 138–144.

47. Letter of N. C. Kingsbury, Vice-President of AT&T, to Attorney General J. C. Reynolds, reprinted in FCC, *Telephone Investigation,* 139–141; Brooks, *Telephone,* 136–165.

48. The maintenance of legal barriers between communications fields represented a victory of antitrust principles over technology and, to some degree, commerce. One reason why AT&T absorbed Western Union was to use its facilities for long-distance service. The technical possibility of multiplexing voice and telegraphic code on the same line was demonstrated about 1910, the same time that AT&T bought Western Union. There was no compelling technical reason to prevent telegraphy and telephony from using the same set of lines. Pool, *Forecasting the Telephone,* 109.

49. U.S. House, 65th Congress, 2d Session, Committee on Interstate and Foreign Commerce, Hearings on H.J. Res. 309, July 2, 1918.

50. For terms of compensation contract, Federal Communications Commission, exhibit 2096-B, *Control of Telephone Communications,* Appendix A, *Data Relating to Federal Control of the Bell Telephone System, August 1, 1918 to July 31, 1919* (Washington, DC: Government Printing Office, 1919). Cited in Danielian, *AT&T,* 250–253.

51. Danielian, *AT&T,* 260.

52. Dakota Central Telephone Co. v. State of South Dakota ex rel. Payne, Attorney General, 250 U.S. 163 (1919).

53. Public Law No. 9, 41 Stat. 157, July 11, 1919. One of the conditions of the reprivatization was that the federally mandated rate hikes remain in force for a period not exceeding four months.

54. Willis-Graham Act, 42 Stat. 27, June 10, 1921.

55. For example, the Senate Commerce Committee declared in 1921 that "telephoning is a natural monopoly." U.S. Senate, 67th Congress, 1st Session, Committee on Interstate Commerce, S. Rep. No. 75, *Amending the Transportation Act of 1920* (Washington, DC: Government Printing Office, 1921), at 1.

The primary visible push for Willis-Graham came from the independent telephone companies. (AT&T was publicly neutral.) Bell's implementation of several inventions made long-distance service more reliable after 1915. Bell's ability to offer connections to the nation's major cities had made the independents' efforts to construct their own system largely futile. The independents thereafter changed their strategy to one of supervised interconnections with the Bell System. Many independents were in severe financial difficulties in the teens. Loeb, "The Communications Act Policy Toward Competition," 13–14; Bornholz & Evans, "The Early History of Competition in the Telephone Industry," 33.

56. From the time of the Willis-Graham Act until the Communications Act (thirteen years), the percentage of all telephones operated by independent telephone companies declined from 36 percent to 21 percent. By 1934, virtually all telephones were connected with the Bell System and there was no direct competition with the Bell System. Bornholz & Evans, "The Early History of Competition in the Telephone Industry," 14; FCC, *Telephone Investigation*, 139–143.

57. Loeb argues that even had the ICC wished to exercise greater oversight over communications, it did not have the statutory power to do so. Loeb, "The Communications Act Policy Toward Competition," 17.

58. Sichter, *Separations Procedures in the Telephone Industry*, 11–12.

59. Brock, *The Telecommunications Industry*, 161.

60. Sichter, *Separations Procedures in the Telephone Industry*, 15–16. Sichter cites a 1905 recommendation by the Merchants Association of New York City that the mode of telephone pricing be value of service, despite the fact that this formula typically resulted in higher charges for business than for residential telephone service.

61. This meant the consideration, in the Court's words, "of the original cost of construction, the amount expended in permanent improvements, the amount and market value of its bonds and stock, the present as compared with the original cost of construction, the probable earning capacity of the property under particular rates prescribed by statute, and the sum required to meet operating expenses. . . ." Smythe v. Ames, 169 U.S. 466 (1898) at 546–547.

62. Alfred E. Kahn, *The Economics of Regulation: Principles and Institutions*, Vol. 1 (New York: John Wiley & Sons, 1970), 39, 43.

63. Simpson v. Shepard, 230 U.S. 352 (1913).

64. Sichter, *Separations Procedures in the Telephone Industry*, 47.

65. The following comparison between the percentage of return on net book cost of plant earned by the Bell Operating Companies (BOCs) and Long Lines between 1913 and 1936 are drawn from the Walker Report.

| Period | BOCs | Long Lines |
|---|---|---|
| 1913–1920 | 6.22 | 17.02 |
| 1921–1925 | 7.16 | 19.21 |
| 1926–1930 | 7.60 | 13.34 |
| 1931–1936 | 6.02 | 6.57 |

The decreased rate of return of Long Lines in the 1926–1930 period was due to four voluntary rate reductions. The decreased rate of return in the 1931–1936 period was due to the Depression. FCC, *Telephone Investigation: Proposed Report,* 435.

In a case called *Pacific Telephone and Telegraph Company v. Whitcomb,* the federal district court, while rejecting the state regulatory commission's rate rulings, "conceded that the amount [of parent company materials and assistance] received by the Home Company [an AT&T licensee] is substantially less than the actual cost of supplying the service." 12 F.2d 279 (D.C.W.D. 1926) at 288.

66. Southwestern Bell Telephone Company v. Public Service Commission of Missouri, 262 U.S. 276 (1923).

67. Stehman, *The Financial History of AT&T,* 258–259.

68. Sichter, *Separations Procedures in the Telephone Industry,* 58–59.

69. Smith v. Illinois Bell Telephone Company, 282 U.S. 133 (1930).

70. Hugh G. J. Aitken, *The Continuous Wave: Technology and American Radio, 1900–1932* (Princeton: Princeton University Press, 1985), 226–229.

71. This early history is drawn from several sources, including, among others, Erik Barnouw, *A History of Broadcasting in the United States,* Vol. 1, *A Tower in Babel* (New York: Oxford University Press, 1966); Gleason Archer, *History of Radio to 1926* (New York: American Historical Company, 1938); Sydney Head, *Broadcasting in America* (Boston: Houghton-Mifflin, 1956); Hugh G. J. Aitken, *Syntony and Spark: The Origin of Radio* (New York: John Wiley & Sons, 1976); Czitrom, *Media and the American Mind;* Brian Winston, *Misunderstanding Media* (Cambridge: Harvard University Press, 1986).

72. Aitken, *The Continuous Wave,* 88–95, 255, 192–194; W. Rupert Maclaurin, *Invention and Innovation in the Radio Industry* (New York: Macmillan, 1949), 41, 58–87.

73. The early technology of signaling through wires was to generate waves by means of sparks. A series of sparks in rapid succession created a chain of electromagnetic disturbances that constructed a radio wave. This technology was adequate for the sending and receiving of Morse code, but had several major drawbacks. Spark transmissions were inherently unstable; they did not stay on one frequency and their power dissipated over distance. They were also subject to tremendous interference. The alternative which developed was continuous wave technology. This method of sending signals concentrated energy on a single frequency. See Aitken, *Syntony and Spark.*

74. Leonard S. Reich, "Industrial Research and the Pursuit of Corporate Security: The Early Years of Bell Labs," *Business History Review* 54/4 (Winter 1980), 504–529.

75. Reich, "Industrial Research and the Pursuit of Corporate Security," 520–521; Danielian, *AT&T,* 102–119; Aitken, *The Continuous Wave,* 246–247. The reasons for the incursion into radio research were explained by Frank Jewett, president of Bell Laboratories, in a letter dated March 9, 1932. He wrote, "[I]t was early clear to the American Telephone and Telegraph Co., and to all in the Bell System, that a thorough, and complete understanding of radio must be had at all times if the art of telephony and the business of the Associated Companies in the giving of telephone service was to be advanced and the money invested in that service safeguarded." Cited in Danielian, *AT&T,* 106.

76. Danielian, *AT&T,* 109; Maclaurin, *Invention and Innovation in the Radio Industry,* 95–98.

77. Federal Trade Commission, Report, *The Radio Industry* (Washington, DC: Government Printing Office, 1923), 24.

78. Josephus Daniels, Woodrow Wilson's Secretary of the Navy, saw communication as a governmental function. He was a vociferous advocate of government ownership of wireless. See Josephus Daniels, *The Wilson Era: Years of War and After, 1917–1923* (Chapel Hill: University of North Carolina Press, 1946).

79. Jeremy Tunstall, *The Media Are American: Anglo-American Media in the World* (New York: Columbia University Press, 1977), 28–30; Anthony Smith, *The Geopolitics of Information: How Western Culture Dominates the World* (New York: Oxford University Press, 1980), 44.

80. This description of the politics of undersea cables draws heavily from Aitken, *The Continuous Wave,* 250–262. See also Daniel R. Headrick, *The Tools of Empire: Technology and European Imperialism in the Nineteenth Century* (New York: Oxford University Press, 1981), 157–164.

81. U.S. Senate, 66th Congress, 3rd Session, Subcommittee of the Committee on Interstate Commerce, Hearings on S. 4301, *A Bill to Prevent the Unauthorized Landing of Submarine Cables in the United States,* testimony of Walter S. Rogers (Washington, DC: Government Printing Office, 1921), 37–52.

82. H. R. 13159 and S. 5036, 65th Congress, 2nd Session, 1919. Head claims that the bill was badly drawn and was ineptly defended by witnesses at the hearings. Barnouw infers that Congressional antipathy toward monopoly and "autocracy," along with the opposition from amateurs were key factors in defeating the Navy bid to nationalize radio. Head, *Broadcasting in America,* 111; Barnouw, *A Tower in Babel,* 54–55.

83. Navy Secretary Daniels' advocacy of government ownership was not shared by all in the Wilson Administration, but the underlying reasons for such a strategy *were* acknowledged by all relevant Wilson officials. Wilson's Postmaster General, A. S. Burleson, advising the President on post-war undersea cable negotiations, argued for a sort of American-based free flow of information policy for post-war communications. Burleson recognized the importance of international communications for American commerce, claiming, "The world system of international electric communication has been built up in order to connect the old world commercial centers with that world business. The United States is connected on one side only. A new system should be developed with the United States as a center." Cable, Burelson to Wilson (forwarded through Secretary Tumulty, March 14, 1919). Cited in Ray Stannard Baker, *Woodrow Wilson and World Settlement,* 3 vols. (New York: Doubleday, Page & Co., 1922), Vol. 3, 426.

Some in the Commerce Department saw international communications as vitally important for post-war international economic competition. Burwell S. Cutler, director of Commerce's Bureau of Foreign and Domestic Commerce, was convinced that "the Departments of Commerce, State, and Navy should take united action" and "give the necessary assistance to some private corporation which may be selected to operate more or less in silent partnership with the Government as the provider of purely American wireless communication throughout the world for the benefit of American commercial and military interests." Burwell S. Cutler, Chief, Bureau of Foreign and Domestic Commerce, to William C. Redfield, Secretary of Commerce, June 26, 1919; Redfield to Daniels, June 26, 1919, File 7534/20, Record Group 40, General Correspondence of the Office of the Secretary of Commerce (Washington, DC: National Archives and Records Service), cited in John P. Rossi, "A 'Silent Partnership'?: The U.S. Government, RCA, and Radio Communications with East Asia, 1919–1928," *Radical History Review* 33 (1985), 36.

84. Aitken, *The Continuous Wave,* 292–295.

85. President Woodrow Wilson personally worried about the expansion of British domination of world communications through the Marconi Company's hold on wireless. According to Owen D. Young of General Electric, Wilson delegated Admiral William H. G. Bullard, Director of Naval Communications, to meet with General Electric in order to prevent the sale of its Alexanderson alternator to Marconi. Bullard had been exhaustively briefed about wireless in general, and specifically on Marconi's designs on GE's alternator by Lieutenant Commander Stanford Hooper, the Navy's key man in its Radio Division.

In Young's account, "[Bullard] told me that the President had learned that the Marconi Company was eager to acquire the exclusive use of the Alexandersen (sic) alternator . . . . The wireless telegraph was beginning to threaten the long reign of the cables, but if Britain could also control this younger prodigy, she would own at the out set two of the three essentials for world dominance. So the President asked Admiral Bullard to say that in the interest of America he hoped we would not transfer exclusive rights to the alternator to any other country. He based his appeal quite frankly on patriotic grounds . . . . Admiral Bullard warned me that the decision might change the whole trend of world affairs." U.S. Senate, 71st Congress, 1st Session, Committee on Interstate Commerce, Hearings on S. 6: Comission on Communications, July 9, 1929 (Washington, DC: Government Printing Office, 1929), at 1100–1101.

86. Aitken, *The Continuous Wave,* 322–344.

87. The Navy's promise of a government-sanctioned monopoly did not survive politically. Interestingly, it was General Electric which removed such language from the final contract, because the corporation believed any provision of monopoly rights were doomed in Congress and would raise tremendous antitrust sentiment against the company. Aitken, *The Continuous Wave,* 349–350.

88. Danielian, *AT&T,* 109–110.

89. Maclaurin, *Invention and Innovation in the Radio Industry,* 102–107; Gleason Archer, *Big Business and Radio* (New York: American Historical Society, 1939), 9–11; Danielian, *AT&T,* 111; Brock, *The Telecommunications Industry,* 166–167.

90. Radio Act of 1912, Public Law No. 264, 62nd Congress, 2nd Session, August 13, 1912.

91. Barnouw, *A Tower in Babel,* 76, 102; Archer, *History of Radio,* 284–287.

92. Bureau of Navigation, Department of Commerce, *Radio Service Bulletin,* Recommendations of the National Radio Committee (Washington, DC: Government Printing Office, 1923), 7.

93. Head, *Broadcasting in America,* 108–109.

94. RCA annual reports give some indication of the boom's rapidity and depth. Gross sales of RCA radio apparatus and radio sets for 1921 were $1.47 million; for 1922, $11.29 million; for 1923, $22.46 million; for 1924, $50.75 million. Archer, *Big Business and Radio,* 139, 200.

95. Christopher Sterling, "Television and Radio Broadcasting," in *Who Owns the Media? Concentration of Ownership in the Mass Communications Industry,* Benjamin M. Compaine (ed.) (New York: Harmony Books, 1979), 62–63; Head, *Broadcasting in America,* 109.

96. Archer, *Big Business and Radio,* 27–28, 40–48, 50–68.

97. Brooks, *Telephone,* 163–165.

98. Danielian, *AT&T,* 112–137.

99. David Sarnoff, Letter of June 17, 1922. Cited in Archer, *Big Business and Radio,* 30–31.

100. U.S. Department of Commerce, *Recommendations for Regulation of Radio,* adopted by the Third National Radio Conference, October 6–10, 1924 (Washington, DC: Government Printing Office, 1924), 4.

101. Don R. Le Duc, *Cable Television and the FCC: A Crisis in Media Control* (Philadelphia: Temple University Press, 1973), 45.

102. Barnouw, *A Tower in Babel,* 106–107.

103. Archer, *Big Business and Radio,* 137–138, 167–168; William Peck Banning, *Commercial Broadcasting Pioneer: The WEAF Experiment, 1922–1926* (Cambridge: Harvard University Press, 1946), 265.

104. I owe this point to Susan Smulyan, *"And Now a Word From Our Sponsors. . ."* *Commercialization of American Broadcast Radio, 1920–1934,* unpublished Ph.D. Dissertation, Department of American Studies, Yale University, 1985.

Radio itself, apart from the content carried by it, constituted a spectacle, which accounts for radio's early placement in department stores—it attracted considerable attention and thus was a boon to sales. Unlike the telegraph or telephone, which developed originally as technologies for business communications, radio developed instantly as a technology of mass consumption. This consumption took place at many different levels. Radio sets themselves were items of mass consumption. Early broadcasting was an important means for the consumption of culture. Broadcasting validated certain aspects and types of culture as good or acceptable. Finally, as advertising took hold, broadcasting became perhaps the most significant means of promoting the consumption of commodities.

The enthusiastic reception of a disembodied star system signified an important cultural shift from social communication rooted in the traditional face-to-face institutions of church, family, school, and settled community to one of an objectively impersonal (yet personalized through known performers and commentators) mass medium transmitted to individual homes. That radio broadcasting became instantly popular gives rise to sociological speculation as to the changed public sphere in a period of the emergence of monopoly capitalism, in which a communication mode which Raymond Williams calls "mobile privatization" found an important niche in augmenting or replacing those declining models of social interaction. In Williams' formulation, broadcasting became the main mode in which social integration—hence control—came to be exercised, because it filled in the gaps created by social and geographic mobility. Raymond Williams, *Television: Technology and Cultural Form* (New York: Schocken Press, 1975), 9–31.

105. Tunstall, *The Media Are American,* 70.

106. Archer, *A History of Radio to 1926,* 317–319. Furthermore, the emergence of two frequencies highlighted a new problem for the industry. An absence of technical standards for receivers meant that many owners of radios were incapable of receiving the two signals without mutual interference. The technical problem of receiver capability grew with each tentative solution to the transmission interference problem. In the summer of 1923 the Commerce Department reassigned frequencies to practically all broadcast stations, creating 86 different channels with 10 to 50 kilocycle separations between stations, depending upon geographic zone. Reception of these new frequencies, however, was difficult without an up-to-date, factory-produced radio set. The millions of homemade crystal sets soon would become largely outmoded. Thus as radio became more and more popular, technical, financial, and political constraints tended to push the industry away from its amateur roots and toward big business. Laurence F. Schmeckebier, *The Federal Radio Commission: Its History, Activities and Organization,* Institute for Government Research, Service Monographs of the United States Government, No. 65 (Washington, DC: Brookings Institution, 1932), 11; Archer, *History of Radio,* 293–294, 319, 355; U.S. Department of Commerce, *Recommendations for the Regulation of Radio* (Washington, DC: Government Printing Office, 1924), 13. *Radio Service Bulletin,* No. 72 (April 2, 1923), 9–13.

107. *The New York Times,* cited in Archer, *History of Radio,* 304, 343.

108. As an early commentator asserted in a 1925 issue of *Radio Broadcast* magazine, harried station managers found that sponsored programs filled radio time with little station effort and improved program quality by featuring professional performers. James C. Young, "New Fashions in Radio Programs," *Radio Broadcast* 7/1 (May 1925), 83–89. A 1927 survey conducted by *Radio Broadcast* found the most popular shows were sponsored. Specifically, the "hour" of greatest popularity was always the one which was broadcast over the

largest number of stations. John Wallace, "What the Listener Likes and How He Likes It," *Radio Broadcast* 11/1 (May 1927), 32.

109. Hiram L. Jome, *Economics of the Radio Industry* (Chicago: A. W. Shaw, 1925; reprinted, New York: Arno Press, 1971), 174; Robert B. Summers and Harrison B. Summers, *Broadcasting and the Public*, 2nd ed. (Belmont: Wadsworth, 1978), 34; Barnouw, *A Tower in Babel*, 173.

110. *Proceedings of the Fourth National Radio Conference and Recommendations for Regulation of Radio*, November 9–11, 1925 (Washington, DC: Government Printing Office, 1926), 5.

111. *Proceedings of the Fourth National Radio Conference*, 18.

112. Ellis Hawley, "Three Facets of Hooverian Associationalism: Lumber, Aviation, and Movies, 1921–1930," *Regulation in Perspective*, Thomas K. McCraw (ed.) (Cambridge: Harvard University Press, 1981), 95–123.

113. Czitrom, *Media and the American Mind*, 79. In addition, the next step in dealing with the interference problem—the decision of the Department of Commerce to limit the issuance of new broadcast licenses—set off a spree of trafficking in licenses. Trafficking clearly was a process which treated the airwaves as private property. Barnouw, *A Tower in Babel*, 173–179.

114. David Sarnoff, Memorandum date March, 1925. The memorandum read: "In order to make this [national broadcasting company] plan commercially practicable, it is suggested that all rights to broadcast transmission for tolls or pay be exclusively vested in this company, the proceeds to be used in the public interest by providing the best possible programs." Cited in Archer, *Big Business and Radio*, 187–188.

115. Danielian, *AT&T*, 126–132.

116. United States v. Zenith Radio Corp., 12 F.2d 614 (N.D. Ill. 1926). An earlier decision undermined the Commerce Secretary's authority to refuse licenses: Hoover, Secretary of Commerce v. Intercity Radio Co., Inc., 286 F. 1003 (D.C. Cir. 1923). The Attorney General declined to appeal *Zenith*, conceding that the Radio Act of 1912 did not give the Secretary of Commerce the powers he had been exercising. 35 Opinions of Attorney General 126 (July 8, 1926).

117. Francis Chase, Jr. described the mid-1920s period as one when "chaos rode the air waves, pandemonium filled every loudspeaker and the twentieth century Tower of Babel was made in the image of the antenna towers of some thousand broadcasters who, like the Kilkenny cats, were about to eat each other up." *Sound and Fury: An Informal History of Broadcasting* (New York: Harper, 1942), 42.

118. Carl Friedrich and Evelyn Sternberg, "Congress and the Control of Radio Broadcasting," *American Political Science Review* 37/5 (October 1943), 797–818.

119. See the comments and entries made by Senator Bingham, 67 *Congressional Record*, 69th Congress, 1st Session, 12497–12501 (1926). The comments of Senator Blease are typical: "I have taken the position heretofore, and I take it now, that we have commissions enough in this country to dictate to the people what to do. We have planks in our platforms against commissions, but we come here and ourselves take part in creating other commissions. The air belongs to the people, and I do not see how Congress has any right to say who shall talk and who shall not talk and who shall have a radio and who shall not have one. Nor can I see why a board to be appointed by the President of the United States has any right to say anything about whether one man shall make a speech over the radio for the Democratic Party or another man shall make a speech over the radio for the Republican Party" (at 12503).

120. See the debates over and ultimate defeat of the many amendments offered by the

most active and vociferous of the anti-monopolists in the House, Congressman Edwin L. Davis of Tennessee. 67 *Congressional Record,* 69th Congress, 1st Session, 5481–5504, 5555–5576 (1926). In many of these debates, the word "monopoly" generally was a code word for AT&T. But populists like Davis were already concerned with the power of established commercial broadcasters.

121. 67 *Congressional Record* 12503 (1926). See also H. R. Report No. 404, 69th Congress, 1st Session, 18 (minority report).

122. 67 *Congressional Record* 12503–12504 (1926).

123. Radio Act of 1927, Public Law 632, 69th Congress, February 23, 1927; reprinted, *Documents of American Broadcasting,* Frank J. Kahn (ed.) (Englewood Cliffs, NJ: Prentice-Hall, 1984), 40–56.

124. 67 *Congressional Record* 5481–5485, 5557 (1926). Also, the provision which permitted revocation of a radio license limited such action to those parties judged guilty in federal court of violating the antitrust laws. Presumably this would not apply to consent decrees, and Davis pressed unsuccessfully for stronger language. His fears did not go unfounded. In 1932 RCA, GE, and Westinghouse accepted a consent decree in the Justice Department's anti-trust action against them, which had alleged unlawful combination and conspiracy in restraint of trade in both foreign and domestic commerce. The consent decree stipulated that GE and Westinghouse dispose their holdings in RCA and make non-exclusive all of the cross-licensing agreements recast in 1926. Neither RCA nor Westinghouse was made to forfeit their broadcast licenses, however. Moreover, changing the exclusive provisions of the 1926 License Agreement to non-exclusive provisions did not significantly alter the division of industry. United States v. Radio Corporation of America et al., U.S. District Court Delaware, consent decree, November 21, 1932.

125. National Broadcasting Co. v. United States, 319 U.S. 190 (1943); Red Lion Broadcasting Co. v. Federal Communications Commission, 395 U.S. 397 (1969).

126. Mutual Film Corp. v. Ohio Industrial Commission, 236 U.S. 230 (1915); Mutual Film Corp. v. Industrial Commission of Ohio, 236 U.S. 247 (1915); Mutual Film Corp. v. Kansas, 236 U.S. 248 (1915). I owe this point to Lucas Powe, Jr., *American Broadcasting and the First Amendment* (Berkeley: University of California Press, 1987), 12, 28–30.

127. See Jack J. Roth, *World War I: A Turning Point in Modern History* (New York: Knopf, 1967); Harold D. Lasswell, *Propaganda Technique in the World War* (New York: Knopf, 1927).

128. In the mid-1920s, vehement public criticism of motion pictures pressured the Motion Picture Research Council to sponsor research on the influence of movies on children. The investigations, conducted between 1929 and 1932, became known as the Payne Fund Studies.

129. See Shearon Lowery and Melvin L. DeFleur, *Milestones in Mass Communications Research: Media Effects* (New York: Longmans, 1983); Leon Bramson, *The Political Context of Sociology* (Princeton: Princeton University Press, 1961).

130. Barnouw, *A Tower in Babel,* 199.

131. Summers and Summers, *Broadcasting and the Public,* 44.

132. Friedrich and Sternberg, "Congress and the Control of Radio Broadcasting."

133. The one important amendment that Congressman Davis succeeded in pushing through Congress, called the Davis amendment, was at once a populist and sectional attempt to equalize broadcast facilities throughout the nation. The amendment called on the FRC to apportion radio frequencies and facilities equally among the five communication "regions." The amendment was repealed in 1936 because it was virtually impossible to administer technically.

134. According to the memoirs of FRC Commissioner Orestes Caldwell, there was an

obsession to avoid litigation before an assignment system was in operation. This meant a certain amount of compromising with stations which could afford to lobby the FRC. Thus, the assignment shuffles of 1927–28 reflected both the difficult technical provisions of implementing the Davis amendment and the power of the big broadcasters. For the original FRC assignment system to function, the number of stations had to be reduced, and many stations would have to surrender their frequencies. In these decisions, the FRC gave special attention to technical standards as a criterion for elimination. Not surprisingly, this would tend to favor large commercial broadcasters. The Commission removed 109 stations from the air, reducing the total to about 590. Of 24 clear channels sanctioned by the FRC, 21 went to network stations; virtually all stations operated by educational institutions were relegated to part-time, daytime-only hours. Commercial stations continually petitioned the FRC for more air time— at the expense of the university stations. Orestes Hampton Caldwell, *Reminiscences,* unpublished, cited in Barnouw, *A Tower in Babel,* 215–218.

Clear channels were frequencies kept free of local signals at night. High-powered transmissions could travel great distances at night, utilizing the propagation technique known as "skywave." The wavelengths in the middle of the standard broadcast band through the shortwave band are such that signals bounce off the ionosphere and travel back to the earth at calculable intervals. Thus clear channels were one method of providing national service (and also one way of alleviating the rural service gap). Le Duc, *Cable Television and the FCC,* 45.

135. See Richard Polenberg, *Reorganizing Roosevelt's Government, 1936–39* (Cambridge: Harvard University Press, 1966).

136. Rayburn said, "I think it is also a fair statement to make that the bill [S. 3285] as a whole does not change existing law, not only with reference to radio but with reference to telegraph, telephone, and cable, except in the transfer of jurisdiction and such minor amendments as to make that transfer effective." 78 *Congressional Record,* 73rd Congress, 2nd Session, 10313 (1934).

137. 78 *Congressional Record* 8828–8829 (1934). The backers of the Wagner-Hatfield amendment seemed to be an amalgam of anti-monopolists, supporters of religion and education, and some cultural conservatives who wanted to keep radio from repeating the "failures" of the motion-picture industry.

138. *Variety,* May 8, 1934, cited in Friedrich and Sternberg, "Congress and the Control of Radio Broadcasting."

139. U.S. Senate, 72nd Congress, 1st Session, "Commercial Radio Advertising," Letter from the Chairman of the Federal Radio Commission, Document No. 137 (Washington, DC: Government Printing Office, 1932), at 34.

140. Communications Act of 1934, Public Law No. 416, 73d Congress, June 19, 1934, Title 1, Section 1.

141. As Congressman Rayburn said, "We did not think we should go into a revision of the radio law, and I think personally it is much better to go ahead and formulate this commission and let them [sic] study all these questions and make their recommendations in the light of their study." 78 *Congressional Record* 10316 (1934).

142. See Hearings on H. R. 8301, 73rd Congress, 2nd Session (introduced Feb. 27, 1934).

143. This is how Raymond Williams formulates it in *Television,* 35.

144. I owe this formulation to Ithiel de Sola Pool, *Technologies of Freedom* (Cambridge: Harvard University Press, 1983), 23.

## Chapter 5. "One Policy, One System, and Universal Service"

1. The implicit assumption here, that the FCC constitutes an identifiable identical "subject" over time, despite changes in its personnel, political coloration, and responsibilities,

poses an epistemological problem the discussion of which cannot really be pursued here. And yet, in a sense, the entire argument of how regulation works poses an answer to this epistemological problem. Suffice it to say that, in the perspective of this study, the identity of the organization over time is assumed because of the history of the organization—including its legislative mandate, the types of general problems it faces, the types of specific responsibilities with which it is charged, the policies and procedures it inherits.

2. U.S. House of Representatives, 74th Congress, 1st Session, Document No. 83, *Recommendations of Three Proposed Amendments to the Communications Act of 1934*, Letter from the Chairman of the Federal Communications Commission, Dated January 21, 1935 (Washington, DC: Government Printing Office, 1935).

The FCC submitted a *Report on the Telegraph Industry* to the Senate Committee on Interstate Commerce on December 23, 1939, and a *Supplemental Report on the Telegraph Industry* on February 21, 1940.

3. House Document No. 83, at 5.

4. U.S. Senate, Subcommittee of the Committee on Interstate Commerce, 77th Congress, 1st Session, Hearings on S. 2445, *A Bill to Amend the Communications Act of 1934, as Amended, to Permit Consolidations and Mergers of Telegraph Operations, and for Other Purposes*, April 23, 24, 29, 30, May 5, 7, 8, and 13, 1942 (Washington, DC: Government Printing Office, 1942), at 7.

6. In the Matter of the Application for Merger of the Western Union Telegraph Company and Postal Telegraph, Inc., 10 FCC 148 (1943), at 162.

7. Id., at 163.

8. 88 Congressional Record, 77th Congress, 2nd Session, 5417 (1942).

9. Notwithstanding this intention, it was not until January 15, 1969, that Western Union and AT&T agreed to the conditions over the sale of TWX. Part of this long delay can be attributed to Western Union's financial weakness. But part of the delay inheres in the longstanding power of AT&T vis-à-vis the FCC. AT&T never accepted a hard and fast regulatory separation between voice and record services, and agreed to sell TWX only on the condition that such a sale did not construe that AT&T accepted such a separation. The FCC itself, in a April 29, 1966, report of its Telephone and Telegraph Committees, stated that a policy of domestic voice/record separation was not justified and that such a policy might not serve the public interest. See, Kurt Borchardt, *Structure and Performance of the U.S. Communications Industry* (Boston: Graduate School of Business Administration, Harvard University, 1970), 26–29. Nonetheless, the Commission to some degree acted to maintain the independence of the telegraph system and the viability of Western Union.

10. Anthony G. Oettinger and Paul J. Berman, ''The Medium and the Telephone: The Politics of Information Resources,'' in *High and Low Politics: Information Resources for the 80s*, Anthony G. Oettinger, Paul J. Berman, and William H. Read (eds.) (Cambridge: Ballinger, 1977), 56–58.

11. Smith v. Illinois Bell Telephone Company, 282 U.S. 133 (1930); Lindheimer v. Illinois Bell Telephone Company, 292 U.S. 151 (1934).

12. James W. Sichter, *Separations Procedures in the Telephone Industry: The Historical Origins of a Public Policy* (Cambridge: Program on Information Resources Policy, Harvard University, 1977).

13. The reduction of interstate rates created a rate disparity between AT&T Long Lines and the six multistate BOCs which conducted interstate toll service within their own operating areas under their own tariffs. Thus, without clear, formal procedures over rates, the reduction of Long Lines' rates resulted in inadvertent rate discrimination. Sichter, *Separations Procedures in the Telephone Industry*, 107–110.

Gerald Brock claims that though the FCC claimed credit for the interstate rate reductions, it is just as plausible that the reductions reflected a normal response to changing market conditions given technological progress and a time of falling prices generally. Gerald W. Brock, *The Telecommunications Industry: The Dynamics of Market Structure* (Cambridge: Harvard University Press, 1981), 179.

14. Department of Public Service of Washington v. The Pacific Telephone and Telegraph Company, 37 Public Utilities Reports (New Series) 321 (1941); Sichter, *Separations Procedures in the Telephone Industry,* 110.

15. Bernard Strassburg, interview with author, March 25, 1985.

16. Federal Communications Commission, in the Matter of Methods for Separating Telephone Property, Revenues, and Expenses, Docket 6328, inquiry opened June 9, 1942, FCC *Annual Report,* 1942, 26–27.

17. Oettinger & Berman, "The Medium and the Telephone," 59–61.

18. Since 1949, the Rural Electrification Administration provided over $4.6 billion in long-term low and reduced interest loans to rural telephone companies to assist them in providing service to over 4.1 million customers. Nina W. Cornell, Daniel Kelley, and Peter R. Greenhalgh, "Social Objectives and Competition in Common Carrier Communications: Incompatible or Inseparable?" (Washington, DC: Federal Communications Commission, Office of Plans and Policy, 1980), 14.

19. National Association of Regulatory Utilities Commissioners v. Federal Communications Commission, U.S. Court of Appeals, No. 83–1225, (D.C. Cir. 1983), at 23–24.

20. *NARUC v. FCC,* at 23. FX service worked as follows: a Washington, DC, business buying Washington-New York FX service with a closed end in Washington can call any telephone subscriber in New York without paying an additional per-call charge. Any New York telephone subscriber can call the business in Washington for the price of a local call. Common Control Switching Arrangement (CCSA), another private line service, involves a network of private lines linked through switches at a local telephone company's premises.

21. Harvey Averch and Leland L. Johnson, "Behavior of the Firm Under Regulatory Constraint," *The American Economic Review* 52/5 (1952); Stanislaw H. Wellisz, "Regulation of Natural Gas Pipeline Companies: An Economic Analysis," *Journal of Political Economy* 71/1 (February 1963), 30–43; Nina W. Cornell, Michael Pelcovits, and S. Brenner, "A Legacy of Regulatory Failure," *Regulation* 7/4 (1983).

22. Federal Communications Commission, *Investigation of the Telephone Industry in the United States* [Pursuant to Public Resolution No. 8, 74th Congress] (Washington, DC: Government Printing Office, 1939), 587.

Two versions of the investigation were released. The *Proposed Report,* or "Walker Report," representing the work of Commissioner Walker and his vast staff, was published in 1938. The Final Report, which essentially replicated the findings of the *Proposed Report* but altered its summaries and conclusions, was published by the full Commission in 1939.

23. Id., 301. As the *Proposed Report* said of the Western Electric problem: "Unregulated and artificially controlled Western Electric prices for telephone apparatus and equipment lead to an unregulated rate base and hence to unregulated rates for the operating companies subject to State jurisdiction. . . . All efforts to obtain manufacturing costs of Western on materials constituting the plant of a telephone company have been thwarted by the American Co. notwithstanding the decision of the decision of the United States Supreme Court in the case of *Smith vs. Illinois Bell Telephone Co.,* in which the Court held that Western's profit on its sales to the Illinois Bell Telephone Co. must be shown to be reasonable. . . . It is significant of the American Co.'s policy that the Western Electric Company is perhaps the only large manufacturer which keeps no records of the true costs of any of its

products, keeps no direct record of the cost of sales, and maintains such a voluminous, intricate, and unreliable mass of records and estimates as a substitute for a cost accounting system that the determination of true and actual costs therefrom is an impossibility." FCC, *Proposed Report: Telephone Investigation,* 682.

24. John Brooks, *Telephone: The First Hundred Years* (New York: Harper & Row, 1975), 198.

25. Merle Fainsod, Lincoln Gordon, and Joseph C. Palamountain, Jr., *Government and the American Economy,* Third Edition (New York: W. W. Norton, 1959), 380.

26. The *Proposed Report* recommended that the statutory basis of valuation of the rate base should be the actual original cost less depreciation reserve. The Bell System relied on a theory of "observed depreciation." See the discussion of depreciation in the FCC's Final Report, *Investigation of the Telephone Industry in the United States,* 325–349, 589–590. AT&T had been upheld in utilizing such a theory in a couple of Court decisions. In Pacific Gas and Electric Company v. San Francisco, 265 U.S. 403 (1924), the Court stated that "facts shown by reliable evidence were preferable to averages based upon assumed probabilities" (at 406).

27. *Proposed Report: Telephone Investigation,* 686–687. It is striking that the *Proposed Report* advocated making explicit a national policy with respect to national wire communications service. That policy was articulated as the "development of a progressively increasing volume and constantly improving quality of national wire communications service at a progressively decreasing unit cost" (at 687).

28. Id., 699–702.

29. Brooks, *Telephone,* 198. AT&T railed at the fact that counsel for the Bell System were not permitted to cross-examine witnesses or present witnesses of their own. The only witnesses to testify were those summoned by the FCC.

30. FCC, *Investigation of the Telephone Industry in the United States,* 597–602.

31. FCC, *Annual Report,* 1949, 104; *Annual Report,* 1954, 40.

32. Booz-Allen & Hamilton, Inc., *Organization and Management Survey of the Federal Communications Commission for the Bureau of the Budget* (Chicago: Booz-Allen & Hamilton, 1962), Vol. I, 285.

This assessment was confirmed over the years by FCC Common Carrier Bureau personnel themselves. Walter Hinchman, Chief of the Common Carrier Bureau between 1974 and 1978, asserted in a public paper delivered in 1981 that "the FCC has never been able to hold Bell accountable to the just, reasonable, and nondiscriminatory standards of the Communications Act." "The Future of AT&T: For Whom *Does* The Bell Toll?," remarks before the Communications Networks Town Meeting, Houston, January 13, 1981. Cited in Martha Derthick and Paul J. Quirk, *The Politics of Deregulation* (Washington, DC: The Brookings Institution, 1985), 81.

33. FCC, in the Matter of American Telephone and Telegraph Co. and Associated Bell System Companies, Charges for Interstate and Foreign Communication Service, Docket 16258, 2 FCC 2d 142 (1965). Consolidated into Amer. Tel. & Tel. Co. Long Line Dept. revisions of Tariff FCC No. 260 Private Line Service Series 5000 (TELPAK), Docket 18128, 61 FCC 2d 587 (1976); Phillip Verveer, "Regulation and the Access Problem: What's Happened and Where We Are Now," *Telecommunications Access and Public Policy,* Alan Baughcum and Gerald Faulhaber (eds.) (Norwood, NJ: Ablex Publishing Corp., 1984), 84.

34. Joseph C. Goulden, *Monopoly* (New York: G. P. Putnam's Sons, 1968), 325–326. This study, though it suffers from a popularistic, naively populist style, is nonetheless extremely good on many points.

35. *Ibid.,* 326–328.

36. *Ibid.,* 332–336.

37. One reason why the Western Electric antitrust problem did not "go away" was that Holmes Baldridge, who had served as the principal attorney for the Walker investigation, subsequently became chief of the general litigation section of the Justice Department's antitrust division. Goulden, *Monopoly,* 87.

38. Charles Zerner, "U.S. Sues to Force AT&T to Drop Western Electric Co.," *The New York Times,* January 15, 1949, 1, 30.

39. Anthony Lewis, "AT&T Settles Antitrust Case; Shares Patents," *The New York Times,* January 25, 1956, 1, 16; United States v. Western Electric Co., Trade Case 71,134 (New Jersey Cir.), consent decree (1956); Gerald F. George, "The Federal Communications Commission and the Bell System: Abdication of Regulatory Responsibility," *Indiana Law Journal,* 44/3 (Spring 1969), 459–477.

40. Richard J. Solomon, "What Happened After Bell Spilled the Acid?—Telecommunications History: A View Through the Literature," *Telecommunications Policy* 2/2 (1978), 146–157.

41. Cited in U.S. Senate, 97th Congress, 1st and 2nd Sessions, Committee on the Judiciary, *The Department of Justice Oversight of the United States versus American Telephone and Telegraph Lawsuit Hearings,* August 6, 1981, and January 25, 1982 (Serial No. J-97-53), part 1 (Washington, DC: Government Printing Office, 1982), 1.

42. U.S. House of Representatives, 85th Congress, 2nd Session, Committee on the Judiciary, Antitrust Subcommittee (Subcommittee No. 5), *Consent Decree Program of the Department of Justice Hearings,* March 25–May 22, 1958 (Serial No. 9) (Washington, DC: Government Printing Office, 1958), 2026–2027.

43. Brooks, *Telephone,* 237, 253; M. D. Fagen (ed.), *A History of Engineering and Science in the Bell System: National Service in War and Peace, 1925–1975* (New York: Bell Telephone Laboratories, Inc., 1978), 163, 384–386, 461–463.

44. Bernard Strassburg, interview with author, March 25, 1985. Strassburg's original letter read, in part: "[I]t would appear that adequate powers reside in the regulatory authorities to deal with the matter of Western's prices and profits, insofar as they may affect the investment and expenses of affiliated companies. It must be recognized, however, that the degree of effective regulation of these powers is largely dependent upon the resources of the respective regulatory authorities to examine and evaluate all of the matters necessary to an informed determination of the reasonableness of Western's prices and profits." The letter as sent excised the last sentence and thus significantly distorted the highly qualified assertion that the FCC could effectively regulate Western Electric. Cited in Goulden, *Monopoly,* 99.

45. K. E. Madsen, "Antitrust: Consent Decree: The History and Effect of Western Electric Co. v. United States, 1956 Trade Cas. 71,134 (D.C.N.J. 1956)," *Cornell Law Quarterly* 45/1 (1959), 88–96.

46. AT&T, *Annual Report,* 1954.

47. C. D. Hanscom, *Dates in American Telephone Technology* (New York: Bell Telephone Laboratories, Inc., 1961); Gerald W. Brock, *The U.S. Computer Industry: A Study of Market Power* (Cambridge: Ballinger, 1975), 14, 91; Katherine D. Fishman, *The Computer Establishment* (New York: Harper & Row, 1981), 295.

48. Fagen (ed.), *A History of Engineering and Science in the Bell System,* 549, 621.

49. Cited in S. L. Mathison and Phillip M. Walker, *Computers and Telecommunications: Issues in Public Policy* (Englewood Cliffs: Prentice-Hall, 1970), 6.

50. "One of the Great Miscalculations in IBM History," advertisement *The New York Times Magazine,* May 4, 1980, 127.

51. W. F. Sharpe, *The Economics of Computers* (New York: Columbia University Press, 1969), 186, 193.

52. Outstanding requests for telephone service on the Bell System from 1949–1954 were:

|            |           |
|------------|-----------|
| July 1949  | 1,000,000 |
| January 1950 | 750,000 |
| January 1951 | 800,000 |
| July 1952  | 718,000   |
| July 1953  | 605,000   |
| July 1954  | 307,000   |

Requests for regrades in existing service were:

|           |           |
|-----------|-----------|
| July 1952 | 1,606,000 |
| July 1953 | 1,300,000 |
| July 1954 | 762,000   |

AT&T, *Annual Reports*, 1948–1957; FCC, *Annual Reports*, 1949–1956.

53. Donald C. Beelar, "Cables in the Sky and the Struggle for Their Control," *Federal Communications Bar Journal* 21/1 (1967), 26–41; Federal Communications Commission, Network Inquiry Special Staff, *Preliminary Report on Prospects for Additional Networks*, Preliminary Draft, "Video Interconnection: Technology, Costs and Regulatory Policies" (Washington, DC: Federal Communications Commission, 1980), 80–95.

54. In the matter of American Telephone & Telegraph Co. and the Western Union Telegraph Co. Charges and Regulations for Television Transmission Services and Facilities, Docket No. 8963, 42 FCC 1 (1949), at 12–13.

AT&T first introduced the "cream-skimming" argument in this context. "Experience has shown that where others are free to furnish parts of the service offered by a communications carrier they are naturally attracted to those areas or part of the service which are less costly or more remunerative, leaving the common carrier to more costly and less profitable portions. Since the common carrier which undertakes to furnish a full service must meet the reasonable demands of all comers, without discrimination, furnishing service on both the heavy and the lean routes, the inevitable effect is to increase the cost of the service left to it" (at 12–13).

55. In the Matter of Allocation of Frequencies to the Various Classes of Non-Government Services in the Radio Spectrum from 10 Kilocycles to 30,000 Kilocycles, Report of the Commission with Respect to Frequency Service-Allocations to the Non-Government Fixed and Mobile Services Between 1000 Mc and 13200 Mc, Docket No. 6651, 39 FCC 298 (1948).

56. Brock, *The Telecommunications Industry*, 183.

57. As the FCC decision stated, "[T]he limitations thus imposed on private intercity TV relaying result from the concrete fact that there is insufficient space in the radio spectrum to accommodate fully all the desirable radio services, and that common carrier operation in general is more flexible and economical with respect to frequency utilization than would be private operations in this particular field." In the Matter of American Telephone & Telegraph Co. and the Western Union Telegraph Co. Charges and Regulations for Television Transmission Services and Facilities, 42 FCC 1 (1949), at 31.

58. In September 1948 AT&T refused to relay an NBC program because that program had first been relayed over the Philco system. Philco filed suit against AT&T and requested an injunction requiring AT&T to provide the services. The court declared itself without jurisdiction until the FCC had acted. The FCC implicitly accepted AT&Ts argument that at common law a carrier could not, in the absence of a statute, be required to connect its

facilities with those of others, even with those of another common carrier. After a twenty-month investigation, the FCC reached a decision which required interconnection with broadcast company systems only. Philco Corporation et al. v. American Telephone and Telegraph Company, 80 F. Supp. 397 (1948). Cited in Brock, *The Telecommunications Industry,* 184–185.

59. In the Matter of Establishment of Physical Connections and Through Routes and Charges Applicable Thereto, Pursuant to Section 201(a) of the Communications Act of 1934, as Amended, with Respect to Intercity Video Transmission Service, 6 R.R. 1157 (1952) at 1180.

60. Given the gross disparity in financial viability between Western Union and AT&T, the protection of AT&T from Western Union competition in intercity video carriage seems ludicrous. Indeed, after World War II, Western Union began to lease circuits from AT&T to render telegraph service, because its own intercity lines were obsolete. In the peak year of 1963, the ratio of Western Union leased to owned facilities was 70:30. Borchardt, *Structure and Performance of the U.S. Communications Industry,* 26.

61. A 1958 rule making which granted permanent authorization of private broadcast interconnection facilities—irrespective of the availability of common carrier facilities—was based upon the petition of a small market television station which claimed it could not afford AT&T facilities at prevailing rates and could build and operate private system links at substantially less cost. The open-entry policy was limited to the lower quality technique of picking off-the-air signals of other television stations. It did not permit interconnection with AT&T facilities. Beelar, "Cables in the Sky," 36–37.

62. Federal Communications Commission v. RCA Communications, Inc., 346 U.S. 86 (1953), at 88–89.

63. *FCC v. RCA,* at 91–92.

64. *FCC v. RCA,* at 97.

65. Goulden, *Monopoly,* 109.

66. Eisenhower statement of December 31, 1959, Department of State Bulletin, January 16, 1961, at 77, cited in Lloyd D. Musolf (ed.), *Communications Satellites in Political Orbit* (San Francisco: Chandler Publishing Co., 1968), 17–18.

67. U.S. House, 87th Congress, 1st Session, Committee on Science and Astronautics, H. Report No. 1279, *Commercial Applications of Space Communications Systems,* October 11, 1961 (Washington, DC: Government Printing Office, 1961).

68. Cited in Musolf, *Communications Satellites in Political Orbit,* 27.

69. Report of the *Ad Hoc* Carrier Committee to the Federal Communications Commission and the Minority Statement of the Western Union Telegraph Company, October 12, 1961, reprinted in U.S. Senate, 87th Congress, 1st Session, Subcommittee on Monopoly of the Select Committee on Small Business, Hearings, *Space Satellite Communications* (Part 2: Review of the Report of the Ad Hoc Carrier Committee), November 8, 9, 1961 (Washington, DC: Government Printing Office, 1961).

70. The four major international carriers were AT&T, International Telephone and Telegraph, Western Union, and RCA Communications. As for AT&Ts dominance, the *Ad Hoc* Carrier Report reveals that AT&T agreed to contribute $65 million toward the new satellite corporation, compared with $13 million from the other companies *combined.* AT&T suggested it would contribute between 75 to 80 percent of total investment. U.S. Senate, 87th Congress, 2nd Session, Judiciary Committee, Hearings, *Antitrust Problems of the Space Satellite Communications System* (Part 1), March 29–30, April 4–5, 1962, Statement of Lee Loevinger, Assistant Attorney General, Antitrust Division, Department of Justice (Washington, DC: Government Printing Office, 1962), 142–144. Cited in Musolf, *Communications Satellites in Political Orbit,* 35.

71. U.S. Senate, 87th Congress, 2nd Session, Subcommittee on Antitrust and Monopoly of the Committee on the Judiciary, Hearings, *Antitrust Problems of the Space Satellite Communications System* (Part 2), testimony of Newton N. Minow, Chairman of the Federal Communications Commission, April 6, 10, 12, 17, 1962 (Washington, DC: Government Printing Office, 1962), 320–321.

The following colloquy between Minow and Bernard Fensterwald, Staff Director of the Senate Subcommittee on Antitrust and Monopoly, provides insight into Minow's (and the FCC generally) logic.

Minow: I wish we could turn it [the satellite system] over to competing firms here. The problem is we can have only one system.

Fensterwald: I thought you did not want any competition in the communication service.

Minow: You cannot have it.

Fensterwald: You could have considerable competition if the Government owned and controlled the satellites.

Minow: I will not personally take any responsibility for Government management of this unless there is a very severe change in the kinds of compensation to which we can pay technical and scientific and professional help. We do not have it. I want this thing to succeed and succeed quickly. The Government cannot do this job with the present limitations. . . . Our view is that business has provided good communication service to the country and, with adequate regulation, will continue to do so.

72. Statement of Lee Loevinger, Assistant Attorney General, Hearings, *Antitrust Problems of the Space Satellite Communications System,* cited in Musolf, *Communications Satellites in Political Orbit,* 34–36.

73. President Kennedy's statement, dated July 24, 1961, cited in U.S. House, 87th Congress, 2nd Session, Committee on Interstate and Foreign Commerce, Hearings, *Communications Satellites* (Part 2), March 13–22, 1962 (Washington, DC: Government Printing Office, 1962), 616–617.

74. Communications Satellite Act of 1962, Public Law 87–624, 76 Stat. 419, approved August 31, 1962.

75. By the 1970s, the two terrestrial links accounted for about 90 percent of the costs of an INTELSAT-connected international telephone call. The space segment amounted to just 10 percent. Jeremy Tunstall, *Communications Deregulation: The Unleashing of America's Communications Industry* (London: Basil Blackwell, 1986), 216, 65–67.

76. Geosynchronous satellites would remain in the same position vis-à-vis the geographic location on earth. AT&T's sponsorship of low-orbital satellites meant that ground stations would have to track moving satellites and continually switch between satellites. Low-orbital satellites made the possibility of a purely domestic satellite service unlikely.

### Chapter 6. "Congress Intended to Leave Competition in the Business of Broadcasting Where It Found It"

1. See David L. Bazelon, "FCC Regulation of the Telecommunications Press," *Duke Law Journal,* 1975/2 (May 1975), 213–251. The term "raised (or lifted) eyebrow" is often attributed to Commissioner John Doerfer in his dissent in Miami Broadcasting Co. (WQAM), 14 Radio Regulations 125 (1956).

2. In Federal Radio Commission v. Nelson Brothers Bond and Mortgage Co., 289 U.S. 266 (1933), the Supreme Court ruled that the FRC had jurisdiction over intrastate radio as ancillary to its authority over interstate radio. The latter authority devolved, of course, from the commerce clause of the Constitution. The Court also ruled that the scope of judicial review of FRC decisions was generally limited to questions of law, not fact.

3. On the advantages of networking, see, among others, Roger G. Noll, Merton J. Peck,

and John J. McGowan, *Economic Aspects of Television Regulation* (Washington, DC: Brookings Institution, 1973); Stanley M. Besen, Thomas G. Krattenmaker, A. Richard Metzger, Jr., and John R. Woodbury, *Misregulating Television: Network Dominance and the FCC* (Chicago: University of Chicago Press, 1984).

The advantages of radio for advertisers quickly became apparent. In 1928, radio accounted for 1 percent of combined gross advertising billings of newspapers, magazines, and radio. By 1945 radio's share had risen to 29 percent—without suffering from cyclical movements in the economy, as did print advertising. Erik Barnouw, *A History of Broadcasting in the United States,* Vol. 2; *The Golden Web* (New York: Oxford University Press, 1968), 111.

Much of this rise might be explained by the historical combination of a shortage of consumer goods following the Depression and during World War II, and a high wartime excess-profits tax which had the effect of sanctioning advertising as a necessary business expense. Together these forces pushed corporations to spend on advertising what otherwise would have gone to taxes. A wartime shortage of newsprint reduced the available amount of hard-copy advertising space—obviously not a problem in electronic communication. And without tangible goods to sell a consuming public, corporations went in for institutional sponsorship, which became a major pattern of programming and advertising. Radio advertising surpassed newspapers as the preeminent *national* advertising medium in 1943.

The Depression economy accelerated radio's popular fortunes (though in purely financial terms, both NBC and CBS profit levels fell in 1932 and 1933). The theater, vaudeville, and recording businesses suffered greatly during the Depression, prompting an influx of that talent to the radio networks. Individual radio stations, also having financial problems, sought to affiliate with the national networks as a way to survive. And for people who had little or no discretionary income to spend on sports events, shows, and movies (not to mention food and shelter), radio grew in importance as a source of "free" entertainment—and was legitimated as such. Barnouw, *The Golden Web,* 165, 214; Christopher Sterling and John M. Kittross, *Stay Tuned: A Concise History of American Broadcasting* (Belmont: Wadsworth, 1978), 211.

4. FRC, in the Matter of the Application of Great Lakes Broadcasting Co., 3 FRC *Annual Report* 32 (1929), at 34.

5. Id.

6. KFKB Broadcasting Association, Inc. v. Federal Radio Commission, 47 F.2d 670 (D.C. Cir. 1931).

7. Trinity Methodist Church, South v. Federal Radio Commission, 62 F.2d 850 (D.C. Cir. 1932) *cert. denied,* 284 U.S. 685 (1932).

8. Examination of the reasons for the approval of license applications in the first year of the FCC's existence is revealing. In one case the Commission looked favorably upon the fact that the applicant had substantial commercial support. "It appears from the record that the applicant will have the financial support of several prominent and wealthy citizens of Newport and that he will have sufficient funds to erect and maintain a station of the kind and class applied for." In Re Application of S. George Webb, Newport, Rhode Island, for Construction Permit, 1 FCC 267 (1934) at 268.

In another case, the availability of local talent culled the Commission's favor. "It appears from the record that there is sufficient program material and talent available to the applicant station from various departments of the State Government, Willamette University, and other sources to maintain a good public service for the additional hours requested." In Re Application of Oregon Radio Inc. (KSLM), Salem, Oregon, for Modification of Construction Permit, 1 FCC 259 (1934) at 260.

Finally, it is instructive how several different factors, including previous broadcasting experience and an experienced staff, are woven together to constitute a showing of the public interest. "The record here showed that the proposed station is to be managed by Mr. George H. Thomas, who resides at Lafayette, and whose previous experience has been as supervisor of programs and studios at Station KFPW, Fort Smith, Arkansas, for 18 months. The applicant, Dean, is a licensed radio operator who will supervise the construction and installation of the proposed equipment and will select a competent engineer to be in charge of the station. The applicant, Thomas, testified that he made a survey of the talent available in the area they propose to serve and that he found there was considerable such talent. It also appears from his testimony that he made a survey of the advertising possibilities in that area and is satisfied that there is sufficient to support a station of the size and character applied for. The station proposes to broadcast programs of local public interest, and to keep the facilities of the station available to all civic, religious, charitable, and educational organizations." In Re Application of Evangeline Broadcasting Company, Lafayette, Louisiana, for Construction Permit, 1 FCC 253 (1934) at 255.

9. In the Matter of the Mayflower Broadcasting Corporation and the Yankee Network, Inc., 8 FCC 333 (1941); In the Matter of Editorializing by Broadcast Licensees, 13 FCC 1246 (1949).

The Fairness Doctrine was given statutory recognition when Congress amended section 315 of the Communications Act in 1959. Thereafter, section 315 stipulated the three most direct content-based rules on broadcast licensees; the Fairness Doctrine, the equal opportunities provision for political candidates to purchase airtime, and the personal attack rules. Equal opportunities is self-explanatory. If a station permits one political candidate to purchase air time, the station must sell time to all political candidates. The personal attack rules require that a station which has attacked an individual provide that person with a transcript of the broadcast, and offer reply time. Public Law No. 274, 86th Congress (1959).

10. Don Lee Broadcasting System v. FCC, 76 F.2d 998 (D.C. Cir. 1935). This general presumption of renewal, in other words, the general presumption that the existing holder of the license is entitled to have the license renewed, has been a basic feature of the licensing procedure. The policy in *Don Lee* was reaffirmed, for instance, in a 1951 case wherein the FCC renewed a radio license due to the station's good past performance. The Commission renewed despite the fact that the challenger demonstrated a better showing on other criteria, such as the integration of ownership and management, and media diversification. Hearst Radio, Inc. (WBAL), 15 FCC 1149 (1951).

11. One study indicated that 78 radio and television licenses were revoked or not renewed between 1934 and 1969, compared with 64 between 1970 and 1978. Multiple grounds were cited for Commission action in the cases between 1934 and 1969, the most common being misrepresentations to the FCC, technical violations, and unauthorized transfer of control. Almost none involved speech grounds. In the 1970s cases, the most common grounds were misrepresentations to the FCC and failure to pursue the renewal procedure. Very few involved speech grounds. John D. Abel, Charles E. Clift III, and Fredric A. Weiss, "Station License Revocations and Denials of Renewal, 1934–69," *Journal of Broadcasting* 14/4 (Fall 1970), 411–421; Fredric A. Weiss, David Ostroff, and Charles E. Clift, III, "Station License Revocations and Denials of Renewal, 1970–78," *Journal of Broadcasting* 24/1 (Winter 1980), 69–77.

The most celebrated of such non-renewal cases was WHDH-TV Boston in 1969. The FCC refused to renew the license of a broadcast station that had an "average" performance record. The main reason the Commission awarded the license to the competing applicant was because *WHDH* was owned by the *Boston Herald Traveler* newspaper. The FCC determined that stripping the *Herald Traveler* of the license would add to the diversity of control over mass communications media in the Boston area. Nonetheless, the FCC's action in WHDH was without precedent and without policy. WHDH, Inc., 16 FCC 2d 1 (1969). The other celebrated non-renewal case, in which the FCC stripped RKO Corporation of its broadcast licenses in 1980, began as a comparative renewal matter over the performance of WNAC-TV Boston. The FCC's decision to strip RKO of its licenses, however, was based on the illegal business activities of RKO's parent company, General Tire and Rubber, Co. Because of the close business ties between RKO and General Tire, the FCC ruled that RKO lacked the character to hold the license for WNAC-TV Boston. RKO General, Inc. (WNAC-TV), 78 FCC 2d 1 (1980).

12. Jack Straw Memorial Foundation, 21 FCC 2d 833 (1970); License Responsibility to Review Records Before Their Broadcast, 28 FCC 2d 409 (1971).

13. In Re Applications of Pacifica Foundation, 36 FCC 147 (1964); Letter to Pacifica Foundations (complaints), 2 FCC 2d 1066 (1965); Citizen's Complaint Against Pacifica Foundation Station WBAI (FM) New York, 56 FCC 2d (1973). The latter case went to the courts as Pacifica Foundation v. FCC, 556 F.2d 9 (D.C. Cir. 1977); FCC v. Pacifica Foundation, 438 U.S. 726 (1978). See the fine discussion of FCC actions in the area of morals and obscenity by Lucas A. Powe, Jr., *American Broadcasting and the First Amendment* (Berkeley: University of California Press, 1987), 162–190.

14. Reginald Stuart, "FCC Acts to Restrict Indecent Programming," *The New York Times,* April 17, 1987, 1, C30.

15. Brandywine-Main Line Radio, Inc., 24 FCC 2d 18 (1970). Even in this case, Fairness Doctrine violations alone did not result in the license revocation. There were additional grounds for nonrenewal.

16. Office of the United Church of Christ v. FCC, 359 F.2d 994 (D.C. Cir. 1966); Office of the United Church of Christ v. FCC, 425 F.2d 543 (D.C. Cir. 1969).

17. The citizens groups involved in the reform of broadcasting had long been critical of conservative FCC actions in the area of license grants and renewals, precisely because such actions maintained a woeful status quo. But, whereas the goal of forcing licensees to improve programming was unimpeachable, the citizens groups sometimes were not sensitive enough to the problem of discretionary authority and the double-edged nature of content and licensee "character" regulations. If, for example, the FCC could easily revoke a license because a broadcaster aired only commercialized programming, the same exercise of discretionary authority might be used to refuse or revoke a license because of provocative programming, or even on the basis of the broadcaster's views. The FCC flirted with regulation based on an applicant's views and character during the McCarthy period. See, for example, In the Matter of Travis Lafferty, 23 FCC 761 (1957), where a licensee was denied renewal because he refused to answer questions about past or present membership in the Communist Party. See also Ralph S. Brown, Jr., "Character and Candor Requirements for FCC Licensees," *Law and Contemporary Problems* 22/4 (Autumn 1957), 644–657.

Such discretionary authority could be used in other ways to chill speech. In an effort to curtail the *Washington Post*'s investigative ardor during the Watergate scandal, the Nixon White House put enormous pressure on the FCC to revoke or delay the renewal of broadcast licenses held by the *Post*. See Thomas Whiteside, "Annals of Television: The Nixon Administration and Television," *The New Yorker,* March 17, 1975, 41–91.

18. Federal Communications Commission, *Public Service Responsibility of Broadcast Licensees* (Washington, DC: FCC, March 7, 1946), at 39.

19. Id., at 55. The legal propriety of the "Blue Book" vis-à-vis the First Amendment would seem to have been resolved by the key, then recently decided case of *National Broadcasting Company v. United States,* in which the Court determined that the FCC was within its jurisdiction to impose other than merely technical rules on broadcasters. Because of the scarcity of the spectrum, a broadcast licensee's rights under the First Amendment were

not absolute. The Court wrote, "But the [Communications] Act does not restrict the Commission merely to supervision of the traffic. It puts upon the Commission the burden of determining the composition of that traffic." 319 U.S. 190 (1943), at 215–216. Notwithstanding the fact that the "Blue Book" for all practical purposes was a dead letter, it was taken to court. In *Bay State Beacon, Inc. v. FCC*, the Court of Appeals found that the "Blue Book" did not violate the Communications Act's prohibition against censorship. 171 F.2d 826 (D.C. Cir. 1948).

20. Though the "Blue Book" was a group effort and was associated with Commissioner Clifford J. Durr, staff member Edward Brecher, and former BBC executive Charles A. Siepmann, the principal author of the document was FCC economist Dallas Smythe. Smythe has since become a major figure in the political-economic study of telecommunications.

21. Barnouw, *The Golden Web*, 229–234; Richard J. Meyer, "Reaction to the Blue Book," *Journal of Broadcasting* 6/4 (Fall 1962), 295–312. *Broadcasting* fulminated against the "Blue Book" from the middle of March through the middle of June 1946. In its first editorial on the "Blue Book," entitled "F(ederal) C(ensorship) C(Commission)," the editors wrote: "Radio censorship is here. . . . The charter upon which it is based was issued ten days ago by the FCC under the title of *Public Service Responsibility of Broadcast Licensees*. To accept lightly that charter, and to blink at its import, one must be blind to the implications within the document itself, and to the devious methods which contrived it. . . . It is as masterfully evasive as it is vicious. It seeks proof for its indictments of American radio in the archives of an art that came into being only 25 years ago. It is soft talk about a serious business, and the issues it projects are larger than broadcasting as a medium; are as large, in fact, as the welfare of democracy. For the meddling of Government in the instruments which enlighten public opinion is contrary to the precepts of the Constitution, and rebuts the fundamental thinking of our leaders from Washington to Truman. . . . How did it come into being? Under a camouflage of innuendo, after the fashion that Hermann Goering built the German air force. . . ." *Broadcasting*, March 18, 1946, 58.

The magazine was not itself short of innuendo. In its May 13, 1946, editorial attacking Commissioner Clifford Durr, *Broadcasting* wrote: "It is now apparent that Clifford J. Durr is the FCC's knight errant. He sets forth with increasing regularity from the Commission's castle on the Potomac to protect the people against the horrible perpetrations of American broadcasters. He enters the joust in righteous splendor, garbed in an academic grey suit and gripping tightly in one hand—the Blue Book. And the banner he bears high—is it the white of purity, or is there a tint of pink?. . . " (at 58).

22. The legacy of the "Blue Book" was revived in a more conservative policy document in 1960. The *Report and Statement of Policy Res.: Commission en banc Programming Inquiry* called for balanced programming and expressed hope that broadcasters would air more local live and public affairs programming. In contrast to the "Blue Book," however, there was little economic analysis as to why such public interest programming is sparse. The 1960 statement was far more aware of the First Amendment dilemma of the Commission imposing government will upon private speech. The statement offered programming objectives toward which the Commission hoped broadcasters would move on their own accord. In this regard, the policy was simply another unenforceable guide to industry self-regulation. However, the policy did introduce a new obligation. It required that broadcasters "ascertain" the tastes, needs, and desires of the people within their service areas. This ascertainment requirement would become one avenue by which activist groups pushed at broadcasters in the 1970s. 44 FCC 2303 (1960).

23. In the Matter of Powell Crosley, Jr., Transferor, and the Aviation Corp., Transferee for Transfer of Control of the Crosley Corp, Licensee, 11 FCC 3 (1945).

24. Public Law 554, 82nd Congress, 1952. The McFarland amendments amended sec-

tion 310(b) of the Communications Act such that in all transfer cases, the Commission was now to dispose of the application "as if the proposed transferee or assignee were making application under section 308 [the section on licensing] for the permit or license in question, but, in acting thereon, the Commission may not consider whether the public interest, convenience, and necessity might be served by the transfer, assignment, or disposal of the permit or license to a person other than the proposed transferee or assignee."

25. Commercial Advertising, 36 FCC 45 (1964); Lawrence D. Longley, "FCC's Attempt to Regulate Commercial Time," *Journal of Broadcasting* 11/1 (Winter 1966–67), 83–89.

The House voted 317 to 43 in favor of the Rogers bill (H.R. 8316). This bill prohibited the FCC from adopting any rules governing the length or frequency of broadcast advertising.

26. James L. Baughman, *Television's Guardians: The FCC and the Politics of Programming, 1958–1967* (Knoxville: University of Tennessee Press, 1985), 44–45, 82–83. Baughman argues convincingly that Minow and the Kennedy liberals on the FCC tried to effect public interest regulations in many areas of broadcast policy, but were consistently unable to galvanize the support of fellow Commissioners or Congress or failed to beat back industry pressure in this endeavor.

27. Baughman, *Television's Guardians*, 105–106; Joseph A. Grundfest, *Citizen Participation in Broadcast Licensing Before the FCC*, R-1896-MF (Santa Monica: Rand, 1976), 15.

Cox, a regulatory activist and liberal, was committed to local, live programming aired during prime time. According to Baughman's account, Cox held to a specific (though, of course, off-the-record and unofficial) percentage that stations should allot for local, live productions.

28. Henry Geller, "A Modest Proposal for Modest Reform of the Federal Communications Commission," *Georgetown Law Journal* 63/3 (February 1973), 705–724.

Another stated purpose in the fostering of local broadcast outlets was to secure the contribution that broadcasting can make to an informed electorate. See W. E. B. DuBois Clubs of America, 22 FCC 2d 678 (1968). Yet the Commission has never denied a license renewal for failure of a licensee to fulfill specific promises of public service programming. See Moline Television Corporation, 31 FCC 2d 263 (1971).

29. Baughman quotes Commissioner Robert E. Lee as saying in 1964 in reference to the issue of license revocation, "One of the tenets of our society is that even a criminal should have a second chance." Baughman, *Television's Guardians*, at 108.

30. In Chicago Federation of Labor v. Federal Radio Commission, 41 F.2d 422 (D.C. Cir. 1930), the appeals court essentially ruled that meritorious stations may not be deprived of their privileges without reasons arising from strong factors of public interest. "It is not consistent with true public convenience, interest, or necessity, that meritorious stations like WBBM and KFAB should be deprived of broadcasting privileges when once granted to them, which they have at great cost prepared themselves to exercise, unless clear and sound reasons of public policy demand such action. The cause of independent broadcasting in general would be seriously endangered and public interests correspondingly prejudiced, if the licenses of established stations should arbitrarily be withdrawn from them, and appropriated to the use of other stations. This statement does not imply any derogation of the controlling rule that all broadcasting privileges are held subject to the reasonable regulatory power of the United States, and that the public convenience, interest, and necessity are the paramount considerations" (at 423).

31. Ben C. Fisher, "Communications Act Amendments, 1952—An Attempt to Legislate Fairness," *Law and Contemporary Problems* 22/4 (Autumn 1957), 672–696. Fisher doesn't comment on the politics of the McFarland amendments. He seems to take at face

value the amendments' goal of making the administrative hearing process more fair. None-theless, his assessment is bald. In Fisher's account, the McFarland amendments did not make the administrative process more fair; they made it more bureaucratic, time-consuming, and inefficient.

32. As one account put it, the McFarland amendments dealt with the minor problem of influence exercised *within* the Commission; they did nothing to address the much more prevalent problem of pressures on the Commission which originated outside the Commission. Frederick F. Blachly and Miriam E. Oatman, "Sabotage of the Administrative Process," *Public Administration Review* 6/3 (Summer 1946), 213–227.

33. 93 Congressional Record, 80th Congress, 1st Session, 5707 (1947).

34. Robert Sears McMahon, *Federal Regulation of the Radio and Television Broadcast Industry in the United States, 1927–1959* (Ph.D. Dissertation, Ohio State University, 1959; reissued, New York: Arno Press, 1979), 168.

35. The comparative hearing for all competing applications for a new broadcast station was mandated by the Supreme Court as a protection of constitutional due process. Ashbacker Radio Corp. v. FCC, 326 U.S. 327 (1945).

36. U.S. House of Representatives, 85th Congress, 2nd Session, Hearings Before a Subcommittee of the Committee on Interstate and Foreign Commerce, *Investigation of Reg-ulatory Commissions and Agencies,* January 27–30, February 3–5, 1958. Memorandum to Hon. Morgan M. Moulder, Chairman, Special Subcommittee on Legislative Oversight, from Dr. Bernard Schwartz, Chief Counsel of the FCC, dated January 4, 1958 (Washington, D.C.: Government Printing Office, 1958), 210.

37. Id., 211. McMahon surveyed several of these cases in his dissertation. Among the more egregious manipulations of licensing criteria was observed in the consistent awarding of television licenses to Republican newspapers in comparative hearings and the equally con-sistent denial of television licenses to Democratic newspapers throughout the 1950s. Nine Democratic papers were denied; 8 Republican papers were approved. McMahon, *Federal Regulation of the Radio and Television Broadcast Industry,* 309–339.

The gross inconsistency of Commission licensing decisions was not confined to com-parative hearings for television licenses in the 1950s. As the 1948 Hoover Commission staff report on the FCC observed of the licensing of stations generally: "Not a single person at the Commission who is concerned with broadcast work will even pretend to demonstrate that the Commission's decisions in these cases have followed a consistent policy, or for that matter, any policy other than the desire to dispose of cases and, if possible, to do so by making grants." Commission on Organization of the Executive Branch of the Government, Commit-tee on Independent Regulatory Commissions, Staff Report on the Federal Communications Commission, prepared for the Committee by William W. Golub, dated September 15, 1948, declassified March 1, 1961 (Washington, DC: Government Printing Office, 1948), Part II, 40.

38. See Powe, *American Broadcasting and the First Amendment,* 74–84.

The *ex parte* contacts of Commissioners did not just encompass the broadcast industry but members of Congress as well. For example, the notorious *ex parte* influence of Senator Joseph McCarthy on Commission licensing decisions in the early 1950s is documented. See the FCC proceedings In Re application of Radio Wisconsin et al., 10 Radio Regulations 1224 (1955).

39. It should be emphasized that the activism of the broadcast reform movement of the 1960s and 1970s did not have much direct or long-lasting effect in altering the regulation of broadcasting. The standard text on broadcast regulation, *The Politics of Broadcast Regula-tion,* by Krasnow, Longley, and Terry, makes the mistake of overemphasizing the victories of the broadcast reform movement. This mistake is indicative of the authors' inadequate

theoretical framework. In formulating a standard and static "interest" theory within a pluralist analysis, the authors pay lip service to structural issues but do not use these to inform their theory. The text posits that all interests in the broadcast regulation game—the FCC, Congress, the executive branch, the industry, the courts, the citizens groups—are relatively equal and possess relatively equivalent influence in shaping policy. This view is patently absurd. Erwin G. Krasnow, Lawrence D. Longley, and Herbert A. Terry, *The Politics of Broadcast Regulation,* Third ed. (New York: St. Martin's Press, 1982).

40. Friedrich and Sternberg's classic description of Congress and the radio industry is worth reviving here. They wrote in 1943: "Although they made a loud noise the number of Congressmen speaking against the radio monopoly was quite small. Those on the other side of the fence were mostly inarticulate because the popular trend was to crusade against monopoly and they saw no need to make themselves unnecessarily popular. But there is little doubt they did a good deal of off-the-record work with the Commission for those who had important financial interests in the industry." Carl J. Friedrich and Evelyn Sternberg, "Congress and the Control of Radio Broadcasting," *American Political Science Review* 37/5 (October 1943), 811.

41. FCC, *Report on Chain Broadcasting,* Pursuant to Commission Order No. 37, Docket No. 5060, May 1941 (Washington, DC: Government Printing Office, 1941), 30–33.

42. *Report on Chain Broadcasting,* 34–44, 51–69. The dependence of individual radio stations on networks was not just a matter of simple economics and coercive contractual practices. The networks—again primarily NBC and CBS—exercised strict control over what could be aired due to their vast ownership of copyrights of recorded music. Moreover, these networks operated talent agencies which tightly bound entertainers to the networks.

43. *Report on Chain Broadcasting,* Appendix B, "Memorandum of Submittal Accompanying Report of Committee on Chain Broadcasting, and Conclusion of the Committee's Report," dated June 2, 1940, 99.

44. Id. at 98.

45. Section 303(i) of The Communications Act gave the FCC "authority to make special regulations applicable to radio stations engaged in chain broadcasting." But it did not appear to give the Commission direct jurisdiction over networks. The "Chain Rules" did facilitate the divestment of the NBC "Blue" network (which became the American Broadcasting Company, ABC), but did so indirectly via the Commission's licensing authority. The Commission did not use the occasion of the "Chain Rules" to broaden its authority over networks.

46. *Report on Chain Broadcasting,* 67. The Chain Rules did not get rid of option time; they only loosened up the practice. The broadcast industry seemingly convinced the Commission that without some version of option time, the practice of networking would be destroyed. Option time was still under discussion at the time of the FCC study on network broadcasting in 1958. See Roscoe L. Barrow, "Network Broadcasting—The Report of the FCC Network Study Staff," *Law and Contemporary Problems* 22/4 (Autumn 1957), 611–625.

47. U.S. Senate, 77th Congress, 1st Session, Committee on Interstate Commerce, Hearings on S. Res. 113, *A Resolution Directing a Study of Certain Rules and Regulations Promulgated by the Federal Communications Commission,* June 2–20, 1941, Testimony of James Lawrence Fly (Washington, DC: Government Printing Office, 1941), 95 (emphasis added).

By the time of the "Chain Rules" the sentiment in Congress had changed. Whereas in the 1930s, calls for investigation of the FCC in reality were attempts to attack the "Radio Trust," by the 1940s the calls for investigation of the FCC were to attack FCC activism.

Representative E. E. Cox of Georgia, instigator of an intensive House investigation of the FCC in the early 1940s, said of Chairman Fly: "He is guilty of a monstrous abuse of power and is rapidly becoming the most dangerous man in the Government. He maintains an active and ambitious Gestapo and is putting shackles on the freedom of thought, press, and speech without restraint . . . . He is taking advantage of the stress of the moment to federalize all means of communication. . . .'' 88 *Congressional Record,* 77th Congress, 2nd Session, (1942), at 794. Cox referred to FCC investigations as ''gestapo''-like, claiming that ''[Fly's] whole outfit now is a nest of reds. . . .'' 89 *Congressional Record,* 78th Congress, 1st Session, (1943), at 235.

48. *Report on Chain Broadcasting,* Additional Views of Commissioners T. A. M. Craven and Norman S. Case in the Matter of Chain Broadcasting, 119. Another likely conservatizing influence in the Chain Rules issues was the Supreme Court's 1940 decision in *Federal Communications Commission v. Sanders Brothers Radio Station.* Though the context of this case was quite different from the ''Chain Report'' (*Sanders* involved the protection of a licensee from competitive injury), the Court clearly wrote that ''the [Communications] Act does not essay to regulate the business of the licensee. The Commission is given no supervisory control of the programs, of business management or of policy.'' The decision even seemed to conclude that the structure of broadcasting was Congressionally mandated. ''Congress intended to leave competition in the business of broadcasting where it found it. . . .'' 309 U.S. 470 (1939), at 475.

49. *Report on Chain Broadcasting,* at 116–117.

50. Fly realized the likely inefficacy of the rules. He testified in the 1941 Senate hearings: ''But I think it would be healthy if we could have as many as six national chains, and then could have more of the substantial regional chains. . . . However, I do not say you will get them. Understand me that no matter how much is said about this being a great reorganization of the industry, I do not want to kid myself or to try to kid you gentlemen. All that we are doing is relaxing a few of these specific restrictive clauses in contracts. Now in talking about a shake-up of the radio industry, that is just so much moonshine. . . .'' Senate Interstate Commerce Committee Hearings on S. Res. 113, at 55.

51. One consequence of this ''middle ground'' between localism and networking was the ''rural service gap.'' The rural service gap describes the problem of a lack of night-time radio service in many rural areas—a situation affecting some 20 million people from the mid-1930s to the mid-1950s.

The policy of localism was inappropriate when applied to geographically large and sparsely populated regions, for the simple reason that such populations generally could not generate the advertising revenues sufficient to cover a local station's operating costs. Such regions received radio service from clear channel signals. But from the mid-1930s on, and especially after the ''Chain Rules,'' the FCC followed a policy of reducing the number of clear channels in favor of increased use of those frequencies for additional local service—a policy whose effect was to increase the number of local urban stations (primarily in the East) and reduce the number and scope of signals receivable in rural areas (primarily across the western prairie and mountain regions).

The solution to the service gap was predicated upon the post-World War II economic boom and the FCC's willingness to create many more local and regional channel classifications. It also illustrates the tension between national networking and the Commission's hopes for local broadcasting. The post-war economic climate induced many applicants (many of whom were returning military personnel with wartime radio experience) willing to accept extreme limitations upon their transmission contours and hours of operation (usually dawn to dusk) in order to obtain a broadcast license. The Commission created these new slots by reducing the power of many older broadcasters and clear channels, and in so doing, effectively transformed the radio industry into one of mainly local broadcasters.

AM radio grew from around 930 to 2,350 stations in the period between 1945 and 1952, primarily in small towns and suburbs. This station growth was accomplished at the cost of interference and the fragmentation of the listening audience and advertiser's dollars. Consequently, programming on these new local and regional stations, partly due to the expense of programming and small audiences, did not serve their local communities along the public service lines envisioned by the Commission's "Blue Book." Rather, they reverted to the practice of the pre-network era, filling empty schedules with recorded music. The Commission's successful late attempt to forge a local system of radio broadcasting served to lessen the importance of national and live programming after World War II. This is not to say, however, that the networks declined. Far from it, but given the tremendous increase of stations in the 1950s, the absolute proportion of network influence declined.

But the decline in national radio programming was precipitated by forces more salient than FCC radio assignment policy. It may be that the Commission was able to restructure radio at least partly due to the fact that the industry's energies were elsewhere, that is, in establishing television. The radio network phenomenon declined very quickly as television became a commercial reality. With audience interest focusing on television, advertisers and popular programs jumped from radio to television in the early 1950s. As early as 1951–1952, chunks of radio time which long had been cleared for network programs were coming back to the affiliate stations for local programming. National advertisers went over to television. Don R. Le Duc, *Cable Television and the FCC: A Crisis in Media Control* (Philadelphia: Temple University Press, 1973), 47–54; Sterling and Kittross, *Stay Tuned,* 253, 262, 510–511.

52. The comment in the FCC's 1947 *Annual Report* is instructive in this regard. The Commission reported that in multiple ownership matters, the "public interest would not be served by adoption of an iron-clad rule defining the extent of overlap of service areas or the degree of common ownership, operation or control that would be deemed to be in contravention to its rules covering standard broadcast, FM and television stations. The Commission announced that it will continue to decide each such case on its own merits" (at 14).

53. In addition to the *Report on Chain Broadcasting,* the "Barrow Report" on network broadcasting strongly recommended limitations on multiple ownership. U.S. House, 85th Congress, 2d Session, Committee on Interstate and Foreign Commerce, *Network Broadcasting,* H.R. No. 1297 (Washington, DC: Government Printing Office, 1958).

54.. In the Matter of Amendment of Section 3.636 of the Commission's Rules and Regulations Relating to Multiple Ownership of Television Broadcast Stations, 43 FCC 2797 (1954). The story of UHF will be told *infra.*

55. However, as will be made clear in the discussion of spectrum allocation *infra,* the most salient factor in the original formation of networks was not necessarily the multiple ownership of stations. Rather, the formation of a viable network was contingent on the ability to line up a large number of technically superior affiliate outlets in the major markets.

56. Commission to Designate for Hearing Applications to Acquire Interests in a Second VHF Station in Major Markets, 45 FCC 1851 (1965).

57. Herbert H. Howard, "Multiple Broadcast Ownership: Regulatory History," *Federal Communications Bar Journal* 27/1 (1974), 1–70; L. A. Powe, Jr., "FCC Determinations on Networking Issues in Multiple Ownership Proceedings," Prepared for the Commercial Television Network Practices Inquiry of the Federal Communications Commission (Washington, DC: FCC, 1980), 60–72.

58. Powe, "FCC Determinations on Networking Issues in Multiple Ownership Proceedings," 85.

59. This assessment of why broadcast programming is the way it is admittedly is a simplification. Obviously, there are more and other factors apart from the structure of the broadcast market which have important bearing on the nature of programming. The economic market model cannot explain why certain programs or genres strike a chord with broadcast

audiences, or why others fail to do so. The most salient other factors are *cultural*. Cultural factors lie at the heart of why, for example, American television seems to be a medium enamored of drama. And cultural factors take into account the professional culture of broadcast production and how network executives construct images and categories of the audience. See, for example, Martin Esslin, *The Age of Television* (San Francisco: W. H. Freeman, 1982), or Todd Gitlin, *Inside Prime Time* (New York: Pantheon, 1983). Cultural analysis is important and lies beyond the scope of this study.

Even the economic factors have nuance. By the late 1970s, pure audience size gave way to demographically identifiable "upscale" audience segments which are more attractive to advertisers. This has some affect on the type of television programs offered. Still, I would argue that the major factor underlying the imitative and inoffensive nature of television broadcast programming has to do with the economic structure of the commercial broadcast market. The same economic factors underlie the *differences* between television and radio. Because there are now so many radio stations and program costs are relatively low, radio sometimes targets specific audiences rather than going after the mass audience. This explains the larger number of different formats in radio and the continued existence of, for example, the left-wing Pacifica stations.

60. See Charles L. Siepmann, *Radio's Second Chance* (Boston: Little, Brown, 1946).

61. Sterling & Kittross, *Stay Tuned,* 143–144. As undisputed industry leader, RCA's active non-support (Armstrong always contended it was outright planned sabotage) could severely limit any innovation's chances for success. Clearly, FM posed a triple threat: (1) to the dominance of AM, (2) to RCA's patent strength, (3) to RCA's hopes for post-war television in terms of competition for spectrum space. It must be noted, however, that television had already garnered tremendous industry and public interest. RCA made an investment decision which reflected its interest in the "future," and in so doing, protected its present investment by consigning FM to the economic and technical hinterland.

62. In the Matter of Aural Broadcasting on Frequencies Above 25,000 Kilocycles Particularly Relating to Frequency Modulation, Docket 5805, May 20, 1940, 39 FCC 29 (1940), at 31.

This analysis of FM's regulatory treatment follows that of Vincent Mosco, *Broadcasting in the United States: Innovative Challenge and Organizational Control* (Norwood: Ablex Publishing Corp., 1979).

63. FCC, *Annual Report,* 1940, 68.

64. Mosco, *Broadcasting in the United States,* 114–115.

65. In the Matter of Aural Broadcasting., 39 FCC 29 (1970), at 30.

66. Mosco, *Broadcasting in the United States,* 55–67.

67. The FCC's successful calling for the radio manufacturers to set up a purely technical planning board in early 1943 underscores the Commission's role as a key rationalizing force of the industry. For the industry composition of the RTPB see the transcripts of the FCC's 1944 Allocation Hearings (Docket No. 6651) compiled by the National Association of Broadcasters. NAB, *Special Allocation Hearings Bulletin,* No. 1, October 13, 1944, 5.

68. In the Matter of Allocation of Frequencies to the Various Classes of Non-Governmental Services in the Radio Spectrum from 10 Kilocycles to 30,000,000 Kilocycles (Docket No. 6651), 39 FCC 68 (1945), at 91–102.

69. Barnouw, *The Golden Web,* 242; FCC, *Annual Report,* 1944, 16; FCC, *Annual Report,* 1945, 20.

70. The Commission's total reliance on Norton's testimony in the face of heated disputation was even more damaging when, in November 1947, Armstrong forced Norton to admit that the technical advice he had given the Commission had been totally in error. W. Rupert

MacLaurin, *Invention and Innovation in the Radio Industry* (New York: Macmillan, 1949), 231.

71. Mosco, *Broadcasting in the United States,* 57; *Business Week,* November 4, 1944, 88.

72. Furthermore, despite the stagnation of FM service in the 1950s, the FCC continued to grant AM "drop-in" stations. Though FM grew again after 1958, this growth was due to increased ownership by AM interests. Assisting in FM's resurgence included authorization to provide specialized services such as Muzak (after 1955), cheaper and more readily available FM receivers (by the mid-1960s), and approval of FM stereo standards (1961). Even so, FM independents generally lost money. Only in 1976 did the FM industry as a whole break into the black financially. See Christopher H. Sterling, "Television and Radio Broadcasting," in *Who Owns the Media?,* Benjamin M. Compaine (ed.) (New York: Harmony Books, 1979), 69. In general, FCC policies resulted in FM serving to strengthen rather than combat monopoly, in duplicating rather than diversifying programming.

73. L. R. Lankes, "Historical Sketch of Television's Progress," in *A Technological History of Motion Pictures and Television,* Raymond Fielding (ed.) (Berkeley: University of California Press, 1967), 227–229; A. G. Jensen, "The Evolution of Modern Television," in Fielding, 235–249; Joseph H. Udelson, *The Great Television Race: A History of the American Television Industry, 1925–1941* (University, Ala.: University of Alabama Press, 1982).

AT&T, as might be expected, claimed that its television research was intended to complement the telephone as a means of two-way communication. But television's technical promise for instantaneous transmission convinced many of those involved with the innovation that it would be a medium of public information and entertainment. As early as 1923, David Sarnoff suggested that television would involve the broadcasting of news and motion pictures for viewing in individual homes and auditoriums. See David Sarnoff, Memorandum, "Radio Broadcasting Activities," to RCA Board of Directors, April 5, 1923, in *Looking Ahead: The Papers of David Sarnoff* (New York: McGraw-Hill, 1968), 88.

74. David Sarnoff, Statement at Hollywood, California, May 18, 1931, in *Looking Ahead,* 97.

75. In 1930, when as part of the consent decree, RCA took over the radio research conducted at GE and Westinghouse, the important television inventor, Vladimir Zwyorkin, went over to RCA. By 1932, RCA had about 60 people working on television. According to RCA data filed with the FCC, RCA put $9.25 million into television research between 1930 and 1939. Maclaurin, *Invention and Innovation in the Radio Industry,* 204, 206.

76. Noran E. Kersta, NBC assistant coordinator for television, wrote in 1940: "[For] three and one-half years, prior to public service in April, 1939, a considerable amount of research was conducted on the advertising aspects of television. In fact, programs thought suitable for advertising purposes, involving products of many different industries, were tried. . . . A considerable number of manufacturing and advertising agencies cooperated in the production of these shows. All this, naturally, was done anticipating that television would eventually become an advertising medium." "The Business Side of Television," *Electronics* 13/2 (March 1940), 90–92, at 90.

77. U.S. Senate, Committee on Interstate Commerce, 76th Congress, 3rd Session, Hearings on S. Res. 251, *Development of Television,* April 10–11, 1940 (Washington, DC: Government Printing Office, 1940), at 48.

Ironically, Sarnoff's advocacy of a private system for television was the opposite of his early proposals for *radio.* In the course of these hearings, several senators seemed to attempt to outdo each other as "advocates of individual initiative." at 47–48.

78. Federal Radio Commission, *Annual Report,* 1928, 21.

79. The FRC stated that "the commission did not recognize visual broadcasting as having developed to the point where it has real entertainment value." Federal Radio Commission, *Annual Report*, 1930, 68.

80. The propagation characteristics of VHF are such that a straight line is required between transmitter and receiver. There can be no possibility of "skywave" service as in AM radio. This would be of great consequence for the future American television system. The propagation characteristics of higher frequencies meant that technically, a nationwide television system could consist only of vast numbers of stations, rather than a few number of high-powered stations.

81. FCC, *Annual Report*, 1937, at 37.

82. See, for example, the FCC *Annual Report* of 1939. Quoting an FCC committee's report on television, the *Annual Report* stated, "[I]t appears that rigid adoption of standards at this state of the art may either 'freeze' the television industry, and thus retard future development, or may result in a high rate of obsolescence of equipment purchased by the public. . . " (at 45).

83. The Commission's most progressive statement about the public interest in television came in a 1937 press release. It stated: "The action taken by the Commission today with respect to television is merely one step of many which are required before television can become a reliable service to the public. Some of these many steps must be taken by the industry in the development of proper standards which in turn the Commission must approve before television can technically be of the greatest use to the public on any scale.

"Also the Commission, at the proper time in the future, must determine the policies which will govern the operation of television service in this country, particularly with reference to those matters which relate to the avoidance of monopolies. And the Commission must also in the future prescribe such rules and policies as will insure the utilization of television stations in a manner conforming to the public interest, convenience and necessity, particularly that phase which will provide television transmission facilities as a medium of public self-expression by all creeds, classes, and social-economic schools of thought.

"The investigations and determinations of the Commission justify the statement that there does not appear to be any immediate outlook for the recognition of television service on a commercial basis. The Commission believes that the general public is entitled to this information for its protection. The Commission will inform the public from time to time with respect to further developments in television." FCC, Press Release No. 23463, October 13, 1937, cited in Frank C. Waldrop and Joseph Borkin, *Television: A Struggle for Power* (New York: William Morrow & Co., 1938, reprinted Arno Press, 1971), 70–71.

Notwithstanding the admirable formulation about the need for diversity and pluralism in television, the press release still does not really contradict the standard Commission line on television. The statement argues that technical standards are not good enough, and there is no *immediate* outlook for commercialization. Such a press release was also consistent with FCC practice. As a press release, provocative pronouncements had no effect as policy or rule.

84. RCA used the 1939 New York World's Fair as a setting to push television. On the fierce intra-industry battles over television, see Waldrop & Borkin, *Television: A Struggle for Power*, Udelson, *The Great Television Race*, and John Michael Kittross, *Television Frequency Allocation Policy in the United States* (New York: Arno Press, 1979).

85. FCC, Order No. 65, March 22, 1940 (Public Notice, March 23, 1940), mimeo 39922; FCC, *Annual Report*, 1940, 71–72.

Early commercialization clearly favored RCA, inasmuch as the corporation held a commanding position in patents and programming. Those New Dealers who still voiced antimonopoly sentiment, most notably FCC Chairman Lawrence Fly, coupled the reticence to allow early commercialization with arguments against monopoly. This coupling is seen in the

FCC press release cited *supra* at note 83. See also, FCC, Report in the Matter of Order 65, Docket No. 5806, May 28, 1940, cited in *Annual Report,* 1940.

86. In so doing, the Commission fulfilled a central obligation to act to rationalize a deeply divided industry. Rupert Maclaurin offered this telling observation on the FCC's role: "I was very much impressed by the quality of co-operation achieved by the National Television Systems Committee. The FCC forced the engineers to work together in a way that would probably not have occurred otherwise. Perhaps because of this, it is my impression that the engineers in the industry were able to come much closer to unanimity of opinion on such matters as FM and television than were the top business executives in the industry." Maclaurin, *Invention and Innovation in the Radio Industry,* 240.

87. FCC, *Annual Report,* 1941, 32–34.

88. IRAC was established in 1922 to assist the executive branch in communications matters. After the creation of the FCC in 1934, IRAC's role devolved slightly. Its responsibilities were to give advice about frequency allocation. Since the Korean War, however, IRAC has been a primary channel for the consolidation of Defense Department communications needs.

89. National Association of Broadcasters, *Special Allocation Hearings Bulletin,* testimony of Paul W. Kesten, (executive vice-president of CBS), No. 2, (October 13, 1944), 12; testimony of Joseph H. Ream (vice-president and secretary of CBS), No. 6, (October 31, 1944), 17–25.

90. National Association of Broadcasters, *Special Allocation Hearings Bulletin,* testimony of Dr. C. B. Jolliffe (chief engineer of RCA Victor division), H. H. Beverage (associate director of RCA Laboratories), E. W. Engstrom (research director of RCA laboratories), No. 8 (November 7, 1944), 1–12.

91. National Association of Broadcasters, *Special Allocation Hearings Bulletin,* testimony of David B. Smith, (chairman of Panel 6 of RTPB on television), No. 1, (October 13, 1944), 14; testimony of David B. Smith, No. 6 (October 31, 1944), 2–8.

The RTPB, upon whose judgment the Commission relied heavily, was sponsored by nine industry associations. It generally was comprised of engineers from the older, more established radio and electronics firms. Thus it is likely that the RTPB was structurally attuned to the RCA position in technical matters.

92. NAB Bulletin No. 1, 12–17.

93. Ibid., 15. This allocation for television meant the shifting of FM radio up the spectrum in order to create another television channel in the lower part of the VHF.

94. In the Matter of Allocation of Frequencies to the Various Classes of Non-Governmental Services in the Radio Spectrum from 10 Kilocycles to 30,000,000 Kilocycles (Docket No. 6651), 39 FCC 68 (1945), at 129–130.

95. Nearly all experts testified that a nationwide, competitive television system required between 25 to 50 channels. Thirty was the most oft-cited number. See NAB Bulletin No. 1, 13–17.

96. FCC, *Annual Report,* 1948, 37–38, 43–45. The televising of the Louis-Wolcott heavyweight boxing championship bout and coverage of the Republican National Convention in the last ten days of June 1948 marked the arrival of television as a cultural force in American life. The FCC *Annual Report* of 1948 estimated that the production rate of receiving sets was approximately 50,000 per month. Total post-war TV receiver output as of June 1948 was 460,000 units, estimated to represent a public investment of $228 million. FCC, *Annual Report,* 1948, 39.

97. The propagation characteristics of the VHF television broadcast signal required strict mileage separations between transmitters operating on co-channel and adjacent channel frequencies. These separations also varied with transmitter power and antenna height. The 1945

allocation plan had ignored the known problem of tropospheric interference when it established guidelines for co-channel separation of 150 miles and adjacent channel separation of 75 miles. At the time, such inadequate separation distances didn't matter because there were so few stations on the air, and Canada and Mexico had not yet entered into television broadcasting. But, because the 1945 assignment plan was based on television demand and market rank, interference quickly became intolerable, especially when New York City was awarded seven assignments in November 1945.

The Commission's ignoring of tropospheric interference might be due to a near total turnover in FCC personnel between 1945 and 1948. But more likely, industry (read, RCA) pressure to begin commercial television and Commission expedience is the better explanation. This is how the matter was posed in a contemporaneous *Fortune* magazine article by the intelligent media analyst, Lawrence P. Lessing. "But the FCC was unaware of this phenomenon [tropospheric interference] only if it couldn't read its own writing. There was everything from its historical report of May, 1945, discussing such interference, to its rule books on standards, giving directions for measuring objectionable levels of it. In addition, the Hoover report [Committee on Independent Regulatory Commissions (1948)] cites the commission for failing to draw upon a mass of tropospheric data then in the hands of the military—an odd oversight, considering the alacrity with which the commission drew upon military data to support its case for moving FM upstairs in 1945.

". . . But what little was known was not applied—and the most plausible reason is that the results would have been unpalatable to the dominant TV interests. For if this interference had been taken into account, the inadequacy of very-high-frequency channels for a good initial service to U.S. cities would have been clearly shown. And this would have opened the pressure valves to move TV into the ultra-highs, with the arguments for finer black and white or color becoming irresistible. . . . RCA and its allies were in haste to catch the postwar market. Whether or not they hoped to put off the tropospheric problem long enough to get established, gambling that the laws of nature might not work out, is the main bone of contention." Lawrence P. Lessing, "The Television Freeze," *Fortune*, November 1949, 158, 162.

98. Third Notice of Further Proposed Rulemaking, Dockets 8736, 8975, 8976, 9175, July 12, 1949.

99. Cited in Sixth Report and Order, 41 FCC 148 (1952), at 167.

100. By way of contrast, changes to AM radio assignments were made through adjudicatory proceedings on individual applications. Changes by rule making effectively made the table of television assignments quite inflexible. In his analysis of the Sixth Report for the Senate Committee on Interstate and Foreign Commerce, Edward L. Bowles suggested that the FCC believed a policy-guided plan would avoid some of the difficulties of the case-by-case radio procedure. United States Senate, 85th Congress, 2d Session, Committee on Interstate and Foreign Commerce, *Allocation of TV Channels,* Report of the Ad Hoc Advisory Committee on Allocations, Committee Print, March 14, 1958 (Washington, DC: Government Printing Office, 1958), at 45. [hereinafter, *Bowles Report*].

101. Sixth Report and Order, 41 FCC 148 (1952), at 167.

102. *Bowles Report,* at 29. This perspective is strongly seconded by, and is the main subject of, Roger G. Noll, Merton J. Peck, and John J. McGowan, *Economic Aspects of Television Regulation* (Washington, DC: Brookings, 1973).

103. See comments of *Barrow Report,* suggesting unduplicated base of 50,000. U.S. House, 85th Congress, 2d Session, Committee on Interstate and Foreign Commerce, *Network Broadcasting,* H.R. No. 1297 (Washington, DC: Government Printing Office, 1958). Le Duc cites statistics of 50,000, and another report which claimed absolute minimum at 25,000. Le Duc, *Cable Television and the FCC,* 65.

104. To provide the state of Wyoming with one television signal, for instance, the FCC required 26 station allocations. Le Duc, *Cable Television and the FCC,* 65. Le Duc argues that such assignments were "obviously only empty gestures, offering service on paper which could never be provided" (at 65).

The irony of the Commission's policy to reserve television frequencies for various communities was that it was based on a misreading of the Communications Act. The Commission claimed that the set of five priorities which legitimated the *Sixth Report and Order* fulfilled Section 307(b) of the Act. That section was taken by the Commission as a mandate to provide "a fair, efficient and equitable distribution of television broadcast *stations* to the several states and communities." 41 FCC 148 (1952) at 167 (emphasis added). But the actual section, as written to apply to radio, mandated the Commission to provide "a fair, efficient, and equitable distribution of radio *service*" to the several states and communities. Communications Act of 1934 (emphasis added). Had the Commission assigned television frequencies on the principle of geographic areas' access to television signals, quite a different television system might have emerged.

105. Appendices of *Sixth Report and Order;* Thomas L. Schuessler, "The Effect of the Federal Communications Commission's Spectrum Management Policies Upon the Number of Television Networks," prepared for the Commercial Television Network Practices Inquiry, Federal Communications Commission (Washington, DC: Federal Communications Commission, 1980), 149–153.

Educational television should be considered in the context. With the strong support of Commissioner Freida Hennock, the *Sixth Report and Order* allocated and reserved television frequencies for noncommercial, educational broadcasting. The reservation of frequencies for educational use, while contributing to the structural limitations on the development of additional commercial networks, was not really significant. As Schuessler shows, had the FCC chosen not to reserve assignments for noncommercial use in the 1952 plan, the number of markets receiving four or more technically comparable assignments would have increased from 10 to 20—not anywhere near enough to allow the possibility of a fourth network. Schuessler, "The Effect of the FCC's Spectrum Management Policies," 174–177.

Interestingly, there was tacit support for educational reservations on the part of the commercial stations already possessing monopoly or near-monopoly position in any particular community. Their reasoning was that the audience for educational television would be small, and at the same time another potential commercial rival would be unable to gain access to that market so long as the reservation for education was in effect. See Kittross, *Television Frequency Allocation Policy in the United States,* 203.

106. CBS Statement Re FCC Report 49–948, Dockets 8736 et al., September 1949, cited in U.S. Senate, 84th Congress, 2d Session, Committee on Interstate and Foreign Commerce, Hearings on the UHF-VHF Allocations Problem (Washington, DC: Government Printing Office, 1956), part 2, at 792.

107. Comments and Proposals of Allen B. DuMont Laboratories, Docket No. 8736 et al., May 7, 1951, at 15–16. Cited in "The Darkened Channels: UHF Television and the FCC," *Harvard Law Review* 75/8 (June 1962), 1580. Though CBS and especially DuMont led the opposition to intermixture, even RCA advised that intermixture be avoided as much as was practical. "The Darkened Channels," 1581, n. 20.

108. Appendices of *Sixth Report and Order*; Schuessler, "The Effect of the FCC's Spectrum Management Policies," 151–152.

109. In 1952, 64 of the 108 original stations were affiliated with NBC. Thirty one were affiliated with CBS. Statistics compiled by Sterling & Kittross, *Stay Tuned,* Appendix C, 517.

Allen B. DuMont's testimony before a Senate subcommittee on communications in 1954 sheds some light on the differential effect of the television freeze: "The 108 stations which were on the air or which went on the air shortly after the freeze were situated in 63 markets— 40 of these 63 markets had only one station; 11 of these 63 markets had only two stations; 8 markets had only three stations and 4 markets had four or more stations. Of the 40 stations in the single station markets, 37 were owned by interests having radio stations. An overwhelming majority of them were affiliated with NBC and CBS radio networks and these affiliations were carried over into affiliation with these two television networks. Of the 22 stations in the two station markets, 21 were owned by radio interests with an overwhelming majority of these having affiliations with NBC and CBS . . . . [This] meant that the freeze reserved to the two networks the almost exclusive right to broadcast in all but 12 of the 63 markets which had television service." U.S. Senate, 83rd Congress, 2d Session, Committee on Interstate and Foreign Commerce, Subcommittee on Communications, Hearings on the Status of TV Stations and S. 3905 (Washington, DC: Government Printing Office, 1954), at 1018.

110. *Bowles Report,* 47–49. Commissioner Robert F. Jones, who voted against the adoption of the *Sixth Report and Order* in 1952, confirmed Bowles' judgment. In a letter to the *Harvard Law Review* Jones wrote: "If I may indulge in reasonable speculation, I would add that existing TV licenses had an influence on the weight given both economic and technical factors. The allocation plan was designed to cause the least disruption to the existing channel assignments of these pre-freeze licensees. Accordingly, practical, rather than optimum, efficiency considerations dictated the minimum mileage separations employed. The power, antenna height, and separations adopted embraced nearly every pre-freeze assignment, and gave each such licensee a tremendous windfall." Letter of Robert F. Jones, October 20, 1961. Cited in "The Darkened Channels," at 1581, n. 24.

111. Bowles lauded the first DuMont plan. He wrote: "The Dumont project was exemplary for its breadth of understanding of the problem and for its professional quality. This comprehensive project, recognizing 1400 communities [the *Sixth Report* embraced some 1200], took into account economic considerations, [and] saw with lucidity the fatal dangers of intermixture. It recognized the principle of reserving space for noncommercial broadcasting by allowing nine channels for this service on a first-come-first-served basis. . . . The plan faced realistically the vital interrelationship of stations and networks and the importance of competition between the networks themselves. It yielded a minimum of four channels, either U or V, not intermixed, in most of the major metropolitan markets. It minimized the intermixture of VHF and UHF assignments. There was but 1 intermixed city among the first 325 in market rank." *Bowles Report,* at 98–99.

112. On the FCC's dismissal of the DuMont allocation plan, see *Sixth Report and Order,* 41 FCC 148 (1952), at 170–172. On its misplaced faith in UHF's ability to compete, see id. at 208. As for technological determinism, the following quotation is indicative: "Further, there is no reason to believe that American science will not produce the equipment necessary for the fullest development of the UHF." Id. at 208.

113. U.S. Senate, 87th Congress, 2d Session, Committee on Interstate and Foreign Commerce, *All-Channel Television,* Report No. 1526 (Washington, DC: Government Printing Office, 1962), at 3. This failure rate of UHFs was astonishing when compared with almost no failures of VHF stations.

In a sample year, 1957, five years after the end of the television freeze, only 10 percent of the pre-freeze stations did not turn a profit, compared with 40 percent of the post-freeze VHF's and 75 percent of UHFs. In 1971, a year in which more than 75 percent of television sets were equipped to receive UHF signals, of 1,185 available UHF frequencies, only 301 stations were operating. In contrast, 598 of 716 VHF reservations were operating (and most of the vacancies were educational reservations). Between the failure of UHF and the scarcity of VHFs, nationwide television coverage was a joke. Only two or fewer television signals were available to roughly 20 percent of the nation's households as late as the early 1970s. Kittross, *Television Frequency Allocation Policy in the United States,* 299–301; FCC, *Annual Report,* 1971, 37; *Television Factbook,* 1973–1974, Vol. 43 (Washington, DC: Television Digest, 1974), 62a–70a.

114. See Schuessler, "The Effect of the FCC's Spectrum Management Policies," 91–112; "The Darkened Channels."

115. FCC, "Preliminary Report of the Federal Communications Commission to the Senate Interstate and Foreign Commerce Committee With Respect to VHF-UHF and Television Network Problems" (March 16, 1955), reprinted in U.S. Senate, 84th Congress, 2d Session, Committee on Interstate and Foreign Commerce, Hearings, *The Television Inquiry: The UHF-VHF Allocation Problem* (Washington, DC: Government Printing Office, 1956), at 260.

116. FCC, Second Report on Deintermixture, 13 Radio Regulations 1571 (1956).

117. Id.; All-Channel Receiver Act, 47 U.S.C. Section 303(s), 330 (1962).

118. "The Darkened Channels," 1586–1591.

119. Baughman, *Television's Guardians,* 92–100.

120. "The Darkened Channels," 1584, 1593.

121. *Television Factbook,* 1970–71, Vol. 40 (Washington, DC: Television Digest, 1971), 66a.

122. J. E. Belknap and Associates, 18 FCC 642 (1954).

123. U.S. Senate, 85th Congress, 2d Session, Committee on Interstate and Foreign Commerce, Hearings pursuant to S. Res. 224 and on S. 376, *Television Inquiry,* Part 6 (Washington, DC: Government Printing Office, 1958).

124. FCC, Inquiry into the Impact of Community Antenna Systems, TV Translators, TV "Satellite" Stations, and TV "Repeaters" on the Orderly Development of Television Broadcasting, 26 FCC 403 (1959), at 435–438 (hereinafter, "Community Antenna Systems). The FCC indicated that it was unable to measure the harm caused by CATV, but determined that the likelihood of severe injury caused by auxiliary services was slight. Studies showed that of 96 stations which had gone off the air since 1952, in only 3 cases was the existence of an auxiliary service mentioned as a factor in the demise (at 415). Notwithstanding an inability to prove a *direct* relation between the rise of CATV systems and the difficulties of small market television stations, it was clear from the "Television Inquiry" hearings that audience fragmentation did pose a genuine threat to rural and small market broadcasters.

125. Id., at 427–429. Le Duc, author of the best work on early cable regulation, makes the case that the Commission wanted to avoid an additional regulatory burden. Le Duc, *Cable Television and the FCC,* 72–73.

The FCC also avoided taking on a new administrative burden in the absence of any Congressional mandate in the matter of CATV. But Congress would be stymied in the area of CATV policy throughout the 1960s and 1970s. No legislation ever made it through Congress.

126. Inquiry into the Impact of Community Antenna Systems, at 430. This was the first indication of the FCC's support of the concept of retransmission consent. In many ways such a policy was in keeping with the Commission's reluctance to regulate CATV. At the same time, the policy would permit *broadcasters* to exercise control over CATV, a result largely in keeping with the protection of broadcasters.

127. Carter Mountain Transmission Corp., 32 FCC 459 (1962), *aff'd,* 321 F.2d 359 (D.C. Cir. 1963), *cert. denied,* 375 U.S. 951 (1963).

128. The Commission reasoned: "A grant of common carrier radio facilities requires a finding that the public interest will be served thereby; certainly the well-being of existing television facilities is an aspect of this public interest. Thus it is not only appropriate, it is necessary that we determine whether the use of the facility applied for would directly or

indirectly bring about the elimination of the only television transmission or reception service to the public. . . . If the CATV pattern is permitted to be altered. . . [the local television station]. . . would find it more difficult to sell its advertising in face of split audience, and this situation. . . results in our judgment that the demise of this local operation would result." Carter Mountain, 32 FCC 459, at 461, 464.

129. Federal Communications Commission v. Sanders Brothers Radio Station, 309 U.S. 470 (1939), at 476.

130. Carroll Broadcasting Co. v. FCC, 258 F.2d 440 (D.C. Cir. 1958), at 443. The specific issue in *Carroll* was the complaint of an existing broadcast licensee that the FCC's proposed grant of a competing license in his market would destroy his ability to perform his public service obligations.

131. Rules re Microwave-Served CATV, 38 FCC 683 (1965). The "must carry" rule presumably protected the local broadcaster by guaranteeing it access to the CATV system. The "nonduplication" rule was imposed to rectify the fact that CATV obtained the signal without consent and had no copyright liability.

132. Id., at 700. Bruce Owen has argued that *Carroll* lies at the heart of FCC treatment of new technologies. One protects existing technologies from competition so that monopoly rents will assure the provision of money-losing public service programs. This then creates an alliance between the government and an artificially small group of media interests, and a vested interest in the scheme of regulation. Owen's solution is the removal of artificial barriers to channel expansion. Bruce M. Owen, *Economics and Freedom of Expression: Media Structure and the First Amendment* (Cambridge: Ballinger, 1975).

133. Second Report and Order, 2 FCC 2d 725 (1966), at 782.

134. The Commission argued that must carry and nonduplication rules "were necessary to ameliorate the risk that the burgeoning CATV industry would have a future adverse impact on television broadcast service, both existing and potential." Second Report and Order, at 736.

135. Martin Seiden, *An Economic Analysis of Community Antenna Television Systems and the Television Broadcasting Industry,* Report to the Federal Communications Commission (Washington, DC: Government Printing Office, 1965).

136. The rules contained within the Second Report and Order were upheld by the Supreme Court in United States v. Southwestern Cable Co., 392 U.S. 157 (1968). Actually, the Court simply acceded FCC jurisdiction over CATV, ruling that the regulation was "reasonably ancillary to the effective performance of the Commission's various responsibilities for the regulation of television broadcasting" (at 178).

137. The anti-siphoning rules included:

1. The so-called "complement of 4" rule, i.e., that only markets with five grade-A commercial signals were eligible for STV;
2. The "one to a community" rule;
3. Most continuous series and feature motion pictures and sporting events that had been typically aired over the past two years on commercial TV could not be shown on STV;
4. STV stations were required to broadcast "conventional" TV without charge for a minimum of 28 hours per week;
5. No series program with interconnected plots or substantially the same cast of characters could be offered on a subscription basis;
6. Not more than 90 percent of the total STV broadcasting hours could consist of feature films and sports events combined;

7. No advertising could be broadcast during subscription operations, except for announcements promoting STV programs.

Rules and Regulations to Provide for Subscription Television Service, 15 FCC 2d 466 (1968); also, Kristin Booth Glen, *Report on Subscription Television,* prepared for the Commercial Television Practices Inquiry of the Federal Communications Commission, Preliminary Report on Prospects for Additional Networks (Washington, DC: FCC, 1980).

138. Memorandum Opinion and Order, 23 FCC 2d 825 (1970).

139. Le Duc, *Cable Television and the FCC,* 135–136.

140. *Ibid.,* 100.

## Chapter 7. The Road to Regulatory Reform

1. Daniel Bell and Virginia Held, "The Community Revolution," *The Public Interest* 16 (Summer 1969), 142–177; Norman Fainstein and Susan Fainstein, *Urban Political Movements: The Search for Power by Minority Groups in American Cities* (Englewood Cliffs, NJ: Prentice-Hall, 1974); Manuel Castells, *The City and the Grassroots: A Cross-Cultural Theory of Urban Social Movements* (Berkeley: University of California Press, 1983).

2. Indeed, some political commentators looked with horror at the increase in political participation and the democratic thrust of political activism. See, for instance, Bell & Held, "The Community Revolution;" Michel J. Crozier, Samuel P. Huntington, and Joji Watanuki, *The Crisis of Democracy: Report on the Governability of Democracies to the Trilateral Commission* (New York: New York University Press, 1975).

3. On the grassroots agitation against corporations see David Vogel, *Lobbying the Corporation: Citizen Challenges to Business Authority* (New York: Basic Books, 1978).

4. Pertschuk identifies the entrepreneurial coalition as consisting of consumer advocates among House and Senate members; a new, or newly flourishing, strain of congressional staff; a newly aggressive core of investigative and advocacy journalists who shared the advocates' view of consumer initiatives as moral imperatives; labor; and the private not-for-profit entrepreneurs, Ralph Nader preeminent among them. Michael Pertschuk, *Revolt Against Regulation: The Rise and Pause of the Consumer Movement* (Berkeley: University of California Press, 1982), 23.

5. See Leonard Silk and David Vogel, *Ethics and Politics: The Crisis of Confidence in American Business* (New York: Simon & Schuster, 1976). Pertschuk describes business during this period as "quiescent."

6. Office of the United Church of Christ v. Federal Communications Commission, 359 F.2d 994 (D.C. Cir. 1966); Scenic Hudson Preservation Conference v. FPC, 354 F.2d 608 (2d Cir. 1965), *cert. denied,* 384 U.S. 941 (1966).

7. As the court wrote in *Scenic Hudson,* "Although a 'case' or 'controversy' which is otherwise lacking cannot be created by statute, a statute may create new interests or rights and thus give standing to one who would otherwise be barred by the lack of a 'case' or 'controversy.' The 'case' or 'controversy' requirement of Article III, Sec. 2 of the Constitution does not require that an 'aggrieved' or 'adversely affected' party have a personal economic interest" (at 615).

In *United Church of Christ* the Court wrote, "The theory that the Commission can always effectively represent the listener interests in a [broadcast license] renewal proceeding without the aid and participation of legitimate listener representatives fulfilling the role of private attorneys general is one of those assumptions we collectively try to work with so long as they are reasonably adequate. When it becomes clear, as it does to us now, that it is no longer a valid assumption which stands up under the realities of actual experience, neither we nor the

Commission can continue to rely on it. The gradual expansion and evolution of concepts of standing in administrative law attests that experience rather than logic or fixed rules has been accepted as the guide" (at 1003–1004).

For the early logic behind the legal movement reconceptualizing property and the expansion of property rights, see the important essays by Charles Reich, "The New Property," *Yale Law Journal* 73/5 (April 1964), 733–787; idem, "Individual Rights and Social Welfare: The Emerging Legal Issues," *Yale Law Journal* 74/7 (June 1965), 1245–1257.

8. The obligation of the agency to consider alternate policy choices in light of their impact on all affected interests was most forcefully stated in the judicial implementation of the National Environmental Policy Act of 1969. As interpreted by the court in *Calvert Cliffs' Coordinating Committee, Inc. v. AEC,* "[The requirements of the Act seek] to ensure that each agency decision maker has before him and takes into account all possible approaches to a particular project (including total abandonment of the project) which would alter the environmental impact and the cost-benefit balance. . . ." 449 F.2d 1109 (D.C. Cir. 1971), at 1114. See the discussion of the "adequate consideration" standard in Richard B. Stewart, "The Reformation of American Administrative Law," *Harvard Law Review* 88/8 (June 1975), 1756–1770, 1781–1790.

9. Indeed, some environmental activists suggested that they acted on behalf of the "rights" of the environment itself. See Christopher D. Stone, *Should Trees Have Standing?* (Los Altos, Calif.: W. Kaufmann, 1974).

10. See, for example, Magnuson-Moss Warranty Act (The Federal Trade Commission Improvement Act of 1975), Public Law No. 93–637, 88 Stat. 2183 (1975); also Robert B. Reich, "Warring Critiques of Regulation," *Regulation,* January/February 1979, 37–42.

The subsidization of public interest representation in regulatory proceedings was prefigured by other like-minded judicial actions. The provisions of the Civil Rights Act of 1964 and Clean Air Act of 1970 allow citizens, acting in the capacity of "private attorneys general," to be compensated for court costs and attorney's fees by the offending parties. Citizen groups which challenged broadcast licensees' renewals in the regulatory arena sometimes negotiated the costs of their participation with the broadcaster.

11. William T. Gormley, Jr., *The Politics of Public Utility Regulation* (Pittsburgh: University of Pittsburgh Press, 1983), 6–36; Paul W. MacAvoy, *The Regulated Industries and the Economy* (New York: WW Norton, 1979), 31–80; Paul L. Joskow, "Inflation and Environmental Concern: Structural Change in the Process of Public Utility Regulation," *Journal of Law and Economics* 17/2 (October 1974), 291–327.

12. See Elizabeth E. Bailey, David R. Graham, and Daniel P. Kaplan, *Deregulating the Airlines* (Cambridge: MIT Press, 1985), 16–19.

13. The national inflation rate had averaged 2.5 percent a year in the 1950s until the late 1960s. It climbed to 5.3 percent in 1971 and averaged 6.7 percent for the decade of the 1970s. At various points in time, the actual inflation rate was in double digits. *Economic Report of the President 1980* (Washington, DC: Government Printing Office, 1980), cited in Thomas K. McCraw, *Prophets of Regulation* (Cambridge: Harvard University Press, 1984), 237.

14. Joskow, "Inflation and Environmental Concern," 323.

15. Id., 313. One traditional pricing structure was the "declining block rate," which meant that as consumption increased, the cost of an additional unit of service declined. In an inflationary period beset by energy shortages, this rate structure would have the affect of encouraging the uneconomic expansion of consumption and unnecessary capacity expansion.

16. MacAvoy claims that regulatory lag increased from an average of 8 months in 1964–1968 to an average of 2 years by 1972–1973. MacAvoy, *The Regulated Industries and the Economy,* 74.

17. *Ibid.*, 67; McCraw, *Prophets of Regulation*, 266. Railroads, of course, had been in trouble for years.

18. Railroads were the primary exception to this pattern. The onus for the long decline of railroads was laid in part at the doorstep of the Interstate Commerce Commission. Thus, widespread industry recognition of the long mal-effects of regulation on the fortunes of railroading made the politics of deregulation of railroads different than those of other infrastructure industries. Railroad corporations and railroad unions largely supported legislation to reform regulation whereas the major corporations and unions in airlines, trucking, and telecommunications vigorously opposed similar reforms in their industries.

Banking was the other industry where the politics of deregulation differed in part from the pattern characteristic of airlines, trucking, and telecommunications. Banking was also characterized by "bypass" incentives. Banking deregulation began when financial services companies such as Merrill Lynch exploited gaps in the bank boundary laws to offer higher than official interest rates and to offer unregulated, bank-like services (partly by means of new communications technologies). But in contrast to the other price-and-entry regulated industries, banking deregulation was supported by big-city money-rich banks and opposed by most other banking institutions. See Robert B. Horwitz, "Understanding Deregulation," *Theory and Society* 15/1–2 (1986), 139–174.

19. Martha Derthick and Paul J. Quirk, *The Politics of Deregulation* (Washington, DC: Brookings Institution, 1985), 58–59; Stephen Breyer, *Regulation and Its Reform* (Cambridge: Harvard University Press, 1982), 208–209.

20. Pertschuk, *Revolt Against Regulation*, 54; Magnuson-Moss Warranty Act, Public Law No. 93-637, 88 Stat. 2183 (1975).

21. See Silk and Vogel, *Ethics and Profits*, especially 42–74.

22. "Business' Most Powerful Lobby in Washington," *Business Week*, December 20, 1976, 63.

The Roundtable was described by David Vogel, perhaps tongue-in-cheek, as a "quasi-Leninist organization," in the sense that it is a hierarchically organized group dedicated to formulating political strategies for "business as a whole." David Vogel, "How Business Responds to Opposition: Corporate Political Strategies in the 1970s," paper delivered to the 1979 Annual Meeting of the American Political Science Association, 22, 24.

23. Pertschuk, *Revolt Against Regulation*, 47–117. As Chairman of the FTC during the Carter Administration, in constant touch with many Congressmen, Pertschuk was in a good position to have a sense of the political agenda and its transformation.

24. Edwin M. Epstein, "An Irony of Electoral Reform," *Regulation*, May/June 1979, 35–41.

By the late 1970s corporations were spending between $850 to $900 million per year on political lobbying. Phyllis S. McGrath, *Redefining Corporate-Federal Relations: A Research Report from the Conference Board* (New York: Conference Board, 1979), 48.

25. Cited in Ann Crittenden, "The Economic Wind's Blowing Toward the Right—For Now," *New York Times*, July 16, 1978, Section 3, at 1. The American Enterprise Institute, shunned for three decades because of its strongly partisan pro-business slant, had 24 employees and a budget of less than $1 million in 1970. By 1978 the staff had grown to 125 with 100 adjunct scholars and a budget of more than $7 million. *Ibid.*, 9.

26. Silk's and Vogel's interviews of chief executive officers in 1974 and 1975 are instructive in this context. Businessmen commonly explained the lack of public confidence in them as a result of their inability to successfully communicate with the public. They saw journalists and university professors as evil culprits in distorting the public's view of business. To rectify that distortion, businessmen saw that it was necessary to enter into the world of ideas—which translated into large corporate outlays to establish what were in effect

institutional bases within academia. *Ethics and Profits,* 102–126; Vogel, "How Business Responds to Opposition," 33–35; also David F. Noble and Nancy E. Pfund, "Business Goes Back to College," *The Nation,* September 20, 1980, 233, 246–252.

27. Some of these AEI studies are cited in chapter 2 at note 48. According to Crittenden, in 1977 AEI held 22 forums and conferences, put out 54 studies, 15 analyses of important legislative proposals, 7 journals and newsletters, a ready-made set of editorials sent regularly to 105 newspapers, public affairs programs carried on more than 300 television stations, and arranged for centers for the display of AEI materials in some 300 college libraries. Crittenden, "The Economic Wind's Blowing Toward the Right," 1, 9.

28. This is not to imply that these economic critiques of regulation were directly "bought," so to speak, by corporate money. What I do wish to convey is that there is a real link between the kinds of academic research which get richly supported and the eventual impact this research has both on the political agenda and on the accepted canons of intellectual discourse. So, while capital did not initiate the reemergence of conservative scholarship, the hefty support of such scholarship assisted its influence and reach immensely. An excellent discussion of this confluence of corporate interests, funding, and academic research—in a different era and concerning a different academic discourse—is Todd Gitlin's analysis of the rise of the dominant paradigm in American communication research. Todd Gitlin, "Media Sociology: The Dominant Paradigm," *Theory and Society* 6 (1978), 205–278.

29. *US News and World Report* claimed that regulation cost $130 billion a year in a 1975 article. " 'The Regulators,' They Cost You $130 Billion a Year," *US News and World Report,* June 30, 1975, 24–25. Though the slightly lower and more widely publicized estimate of $100 billion is normally associated with Murray Weidenbaum, it was reported first in Robert DeFina, *Public and Private Expenditures for Federal Regulation of Business,* Working Paper No. 27, Center for the Study of American Business, washington University, St. Louis, November 1977, mimeo. The estimate later was reworked and included in Murray L. Weidenbaum and Robert DeFina, *The Cost of Federal Regulation of Economic Activity* (Washington, DC: American Enterprise Institute, May 1978), Reprint No. 88.

30. See the connection drawn between regulation and inflation and productivity decline in studies by several influential business policy groups, including the Committee for Economic Development's study, *Fighting Inflation and Promoting Growth: A Statement on National Policy by the Research and Policy Committee of the Committee for Economic Development* (New York: Committee for Economic Development, 1976), 57–59; also the discussion of costs and benefits of regulation in the Conference Board's symposium, *Answers to Inflation and Recession: Economic Policies for a Modern Society,* Albert T. Sommers (ed.) (Washington, DC: The Conference Board, 1975), 65–70.

In 1978 the Business Roundtable retained the accounting firm of Arthur Andersen & Co. to develop a study which measured certain "incremental" costs (i.e., the costs of regulation to society in waste and nonproductiveness) incurred by 48 Business Roundtable member companies in one year to comply with the regulatory requirements of six major federal government agencies and programs. The 1977 incremental costs for 48 companies to comply with just six federal agencies (EPA, EEOC, OSHA, FTC, Department of Energy, and the Employee Retirement Income Security Act) were more than $2.62 billion. Arthur Andersen & Co., *Cost of Government Regulation Study for Business Roundtable* (Chicago: author, 1979).

Whereas these business-funded studies essentially attempted to directly tie regulation with low economic productivity, there is evidence that several Western European nations incurred regulatory and social welfare costs higher on a percentage basis than those of the United States, and whose economic productivity rates were also higher than those of the United States.

31. OMB Watch, "OMB Control of Rulemaking: The End of Public Access" (Wash-

ington, DC: author, 1985); George C. Eads and Michael Fix, *Relief or Reform? Reagan's Regulatory Dilemma* (Washington, DC: Urban Institute Press, 1984).

According to Eads and Fix, the process did have indirect benefits. First, it persuaded EPA (the agency most affected by the Quality of Life Review) that it needed to have its own in-house analytical capacity. Second, the review process induced the agency to become smarter (that is to say, less confrontational) about issuing regulations. That is, it led EPA to begin informal consultation with industry and other affected agencies earlier in the regulatory development process in order to head off controversy at the formal interagency review stage. Eads and Fix, *Relief or Reform?*, 50.

32. Executive Order 11081, November 27, 1974.

33. "White House Conference on Domestic Affairs and Inflation: The President's Remarks at the Conference in Concord, New Hampshire," April 18, 1975, in *Weekly Compilation of Presidential Documents* 11/17 (April 25, 1975), 104. Ford's figures were based on information carelessly thrown together (and subsequently repudiated) by OMB. Eads and Fix, *Relief or Reform?*, 28.

34. See the series of publications of task force reports, study papers, and memoranda on several issues in government regulation edited by Paul W. MacAvoy, under the series title, *Ford Administration Papers on Regulatory Reform*. Individual titles include: *OSHA Safety Regulation: Report of the Presidential Task Force* (Washington, DC: American Enterprise Institute, 1977); *Federal Energy Administration Regulation: Report of the Presidential Task Force* (Washington, DC: American Enterprise Institute, 1977); *Deregulation of Cable Television* (Washington, DC: American Enterprise Institute, 1977).

35. All quotations from Arthur Andersen & Co., *Cost of Government Regulation Study for the Business Roundtable*, at 12-5.

36. On the proposed Consumer Protection Agency, see U.S. House of Representatives, 95th Congress 1st Session, Committee on Government Operations, Subcommittee on Legislation and National Security, Hearings on Proposed Agency for Consumer Protection (H.R. 6116), April 20, 21, 1977 (Washington, DC: Government Printing Office, 1977); also American Enterprise Institute for Public Policy Research, "The Proposed Agency for Consumer Advocacy" (Washington, DC: author, 1975).

On labor law reform, see U.S. Senate, 95th Congress, 2nd Session, Committee on Human Resources, Hearings on Labor Law Reform Act of 1978 (H.R. 8410), June 28, 1978 (Washington, DC: Government Printing Office, 1978); also, American Enterprise Institute for Public Policy Research, "Labor Law Reform?: A Round Table" (Washington, DC: author, 1978).

On Federal Trade Commission Improvement Act of 1980, see account of Pertschuk, *Revolt Against Regulation*.

37. See Executive Order 12044, March 24, 1978.

38. Executive Order No. 12291, issued February 19, 1981, codified at 3 C.F.R. 127 (1982); Executive Order No. 12498, issued January 4, 1985, 50 Fed. Reg. 1036 (1985); Paperwork Reduction Act of 1980, Public Law No. 96–511, 94 Stat. 2812 (1980); "OMB Control of Rulemaking," 5–15.

Budget cuts of regulatory agencies primarily affect enforcement. Thus, even if the agencies retain their mandates, they are often inhibited from carrying them out. On the extent of regulatory rollback consequent to Reagan policies, see Martin Tolchin and Susan Tolchin, *Dismantling America: The Rush to Deregulate* (Boston: Houghton-Mifflin, 1983). However, on the inability of the Reagan Administration to secure any lasting legislation that would deregulate health and safety agencies, see Eads and Fix, *Relief or Reform?*.

39. Interview, Peter Zschiesche, Business Agent, International Association of Machinists, District 50, San Diego, California, March 28, 1986.

Notwithstanding a set of headline-grabbing fines that OSHA imposed on several corporations in 1986–87, many informed observers argue that since the Reagan Administration came to power, OSHA has been gutless in protecting workplace health and safety. Two recent studies of the agency (invited by OSHA itself) concluded that OSHA's rule making faces "total paralysis," and that its enforcement program was characterized by "systemic organizational weaknesses." The big fines imposed on Union Carbide ($1.4 million), Chrysler ($1.5 million) and IBP ($2.59 million) were for recordkeeping violations, not for safety and health violations *per se*. And if all goes to form, those big fines will be settled for less than a third of the original amounts. John Holusha, "US Fines Chrysler $1.5 Million, Citing Workers' Exposure to Peril," *The New York Times,* July 7, 1987, 1, 10; Phillip Shabecoff, "Record Fine Urged on Injury Reports," *The New York Times,* July 22, 1987, 1, 24; William Glaberson, "Is OSHA Falling Down on the Job?," *The New York Times,* August 2, 1987, Sec. 3, 1, 6.

40. See U.S. House, 98th Congress, 1st Session, Committee on Interstate and Foreign Commerce, Subcommittee on Energy Conservation and Power, Hearings on H.R. 2510: *Nuclear Licensing and Regulatory Reform Act of 1983* (Washington, DC: Government Printing Office, 1983).

41. Natural Resources Defense Council, Inc. v. EPA, 683 F.2d 752 (3d Cir. 1982); Farmworker Justice Fund, Inc. v. Brock, 811 F.2d 613 (D.C. Cir. 1987); Union of Concerned Scientists v. Nuclear Regulatory Commission, Nos. 85-1757, 86-1219, U.S. Court of Appeals, District of Columbia Circuit, Slip Opinion, August 4, 1987.

In Natural Resources Defense Council, Inc. v. Herrington, 768 F.2d 1355 (D.C. Cir. 1985), the court vacated the weakened rules the Reagan Department of Energy had promulgated on mandatory energy-efficiency standards in eight types of household appliances. The court held that the agency adopted tests for significant energy savings which violated Congressional intent. The agency failed to determine maximum technologically feasible improvements in efficiency for covered products and limited the technologies it was willing to consider for standards without sufficient explanation. The agency violated the Energy Policy and Conservation Act by refusing to allow interested persons a meaningful opportunity to question Department employees who participated in rule making. The Department's decision not to issue an environmental assessment or environment impact statement was arbitrary and capricious.

In International Brotherhood of Teamsters v. United States, 735 F.2d 1525 (D.C. Cir. 1984), the court vacated part of Federal Highway Administration policy because the agency acted arbitrarily and capriciously in omitting items of information from record-keeping requirements for truck drivers. In Farmers Union Central Exchange, Inc. v. Federal Energy Regulatory Commission, 734 F.2d 1486 (D.C. Cir. 1984), the court remanded FERC-set oil pipeline rate ceilings because the Commission failed both to give due consideration to responsible alternative rate-making methodologies and to offer a reasoned explanation in support of its own chosen methodology.

In Public Citizen v. Steed, 733 F.2d 93 (D.C. Cir. 1984), the court vacated the NHTSA's indefinite suspension of the tire grading program. In stinging language, the court declared the agency's attempt to sabotage the grading program by "compulsive perfectionism" as arbitrary and capricious. In New England Coalition on Nuclear Pollution v. Nuclear Regulatory Commission, 727 F.2d 1127 (D.C. Cir. 1984), the court remanded the NRC's amended rules of practice for domestic licensing proceedings, because they were not supported by accompanying statement of basis and purpose.

In ILGWU v. Donovan, 722 F.2d 795 (D.C. Cir. 1983), the court reversed the Department of Labor's rescission of restrictions on homework in the knitted outerwear industry. The court declared that the Secretary's failure to consider alternatives to the elimination of homework restrictions, failure to give sufficient consideration to the ability of the Department of Labor to enforce the Fair Labor Standards Act without homework restrictions, failure to consider differences between rural and urban areas, and failure to consider adequately the possibility that employment increase resulting from recission would be offset by economic injury to factory workers rendered the Secretary's decision arbitrary and capricious.

In State Farm Mutual Automobile Insurance Co. v. Department of Transportation, 680 F.2d 206 (D.C. Cir. 1982), *vacated on other ground sub nom.* Motor Vehicles Manufacturers Association v. State Farm Mutual Auto Insurance, 463 U.S. 29 (1983), the court vacated as arbitrary and capricious the NHTSA's recision of the passive restraint (auto airbags) standard, because the agency did not clearly justify its shift in regulatory policy. In Action of Smoking and Health v. CAB, 699 F.2d 1209 (1983), the court vacated CAB regulations which relaxed protections afforded nonsmokers aboard aircraft. The court declared that an agency's obligation to explain its actions is not reduced where it rescinds rather than promulgates a regulation, and that the Board failed to state sufficiently its basis for vacating a portion of a prior regulation and rejecting several proposed regulations.

In Environmental Defense Fund, Inc. v. Gorsuch, 713 F.2d 802 (D.C. Cir. 1983), the court vacated a decision of the EPA to defer processing of operating permits for existing hazardous waste incinerators and storage impoundments. The EPA's deferral amounted to a suspension of a regulation without notice or comment in violation of the Administrative Procedure Act.

With the exception of the *State Farm* case, *certiorari* was granted in none of the above cases.

42. Natural Resources Defense Council, Inc. v. EPA, 683 F.2d 752 (3rd Cir. 1982).

43. In *Motor Vehicle Manufacturers Association of United States, Inc. v. State Farm Mutual Automobile Insurance Co.* the Supreme Court held that the arbitrary and capricious standard of judicial review applied to regulation and deregulation alike. 463 U.S. 29 (1982). This meant that judicial review of regulatory inaction and delay would tend to be substantive. That is, the courts would seek to bind the agencies to their mandates and congressional purpose. An agency's findings of fact could be reviewed, its policy choices examined, and its motives questioned. In *Sierra Club v. Gorsuch,* for example, the court opined, in reference to EPA delays, "To accept EPA's proposal for further, indefinite, and virtually open-ended extension of the time for compliance, without a more convincing demonstration of evident impossibility, would be to, in effect, repeal the Congressional mandate." 551 F. Supp. 785 (N.D. Cal. 1982), at 789. See Merrick B. Garland, "Deregulation and Judicial Review," *Harvard Law Review* 98/3 (January 1985), 507–591.

44. ILGWU v. Donovan, 722 F.2d 795 (D.C. Cir. 1983), at 828.

45. Action for Children's Television v. Federal Communications Commission, 821 F.2d 741 (1987).

For court rejection of some New Deal agency deregulation, see, for instance, General Chemical Corp., et al. v. United States, 817 F.2d 844 (D.C. Cir. 1987). In this case, the court ruled that the ICC's determination that railroads were not market dominant in relevant soda ash markets was arbitrary and capricious, because its analysis of geographic competition was internally inconsistent and inadequately explained. In Arizona Public Service Co. v. United States, 742 F.2d 644 (D.C. Cir. 1984), the court vacated an ICC Review Board's decision on market dominance because the decision was "not the product of reasoned decision making required by the Administrative Procedure Act." In Brae Corp. v. United States, 740 F.2d 1023 (D.C. Cir. 1984), the court vacated part of the ICC's implementation of the Staggers Rail Act deregulation on the ground that the Commission "failed to adequately consider" certain facts.

Even the FCC's deregulatory actions, which have fared best of all, have been vacated when they have eliminated record and log keeping. Office of Communication of the United

Church of Christ v. FCC, 707 F.2d 1209 (D.C. Cir. 1983). The courts have vacated FCC deregulatory decisions when these would undermine the Commission's basic requirement to protect the public interest. See, for instance, National Association of Broadcasters v. FCC, 740 F.2d 1190 (D.C. Cir. 1984), and United States Satellite Broadcasting Co. v. FCC, 740 F.2d 1177 (D.C. Cir. 1984), in which the court refused to exempt satellite programming technologies from the broadcast regulations set forth in the Communications Act.

46. See Joan Claybrook et al., *Retreat from Safety: Reagan's Attack on America's Health* (New York: Pantheon, 1984); Tolchin & Tolchin, *Dismantling America.*

47. See, for example, Abner J. Mikva, "How Should the Courts Treat Administrative Agencies?," *The American University Law Review* 36/1 (Fall 1986), 1–10; Kenneth W. Starr, "Judicial Review in the Post-*Chevron* Era," *Yale Journal on Regulation* 3/2 (Spring 1986), 283–312; Symposium on Administrative Law, "The Uneasy Constitutional Status of the Administrative Agencies," *The American University Law Review* 36/2 (Winter 1987).

48. Chevron v. Natural Resources Defense Council, 467 U.S. 837 (1984).

49. See, for instance, Peter Steinfels, *The Neoconservatives: The Men Who Are Changing America's Politics* (New York: Simon & Schuster, 1979).

50. It is in this regard that I believe Michael Pertschuk's analysis is somewhat flawed. Pertschuk asserts that the movement to deregulate rate-regulated industries was an ideological gambit by capital to afix a "public interest face" on anti-regulatory actions that clearly favored business. He implies that the deregulation of airlines and trucking was an easy first step in a carefully mapped-out strategy by capital to dismantle social regulation. Though the deregulation of airlines and trucking may indeed have provided some ideological respectability to subsequent attacks on social regulation, Pertschuk presents no evidence to indicate such a strategy on the part of capital. Some business lobbies did support deregulation—such as the support of airline deregulation by the National Association of Manufacturers and Sears Roebuck. But I see no clear evidence that capital as a whole mobilized against economic regulation. If anything, specific business support for the dismantling of economic regulation fit the traditional pattern of particular businesses fighting for competitive advantage *via* the regulatory or legislative process. Pertschuk, *Revolt Against Regulation*, 62–64, 72.

51. Derthick & Quirk, *The Politics of Deregulation*, 19–28, 237–258.

52. In the Matter of Prescription of Procedures for Separating and Allocating Plant Investment, Operating Expenses, Taxes, and Reserves Between the Intrastate and Interstate Operations of Telephone Companies, 25 FCC 2d 123 (1970). See chapter 8 *infra.*

53. Breyer, *Regulation and Its Reform*, 223; Walter Adams, "The Rocky Road to Deregulation," *Deregulation: Appraisal Before the Fact*, Thomas G. Gies & Werner Sichel (eds.) (Ann Arbor: Graduate School of Business Administration, University of Michigan, 1982), 121–122.

54. Cited in MacAvoy, *The Regulated Industries and the Economy*, 60.

55. The data on the actual number of large shippers that went over to private carriage are not very good. Most of the evidence is anecdotal, but, according to John V. Wells, transportation economist at the General Accounting Office, the general impression of the economists who studied trucking in the 1970s is that private carriage incentives were there and some number of large shippers went over to self-supply. John V. Wells, interview with author, December 10, 1986.

56. Breyer, *Regulation and Its Reform*, 206–209. I must acknowledge that too much can be made of the *rational* nature of administrative behavior. As we saw in earlier empirical chapters on FCC actions, often the Commission made license grants or came to decisions in ways which cannot be explained as protecting the long-term interests of the industry or as maintaining organizational integrity. Derthick and Quirk discuss the shift of some within the

CAB staff to favor deregulation precisely because they were appalled at and frustrated with the bald arbitrariness of many decisions. Derthick & Quirk, 71–95.

57. U.S. Senate, 94th Congress, 1st Session, Committee on the Judiciary, Subcommittee on Administrative Practice and Procedure, *Oversight of Civil Aeronautics Board Practices and Procedures* (Washington, DC: Government Printing Office, 1975), Vol. 1, table at 502.

58. James R. Snitzler and Robert J. Byrnes, "Interstate Trucking of Fresh and Frozen Poultry Under Agricultural Exemption," U.S. Department of Agriculture (Washington, DC: Government Printing Office, 1958).

59. Derthick and Quirk put it thus: "What ultimately, in the mid-1970s, made the economists' arguments relevant to politics were events that no one could have foreseen: the development of severe inflation, the rise of consumerism, and a vague but widely diffused disaffection with a government that seemed to grow uncontrollably and irreversibly." *The Politics of Deregulation,* at 56.

60. *Ibid.,* 106.

61. *Oversight of Civil Aeronautics Board Practices and Procedures,* Vol. 1, at 1.

62. See especially the Air Transport Association of America's exhibits on "The Consequences of Deregulation," in *Oversight of Civil Aeronautics Board Practices and Procedures,* Vol. 1, 122–380; also, Derthick & Quirk, *The Politics of Deregulation,* 122.

63. McCraw, *Prophets of Regulation,* 273–282; Bradley Behrman, "Civil Aeronautics Board," *The Politics of Regulation,* James Q. Wilson, (ed.) (New York: Basic Books, 1980), 75–120; Derthick and Quirk, *The Politics of Deregulation,* 58–95, 148–164; Bailey, Graham & Kaplan, *Deregulating the Airlines,* 12–37.

64. Airline Deregulation Act of 1978, Public Law No. 95-504, 92 Stat. 1705. Legislation to deregulate trucking passed in 1980. Motor Carrier Act of 1980, Public Law No. 96-296, 94 Stat. 793. Legislation to deregulate aspects of banking passed in 1980. Depository Institutions Deregulation and Monetary Control Act of 1980, Public Law No. 96-221, 94 Stat. 132.

65. John E. Moss et al v. Civil Aeronautics Board, 430 F.2d 891 (D.C. Cir. 1970), at 893.

66. Id., at 900.

67. Continental Airlines v. Civil Aeronautics Board, 519 F.2d 944 (D.C. Cir. 1975), at 944.

68. P. C. White Truck Line v. ICC, 551 F.2d 1326 (D.C. Cir. 1977).

69. See, for instance, Office of Communication of the United Church of Christ v. Federal Communications Commission, 707 F.2d 1413 (D.C. Cir. 1983), a decision in which the Court of Appeals approved the deregulation of commercial radio in favor of marketplace forces. And in FCC v. WNCN Listeners Guild, 450 U.S. 582 (1981), the Supreme Court upheld FCC policy (against a long series of Court of Appeals reversals) not to interfere with licensee discretion and market forces regarding radio station formats.

## Chapter 8. The Deregulation of Telecommunications

1. Remark attributed to FCC Chairman Richard Wiley by Henry Geller (FCC General Counsel, appointed 1964; Assistant Secretary for Communications and Information, and Administrator of National Telecommunications and Information Administration, appointed 1977). Geller interview with author, March 24, 1985. The remark seems apropos as an entrée into the black hole of common carrier matters.

2. Gerald W. Brock, *The Telecommunications Industry: The Dynamics of Market Structure* (Cambridge: Harvard University Press, 1981), 201.

3. FCC, *Network Broadcasting,* published as U.S. House of Representatives, 85th Con-

gress, 2d Session, Report No. 1297 (Washington, DC: Government Printing Office, 1958), Ch 11; FCC, *Annual Report,* 1951: 42–43. Also recall that AT&T had difficulty meeting the demand for new telephone service and service regrades through the middle 1950s.

4. Many of these observations were introduced into scholarly discussion by Dan Schiller in his fine book, *Telematics and Government* (Norwood, NJ: Ablex Publishing Co., 1982).

5. Id.

6. In the Matter of Allocation of Microwave Frequencies in the Band Above 890 Mc, 27 FCC 359 (1959), at 388. (Hereinafter, *Above 890.*) In the reconsideration, AT&T argued that frequency allocations should for private users should be suspended until the frequencies needed for nascent space communications became known.

7. Id., at 412.

8. Id. at 414.

9. In the Matter of Amer. Tel. & Tel. Co. Long Line Dept. revisions of Tariff FCC No. 260 Private Line Service Series 5000 (TELPAK), FCC Docket No. 18128, 61 FCC 2d 587 (1976), recon., 64 FCC 2d 971 (1977), further recon., 67 FCC 2d 1414 (1978).

Former FCC Commissioner Kenneth Cox, testifying before a House subcommittee in his new capacity as vice-president of MCI, asserted that TELPAK bulk discounts ran from 51 to 85 percent off. The discount was so great for large private line systems that there was no incentive to build one's own. U.S. House, 94th Congress, 1st Session, Committee on Interstate and Foreign Commerce, Subcommittee on Communications, *Domestic Common Carrier Regulation,* Hearings, November 10, 11, 13, 18, 1975 (Washington, DC: Government Printing Office, 1975), at 122.

TELPAK and other associated corporate moves later would be seen as part of the company's efforts to illegally thwart competition, and would constitute evidence in the government's 1974 antitrust suit against AT&T. For instance, an August 1964 study showed that TELPAK was the least profitable of AT&Ts various long-distance services. It earned 0.3 percent in contrast to the 10 percent earned by the main long-distance services. Cited in Brock, *The Telecommunications Industry,* 210.

10. In Re Applications of Microwave Communications, Inc., 18 FCC 2d 953 (1969), recon. denied, 21 FCC 2d 825 (1970), at 965.

11. Joseph C. Goulden, *Monopoly* (New York: George Putnam's Sons, 1968); John Patrick Phillips, *Ma Bell's Millions* (New York: Vantage Press, 1970).

12. MCI's role—and duplicity—in the breakup of AT&T is a main focus of Steve Coll's book, *The Deal of the Century: The Breakup of AT&T* (New York: Atheneum, 1986). Coll argues that William McGowan, an ambitious and tough entrepreneur, bought MCI in 1968 with the clear intention of breaking AT&T's legal monopoly in long-distance service. In Coll's history, McGowan retained an "army" of insider Washington lawyers in the effort to stage a three-front attack (Congress, the FCC, and the courts) on AT&T. And notwithstanding the David vs. Goliath image, MCI had significant financial backing by investment banks and telecommunications equipment suppliers.

13. Concurring statement of Commissioner Nicholas Johnson, 18 FCC 2d 953 (1969), at 978. Johnson's animosity toward AT&T was quite strong. In a 1969 decision to reduce AT&T long-distance tariffs, Johnson cast the lone dissent because he thought the reduction should have been greater. He bitterly denounced the Commission's policy of continuing surveillance. In the Matter of AT&T Revisions to AT&T Tariff FCC No. 263, Long-Distance Message Telecommunications Service, 20 FCC 2d 886 (1969). His bitter dissent brought a nasty rebuke from fellow Commission liberal, Kenneth Cox.

However, Johnson's support of MCI cannot be attributed solely to his populistic antipathy to AT&T. This was not the only instance of Johnson's defection from regulatory protectionism. As we shall see in the text *infra,* Johnson supported the liberalization of entry for cable television in 1970.

14. In the Matter of Establishment of Policies and Procedures for Consideration of Applications to Provide Specialized Common Carrier Services in the Domestic Public Point-to-Point Microwave Radio Service and Proposed Amendments to parts 21, 43 and 61 of the Commission's Rules, 29 FCC 2d 870 (1971), recon. denied, 31 FCC 2d 1106 (1971), at 910.

15. Bell System Offerings, 46 FCC 2d 413 (1974), *aff'd sub nom.* Bell Tel. Co. v. FCC, 503 F.2d 1250 (3rd Cir. 1974), *cert. denied,* 422 U.S. 1026 (1975).

The ruling which mandated interconnection was in keeping with the traditional non-discrimination principle of common carrier law. Again, these restrictive actions on the part of AT&T were used as evidence of the corporation's violation of the antitrust laws in the suit which commenced in 1974.

16. Packet Communications Inc., 43 FCC 2d 922 (1973); Graphnet Systems Inc., 44 FCC 2d 800 (1974); Telenet Communications Corp., 46 FCC 2d 680 (1974); In the Matter of Regulatory Policies Concerning Resale and Shared Use of Common Carrier Services and Facilities, 60 FCC 2d 261 (1976), recon. 62 FCC 2d 588 (1977), *aff'd sub nom.* AT&T v. FCC, 572 F.2d 17 (2nd Cir. 1978), *cert. denied,* 439 U.S. 875 (1978).

17. This is one of Dan Schiller's central points in *Telematics and Government.* And while the point is unimpeachable, the inferences Schiller draws from it underscore what I consider to be a weakness in his overall argument. Schiller takes the breakup of AT&T to be primarily a function of large telecommunications users' ultimate victory over AT&T. The only way a corporation as powerful as AT&T can be defeated is to be battled by a larger coalition of powerful corporations. The regulatory arena is taken as merely an arena for corporate struggle. While this conception of the regulatory arena may be true to a significant degree, I believe it slights both the organizational autonomy of the FCC and the salience of the interrelated issues that dogged regulation from the beginning, namely, the antitrust problems and the rate-making quandaries. It tends to reduce the complex interrelation of forces and constraints and court decisions and accidents into a single coherent cause. If the problem with Derthick's and Quirk's account of deregulation in *The Politics of Deregulation* is that they incorrectly downplay the economic (and other) underpinnings of political choice, the problem with Schiller's analysis is that the economic underpinnings become primary and controlling. Political choices essentially become stand-ins, smokescreens for economic battles.

18. This is essentially the position of the British Telecommunications Union Committee in its pamphlet, *The American Experience . . . A Report on the Dilemma of Telecommunications in the USA* (London: author, 1983).

19. Domestic Communications-Satellite Facilities ("DOMSAT"), First Report and Order, 22 FCC 2d 86 (1970); Second Report and Order, 35 FCC 2d 844 (1972), *aff'd sub nom.* Network Project v. FCC, 511 F.2d 786 (D.C. Cir. 1975).

20. Fred Friendly, *Due to Circumstances Beyond Our Control. . .* (New York: Vintage Books, 1967), 309.

21. *Ibid.,* 309–318. Educational television was unable to afford AT&T signal carriage, hence it could not constitute a network.

22. Hush-a-Phone Corp. v. United States, 238 F.2d 266 (D.C. Cir. 1956). Interestingly, once again this was a decision of the DC Circuit Court of Appeals, written by Judge David Bazelon.

23. In the Matter of Use of the Carterfone Device in Message Toll Telephone Service, 13 FCC 2d 420 (1968), recon. denied, 14 FCC 2d 571 (1968).

24. *Hush-a-Phone Corp. v. United States,* at 269.

25. Hannibal and Saint Joseph Railroad Co. v. Swift, 12 Wall 262 (1870); Philadelphia and Reading Railroad Co. v. Derby, 14 How. 468 (1852).

Moreover, the separation between medium and use seems a reasonable extension of the principle of the separation between medium and message—a principle which embodies the traditional concern with the protection of freedom of speech.

26. The other legal foundation underlying Hush-a-Phone was a 1936 antitrust decision which declared illegal IBM's compulsory tie-in between its tabulating cards and tabulating machines. International Business Machines Corp. v. U.S., 298 U.S. 131 (1936).

27. President's Task Force on Communications Policy, *Final Report* (Washington, DC: Government Printing Office, 1968).

28. The Network Project, *OTP*, Notebook No. 4, (New York: author, 1973), 14–17.

Commissioner Kenneth Cox claimed that the White House memorandum on domestic satellites had changed the thinking of both FCC staff and commissioners. Bruce Thorpe, "Office of Telecommunications Policy Speaks For President," *National Journal* 3/7 (February 13, 1971), 345.

29. Note, for instance, the alliance between consumer groups and new telecommunications companies to lower AT&T's rate of return. In this case, the FCC agreed that AT&T had not demonstrated that it required a rate of return of 9.5 percent. The FCC reduced the percentage to 8.25. In the Matter of AT&T Charges for Interstate Telephone Service, ATT Transmittals 10989 and 11027, 41 FCC 2d 389 (1973). Nonetheless, both Ralph Nader and the MCI Corporation appealed this case to the DC Court of Appeals. Nader's appeal brought front and center the Western Electric issue once again, claiming that the FCC had refused to account for the earnings of Western Electric in calculating AT&Ts overall rate of return. MCI claimed that the FCC abused its discretion in several instances. Nader v. Federal Communications Commission, 520 F.2d 182 (D.C. Cir. 1975).

In partial support of Steve Coll's contention that MCI waged primarily a legal, rather than an economic, battle against AT&T, see the Court's dismissal of MCI's arguments. The Court describes MCI's brief as "singularly unenlightening," "virtually devoid of authority" (at 198).

30. In the Matter of MCI Telecommunications Corp., 34 R.R. 2d 539 (1975), 37 R.R. 2d 1339 (1976), *rev'd sub nom.* MCI Telecommunications Corp. v. FCC, 561 F.2d 356 (D.C. Cir. 1977), *cert. denied sub nom.* FCC v. MCI Telecommunications Corp., 434 U.S. 1040 (1978).

31. MCI Telecommunications Corp v. FCC, 561 F.2d 356 (D.C. Cir. 1977), at 379.

32. Id., at 380.

33. Id., at 380. Note, again, the tone of the decision. Like *Moss v. CAB* and others of this period, the court clearly intimates that the historically close relation between the regulatory agency and the regulated industry may border on capture and is contrary to the public interest. Moss v. CAB, 430 F.2d 891 (D.C. Cir. 1970).

34. This point was emphasized in interviews by both Henry Geller (FCC General Counsel, appointed 1964; Assistant Secretary for Communications and Information, and Administrator of National Telecommunications and Information Administration, appointed 1977) and Bernard Strassburg (Chief FCC Common Carrier Bureau, 1966–1973). Geller interview with author, March 24, 1985; Strassburg interview with author, March 25, 1985.

35. In the Matter of Prescription of Procedures for Separating and Allocating Plant Investment, Operating Expenses, Taxes, and Reserves Between the Intrastate and Interstate Operations of Telephone Companies, Petition of the National Association of Regulatory Utility Commissioners to Amend Part 67 of the Code of Federal Regulations, 25 FCC 2d 123 (1970).

The Ozark formula shifted about 1 percent per year of non-traffic sensitive costs to toll from 1971 to 1984. As a result, the increase in local telephone rates from 1967 to 1984 was the fourth lowest among all goods surveyed in the Consumer Price Index.

36. In the Matter of Regulatory and Policy Problems Presented by the Interdependence of Computer and Communications Services and Facilities, First Computer Inquiry, FCC Docket No. 16979 (Notice of inquiry November 10, 1966), final decision 28 FCC 2d 267 (1971), *aff'd in part sub nom.* GTE Service Corp. v. FCC, 474 F.2d 724 (2nd Cir. 1973).

37. In the Matter of Amendment of Section 64.702 of the Commission's Rules and Regulations, Second Computer Inquiry, Docket No. 20828 (Notice of inquiry and proposed rulemaking 1976), final decision, 77 FCC 2d 384 (1980); R. M. Frieden, "The Computer Inquiries: Mapping the Communications/Data Processing Terrain," *Federal Communications Law Journal* 33/1 (Winter 1981), 55–115.

38. In the Matter of Amer. Tel. & Tel. Co. Long Line Dept. Revisions of Tariff FCC No. 260 Private Line Service Series 5000 (TELPAK), 61 FCC 2d 587 (1976), recon., 64 FCC 2d 971 (1977), further recon., 67 FCC 2d 1414 (1978).

39. Leland L. Johnson, "Monopoly and Regulation in Telecommunications," in *Communications for Tomorrow: Policy Perspectives for the 1980s,* Glen O. Robinson (ed.) (New York: Praeger, 1978), at 140. Echoing this conclusion was the Justice Department in the presentation of its case against AT&T in the government's 1974 antitrust case. Justice pointed to AT&T's control over cost information and its demonstrated ability to frustrate any attempt to penetrate the relationship between its costs, by whatever definition, and its prices. United States Department of Justice, Plaintiff's Memorandum in Opposition to Defendants' Motion for Involuntary Dismissal Under Rule 41 (b) in United States v. American Telephone and Telegraph Company, Civil Action No. 74–1698, August 16, 1981. Cited in *Decision to Divest: Major Documents in U.S. v. AT&T, 1974–1984,* Christopher H. Sterling, Jill F. Kasle, and Katherine T. Glakas (eds.) (Washington, DC: Communications Press, Inc., 1986), Vol. 2, 757–857.

40. Justice Department career lawyers felt the case could be reopened. Justice held meetings with Hart's subcommittee staff. See the extremely interesting, though somewhat anecdotal account of Steve Coll, *The Deal of the Century,* 53–72.

41. In the Matter of Amendment of Section 64.702 of the Commission's Rules and Regulations (Second Computer Inquiry), 77 FCC 2d 384 (1980). See the excellent discussion of this in Schiller, *Telematics and Government,* 84–90.

42. John deButts, address to the 1973 annual convention of the National Association of Regulatory Utility Commissioners, Seattle, Washington, September 20, 1973, entitled, "An Unusual Obligation." Printed in Alvin von Auw, *Heritage and Destiny: Reflections on the Bell System in Transition* (New York: Praeger, 1983), 422–432.

43. FCC, *Report by the Federal Communications Commission on Domestic Telecommunications Policies,* September 27, 1976 (Washington, DC: FCC, 1976).

44. Ferris enlarged the functions of the FCC's Office of Plans and Policy. Nina Cornell, an economist critical of traditional public utility regulation, headed that office. Philip L. Verveer, who initially drafted the Justice Department's lawsuit against AT&T and had been lead counsel for Justice in the preparation of the suit, was named chief of the Common Carrier Bureau in 1979.

45. *Telecommunications Reports,* Vol. 45, November 12, 1979, 5. Cited in Derthick and Quirk, *The Politics of Deregulation,* 89.

46. deButts, "An Unusual Obligation."

47. See Jeremy Tunstall, *Communications Deregulation: The Unleashing of America's Communications Industry* (London: Basil Blackwell, 1986), 99–101, 228–229. Tunstall's analysis of the breakup of AT&T and of telecommunications deregulation in general, while perceptive in parts, is conducted at too anecdotal a level to be really instructive. The large

number of interviews of Washington "insiders" has limited value because Tunstall fails to develop an adequate theoretical structure of regulation or the politics of deregulation. *Communications Deregulation* provides no sense as to how and why deregulation in telecommunications was related to deregulation in other fields. Because of this, the reader is left with a mistaken impression that deregulation was largely a matter of the politics of personalities. The same problem also characterizes Steve Coll's *The Deal of the Century*, but that book uses its interviews so well that it illuminates many of the details around the Justice Department's antitrust suit and subsequent consent decree agreement with AT&T.

48. See, for example, the testimony given against AT&T and the restoration of monopoly in telecommunications by liberal Congressmen such as Senator Gary Hart, FCC members, corporate executives, academicians, and a spokesman for the Consumer Federation of America in U.S. Senate, 95th Congress, 1st Session, Committee on Commerce, Science, and Transportation, Subcommittee on Communications, Hearings on *Domestic Telecommunications Common Carrier Policies,* March 21, 22, 23, 28, 1977 (Washington, DC: Government Printing Office, 1977).

49. U.S. House, 95th Congress, 1st Session, Committee on Interstate and Foreign Commerce, Subcommittee on Communications, *Options Papers Prepared by the Staff for Use by the Subcommittee on Communications,* Committee Print 95-13 (Washington, DC: Government Printing Office, 1977).

50. The settlement exploration of 1979 foundered on internal Justice Department squabbles over turf. The 1980 talks fell through in part because of timing. Judge Harold Greene, the Federal District Court Judge in whose court the *U.S. v. AT&T* case would be tried, denied the parties' request to postpone the trial (whose start was literally days away). Justice and AT&T needed additional time to hammer out the actual terms and details of a settlement agreement. But Judge Greene, who inherited the case in August 1978, after a 3-year jurisdictional battle that resolved that the case should be tried in federal court (rather than at the FCC, as AT&T had maintained), was committed to a speedy trial. The Justice Department could not guarantee that a settlement would be reached, and the incoming Reagan Administration might scotch the deal anyway. Nonetheless, the settlement talks proceeded through the start of the trial. The Justice Department withdrew from the deal when the top Justice lawyers (including incoming Antitrust division chief William F. Baxter) became convinced that the equal access rules for interconnection could not work. Baxter, a conservative law professor, but, crucially (and in keeping with the deregulation pattern), a free-market ideologue, asserted to reporters that he would litigate the case "to the eyeballs," because separating the regulated from unregulated portions of an industry was economically "correct." This put Baxter totally at odds with many key members of the Reagan Administration vis-à-vis the AT&T case. See the marvelous recounting of these events in Coll, *The Deal of the Century,* 135–189; also Judge Greene's history of the case in his Opinion on the Modification of Final Judgment, U.S. v. AT&T, 552 F. Supp. 131 (D.D.C. 1982).

51. U.S. Senate, 97th Congress, 1st & 2nd Sessions, Committee on the Judiciary, Hearings on *The Department of Justice Oversight of the United States v. American Telephone and Telegraph Lawsuit,* August 6, 1981, and January 25, 1982 (Serial No. J-97-53), part 1 (Washington, DC: Government Printing Office, 1982), statement of Malcolm Baldridge, at 11.

52. Id., statement of William H. Taft, IV, at 51-52.

53. U.S. Senate, 97th Congress, 2nd Session, Committee on Commerce, Science and Transportation, Hearings on *AT&T Proposed Settlement,* January 25 and February 4, 1982 (Washington, DC: Government Printing Office, 1982), at 39–42.

54. Coll, *The Deal of the Century,* 211–229. Note, again, the consequential differences between normal business Republicanism's antagonism toward regulation (in the personage of

Secretary of Commerce Malcolm Baldridge) and the hostility toward regulation by free-market economist ideologues (in the personage of Antitrust chief William Baxter).

55. Greene opined, "The testimony and the documentary evidence adduced by the government demonstrate that the Bell System has violated the antitrust laws in a number of ways over a lengthy period of time." United States v. American Telephone and Telegraph Co., 524 F. Supp. 1336 (D.D.C. 1981), at 1381.

56. See Greene's Opinion denying the motion to dismiss, 524 F. Supp. 1336 (D.D.C. 1981); also Coll, *The Deal of the Century*, 288–290.

57. U.S. Senate, 97th Congress, 1st and 2nd Sessions, Committee on the Judiciary, Hearings on *The Department of Justice Oversight of the United States v. American Telephone and Telegraph Lawsuit*, August 6, 1981, and January 25, 1982 (Washington, DC: Government Printing Office, 1982), statement of William F. Baxter, at 28, 73.

58. U.S. District Court, District of Columbia, Modification of Final Judgment, United States v. Western Electric Co., Inc. & American Telephone and Telegraph Co., Civil Action No. 82-01982, August 24, 1982, Section IB.

In fact, AT&T is able to provide the very end-to-end telecommunications services the settlement was designed to disallow, so long as those services meet certain national security needs. Claudia Ricci, "AT&T Will Seek Waiver to Offer Services to US," *The Wall Street Journal*, April 2, 1984, 3.

59. Indeed, the original settlement, "unmodified" by Judge Greene, underscores how well AT&T's and Justice's interests meshed—to the detriment of the divested local telephone companies. The financial viability of the divested BOCs was not a major concern in the original settlement. It was only Judge Greene's post-Decree intervention which took away Yellow Pages (producing $3 billion in revenues annually) from AT&T and gave the service to the BOCs. This intervention also limited the share of debt each BOC would have to bear post-divestiture. Finally, Judge Greene permitted the BOCs to market telephone equipment so long as it was manufactured by some other entity.

Compare Greene's Modification of Final Judgment, United States v. Western Electric Co. and American Telephone and Telegraph Co., Civil Action No. 82-0192, August 24, 1982, to the original agreement between the Justice Department and AT&T, known formally as the Stipulation for Voluntary Dismissal, United States District Court, District of New Jersey, United States v. Western Electric Co. Inc., & American Telephone & Telegraph Co., Civil Action No. 17-49. Collected in *Decision to Divest*, Vol. 2, 900–923, 1294–1302.

60. In his speech before the shareholders in 1981, Charles L. Brown said that AT&T's "long distance services must be relieved of the burden of contributing to the support of local service." Brown outlined AT&T's "Statement of Policy," which claimed that increasing local rates was the key to enabling AT&T expansion into data processing and related fields. "AT&T Lifts Earnings 11.1%, Calls For Higher Local Rates," *The New York Times*, April 16, 1981, D5.

In another context, Brown as much as admitted that divestiture was necessary. In an address at AT&T's annual meeting in 1982, he stated, "Slowly, indeed painfully, it had become clear over the last few years that the Bell System would have to be significantly restructured. And it had become clear that the choice was not between preserving the Bell System as it is today or restructuring it in some new way . . . . The real issue was how and when to undertake a radical transformation." "Ma Bell Speaking," *The New York Times*, April 25, 1982, Sec. 3, 2.

Coll argues that with Brown at the helm, AT&T executives, needing to cover all contingencies, began talking about an "interexchange-intraexchange" split in the fall of 1980. Coll, *The Deal of the Century*, 268–281.

61. For all of the analysis which claims that divestiture was a good move for AT&T, a

couple of caveats need to be acknowledged. At least for the short term in the domestic arena, divestiture will not be easy for the company. It is not accustomed to having to compete in an open marketplace. And deregulation is by no means complete. The FCC still exercises oversight over long-distance and private line rates. This rate oversight has enormous bearing on the determination of market share among the competitive interexchange carriers. Hence, divestiture may not mean the end of regulation at all—at least for the short term it signals the emergence of an *ad hoc* form of regulated competition.

Though divestiture allows AT&T to enter the computer market, its actions have been cautious and conservative. The introduction of AT&T's personal computer in June 1984 confirmed this. Rather than come out with a major new product, the AT&T model 6300 was another IBM-compatible computer. For all the hoopla, AT&T has barely figured in the computer market.

62. Cited in Bernard D. Nossiter, "The FCC's Big Giveaway Show," *The Nation*, October 26, 1985, 402–404, at 402.

63. Office of Communication of the United Church of Christ v. FCC, 359 F.2d 994 (D.C. Cir. 1966).

64. When I speak of the "broadcast reform movement" *qua* movement, I do not mean to infer that this was a broad, unified, coherent set of organizations. If anything, the broadcast reform movement was a loose confederation of voluntary citizens' groups which garnered implicit support from people critical of the commercial broadcast system. For the most part, the groups were locally oriented—precisely because the easiest reform strategy was to go after *local* broadcast licensees. Thus the structure of the regulatory system in part structured the pattern of reformist activism. The movement never gained the discipline or organizational coherence to become a truly effective national lobby, and a case can be made that its reform agenda was coopted by superficial regulatory changes. One of the most incisive analyses of the broadcast reform movement is Willard D. Rowland, Jr., "The Illusion of Fulfillment: The Broadcast Reform Movement," *Journalism Monographs*, No. 79 (December 1982).

65. Between 1971 and 1973, for example, renewal denial petitions were filed against 342 stations. The FCC delayed action in so many cases that by August 1975 the Commission had a backlog of over 200 unsettled petitions. Joseph A. Grundfest, *Citizen Participation in Broadcast Licensing Before the FCC*, R-1896-MF (Santa Monica: Rand, 1976), 62, v.; also Rowland, "The Illusion of Fulfillment," 11–15.

The Commission's active attempts to block greater participation by citizen groups were decisively rebuffed by the courts. Office of Communication of the United Church of Christ v. FCC, 425 F.2d 543 (D.C. Cir. 1969); Office of Communication of the United Church of Christ v. FCC, 465 F.2d 519 (D.C. Cir. 1972).

66. WHDH, Inc., 16 FCC 2d 1 (1969).

67. See Barry Cole and Mal Oettinger, *Reluctant Regulators* (Reading, Mass: Addison-Wesley, 1978); Grundfest, *Citizen Participation*, 39–56.

68. Primer on Ascertainment of Community Problems by Broadcast Applicants, 27 FCC 2d 650 (1971); Ascertainment of Community Problems by Broadcast Applicants, 57 FCC 2d 418 (1976).

This policy was in a sense prefigured by the 1960 programming policy statement, which called for "assiduous planning and consultation" by the licensee in its community. Report and Statements of Policy Res.: Commission *en banc* Programming Inquiry, 44 FCC 2303 (1960).

69. See First Report and Order on Ascertainment of Community Problems by Broadcast Applicants, 57 FCC 2d 460 (1976).

Some broadcast reform movement actors have acknowledged their lack of efficacy. See

William E. Hanks and Terry A. Pickett, "Influence of Community-Based Citizens Groups on Television Broadcasters in Five Eastern Cities: An Exploratory Study," *Proceedings of the Sixth Annual Telecommunications Policy Research Conference*, Herbert A. Dordick (ed.) (Lexington, Mass.: DC Heath & Co., 1979), 105–133.

70. Red Lion Broadcasting Company v. Federal Communications Commission, 395 U.S. 387 (1969). The Court wrote that "the First Amendment confers no right on licensees to prevent others from broadcasting on 'their' frequencies," because "it is the right of the viewers and listeners, not the right of the broadcasters, which is paramount" (at 391, 390).

71. Banzhaf v. Federal Communications Commission, 405 F.2d 1082 (D.C. Cir. 1968), *cert. denied,* 396 U.S. 842 (1969).

The potential effectiveness of the "counter commercials" raised deep anxiety in the tobacco industry, because the counter commercials constituted a direct and mirror-like contestation of cigarette ad representations. Counter commercials in effect deconstructed tobacco ads. The tobacco industry was more than a little relieved when in 1969 Congress banned cigarette advertising from the airwaves after January 1, 1971, 15 U.S.C. §1335.

72. Friends of the Earth v. Federal Communications Commission, 449 F.2d 1164 (D.C. Cir. 1971).

73. Public Interest Research Group v. Federal Communications Commission, 522 F.2d 1060 (1st Cir. 1975), *cert. denied,* 424 U.S. 965 (1976). This case involved a Maine citizens group which desired to air, in response to television ads for snowmobiles, its view that such vehicles were dangerous and destructive to the environment. The FCC ruled that the Fairness Doctrine did not apply and the courts ruled that the Commission had not acted arbitrarily or capriciously.

74. Jerome A. Barron, "Access to the Press—A New First Amendment Right," *Harvard Law Review* 80/8 (June 1967), 1641–1678; idem, *Freedom of the Press for Whom?: The Right of Access to Mass Media* (Bloomington: Indiana University Press, 1973).

75. Columbia Broadcasting System v. Democratic National Committee, 412 U.S. 94 (1973); Miami Herald Publishing Co. v. Tornillo, 418 U.S. 258 (1974). The *Miami Herald* decision, astonishingly, did not even mention *Red Lion*. Red Lion Broadcasting Company v. Federal Communications Commission, 395 U.S. 387 (1969). For interesting discussions of these issues, see Benno C. Schmidt, Jr., *Freedom of the Press vs. Public Access* (New York: Praeger, 1976); William W. Van Alstyne, *Interpretations of the First Amendment* (Durham, NC: Duke University Press, 1984); Daniel L. Brenner and William L. Rivers (eds.), *Free But Regulated: Conflicting Traditions in Media Law* (Ames, Iowa: Iowa State University Press, 1982).

76. Columbia Broadcasting System v. Democratic National Committee, 412 U.S. 94 (1973), at 131.

77. Public Broadcasting Act of 1967, Public Law No. 90-129, Stat. 365 [codified as amended at 47 U.S.C. §§ 390–399 (1976)].

There was not much opposition to the Act, in part because the effort was so modest. The Act did not secure a permanent source of funding for the network (such as the proposed tax on television receivers). Commercial broadcasters did not put up much opposition because they didn't have to give anything up. The educational frequencies were already allocated, and the industry believed that the public television audience would be so small that a public network posed little competitive threat. See Robert M. Pepper, *The Formation of the Public Broadcasting Service,* Ph.D. Dissertation, Department of Communications Arts, University of Wisconsin, Madison, 1975, reprinted (new York: Arno Press, 1979); James L. Baughman, *Television's Guardians: The FCC and the Politics of Programming, 1958–1967* (Knoxville: University of Tennessee Press, 1985), 153–165.

78. Aspects of this discussion draw upon Thomas Streeter, "The Cable Fable Revisited: Discourse, Policy, and the Making of Cable Television," *Critical Studies in Mass Communication* 4/2 (June 1987), 174–200.

The emergence of this new discourse of the unbounded liberatory promise of new technologies is a recurring feature in the social history of technology in America, particularly communication technologies. The telegraph was accompanied by breathless excitement, replete with learned commentators gushing over the technology's expected ushering-in of world peace through its breakdown of cultural and geographic boundaries. Radio received similar treatment. See, among others, Daniel J. Czitrom, *Media and the American Mind: From Morse to McLuhan* (Chapel Hill: University of North Carolina Press, 1982).

79. The quasi-utopian embrace of cable earned the label "blue sky." For published examples of the embrace of cable by liberals and the broadcast reform movement, see, among others, Fred Friendly, "Asleep at the Switch of the Wired City," *Saturday Review* (October 10, 1970), 58–60; Ralph Lee Smith, "The Wired Nation," *The Nation* (May 18, 1970); idem, *The Wired Nation—Cable TV: The Electronic Communications Highway* (New York: Harper & Row, 1972); Harold J. Barnett and Edward Greenberg, "On the Economics of Wired City Television," *American Economic Review* 58/3 (June 1968), 503–508; Don R. Le Duc, *Cable Televisions and the FCC: A A Crisis in Media Control* (Philadelphia: Temple University Press, 1973). For a nice discussion of cable issues, see Lewis A. Friedland, *Cable-Broadband Communications: The Control of Information in Post-Industrial Society*, unpublished Ph.D. dissertation, Department of Sociology, Brandeis University, 1985.

80. U.S., President's Task Force on Communications Policy, *Final Report* (Washington, DC: Government Printing Office, 1968).

81. Nixon's Cabinet Committee on Cable Communications, in addition to its manifest tasks, also constituted one part of the Nixon Administration's political assault on broadcasters. The three networks in particular were vilified by the Nixon Administration as an elitist "liberal Eastern establishment" which controlled the media and injected ideological bias into program and news content. Nixon's Office of Telecommunications Policy, for whatever else it did, functioned as a Presidential tool in the effort to control broadcasters. Vice President Agnew's famous inflammatory alliterative speeches against the press constituted but a rhetorical moment to the extensive behind-the-scenes pressures on broadcasters and on the FCC to deny the license renewals of certain media corporations. Nixon Administration flirtatious support of cable TV had the added benefit of raising an additional economic threat to broadcasters. See David L. Bazelon, "FCC Regulation of the Telecommunications Press," *Duke Law Journal* 1975/2 (May 1975), 213–251; Thomas Whiteside, "Annals of Television (The Nixon Administration and Television)," *The New Yorker* (March 17, 1975), 41–91; William E. Porter, *Assault on the Media: The Nixon Years* (Ann Arbor: University of Michigan Press, 1976).

The Ford Administration's Domestic Council Review Group on Regulatory Reform specifically and concretely addressed the possibilities for the deregulation of cable television. See Paul W. MacAvoy (ed.), *Deregulation of Cable Television: Ford Administration Papers on Regulatory Reform* (Washington, DC: American Enterprise Institute, 1977).

82. Walter S. Baer, *Interactive Television: Prospects for Two-Way Services on Cable*, Rand Memorandum R-888-MF (Santa Monica: Rand Corporation, 1971); Leland L. Johnson, *The Future of Cable Television: Some Problems of Federal Regulation*, Rand Memorandum RM-6199-FF (Santa Monica: Rand Corporation, 1970); Rolla E. Park, *Potential Impact of Cable Growth on Television Broadcasting*, Rand Memorandum R-587-FF (Santa Monica: Rand Corporation, 1970); idem, "Cable Television, UHF Broadcasting, and FCC Regulatory Policy," *Journal of Law and Economics* 15/1 (April 1972), 207–232; Richard A. Posner,

"The Appropriate Scope of Regulation in the Cable Television Industry," *Bell Journal of Economics and Management Science* 3/1 (Spring 1972), 98–129.

83. Sloan Commission of Cable Communications, *On the Cable: The Television of Abundance* (New York: McGraw-Hill, 1971). Also, the Conference Board, *Information Technology: Some Critical Implications for Decision Makers*, Report 537 (New York: author, 1972); Committee for Economic Development, *Broadcasting and Cable Television: Policies for Diversity and Change* (New York: author, 1975).

It should be acknowledged that while the Sloan and CED studies (and, for that matter, the Cabinet Committee on Cable Communication Report, delivered in 1974) criticized FCC restriction of cable, the studies did not advance the notion that the cable operator be freed from all regulation. All these studies argued that cable be placed under some kind of common carrier status.

84. Again, the fundamental differences between the free market critics of regulation and the main industrial beneficiary of restrictive cable regulation—the broadcast industry—must be noted.

85. The transformation of Commissioner Nicholas Johnson is interesting in this context. Johnson, an articulate liberal long supportive of the restrictions on cable, began to reflect the progressive "blue sky" pronouncements of the broadcast reform groups by 1970. He voted in favor of a proposal that would end the 1968 restrictions on major market cable systems. Notice of Proposed Rulemaking in Docket 18397A, 24 FCC 2d 580 (1970); Streeter, "The Cable Fable Revisited," 189–190.

86. Growth of the cable television industry:

| Year | Number of systems | Number of subscribers |
|------|-------------------|----------------------|
| 1955 | 400 | 150,000 |
| 1960 | 640 | 650,000 |
| 1965 | 1325 | 1,275,000 |
| 1970 | 2490 | 4,500,000 |
| 1975 | 3506 | 9,800,000 |

*Television Factbook*, 1981–82, Vol. 50 (Washington, DC: Television Digest, 1981), 83a.

87. Yale M. Braunstein, "Recent Trends in Cable Television Related to the Prospects for New Television Networks," prepared for the Commercial Television Practices Inquiry of the Federal Communications Commission, *Preliminary Report on Prospects for Additional Networks* (Washington, DC: FCC, 1979), 12–21.

88. See Christopher H. Sterling, "Cable and Pay Television," *Who Owns the Media?: Concentration of Ownership in the Mass Communications Industry*, Benjamin M. Compaine (ed.) (New York: Harmony Books, 1979), 302–303.

89. Glen O. Robinson, "The Federal Communications Commission," in *Communications for Tomorrow: Policy Perspectives for the 1980s*, Glen O. Robinson (ed.) (New York: Praeger, 1978), 353–400, quote at 378–379.

90. Nicholas Johnson and John Jay Dystel, "A Day in the Life: The Federal Communications Commission," *Yale Law Journal* 82/8 (July 1973), 1575–1634, quote at 1596.

91. The Supreme Court ruled in *Fortnightly Corp. v. United Artists Television, Inc.* that retransmission of broadcast television signals via cable television did not constitute a "public performance for profit" within the narrow meaning of the Copyright Act of 1909. Thus cable did not incur copyright liability. 392 U.S. 390 (1968).

92. Commission Proposals for Regulation of Cable Television, 31 FCC 2d 115 (1971).

93. Cable Television Report and Order, 36 FCC 2d 143 (1972). This subsection on the 1972 cable rules and their aftermath draws on Braunstein, "Recent Trends in Cable Television"; Stanley M. Besen and Robert W. Crandall, "The Deregulation of Cable Television," *Law and Contemporary Problems* 44/1 (Winter 1981), 77–124; Le Duc, *Cable Television and the FCC.*

94. The network stations imported by cable operator had to be the closest network affiliates. The cable operator could import two independent stations, but if they were from the top 25 markets, they had to be from one or both of the closest top 25 markets. If the cable operator was allowed to import a third independent signal, that signal had to be a UHF station from within 200 miles, or a VHF station within 200 miles, or any other UHF—in that order of priority. Braunstein, "Recent Trends in Cable Television," 63–64.

95. The Commission had ordered that "cablecasting," that is, local origination of programming by cable operators, was in the public interest already in 1969. First Report and Order, 20 FCC 2d 201 (1969), Memorandum Opinion and Order, 23 FCC 2d 825 (1970).

96. Braunstein, "Recent Trends in Cable Television," 105.

97. Rules and Regulations Relative to Carriage of Late Night Television Programming by Cable Systems, 48 FCC 2d 699 (1974), at 699.

The Commission, not surprisingly, retained its protectionistic out. "But. . . where a station can demonstrate actual harm from importation of late night programming, of course, we will consider granting special relief. . ." (at 707).

98. Id., 707.

99. Interview, Henry Geller, March 24, 1985.

100. Interview, Richard Wiley and Lawrence Secrest, III, March 24, 1985.

101. Rules and Regulations with Respect to Selection of Television Signals for Cable Television Carriage, 57 FCC 2d 625 (1976).

102. Regulatory Policies Concerning Resale and Shared Use of Common Carrier Services and Facilities, 60 FCC 2d 261 (1976).

103. Southern Satellite System, 62 FCC 2d 153 (1976). Ted Turner essentially formed a carriage company to purchase transponder space on RCA Satcom I—the same satellite the Home Box Office (HBO) corporation had designated in late 1975 as the carrier to deliver its programming of first-run feature films.

104. ABC, no doubt hoping to slow cable-satellite growth, claimed that small satellite receiving dishes would ultimately lead to inefficient satellite band use. The Commission did not agree with this presumptive reasoning, stating, "[W]e decided that the public interest would be best served by providing potential users as wide a degree of flexibility as practical to develop and utilize domestic satellite facilities for existing and new types of services." American Broadcasting, Inc., 62 FCC 2d 901 (1977), at 916.

Satellite receiving dishes had been standard at 9 meters, and cost between $100,000 and $150,000. The 4.5 meter dishes instantly slashed the cost for a dish to $20,000–$25,000. This put receive-only satellite dishes within the reach of many smaller cable systems. Braunstein, "Recent Trends in Cable Television," 67.

105. See Federal Communications Commission, Network Inquiry Special Staff, "Video Interconnection: Technology, Costs and Regulatory Policies," prepared for the Commercial Television Practices Inquiry of the Federal Communications Commission, *Preliminary Report on Prospects for Additional Networks* (Washington, DC: author, 1980).

106. Besen and Crandall, "The Deregulation of Cable Television," 100.

107. When he came on board as Commission Chairman, Ferris said he found the views of Commission bureaucrats "dated," and commissioners to be generally "broadcast-oriented and protectionistic." Ferris described himself, on the other hand, as "open." Because

he was not from the industry, he had "no debts to pay." Interview, Charles Ferris, March 25, 1985.

108. Notice of Inquiry in Docket 21284, 65 FCC 2d 9 (1977).

109. The inquiry resulted in a rulemaking which removed distant signal carriage and syndicated exclusivity rules. Report and Order on Cable Television Syndicated Exclusivity Rules, 79 FCC 2d 663 (1980).

110. Arlington Telecommunications Corp. (ARTEC), 65 FCC 2d 469 (1977), recon. 69 FCC 2d 1923 (1978), at 1941, note 46.

111. See the opinions and writings of Judge Harold Leventhal, the Judge on the DC Court of Appeals who originally formulated the "hard look" standard of judicial review. Harold Leventhal, "Environmental Decisionmaking and the Role of the Courts," *University of Pennsylvania Law Review* 122/3 (January 1974), 509–555; Greater Boston Television Corp. v. FCC, 444 F. 2d 841 (D.C. Cir. 1970). Also see Richard B. Stewart, "The Reformation of American Administrative Law," *Harvard Law Review* 88/8 (June 1975), 1669–1813; Merrick B. Garland, "Deregulation and Judicial Review," *Harvard Law Review* 98/3 (January 1985), 525–542.

112. "The First Amendment theory espoused in National Broadcasting Co. and Red Lion Broadcasting cannot be directly applied to cable television since an essential precondition of that theory—physical interference and scarcity requiring an umpiring role for the government—is absent." Home Box Office Inc. v. Federal Communications Commission, 567 F.2d 9 (D.C. Cir. 1977), at 44–45, *cert. denied,* 434 U.S. 829 (1977).

113. "The Commission has in no way justified its position that cable television must be supplement to, rather than an equal of, broadcast television. Such an artificial narrowing of the scope of the regulatory problem is itself arbitrary and capricious and is ground for reversal." Id., at 36.

114. United States v. Midwest Video Corp., 406 U.S. 649 (1972).

115. Cablecasting Rules, 47 FCC 2d 1004 (1975); Cable Television Report and Order, 59 FCC 2d 294 (1976).

116. United States v. Midwest Video Corp., 440 U.S. 689 (1979).

117. Cable Communications Policy Act of 1984, 47 U.S.C. §601 (1984).

118. The most telling example of self-indictment was the Commission's Network Inquiry, conducted during the time when the FCC was chaired by Carter appointee Charles Ferris. The report critically reviewed past Commission policies, holding them responsible for network dominance of television. The economically oriented report recommended entry liberalization. Network Inquiry Special Staff, *New Television Networks: Entry, Jurisdiction, Ownership and Regulation: Final Report* (Washington, DC: FCC, 1980).

119. In Ferris' words, "The [Commission's] attitude [not to restrict technologies] created the environment that attracted the capital the new technologies needed." Cited in *Broadcasting,* January 19, 1981, at 42.

Direct broadcast satellite is a system of broadcasting directly from studio to home via a high-power satellite and small antenna. Multi-point distribution service transmits microwave signals over super high frequencies within a range of 25 miles. Low-power television is self-explanatory. These stations operate at a power sufficient to reach viewers within a radius of 10 to 15 miles, so long as they do not interfere with existing stations. Low Power Television Service, 51 Radio Regulations 2d 476 (1982); Direct Broadcast Satellites, 90 FCC 2d 676 (1982). The Commission preempted state and local regulation that might hinder the development of MDS in a 1977 decision. This was affirmed in New York State Commission on Cable Television v. Federal Communications Commission, 669 F.2d 58 (2d Cir. 1982).

120. See, for instance, the address by Richard Neustadt (associate director of President

Carter's Domestic Policy Staff) to an October 1980 conference on access to broadcasting held at the Massachusetts Institute of Technology. Neustadt claimed that the White House and the FCC had won an "intense struggle" to lift restrictions that had protected the networks' dominion over the airwaves. Minority groups and nonprofit organizations would be given preference in ownership applications for the new services of low-power television and additional AM radio slots. Neustadt strongly urged minority and nonprofit groups to "reach out and grab the opportunities" posed by the new broadcast outlets. Cited in *Broadcasting,* November 3, 1980, at 63. Also see Minority Ownership of Broadcasting Facilities, 68 FCC 2d 979 (1978).

121. Cited in *Broadcasting,* Interview of Charles Ferris, January 19, 1981, 37–42, at 37.

122. Notice of Inquiry and Proposed Rulemaking, Deregulation of Radio, 733 FCC 2d 457 (1979), at 458.

123. Office of Communication of the United Church of Christ v. Federal Communications Commission, 707 F.2d 1413 (D.C. Cir. 1983). The Court did remand to the FCC the part of radio deregulation that had relieved broadcasters from keeping programming logs.

124. Cited in *Broadcasting,* April 30, 1984, 112. For a theoretical statement, see Mark S. Fowler and Daniel L. Brenner, "A Marketplace Approach to Broadcast Regulation," *Texas Law Review* 60/2 (February 1982), 207–257.

125. See Willard D. Rowland, Jr., "The Process of Reification: Recent Trends in Communications Legislation and Policy-Making," *Journal of Communication* 32/4 (Autumn 1982), 114–136.

126. Postcard Renewal, 87 FCC 2d 1127 (1981), *aff'd* Black Citizens for a Fair Media v. FCC, 719 F.2d 407 (D.C. Cir. 1983).

127. Thomas B. Rosenstiel and Penny Pagano, "FCC to Review Rule on Media Ownership," *Los Angeles Times,* January 16, 1987, Part IV, 2.

128. Deregulation of Commercial Television, 98 FCC 2d 1076 (1984) (appeals pending). The old content rules specified that a television licensee had to air a minimum of 5 percent information, 5 percent locally produced, and a total of 10 percent nonentertainment programming.

129. Office of Communication of the United Church of Christ v. Federal Communications Commission, 779 F.2d 702, (D.C. Cir. 1985).

130. Children's Television Programming, 55 Radio Regulations 2d 199 (1984), *aff'd* Action for Children's Television v. Federal Communications Commission, 756 F.2d 899 (D.C. Cir. 1985).

131. Applications for Voluntary Assignments or Transfer of Control, 52 Radio Regulations 2d 1081 (1982).

132. "FCC Says Licensing Policy Favoring Minorities Should Be Eliminated," *Los Angeles Times,* September 16, 1986, 14.

133. In *FCC v. Pacifica Foundation,* a case concerning indecent and obscene language on the airwaves, the Supreme Court put forward a rationale for the regulation of broadcasting which did *not* rest on the scarcity argument. Instead, the Court declared that the FCC may regulate broadcasting due to the "uniquely pervasive" nature of the medium. Radio, the Court wrote, is a kind of "intruder" in the home, "uniquely accessible to children." 438 U.S. 726 (1978), at 748, 749. "Uniquely pervasive" rests not upon a technological distinction, but upon a perception of the *power* of the broadcast medium. It is unclear, however, if this decision and its rationale have any precedential import.

## Chapter 9. Conclusion: From Deregulation to Reregulation?

1. See the cases discussed in chapter 7, footnotes 41 and 45.

2. U.S. General Accounting Office, *Deregulation: Increased Competition Is Making*

*Airlines More Efficient and Responsive to Consumers,* GAO/RCED-86-26 (Washington, DC: GAO, November 6, 1985), 12–14.

3. Douglas W. Caves, Laurits R. Chrisensen, and Michael W. Tretheway, "Airline Productivity Under Deregulation," *Regulation* (November/December 1982), 25–28.

4. For instance, in 1983 American Airlines placed a large order for the new, cost-efficient McDonnell-Douglas MD-80 jetliner in its bid to challenge United Airlines as the nation's preeminent air carrier. Agis Salpukas, "Airlines Adapt to Decontrol," *The New York Times,* December 8, 1983, D1. Sharon Warren Walsh and Martha M. Hamilton, "FTC Hails Deregulation of Airlines," *The Washington Post,* February 9, 1988, C1.

5. Statistics cited in "Is Deregulation Working?," *Business Week,* December 22, 1986, 50–55, at 50; These figures, though impressive, are logically arbitrary. The comparison of contemporary, market-determined airline fares is made to what airline fares "would have risen" under continued CAB regulation—a hypothesis, based on speculative data.

6. Brookings statistics cited in Robert E. Dallos and Lee May, "Debate Still Rages Over Deregulation," *Los Angeles Times,* November 2, 1986, 1, 20–22; Nathaniel C. Nash, "Assessing the Effects of Airline Deregulation," *The New York Times,* March 20, 1988, E5; traffic statistics cited in Peter S. Greenberg, "Congress Considering Re-Regulation of Airlines," *Los Angeles Times,* October 18, 1987, Part VII, 2, 8.

7. Stephen Phillips, "Continental Cuts Fares; Other Airlines to Follow," *The New York Times,* November 12, 1986, 25.

8. GAO, *Deregulation,* 29. Congress in effect has acted to recreate a subsidy system by passing the Essential Air Services program. That program insures that airlines maintain service to some 150 small communities.

9. Several airlines have won the right to hire new employees at much lower wages than senior workers, creating a "two-tier" wage system. The companies also have won the right to hire more part-time help, and to allow management to "cross-utilize," or shift workers to different jobs. The number of workers on the lower wage tier at American Airlines, for example, is approximately 40 percent of American's workforce. Dallos & May, "Debate Still Rages Over Deregulation," 1.

10. Labor Research Association, "Economic Notes," 54/9 (October 1986), 6; Frederick C. Thayer, "The Emerging Dangers of Deregulation," *The New York Times,* February 23, 1986, Sec. 3, 3; "Airline Pilots Link Decline in Safety to Deregulation," *Los Angeles Times,* December 16, 1985, Part I, 4.

The raw statistical data *per se* do not support the claim that deregulation has eroded air safety. In fact, 1986 turned out to be a good year for air safety. However, and this may be the most important point, most air safety experts agree that the margin of safety vis-à-vis government-mandated minimum safety standards has diminished considerably. Those who raised the safety issue in the debates over deregulation have been proved correct. Richard Witkin, "Safety Record of US Airlines Shows Big Gain," *The New York Times,* January 13, 1987, 1, 12; Robert Reed Gray, "Aviation Safety: Fact or Fiction," *Technology Review,* August-September 1987, 32–40.

11. The GAO report lists 27 carriers that went belly-up as of November 1984. GAO, *Deregulation,* 41.

12. Agis Salpukas, "Airline Deregulation Costly to Small Competitors, *The New York Times,* December 29, 1986, 26; "Is Deregulation Working?," *Business Week,* 52; Agis Salpukas, "Climbing Air Fares Increase Worries of Price-Setting," *The New York Times,* September 9, 1987, 1, 28.

13. D. A. Vise and P. Behr, "When the Airline's Dogfight Is Over, How Many Dogs Will Be Left?," *Washington Post National Weekly Edition,* March 17, 1986, 19–20; Agis Salpukas, "Continental Is Buying Presidential Air's Gates," *The New York Times,* January

13, 1987, 28; Debra Whitefield, "Pan Am Stock Active as Rumors Point to Merger With American," *Los Angeles Times,* January 16, 1987, Part IV, 1, 2; Salpukas, "Climbing Air Fares Increase Worries of Price-Setting."

14. "Is Deregulation Working?," *Business Week,* 52–53. For instance, TWA accounts for 82.3 percent of the passengers emplaning at St. Louis. American handles 63.4 percent of the traffic at the Dallas-Fort Worth airport. At Pittsburgh the figure for US Air is nearly 83 percent. Northwest holds 83 percent of the air traffic in Minneapolis, almost 65 percent at Detroit's Metropolitan Airport, and 86.6 percent of the traffic at Memphis International Airport. Salpukas, "Airline Deregulation Costly to Small Competitors;" Ernest Conine, "More and More, Deregulation Won't Fly," *Los Angeles Times,* July 28, 1987, Part II, 9; Salpukas, "Climbing Air Fares Increase Worries of Price-Setting;" idem, "The Crunch at Airlines' Hubs," *The New York Times,* October 12, 1987, 23, 27.

15. U.S. General Accounting Office, *Airline Competition: Impact of Computerized Reservation Systems,* GAO/RCED-86-74 (Washington, DC: GAO, May, 1986).

16. Agis Salpukas, "Trucking's Great Shakeout," *The New York Times,* December 13, 1983, D1, 2; D. Machalaba, "Trucking Association, Powerful for Decades, Has Load of Trouble," *Wall Street Journal,* February 21, 1984, 1, 12.

17. David Henry, "Surface Transportation," 38th Annual Report on American Industry, *Forbes,* January 13, 1986, 208–209; "Is Deregulation Working?," 52.

18. John V. Wells, transportation economist, U.S. General Accounting Office, Interview with author, December 10, 1986.

19. U.S. General Accounting Office, Statement of Herbert R. McLure, Associate Director, Resources, Community, and Economic Development Division, U.S. GAO, before the Subcommittee on Surface Transportation, Committee on Public Works and Transportation, House of Representatives, Hearings on Predatory Pricing and Antitrust Enforcement in the Trucking Industry (Washington, DC: GAO, November 7, 1985).

20. Id.; "Truckers Brace for Plenty of Head-On Collisions," *Business Week,* January 12, 1987, 99. The data on trucking are not very good, and one reason for this is that without regulation, there is no compulsion for businesses to report information. The Labor Research Association's "Economic Notes" asserts that on an industry-wide basis, the top ten carriers now account for 50 percent of all trucking industry profits, while half the carriers are operating at a loss. "Economic Notes," 8.

21. John V. Wells, transportation economist, U.S. General Accounting Office, Interview with author, December 10, 1986; "Is Deregulation Working?," 53.

22. William E. Schmidt, "Sharp Rise in Truck Crashes Prompts Action Across US," *The New York Times,* December 7, 1986, 1, 15. There is some reason to be wary of such statistics, however. The Department of Transportation asserts that the accident data is distorted over time because accident reports are filed only if over $2500 worth of damage ensues. Hence, with inflation, the number of accident reports goes up. DOT reported a *decline* in accidents involving trucks between 1980 and 1983, and a rise in 1984 and 1985. John V. Wells, interview with author.

23. Alfred E. Kahn, "The Passing of the Public Utility Concept: A Reprise," in Eli Noam (ed.), *Telecommunications Regulation Today and Tomorrow* (New York: Law and Business, Inc., 1983), 18–19.

24. See Martha M. Hamilton, "You Can't Get Here from There: Deregulation Is Leaving Rural Communities Stranded," *Washington Post National Weekly Edition,* July 21, 1986, 6–7; statistics cited in Dallos & May, "Debate Still Rages Over Deregulation," 1.

25. Oswald Johnston, "Greyhound to Buy Routes, Assets of Trailways Corp.," *The Los Angeles Times,* June 20, 1987, 1, 20.

26. Henry, "Surface Transportation," 209.

27. "Is Deregulation Working?," *Business Week,* 52, 54; Hamilton, "You Can't Get Here From There." *Business Week* cites an unreleased March 1986 report by the Interior Department on Wyoming and Montana coalfields which concluded that rates charged utility buyers by Burlington Northern Inc., the only railroad serving much of the region, were "monopolistic."

28. Robert A. Bennett, "Deregulation Affects Banking," *The New York Times,* December 5, 1983, 29, 25; idem, "A Banking Puzzle: Mixing Freedom and Protection," *The New York Times,* February 19, 1984, Sec. 3, 1, 12–13; idem, "Deregulation's Effect at Banks," *The New York Times,* March 16, 1984, 30.

29. Lowell L. Bryan, "The Credit Bomb in Our Financial Future," *Harvard Business Review* 87/1 (January/February 1987), 45–51; Nathaniel C. Nash, "Record Loss for Savings Industry," *The New York Times,* March 25, 1988, 25, 43.

30. Bill Sing, "Banks Face a Crisis of Confidence," *Los Angeles Times,* June 3, 1984, 1, 18–19; Eric N. Berg, "Bank Deregulation Crossroads," *The New York Times,* May 3, 1986, 21, 24; Kathleen Day, "Re-Regulating the Savings and Loans," *The Washington Post National Weekly Edition,* May 26, 1986, 6–7.

31. Herbert S. Dordick, H. G. Bradley, and B. Nanus, *The Emerging Network Marketplace* (Norwood, NJ: Ablex Publishing Co., 1981), 204–210.

32. For example, the Goldome Savings Bank, established in the 19th century as a not-for-profit haven for workers' savings, introduced a $5 monthly fee on savings accounts for the customer who fails to keep at least $20,000 in the bank. The bank is trying to make these accounts more profitable, or get rid of customers who resist the fee. Robert A. Bennett, "Now, the Age of Fast-Buck Banking," *The New York Times,* December 14, 1986, Sec. 3, 1, 8.

Banking deregulation has been cited in the recent widening of income differentials. As Robert L. Thaler, executive vice-president in charge of planning for Los Angeles' Security Pacific Corporation, claims, "The deregulation of banking is an enormous transfer of resources from the less affluent in our population to the more affluent." Cited in James Flanigan, "The Gap Between Rich and Poor is Widening," *Los Angeles Times,* December 4, 1983, Business section, 1.

33. Cited in Robert A. Bennett, "Specter at Continental," *The New York Times,* May 20, 1984, Sec. 3, 8.

34. See, for example, Barry Bluestone and Bennett Harrison, *The Deindustrialization of America: Plant Closings, Community Abandonment, and the Dismantling of Basic Industry* (New York: Basic Books, 1982).

35. Statistic provided by Dennis Patrick, Commissioner, Federal Communications Commission, address before Emerging Issues Program for State Legislative Leaders on Telecommunications Policy, UCLA, September 4, 1986.

36. Statistics cited in Letter, *The New York Times,* March 2, 1987, 18.

37. Statistic on long-distance rate reductions provided by Dennis Patrick, address before Emerging Issues Program for State Legislative Leaders on Telecommunications Policy; American Telephone and Telegraph Co., "Competition in Telecommunications: A Matter of Public Interest," pamphlet (New York: author, 1984).

38. In some cases, the local telephone monopoly bypasses its own central office in order to provide services to large users who might otherwise build their own systems. Eric N. Berg, "New Phone Company Twist," *The New York Times,* March 11, 1985, 21, 24.

39. Pacific Telesis, for instance, has built a fiber optic ring around San Francisco's financial district to prevent banks from constructing bypass systems.

40. See U.S. House of Representatives, 97th Congress, 2nd Session, Committee on Government Operations, *Seventh Report* (Washington, DC: Government Printing Office,

1983); California PUC Decision 83-12-024, Applications 82-11-07; 83-01-22; OII 83-04-02; and 83-06-65; Case 82-10-09; issued December 7, 1983.

41. U.S. General Accounting Office, *Telephone Communications: Bypass of the Local Telephone Companies—A Report to Congress,* GAO/RCED-86-66 (Washington, DC: GAO, August 1986), 2-4; see also the monumental report on post-divestiture telecommunications put together under the auspices of the Washington Program of the Annenberg School of Communications, *Telecommunications Policy for the 1980s: The Transition to Competition,* Walter G. Bolter (ed.) (Englewood Cliffs, NJ: Prentice-Hall, 1984).

42. "The World on the Line," *The Economist,* November 23, 1985, 5-40; "The Small Fry in Phones Are Getting Cut Off," *Business Week,* November 4, 1985, 98; "As the Big Get Bigger, the Small May Disappear," *Business Week,* January 12, 1987, 90.

43. Victor J. Toth, attorney on regulatory matters of the Society of Telecommunications Consultants, address to the Society's annual meeting, San Diego, California, November 22, 1986; "Ratifying a Winner in the Phone Vote," *Time,* August 25, 1986, 44-45; Barnaby J. Feder, "MCI Plans 4th-Quarter Write-Off," *The New York Times,* December 3, 1986, 33.

44. Calvin Sims, "FCC's Phone Rate Plan Is Under Attack in Congress," *The New York Times,* April 2, 1988, 17, 19. MCI earned a profit of $88 million in 1987 largely through cost-cutting measures.

45. Kenneth B. Noble, "FCC Proposing Wide Shifts in Long-Distance Rate Rules," *The New York Times,* August 5, 1987, 1, 38.

46. U.S. Department of Justice, *Report and Recommendations of the United States Concerning the Lines of Business Restrictions Imposed on the Bell Operating Companies by the Modification of Final Judgment,* United States v. Western Electric Company, Inc. and American Telephone and Telegraph Co., Civil Action No. 82-0192 (Washington, DC: author, released February 2, 1987).

47. Peter Huber, *The Geodesic Network: 1987 Report on Competition in the Telephone Industry,* Report to U.S. Department of Justice (Washington, DC: Government Printing Office, 1987); U.S. Department of Justice, *Report and Recommendations of the United States Concerning the Lines of Business Restrictions Imposed on the Bell Operating Companies by the Modification of Final Judgment,* 97-103.

48. In the Third Computer Inquiry (Computer III), the FCC ruled that it would allow AT&T and the BOCs to provide enhanced services without structural separation, but only if they complied with newly developed Comparably Efficient Interconnection ("CEI") and Open Network Architecture ("ONA") requirements. These are designed to ensure that all enhanced service providers receive equal access to basic network facilities. Companies also would be required to issue reports to document nondiscrimination. FCC, *Amendment of Section 64.702 of the Commission's Rules and Regulations (Third Computer Inquiry),* CC Docket No. 85-229, FCC 86-252 (released June 16, 1986).

49. Calvin Sims, "Curbs on Phone Companies Kept," *The New York Times,* September 11, 1987, 1, 26; idem, "Judge Lets 'Baby Bells' Offer Some Information Services," *The New York Times,* March 8, 1988, 27-28.

50. The RBOCs, not surprisingly, criticized Judge Greene's decision, as did members of the Departments of Justice and Commerce. Interestingly, the ruling was denounced by Representative John D. Dingell, chairman of the House Committee on Energy and Commerce, and generally a strong proponent of regulation. Dingell's counterpart in the Senate, Ernest Hollings, said through a spokesman that the Senate Committee on Commerce, Science and Transportation would hold hearings on the decision. "Curbs on Phone Companies Kept," 26.

51. Robert Pepper, "Competition in Local Distribution: The Cable Television Indus-

try," *Understanding New Media: Trends and Issues in Electronic Distribution of Information,* Benjamin M. Compaine (ed.) (Cambridge: Ballinger Publishing Co., 1984), 147–194.

52. DTS is wide-band microwave service for data communications intended to provide the local connection for long-haul networks. An experiment in November 1981 involving Satellite Business Systems, Tymnet, Local Digital Distribution Company, Manhattan Cable Television, and Viacom transmitted data between New York and San Francisco using an SBS satellite channel connected with a local cable television channel in New York and cable and microwave DTS channels in San Francisco. The connection entirely bypassed the local telephone operating companies. The experiment reportedly demonstrated that such DTS and cable local distribution can provide greater bandwidth at lower price than AT&T's Dataphone Digital Service. Cited in Pepper, "Competition in Local Distribution," 165–166.

53. "The Baby Bells: Special Report," *Business Week,* December 2, 1985, 94–106.

54. Andrew Pollack, "Omens for Phone Technology," *The New York Times,* February 18, 1984, 29, 31; Frederick C. Thayer, *Rebuilding America: The Case for Economic Regulation* (New York: Praeger, 1984), 110–115.

55. Jeremy Tunstall, *Communications Deregulation: The Unleashing of America's Communications Industry* (London: Basil Blackwell, 1986), 121, 129, " '87 Field Guide to the Electronic Environment," *Channels,* January 1987, 68; " '88 Field Guide to the Electronic Environment," *Channels,* January 1988, 100–101.

56. " '87 Field Guide to the Electronic Environment," *Channels,* 41.

57. Figures cited in James Flanigan, "Networks Will Emerge on Top in TV Shakeout," *Los Angeles Times,* January 9, 1987, Part IV, 1, 3.

58. See, for example, Peter J. Boyer, "Trauma Time on Network TV," *The New York Times,* November 2, 1986, Sec. 3, 1, 28; Burton Benjamin, "Technology and the Bottom Line Create Profound Challenges," *The New York Times,* August 17, 1986, Sec. 2, 1, 25.

59. Paul Richter, "Networks Send Upsetting Signal to Local Stations," *Los Angeles Times,* December 28, 1986, Part IV, 1, 5.

60. Steven Rattner, "Broadcast Deregulation on Wall Street," *Gannett Center Journal,* 2/1 (Winter 1988), 1–15.

61. Paul Richter and Kathryn Harris, "MCA Write-Off May Signal Independent TV Shakeout," *Los Angeles Times,* January 17, 1987, 1, 25. See *Broadcasting Yearbook,* January 1987; *Channels,* " '87 Field Guide to the Electronic Media."

62. Tunstall, *Communications Deregulation,* 123; Geraldine Fabrikant, "2 Cable Companies Set $1.6 Billion Merger," *The New York Times,* March 10, 1988, 29, 33. TCI, the largest cable MSO, owns and operates hundreds of cable systems, with nearly 8 million subscribers. "The King of Cable TV," *Business Week,* October 26, 1987, 88–96.

63. " '87 Field Guide to the Electronic Media," 34–36. Finally, in cable there is the problem that the cable operator, a local monopolist, controls both conduit and content. The ongoing deregulation of cable has meant the dropping of "must carry" provisions. Cable no longer has a legal obligation to carry the local, over-the-air broadcast signals in its service area, though this is still unresolved.

64. Tunstall, *Communications Deregulation,* 152–153.

65. Theodore L. Glasser, "Competition and Diversity Among Radio Formats: Legal and Structural Issues," *Mass Communication Review Yearbook,* Michael Gurevitch and Mark R. Levy (eds.), Vol. 5 (1985), 547–562.

66. *Ibid.,* at 560.

67. Associated Press v. United States, 326 U.S. 1 (1945), at 20.

68. Citizens Committee to Save WEFM v. Federal Communications Commission, 506

F.2d 246 (D.C. Cir. 1974). The Court wrote: "When faced with a proposed license assign-ment encompassing a format change, Federal Communications Commission is obliged to determine whether format to be lost is unique or otherwise serves a specialized audience that would feel its loss, and if endangered format is of such variety, Commission must affirma-tively consider whether public interest would be served by approving proposed assignment, which may, if there are substantial questions of fact or inadequate data in application or other officially noticeable materials, necessitate conducting a public hearing in order to resolve factual issues or assist Commission in discerning public interest. . . . It is not sufficient justification for approving application for a license assignment encompassing a format change that assignor had asserted financial losses in providing special format; those losses must be attributable to format itself in order logically to support an assignment that occasions a loss of format" (at 247).

After years of FCC avoidance of this Appellate Court directive, the Supreme Court essentially trashed this logic and reversed the Appeals Court in Federal Communications Commission v. WNCN Listeners Guild et al., 450 U.S. 582 (1981).

69. Bob Davis, "Broadcasters, Absent Regulation, Kill News Shows—But Is That Bad?," *The Wall Street Journal,* October 16, 1986, Sec. 2, 1.

70. *Broadcasting/Cablecasting Yearbook 1987,* C-10.

71. Jerome A. Barron, "Access to the Press—A New First Amendment Right," *Harvard Law Review* 80/8 (June 1967), 1641–1678; idem, *Freedom of the Press for Whom?: The Right of Access to Mass Media* (Bloomington: Indiana Univeristy Press, 1973). Also see the superb review essay dealing with Ithiel de Sola Pool's *Technologies of Freedom* by Stephen Carter, "Technology, Democracy, and the Manipulation of Consent," *Yale Law Journal* 93/3 (January 1984), 581–607.

72. See, for example, the attempts by Senator Robert Packwood to eliminate all broad-cast regulations, because of the end of the scarcity rationale. U.S. Senate, 98th Congress, 1st Session, Committee on Commerce, Science, and Transportation, *Print and Electronic Me-dia: The Case for First Amendment Parity,* Committee Print 98–50, May 3, 1983 (Wash-ington, DC: Government Printing Office, 1983). Also, Ithiel de Sola Pool, *Technologies of Freedom* (Cambridge: Harvard University Press, 1983); Edwin Diamond, Norman Sandler, and Milton Mueller, *Telecommunications in Crisis: The First Amendment, Technology, and Deregulation* (Washington, DC: The Cato Institute, 1983); Lucas A. Powe, Jr., *Amer-ican Broadcasting and the First Amendment* (Berkeley: University of California Press, 1987).

73. In September 1986, the District of Columbia Court of Appeals ruled that the Fairness Doctrine was not a binding statutory obligation. Rather, the Court declared the doctrine was an administrative construction designed to fulfill the public interest. That opinion gave the Commission the legal clearance it needed to do away with the Fairness Doctrine. Telecom-munications Research and Action Center v. Federal Communications Commission, 801 F.2d 501 (D.C. Cir. 1986).

74. "Excerpts of Statement by the FCC Counsel," *The New York Times,* August 5, 1987, 20. Following the FCC's action, Congress voted to legislate the Fairness Doctrine. President Reagan vetoed that legislation.

75. Labor Research Association, "Economic Notes," 8.

76. Martin Tolchin and Susan Tolchin, *Dismantling American: The Rush to Deregulate* (Boston: Houghton Mifflin, 1983), 247.

77. According to Congressional Research Service, a comparison of the average annual pre-deregulation wages of unionized Eastern Airlines and non-unionized New York Air showed the following:

| | **Eastern** | **New York Air** |
|---|---|---|
| Pilots & Co- | $83,530 | $28,500 |
| Pilots | 22,661 | 12,559 |
| Cabin Attendants | 23,819 | 23,442 |
| Maintenance | 23,318 | 12,800 |
| Ticketing & Sales | | |

(cited in Labor Research Association, "Economic Notes," 7).

78. Bill Keller, "A Union Copes With Deregulation," *The New York Times,* November 18, 1984, Sec. 3, 4.

79. Paul Richter, "AT&T Planning Big Write Off, 27,000 Job Cut," *Los Angeles Times,* December 19, 1986, 1, 32.

80. Agis Salpukas, "Greyhound Selling Its Bus Operations," *The New York Times,* December 24, 1986, 29, 40.

81. Labor Research Association, "Economic Notes," 6.

82. In 1987 the Department of Transportation announced a "truth in scheduling" rule that requires 14 large air carriers to publicly disclose key information about flight delays and baggage problems. Congress is moving toward legislation thet would compel airlines to pay monetary penalties to delayed passengers and require that the DOT publish a monthly report detailing on-time performance, baggage misdeeds, canceled flights, bumping, and passenger complaints.

# Bibliography

**Books and Articles**

Abel, John D., Charles E. Clift III and Fredric A. Weiss, "Station License Revocations and Denials of Renewal, 1934–1969," *Journal of Broadcasting* 14/4 (Fall 1970), 411–421.

Adams, Walter, "The Rocky Road to Deregulation," *Deregulation: Appraisal Before the Fact*, Thomas G. Gies & Werner Sichel (eds.) (Ann Arbor: Graduate School of Business Administration, University of Michigan, 1982), 119–126.

"Airline Pilots Link Decline in Safety to Deregulation," *Los Angeles Times*, December 16, 1985, Part I, 4.

Aitken, Hugh G. J., *Syntony and Spark: The Origin of Radio* (New York: John Wiley & Sons, 1976).

———,*The Continuous Wave: Technology and American Radio, 1900–1932* (Princeton: Princeton University Press, 1985).

American Enterprise Institute for Public Policy Research, "Labor Law Reform?: A Round Table" (Washington, DC: author, 1978).

———, "The Proposed Agency for Consumer Advocacy" (Washington, DC: author, 1975).

American Telephone and Telegraph Co., "Competition in Telecommunications: A Matter of Public Interest," pamphlet (New York: author, 1984).

Angell, Joseph K., *A Treatise on the Law of Carriers*, 5th Edition (Boston: Little, Brown, 1877).

Archer, Gleason, *Big Business and Radio* (New York: American Historical Society, 1939).

———, *History of Radio to 1926* (New York: American Historical Company, 1938).

Aronson, Sidney H., "Bell's Electrical Toy: What's the Use? The Sociology of Early Telephone Usage," *Social Impact of the Telephone*, Ithiel de Sola Pool (ed.) (Cambridge: MIT Press, 1977), 15–39.

Arthur Andersen & Co., *Cost of Government Regulation Study for Business Roundtable* (Chicago: author, 1979).

"As the Big Get Bigger, the Small May Disappear," *Business Week,* January 12, 1987, 90.

"AT&T Lifts Earnings 11.1%, Calls for Higher Local Rates," *The New York Times,* April 16, 1981, D5.

Averch, Harvey, and Leland J. Johnson, "Behavior of the Firm Under Regulatory Constraint," *American Economic Review* 52/5 (December 1962), 1052–1069.

"The Baby Bells: Special Report," *Business Week,* December 2, 1985, 94–106.

Baer, Walter S., *Interactive Television: Prospects for Two-Way Services on Cable,* Rand Memorandum R-888-MF (Santa Monica: Rand Corporation, 1971).

Bailey, Elizabeth E., David R. Graham, and Daniel P. Kaplan, *Deregulating the Airlines* (Cambridge: MIT Press, 1985).

Baker, Ray Stannard, *Woodrow Wilson and World Settlement,* 3 vols. (New York: Doubleday, Page & Co., 1922).

Banning, William Peck, *Commercial Broadcasting Pioneer: The WEAF Experiment, 1922– 1926* (Cambridge: Harvard University Press, 1946).

Bardach, Eugene, and Robert A. Kagan, *Going by the Book: The Problem of Regulatory Unreasonableness* (Philadelphia: Temple University Press, 1982).

———, *Social Regulation: Strategies for Reform* (San Francisco: Institute for Contemporary Studies, 1982).

Barnett, Harold J., and Edward Greenberg, "On the Economics of Wired City Television," *American Economic Review* 58/3 (June 1968), 503–508.

Barnouw, Erik, *A History of Broadcasting in the United States.* Vol. 1: *A Tower in Babel* (1966); Vol. 2: *The Golden Web* (1968); Vol. 3: *The Image Empire* (1970) (New York: Oxford University Press).

Barron, Jerome A., "Access to the Press—A New First Amendment Right," *Harvard Law Review* 80/8 (June 1967), 1641–1678.

———, *Freedom of the Press for Whom?: The Right of Access to Mass Media* (Bloomington: Indiana University Press, 1973).

Barrow, Roscoe L., "Network Broadcasting—The Report of the FCC Network Study Staff," *Law and Contemporary Problems* 22/4 (Autumn 1957), 611–625.

Baughman, James L., *Television's Guardians: The FCC and the Politics of Programming, 1958–1967* (Knoxville: University of Tennessee Press, 1985).

Baumol, William J., and Alvin K. Klevorick, "Input Choices and Rate-of-Return Regulation: An Overview of the Discussion," *Bell Journal of Economics and Management Science* 1/2 (Autumn 1970), 162–190.

Bazelon, David L., "FCC Regulation of the Telecommunications Press," *Duke Law Journal* 1975/2 (May 1975), 213–251.

Beard, Charles, and Mary Beard, *The Rise of American Civilization* (New York: Macmillan, 1933).

Beelar, Donald C., "Cables in the Sky and the Struggle for Their Control," *Federal Communications Bar Journal* 21/1 (1967), 26–41.

Beer, Samuel, "The Modernization of American Federalism," *Publius* 3/2 (Fall 1973), 49– 95.

Behrman, Bradley, "Civil Aeronautics Board," *The Politics of Regulation,* James Q. Wilson, (ed.) (New York: Basic Books, 1980), 75–120.

Benjamin, Burton, "Technology and the Bottom Line Create Profound Challenges," *The New York Times,* August 17, 1986, Sec. 2, 1, 25.

Benjamin, Walter, "Theses on the Philosophy of History," *Illuminations,* Hannah Arendt (ed.) (New York: Schocken Books, 1969), 253–264.

Bennett, Robert A., "Deregulation Affects Banking," *The New York Times*, December 5, 1983, 29, 25.

———, "Specter at Continental," *The New York Times*, May 20, 1984, Sec. 3, 8.

———, "Now, the Age of Fast-Buck Banking," *The New York Times*, December 14, 1986, Sec. 3, 1, 8.

———, "A Banking Puzzle: Mixing Freedom and Protection," *The New York Times*, February 19, 1984, Sec. 3, 1, 12–13.

———, "Deregulation's Effect at Banks," *The New York Times*, March 16, 1984, 30.

Bell, Daniel, and Virginia Held, "The Community Revolution," *The Public Interest* 16 (Summer 1969), 142–177.

Benson, Lee, *Merchants, Farmers, and Railroads: Railroad Regulation and New York Politics, 1850–1887* (Cambridge: Harvard University Press, 1955).

Berg, Eric N., "New Phone Company Twist," *The New York Times*, March 11, 1985, 21, 24.

———, "Bank Deregulation Crossroads," *The New York Times*, May 3, 1986, 21, 24.

Bernstein, Marver H., *Regulating Business by Independent Commission* (Princeton: Princeton University Press, 1955).

Besen, Stanley M., Thomas G. Krattenmaker, A. Richard Metzger, Jr., and John R. Woodbury, *Misregulating Television: Network Dominance and the FCC* (Chicago: University of Chicago Press, 1984).

Besen, Stanley M., and Robert W. Crandall, "The Deregulation of Cable Television," *Law and Contemporary Problems*, 44/1 (Winter 1981), 77–124.

Blachly, Frederick F., and Miriam E. Oatman, "Sabotage of the Administrative Process," *Public Administration Review* 6/3 (Summer 1946), 213–227.

Block, Fred, "The Ruling Class Does Not Rule: Notes on the Marxist Theory of the State," *Socialist Revolution* 7/3 (May–June 1977), 6–28.

Bluestone, Barry, and Bennett Harrison, *The Deindustrialization of America: Plant Closings, Community Abandonment, and the Dismantling of Basic Industry* (New York: Basic Books, 1982).

Bolter, Walter G. (ed.), *Telecommunications Policy for the 1980s: The Transition to Competition* (Englewood Cliffs, NJ: Prentice-Hall, 1984).

Bonbright, J. C., *Principles of Public Utility Rates* (New York: Columbia University Press, 1961).

Booz-Allen & Hamilton, *Organization and Management Survey of the FCC;* United States, Commission on Organization of the Executive Branch of the Government (Washington, DC: Government printing Office, 1949).

Booz-Allen & Hamilton, Inc., *Organization and Management Survey of the Federal Communications Commission for the Bureau of the Budget* (Chicago: Booz-Allen & Hamilton, 1962).

Borchardt, Kurt, *Structure and Performance of the U.S. Communications Industry* (Boston: Graduate School of Business Administration, Harvard University 1970).

Bornholz, Robert, and David S. Evans, "The Early History of Competition in the Telephone Industry," in *Breaking Up Bell: Essays on Industrial Organization and Regulation*, David S. Evans (ed.) (New York: North-Holland, 1983), 7–40.

Boyer, Peter J., "Trauma Time on Network TV," *The New York Times*, November 2, 1986, Sec. 3, 1, 28.

Bramson, Leon, *The Political Context of Sociology* (Princeton: Princeton University Press, 1961).

Braunstein, Yale M., "Recent Trends in Cable Television Related to the Prospects for New Television Networks," prepared for the Commercial Television Practices Inquiry of the Federal Communications Commission, *Preliminary Report on Prospects for Additional Networks* (Washington, DC: FCC, 1979).

Brenner, Daniel L., and William L. Rivers (eds.), *Free but Regulated: Conflicting Traditions in Media Law* (Ames, Iowa: Iowa State University Press, 1982).

Breyer, Stephen, *Regulation and Its Reform* (Cambridge: Harvard University Press, 1982).

————, and Richard B. Stewart, *Administrative Law and Regulatory Policy* (Boston: Little, Brown & Co., 1979).

Briggs, B. Bruce (ed.), *The New Class* (New Brunswick: Transaction Books, 1979).

British Telecommunications Union Committee, *The American Experience . . . A Report on the Dilemma of Telecommunications in the USA* (London: author, 1983).

Brock, Gerald W., *The Telecommunications Industry: The Dynamics of Market Structure* (Cambridge: Harvard University Press, 1981).

————, *The U.S. Computer Industry: A Study of Market Power* (Cambridge: Ballinger, 1975).

Brooks, John, *Telephone: The First Hundred Years* (New York: Harper & Row, 1975).

Brown, Ralph S., Jr., "Character and Candor Requirements for FCC Licensees," *Law and Contemporary Problems* 22/4 (Autumn 1957), 644–657.

Bryan, Lowell L. "The Credit Bomb in Our Financial Future," *Harvard Business Review* 87/1 (January/February 1987), 45–51.

Buchanan, James M., *The Demand and Supply of Public Goods* (Chicago: Rand McNally, 1968).

————, and Gordon Tullock, *The Calculus of Consent: Logical Foundations of Constitutional Democracy* (Ann Arbor: University of Michigan Press, 1962).

Buck, Solon Justus, *The Granger Movement: A Study of Agricultural Organization and Its Political, Economic and Social Manifestations, 1870–1880* (Cambridge: Harvard University Press, 1913).

"Business' Most Powerful Lobby in Washington," *Business Week,* December 20, 1976.

Carson, Rachel, *Silent Spring* (New York: Fawcett Crest, 1962).

Carter, Stephen, "Technology, Democracy, and the Manipulation of Consent," *Yale Law Journal* 93/3 (January 1984), 581–607.

Cary, William L., *Politics and the Regulatory Agencies* (New York: McGraw-Hill, 1967).

Castells, Manuel, *The City and the Grassroots: A Cross-Cultural Theory of Urban Social Movements* (Berkeley: University of California Press, 1983).

Caves, Douglas W., Laurits R. Christensen, and Michael W. Tretheway, "Airline Productivity Under Deregulation," *Regulation* (November/December 1982), 25–28.

Caves, Richard E., *Air Transport and Its Regulators* (Cambridge: Harvard University Press, 1962).

Chandler, Alfred D., Jr., *The Visible Hand: The Managerial Revolution in American Business* (Cambridge: Harvard University Press, 1977).

"*Channels* '87 Field Guide to the Electronic Environment," *Channels,* January 1987.

"*Channels* '88 Field Guide to the Electronic Environment," *Channels,* January 1988.

Chase, Francis, Jr., *Sound and Fury: An Informal History of Broadcasting* (New York: Harper, 1942).

Chatov, Robert, "Government Regulation: Process and Substantive Impacts," *Research in Corporate Social Performance and Policy,* Lee E. Preston (ed.), Vol. 1 (Greenwich, Conn.: JAI Press, Inc., 1978), 223–254.

Childs, William R., *Trucking and the Public Interest: The Emergence of Federal Regulation, 1914–1940* (Knoxville: University of Tennessee Press, 1985).

Clark, John B., and John M. Clark, *The Control of Trusts* (New York: Macmillan, 1912).

Claybrook, Joan, et al., *Retreat from Safety: Reagan's Attack on America's Health* (New York: Pantheon, 1984).

Coase, Ronald H., "The Problem of Social Cost," *Journal of Law and Economics* 3/1 (October 1960), 1–44.

Cochran, Thomas C., *Railroad Leaders, 1845–1890: The Business Mind in Action* (Cambridge: Harvard University Press, 1953).

Cole, Barry, and Mal Oettinger, *Reluctant Regulators: The FCC and the Broadcast Audience* (Reading, Mass: Addison-Wesley, 1978).

Coll, Steve, *The Deal of the Century: The Breakup of AT&T* (New York: Atheneum, 1986).

Committee for Economic Development, *Broadcasting and Cable Television: Policies for Diversity and Change* (New York: author, 1975).

———, *Fighting Inflation and Promoting Growth: A Statement on National Policy by the Research and Policy Committee of the Committee for Economic Development* (New York: Committee for Economic Development, 1976).

Common Cause, *Serving Two Masters: A Common Cause Study of Conflicts of Interest in the Executive Branch* (Washington, DC: Common Cause, 1976).

Conference Board, *Answers to Inflation and Recession: Economic Policies for a Modern Society*, Albert T. Sommers (ed.) (Washington, DC: The Conference Board, 1975).

———, *Information Technology: Some Critical Implications for Decision Makers*, Report 537 (New York: author, 1972).

Congressional Quarterly, *Federal Regulatory Directory, 1983–84* (Washington, DC: Congressional Quarterly, Inc., 1984).

Conine, Ernest, "More and More, Deregulation Won't Fly," *Los Angeles Times*, July 28, 1987, Part II, 9.

Cooley, Thomas, *A Treatise on Constitutional Limitations*, 2nd Ed. (Boston: Little, Brown, 1871).

Coon, Horace, *American Tel & Tel: The Story of a Great Monopoly* (New York: Longmans, Green & Co., 1939).

Cornell, Nina W., Daniel Kelley, and Peter R. Greenhalgh, "Social Objectives and Competition in Common Carrier Communications: Incompatible or Inseparable?" (Washington, DC: Federal Communications Commission, Office of Plans and Policy, 1980).

Cornell, Nina W., Michael Pelcovits, and S. Brenner, "A Legacy of Regulatory Failure," *Regulation* 7/4 (1983).

Crandall, Robert W., *Controlling Industrial Pollution: The Economics and Politics of Clean Air* (Washington, DC: Brookings Institution, 1983).

Crittenden, Ann, "The Economic Wind's Blowing Toward the Right—For Now," *The New York Times*, July 16, 1978, Section 3, at 1.

Croly, Herbert, *The Promise of American Life* (New York: Macmillan, 1909).

Crozier, Michel J., Samuel P. Huntington, and Joji Watanuki, *The Crisis of Democracy: Report on the Governability of Democracies to the Trilateral Commission* (New York: New York University Press, 1975).

Cushman, Robert E., *The Independent Regulatory Commissions* (New York: Octagon Books, 1972).

Czitrom, Daniel J., *Media and the American Mind: From Morse to McLuhan* (Chapel Hill: University of North Carolina Press, 1982).

Dallos, Robert E., and Lee May, "Debate Still Rages Over Deregulation," *Los Angeles Times*, November 2, 1986, 1, 20–22.

Danielian, N. R., *AT&T: The Story of Industrial Conquest* (New York: Vanguard Press, 1939).

Daniels, Josephus, *The Wilson Era: Years of War and After, 1917–1923* (Chapel Hill: University of North Carolina Press, 1946).

"The Darkened Channels: UHF Television and the FCC," *Harvard Law Review* 75/8 (June 1962), 1578–1607.

Davis, Bob, "Broadcasters, Absent Regulation, Kill News Shows—But Is That Bad?," *The Wall Street Journal*, October 16, 1986, Sec. 2, 1.

Davis, G. Cullom, "The Transformation of the Federal Trade Commission, 1914–1929," *Mississippi Valley History Review* XLIV (December 1962), 437–455.

Davis, Kenneth Culp, *Administrative Law Treatise* (St. Paul: West Publishing Co., 1958).

———, *Discretionary Justice: A Preliminary Inquiry* (Urbana: University of Illinois Press, 1977).

Day, Kathleen, "Re-Regulating the Savings and Loans," *The Washington Post National Weekly Edition*, May 26, 1986, 6–7.

DeFina, Robert, *Public and Private Expenditures for Federal Regulation of Business*, Working Paper No. 27, Center for the Study of American Business, Washington University, St. Louis, November 1977, mimeo.

Derthick, Martha, and Paul J. Quirk, *The Politics of Deregulation* (Washington, DC: The Brookings Institution, 1985).

De Witt, Benjamin Parke, *The Progressive Movement* (New York: Macmillan, 1915).

Diamond, Edwin, Norman Sandler, and Milton Mueller, *Telecommunications in Crisis: The First Amendment, Technology, and Deregulation* (Washington, DC: The Cato Institute, 1983).

Dillon, John F., *Treatise on Municipal Corporations* (1872).

DiPietro, Aldon, "An Analysis of the OSHA Inspection Program in Manufacturing Industries, 1972–73," Draft Technical Analysis Paper, US Department of Labor (Washington, DC: Government Printing Office, August 1976).

Domhoff, G. William, *The Powers That Be: Processes of Ruling Class Domination in America* (New York: Vintage Press, 1978).

Dordick, Herbert S., H. G. Bradley, and B. Nanus, *The Emerging Network Marketplace* (Norwood, NJ: Ablex Publishing Co., 1981).

Douglas, George W., and James C. Miller III, *Economic Regulation of Domestic Air Transport* (Washington, DC: Brookings Institution, 1974).

Douglas, Mary, and Aaron Wildavsky, *Risk and Culture* (Berkeley: University of California Press, 1982).

Downs, Anthony, *An Economic Theory of Democracy* (New York: Harper and Row, 1957).

———, *Inside Bureaucracy* (Boston: Little, Brown, 1967).

DuBoff, Richard B., "Business Demand and the Development of the Telegraph in the United States," *Business History Review* 54/4 (Winter 1980), 459–479.

———, "The Rise of Communications Regulation: The Telegraph Industry, 1844–1880," *Journal of Communication* 34/3 (Summer 1984), 52–66.

———, "The Telegraph and the Structure of Markets in the United States, 1845–1890," *Research in Economic History* 8 (1983), 253–277.

———, "The Telegraph in Nineteenth-Century America: Technology and Monopoly," *Comparative Studies in Society and History* 26/4 (October 1984), 571–586.

Dubofsky, Melvyn, *Industrialism and the American Worker, 1865–1920* (Arlington Heights: AHM Publishing Co, 1975).

Eads, George C., and Michael Fix, *Relief or Reform? Reagan's Regulatory Dilemma* (Washington, DC: The Urban Institute Press, 1984).

Emery, Walter, *Broadcasting and the Government: Responsibilities and Regulation* (East Lansing: Michigan State University Press, 1971).

Engerman, Stanley L, and Robert E. Gallman, "US Economic Growth, 1763–1860," *Research in Economic History* 8 (1983), 1–46.

Epstein, Edwin M., "An Irony of Electoral Reform," *Regulation,* May/June 1979, 35–41.

Esslin, Martin, *The Age of Television* (San Francisco: W. H. Freeman, 1982).

"Excerpts of Statement by the FCC Counsel," *The New York Times,* August 5, 1987, 20.

Fabrikant, Geraldine, "2 Cable Companies Set $1.6 Billion Merger," *The New York Times,* March 10, 1988, 29, 33.

Fagen, M. D. (ed.), *A History of Engineering and Science in the Bell System: National Service in War and Peace, 1925–1975* (New York: Bell Telephone Laboratories, Inc., 1978).

Fainsod, Merle, "Some Reflections on the Nature of the Regulatory Process," *Public Policy,* C. J. Friedrich and Edward S. Mason (eds.) (Cambridge: Harvard University Press, 1940), 297–323.

————, and Lincoln Gordon, *Government and the American Economy,* 3rd ed. (New York: Norton, 1941).

Fainstein, Norman, and Susan Fainstein, *Urban Political Movements: The Search for Power by Minority Groups in American Cities* (Englewood Cliffs, NJ: Prentice-Hall, 1974).

Faulkner, Harold U., *The Decline of Laissez-Faire, 1897–1917* (New York: Rinehart, 1951).

"FCC Says Licensing Policy Favoring Minorities Should Be Eliminated," *Los Angeles Times,* September 16, 1986, 14.

Feder, Barnaby J., "MCI Plans 4th-Quarter Write-Off," *The New York Times,* December 3, 1986, 33.

Fellmeth, Robert C., *The Interstate Commerce Omission: The Public Interest and the ICC* (New York: Grossman, 1970).

Fiorina, Morris P., *Congress: Keystone of the Washington Establishment* (New Haven: Yale University Press, 1977).

————, and Roger G. Noll, "Voters, Bureaucrats and Legislators," *Journal of Public Economics* 9/2 (April 1978), 239–254.

Fisher, Ben C., "Communications Act Amendments, 1952—An Attempt to Legislate Fairness," *Law and Contemporary Problems* 22/4 (Autumn 1957), 672–696.

Fishman, Katherine D., *The Computer Establishment* (New York: Harper & Row, 1981).

Flanigan, James, "The Gap Between Rich and Poor Is Widening," *Los Angeles Times,* December 4, 1983, Business section, 1.

————, "Networks Will Emerge on Top in TV Shakeout," *Los Angeles Times,* January 9, 1987, Part IV, 1, 3.

Fowler, Mark S., and Daniel L. Brenner, "A Marketplace Approach to Broadcast Regulation," *Texas Law Review* 60/2 (February 1982), 207–257.

Frieden, R. M., "The Computer Inquiries: Mapping the Communications/Data Processing Terrain," *Federal Communications Law Journal* 33/1 (Winter 1981), 55–115.

Friedland, Lewis A., *Cable-Broadband Communications: The Control of Information in Post-Industrial Society,* unpublished Ph.D. dissertation, Department of Sociology, Brandeis University, 1985.

Friedman, Lawrence M., *A History of American Law* (New York: Simon and Schuster, 1973).

————, and Jack Ladinsky, "Social Change and the Law of Industrial Accidents," *Columbia Law Review* 67/1 (January 1967), 50–82.

Friedrich, Carl, and Evelyn Sternberg, "Congress and the Control of Radio Broadcasting," *American Political Science Review* 37/5 (October 1943), 797–818.

Friendly, Fred, *Due to Circumstances Beyond Our Control. . .* (New York: Vintage Books, 1967).

———, "Asleep at the Switch of the Wired City," *Saturday Review* (October 10, 1970), 58–60.

Friendly, Henry, *The Federal Administrative Agencies: The Need for Better Definition of Standards* (Cambridge: Harvard University Press, 1962).

Gabel, Richard, "The Early Competitive Era in Telephone Communication, 1893–1920," *Law and Contemporary Problems* 34/2 (Spring 1969), 340–359.

Galbraith, John Kenneth, *American Capitalism: The Concept of Countervailing Power* (Boston: Houghton-Mifflin, 1956).

———, *The Great Crash* (New York: Houghton-Mifflin, 1955).

Garland, Merrick B., "Deregulation and Judicial Review," *Harvard Law Review* 98/3 (January 1985), 507–591.

Geller, Henry, "A Modest Proposal for Modest Reform of the Federal Communications Commission," *Georgetown Law Journal* 63/3 (February 1973), 705–724.

George, Gerald F., "The Federal Communications Commission and the Bell System: Abdication of Regulatory Responsibility," *Indiana Law Journal* 44/3 (Spring 1969), 459–477.

Gilmore, Grant, *The Ages of American Law* (New Haven: Yale University Press, 1977).

———, *The Death of Contract* (Columbus: Ohio State University Press, 1974).

Gitlin, Todd, *Inside Prime Time* (New York: Pantheon, 1983).

———, "Media Sociology: The Dominant Paradigm," *Theory and Society* 6 (1978), 205–253.

Glaberson, William, "Is OSHA Falling Down on the Job?," *The New York Times,* August 2, 1987, Sec. 3, 1, 6.

Glasser, Theodore L., "Competition and Diversity Among Radio Formats: Legal and Structural Issues," *Mass Communication Review Yearbook,* Michael Gurevitch and Mark R. Levy (eds.), Vol. 5 (1985), 547–562.

Glen, Kristin Booth, *Report on Subscription Television,* prepared for the Commercial Television Practices Inquiry of the Federal Communications Commission, *Preliminary Report on Prospects for Additional Networks* (Washington, DC: FCC, 1980).

Goodrich, Carter, *Government Promotion of American Canals and Railroads, 1800–1890* (New York: Columbia University Press, 1960).

———, "The Revulsion Against Internal Improvements," *Journal of Economic History* 10 (November 1950), 145–169.

Gormley, William T., Jr., *The Politics of Public Utility Regulation* (Pittsburgh: University of Pittsburgh, 1983).

Goulden, Joseph C., *Monopoly* (New York: G. P. Putnam's Sons, 1968).

"Government Sues Telephone Trust," *The New York Times,* July 25, 1913, 1.

Graebner, William, "Federalism in the Progressive Era: A Structural Interpretation of Reform," *Journal of American History* 44/2 (September 1977), 331–357.

Gray, Horace M., "The Passing of the Public Utility Concept," *Journal of Land and Public Utility Economics* 16/1 (February 1940), 1–20.

Gray, Robert Reed, "Aviation Safety: Fact or Fiction," *Technology Review,* August–September 1987, 32–40.

Graham, Otis L. (ed.), *From Roosevelt to Roosevelt: American Politics and Diplomacy, 1901–1941* (New York: Appleton-Century-Crofts, 1971).

Green, Mark J. (ed.), *The Monopoly Makers* (New York: Grossman, 1973).

———, and Ralph Nader, "Economic Regulation vs Competition: Uncle Sam the Monopoly Man," *Yale Law Journal* 82/5 (April 1973), 871–889.

Greenberg, Peter S., "Congress Considering Re-Regulation of Airlines," *Los Angeles Times,* October 18, 1987, Part VII, 2, 8.

Grundfest, Joseph A., *Citizen Participation in Broadcast Licensing Before the FCC*, R-1896-MF (Santa Monica: Rand, 1976).

Gutman, Herbert G., *Work, Culture and Society in Industrializing America: Essays in American Working-Class and Social History* (New York: Vintage Books, 1977).

Haar, Charles M., and Daniel William Fessler, *The Wrong Side of the Tracks* (New York: Simon & Schuster, 1986).

Haber, Samuel, *Efficiency and Uplift: Scientific Management in the Progressive Era, 1890–1920* (Chicago: University of Chicago Press, 1964).

Habermas, Jürgen, *Legitimation Crisis* (Boston, Beacon Press, 1975).

———, *Strukturwandel der Offentlichkeit* (Neuwied: Luchterhand, 1962).

———, "The Public Sphere: An Encyclopedia Article," *New German Critique* 1/3 (Fall 1974), 49–55.

Hamilton, Martha M., "You Can't Get Here from There: Deregulation Is Leaving Rural Communities Stranded," *Washington Post National Weekly Edition*, July 21, 1986, 6–7.

Handlin, Oscar, "The Development of the Corporation," in *The Corporation: A Theological Inquiry*, Michael Novak and John W. Cooper (eds.) (Washington, DC: American Enterprise Institute for Public Policy Research, 1981), 1–16.

Haney, Lewis H., *A Congressional History of Railways in the United States* (Madison, Wis.: University of Wisconsin Press, 1908; reprinted, New York: Augustus M. Kelley, 1968).

Hanks, William E. and Terry A. Pickett, "Influence of Community-Based Citizens Groups on Television Broadcasters in Five Eastern Cities: An Exploratory Study," *Proceedings of the Sixth Annual Telecommunications Policy Research Conference*, Herbert A. Dordick (ed.) (Lexington, Mass.: DC Heath & Co., 1979), 105–133.

Hanscom, C. D., *Dates in American Telephone Technology* (New York: Bell Telephone Laboratories, Inc., 1961).

Harbeson, Robert W., "Railroads and Regulation, 1877–1916: Conspiracy or Public Interest?," *Journal of Economic History* 27/2 (June 1967), 230–242.

Harlow, Alvin F., *Old Wires and New Waves: The History of the Telegraph, Telephone, and Wireless* (New York: D. Appleton-Century Company, 1936).

Hartz, Louis, *Economic Policy and Democratic Thought* (Cambridge: Harvard University Press, 1948).

———, *The Liberal Tradition in America: An Interpretation of American Political Thought Since the Revolution* (New York: Harcourt Brace Jovanovich, 1955).

Hays, Samuel P., *Conservation and the Gospel of Efficiency* (Cambridge: Harvard University Press, 1959).

———, *The Response to Industrialism, 1885–1914* (Chicago: University of Chicago Press, 1957).

———, "The Politics of Reform in Municipal Government in the Progressive Era," *Pacific Northwest Quarterly* 55/4 (October 1964), 157–169.

———, "Political Parties and the Community-Society Continuum," in *The American Party Systems: Stages of Political Development*, William Nisbet Chambers and Walter Dean Burnham (eds.) (New York: Oxford University Press, 1967), 169–177.

———, "Political Choice in Regulatory Administration," in *Regulation in Perspective*, Thomas K. McCraw (ed.), (Cambridge: Harvard Business School, 1981), 124–154.

Hawley, Ellis W., *The New Deal and the Problem of Monopoly* (Princeton: Princeton University Press, 1966).

———, "Three Facets of Hooverian Associationalism: Lumber, Aviation, and Movies, 1921–1930," *Regulation in Perspective*, Thomas K. McCraw (ed.) (Cambridge: Harvard Business School, 1981), 95–123.

Head, Sydney, *Broadcasting in America* (Boston: Houghton-Mifflin, 1956).

Headrick, Daniel R., *The Tools of Empire: Technology and European Imperialism in the Nineteenth Century* (New York: Oxford University Press, 1981).

Heckscher, Eli F., *Mercantilism* (New York: Macmillan, 1935).

Hector, Louis, "Problems of the CAB and the Independent Regulatory Commissions," *Yale Law Journal* 69/6 (May 1960), 931–964.

Henry, David, "Surface Transportation," 38th Annual Report on American Industry, *Forbes,* January 13, 1986, 208–209.

Herring, James M., and Gerald C. Gross, *Telecommunications: Economics and Regulation* (New York: McGraw-Hill, 1936; reprinted Arno Press, 1974).

Hilton, George W., "The Consistency of the Interstate Commerce Act," *Journal of Law and Economics* 9 (October 1966), 87–113.

Hofstadter, Richard (ed.), *The Progressive Movement, 1900–1915* (Englewood Cliffs: Prentice-Hall, 1963).

Holmes, Oliver Wendell, *The Common Law* (Boston: Little, Brown, 1951).

Holusha, John, "US Fines Chrysler $1.5 Million, Citing Workers' Exposure to Peril," *The New York Times,* July 7, 1987, 1, 10.

Horwitz, Morton J., *The Transformation of American Law, 1780–1860* (Cambridge: Harvard University Press, 1977).

Horwitz, Robert B., "Understanding Deregulation," *Theory and Society* 15/1–2 (1986), 139–174.

Howard, Herbert H., "Multiple Broadcast Ownership: Regulatory History," *Federal Communications Bar Journal* 27/1 (1974), 1–70.

Huber, Peter, *The Geodesic Network: 1987 Report on Competition in the Telephone Industry,* Report to US Dept. of Justice (Washington, DC: Government Printing Office, 1987).

Hudson, James, *Railways and the Republic* (New York: Harper & Brothers, 1886).

Huntington, Samuel P., *Political Order in Changing Societies* (New Haven: Yale University Press, 1968).

———, "The Marasmus of the ICC: The Commission, the Railroads, and the Public Interest," *Yale Law Journal* 61/4 (April 1952), 467–509.

Hurst, James Willard, *Law and the Conditions of Freedom in the Nineteenth Century United States* (Madison: University of Wisconsin Press, 1964).

"Is Deregulation Working?," *Business Week,* December 22, 1986, 50–55.

Jackson, Charles O., *Food and Drug Legislation in the New Deal* (Princeton: Princeton University Press, 1970).

Jacobs, Clyde E., *Law Writers and the Courts: The Influence of Thomas M. Cooley, Christopher G. Tiedeman, and John F. Dillon Upon American Constitutional Law* (Berkeley: University of California Press, 1954).

Jaffe, Louis L., "The Effective Limits of the Administrative Process," *Harvard Law Review* 67/7 (May 1954), 1105–1135.

———, "The Independent Agency—A New Scapegoat," [review of Bernstein's *Regulating Business by Independent Commission], Yale Law Journal* 65/7 (June 1956), 1068–1076.

Jensen, A. G., "The Evolution of Modern Television," in *A Technological History of Motion Pictures and Television,* Raymond Fielding (ed.) (Berkeley: University of California Press, 1967), 235–249.

Johnson, Leland L., "Monopoly and Regulation in Telecommunications," in Glenn O. Robinson (ed.), *Communications for Tomorrow: Policy Perspectives for the 1980s* (New York: Praeger, 1978), 127–155.

———, *The Future of Cable Television: Some Problems of Federal Regulation,* Rand Memorandum RM-6199-FF (Santa Monica: Rand Corporation, 1970).

Johnson, Nicholas, and John Jay Dystel, "A Day in the Life: The Federal Communications Commission," *Yale Law Journal* 82/8 (July 1973), 1575–1634.

Johnston, Oswald, "Greyhound to Buy Routes, Assets of Trailways Corp.," *Los Angeles Times*, June 20, 1987, 1, 20.

Jome, Hiram L., *Economics of the Radio Industry* (Chicago: A. W. Shaw, 1925; reprinted, New York: Arno Press, 1971).

Jones, Sir William, *An Essay on the Law of Bailments*, 4th English Edition (London: S. Sweet, 1833).

Jordan, William A., *Airline Regulation in America* (Baltimore: Johns Hopkins Press, 1970).

———, "Producer Protection, Prior Market Structure and the Effects of Government Regulation," *Journal of Law and Economics* 15/1 (April 1972), 151–76.

Josephson, Matthew, *The Politicos, 1865–1896* (New York: Harcourt Brace & Co., 1938).

Joskow, Paul L., "Inflation and Environmental Concern: Structural Change in the Process of Public Utility Price Regulation," *Journal of Law and Economics* 17/2 (October 1974), 291–327.

———, "Pricing Decisions of Regulated Firms, A Behavioral Approach," *Bell Journal of Economics and Management Science* 4/1 (Spring 1973), 118–140.

Kahn, Alfred E., *The Economics of Regulation: Principles and Institutions* (New York: John Wiley & Sons, 1970).

———, "The Passing of the Public Utility Concept: A Reprise," in Eli Noam (ed.), *Telecommunications Regulation Today and Tomorrow* (New York: Law and Business, Inc., 1983), 3–37.

Kahn, Frank J. (ed.), *Documents of American Broadcasting* (Englewood Cliffs, NJ: Prentice-Hall, 1984).

Keeler, Theodore E., "Airline Regulation and Market Performance," *Bell Journal of Economics and Management Science* 3/2 (Autumn 1972), 399–424.

Keller, Bill, "A Union Copes With Deregulation," *The New York Times*, November 18, 1984, Sec. 3, 4.

Keller, Morton, "The Pluralist State: American Economic Regulation in Comparative Perspective, 1900–1930," in *Regulation in Perspective*, Thomas K. McCraw, (ed.) (Cambridge: Harvard Business School, 1981), 56–94.

Kennedy, David M. (ed), *Progressivism: The Critical Issues* (Boston: Little, Brown, 1971).

Kersta, Noran E., "The Business Side of Television," *Electronics* 13/2 (March 1940), 90–92.

"The King of Cable TV," *Business Week*, October 26, 1987, 88–96.

Kitch, Edmund W., "Regulation and the American Common Market," in *Regulation, Federalism, and Interstate Commerce*, A. Dan Tarlock (ed.) (Cambridge: Oelgeschlager, Gunn & Hain, Pulishers, 1981), 7–56.

Kittross, John M., *Television Frequency Allocation Policy in the United States* (New York: Arno Press, 1979).

Kohlmeier, Louis M., Jr., *The Regulators: Watchdog Agencies and the Public Interest* (New York: Harper and Row, 1969).

Kolko, Gabriel, *The Triumph of Conservatism: A Reinterpretation of American History, 1900–1916* (New York: Free Press, 1963).

———, *Railroads and Regulation, 1877–1916* (Princeton: Princeton University Press, 1965).

Krasnow, Erwin G., Lawrence D. Longley, and Herbert A. Terry, *The Politics of Broadcast Regulation*, Third Ed. (New York: St. Martin's Press, 1982).

Kristol, Irving, "A Regulated Society?," *Regulation* 1/1 (July/August 1977), 12–13.

Labor Research Association, "Economic Notes," 54/9 (October 1986).

Landis, James M., *The Administrative Process* (New Haven: Yale University Press, 1938).

———, *President's Committee on Administrative Management, Report With Special Studies* (Washington, DC: Government Printing Office, 1937).

———, *Report on Regulatory Agencies to the President-Elect* (Washington, DC: Government Printing Office, 1960).

Lankes, L. R., "Historical Sketch of Television's Progress," in *A Technological History of Motion Pictures and Television,* Raymond Fielding (ed.) (Berkeley: University of California Press, 1967), 227–229.

Larrabee, William, *The Railroad Question* (Chicago: The Schulte Publishing Co., 1893).

Lasswell, Harold D., *Propaganda Technique in the World War* (New York: Knopf, 1927).

Lave, Lester B., *The Strategy of Social Regulation* (Washington, DC: Brookings Institution, 1981).

Le Duc, Don R., *Cable Television and the FCC: A Crisis in Media Control* (Philadelphia: Temple University Press, 1973).

Lessing, Louis, "The Television Freeze," *Fortune* XXXX (November 1949).

Letwin, William, "Congress and the Sherman Antitrust Law," *The University of Chicago Law Review* 23/1 (Autumn 1955), 221–256.

Leuchtenberg, William E., *Franklin D. Roosevelt and the New Deal, 1932–1940* (New York: Harper & Row, 1963).

Leventhal, Harold, "Environmental Decisionmaking and the Role of the Courts," *University of Pennsylvania Law Review* 122/3 (January 1974), 509–555.

Levine, Michael E., "Is Regulation Necessary? California Air Transportation and National Regulatory Policy," *Yale Law Journal* 74/8 (July 1965), 1416–1447.

Lewis, Anthony, "AT&T Settles Antitrust Case; Shares Patents," *The New York Times,* January 25, 1956, 1, 16.

Lichty, Lawrence W., "Members of the Federal Radio Commission and Federal Communications Commission, 1927–61," *Journal of Broadcasting* 6/1 (Winter 1961–62), 23–34.

———, "The Impact of FRC and FCC Commissioners' Backgrounds on the Regulation of Broadcasting," *Journal of Broadcasting* 6/2 (Spring 1962), 97–110.

Lilley, William, and James C. Miller III, "The New 'Social Regulation,'" *The Public Interest* 47 (Spring 1977), 49–61.

Lindblom, Charles E., *Politics and Markets: The World's Political-Economic Systems* (New York: Basic Books, 1977).

Lindley, Lester, G., *The Constitution Faces Technology: The Relationship of the National Government to the Telegraph, 1866–1884* (New York: Arno Press, 1975).

Lippmann, Walter, *Drift and Mastery* (New York: M. Kennerley, 1914).

Loeb, G. Hamilton, "The Communications Act Policy Toward Competition: A Failure to Communicate," *Duke Law Journal* 1978/1 (March 1978), 1–56.

Longley, Lawrence D., "FCC's Attempt to Regulate Commercial Time," *Journal of Broadcasting* 11/1 (Winter 1966–67), 83–89.

Lowery, Shearon, and Melvin L. DeFleur, *Milestones in Mass Communications Research: Media Effects* (New York: Longmans, 1983).

Lowi, Theodore J., "Four Systems of Policy, Politics and Choice," *Public Administration Review* 32/4 (July/August 1972), 298–310.

———, *The End of Liberalism: Ideology, Policy, and the Crisis of Public Authority* (New York: Norton, 1969); idem, *The End of Liberalism: The Second Republic of the United States* (2d. ed. 1979).

———, "The State in Politics: The Relation Between Policy and Administration," in *Regulatory Policy and the Social Sciences,* Roger G. Noll (ed.) (Berkeley: University of California Press, 1985), 67–105.

"Ma Bell Speaking," *The New York Times,* April 25, 1982, Sec. 3, 2.

MacAvoy, Paul W., *The Economic Effects of Regulation: The Trunk Line Railroad Cartels and the Interstate Commerce Commission Before 1900* (Cambridge: Harvard University Press, 1965).

———, (ed.), *Ford Administration Papers on Regulatory Reform.* Individual titles include: *OSHA Safety Regulation: Report of the Presidential Task Force; Federal Energy Administration Regulation: Report of the Presidential Task Force; Deregulation of Cable Television* (all: Washington, DC: American Enterprise Institute, 1977).

———, (ed.), *Unsettled Questions on Regulatory Reform* (Washington, DC: American Enterprise Institute, 1977).

———, "The Regulation-Induced Shortage of Natural Gas," *Journal of Law and Economics* XIV (April 1971), 167–199.

———, *The Regulated Industries and the Economy* (New York: Norton, 1979).

———, and Roger G. Noll, "Relative Prices on Regulated Transactions of the Natural Gas Pipelines," *Bell Journal of Economics and Management Science* 4/1 (Spring 1973), 212–234.

McCaffrey, David, P., *OSHA and the Politics of Health Regulation* (New York and London: Plenum Press, 1982).

McConnell, Grant, *Private Power and American Democracy* (New York: Vintage Books, 1966).

McCraw, Thomas K., "Regulation in America: A Review Article," *Business History Review* 49/2 (Summer 1975), 159–183.

———, *Prophets of Regulation* (Cambridge: Harvard University Press, 1984).

Machalaba, D. "Trucking Association, Powerful for Decades, Has Load of Trouble," *Wall Street Journal,* February 21, 1984, 1, 12.

McGarity, Thomas O., "Regulatory Reform and the Positive State: An Historical Overview," *Administrative Law Review* 38/4 (Fall 1986), 399–425.

McGowan, Carl, "A Reply to *Judicialization,*" *Duke Law Journal* 1986/2 (April 1986).

McGrath, Phyllis S., *Redefining Corporate-Federal Relations: A Research Report from the Conference Board* (New York: Conference Board, 1979).

McKie, James W., "Regulation and the Free Market: The Problem of Boundaries," *Bell Journal of Economics and Management Science* 1/1 (Spring 1970), 6–26.

Maclaurin, W. Rupert, *Invention and Innovation in the Radio Industry* (New York: Macmillan, 1949).

McMahon, Robert Sears, *Federal Regulation of the Radio and Television Broadcast Industry in the United States, 1927–1959* (Ph.D. Dissertation, Ohio State University, 1959; reissued, New York: Arno Press, 1979).

Madsen, K. E., "Antitrust: Consent Decree: The History and Effect of Western Electric Co. v. United States, 1956 Trade Cas. 71,134 (D.C.N.J. 1956)," *Cornell Law Quarterly* 45/1 (1959).

Manne, H. G., and R. M. Miller (eds.), *Auto Safety Regulation: The Cure or the Problem?* (Glen Ridge, NJ: Thomas Horton, 1976).

Mansfield, Edward, "Federal Maritime Commission," in *The Politics of Regulation,* James Q. Wilson (ed.) (New York: Basic Books, 1980), 42–74.

Martin, Albro, *Enterprise Denied: Origins of the Decline of American Railroads, 1887–1917* (New York: Columbia University Press, 1971).

Mathison, S. L., and Phillip M. Walker, *Computers and Telecommunications: Issues in Public Policy* (Englewood Cliffs, NJ: Prentice-Hall, 1970).

Meier, Kenneth J., and John Plumlee, "Regulatory Administration and Organizational Rigidity," *The Western Political Quarterly* XXXI/1 (March 1978), 80–95.

Meyer, Richard J., "Reaction to the Blue Book," *Journal of Broadcasting* 6/4 (Fall 1962), 295–312.

Michael, James R. (ed.), *Working on the System: A Comprehensive Manual for Citizen Access to Federal Agencies* (New York: Basic Books, 1974).

Mikva, Abner J., "How Should the Courts Treat Administrative Agencies?," *The American University Law Review* 36/1 (Fall 1986), 1–10.

Mill, John Stuart, *On Liberty,* Currin V. Shields (ed.) (Indianapolis: Bobbs-Merrill Co., 1956).

Miller, George H., *Railroads and Granger Laws* (Madison: University of Wisconsin Press, 1971).

Mitford, Jessica, *The American Way of Death* (New York: Simon & Schuster, 1963).

Mitnick, Barry M., *The Political Economy of Regulation* (New York: Columbia University Press, 1980).

Mosco, Vincent, *Broadcasting in the United States: Innovative Challenge and Organizational Control* (Norwood, NJ: Ablex, 1979).

Musolf, Lloyd D. (ed.), *Communications Satellites in Political Orbit* (San Francisco: Chandler Publishing Co., 1968).

Nader, Ralph, *Unsafe at Any Speed: The Designed-in Dangers of the American Automobile* (New York: Grossman, 1965).

Nash, Gerald D., "Origins of the Interstate Commerce Act of 1887," *Pennsylvania History* XXIV (July 1957), 181–190.

Nash, Nathaniel C., "Assessing the Effects of Airline Deregulation," *The New York Times,* March 20, 1988, Section E, 5.

———, "Record Loss for Savings Industry," *The New York Times,* March 25, 1988, 25, 43.

National Association of Broadcasters, *Special Allocation Hearings Bulletin,* Nos. 1–12, October/November 1944.

Nichols, A. L., and Richard Zeckhauser, "Government Comes to the Workplace: An Assessment of OSHA," *The Public Interest* 49 (Fall 1977), 39–69.

Niskanen, William, "Bureaucrats and Politicians," *Journal of Law and Economics* 18/3 (December 1975), 617–643.

———, *Bureaucracy and Representative Government* (Chicago: Aldine-Atherton, 1971).

Noble, David F., and Nancy E. Pfund, "Business Goes Back to College," *The Nation,* September 20, 1980, 233, 246–252.

Noble, David W., *The Paradox of Progressive Thought* (Minneapolis: University of Minnesota Press, 1958).

Noble, Kenneth B., "FCC Proposing Wide Shifts in Long-Distance Rate Rules," *The New York Times,* August 5, 1987, 1, 38.

Noll, Roger G., *Reforming Regulation: An Evaluation of the Ash Council Proposals* (Washington, DC: Brookings Institution, 1971).

———, "The Behavior of Regulatory Agencies," *Review of Social Economy* 29/9 (March 1971), 15–19.

———, and Morris Fiorina, "Majority Rule Models and Legislative Elections," *Journal of Politics* 41/4 (November 1979), 1081–1104.

Noll, Roger G., Merton J. Peck, and John J. McGowan, *Economic Aspects of Television Regulation* (Washington, DC: Brookings Institution, 1973).

Nordhauser, Norman, "Origins of Federal Oil Regulation in the 1920s," *Business History Review* XLVII (Spring 1973), 54–71.

Nossiter, Bernard D., "The FCC's Big Giveaway Show," *The Nation,* October 26, 1985, 402–404.

Novak, Michael, *The American Vision* (Washington, DC: American Enterprise Institute, 1978).

O'Connor, James, *The Fiscal Crisis of the State* (New York: St. Martin's Press, 1973).

Oettinger, Anthony G., and Paul J. Berman, "The Medium and the Telephone: The Politics of Information Resources," in *High and Low Politics: Information Resources for the 80s*, Anthony G. Oettinger, Paul J. Berman, and William H. Read (eds.) (Cambridge: Ballinger, 1977), 1–145.

Offe, Claus, "Structural Problems of the Capitalist State," in *German Political Studies*, I, Klaus von Beyme (ed.) (Beverly Hills: Sage Publishing Co., 1974), 31–57.

————, "The Theory of the Capitalist State and the Problem of Policy Formation," in *Stress and Contradiction in Modern Capitalism*, Leon Lindberg at al. (eds.) (Lexington: D.C. Heath, 1975), 125–144.

————, "Crises of 'Crisis Management': Elements of a Political Crisis Theory," *International Journal of Politics* 6, (1976), 29–67.

Olson, C. Vincent, and John Trapani III, "Who Has Benefitted from Regulation of the Airline Industry?," *Journal of Law and Economics* 24/1 (April 1981), 75–93.

Olson, Mancur, Jr., *The Logic of Collective Action: Public Goods and the Theory of Groups* (New York: Harvard University Press and Schocken Books, 1965.

OMB Watch, "OMB Control of Rulemaking: The End of Public Access" (Washington, DC: author, 1985).

"One of the Great Miscalculations in IBM History," advertisement, *The New York Times Magazine*, May 4, 1980, 127.

Owen, Bruce M., *Economics and Freedom of Expression: Media Structure and the First Amendment* (Cambridge: Ballinger, 1975).

————, and Ronald Braeutigam, *The Regulation Game* (Cambridge: Ballinger Publishing Co., 1978).

Park, Rolla E., *Potential Impact of Cable Growth on Television Broadcasting*, Rand Memorandum R-587-FF (Santa Monica: Rand Corporation, 1970).

————, "Cable Television, UHF Broadcasting, and FCC Regulatory Policy," *Journal of Law and Economics* 15/1 (April, 1972), 207–232.

Parrington, Vernon L., *Main Currents of American Thought* (New York: Harcourt, Brace, 1927).

Parrish, Michael E., *Securities Regulation and the New Deal* (New Haven: Yale University Press, 1970).

Paul, Arnold M., *Conservative Crisis and the Rule of Law: Attitudes of Bar and Bench, 1887–1895* (Gloucester: Peter Smith, 1976).

Peltzman, Sam, *Regulation of Automobile Safety* (Washington, DC: American Enterprise Institute, 1975).

————, "Toward a More General Theory of Regulation," *Journal of Law and Economics* 19/2 (August 1976), 211–240.

Penoyer, Ronald (compiler), *Directory of Federal Regulatory Agencies*, 3rd Edition (St. Louis: Center for the Study of American Business, 1981).

Pepper, Robert M., *The Formation of the Public Broadcasting Service*, Ph.D. Dissertation, Department of Communications Arts, University of Wisconsin, Madison, 1975, reprinted (New York: Arno Press, 1979).

————, "Competition in Local Distribution: The Cable Television Industry," in *Understanding New Media: Trends and Issues in Electronic Distribution of Information*, Benjamin M. Compaine (ed.) (Cambridge: Ballinger Publishing Co., 1984), 147–194.

Pertschuk, Michael, *Revolt Against Regulation: The Rise and Pause of the Consumer Movement* (Berkeley: University of California Press, 1982).

Phillips, John Patrick, *Ma Bell's Millions* (New York: Vantage Press, 1970).

Phillips, Stephen, "Continental Cuts Fares: Other Airlines to Follow," *The New York Times,* November 12, 1986, 25.

Piven, Francis Fox, and Richard A. Cloward, *Regulating the Poor: The Functions of Public Welfare* (New York: Pantheon Books, 1971).

Polanyi, Karl, *The Great Transformation* (Boston: Beacon Press, 1944).

Polenberg, Richard, *Reorganizing Roosevelt's Government: The Controversy Over Executive Reorganization, 1936–1939* (Cambridge: Harvard University Press, 1966).

Pollack, Andrew, "Omens for Phone Technology," *The New York Times,* February 18, 1984, 29, 31.

Pool, Ithiel de Sola, *Forecasting the Telephone: A Retrospective Technology Assessment of the Telephone* (Norwood: Ablex Publishing Co., 1983).

———, *Technologies of Freedom* (Cambridge: Harvard University Press, 1983).

Porter, P. Glenn, *The Rise of Big Business, 1860–1910* (New York: 1973).

Porter, William E., *Assault on the Media: The Nixon Years* (Ann Arbor: University of Michigan Press, 1976).

Posner, Richard A., "Taxation by Regulation," *Bell Journal of Economics and Management Science* 2/1 (Spring 1971), 22–50.

———, "Theories of Economic Regulation," *Bell Journal of Economics and Management Science* 5/2 (Autumn 1974), 335–358.

———, "The Appropriate Scope of Regulation in the Cable Television Industry," *Bell Journal of Economics and Management Science* 3/1 (Spring 1972), 98–129.

Poulantzas, Nicos, *State, Power, Socialism* (London: New Left Books, 1978).

Powe, Lucas A., Jr., *American Broadcasting and the First Amendment* (Berkeley: University of California Press, 1987).

———, "FCC Determinations on Networking Issues in Multiple Ownership Proceedings," Prepared for the Commercial Television Network Practices Inquiry of the Federal Communications Commission, (Washington, DC: FCC, 1980).

*Proceedings of the Fourth National Radio Conference and Recommendations for Regulation of Radio,* November 9–11, 1925 (Washington, DC: Government Printing Office, 1926).

"Ratifying a Winner in the Phone Vote," *Time,* August 25, 1986, 44–45.

Rattner, Steven, "Broadcast Deregulation on Wall Street," *Gannett Center Journal,* 2/1 (Winter 1988), 1–15.

" 'The Regulators', They Cost You $130 Billion a Year," *US News and World Report,* June 30, 1975.

Reich, Charles, "The New Property," *Yale Law Journal* 73/5 (April 1964), 733–787.

———, "Individual Rights and Social Welfare: The Emerging Legal Issues," *Yale Law Journal* 74/7 (June 1965), 1245–1257.

Reich, Leonard S., "Industrial Research and the Pursuit of Corporate Security: The Early Years of Bell Labs," *Business History Review* 54/4 (Winter 1980), 504–529.

Reich, Robert B., "Warring Critiques of Regulation," *Regulation,* January/February 1979, 37–42.

Ricci, Claudis, "AT&T Will Seek Waiver to Offer Services to US," *The Wall Street Journal,* April 2, 1984, 3.

Richter, Paul, "AT&T Planning Big Write-Off, 27,000 Job Cut," *Los Angeles Times,* December 19, 1986, 1, 32.

———, "Networks Send Upsetting Signal to Local Stations," *Los Angeles Times,* December 28, 1986, Part IV, 1, 5.

———, and Kathryn Harris, "MCA Write-Off May Signal Independent TV Shakeout," *Los Angeles Times,* January 17, 1987, 1, 25.

Robinson, Glen O., "The Federal Communications Commission," in *Communications for Tomorrow: Policy Perspectives for the 1980s,* Glen O. Robinson (ed.) (New York: Praeger, 1978), 353–400.

Rosenbaum, Irwin S., "The Common Carrier-Public Utility Concept: A Legal-Industrial View," *The Journal of Land and Public Utility Economics* 7/2 (May 1931), 155–168.

Rosenstiel, Thomas B. and Penny Pagano, "FCC to Review Rule on Media Ownership," *Los Angeles Times,* January 16, 1987, Part IV, 2.

Rossi, John P., "A 'Silent Partnership'?: The U.S. Government, RCA, and Radio Communications with East Asia, 1919–1928," *Radical History Review* 33 (1985).

Roth, Jack J., *World War I: A Turning Point in Modern History* (New York: Knopf, 1967).

Rowland, Willard D., Jr., "The Illusion of Fulfillment: The Broadcast Reform Movement," *Journalism Monographs,* No. 79 (December 1982).

———, "The Process of Reification: Recent Trends in Communications Legislation and Policy-Making," *Journal of Communication* 32/4 (Autumn 1982), 114–136.

Salpukas, Agis, "Airlines Adapt to Decontrol," *The New York Times,* December 8, 1983, D1.

———, "Airline Deregulation Costly to Small Competitors, *The New York Times,* December 29, 1986, 26.

———, "Climbing Air Fares Increase Worries of Price-Setting," *The New York Times,* September 9, 1987, 1, 28.

———, "Continental Is Buying Presidential Air's Gates," *The New York Times,* January 13, 1987, 28.

———, "Greyhound Selling Its Bus Operations," *The New York Times,* December 24, 1986, 29, 40.

———, "The Crunch at A rlines' Hubs," *The New York Times,* October 12, 1987, 23, 27.

———, "Trucking's Great Shakeout," *The New York Times,* December 13, 1983, D1, 2.

Sands, Paul E., "How Effective Is Safety Legislation?," *Journal of Law and Economics* 11/1 (April 1968), 165–179.

Sarnoff, David, *Looking Ahead: The Papers of David Sarnoff* (New York: McGraw-Hill, 1968).

Scheiber, Harry N., "The Road to *Munn:* Eminent Domain and the Concept of Public Purpose in the State Courts," *Perspectives in American History,* Vol. 5 (1971), 329–404.

Schlesinger, Arthur M., Jr., *The Age of Roosevelt.* Vol. I, *The Crisis of the Old Order: 1919–1933* (1957); Vol. II, *The Coming of the New Deal* (1959); Vol. III, *The Politics of Upheaval* (1960) (Boston: Houghton Mifflin).

Schiller, Dan, *Telematics and Government* (Norwood, NJ: Ablex Publishing Co., 1982).

Schmeckebier, Laurence F., *The Federal Radio Commission: Its History, Activities and Organization,* Institute for Government Research, Service Monographs of the United States Government, No. 65 (Washington, DC: Brookings Institution, 1932).

Schmidt, Benno C., Jr., *Freedom of the Press vs. Public Access* (New York: Praeger, 1976).

Schmidt, William E., "Sharp Rise in Truck Crashes Prompts Action Across US," *The New York Times,* December 7, 1986, 1, 15.

Schuessler, Thomas L., "The Effect of the Federal Communications Commission's Spectrum Management Policies Upon the Number of Television Networks," prepared for the Commercial Television Network Practices Inquiry of the Federal Communications Commission (Washington, DC: Federal Communications Commission, 1980).

Seiden, Martin, *An Economic Analysis of Community Antenna Television Systems and the Television Broadcasting Industry,* Report to the Federal Communications Commission (Washington, DC: Government Printing Office, 1965).

Shabecoff, Philip, "Record Fine Urged on Injury Reports," *The New York Times,* July 22, 1987, 1, 24.

Shapiro, Martin, "On Predicting the Future of Administrative Law," *Regulation* (May/June 1982), 18–25.

Sharfman, I. Leo, *The Interstate Commerce Commission* (New York: The Commonwealth Fund, 1931).

Sharpe, W. F., *The Economics of Computers* (New York: Columbia University Press, 1969).

Shefter, Martin, "Party, Bureaucracy, and Political Change in the United States," Department of Politics, Cornell University, unpublished manuscript.

Sichter, James W., *Separations Procedures in the Telephone Industry: The Historical Origins of a Public Policy* (Cambridge: Program on Information Resources Policy, 1977).

Siepmann, Charles A., *Radio's Second Chance* (Boston: Little, Brown, 1946).

Silk, Leonard, and David Vogel, *Ethics and Profits: The Crisis of Confidence in American Business* (New York: Simon & Schuster, 1976).

Sims, Calvin, "FCC'S Phone Rate Plan Is Under Attack in Congress," *The New York Times,* April 2, 1988, 17, 19.

———, "Curbs on Phone Companies Kept," *The New York Times,* September 11, 1987, 1, 26.

———, "Judge Lets 'Baby Bells' Offer Some Information Services," *The New York Times,* March 8, 1988, 27–28.

Sing, Bill, "Banks Face a Crisis of Confidence," *Los Angeles Times,* June 3, 1984, 1, 18–19.

Skowronek, Stephen, *Building a New American State: The Expansion of National Administrative Capacities, 1877–1920* (Cambridge: Cambridge University Press, 1982).

Sloan Commission on Cable Communications, *On the Cable: The Television of Abundance* (New York: McGraw-Hill, 1971).

"The Small Fry in Phones Are Getting Cut Off," *Business Week,* November 4, 1985, 98.

Smith, Anthony, *The Geopolitics of Information: How Western Culture Dominates the World* (New York: Oxford University Press, 1980).

Smith, Ralph Lee, "The Wired Nation," *The Nation* (May 18, 1970).

———, *The Wired Nation—Cable TV: The Electronic Communications Highway* (New York: Harper & Row, 1972).

Smulyan, Susan, *"And Now a Word From Our Sponsors. . ." Commercialization of American Broadcast Radio, 1920–1934,* unpublished Ph.D. Dissertation, Department of American Studies, Yale University, 1985.

Spann, Richard, and Edward W. Erickson, "The Economics of Railroading: The Beginning of Cartelization and Regulation," *Bell Journal of Economics and Management Science* 1/2 (Autumn 1970), 227–244.

Snitzler, James R., and Robert J. Byrnes, "Interstate Trucking of Fresh and Frozen Poultry Under Agricultural Exemption," U.S. Department of Agriculture (Washington, DC: Government Printing Office, 1958).

Solomon, Richard J., "What Happened After Bell Spilled the Acid?—Telecommunications

History: A View Through the Literature," *Telecommunications Policy* 2/2 (1978), 146–157.

Spievack, Edwin B., "Presidential Assault on Telecommunications," *Federal Communications Bar Journal* 23/3 (1969), 155–181.

Starr, Kenneth W., "Judicial Review in the Post-*Chevron* Era," *Yale Journal on Regulation* 3/2 (Spring, 1986), 283–312.

Stehman, J. Warren, *The Financial History of the American Telephone and Telegraph Company* (Boston: Houghton Mifflin Co., 1925; reprinted, Augustus M. Kelley, 1967).

Steinfels, Peter, *The Neoconservatives: The Men Who Are Changing America's Politics* (New York: Simon & Schuster, 1979).

Sterling, Christopher, "Cable and Pay Television" and "Television and Radio Broadcasting," in *Who Owns the Media? Concentration of Ownership in the Mass Communications Industry,* Benjamin M. Compaine (ed.) (New York: Harmony Books, 1979), 293–327, 61–125.

———, and John M. Kittross, *Stay Tuned: A Concise History of American Broadcasting* (Belmont: Wadsworth, 1978).

Sterling, Christopher, Jill F. Kasle, and Katherine T. Glakas (eds.), *Decision to Divest: Major Documents in U.S. v. AT&T, 1974–1984* (Washington, DC: Communications Press, Inc., 1986).

Stewart, Richard B., "The Reformation of American Administrative Law," *Harvard Law Review* 88/5 (June 1975), 1669–1813.

Stewart, Robert, *The Occupational Safety and Health Act* (Washington, DC: American Enterprise Institute for Public Policy Research, 1976).

Stigler, George J., "The Theory of Economic Regulation," *Bell Journal of Economics and Management Science* 2/1 (Spring 1971), 3–21.

———, and Claire Friedland, "What Can Regulators Regulate? The Case of Electricity," *Journal of Law and Economics* 5 (October 1962), 1–16.

Stone, Christopher D., *Should Trees Have Standing?* (Los Altos, Calif.: W. Kaufmann, 1974).

Story, Justice Joseph, *Commentaries on the Law of Bailments, With Illustrations from the Civil and Foreign Law,* 4th Edition (1846).

Streeter, Thomas, "The Cable Fable Revisited: Discourse, Policy, and the Making of Cable Television," *Critical Studies in Mass Communication* 4/2 (June 1987), 174–200.

Stuart, Reginald, "FCC Acts to Restrict Indecent Programming," *The New York Times,* April 17, 1987, 1, C30.

Summers, Robert B., and Harrison B. Summers, *Broadcasting and the Public,* 2nd ed. (Belmont: Wadsworth, 1978).

Thayer, Frederick C., *Rebuilding America: The Case for Economic Regulation* (New York: Praeger, 1984).

———, "The Emerging Dangers of Deregulation," *The New York Times,* February 23, 1986, Sec. 3, 3.

Thompson, Robert Luther, *Wiring a Continent: The History of the Telegraph Industry in the United States, 1832–1866* (Princeton: Princeton University Press, 1947).

Tiedeman, Christopher G., *A Treatise on the Limitations of the Police Power in the United States* (1886; reprinted, New York: Da Capo Press, 1971).

Tolchin, Martin, and Susan Tolchin, *Dismantling America: The Rush to Deregulate* (Boston: Houghton Mifflin, 1983).

Trebing, Harry M., "Common Carrier Regulation—The Silent Crisis," *Law and Contemporary Problems* 34/2 (Spring 1969), 302–309.

Tribe, Laurence H., *American Constitutional Law* (Mineola: The Foundation Press, 1978).

"Truckers Brace for Plenty of Head-On Collisions," *Business Week,* January 12, 1987, 99.

Tunstall, Jeremy, *Communications Deregulation: The Unleashing of America's Communications Industry* (London: Basil Blackwell, 1986).

———, *The Media Are American: Anglo-American Media in the World* (New York: Columbia University Press, 1977).

Turner, James, *The Chemical Feast* (New York: Grossman, 1970).

Udelson, Joseph, H., *The Great Television Race: A History of the American Television Industry, 1925–1941* (University, Ala.: University of Alabama Press, 1982).

"The Uneasy Constitutional Status of the Administrative Agencies," Symposium on Administrative Law, *The American University Law Review* 36/2 (Winter 1987).

Van Alstyne, William W., *Interpretations of the First Amendment* (Durham, NC: Duke University Press, 1984).

Verveer, Phillip, "Regulation and the Access Problem: What's Happened and Where We Are Now," *Telecommunications Access and Public Policy,* Alan Baughcum and Gerald Faulhaber, (eds.) (Norwood, NJ: Ablex Publishing Corp, 1984), 83–88.

Vietor, Richard H. K., "Businessmen and the Political Economy: The Railroad Rate Controversy of 1905," *Journal of American History* LXIV/1 (June 1977), 47–66.

Vise, D. A., and P. Behr, "When the Airline's Dogfight Is Over, How Many Dogs Will Be Left?," *Washington Post National Weekly Edition,* March 17, 1986, 19–20.

Vogel, David, *Lobbying the Corporation: Citizen Challenges to Business Authority* (New York: Basic Books, 1979).

———, "The 'New' Social Regulation in Historical and Comparative Perspective," in *Regulation in Perspective,* Thomas McCraw (ed.) (Cambridge: Harvard Business School, 1981), 155–185.

———, "How Business Responds to Opposition: Corporate Political Strategies During the 1970s," paper delivered to the 1979 Annual Meeting of the American Political Science Association, August 31–September 3, 1979.

von Auw, Alvin, *Heritage and Destiny: Reflections on the Bell System in Transition* (New York: Praeger, 1983).

Waldrop, Frank C., and Joseph Borkin, *Television: A Struggle for Power* (New York: William Morrow & Co., 1938; reprinted, Arno Press, 1971).

Wallace, John, "What the Listener Likes and How He Likes It," *Radio Broadcast* 11/1 (May 1927), 32.

Walsh, Sharon Warren, and Martha M. Hamilton, "FTC Hails Deregulation of Airlines," *The Washington Post,* February 8, 1988, C1.

Weaver, Suzanne, "Antitrust Division of the Department of Justice," in *The Politics of Regulation,* James Q. Wilson (ed.) (New York: Basic Books, 1980), 123–151.

Weber, Max, *On Law in Economy and Society,* Max Rheinstein (ed.) (New York: Simon and Schuster, 1954).

Weidenbaum, Murray, and Robert DeFina, *The Costs of Federal Regulation of Economic Activity* (Washington, DC: American Enterprise Institute, Reprint No. 88, May 1978).

Weingast, Barry R., "Congress, Regulation, and the Decline of Nuclear Power," *Public Policy* 28/2 (Spring 1980), 231–255.

———, "Regulation, Reregulation, and Deregulation: The Political Foundations of Agency-Clientele Relationships," *Law and Contemporary Problems* 44/1 (Winter 1981), 147–178.

Weinstein, James, *The Corporate Ideal in the Liberal State, 1900–1918* (Boston: Beacon Press, 1968).

Weiss, Fredric A., David Ostroff, and Charles E. Clift III, "Station License Revocations and

Denials of Renewal, 1970–78,'' *Journal of Broadcasting* 24/1 (Winter 1980), 69–77.

Wellisz, Stanislaw H., "Regulation of Natural Gas Pipeline Companies: An Economic Analysis," *Journal of Political Economy* 71/1 (February 1963), 30–43.

Weyl, Walter S., *The New Democracy* (New York: Macmillan, 1912).

White, Lawrence J., "Quality Variation When Prices Are Regulated," *Bell Journal of Economics and Management Science* 3/2 (Autumn 1972), 425–436.

White, William Allen, *The Old Order Changeth* (New York, Macmillan, 1910).

Whitefield, Debra, "Pan Am Stock Active as Rumors Point to Merger With American," *Los Angeles Times,* January 16, 1987, Part IV, 1, 2.

Whiteside, Thomas, "Annals of Television (The Nixon Administration and Television)," *The New Yorker,* March 17, 1975, 41–91.

Wiebe, Robert H., *The Search for Order, 1877–1920* (New York: Hill and Wang, 1967).

Williams, Raymond, *Television: Technology and Cultural Form* (New York: Schocken Press, 1975).

Wilson, James Q., "The Politics of Regulation," in *The Politics of Regulation,* James Q. Wilson, (ed.) (New York: Basic Books, 1980), 357–394.

———, "The Dead Hand of Regulation," *The Public Interest* 25 (Fall 1971), 39–58.

———, "The Bureaucracy Problem," *The Public Interest* 6 (Winter 1967), 3–9.

Winner, Langdon, "Do Artifacts Have Politics?," *Daedalus* 109 (Winter 1980), 121–136.

Winston, Brian, *Misunderstanding Media* (Cambridge: Harvard University Press, 1986).

Witkin, Richard, "Safety Record of US Airlines Shows Big Gain," *The New York Times,* January 13, 1987, 1, 12.

Wolfe, Alan, *The Limits of Legitimacy: Political Contradictions of Contemporary Capitalism* (New York: Free Press, 1977).

"The World on the Line," *The Economist,* November 23, 1985, 5–40.

Wyman, Bruce, *The Special Law Governing Public Service Corporations and All Others Engaged in Public Employment,* 2 vols. (New York: Baker, Voorhis & Co., 1911).

Young, James C., "New Fashions in Radio Programs," *Radio Broadcast* 7/1 (May 1925), 83–89.

Zerner, Charles, "U.S. Sues to Force AT&T to Drop Western Electric Co.," *The New York Times,* January 15, 1949, 1, 30.

## Government Documents

[*Note:* The many citations to FCC decisions and policies are not listed individually in this bibliography because they can be found in two "corporate" sources, FCC Reports and FCC Annual Reports. Those FCC documents that were published separately are listed below.]

U.S. National Commission on Air Quality, *To Breathe Clean Air* (Washington, DC: Government Printing Office, 1981).

U.S. Commission on Organization of the Executive Branch of the Government, Committee on Independent Regulatory Commissions, Staff Report on the Federal Communications Commission, prepared for the Committee by William W. Golub, dated September 15, 1948, declassified March 1, 1961.

U.S. Commission on Organization of the Executive Branch of the Government [the first Hoover Commission Report] (Washington, DC: Government Printing Office, 1949).

U.S. Commission on Organization of the Executive Branch of the Government [the second Hoover Commission Report] (Washington, DC: Government Printing Office, 1955).

U.S. Department of Commerce, Bureau of Navigation, *Radio Service Bulletin,* Recommendations of the National Radio Committee (Washington, DC: Government Printing Office, 1923).

U.S. Department of Commerce, *Recommendations For Regulation of Radio,* adopted by the

Third National Radio Conference, October 6–10, 1924 (Washington, DC: Government Printing Office, 1924).

U.S. Department of Justice, Plaintiff's Memorandum in Opposition to Defendants' Motion for Involuntary Dismissal Under Rule 41 (b) in United States v. American Telephone and Telegraph Company, Civil Action No. 74–1698, August 16, 1981.

U.S. Department of Justice, *Report and Recommendations of the United States Concerning the Lines of Business Restrictions Imposed on the Bell Operating Companies by the Modification of Final Judgment,* United States v. Western Electric Company, Inc. and American Telephone and Telegraph Co., Civil Action No. 82-0192 (Washington, DC: author, released February 2, 1987).

U.S. District Court, District of Columbia, Modification of Final Judgment, United States v. Western Electric Co., Inc. & American Telephone and Telegraph Co., Civil Action No. 82-01982, August 24, 1982.

U.S. Federal Communications Commission, *Telephone Investigation: Proposed Report* ["Walker Report"] (Pursuant to Public Resolution No. 8, 74th Congress) (Washington, DC: Government Printing Office, 1938).

U.S. Federal Communications Commission, *Investigation of the Telephone Industry in the United States* ["Final Report"] (Washington, DC: Government Printing Office, 1939).

U.S. Federal Communications Commission, Network Inquiry Special Staff, *Preliminary Report on Prospects for Additional Networks,* Preliminary Draft, "Video Interconnection: Technology, Costs and Regulatory Policies" (Washington, DC: Federal Communications Commission, 1980).

U.S. Federal Communications Commission, Network Inquiry Special Staff, Final Report, *New Television Networks: Entry, Jurisdiction, Ownership and Regulation* (Washington, DC: FCC, 1980).

U.S. Federal Communications Commission, *Public Service Responsibility of Broadcast Licensees* (Washington, DC: FCC, March 7, 1946).

U.S. Federal Communications Commission, *Report on Chain Broadcasting,* Pursuant to Commission Order No. 37, Docket No. 5060, May 1941 (Washington, DC: Government Printing Office, 1941).

U.S. Federal Communications Commission, *Report by the Federal Communications Commission on Domestic Telecommunications Policies,* September 27, 1976 (Washington, DC: FCC, 1976).

U.S. Federal Trade Commission, Report, *The Radio Industry* (Washington, DC: Government Printing Office, 1923).

U.S. General Accounting Office, Statement of Herbert R. McLure, Associate Director, Resources, Community, and Economic Development Division, US GAO, before the Subcommittee on Surface Transportation, Committee on Public Works and Transportation, House of Representatives, on Predatory Pricing and Antitrust Enforcement in the Trucking Industry (Washington, DC: GAO, November 7, 1985).

U.S. General Accounting Office, *Deregulation: Increased Competition Is Making Airlines More Efficient and Responsive to Consumers,* GAO/RCED-86-26 (Washington, DC: GAO, November 6, 1985).

U.S. General Accounting Office, *Airline Competition: Impact of Computerized Reservation Systems,* GAO/RCED-86-74 (Washington, DC: GAO, May 1986).

U.S. General Accounting Office, *Telephone Communications: Bypass of the Local Telephone Companies—A Report to Congress,* GAO/RCED-86-66 (Washington, DC: GAO, August 1986).

U.S. House of Representatives, 65th Congress, 2d Session, Committee on Interstate and Foreign Commerce, Hearings on H.J. Res. 309, July 2, 1918.

U.S. House of Representatives, 74th Congress, 1st Session, Document No. 83, *Recommendations of Three Proposed Amendments to the Communications Act of 1934*, Letter from the Chairman of the Federal Communications Commission, Dated January 21, 1935 (Washington, DC: Government Printing Office, 1935).

U.S. House of Representatives, 85th Congress, 2nd Session, Subcommittee of the Committee on Interstate and Foreign Commerce, Hearings on *Investigation of Regulatory Commissions and Agencies*, January 27–30, February 3–5, 1958. Memorandum to Hon. Morgan M. Moulder, Chairman, Special Subcommittee on Legislative Oversight, from Dr. Bernard Schwartz, Chief Counsel of the FCC, dated January 4, 1958 (Washington, DC: Government Printing Office, 1958).

U.S. House of Representatives, 85th Congress, 2nd Session, Committee on the Judiciary, Antitrust Subcommittee (Subcommittee No. 5), *Consent Decree Program of the Department of Justice Hearings*, March 25–May 22, 1958 (Serial No. 9) (Washington, DC: Government Printing Office, 1958).

U.S. House of Representatives, 85th Congress, 2d Session, Committee on Interstate and Foreign Commerce, *Network Broadcasting*, H.R. No. 1297 ["Barrow Report"] (Washington, DC: Government Printing Office, 1958).

U.S. House of Representatives, 87th Congress, 1st Session, Committee on Science and Astronautics, *Commercial Applications of Space Communications Systems*, H. Report No. 1279, October 11, 1961 (Washington, DC: Government Printing Office, 1961).

U.S. House of Representatives, 87th Congress, 2nd Session, Committee on Interstate and Foreign Commerce, Hearings, *Communications Satellites* (Part 2), March 13–22, 1962 (Washington, DC: Government Printing Office, 1962).

U.S. House of Representatives, 94th Congress, 1st Session, Committee on Interstate and Foreign Commerce, Subcommittee on Communications, *Domestic Common Carrier Regulation*, Hearings, November 10, 11, 13, 18, 1975 (Washington, DC: Government Printing Office, 1975).

U.S. House of Representatives, 94th Congress, 2d Session, Subcommittee of the Committee on Appropriations, Hearings, *Department of Transportation and Related Agencies Appropriations for 1977*, March 1, 1976, Part 2 (Washington, DC: Government Printing Office, 1976).

U.S. House of Representatives, 95th Congress 1st Session, Committee on Government Operations, Subcommittee on Legislation and National Security, Hearings on *Proposed Agency for Consumer Protection* (H.R. 6116), April 20, 21, 1977 (Washington, DC: Government Printing Office, 1977).

U.S. House of Representatives, 95th Congress, 1st Session, Committee on Interstate and Foreign Commerce, Subcommittee on Communications, *Options Papers Prepared by the Staff for Use by the Subcommittee on Communications*, Committee Print 95-13 (Washington, DC: Government Printing Office, 1977).

U.S. House of Representatives, 98th Congress, 1st Session, Committee on Interstate and Foreign Commerce, Subcommittee on Energy Conservation and Power, Hearings on H.R. 2510: *Nuclear Licensing and Regulatory Reform Act of 1983* (Washington, DC: Government Printing Office, 1983).

U.S. House of Representatives, 97th Congress, Congress, 2nd Session, Committee on Government Operations, *Seventh Report* (Washington, DC: Government Printing Office, 1983).

U.S. *Report of the President's Committee on Administrative Management* (Washington, DC: Government Printing Office, 1937).

U.S. The President's Advisory Council on Executive Organization, *A New Regulatory Framework: Report on Selected Independent Regulatory Agencies* ["Ash Council Report"] (Washington, DC: Government Printing Office, 1971).

U.S. President's Task Force on Communications Policy, *Final Report* (Washington, DC: Government Printing Office, 1968).

U.S. Senate, 49th Congress, 1st Session, Committee on Interstate Commerce, *Report of the Select Committee on Interstate Commerce* [known as the Cullom Committee Report], S. Rep. No. 46 (Washington, DC: Government Printing Office, 1886).

U.S. Senate, 63rd Congress, 2d Session, Senate Document 399, *Government Ownership of Electrical Means of Communication,* (Washington, DC: Government Printing Office, 1914).

U.S. Senate, 66th Congress, 3rd Session, Subcommittee of the Committee on Interstate Commerce, Hearings on S. 4301, *A Bill to Prevent the Unauthorized Landing of Submarine Cables in the United States* (Washington, DC: Government Printing Office, 1921).

U.S. Senate, 67th Congress, 1st Session, Committee on Interstate and Foreign Commerce, S. Rep. No. 75, *Amending the Transportation Act of 1920* (Washington, DC: Government Printing Office, 1921).

U.S. Senate, 71st Congress, 1st Session, Committee on Interstate Commerce, Hearings on S. 6, *Commission on Communications,* July 9, 1929 (Washington, DC: Government Printing Office, 1929).

U.S. Senate, 72nd Congress, 1st Session, "Commercial Radio Advertising," Letter from the Chairman of the Federal Radio Commission, Document No. 137 (Washington, DC: Government Printing Office, 1932).

U.S. Senate, 76th Congress, 3rd Session, Committee on Interstate Commerce, Hearings on S. Res. 251, *Development of Television,* April 10–11, 1940.

U.S. Senate, 77th Congress, 1st Session, Subcommittee of the Committee on Interstate Commerce, Hearings on S. 2445, *A Bill to Amend the Communications Act of 1934, as Amended, to Permit Consolidations and Mergers of Telegraph Operations, and for Other Purposes,* April 23, 24, 29, 30, May 5, 7, 8, and 13, 1942 (Washington, DC: Government Printing Office, 1942).

U.S. Senate, 77th Congress, 1st Session, Committee on Interstate Commerce, Hearings on S. Res. 113, *A Resolution Directing a Study of Certain Rules and Regulations Promulgated by the Federal Communications Commission,* June 2–20, 1941 (Washington, DC: Government Printing Office, 1941).

U.S. Senate, 83rd Congress, 2d Session, Committee on Interstate and Foreign Commerce, Subcommittee on Communications, Hearings on the Status of TV Stations and S. 3905 (Washington, DC: Government Printing Office, 1954).

U.S. Senate, 84th Congress, 2d Session, Committee on Interstate and Foreign Commerce, Hearings on *The Television Inquiry: The UHF-VHF Allocation Problem* (Washington, DC: Government Printing Office, 1956).

U.S. Senate, 85th Congress, 2d Session, Committee on Interstate and Foreign Commerce, Hearings pursuant to S. Res. 224 and on S. 376, *Television Inquiry,* Part 6 (Washington, DC: Government Printing Office, 1958).

U.S. Senate, 85th Congress, 2d Session, Committee on Interstate and Foreign Commerce, *Allocation of TV Channels,* Report of the Ad Hoc Advisory Committee on Allocations, Committee Print, March 14, 1958 (Washington, DC: Government Printing Office, 1958) ["Bowles Report"].

U.S. Senate, 87th Congress, 2d Session, Committee on Interstate and Foreign Commerce, *All-Channel Television,* Report No. 1526 (Washington, DC: Government Printing Office, 1962).

U.S. Senate, 87th Congress, 1st Session, Subcommittee on Monopoly of the Select Committee on Small Business, Hearings, *Space Satellite Communications* (Part 2: Review of the Report of the Ad Hoc Carrier Committee), November 8, 9, 1961 (Washington, DC: Government Printing Office, 1961).

U.S. Senate, 87th Congress, 2nd Session, Judiciary Committee, Hearings, *Antitrust Problems of the Space Satellite Communications System* (Part 1), March 29–30, April 4–5, 1962 (Washington, DC: Government Printing Office, 1962).

U.S. Senate, 87th Congress, 2nd Session, Subcommittee on Antitrust and Monopoly of the Committee on the Judiciary, Hearings, *Antitrust Problems of the Space Satellite Communications System* (Part 2), April 6, 10, 12, 17, 1962 (Washington, DC: Government Printing Office, 1962).

U.S. Senate, 94th Congress, 1st Session, Committee on the Judiciary, Subcommittee on Administrative Practice and Procedure, *Oversight of Civil Aeronautics Board Practices and Procedures* (Washington, DC: Government Printing Office, 1975).

U.S. Senate, 95th Congress, 1st Session, Committee on Commerce, Science, and Transportation, Subcommittee on Communications, Hearings on *Domestic Telecommunications Common Carrier Policies,* March 21, 22, 23, 28, 1977 (Washington, DC: Government Printing Office, 1977).

U.S. Senate, 95th Congress, 2nd Session, Committee on Human Resources, Hearings on H.R. 8410, *Labor Law Reform Act of 1978,* June 28, 1978 (Washington, DC: Government Printing Office, 1978).

U.S. Senate, 96th Congress, 2nd Session, Judiciary Committee, *Reform of Federal Regulation,* Joint Report of the Senate Committee on Governmental Affairs and the Committee on the Judiciary, Senate Report 96-1018 part 2 (Washington, DC: Government Printing Office, 1980).

U.S. Senate, 97th Congress, 1st & 2nd Sessions, Committee on the Judiciary, *The Department of Justice Oversight of the United States v. American Telephone and Telegraph Lawsuit,* Hearings, August 6, 1981, and January 25, 1982 (Serial No. J-97-53), part 1 (Washington, DC: Government Printing Office, 1982).

U.S. Senate, 97th Congress, 2nd Session, Committee on Commerce, Science and Transportation, Hearings, *AT&T Proposed Settlement,* January 25 and February 4, 1982 (Washington, DC: Government Printing Office, 1982).

U.S. Senate, 98th Congress, 1st Session, Committee on Commerce, Science, and Transportation, *Print and Electronic Media: The Case for First Amendment Parity,* Committee Print 98-50, May 3, 1983 (Washington, DC: Government Printing Office, 1983).

## Corporate Sources

American and Telegraph Company Annual Reports.

*Broadcasting.*

*Broadcasting/Cablecasting Yearbook.*

Congressional Record.

Federal Communications Commission Annual Reports.

Federal Communications Commission Reports, 2 Series.

Federal Radio Commission Annual Reports, Numbers 1–7, 1927–1933 (reprinted New York: Arno Press, 1971).

Federal Register.

Federal Reports.

Federal Supplement.

Pike and Fisher Radio Regulations.

Public Utilities Reports.

*Television Factbook.*

United States Code.

United States Reports.
Weekly Compilation of Presidential Documents.

## Interviews

Daniel L. Brenner, Legal Assistant to the Chairman, Federal Communications Commission, 1977–1985. March 25, 1985.

Charles Ferris, Chairman, Federal Communications Commission, 1977–1981. March 25, 1985.

Henry Geller, General Counsel, Federal Communications Commission, 1964–1971; Assistant Secretary for Communications and Information, Commerce Department and Director of National Telecommunications and Information Administration, 1977–1981. June 19, 1984, and March 24, 1985.

Michael Pertschuk, Chairman, Federal Trade Commission, 1978–1981; Commissioner, Federal Trade Commission, 1982–1984. June 20, 1984.

Lawrence Secrest, III, Deputy General Counsel, Federal Communications Commission, 1977–1978. March 25, 1985.

Sam Simon, Director, Telecommunications Research and Action Center. June 19, 1984.

Thomas C. Spavins, Deputy Chief, Office of Plans and Policy, Federal Communications Commission. June 20, 1984.

Bernard Strassburg, Chief, Federal Communications Commission Common Carrier Division, 1964–1973. March 25, 1985.

John V. Wells, Transportation Economist, U.S. General Accounting Office. December 10, 1986.

Richard E. Wiley, Commissioner, Federal Communications Commission, 1972–1974, Chairman, Federal Communications Commission, 1974–1977. March 25, 1985.

Peter Zschiesche, Business Agent, International Association of Machinists, District 50, San Diego, California. March 28, 1986.

# Index